THE PAPERS OF DANIEL WEBSTER

CHARLES M. WILTSE, EDITOR-IN-CHIEF

SERIES ONE: CORRESPONDENCE

THE UNIVERSITY PRESS

OF NEW ENGLAND

Sponsoring Institutions

BRANDEIS UNIVERSITY

CLARK UNIVERSITY

DARTMOUTH COLLEGE

UNIVERSITY OF NEW HAMPSHIRE

UNIVERSITY OF RHODE ISLAND

TUFTS UNIVERSITY

UNIVERSITY OF VERMONT

The Papers of
Daniel Webster

Correspondence, Volume 4

1835-1839

CHARLES M. WILTSE AND

HAROLD D. MOSER, EDITORS

PUBLISHED FOR

DARTMOUTH COLLEGE BY THE

UNIVERSITY PRESS OF NEW ENGLAND

HANOVER, NEW HAMPSHIRE AND

LONDON, ENGLAND 1980

*The edition of the Papers of Daniel Webster, of which this is volume
four in the Correspondence series, has been made possible through
grants from the Program for Editions of the National Endowment for
the Humanities, an independent Federal agency; and through the continuing support, both administrative and financial, of the National
Historical Publications and Records Commission. The edition is spon-
sored and published by Dartmouth College.*

Acknowledgments

The deep indebtedness of the editors to libraries, archives, historical societies, and individual collectors has been many times acknowledged as new volumes of Webster Papers have appeared. As in earlier volumes the source of each individual letter printed or calendared is indicated by the standard location symbol; to each of these depositories, and to the patient men and women who administer them, our most sincere thanks are once again extended. A small sampling of major institutions has continued to supply documents and to answer questions as we have called upon them. These are the Library of Congress, where Manuscript Historian John McDonough has been most helpful; the National Archives, where we are under special obligation to Mary A. Giunta and Richard N. Sheldon; the Massachusetts Historical Society; the New Hampshire Historical Society; and, most important of all, Baker Library of Dartmouth College. Our obligation at Baker, where the project itself is housed, extends to virtually every member of the staff, but is greatest to Virginia Close, Reference Librarian; Patricia A. Carter, Interlibrary Loan Officer; Walter W. Wright, Chief of Special Collections; and Kenneth C. Cramer, Archivist.

To those who have supplied the generous financial support that has kept us working, our obligation is certainly of equal magnitude: Dartmouth College, the National Endowment for the Humanities, the National Historical Publications and Records Commission, and a handful of individual donors. Among the latter we are especially grateful at this time to Mr. John S. Hodel, Dartmouth 1941, of Deer Harbor, Washington.

To various other individuals who have contributed in countless tangible and intangible ways, we may single out for particular mention Leonard M. Rieser, Dartmouth Provost and Dean of the Faculty of Arts and Sciences, who has added the administration of the Webster Papers to an already overwhelming schedule; William B. Durant, Executive Officer to the Faculty of Arts and Sciences, who has from the inception of the project handled our finances; George F. Farr, Jr., Assistant Director of the Research Materials Program, National Endowment for the Humanities; James B. Rhoads, Archivist of the United States and Chairman of the National Historical Publications and Records Commission; and Roger Bruns, its Publication Program Director.

Finally, we must acknowledge the contribution by staff members of the Webster Papers, other than those specifically responsible for this volume. We have at all times been able to call upon the special skills of Legal Editors Alfred S. Konefsky and Andrew J. King, Diplomatic Editor Kenneth E. Shewmaker, and Assistant Editor Rexford G. Sherman. Mary V. Anstruther, who combines the roles of Research Assistant and Office Manager, has consistently transcended her job description.

Contents

For the page number on which each document of
the Papers begins, see the Calendar.

A section of illustrations follows page 282

Introduction

This fourth volume of Webster's Correspondence begins with his nomination by the Massachusetts legislature for the Presidency of the United States, although the election of 1836 was still almost two years distant. Close to the end of the volume we print his formal withdrawal from the succeeding presidential contest, again well over a year before the election. In the correspondence of the intervening years there is surprisingly little of presidential politics but a vast deal of speculation in Western lands, most of it with borrowed money and all of it on faith in the judgment of others.

At no period of his life is Webster's ambivalence more clearly revealed. He wanted very much to be President; but he wanted also—perhaps even more—to amass a fortune and to live as the Boston and New York merchants, manufacturers, and bankers who were his clients lived. To a large extent these men financed both his political career and his speculations, and he in turn represented their interests, faithfully and well, in the Senate and before the Courts. It was an almost symbiotic relationship, necessary to the fulfillment of each party. But Webster wanted more; he wanted to be not merely the hireling of wealth but the possessor of it, not alone the cunning advocate of power but its very fountainhead.

There was an abrupt awakening after the Panic of 1837 closed banks, froze credit, and plunged the country into a major depression. Webster should have seen it coming, but the lure of fortune blinded him to everything else. One feels in the correspondence of 1836 and the early months of the following year the excitement, rising to fever, of land speculation in the West; and through these case records more clearly than through statistical summations one sees the phenomenal growth that made it possible. Still clinging to his fantasy, and even toying with the notion of settling in Illinois, Webster's indebtedness, to banks and to individuals, was at its greatest extent just before the crash came in the spring of 1837. Our records are not complete, so that we do not know precisely how heavily in debt he was, but based on the materials selectively reproduced in this volume, the sum was enormous for that day—certainly not less than $200,000, secured by lands whose value fell day by day; lands, moreover, to which Webster's agents, chief among them his son Daniel Fletcher Webster, had often failed to secure proper titles, or which occasionally, upon inspection, proved to be swamp or lake bottom.

Webster's holdings were largely concentrated in the upper Midwest: Ohio, Indiana, Michigan, Illinois, Wisconsin, Missouri; but there were also "investments" in Tennessee, Texas, Maine, and New Hampshire. Some purchases were financed with his personal credit; others were made in conjunction with wealthier friends such as Governor John Davis and Thomas Handasyd Perkins; and still others were handled through joint stock companies like the Clamorgan Land Company and the Ellsworth Land and Lumber Company, or through corporations like the Maryland Mining Company. Investment was at first in government lands, located by agents and agents of agents, and obtained through public land offices. After the Specie Circular of 1836 put an end to the sale of government lands except for an equivalent of gold or silver currency, speculations turned to "second-hand" lands—those already in private hands, sold and resold for progressively higher sums in bank paper or in promissory notes. Still optimistic even into the summer of 1837, Webster visited the West and glowed with enthusiasm for the future of his properties, especially for his farm at Peru, Illinois, which Fletcher was then managing.

By the time he returned to the East, however, his drafts were being protested, those who had freely loaned him money wanted payment, and his professional practice, neglected while he pursued the phantom of quick riches, brought sharply contracted income. The Boston capitalists who had shared some of his ventures quietly wrote off their losses and turned to such other forms of investment as transportation and manufacturing, but Webster had no such options. He had no capital to invest—only a mountain of debt. He began to hint at resigning his Senate seat, but he was not serious, nor did his political and financial backers believe he was. They still needed each other, perhaps more than ever. Van Buren's program to combat the depression included Jackson's projected Independent Treasury, functioning through "subtreasuries"— customs offices and other government financial agencies around the country—to collect revenue and disburse income in lieu of the now defunct Bank of the United States. It was a system abhorrent to the business community, and so Webster stood forth as its leading opponent, concentrating his efforts toward banking and bankruptcy legislation. There are no references to the rising tide of sentiment for the abolition of slavery, or to the violence of antiabolitionist mobs, particularly in Philadelphia and in his own Boston. There is no mention of the mob-murder of abolitionist editor Elijah Lovejoy in Alton, Illinois; nor of the gag rule passed by the House of Representatives to forestall debate on the slavery issue. He was among those presenting petitions for the abolition of slavery and the slave trade in the District of Columbia, but except to affirm his belief that the petitioners were asking nothing not in the constitutional power of Congress to grant, he went along with the Senate conspiracy of silence.

After 1837, Webster's personal drive was toward paying off the debts accumulated in his land speculations. Not even his rivalry with Clay and Harrison for leadership of the Whig party, nor Calhoun's defection to the Democrats, diverted him more than peripherally from this goal; for though he did not commit his convictions to paper, he knew well that his own political advancement must come, if it came at all, with clean hands. As lawyer and legislator he concerned himself with economic development, especially with transportation, manufacturing, trade, and banking. Boston, suffering increasingly from the competition of New York, Philadelphia, and Baltimore, sought to tap the growing volume of Western commerce, and despite the financial stringency made good progress in these years toward completion of a rail connection with the Hudson River. (The western extension of the Boston and Worcester Railroad was opened to Albany in 1841.) But though Webster shared indirectly in the returns from Boston's economic growth, he was no longer willing to rely predominantly upon that city, or even on New England, for the advancement of his own fortunes. He expanded his law practice in New York and in other cities, and began to look beyond even the confines of the United States for sources of profit and power.

The "Aroostook War," involving lumbering interests in Maine and New Brunswick, forced Van Buren by 1838 to reconsider the still undetermined boundary between the United States and Canada, along with other sources of friction arising for the most part from overt American support of the Canadian rebels of 1836. For a time Webster, encouraged by Secretary of War Joel Roberts Poinsett, hoped he might be sent as special envoy to England, where incidentally he might dispose of some of his own Western lands. The President, needless to say, had no thought of bestowing so potentially rewarding a mission upon a political opponent, but Webster managed to make the trip anyway, without official title or support. Both Massachusetts and New York engaged him to offer their state bonds to British investors. Nicholas Biddle, for the Pennsylvania Bank of the United States and the Baring Brothers of London, engaged his services, and his father-in-law contributed a substantial sum.

The trip to England, lasting from June to December 1839, makes up the latter portion of this volume. It was from London that he withdrew his candidacy for the 1840 Whig presidential nomination; and it was there that he tested his own diplomatic skills. He was indeed successful in disposing of a considerable volume of the State bonds entrusted to his care; successful also in unloading some of his personal holdings; but the most important result of the trip was intangible. It made him favorably known to leading British statesmen and prepared the way for the later peaceful settlement of the northeastern boundary question.

PLAN OF WORK

From its inception the Papers of Daniel Webster was planned as an integrated project, using both microfilm and letterpress publication. The persistent pressure of time and the steadily rising cost of book publication were important factors in the choice of the dual media, but the overriding consideration was the desire to bring all of Webster together, without abridgment or gloss, for those who were equipped to use it that way, while providing the less dedicated scholar and the general reader with the essential Webster in convenient annotated form. The microfilm edition, in four different groupings, is as complete as the surviving records permit. Webster's correspondence, including letters received as well as letters sent, together with miscellaneous notes, memoranda, briefs, drafts, formal writings, reports, petitions, and business papers have been issued with printed guide and index as *The Papers of Daniel Webster* by University Microfilms, Ann Arbor, Michigan. *The Legal Papers of Daniel Webster*, also issued with guide and alphabetical list of cases by University Microfilms, consists of records drawn primarily from the county courts of New Hampshire and Massachusetts and from the state and lower federal courts in New England. Records of the Department of State and of the Supreme Court are available on film from the National Archives and Records Service of the General Services Administration, but the user must select for himself the reels that may contain Webster material.

The value of this film, including as it does virtually all known Webster papers, cannot be overstated; but its very magnitude makes it unmanageable. It is relatively expensive, requires special equipment to use, is hard on the eyes, and effectively buries the grains of wheat by mixing them unevenly with an enormous amount of chaff. The user of the film, moreover, must decipher for himself often difficult or faded handwriting. He must search out the identity of persons and the nature of events alluded to, and finally he must rely upon his own judgment as to the significance of the given document. In the letterpress edition all this has been done for him, even to the selection of documents in terms of their significance, by editors totally immersed in the time and place and almost as familiar with the central characters as was Webster himself.

The letterpress edition in effect complements and renders more useful these various microfilm collections, whose very existence has made it possible to select more rigorously the documents important enough to be offered to the larger audience reached by the printed book. Each volume of correspondence, moreover, includes a calendar of letters written in the same time period but not selected for publication. For each of these the microfilm frame number is cited, as is volume and page citation for any document now available only in a printed version. Footnote references are also made to the film wherever appropriate. Items found subsequent to publication of the appropriate volume will be calendared at the end of the *Correspondence* Series. For the general reader and for the student of the period rather than of the man, the editors believe the selection of items printed will be ample. The biographer, and the scholar pursuing an in-depth study of some segment of the times, will need the film, to which he will find the printed volumes an indispensable annotated guide.

The letterpress edition is being published in four different series, overlapping in time but not in content, in order to make maximum use of subject matter specialists as technical editors. The edition was originally planned to fill a total of fourteen volumes, of which seven were to be correspondence, three were to be legal papers, two were diplomatic papers, and two were speeches and formal writings. The legal papers have since been reorganized for publication in two rather than three volumes, although the combined length of the two will be not much if any less than that of the planned three. The change merely accommodates to a more logical division of material.

The present volume, including the period 1835–1839, is the fourth in the Correspondence series.

EDITORIAL METHOD

Letters and other documents included in this volume are arranged in chronological sequence, irrespective of whether Webster was the writer or the recipient. The only exception is for letters that were sent as enclosures in later correspondence. These have been placed immediately after the document which they accompanied. Date and point of origin have been placed at the upper right of each letter. If all or part of this information has been supplied by the editors, it appears in square brackets, with a question mark if conjecture. The complimentary close, which in the original manuscripts often takes up three or four lines, has been run continuously with the last line of the text.

All letters are reproduced in full except in rare instances where the only surviving text is incomplete or is from a printed source which did not reproduce it in its entirety. Needless to say, texts from printed sources are used only when the original manuscript has not been found, but the letter is of sufficient importance to warrant its inclusion.

The letters themselves have been reproduced in type as nearly as possible the way they were written. Misspellings have been retained without the annoyingly obtrusive "(sic)"; and abbreviations and contractions have been allowed to stand unless the editor feels they will not be readily understood by a present-day reader. In such cases the abbreviation has been expanded, with square brackets enclosing the letters supplied. Punctuation, too, has been left as Webster and his correspondents used it, save only that dashes clearly intended as periods are so written. Superscript letters in abbreviations or contractions have been brought down, but a period is supplied only if the last letter of the abbreviation is not the last letter of the word abbreviated. In all other cases, periods, apostrophes, dashes, and other forms of punctuation have been left as Webster and his contemporaries used them. The ampersand, far more frequently used than the spelled out "and," has been retained, but diacritical marks over contractions have been omitted even where the contraction itself is retained.

Canceled words or passages that are obvious slips, immediately corrected, have been left out altogether; those which show some change of thought or attitude or have stylistic or psychological implications have been included between angled brackets. Interlineations by the author have been incorporated into the text, but marginal passages, again if by the author, have been treated as postscripts and placed below the signature.

In order to keep explanatory footnotes to a minimum, general notes have been interspersed from time to time with the letters that constitute the text of the volume. These serve to indicate what Webster was doing at a particular time or to explain a sequence of events that may help to clarify subsequent correspondence. Footnotes are used to identify persons, places, events, situations, problems, or other matters that help to understand the context of a particular reference.

Individuals are identified only once, generally the first time they are mentioned. For the convenience of the reader who may have missed this first reference, the appropriate index entry is printed in bold face type. Well-known individuals—those in the *Dictionary of American Biography* or the *Biographical Directory of the American Congress*—have not been identified at all unless the context seems to require it. For those in the DAB the index entry is marked with an asterisk, and with a dagger for those in the BDAC. The extent of footnoting has been reduced by adding given names and initials in square brackets where text references are to surnames only.

Immediately following each document is an unnumbered note indicating the provenance of the document and if appropriate, giving some information about the writer or recipient. Symbols used in these provenance notes are the standard descriptive symbols and the location symbols developed by the Union Catalog Division of the Library of Congress. Those appearing in the present volume have been listed under Abbreviations and Symbols below.

Webster Chronology, 1835–1839

1835

January 21	Webster nominated by Massachusetts legislature for President of the United States.
February 16	Speaks in Senate on abuse of Executive patronage.
March 17–27	Visits Harrisburg, Lancaster, Philadelphia and other Pennsylvania cities electioneering.
May 20	Democratic national convention nominates Van Buren for President and Richard M. Johnson of Kentucky for Vice President.
May 28	Whig rally in Faneuil Hall unanimously endorses DW's nomination for President.
July 2	Suggests that General Harrison be toasted "on the 4th, in various places, as Whig candidate for Vice President."
July 6	Chief Justice John Marshall dies.
July 29	Abolitionist literature taken by a mob from the Charleston, S.C., Post Office and publicly burned.
September 14	Contracts with John Taylor, Jr., to manage The Elms, Franklin, N.H.
October 21	William Lloyd Garrison, abolitionist editor, attacked by Boston mob.
November 28	States views on Masonry in cautiously worded reply to enquiry from Pennsylvania Antimasons.
December 17	Pennsylvania Antimasons nominate Harrison for President, Francis Granger for Vice President, ending DW's hopes.

1836

January 18	President Jackson calls for nonimportation against France, increased naval appropriation.
January 27	British offer mediation in dispute with France.
February 27	Withdraws from Presidential contest.
March 2	Texas declares independence.
March 6	Massacre at the Alamo spurs Texas revolution.
March 15	Roger B. Taney of Maryland confirmed as Chief Justice.
March–April	Begins heavy speculation in western lands.
May	Joins with Thomas Handasyd Perkins for land speculation through agents.
May 26	"Gag Rule" adopted by House of Representatives.
June	Invests in Winnebago City, Wisconsin, a "paper" town.
June 28	James Madison dies.
July 11	Jackson issues Specie Circular, requiring land offices to accept only gold, silver, or notes of specie-paying banks in payment for public lands.
July 16	Webster invests in Gibraltar and Flat Rock Company near Detroit.
July 18	Makes major investment in land near Peru, La Salle County, Illinois.
October 22	Sam Houston chosen first President of Republic of Texas.
November 27	Daniel Fletcher Webster marries Caroline White.
December 7	Final returns give Van Buren a sweeping electoral victory over Webster, White, and Harrison.

1837

January 23	Chosen a director of the Ellsworth (Maine) Land and Lumber Company.

January 24–27	Argued before the Supreme Court for the Appellants in Charles River Bridge case, decided against his client February 14.
February 13	Invests approximately $60,000 in Rock Island City, Illinois, lands.
February 21	Initiated speculation in lands of the Clamorgan Grant in Arkansas and Missouri; named a director of the Clamorgan Land Association.
March 4	Van Buren inaugurated.
March 5	The United States recognizes the Republic of Texas.
March 15	Webster states his political platform in a speech at Niblo's Garden, New York City.
May 10	New York banks suspend specie payments, precipitating the Panic of 1837.
May 15	Van Buren calls a special session of Congress to deal with the financial crisis.
May-July	Webster makes his second western tour, visiting Cincinnati, Louisville, St. Louis, Chicago, Detroit, and Toledo among other cities.
September 4	Congress meets in special session.
September 18	In a speech supporting the Subtreasury, Calhoun rejoins the Democratic Party, destroying the Whig coalition and giving Van Buren control of Congress.
September	Samuel F. B. Morse files for a patent on the magnetic telegraph.
November 7	Abolitionist editor Elijah Lovejoy killed by a mob in Alton, Illinois.
December 29	The *Caroline*, American-owned vessel supplying Canadian rebels, burned at her Buffalo pier by Canadian officials; an American citizen killed.

1838

January 26	Webster represents Massachusetts before the Supreme Court in boundary dispute with Rhode Island.

February 24	Representative Jonathan Cilley of Maine killed in a duel with Representative William Graves of Kentucky.
March 12	Webster delivers major speech against the Sub-treasury.
October 12	Texas withdraws request for annexation.

1839

January 17	Webster reelected to U. S. Senate.
February 9	Argues before Supreme Court for appellants in *Bank of the United States* v. *Primrose*; decided March 9 for DW's client.
February 12– March 25	Controversy between Maine and New Brunswick, known as the "Aroostook War," makes northeast boundary settlement imperative.
May 18– December 29	Webster visits England and the Continent.
May?	Publication of *American Slavery as it Is*, by Theodore Dwight Weld—most influential of all antislavery tracts.
June 17	Webster and party attend Royal Ball at Buckingham Palace and are presented to Queen Victoria.
July 18	Speaks at Oxford before Royal Agricultural Society of England.
August 5	Webster and party dine with the Queen, whom DW finds to be "intelligent and agreeable."
August 25	The *Amistad*, a Spanish vessel manned by mutinied slaves, taken into custody on Long Island.
September 24	Julia Webster marries Samuel Appleton Appleton in London.
October 16	Advises Baring Brothers that the American States have "legal and constitutional power to contract loans at home and abroad."
December 4–7	Whig National Convention nominates Harrison and Tyler.

Abbreviations and Symbols

In	Indiana State Library, Indianapolis
MAJ	Jones Library, Amherst, Mass.
MB	Boston Public Library
MBAt	Boston Athenaeum
MBBA	Boston Bar Association
MBBS	Bostonian Society
MBU	Boston University
MBevHi	Beverly Historical Society, Beverly, Mass.
MDeeP	Pocumtuck Valley Memorial Association, Deerfield, Mass.
MDuHi	Duxbury Rural and Historical Society, Duxbury, Mass.
MH	Harvard University
MH-H	Harvard University, Houghton Library
MHaDP	Porter-Phelps-Huntington Foundation, Hadley, Mass.
MHi	Massachusetts Historical Society, Boston, Mass.
MLexHi	Lexington Historical Society, Lexington, Mass.
MMarsW	Historic Winslow House, Marshfield, Mass.
MNS	Smith College
MSaE	Essex Institute, Salem, Mass.
MWA	American Antiquarian Society, Worcester, Mass.
MWalB	Brandeis University
MdBP	Enoch Pratt Free Library, George Peabody Branch, Baltimore, Md.
MdHi	Maryland Historical Society, Baltimore
MeB	Bowdoin College
MeEL	William Fogg Memorial Library, Eliot, Me.
MeHi	Maine Historical Society, Portland
MiD-B	Detroit Public Library, Burton Historical Collection
MiU-C	University of Michigan, William L. Clements Library
MnHI	Minnesota Historical Society, St. Paul
MnM	Minneapolis Public Library
MoSW	Washington University, St. Louis, Mo.
N	New York State Library, Albany
NBLiHi	Long Island Historical Society, Brooklyn, N.Y.
NBuHi	Buffalo and Erie County Historical Society
NCanHi	Ontario County Historical Society, Canandaigua, N.Y.
NHi	New-York Historical Society, New York City
NIC	Cornell University
NN	New York Public Library
NNC	Columbia University
NNPM	Pierpont Morgan Library, New York City
NNU	New York University
NNU-F	New York University, Fales Collection

NNebgWM	Washington's Headquarters Museum, Newburgh, N.Y.
NRU	University of Rochester
NSyU	Syracuse University
NcD	Duke University
NcU	University of North Carolina, Chapel Hill
NeAA	Gemeente Archief van Amsterdam, Amsterdam, The Netherlands
NhD	Dartmouth College
NhExP	Phillips Exeter Academy, Exeter, N.H.
NhFr	Franklin Public Library, Franklin, N.H.
NhHi	New Hampshire Historical Society, Concord
NjHi	New Jersey Historical Society, Newark
NjMoHP	Morristown National Historical Park, Morristown, N.J.
NjP	Princeton University
OCHP	Cincinnati Historical Society
OT	Toledo-Lucas County Public Library, Toledo, Ohio
PBL	Lehigh University
PCarlD	Dickinson College
PErHi	Erie County Historical Society, Erie, Pa.
PHi	Historical Society of Pennsylvania, Philadelphia
PLF	Franklin and Marshall College
PMedS	Delaware County Institute of Science, Media, Pa.
PP	Free Library of Philadelphia
PPiHi	Historical Society of Western Pennsylvania, Pittsburgh
PPAmP	American Philosophical Society, Philadelphia
PPL	Library Company of Philadelphia
RNHi	Newport Historical Society, Newport, R.I.
ScCleU	Clemson University
ScHi	South Carolina Historical Society, Charleston
T	Tennessee State Library and Archives, Nashville
TxU	University of Texas
UkBelQU	Queen's University of Belfast
UkENL	National Library of Scotland, Edinburgh
UkLiU	University of Liverpool
UkWC-A	Windsor Castle, Royal Archives
ViU	University of Virginia
WGrNM	Neville Public Museum, Green Bay, Wis.
WHi	State Historical Society of Wisconsin, Madison
WaU	University of Washington, Seattle

SHORT TITLES

Correspondence	Charles M. Wiltse and Harold D. Moser, eds., *The Papers of Daniel Webster, Correspondence*, vols. 1, 2; Wiltse and David G. Allen, eds., vol. 3 (Hanover, 1974, 1976, 1977).
Curtis	George Ticknor Curtis, *Life of Daniel Webster* (2 vols., New York, 1870).
Fuess, *Cushing*	Claude Moore Fuess, *The Life of Caleb Cushing* (2 vols., New York, 1923).
McGrane, *Correspondence of Nicholas Biddle*	Reginald C. McGrane, ed., *The Correspondence of Nicholas Biddle dealing with National Affairs, 1807–1844* (Boston and New York, 1919).
Mason, *Memoir and Correspondence*	Robert Means Mason and G. S. Hilliard, eds., *Memoir and Correspondence of Jeremiah Mason* (Cambridge, Mass., 1873).
MHi Proc.	*Proceedings of the Massachusetts Historical Society.*
mDW	Microfilm Edition of the Papers of Daniel Webster (Ann Arbor, 1971). References followed by frame numbers.
mDWs	Microfilm Edition of the Papers of Daniel Webster, Supplementary Reel.
PC	Fletcher Webster, ed., *The Private Correspondence of Daniel Webster* (2 vols., Boston, 1856).
Speeches and Forensic Arguments	Daniel Webster, *Speeches and Forensic Arguments* (3 vols., Boston, 1830, 1835, 1843).
Van Tyne	Claude H. Van Tyne, ed., *The Letters of Daniel Webster* (New York, 1902).
W & S	James W. McIntyre, ed., *The Writings and Speeches of Daniel Webster* (National Edition, 18 vols., New York, 1903).

SERIES ONE: CORRESPONDENCE

VOLUME FOUR: 1835–1839

The Papers, 1835–1839

TO ISRAEL WEBSTER KELLY

Washington Jan. 1. 1835

My Dear Sir,

I recd yours of the 22d, not until yesterday. I wrote you, from Baltimore, about the 26th which I hope you received.[1] I trust you are well assured of my sympathy with you, for the loss of your son, & the illness of so many others of your family. It is a great consolation to know that William died with an untroubled & tranquil mind.[2] I fervently pray that the rest of your children may be soon restored to the enjoyment of perfect health.

I now enclose for Mr. [Benjamin] Shaw three notes of $500 each, & one check for $168.00.[3]

You will of course see the business done, as it ought to be. I should prefer to have the whole of the land; but if the part belonging to Mr [Samuel] Quimby[4] is not to be had, at present, then you must take the rest, & make an indorsement on the notes, as you propose.

I will thank you to attend to this, as soon as may be, & let me know the result.

If Mr Shaw *asks* for a mortgage, or for an earlier day of payment, he may have both or either. I should like to have the bargain *closed* & *finished*. If he wants money, instead of the check, you must get it for him of Mr [William A.] Kent.[5]

Let me hear from you, on receipt of this.

We are all well, & Mrs W. & Julia desire their kindest regards.[6]

Danl. Webster

ALS. NhHi. Excerpt published in Van Tyne, p. 622. Kelly (1778–1857), sheriff of Hillsborough County, New Hampshire, judge of the Court of Sessions, was Webster's brother-in-law. In 1801, he married Rebecca, Grace Fletcher Webster's sister.

1. Neither letter found.

2. Kelly's son, William, had died December 27, 1834, at the age of twenty-two.

3. Shaw (1791–1846), a resident of Salisbury, New Hampshire, from whom Webster had bought land. Notes and check not found.

4. Quimby (1789–1878?), a blacksmith in Franklin, New Hampshire.

5. Kent (1765–1840), a Concord, New Hampshire, merchant and banker. Webster was purchasing property adjacent to The Elms in Franklin. See Deed Book, 39: 498; 41: 330; 43: 13, Office of the Register of Deeds, Merrimack County, Concord, New Hampshire, mDWs.

6. Caroline Le Roy (1797–1882),

whom Webster had married on December 12, 1829; and Julia (1818– 1848), Webster's daughter by his first marriage.

As the newly fledged Whig party prepared to contest its first presidential election, its leaders found themselves as much at odds as the disparate elements that composed the party had been before a common distaste for Andrew Jackson's use of executive power had driven them to unite. Before the end of 1834 the potential candidates were in the field, on their own initiative or by the promotion of their "friends"; but there were too many of them. In addition to Webster, who was formally nominated by the Massachusetts legislature on January 21, 1835, there were Henry Clay, now seeking to represent his third party in a dozen years; Justice John McLean of Ohio, another hardy perennial in presidential politics; Senator Hugh Lawson White of Tennessee, once friend and supporter of Jackson; and General William Henry Harrison, Ohio-based scion of an old Virginia family, who shared with Jackson the distinction of military success in the War of 1812. Among these, not surprisingly, a party loosely compounded of National Republicans, old Federalists, States Rights Democrats, and Anti-Masons could make no choice.

Webster's correspondence through 1835, when it touched upon presidential politics at all, was primarily concerned with unsuccessful efforts to broaden the basis of his support. Other Whig contenders did little better. By the end of the year Clay and McLean had been forced from the field and party strategists prepared to oppose Martin Van Buren with three regional candidates—Webster, Harrison, and White—in hopes of throwing the election into the House of Representatives. See Correspondence, *3: 360, 379–380.*

TO JEREMIAH MASON

Washington, January 1, 1835.

Dear Sir:

Whether it is or will be best for Massachusetts to act at all on the subject of a nomination, is a question which I leave entirely to the judgment of others. I cannot say that I have any personal wishes about it, either one way or the other. A nomination by Massachusetts would certainly be one of the highest proofs of regard which any citizen can receive. As such, I should most undoubtedly esteem it. But, in the present condition of things, and with the prospects which are before us, a nomination is a questionable thing to one who is more desirous of preserving what little reputation he has than anxious to grasp at further distinction. I have made up my mind, however, to be passive, and shall be satisfied with any result.

But I have a clear opinion on one point; and, as I promised you to communicate my sentiments freely, I will state that opinion frankly. It is, that if Massachusetts is to act at all, *the time has come*. I think the proceeding, if one is to be had, should be one of the first objects of attention when the Legislature assembles. In Ohio, Mr. [John] McLean is already nominated, I presume, according to late accounts.[1] Many Whigs, who do not prefer him, fall into the measure (in Ohio) simply because they have no other choice. It is expected, or at least hoped, that New Jersey will second this nomination. Movements are in preparation in other places; but, as far as I know, nothing is yet proposed anywhere in which there could be a general union, or in which Massachusetts would be likely to agree.

If a resolution to make a movement in Massachusetts should be adopted, not only should the thing itself be done as soon as practicable, but in the mean time notice of the intention should be given to friends in the neighboring States, and especially in New York, that they may prepare for it. Let us know *here* the moment any thing is determined on.

It looks at present as if Mr. [Henry] Clay would not do or say any thing. He declares himself in nobody's way; but still it is evident that his particular friends are not prepared to act heartily and efficiently for anybody else.[2]

Be sure to *burn* this letter, and assure yourself also that I write such letters to nobody else. Your truly,   D. Webster.

The committee of the House of Representatives will not report in conformity to the recommendation of the message on French affairs. Probably no report will be made, till further intelligence from France.[3]

Text from Curtis, 1: 503. Original not found.

1. On Webster's candidacy in Massachusetts in late 1834, see *Correspondence*, 3: 360, 379–380. McLean had received the Ohio nomination in December 1834, but withdrew from the canvass on August 31, 1835. Francis P. Weisenburger, *The Life of John McLean: A Politician on the United States Supreme Court* (Columbus, 1937), pp. 91–93.

2. Clay's withdrawal from the race came on December 26, 1835. Glyndon G. Van Deusen, *The Life of Henry Clay* (Boston, 1937), p. 298.

3. In his sixth Annual Message to Congress on December 1, 1834, Jackson had urged Congress to pass laws authorizing seizure of French property in reprisal for France's failure to appropriate the funds necessary to fulfill the Indemnity Treaty of July 4, 1831. Contrary to Webster's prediction, the Committee on Foreign Relations of both the House and the Senate issued reports, and the House report sustained Jackson's recommendation. But neither house passed legislation authorizing reprisals. James D. Richardson, *A Compilation of the Messages and Papers of the Presidents, 1789–1897* (10 vols.; Washington, 1900), 3: 100–107; *Senate Documents*, 23d Cong., 2d sess., Serial 268, Document No. 40; *Reports of Committees*, 23d Cong., 2d sess., Serial 276, Report No. 133.

*The French Spoliations Commission, created by Congress in 1831 to set-
tle claims against France arising after 1800, was still sitting when Webster championed in the Senate the appropriation of $5,000,000 to settle
claims arising before 1800. Democratic senators promptly charged that
Webster and James H. Causten, agent of the Baltimore Life Insurance
Company and lobbyist for many of the claimants, were themselves speculating in the claims. Though vigorously denied, rumor persisted and
may have influenced the House to set aside the pending appropriation
after it had passed the Senate. Webster no doubt anticipated a share of
the business. Before the commission on French spoliations, which
sat from 1832 to 1836 and for which the French Assembly granted 25
million francs under the reparations treaty, he represented claims
amounting to more than $108,000, on which he received an average
commission of 5 percent. Something less than a quarter of these claims
were probably speculative ventures. (See* Correspondence, *3: 377–378;*
Congressional Globe, *23d Cong., 2d sess., pp. 45, 190;* House Journal,
23d Cong., 2d sess., Serial 270, p. 425.)

FROM JAMES H. CAUSTEN

Washington Jany 1. 1835

Dr Sir,

In the recent discussions, in the Senate, on the Bill for the relief of
the sufferers by French spoliations prior to Sep 30. 1800, some opposition has been manifested on the supposed ground that the parties interested have employed an agent for a "moiety" to prosecute the claims,
and that they are in the hands of speculators but set forth in the names
of Widows and orphans, in order to profit by the sympathy of Congress
&c.[1]

Being the sole agent of the claimants for the last twelve years, it is
impossible that I should be insensible to these unfounded charges, or
unfaithful to my duty by not offering a prompt and distinct denial of
them. In preferring this denial to you, as chairman of the Committee
having the Bill in charge, I have sought for the proper channel, but in
any event I rely on your kind indulgence.

For your information I take the occasion to say, that my sole Commission is only one half the usual compensation for the most plain and
ordinary prompt claims—it is two and a half percent, and that con-
tingent.

In some three or four instances, I was applied to by obscure and im-
poverished individuals to find purchasers for small claims, which were
derivitive as heirs, and whose wants pressed heavily. My answer was
uniform—"I know of no purchasers, and would not point them out if I

knew such—do not sell your claim, because it would yield little for your relief, and because Congress will eventually do you justice—but I cannot aid you in that shape, as such an act would (justly or otherwise) materially impair the inducement which happily exists to indemnify the claimants."

Subsequently, a remark in the House of Representatives gave rise to an impression that the claimants, or some of them, were such on speculation. I forthwith addressed a circular letter to the claimants in all parts of the United States, setting forth that impression, and requiring the fact: by the answers, extending to some hundreds, I found not a single case of sale or purchase, but some assignments in Bankrupt and other analogous cases.

Perhaps there has been few subjects before Congress in which Widows and orphans are so generally the complainants; the mere lapse of time and course of nature has placed them in the situation they are now found without any act or effort of their own. But such persons do not make themselves conspicuous; nor in this case have they been put forward, either properly or improperly, since few of them are seen upon the Memorials; and all the petitions and arguments offered, refer to the naked justice of the claim: And, for the truth of this assertion, I can safely appeal to the files of the Senate and to the recollection of every senator with whom I have had intercourse.

I give you this information on the responsibility of my name, to be used in any manner you may deem proper.

I may be permitted to add, that no Counsel, auxiliary, or aid of any kind has been employed or contemplated—the claimants have selected for their agent a plain and unpretending citizen (not even a Lawyer), with the only qualification of patiently enduring protracted labor. His high respect for the body with whom his duty calls him to act, added to self respect, has marked the exercise of his functions with all the studied delicacy of which he is capable.

I am, dear Sir, with great respect, Your Obedient Servant [2]

James H. Causten

ALS copy (by Causten). H. Bartholomew Cox, Oxon Hill, Maryland.

1. Causten was specifically referring to Isaac Hill's comments in the Senate on December 23, 1834. (*Congressional Globe*, 23d Cong., 2d sess., p. 68.)

2. Causten explained this second effort to deny the charge of speculation in his endorsement on the letter:

"Note. It was again and again hinted on the floor of the Senate (and probably well founded) that Mr. Webster had himself made speculation in these claims, and in consequence thereof he requested of me a letter to counteract such report. I wrote the letter to him of Jany 1, 1835 (copy enclosed herein) which he returned with this letter, in which he enclosed the draft (A) of a modified letter for me to copy and sign—as I did, and forwarded it to him. The draft A is in his hand writing.

"It will be seen that my letter of Jany 1/35 had a two fold object, to shield Mr. Webster and to shield myself—but his draft A is made to shield himself only, leaving myself and the cause without notice. It was a selfish and heartless act on his part—and I take no credit to myself for yielding to the modification. It was not my judgement, but sound policy that thus yielded. JHC"

TO [JAMES H. CAUSTEN], WITH ENCLOSURE

[c. January 1, 1835]

Dr Sir

Yr letter is too long. We want something like the enclosed.

AL. H. Bartholomew Cox, Oxon Hill, Maryland.

ENCLOSURE: FROM JAMES H. CAUSTEN (IN WEBSTER'S HAND)

A

I see, with much regret, that an objection is made to the claims for French Spoliations before 1800, on the supposition that a large portion of these claims have been purchased up, & are holden by Speculators. This is certainly a great mistake. My means of information are such, that I think I cannot be misled on this subject; & I assure you I am fully convinced that the idea of extensive speculation in these claims is founded in error. I have known no transfers, except in the ordinary settlement of estates, or by insolvents, to pay or secure debts; & am perfectly sure that a vast majority of the whole still remains in the hands of the original holders, their heirs & representatives.

If you think it would be useful, you may communicate this to the members of the Com[mitt]ee or others. Yours &c.

AL draft. NhD.

FROM CALEB CUSHING

Newbury Port, Jan. 3rd 1835.

My dear sir:

The tempestuous weather detained me at New York three days, and somewhat interfered with my plans of usefulness in Boston; as I had professional engagements requiring me to be here today and Monday. But I shall return to Boston on Tuesday.

Meanwhile, upon my own reflection and upon conversation with such gentlemen of our friends as I have seen, I am satisfied that if the Legislature will cordially make a nomination, there is a great *net balance* of argument in favor of its being done. And that if proposed, it can be carried, seems to be certain. The point now is, to have it done handsomely and con amore.

The first point to be touched is the press. The Atlas has got the lead by its superior decision and firmness, and I doubt not will keep it.[1] I have conferred with Mr [Joseph T.] B[uckingham] of the Courier, and he is also sure. The letter from Washington signed 'Moth' expresses *his personal* sentiments.[2] He is to publish on Tuesday an editorial article written by me;[3] and to follow it up if occasion prompts; so as to pledge the Courier to a nomination. I wrote a letter from Washington to Mr [Joseph T.] A[dams] of the Centinel;[4] but did not meet him yesterday, although I mean to have a conference with him on Tuesday. I have no intimate acquaintance with the conductors of the Gazette;[5] and could not advantageously interfere in that quarter. I will also confer with the editors in this District in person or by letters.

Mr Buckingham, in the course of our interview, threw in the remark that he had not heard from you this session, in a manner of quasi-complaint, although good humoredly enough.

There is extreme diversity of wish & opinion in the matter of Senator in the place of Mr [Nathaniel] Silsbee. Mr [John Quincy] Adams, Mr E[dward] Everett, Mr [Isaac Chapman] Bates, Mr [Levi] Lincoln, Gov. [John] Davis, each have warm supporters. The opinion is current among well informed persons that Gov. Davis would prefer going into the Senate to remaining where he is. I have only one predominant wish in reference to the whole question, and that is to see Mr Everett either stably fixed in the Senate for six years, or placed in the Governor's chair.

I shall write to you again in a few days, when the Legislature will be together, and I shall gather a more distinct knowledge of the purposes of gentlemen, than it is possible to do at present; expecting also by Tuesday or Wednesday to hear from Mr Everett on the subject of addressing the delegation in Congress. Very respectfully & faithfully yours &c

C. Cushing

ALS. DLC. Published in Fuess, *Cushing*, 1: 168–169.
   1. On December 17, 1834, the *Boston Atlas* endorsed Webster for the Presidency. See *Correspondence*, 3: 379–381.
   2. For the letter of "Moth," see

Boston Courier, January 1, 1835.
   3. Cushing's editorial, entitled "Virginia Whigism," appeared in the *Boston Courier*, January 6, 1835.
   4. Adams (1796–1878) was editor of the *Columbian Centinel*.
   5. W. W. Clapp.

TO CHARLES HENRY THOMAS

Washington
Jan. 5. 1835

Dear Henry,

I have recd your letter of Decr. 31,[1] giving an account of the high tide & storm, & of the breaking away of the Dyke. I regret the occurrence;

but it is no occasion for repining or complaint. It has happened, that in a course of high tides, and at the moment of a violent East wind, the sea has invaded the land, with such violence as to overcome the barriers which man had erected against its encroachments—very well. This is an event, beyond human foresight, or, at least, beyond the power of human prevention; & is therefore no cause of remorse, although it may occasion regret. No wise man supposes, that the agencies of nature, or the power of physical causes, will fail to have their full effect & operation, always. If high tides, & a strong wind from the sea, concur, & cooperate, the land will be, to some extent, unusually overflowed; & both the just & the unjust must bear alike the consequences. In all this, there is nothing wrong, nothing to complain of, nothing to repine at. Whatsoever Providence orders, is right; and the violent convulsions & agitations of the elements, are but processes, in the general administration of Providence. The winds, the sea, the clouds, commit no mistake. If our new barn (if I may illustrate sentiment by so coarse an example) were to be blown away by the winds, (like one of its predecessors) or burnt up, by lightning, it would not cause me a moment's pain. Nothing would remain, but to rebuild it. But if it were to be burnt, thro' the carelessness of a careless man, I should, I confess, be angry enough—*almost*—to wish that he, himself, had been a *little scorched*, in the same fire. Therefore, My Dear Henry, go to work—repair, or rebuild, the dyke. If any of the trees are killed, let them die, & set out others. If the English meadow be injured, remedy the injury, as best you may; and guard, as well as you can, against future casualties. The sea, tho the instrument of Providence, is not Providence. You may, therefore, war against it, without irreverence; & if you can so far shut it out, restrain it, & get the mastery of it, as to be able to say that hitherto it shall come, but no farther, there is no impiety in so saying. Give the Atlantic, then, to understand, that hereafter you do not expect to see its unwelcome & officious waves, overflowing our meadow, interfering with our belt, & spoiling our orchard. Yrs truly   Danl Webster

ALS. NhD. Published in Gershom Bradford, "The Unknown Webster," *Old-Time New England*, 44 (Fall 1953): 59–60. Charles Henry Thomas (1807–1894) was the son of John Thomas (1764–1837), from whom Webster purchased the Marshfield farm. From 1832 until his death, Webster relied upon Henry to manage the property.

1. Not found.

FROM ABBOTT LAWRENCE

Boston, January 5, 1835.

My Dear Sir:

I wish I could see you for ten minutes, that I might say to you many things that cannot be written. Yet, I cannot omit the present time to say that I have been called upon within the last few days by many prominent individuals (your particular friends), who would be glad to know your wishes in relation to the future.

There is a strong disposition to make a nomination early, by a Legislative caucus, of President of the United States. This will take place beyond a doubt, and it is to be hoped other States may follow in the course of the winter. Supposing such an event to take place, is it your intention to resign your seat in the Senate? If you have not made up your mind on this point, your friends here hope you will not do so without very mature deliberation, as your services in the Senate appear to be almost indispensable during this and the next session of Congress. I know full well that your sacrifices have been great, and I am the last individual to require of you a continuance of them if, in your judgment, your interests are to be promoted by retirement; at present I am not clear upon this point. There is hardly any thing, I believe, that your friends will not be ready to do in either case, whether you remain or whether you retire. I ask now, in candor and frankness, and in perfect confidence, as I have consulted with but one individual, in case your sacrifices *professionally* can be made more *reasonable*,[1] whether you do not think it will be best, all things considered, to remain in your present situation till we see how matters stand a year hence, and then take such a course as circumstances may make expedient. I do not see that it is incumbent on you to resign in consequence of your nomination; perhaps, however, I may not see the whole ground. Others, I find, have the same opinion.

You have doubtless marked out a course of action for yourself. I would not certainly undertake to divert you from it, as you have much more practical wisdom upon these matters than myself. I esteem the point at which you have arrived. however, one of vast moment to the country as well as to yourself, and feel an indescribable interest, that nothing should be done by which yourself or your friends shall hereafter feel that a mistake was made at this particular period of your political life.

If you can do yourself politically more good by retirement, you can promote the good of the country by the same course. I leave the subject with a hope that, whatever your decision may be, it will be one which will lead to a life devoted to the public interest. This should be your *destiny*, and your friends ought in justice to do for you all that may be required.

I remain, dear sir, Truly yours,   A. L.

Text from Curtis, 1: 503–504. Original not found.

1. Whether Webster's friends and supporters raised a fund for him about this time has not been determined. If they did so, it was probably

not the first time, nor would it be the last. There is, for example, a draft of a letter from Edward Everett to Thomas Wren Ward, dated February 18, 1834—a time when Webster seemed the last bulwark of the conservative financial community against the expropriations of the Jacksonians—proposing just such a fund. It was to be, according to Everett, "not less than one hundred thousand dollars," and its purpose was to be "first & foremost to release Mr W. from the necessity of employing in the drudgery of the Courts that time, which is all wanted for the public service, & secondly to sustain an independent press & circulate information & truth among the people." Ward Papers, MHi.

TO EDWARD EVERETT

[January 7, 1835]

Dear Sir—

I could not get these ready, last Eve'. I now send three copies, in the *plural*—thinking it might perhaps be well for Mr [John] Reed & Mr [Levi] Lincoln to sign with you.[1]

These might go to "Peter Hitchcock, Speaker of the Senate," & Jno. M. Creed,[2] Speaker of the House of Representatives, of the Legislature of Ohio at Columbus—& to Bellamy Storer, Cincinnati.

I will have some singular ones ready, by Eve'.

If your fingers are not worn out, it would be well to write to Mr [Elihu] Chauncey,[3] intimating the propriety & necessity of two things.

1. To inform his friends at Harrisburg of what may be expected soon, & to admonish them to be on the alert.
2. To see if he cannot move the Pa. *press*, more or less, to be breaking ground.

Yrs—D.W.

If you should not be engaged, suppose we spend an hour together, this Eve, on the subject of the Resolutions.[4]

ALS. MHi.

1. The material referred to concerned John McLean's nomination for the Presidency and involved an attempt to influence Ohio Whigs. See Entry of January 7, 1835, Edward Everett Diary (Reel 36), Everett Papers, MHi (Microfilm).

2. Creed, speaker pro tempore of the Ohio House of Representatives, had at first refused to endorse McLean, contending that Ohio should postpone a nomination until southern states had settled upon someone who could win the support of former Jacksonians. But in December 1834, he had finally agreed to McLean's nomination.

3. Chauncey (1779–1847; Yale 1796) was an influential Philadelphia lawyer and financier.

4. The resolutions were probably those to be presented to the Whig caucus of Massachusetts legislators nominating Webster for the Presidency.

FROM JEREMIAH MASON

Boston, January 8, 1835.

Dear Sir,

The Legislature was organized yesterday. A nomination will be made within a few days, unless some unforeseen obstacle comes in the way. I have seen Governor [John] Davis, whose feelings and opinions are, as always, entirely right. Mr. [Nathan] Hale, and perhaps, some others, who are rightly inclined, but habitually slow in action, seem desirous of having a more formal communication with the Massachusetts Representatives, at Washington, on the subject. Letters have been sent to Washington, but, I think, answers will not be waited for. One difficulty suggested against the movement is, that a nomination would cause your resignation of your seat in the Senate, at the end of the present session. This is stated vaguely, on the authority of a supposed intimation made by you. This, some of your friends have denied. I do not think that a nomination would create any necessity for a resignation. Indeed, I think a resignation of your place in the Senate, for this cause, would be considered as false delicacy. In this I know many of your best and soundest friends concur. It would cause universal regret. At all events, it seems to me there is no necessity for making such a determination at this time. If the election is to be finally determined in the House of Representatives, the presence of a candidate at Washington, without exerting any improper influence, will be advantageous.

As to personal considerations for your resignation, I hope arrangements can be made to counteract their influence. Some individuals here, who have a right to speak with authority, say such arrangements can and shall be made.[1] Truly yours,   J. Mason.

Text from Mason, *Memoir and Correspondence*, p. 354. Original not found.

1. See above, Abbott Lawrence to DW, January 5, 1835.

FROM CALEB CUSHING

Boston Jan. 9. 1835

My dear sir:

It gives me great pleasure to find that the disposition to make an early nomination gains ground among the members of the Legislature; and I cannot doubt that it will be done cordially and spiritedly. This I gather from the representations & opinions of many intelligent members.

I conversed wth Mr Abbott Lawrence on Tuesday, and discovered that he did not mean to be understood, as a general expression in his letter to Mr [Theophilus] P[arsons] implied, that is, as averse to a nomination; he is in favor of its being made.

From all quarters, also, I hear of a strong purpose to elect Gov. [John] Davis to supply Mr [Nathaniel] Silsbee's place. And in that event, it is admitted that no gentleman has a better chance to succeed Gov. Davis than Mr E. Everett. At the westward, however, they talk considerably of Mr [Isaac Chapman] Bates. If, as you have sometimes intimated, you should resign your seat, that might lead the public mind to a different result as to the place of Governor.

But, as to this last thing, your quitting the Senate, I think, in the present state of public affairs, it would be unequivocally a national calamity; and I hope you will not do it, or express any formed intention to do it, without very full consideration of the for and against appertaining to the question.

I have not yet heard from Mr Everett as to obtaining some ac[coun]t of the State Delegation in Congress. Although I continue to think it desirable, yet I do not believe the want of it, or even a difference of opinion in the Delegation, will seriously impair the harmony of proceedings here. Yet still I hope the Delegation may be induced to act.

The press, I think, will do well; but some of the editors either have or profess to have doubting correspondents at W[ashington]. "Our doubts are traitors."

Ever & faithfully your ob. servt.   C. Cushing.

ALS. DLC. Published in Fuess, *Cushing*, 1 : 169–170.

FROM CALEB CUSHING

Boston Jan 16. 1835

Dear Sir:

There was a preliminary meeting of members of the Legislature this evening to consider the question of a nomination, at which it was determined to have a general meeting next Wednesday for that purpose. I understand the measure was opposed by only one gentleman; and *him* I was extremely sorry to find of an adverse opinion.

Although by common accord the serious discussion of who shall be Mr Silsbee's successor is deferred until after the nomination is disposed of, yet it continues of course to be a subject of speculation. And I think there is a growing disinclination to remove Gov. Davis, in the fear that it may unsettle our State politics, especially as the Antimasonic & Jackson parties manifest a willingness to vote for Gov. D., or at least to further his election, for the very purpose of making a clear field in Massachusetts. And concurrently with their views, I think the cause of Mr H[enry] Shaw is coming to be talked of somewhat familiarly. I regret this in so far as it may tend to postpone the return of Mr E. to office.

I am collecting materials for a magazine analysis & possibly pamphlet, on your speeches &c during & connected with the war.[1] Mr [Jeremiah] Mason has told me that there was a proceeding of yours in New Hampshire in reference to this matter, advantageous to be used; & this prompted me to ask you, at your leisure, to indicate to Mr [Richard] Fletcher or to me, where to find any particulars to my purpose.[2]

It has given me pleasure to hear today that Mr Clay has wisely resolved to give way, and to act, as alone he can honorably do, in concert with your friends. I sincerely hope the intelligence is sure.

I remain, very truly & respectfully Your ob sert   C. Cushing.

ALS. DLC. Published in Fuess, *Cushing*, 1: 170–171.

1. Cushing was most likely preparing his unsigned essay, "Mr. Webster," which appeared in the *New England Magazine*, 8 (March 1835): 220–228. Later in the year, Cushing used again the materials he had collected for the "Mr. Webster" article, this time responding to *Extracts from the Writings and Speeches of Daniel Webster, and from a Paper Sustained by his Endorsements, Called the Massachusetts Journal* (n.p., n.d.). In the *National Intelligencer*, December 2, 1835, Cushing presented the "truth" about Webster in the "recent war" and offered a point-by-point refutation of the "damaging" comments printed in the *Extracts* pamphlet. See Caleb Cushing to DW, December 2, 1835, and DW to Cushing, December 6, 1835, below.

2. Cushing was probably alluding to the document emanating from the Portsmouth Committee of Defence, a committee that Webster chaired. For that document, see *Correspondence*, 1: 169–170.

FROM HENRY WILLIS KINSMAN

Jany. 18/35

Dear Sir

I will give you a little chapter of the secret history of matters here. There are, as you are probably aware, among the whigs three parties, viz—Those who are more friendly to Mr. Clay as a candidate than to yourself; Those who prefer you & wish to make a nomination forthwith; and, Those, who, although you would be their first preference, yet wish to wait to take up the strongest whig candidate who may appear in the field. These are all honest, sincere whigs. There is, however, besides, a set of *waiters upon Providence* who at present hail from the whig party, but who are ready to attach themselves to any party in which they can become conspicuous; these last are generally opposed to you at heart, although they do not deem it prudent to say so openly, & they have occasioned us considerable embarrassment by their management & secret whisperings with the first & last mentioned portions of the Whig party. All the delay in our proceedings has arisen from this source. At the preliminary meeting on Friday evening, which I mentioned in my last,[1] your immediate nomination was advocated by T[heophilus] Parsons, F[ranklin] Dexter & Mr. N[athan] Hale & also by Mr. [John C.] Gray² & Mr. [Francis] Baylies. It was opposed by A[lexander] H. Everett, who said that your prospect was hopeless; that we, by nominating you should take a course fatal to the influence of the State, & perhaps ruinous to the cause; that unquestionably some more popular candidate would be taken up by the whigs, & we should then, being pledged to support you, & not being able to recede, be placed in a very embarrassing situation; he affected to doubt, notwithstanding his brother's letters were read, whether Mr. Clay had yet declined &c. &c. [Henry] Chapman of Green-field,³ also opposed an immediate nomination; he is, I think, a good whig, but his *bummp of self-esteem* is very strongly developped, as the Phrenologists would say; his ground was that Mr. Clay could not have declined—he said he had recently been at Washington, had frequently seen Mr. Clay, & conversed with him, & that that gentleman had not mentioned to him (Mr. Chapman) that he intended to decline being a candidate, he therefore could not believe it &c &c.

[David] Roberts of Salem,⁴ was also inclined to the opposition, he is also a good whig, but a very soft one, his whig principles are not yet burnt into him, & hardly any other principles, & he has withal such a desire to appear honest, fair & courteous, that he is almost willing to yield the very question in dispute to his adversary, for the sake of being called generous & candid. From this description you will perceive, that it was better for us that he should *begin* on the other side, as he did, & come over to us in a *candid, fair, courteous & gentlemanly manner*, as he also did. It was with a view to make these men operate in our favour by putting them into a conspicuous situation, that they were all, with Mr. [Henry] Shaw who professes to be favourable, put on the Commit-tee so that they cannot bolt, or get out of the traces, without being no-ticed, although I am apprehensive that this policy was carried too far. The Committee ought to have been so numerous, as to have given us a majority of assured friends. We hope, however, by keeping a vigilent eye upon their proceedings, that we shall be able to finish the business this week, and if there is any flinching, any hesitation on the part of the Committee, in calling the proposed meeting, it will be called never-theless by others.

In this state of things we were much troubled by the premature as-signment of a time for the election of a Senator, a movement which has every appearance of having been concerted.

Our present plan is, to have a meeting Tuesday or Wednesday Eve-ning, at which the President of the Senate is to be made Prest. & the

Speaker Vice Prest., & if every thing goes on according to present expectation you will hear by the last of this week the result. Yrs

H. W. Kinsman

ALS. NhHi. Published in Van Tyne, pp. 191–193. Kinsman (1803–1859; Dartmouth 1822), a native of Portland, Maine, had read law with Webster and succeeded Alexander Bliss as an associate in Webster's office. At this time he was a Boston delegate to the Massachusetts legislature. In 1837, he left Webster's office to move to Newburyport, where he subsequently represented that town in the state legislature. (Kinsman's dates were printed incorrectly in *Correspondence*, 2: 231.)

1. According to an entry in his letterbook, Kinsman wrote Webster on January 17. That letter has not been found. The *Columbian Centinel*, January 17, 1835, which copied a report of the proceedings Kinsman describes from the *Boston Advocate*, stated that the meeting occurred on Thursday evening, January 8.

2. Gray (1793–1881; Harvard 1811) was a Boston lawyer and long-time member of the Massachusetts legislature.

3. Chapman (?–1875) was a lawyer and member of the Massachusetts legislature from 1833 to 1837.

4. Roberts (1804–1879; Harvard 1824) was also a lawyer and member of the Massachusetts legislature.

TO JEREMIAH MASON

Jan. 22. 1835

Private

Dr Sir

I have recd yours of the 17th.[1] There has been some impatience here, in regard to proceedings in Boston, on account of the daily inquiries by friends in other quarters, as to what might be expected; but I presume things have gone on as fast as they well could.

Mr McLean's nomination appears to take but little. It is coldly recd, even in Ohio; so much so, indeed, that Genl [William Henry] Harrison's friends are holding meetings in that State, for the purpose of bringing *him* forward. Letters recd today, from Columbus & Cincinnati, ask urgently what is doing or to be done in Mass.

The *Schism* in the Jackson party proceeds. It appears [to] me, that nothing is likely to stop its progress.[2] If we *Whigs* had union & energy, we have now before us a prospect, no way discouraging.

You will have heard of a duel today, between Mr [Henry A.] Wise, of Va. & his predecessor Mr [Richard] Coke[, Jr.]. I hear the former is badly wounded.[3]

I am busy in the Court. Mr. [Roger Brooke] Taney is yet before us. *Probably* will not be confirmed; but that is not certain.[4]

Yrs truly   D Webster

ALS. DLC. Published in Curtis, 1: 506.

1. Not found.

2. Webster was probably referring to Hugh Lawson White's recent break with Jackson and to the Tennessee legislature's nomination of White for the Presidency.

3. The duel, in which neither was seriously wounded, had arisen out of the campaign.

4. On January 15, 1835, Jackson had nominated Taney to the Supreme Court, but the Senate voted, on March 3, with DW leading the opposition, to postpone the confirmation (see DW to Warren Dutton, January 30, 1835, below). Subsequent to Chief Justice John Marshall's death on July 6, 1835, Jackson renominated Taney, this time for Chief Justice, and on March 15, 1836, over Whig opposition, the Senate confirmed.

TO ABRAHAM G. STEVENS

Washington Jan. 24. '35

Dear Sir,

I have written to you & Mr [Israel W.] Kelley, heretofore, fully, in respect to the repairs of the House;[1] & I wish the repairs to go on, according to what I have before mentioned. I cannot consent that wood sheds, pig pens, & all other such things should remain attached to the dwelling house. I desire things to be placed on a more neat & snug establishment. It is not very inconvenient to go out doors, to feed the pigs, or bring the wood; on the other hand, it is slovenly & uncleanly to have such huge & dirty sheds connected with the house. You want a small wood house, & a small pig pen. These may be in the same building, if you please, placed at any convenient distance from the House. And distinct from both these, though as much hidden as may be by other buildings, must be the Privy.

All that belongs to the House, properly, must be painted, with the House. The Privy should be painted. The wood-house may be whitewashed, or left as the boards leave it. I wish the outhouse to be comfortable, but am utterly opposed to such great wooden buildings, going yearly to decay. Let the sashes, doors, &c be made this winter, & every thing got ready, as far as may be, to go thro' the work in the Spring, in the shortest time possible. I pray you to consider the plan of the repairs as settled, & go on & see it executed. As to the place, in which the out buildings ought to stand; if I am not at home in season to consult about it, I shall write you upon it.

Mrs Webster & Julia, as well myself, have good health at present. They desire to be remembered to your family. Yrs respectfully

Danl Webster

ALS. Carlos G. Wright, Riverside, R. I. Stevens (1778–1864) was for twelve years overseer on Webster's farm in Franklin, the Elms, which Webster had bought from Ezekiel Webster's heirs.

1. Letters not found.

In deep debt to Nicholas Biddle and the Bank of the United States, who were pressuring him for payment, James Watson Webb approached Webster in mid-January 1835 asking for financial assistance and offering in return strong support for Webster's candidacy in the New York Courier and Enquirer *(see Webb to DW, January 20, 1835, mDW 12235). Webster responded that he would do what he could for Webb if Webb could not raise money in any other way (see mDW 12241). As Webb reports below and in his letter of April 9, he was able in part to make arrangements through Roswell L.* Colt *(1779–1856), a merchant and banker in New York City, a director of the Savings Bank of Baltimore, and close friend of Webster. Whether Webster had approached Colt on Webb's behalf has not been determined, but the* Courier and Enquirer *was soon enthusiastically backing Webster. See the* New York Courier and Enquirer, *February 6, 9, 28, March 16, 18, April 11, 1835. For a discussion of Webb's financial difficulties and his support of Webster, see James L. Crouthamel,* James Watson Webb, A Biography *(Middletown, Conn., 1969), pp. 52–53, 60.*

FROM JAMES WATSON WEBB

Philadelphia January 25th. 1835

(*Confidential*)

My Dear Sir

I am in the rect of yours of the 22d,[1] which came to hand this morning, and as you may easily imagine, its contents are not very cheering. But I am not to be deterred by small obstacles. The object we have in view is one of too great magnitude, and too vitally important to the welfare of the Country. And withal, my feelings have become too warmly interested in its success to enable me to brook disappointment. I must abandon the plan of compromising my debts at *present*, and raise a sum barely sufficient to make such payments on the claims of two of my investors in New York as will induce them to look quietly on my course. The Bank of Mr [Roswell L.] Colt & his friends, will remain perfectly quiet and be pleased with my course in your favour.

I can raise in short time on my own paper in New York, subject to renewal, from 8 to 10,000 $ and you must induce some of your friends to loan me the same amt ($10,000) on my note for one year subject to renewal for one half at the expiration of that time. With these funds I can accomplish my object. This loan I'll consider a debt of *honor* and if they wish at any time within the year they may add $40,000 to it and receive a mortgage on the terms specified in my last. I think you will not meet with any difficulty in arranging this, and to make them doubly secure against loss I will, if they wish it, give them a second Mortgage on my farm which has cost me $7,500 more than it is mortgaged for, and which is worth $15,000 more than I gave for it. This proposition reduces the whole matter to a simple accommodation for $10,000 and in such a crisis, surely some one of your friends will not hesitate.

I have just had [Robert] Morris of the Pennsylvania Enquirer[2] with me. We have always acted in concert, & he has promised whenever I move to follow it up very closely and prompt some of the papers in the interior to unite with him. He is decidedly of opinion that no man except John McLean can do as well as you in this State, and says that your nomination by the Legislature of Massachusetts is well recd. & that every thing is ripe for action, and we should endeavor to get matters so far *advanced* before news of character calculated to produce war arrives from France, as to render it impossible for our friend from the West to take the field on the supposition that he may *then* succeed. He looks confidently to such a contingency as rendering his success certain.

It is impossible for me to get a Dollar more from the U.S. B[ank] and indeed I would not ask it when they now have a proposition before them to compromise the $18,000 which I owe them. But Biddle is very desirous that I should succeed in my object as *you* are decidedly his candidate. In the whole of this movement I am the only person who hazzards any thing, and when you lay it properly before any one of your friends I doubt not but the loan can be secured. I am almost prepared to say that I shall proceed whether I get the loan or not; but such a course would not be prudent, and might eventually destroy all my ability to serve either you or myself.

Please write me as soon as possible,[3] and do not I beg of you, decide that this proposition cannot be arranged for, without fully & clearly ascertaining the utter impossibility of doing so. In raising the 8. or $10,000 on my personal credit in New York, I undertake to perform *all* that it is in my power to accomplish, and for the rest must look elsewhere. Yours truly   W.

ALS. DLC.
1. See mDW 12241.
2. Morris (1809–1874) was the editor of the *Pennsylvania Inquirer* and later president of the Commonwealth Bank of Pennsylvania.
3. Webster's response, if he made one, has not been found.

FROM CHARLES PELHAM CURTIS

[January 26, 1835]

My dear Sir

Will you let your servant take the enclosed to Judge [Joseph] Story.[1]

You have before this, received the information of the proceedings of the Legislative caucus held here on 21st.; I wish I could have been entitled to join in a nomination from which I believe such glorious consequences may flow, but in my private sphere I contributed what I could to it as you will readily suppose, and it so happened that on the very day of the caucus, at 1 o'clock, a *knot* was found which I was told that I alone could *gnaw* off. Whether this was true or not, I gladly embraced the chance of aiding in the good work "unguibus et nostro" & the knot was removed.

(I do not state this as a foundation for any claims to office, for I have such a horror of the dependence of an officeholder that there is no place in the gift of the U States, that I would take—Amen.)

I hope Mrs W. is with you & enjoys good health—my wife feels a warm attachment to her, and if she knew I was writing would desire me to join her regards to mine for her kindness to us last Spring.

Send me a copy of Mr [John Quincy] Adams' Address if you have any to spare.[2]

He, Mr A. is pretty prominent among the Candidates for the Senate; [Henry] Shaw, of Lanesboro, has but little chance I think, & *hope*. He was a doughface in 1819. There is general feeling that it would be suicidal in the Whigs to take "the Governour" away from that place.

I shall not be surprized if it settles down between Gov Lincoln & W[illia]m Baylies—which is the best? If you answer, you may do it without fear of being named, but give me your reasons that if I have opportunity I may use them. "May you live a thousand years." Yours truly

C P Curtis

ALS. DLC. Curtis (1792–1864; Harvard 1811) was a Boston lawyer, member of the Common Council, 1823–1826, and state representative in 1842.

1. Enclosure not found.
2. Curtis probably wanted a copy of Adams's speech in Congress on the life and character of Lafayette.

TO EDWARD CURTIS

Washington, January 26. 1835.

My Dear Sir,

I have made the acquaintance, within the last month, of Mr. K[emp] P. Willis, of North Carolina. He appears to be a Gentleman of intelligence, and is regarded, at home, not only as a man of large property, but as a man of honor and character; as you will perceive by the letters addressed to me by Mr. [Willie Person] Mangum and Mr. [James] Graham, members of Congress.[1] Mr. Willis is desirous of inviting northern capital into mining operations, in the gold region of North Carolina.

His tracts of gold land are extensive, and some of them thought capable of immediate and profitable development. He has obtained a Charter from the Legislature of North Carolina, of which he will show you a copy and his present object is, that a company should be formed, under this Charter to buy some part of his mines and put them into operation, he himself taking a large share, of the stock of the company.[2] I have felt some inclination to· become interested in some small degree, in this Corporation, if the stock should be mainly taken by Gentlemen, known to each other, and disposed to make a business matter of it. It would be convenient, if practicable, to have the whole stock, except Mr. Willis' part, owned by persons residing in the same place, so that they could readily confer and all be kept acquainted with the proceedings of Agents.

If you and other friends in New York should incline to take the subject into consideration, I am prepared to join in taking the first necessary step; that is, to send an Agent, or Agents, to North Carolina, to examine the Mine and report thereon. I suppose some persons fit for this purpose could be readily found in New York. Mr Willis will explain his views to you fully, on this and other parts of his plan. If you could go to Carolina, yourself, and survey the whole ground, I should not doubt that something profitable might be accomplished.

It is another object of Mr. Willis to raise the sum of 5000 $, to put in motion some of his mines, on his own account, or to prepare the way for the operations of the company. He offers security, on the land itself, and adds that he can obtain the guarantee of Mr. Mangum. This would be perfectly good. If I were at home, or any where, where I could assist Mr. Willis in this respect, I should readily do it; but Washington is not a place for raising money. He will confer with you on the subject, and if you can see how the cash may be had, it will be easy to write to me here, for Mr. Mangum's guaranty.[3] Yours with much regard   Danl Webster

LS. NhD.

1. Letters not found.

2. Kemp P. Willis incorporated the Burke County Gold Mining Company with Oscar Willis and others in 1834. The company was capitalized at $100,000, with shares selling for $100 each. See *Acts Passed by the General Assembly . . . of North Carolina . . . 1834–35* (Raleigh, 1835),

pp. 26–28; and Edward W. Phifer, "Champagne at Brindletown: The Story of the Burke County Gold Rush, 1829–1833," *North Carolina Historical Review*, 40 (October 1963): 498.

3. It has not been determined whether either Webster or Curtis bought stock in Willis's mine.

TO ISRAEL WEBSTER KELLY

Washington Jan. 29. 1835

Dear Sir,

Your two missing letters were brought to me yesterday.[1] One, a letter about Family affairs, the other a letter about the land, enclosing, or enclosed with, a mortgage deed, three notes, a rough sketch of the land &c. From circumstances, I incline to think these letters were mislaid in the Post office here. As you will have recd. the other mortgage deed, & notes, I need not execute this, as I presume.

By the description in this deed, & the plan, I see how the land lies. I am quite satisfied with the bargain. I think I have been fortunate in getting a good pasture.

I am inclined to buy Mr. [Samuel] Quimby's, if he should be disposed to sell, as I should think he would be, rather than to make so much fence.[2] You may manage with him, as you see fit, & get the land, if you can, at a fair rate. Give him to understand at once, that we must fence, if he does not sell. I would give him something more, per acre, than we gave Mr. [Benjamin] Shaw,[3] rather than not get it—but would not give an extravagant price. If you find him disposed to make a bargain, which you think it for my interest to comply with, you may conclude it, at once, without further reference to me. Name a day, when the money shall be paid, & the deed executed; & put it just so far ahead that you can write to me—& I will send a check for the cash. Put the bargain at once into writing, & sign it, as my agent—or, what will be shorter—go to Mr [George W.] Nesmith,[4] have the deed made out & executed, & left with him, till you bring the money. I should think he would rather sell, for a little something more per acre than was given to Mr Shaw, rather than make 300 rods of fence, to enclose only 28 acres of land.

Manage the matter, as well as you can.

I do not know whether the Widow Tandy's[5] dower land, is for sale or not.

It is an awkward piece, to lie in the middle of our pasture, but as it is a wood lot, I suppose it will not create any necessity of fencing. I suppose she has but a life estate in the land: who owns the reversion?

Since writing you the other day, I have heard from Capt. [Abraham G.] Stevens,[6] respecting the House, &c—& shall write him, this mail or the next. Yrs with regard   Danl Webster

ALS. NhHi. Published in Van Tyne, pp. 722–723.

1. Not found.
2. Webster completed the purchase of the Quimby land on May 5, 1835. For the deed of conveyance, see Deed Book 41: 330, Office of the Register of Deeds, Merrimack County, Con-

cord, New Hampshire, mDWs.

3. The deed transferring the Shaw property to DW had been recorded on January 1, 1835. See Deed Book 39: 498, Office of the Register of Deeds, Merrimack County, Concord, New Hampshire, mDWs.

4. Nesmith (1800–1890; Dart-mouth 1820) practiced law first in Salisbury and later in Franklin. A state legislator and banker, a long-time friend of Webster, he was appointed a justice of the Superior Court in 1859.

5. Not identified.

6. Letter not found.

TO WARREN DUTTON

Washington Jan. 30. 35

Dear Sir

Since I wrote you, four or five days ago, appearances have changed again.[1] It looks now as if Mr Taney would not be appointed Judge, at least not soon. You may rest in peace, therefore, for the present.

Is there any chance for a compromise?

So far as I express any opinion about Mr Taney's confirmation, I hope you will consider it closely confidential. I have in contemplation a movement, which will, if successful, supersede his nomination. It is, to unite Delaware & Maryland to the third Circuit, & fill the vacant seat by an appointment in *the West*. Five Judges will do very well for the Atlantic States—*tace*. Yrs   D. Webster

ALS. NhD. Dutton (1774–1857; Yale 1797) was a newspaper editor, lawyer, and Massachusetts legislator.

1. See DW to Warren Dutton, January 26, 1835, mDW 12259.

TO JEREMIAH MASON

Washington, February 1, 1835.

My Dear Sir,

I received your letter yesterday,[1] and the mail of to-day brings intelligence verifying your prediction that Mr. [John] Davis would be elected Senator. So far as regards the filling up the vacant seat in the Senate, nothing could be better. I hope all the evil will not happen, which is expected or feared, arising from the difficulty of finding him a successor in the administration of the executive government of the State. I do not think Mr. Adams will ever again consent to be [a] candidate; certainly not against Mr. Everett; and Mr. Everett and Mr. [Isaac Chapman] Bates are not men to suffer the harmony of the State to be disturbed by a controversy among their personal friends. I am still most anxious that all fair means should be used to settle this masonic and anti-masonic quarrel in Massachusetts. You have little idea how much it retards operations elsewhere. The reported debate in the Whig Caucus, on the subject of the Bristol Senators, is industriously sent to every anti-masonic quarter of the Union, and has excited much unkind feeling, and thereby done mischief.[2] We are endeavoring here to make the best of [Nathaniel Briggs] Borden. Our anti-masonic friends in Congress will write to him, advising him not to commit himself to any course of public conduct, till he shall come here and see the whole ground. The nomination appears to have been done as well as it could be. I mean, of course, in the manner of it. No fault is found with it by our friends, so far as I know. Measures are in train to produce a correspondent feeling and action, in New York, Vermont, and some other States. The Legislature of Maryland is now in session, and I have seen a letter to-day, which says, that if Mr. Clay were fairly out of the way, that Legislature would immediately second the Massachusetts nomination. Mr. Clay does nothing, and will do nothing, at present. He thinks—or perhaps it is his friends who think —that *something* may yet occur, perhaps a war, which may, in *some* way, cause a general rally round him. Besides, sundry of the members of Congress from Kentucky, in addition to their own merits, rely not a little on Mr. Clay's popularity, to insure their reelection next August. They have been, therefore, altogether opposed to bringing forward any other man at present. Public opinion will, in the end, bring out these things straight. If Massachusetts stands steady, and our friends act with prudence, the union of the whole Whig and anti-masonic strength is certain. Everything indicates that result. Judge McLean already talks of retiring. His nomination seems coldly received everywhere. Unless Indiana should come out for him, I see no probability of any other movement in his favor. Mr. [Hugh Lawson] White's nomination is likely to be persisted in. Neither you nor I have ever believed it would be easy to get Southern votes for *any* Northern man; and I think the prospect now is, that Mr. Van Buren will lose the whole South. This schism is calculated to give much additional strength to our party. If Mr. W[hite] appear likely to take the South, it will be seen that Mr. Van Buren cannot be chosen by the people; and as it will be understood that Mr. White's supporters are quite as likely to come to us, in the end, as to go to Van Buren, his course will lose the powerful support which it derives, or has derived, from an assured hope of success. The effect of those apprehensions is already visible. The recent attempt to shoot the President is much to be lamented. Thousands will believe there was plot in it; and many more thousands will see in it new proof, that he is especially favored and protected by Heaven.[3] He keeps close as to the question between White and Van Buren. I have omitted to do what I intended, that is, to say a few words upon that part of your letter which relates to myself, more directly. In a day or two I will make another attempt to accomplish that purpose. Mr. Taney's case is not yet decided. A movement is contemplated to annex Delaware and Maryland to Judge [Henry] Baldwin's circuit, and make a circuit in the West for the judge now to be appointed. If we could get rid of Mr. Taney, on this ground, well and good; if not, it will be a close vote. We shall have a warm debate on the Post Office Report,⁴ the Alabama resolutions,⁵ and other matters; but I think my course is to take no prominent part in any of them. I may say something against expunging the Journal. Yours truly,   D. Webster

Text from Mason, *Memoir and Correspondence*, pp. 355–357. Original not found.

1. Not found.

2. Instead of supporting Anti-Masonic candidates for the Bristol vacancies, the Whig caucus had agreed to vote for three "sound Whigs," who were elected. *Columbian Centinel*, January 10, 1835.

3. On January 29, just as President Jackson was passing from the rotunda of the Capitol after attending the funeral of South Carolina Representative Warren R. Davis, Richard Lawrence had fired two pistols at Jackson from point-blank range, neither of which went off.

4. Senator Thomas Ewing's Post Office report of January 27, showing that approximately 30 percent of the Post Office funds were unaccounted for, was a general attack upon Jackson's use of patronage. *Senate Documents*, 23d Cong., 2d sess., Doc. No. 86 (Serial 268).

5. The Alabama legislature had passed resolves instructing its senators to expunge from the Senate Journal the resolutions of the previous session censuring the President for the removal of the deposits. *National Intelligencer*, January 31, 1835. On the issue of the removal of the deposits, see *Correspondence*, 3: 225–334 *passim*.

TO JEREMIAH MASON

Washington Feb. 6. 1835

Private

My Dear Sir,

It is true that I have looked forward to the events which the approaching election might bring about, as likely to furnish a fit occasion for my retirement from the Senate. I have fixed on no particular time, nor made, indeed, any such determination as may not be changed, by the advice or the wishes of friends. As I am now placed, I shall certainly not leave my place, till the time arrives when I may think that its relinquishment will not be unsatisfactory to *Massachusetts*.

I do not affect, My Dear Sir, to desire to retire from public life, & to resume my profession. My habits, I must confess, & the nature of my pursuits for some years, render it more agreeable to me to <follow> attend to political than to professional subjects. But I have not lost all relish for the bar; I can still make something by the practice, & by remaining in the Senate, I am making sacrifices which my circumstances do not justify. My residence here so many months every year greatly increases my expenses, & greatly reduces my income. You know the charge of living here, with a family; & I cannot leave my wife & daughter at home, & come here & go into a "mess," at 10 Dollars a week.

I find it inconvenient to push my practice in the Supreme Court, while a member of the Senate; & am inclined, under any view of the future, to decline engagements hereafter, in that Court, unless under special circumstances. These are the reasons that have led me to *hope* for a fit occasion of leaving the Senate; & when I can quit, with the approbation of friends, *I* shall eagerly embrace the opportunity. In the meantime, I shall say nothing about it.[1]

I ought, this Spring to go to the West, as far at least as Ken. & Indiana. I am fully persuaded it would be a highly useful thing. My friends urge it upon me, incessantly; & I hold back from promising compliance with their wishes only from an unwillingness to lose six weeks more, after the session closes. On this point, however, as nothing is decided, I say nothing at present. There will be no cause in Court, I think, to detain me after the 3rd of March.

We have nothing new here. A base attempt has been made to ascribe the *madness* of [Richard] Lawrence to the Speeches &c of the Senate. An inquisition, if it may be so called, has been had upon Lawrence, by two physicians, who have signed a report, & returned it to the Marshall. It proves a clear case of insanity. The Report will not be published, so long as the publication can be withheld.

We shall pass thro' the Senate, a pretty good Bill for reorganizing the Post Office.

I saw lately a strange letter from Washington in the Boston Gazette, about an express from the N. Y. Whigs, & a coldness between Mr W[ebster] & Mr. Clay. Both stories are equally & entirely groundless. There has been no express here, from N.Y. On the contrary, *all* the Whig papers of the City, (except [Mordecai M.] Noahs)[2] will soon be out, (or we are misinformed) in the direction you would desire. Yrs truly   D. Webster

ALS. DLC. Published in Curtis, 1: 506–507.
  1. See above, Abbott Lawrence to

DW, January 5, 1835, note 1.
  2. The *New York Evening Star*, founded in 1834.

FROM CALEB CUSHING

                             Newbury Port Feb. 9th 1835
Private.
Dear Sir:
    Two or three times this winter, I have had conversation with Mr Jere-

miah Mason with regard to the probable successor of Gov. Davis, in the event of his being transferred to the Senate. I find that Mr M., although he avows the highest respect and esteem for Mr Everett, yet has not made up his mind to enter cordially into the plan of supporting Mr E. He is an auxiliary, whom, as well on his own account as of his weight with others, we ought not to lose to that enterprise. Might not a line from you to him on the subject be useful, as in his hands it certainly would be safe? I beg of you to excuse the liberty I take in making this suggestion; which I have marked *private*,—both out of consideration for Mr M., whose remarks upon such a subject I should never think of communicating to any person except in this way,—and of consideration for Mr E., who I trust will have no occasion to hear of the doubts of Mr M.

Everything continues to stand as well as possible in this State, in relation to the presidency.

Very truly & respectfully, Your ob. servt.   C. Cushing.

ALS. DLC. Published in Fuess, *Cushing*, 1: 171.

FROM JOHN DAVIS (1787–1854)

Boston Feby 11th 1835

Confidential

My Dear Sir,

The vote of the senate you will see before this reaches you. I have been a silent spectator of these painful scenes but matters have now arrived at a crisis that I may speak, but in the closest confidence. I can never be taught to bear with complacency disgrace & I cannot help looking upon this vote of a body calling themselves whigs as such. I neither sought for nor desired the Office nor did I look for it, but it was the pleasure of the house to take their own course and after I was placed in this connexion with the public, is it not insulting for a body who profess to believe me to be qualified for the station to veto the act of the house? Can I after this, consistent with a proper regard for my own character take a nomination from this body for reelection or consent to serve in any way? What if the Election should come to the senate? If political Expediency required in their judgment the support of another candidate it would be accorded to him. Can one serve where there is so little good faith—so little cohesion among friends? [1]

My present purpose is to withdraw from the canvass for senator if my friends will permit it, & to go home to my family at the end of the year from which I was literally torne and forced into this place by the men who now sustain these repeated votes. I would not trouble you with these remarks but I wish to do no rash act—none that may injure others and as you have allowed me to consult you as a friend I now come in that capacity & desire you after reading & burning this to write me freely & fully.[2] I wish your opinions for the guidance of no one but myself. They may therefore be the most confidential. That I feel wounded & mortified I need not say nor need I add it will be decidedly most agreeable to me to return to private life where I have little to fear having long since learned to live upon a crust of bread & a cup of water.

I am very truly yours   J. Davis

ALS. DLC.

1. By mid-January 1835, John Davis and John Quincy Adams had become the leading contenders for Massachusetts' second Senate seat. On January 28, the state House of Representatives had nominated Davis, but the Senate, on February 10, voted for Adams's election. Adams weakened his chances by coming out in favor of Jackson's French policy, and Davis eventually won the seat. *Columbian Centinel*, January 31, February 11, 17, 21, 1835; Arthur B. Darling, *Political Changes in Massachusetts, 1828–1848* (New Haven, 1925), pp. 184–185; Samuel Flagg Bemis, *John Quincy Adams and the Union* (New York, 1956), pp. 313–314.

2. Webster's reply has not been found.

TO CHARLES HENRY THOMAS

Washington Feb. 16. [1835]

Dear Henry,

I like most of your ideas about the farming operations of the year very well. On one or two points, I differ. I do not think it best to sow or plant the piece where the corn grew last year, any further than we can dress it. In the first place, it is ag[ains]t all rule for corn to follow corn; & in the next place I think it would injure the land, to take from it another exhausting crop without manure. It seems to me the better way will be to plough up the whole field, as early as may be. Then sow oats, on the Eastern side, as far as we can manure. Let the rest lie fallow, & ploughed. Possibly in June or July we may find some manure for part of it, on which we may sow turnips. If not, possibly we get rock weed, kelp, or muscles, by Septr, so as to put in a crop of winter rye. If neither happens, the ground will be in good condition to receive kelp next winter.

I do not want to raise any penny-royal corn.

As to the little piece near Cherry Hill, I thought we might as well lay it down, perhaps with barley, & grass seed. All the rest of yr. suggestions I like. We shall have but a small parcel of corn, upon my plan. Still, I do not think it worth while to labor on poor land. As corn will be rather scant, we must calculate on potatos, carrots, & turnips, & pumpkins for the stock.

I hope you will look well to the Luzerne. We must diminish the number of our cows, & keep them better.

I intend next year to take up 5 or 6 acres of ground, somewhere, & go thro' a regular process of English husbandry with it, beginning with the Summer fallow. I do not know whether I shall take the lower part of Slaughter Island, or a piece on the Soule farm. I wish to proceed with it, in order, till it is as good as the garden.

Has Lowrie [1] smoothed off his field, down by the marsh? Is the turf off the meadow? Are all the bushes grubbed up?

Congress rises one fortnight from tomorrow. I believe I shall push direct for home—& hope to see you before March is out. Yrs   D. Webster

ALS. MHi.
   1. Lowrie, an employee on the Webster property at Marshfield, later worked at Webster's farm, "Salisbury," in Peru, Illinois.

TO SAMUEL FROTHINGHAM

Washington Feb. 21. 35

Dear Sir,

Messrs [Herman] Le Roy & Co's acceptance of my other draft falls due Feb. 28—& Mar. 3.[1]

I now enclose another draft, on them which [I] will thank you to get discounted; & remit *to them* $2.000, on my acct. in season. I propose you would remit to *them*, as there will be hardly time for the check to go thro my hands. Their address is "Le Roy & Co. Wall Street, N. York."

I shall hasten directly *home*, after the rising of Congress, & shall have the pleasure of partaking in the March winds of N. England. Yrs

D. Webster

ALS. PHi. Frothingham (1787–1869) was cashier of the Boston branch of the Bank of the United States.

   1. Le Roy (1758–1841), Webster's father-in-law, was a prominent New York merchant.

FROM WILLIAM SULLIVAN

Feb. 21, 1835

You know by the papers that went last night (if in no other way) that a Senator is chosen. You know probably, to-day, that the ministers are recalled. I am reminded of a country milliner who was called to a duchess; to prepare herself for the interview, she inquired what she must say, and was answered, "Your Grace." Wherefore, on coming into the presence, she courtesied, and said: "God bless us, and what is provided for us!" . . . . There is here to-day much of that sort of feeling which one may suppose to exist among persons who dwell around the base of Vesuvius or Ætna, when the black smoke begins to ascend, and sparks to fly. Our Executive has no *metre*, to announce what is to come next, any more than a burning mountain has, to disclose when the lava will run, in what course, or in what quantity. Deplorable as a war with France would be in the present condition of the world, it is much more to be dreaded from its effects on our own institutions. In the feverish state of the slaveholding South, what will its duties and interests seem *to itself* to be? What is to be the character, and the will, of the military power to be embodied in this country, and by whom is its physical force to be directed, and to what objects? How entirely uncalled for is all this combination of probable evils! You stand acquitted of all responsibility, eminently. If your speech at Worcester, in October, 1832,[1] could have found its way to the understanding of the country, things would not have been as they are. Is there not some reason to fear that restive, unquiet France, and perplexed England, and vindictive Spain, may think a good opportunity has arisen to dispose of that "food for gunpowder" which a long peace necessarily prepares in Europe, and which must be sent abroad, to prevent mischief at home. Then, in what condition is this country for a violent or protracted struggle, even if another class of rulers had the power. This you know better than anybody, but every thinking man in Massachusetts knows that this State was never in a worse condition to meet such a crisis. The pulpit, peace societies—a sickly sort of philanthropy—a bad militia system, mischievously perverted, have combined to extinguish the noble spirit of independence, and to palsy the power of self-defence, which once gave Massachusetts a proud preëminence. Add to this (as I know from what I saw in the long session of the nominating committee at Worcester, October, 1833[2]), there is not a man in the State on whom one-quarter of the qualified voters would combine, and to whom they would give the direction of its affairs. I remember to have heard you say, on one occasion, "Providence may be better to us than our fears"; and, if not, I must again say, with the milliner, "God bless us, and what is provided for us. . . ."

I was interrupted here by an old gentleman named Goodhue,[2] who is one of your admirers, and to whom (he says) you once gave four or five books. He has closed a somewhat long, profitless, and tedious discourse, with a phrase which I think I may well use to close a letter to which, perhaps, you may give a like character: "I hope you will not impute any thing that I have said to any thing worse than weakness."

Your respectful friend, Wm. Sullivan.

Text from Curtis, 1: 515. Original not found.

1. Webster's speech before the Massachusetts National Republican Convention at Worcester on October 12, 1832, is printed in *W & S*, 2: 87–128.

2. Possibly Samuel Goodhue (d. 1846; Dartmouth 1792), lawyer from Brattleboro, Vermont.

TO WILLIAM SULLIVAN

Washington Feb. 23. '35

Dear Sir,

The Bostonians are very sensible on the French question; much more so than some of their acquaintances in Congress. I shall present their memorial this morning;[1] but shall endeavor to avoid discussion, at present. There are three parties in Congress, on this question. The Jackson party proper, which, like its chief feels very warlike; the Southern Anti-Jackson men, who seem to me to be in the other extreme, witness Mr [John C.] Calhoun & Mr [George] Poindexter, who speak of the whole matter only as a *debt*, and recommend an action of assumpsit, instead of war, &c &c &c; & then there is the rest of us, who desire to say & do nothing to encourage France, in her neglect of our rights, & who are not willing, nevertheless, to hazard the peace of the Country, without absolute necessity. We wish to show to France that there is but one sentiment in the U.S. as to the justice of our side of the question; one sentiment as to the propriety of insisting on the fulfilment of the Treaty; but at the same time a great reluctance to come to an open rupture, &, in order to avoid that, a disposition to give France full time to consider well of her course.

No despatches from Mr [Edward] L[ivingston] are yet recd, since the message reached Paris. Today, unluckily, we have no N Y. mail. An Extra Session of Congress is talked of, & perhaps is not unlikely, either to be provided for, by law, or to be called by the President.

I shall depart hence soon after the rising of Congress, but probably shall not be home until the middle of March, or a day or two later. You will do well not to rely on me for any thing in Court. I am pretty much worked out of *all* Courts. If it were not for the two bridges, which are still "hanging bridges" here, I might say, I believe, that I no longer kept company with either Pl[aintif]f or Def[en]d[an]t on the Docket of the Sup. Court here.[2] Perhaps there may be one other exception. This state of things has arisen, partly by design, & partly thro necessity. As I am circumstanced, at present, I cannot practise extensively in the Sup. Court, because I cannot leave the Senate, long enough to go thro' an important cause. *Non possumus omnia.* I must leave off saying "Mr President," or leave off saying "May it please your Honors"; but, My Dear Sir, I shall never leave off saying, that I am, with much sincere regard, Yrs

Danl Webster

ALS. MHi. Published in *PC*, 2: 9–10.

1. The memorial to which Webster referred was probably similar to those Nathaniel Silsbee had presented on February 2 urging nonintercourse with France instead of war. The *Senate Journal* does not record Webster's presentation of the memorial on February 23. *Senate Jour-*

nal, 23d Cong., 2d sess., Serial 265, pp. 178, 183–185.

2. Webster was referring to the case, *Charles River Bridge* v. *Warren Bridge*, 11 Peters 420 (1837). For the origins of the case, see *Correspondence*, 3: 103, 205–206, 389, 391, 393, 397, 413, 418, 420, 451, 453, 505, 506.

FROM DANIEL FLETCHER WEBSTER

Hopkinton Feby 28th. 1835

My dear Father

I should have written you much oftener than I have this winter, did I not feel assured that you have heard of me through my letters to Mother and Julia, and as I have had nothing at all to communicate, of the slightest importance, I have forborne to encumber you with my letters.

I cannot write to you, and you would be by no means pleased to have me, as I can to Julia or Mother, a letter full of talk, the reading of which may be done or left undone and not a consequence of any kind ensue.

Nor have I now any thing in particular to say, but write to you to show that it has not been because my thoughts have not been often with you that you have so seldom heard from me, but because I was afraid to trouble you, with empty letters at a time when I knew you to be so busy. I have been "tearing the law to pieces" these last *seven months* that I have been at Hopkinton, and have arrived to such a degree of proficiency as to be able to take care of almost any business that presents itself at our office.

Mr. [Samuel B.] Walcott[1] was kind enough to say he felt no anxiety about his law affairs when at the Legislature, if I was in the office, and as this is the first thing that sounds any way like a compliment, that I ever received upon my attention to study I'm quite proud of it, and hope to give Mr. W. no reason to take it back again.

Besides my legal acquirements, I have been making favour with the natives, shall be a voter at our "March Meeting" next Monday and have some hopes of the responsible office of field-driver or hog-reeve. I have delivered a long lecture before The Lyceum of the Town and my remarks were so well received by that learned body that I was asked to repeat my lecture and write another in continuation of the subject, which I am now employed upon. Mr. W. has given up all thoughts of leaving town at present, I believe, at least he never speaks of it. I do not think he will for some years yet; his business is all the time increasing, he is getting well known at Middlesex bar and has no inclination to bury himself at Salem I think.

I have been once at Marshfield, found all well there, though it looked pretty bleak. I was at Boston last Tuesday, saw Uncle and Mrs [James William] Paige, Mr. [Stephen] White, Caroline [White], Mr. [Henry Willis] Kinsman and so on; all well.[2] Mr. W. is to start south pretty soon I believe.

I suppose you will hardly go to N. Orleans yourself this spring, at least not before you come home. I hope my engagements will be such as to allow me to accompany you, if you conclude to make the journey. We have plenty of snow on our hills and very good sleighing. Leicester has improved wonderfully and trots down hill under the saddle at full speed.

Please give my love to Mother and Julia, and believe me, my dear Father Your ever affectionate son F. Webster.

ALS. NhHi. Excerpt published in Van Tyne, p. 589. Daniel Fletcher (1813–1862; Harvard 1833) was DW's oldest son.

1. Walcott (1795–1854; Harvard 1819), who had studied law in Webster's office and gained admission to the Suffolk Bar in 1824 before moving to Hopkinton, had tutored Fletcher for Harvard. Now Fletcher was studying law with Walcott.

2. Paige (1792–1868), Grace

Fletcher Webster's half-brother, was a prosperous merchant in Boston and one of Webster's most reliable financial backers. His wife was the former Harriette Story White (1809–1863), daughter of Stephen (1787–1841), a Boston merchant, and Harriet Story (1787–1827). Caroline (1811–1886), another daughter of Stephen and Harriet White, married Daniel Fletcher Webster on November 27, 1836.

FROM STEPHEN WHITE

Boston February 28 1835

Dear Sir

Things are working well here. The nomination by the Whig convention of Mr. Everett will put things on the best footing. The Anti-Masons are well satisfied. If the prevailing cold weather does not freeze up the river I shall leave in the Steam Boat on next wednesday for New York. From thence I go to Washington and shall hope to have the great pleasure of finding yourself and family there. Ever truly yours

Stephen White

ALS. NhHi.

TO CALEB CUSHING

Washington Mar. 5. '35

Dear Sir,

I write you a line, amidst the weariness of the finale of a Session. Hereafter, you will know what that is. I did the needful, in compliance with your last;[1] & all that matter is most happily settled. Nothing remains, so far as Gov. of Mass is concerned, but for Mr Everett to see the people. He must be made a peripatetic, for the whole summer. He must verify the geographical descriptions of some of the old stanzas of Yankee doodle, & learn, for himself, that

"Marblehead's a rocky place,
Cape Cod is sandy," &c &c &c.

I have found you out, in the Magazine.[2] All that I wonder at, is, that your conscience did not sometimes give you such a pang, that your friendship could not allay the grief of it.

Mr Everett sent you some time since, a communication to me from Mr. Noah Webster.[3] The writer wishes it, as he kept no copy. Will you enclose it, very carefully, & address it to me at New York. If you will let your clerk first make a copy of it for me, it will be an additional favor.

I stay here two or three days longer, & then go home by way of Harrisburg & Lancaster. Yrs truly   Danl. Webster

ALS. NN. Published in part in Fuess, *Cushing*, 1: 172.

1. Cushing had asked DW to write Jeremiah Mason on supporting Everett for governor (see above, Cushing to DW, February 9, 1835). Webster's letter to Mason and Mason's reply have not been found.

2. DW was probably referring to Cushing's essay, "Mr. Webster," which appeared in the *New England Magazine*, 8 (March 1835): 220–228.

3. DW had been corresponding with Noah Webster on the "first proposal" for the Hartford Convention (see Noah Webster to DW, February 9, 1835, mDW 12308). DW's letter to Noah Webster has not been found.

In March 1835 Webster stepped up the tempo of his campaign for the Presidency. When the second session of the Twenty-third Congress adjourned on the third, he remained in Washington for a few days to defend in editorials his action on the French reparations question (see mDW 12378, 12407, 12411), on the Fortification Bill (see mDW 12382), and on Taney's rejection as Associate Justice of the Supreme Court (see DW to Joseph Gales and W. W. Seaton, [March 8], below). From Washington he left for Boston, swinging first through Baltimore and then into central Pennsylvania, courting the support of state legislators in Harris-

burg and of local politicians in York and in Lancaster, where he was honored with a public dinner. Following a conference with Nicholas Biddle and other friends in Philadelphia, he made his way on to Boston, arriving in mid-April in time to attend the Lexington celebration on the twenty-second and to witness the publication of a second volume and a reprint of the first volume of his Speeches and Forensic Arguments. *In late May, his friends presented him with a $1,500 vase to show their appreciation for his services.* Columbian Centinel, *March 25, 28, April 18, 22, May 30, 1835;* Niles' Register, *48 (May 23, 1835): 202.*

TO STEPHEN WHITE

Washington, March 5. [1835]

Dear Sir,

I received yours of the 28 of Feb. yesterday,[1] & am delighted to learn that you are coming this way. I fear however the cold weather will detain you, so that I hardly know where to send this letter with best chance of meeting you. I hope you will hasten on, so as to be, at least, at Baltimore on Monday Eve, else we may cross each other. My plan at present is to leave Washington Monday, & go to Baltimore, on Tuesday go to York, then to Harrisburg & Lancaster, & reach Philadelphia about Friday or Saturday, the 13th or 14th, & then home with little delay. I shall make two copies of this, so that one of the three may probably reach you. We have broken up here leaving much undone. Yours   Danl. Webster

LS. MH-H.
1. See above.

TO [JOSEPH GALES AND W. W. SEATON]

[March 8, 1835]

The real secret history, I take to be this—

—The Senate p[ost]p[one]d indefinitely, R. B. Taney.

—In the regular course, another nomination should then have been made—it being equivalent to a rejection.

—The Sec. carried this minute to the Pres[iden]t—

It was *near* 12 oclock—

—The President did not wish to nominate another Judge—

—Whereupon he chose to consider it past 12, & to go away. He did so, telling [Walter] Lowrie he would receive no communication from the Senate, at that hour—

—He went away. Van Buren & [John] Forsyth went from Presidents room to H. of R.—

—In two minutes [Churchill Caldom] Cambreleng came in—

—*They* dissuaded him from Reporting—

—The probable reason, is, that they wished to avoid throwing the responsibility of losing the Bill, on Prest.

—to affect [Hugh Lawson] White, might be another motive—[1]

AL. NhD.
1. White, an old friend and supporter of Andrew Jackson, was now running for the Presidency as a Whig. Webster's comments on the judiciary reorganization bill and Taney's nomination above formed the basis of an article appearing in Gales's and Seaton's *National Intelligencer*, March 10, 1835.

TO CHARLES HANDY RUSSELL

Washington Mar. 10. 1835

Private & Confidential
Dear Sir

I know not what I can better do with this letter[1] than to send it to you, to be used confidentially. I need not suggest to you the *great* importance of the election of a Senator in R. Island.[2] Friends in Mass will do what they can to accomodate the difficulty with the Anti Masons, but I know not with what success. I pray you, with other friends, to take such steps for the furtherance of the common object, as you may judge most expedient.

I am, with entire regard, Yours   Danl Webster

ALS. NhD. Charles Handy Russell (1796–1884), born in Newport, Rhode Island, was a prominent merchant in New York City.
1. Enclosure not found.

2. The Rhode Island legislature reelected Nehemiah Rice Knight, a Democrat, to the United States Senate in 1835.

TO CHARLES HENRY THOMAS

Harrisburg, Pa. Mar. 19. '35

Dear Henry,

We left Washington last friday—staid a day or two at Baltimore—arrived here on Tuesday, & go to Lancaster, on our way to Philadelphia, tomorrow. We have had sad & sorry weather, all the time, till this morning, when the sun comes out. Last night we had a fall of snow. I shall hardly reach home before April, but will write you particularly from N. York. Meantime, one or two things occur to me.

1. Lime. If there be lime afloat at Boston, & rather cheap, buy a considerable quantity, say 100 bushels; have it sent down, & drawn home. We will, at the proper time, mix it with the manure for the land next to Mr. [Joseph Phillips] Cushmans,[1] & other places.

I presume there has been no chance for kelp. Can any thing be done in the way of muscles? It would be a great thing if we could get muscles, for a part of the land where the corn grew last year. Suppose a gang of hands should try, for once, the muscle bed, in Duxbury bay, with both Gondolas. If you get any, put them on thick; so that the land may be made rich, so far as they go.

If you can sell any of the oxen, or cows, for fair prices, I hope you will do so, as we are overstocked. We do not want more than 5 or 6 cows at home, & those we must continue to *feed*. I was ashamed of our cows last year. Three good cows, well kept, would have been worth more than all of them. Keep the bulls up, & be sure to keep them from the young heifers. Perfect care must be used, in this respect.

I have seen some of the handsomest cattle, in this State, that I ever did see; they are of the Durham breed.

Remember the Lucerne. Get enough seed to sow quite or near an acre. Yrs   D.W.

ALS. MHi.
1. Cushman (b. 1785) was one of DW's Marshfield neighbors.

TO JAMES BUCHANAN

Saturday Mar. 21. [1835]
Dear Sir

My wife may like to go to Meeting, or Church, tomorrow, in the P.M. Would it not be better, for that reason, that we taste your wine at a later hour than that proposed? Yrs truly   D. Webster

ALS. PHi. Published in *The Works of*   Moore (12 vols.; Philadelphia, 1908–
James Buchanan, ed. John Bassett   1911), 2: 442.

TO [EDWARD EVERETT]

N York, April 2. 1835
Dear Sir,

The present weather continuing, I shall be home, as I trust, on Saturday; but I have thought it worth while, nevertheless, to trouble you with this line for one particular purpose.

Friends in Philadelphia suggested the importance of the expression of opinions, by local meetings, as often as convenient; as such things usually get into circulation, and are more read than mere paragraphs. Mr [Joseph] McIlvaine[1] thought he should write you, on that point. Since I left Philadelphia, I have seen a meeting called in Franklin Co., Mass; & it has occurred to me that it might be well for you to write a line

to Mr. [George] Grennell[, Jr]. In Pa. all things look exceedingly well.
Yrs   D. Webster

ALS. MHi.
1. McIlvaine (d. 1838) was a Phil-

adelphia Whig, state legislator, and
lobbyist for Nicholas Biddle.

FROM NICHOLAS BIDDLE

Phila. April 6th 1835

My dear Sir

I send as you requested a copy of your speech of the 26th. of Feby last,[1] and will repeat in a few words what I stated to you in conversation.

The objection to it in its present form is, that it states as a fact, without qualification, that the people had decided against the Bank—that public opinion had decided against it, without implying any doubt of the correctness of that opinion except that it is called unfortunate.

Now I doubt very much whether public opinion can be said to have declared against the Bank—but supposing it to be so what jarred upon the minds of the friends of the Bank as well as your own personal friends, was that you should have pronounced such a sentence. It seemed to imply an indifference—a coldness—an alienation from the Bank— and a desire to disconnect yourself with it. Such impressions are unjust to you as well as to your friends in the Bank, and the best mode of rectifying them would probably be a revision of the speech. You can do this with more freedom, because Mr. [Samuel] Jaudon[2] tells me that when the speech appeared while he was in Washington, he mentioned to you that it was not what you said. Remember then what you did say and I think you will fall into this train of thought. In the first paragraph, after remarking that you considered the question settled, say

You consider this an unfortunate result—and an unjust one. The Bank had accomplished all the objects designed by its establishment— reformed the currency—regulated the exchanges and built up a system of facilities for internal commerce between the States such as did not exist before, and does not exist in any other country. That it had been ably and purely administered. Say all the good you can with a good conscience of the Directors and of the Officers of the Bank. It was remarkable, as the Report of the Senate Comm[itt]ee proved, that while the whole country was filled with partizan clamors against these Officers, they never suffered themselves to be seduced or frightened from their great duty to the country—their whole object seems to have been to save the people from the Executive. Nevertheless, such is the blind violence of party which spares nothing that will not yield to its fury, that the very men of the Bank have been perverted into its misfortune. Had its Officers capitulated to power or surrendered their trust to faction, they would have been favored. But its independence renders it no longer tolerable to those in power. No matter. It should be a nobler pride to have fallen rather than to have yielded. Make something like that in your short—sententious—lapidary way and I will accept it as the epitaph of the Bank.

In the 5th paragraph—about the Experiment—

add—The Bank seeing that the charter is to expire, will naturally desire to make the most it can for the interest of the stockholders and will reach the end of its charter with a large amount of loans and of bills in circulation. Until these disappear and are replaced by the new currency, there is no experiment at all. The Bank now is doing as large a business as usual without the deposits—while these deposits have gone to the State Banks to increase their ability—so that thus far there has been no diminution at all. If, after the withdrawal of the bills and the loans of the Bank, it shall appear for some years, that the Bills of the Five or Six hundred Banks are as safe as those of the Bank of the U.S.—that internal exchanges are as low as now,—that there pervades the Union a sound, equal, universally redeemable currency, then, and not 'till then, shall we allow that the experiment has succeeded.

Something which you can readily make out of these hints would answer the purpose, and remove a little soreness, where none ought to exist. Yrs always   N. B.

LC. DLC.

1. Speaking in the Senate on February 26, DW had pronounced the Bank issue dead, declaring that he would not again seek recharter nor the substitution of any other bank, as long as public sentiment opposed. *Congressional Globe*, 23d Cong., 2d sess., p. 296. Biddle had objected to the language and DW had softened it, without changing the sense, before book publication. The revised version, an effort to "remove a little soreness," appeared first in the *National Intelligencer*, March 5, 1835, and a few weeks later in *Speeches and Forensic Arguments*, 2: 478–482.

2. Jaudon (1796–1874) was cashier of the Bank of the United States.

TO TRISTAM BURGES

Boston April 8th [1835]

My Dear Sir,

I recd yr letter[1] only last Eve', & shall this morning lay it before those who *ought* to estimate the importance of its suggestions. The news from Connecticut is so disheartening, I know not whether it is possible to persuade men not to despair.[2]

Yrs, always truly,   Danl Webster

ALS. PBL.

1. Not found.

2. In the Connecticut elections of April 6, the Jacksonians had made a clean sweep, electing the governor and a majority of both houses of the legislature. *Boston Courier*, April 9, 11, 13, 1835.

FROM JAMES WATSON WEBB

Spring-Lawn April 9th. 1835

My Dear Sir

I returned to the City last evening, and having sold my House in Town, found it necessary to come down here immediately to expedite the arrangements making for the reception of my family. It afforded me much pleasure to learn that you had paid this place a visit while in the vicinity, and my only regret is that I was not present to extend to you such little hospitality as under existing circumstances, was practicable. I hope however, that you were sufficiently pleased with its natural beauties to be induced to make it another visit when you will find ready to receive you [one] who will properly appreciate the pleasure of your presence. Indeed, I consider your recent visit, a *pledge* that the first time you and Mrs. Webster visit New York, you will consent to spend a few days with us and partake of such hospitality as it may *then* be in our power to bestow. I am expressly charged by Mrs. *Webb*[1] to say to Mrs. *Webster*, that she shall esteem her company not only an honor and a pleasure, but a very proper species of penance imposed upon both of you for your *"stolen visit"* when every thing was in a state of confusion, and when even the *natural* Beauties of what we consider a very lovely situation, were destroyed by the unfinished labours of *man*.

When I left New York for Philadelphia I was quite certain of meeting with you in that quiet city, and my departure was expedited in the hopes of availing myself of your kind services in my negotiation with the Bank; but unfortunately for me, you left Philadelphia on the same morning. The truth is, all my worst fears of the consequences to myself of breaking ground for the Presidency have been realized, and I was threatened with an application to the chancellor to close the Trust of the Courier & Enquirer under my assignment. I had no alternative therefore, but to commence negotiations with *all* my creditors and simultaneous ones with some capitalists in order to extricate myself. Pending these negotiations, and partly in consequence of an approaching charter election, I thought it best to keep quiet on the subject of my preference for you; but the necessity for doing so, will no longer exist after next week, and then I shall resume the good work with renewed zeal. It is idle at this time to attempt a detail of all I have encountered in getting clear of the *cormorants*. I have suffered both in mind & in *purse*, but I *have* succeeded, and in the satisfaction of having triumphed I already find my reward. For numerous considerations which must at once occur to you, I shall endeavour to avoid calling on you or your friends for aid even to the amount heretofore mentioned; but in case of absolute necessity I shall ask for a loan of $5,000 for one year with the privilege of renewal if necessary. This at all events will be the extent of the accommodation I may require, and even this I may not want. The Bank now has no lien upon my Paper, and this I consider an all-important consideration in the coming contest. I have given them instead, or rather am to give them, a mortgage on 25,000 acres of Land in this state for my note of $18,600. To accomplish even this much, detained me in Philadelphia nearly two weeks, and in consequence I missed the pleasure of seeing you. At this juncture I cannot but consider this unfortunate; but I think you know enough of me, to feel convinced that you may frankly write me all you think and all you require me to do, under a full conviction that neither now nor hereafter, will it ever meet any other eye but mine. I hope then that on rect. of this you will give me at length your views of the existing state of things and your plans for the future, not for the purpose of encouragement or to excite me to perseverance. I have embarked in the contest with all the ardour necessary for success, and under the fullest persuasion that if New England and the Middle states & part of the West will as truly discharge their duty to you and the Country, as the South & South-west will to Judge *White* Van Buren can never succeed. At the same time I verily believe that when the election once gets into the House of Rep. the northern States will *all* vote for you instead of *White*. We have a Party throughout the Country which will increase precisely in the ratio that we exhibit confidence in ourselves, and it is only necessary to impress this *fact* upon the mind of the wavering to ensure a triumph worthy of the Principles we advocate. Your friend

Jas. Watson Webb.

ALS. DLC.
1. Helen Lispenard Webb, née Stewart, whom Webb had married in 1832, was the daughter of a wealthy New York City merchant.

TO SAMUEL LEWIS SOUTHARD

Boston April 28. 1835

Confidential

My Dear Sir,

You have probably had a letter recently from Mr Everett, & learned from him what is the state of things, in this part of the world. In truth, we are rather waiting for manifestations elsewhere. Friends here are ready to act, with as much zeal & spirit as their neighbours; but they think there is a want of *decision*, in other quarters. It appears to them that the time has come, when all friends of the Constitution ought to form *some opinion*, as to the best course for them to pursue. There is no disposition, this way, not the slightest, to join either branch of the Jackson Party. In truth, our Whigs are indignant at the conduct & language, which are manifested by certain Southern supporters of Judge White. They cannot understand upon what principle it is, that the sentiments & opinions of the North are, at this moment, so angrily to be denounced, as they see they are, daily, in the [United States] Telegraph,[1] & other papers.

At this moment, no topic would be more popular here, than the inconsistency, local prejudice, & contempt for others, which have been shown by some of our Southern fellow-laborers. We endeavor, however, to keep cool; but as to changing our own course, it is out of the question. We shall not budge one inch, toward nullification, come what—come may. My only personal consolation, in all this matter, is, that *I have not been cheated*: I am not at all disappointed. Every thing turns out exactly as I expected.

If the Country is to be saved, My Dear Sir, it must be by an undeviating adherence to the Constitution. We must give up nothing—qualify nothing—abandon nothing. We must go for the *whole* Constitution, & for men who will support the *whole* Constitution; for if we cannot have the whole, it is greatly better, I think that we should have no part of it.

Unless I shall learn that Mr Everett has written to you, I will address you again, in a day or two. Mrs Everett[2] has been quite sick, so much so that I have hardly seen Mr. E. for a week. We heard yesterday that she was better.

I have recd. & read your Speech, upon the *Expunging* motion.[3] I need not say I think it able, but I must say I think it altogether unanswerable, & conclusive, upon the whole subject.

With kind regards to Mrs & Miss Southard,[4] I am, Dr Sir, very truly, Your friend,   Danl Webster

ALS. NjP.

1. Duff Green's *United States Telegraph* supported White in the presidential campaign. On March 9, 1835, Green informed Calhoun of a conversation with White. "I told him [White]," Green wrote, "that the N Ham. Patriot had already assailed him as the candidate of the Nullifiers —that he must be aware that if his friends undertook to defend him against that charge in terms that would be offensive to us, it would be repelled, & that it might do him injury. He indicated that the attacks of the Globe would not drive him from the Senate and assured me that I need be under no apprehensions that his friends would assail me or my friends—that day had gone

by." Calhoun Papers, ScCleU.

2. Charlotte Gray Everett, née Brooks, whom Everett had married in 1822, was the daughter of Peter Chardon Brooks.

3. On February 27, 1835, Southard had delivered a long speech to the Senate against Thomas Hart Benton's expunging resolution.

4. Rebecca Southard, née Harrow, of Virginia, whom Southard had married in 1812. Miss Southard, probably a daughter, sister, or niece, has not been further identified.

TO [EDWARD EVERETT]

May 1 [1835]

Dr Sir

Pray remember the importance of R. I.

I go to N. H. this morning. The R. I. Assembly convene on the 6th.[1]

Yrs D. W.

ALS. MHi.

1. See above, DW to Charles Handy Russell, March 10, 1835, for a discussion of the Rhode Island election.

TO [NICHOLAS BIDDLE]

Boston May 9. 1835

Private

My Dear Sir

It appears to me that our political affairs are taking a very decided turn, & that if nothing be done to check the current, Mr. V.B. will be elected President, by a vast majority. It is entirely obvious, I think, that the movement of the Southern Whigs (as they call themselves) in Mr. White's favor, has disgusted, deeply, the whole body of our friends in the North. Such papers as the Richmond Whig & [United States] Telegraph have endeavored to persuade the People that the question is narrowed down to a choice between Judge White & Mr. V. Buren; & if this be the only issue presented, there is already abundant indication that the whole north, east, & middle too, as I believe, will go for V.B. I do not know whether any thing can be done to change the course of things; but I am fully persuaded, that if anything *can* be done, it is be[ing] done in Penna. Your people are awake to political subjects, in consequence of the pendency of an election for Govr. If those who are likely to unite in support of Mr [Joseph] Ritner could unite also in making some demonstration, on National Subjects, & do it immediately, it might hopefully have some effect. Whether this be practicable, is more than I know.

I have thought it right, My Dear Sir, to express to you my opinion, thus freely, on the present state, & apparent tendency, of things. Our friends here receive letters, every day, & from Pa. as well as from other quarters, calling on them to do more, & say more. But they hardly see what more *they* can do, or say. The sentiment of Massachusetts is known; & it would seem to be for the consideration of others, whether it should be seconded.

You will, of course, *burn this*—& let no eye but your own see it. You can judge whether any thing can be usefully done. For my part, I confess, it looks to me as if the whole Whig strength in the Country was either to be frittered away, or melt into the support of Mr V. Buren. Yrs truly ever

AL. DLC. Published in McGrane, *Correspondence of Nicholas Biddle*, pp. 250–251.

TO [NICHOLAS BIDDLE]

Boston May 12. '35

Private

Dr Sir

One word more on political subjects. It seems truly lamentable that the Nat[ional] Intelligencer should be so unwilling to give, or take, tone, on questions most interesting to us, as a party. Cannot this reluctance be overcome? If Messrs G[ales] & S[eaton] are not disposed to support, at present, any named Candidate, they might, at least, preach the necessity of supporting *a* Whig Candidate—*some* Whig Candidate. We are in danger of breaking up, & dividing. Our natural field marshall—he that should rally & encourage us, is the leading paper on our side. But this natural leader seems at present to be without any "object, end, or aim."

I mention this matter to you, because you can judge, as well as any one, whether the subject deserve any attention; & if it do, can, better than any one, give an availing hint, in the right quarter. Yrs ever truly

burn

AL. DLC. Published in McGrane, *Correspondence of Nicholas Biddle,* pp. 251–252.

TO TRISTAM BURGES

Boston May 18. '35

Monday Eve'

Private

My Dear Sir

I have recd. yours of the 16th[1] this moment. So soon as I saw the result of the *choice*, in R. I. I thought I saw at once the whole chain of cause & effect. I still think I comprehend the matter. My engagements, for this week, are very stringent, in their nature. A confidential friend will call on you, on Wednesday, at 12 oclock, with a letter from me.[2] If, after that, you desire to see me, he will arrange with you a time for meeting, at Walpole. Yrs truly   D. Webster

ALS. NhD.   2. Not found.
     1. Not found.

FROM SAMUEL PRENTISS

Montpelier, May 18th. 1835

Dear Sir,

I have received your letter of the 12th. inst.,[1] and in answer to your inquiries have to say, that by the law of this state a divorce *a vinculo* may be granted for impotency, adultery, wilful desertion for three years, absence of seven years if unheard of, or intolerable severity. These are the causes specified in the statute. The one last mentioned is very vague and indefinite, but is understood to comprehend personal abuse and violence, and other gross and long continued ill-treatment. It is immaterial where the marriage was entered into; but the petitioner must have resided one full year in this state next before the filing of the petition, and must also have been an inhabitant of this state at the time the cause assigned for the divorce occurred, or the cause must have happened within this state.

The spring elections, it seems, are unfavourable to a reform in the general government. In Connecticut, all is lost, and Virginia, without doubt, has gone back to the administration.[2] Rhode Island has done better than was expected, but the enemy is strong and the struggle doubtful there. A strange infatuation has seized upon the people. They seem to love delusion, and to yield themselves willing dupes to political demagogues and jackies. The prospect is discouraging enough, but I still hope for the best. Though the public mind is extensively diseased, time may, and I trust will, restore to it a healthy action. In this state, a portion of the antimasonic party are disposed to unite with the Jackson men, and will probably act with them in the election of President. A large majority of that party, however, are opposed to the men in power, and will, I am persuaded, go with the Whigs in supporting you, especially if the antimasons of Massachusetts take that course. Some of the Whigs, despairing of your success, think it will be better, on the score of policy, to vote for the least exceptionable of the other candidates; but from the best information I can obtain, the party in general are inclined to support a man of their own sentiments, and thus uphold and sustain their own principles. This is the ground taken by the Whig paper in this village,[3] and by several other papers of the same political character in the state.

The conductor of the antimasonic paper here [4] publishes articles favourable to you, and no doubt feels so, but is restrained from coming out decidedly in your behalf, by the apprehension of premature decision in the party. A paper to the north of us, early engaged in the antimasonic cause, and heretofore of considerable influence with the party, has already declared against you; [5] and it is probably from a fear of distraction in their ranks, that the conductor[s] of other papers of the party, though favourable to you, are cautious in expressing their opinions and wishes. They will be likely to observe the same caution, until there is an expression, in some form or other, of the general sense of the party. Although no one can tell what may be effected by intrigue and management, or by the influence of party interest, I do not allow myself to doubt, that men agreeing in general politics, though divided on matters of minor importance, will ultimately unite, to sustain their own principles, and preserve the political character of the state.

I am with high respect, your friend and Obedient servant,

Saml. Prentiss

ALS. NhD.
1. Not found.
2. Virginians elected a Jacksonian majority to the state legislature and to Congress. *National Intelligencer*, May 2, 1835.
3. The *Vermont Watchman*, edited

by Ezekiel P. Walton (1789–1855).
4. Chauncey L. Knapp (1809–1868), editor of the *State Journal*.
5. The *North Star*, a Danville paper edited by Ebenezer Eaton (1777–1859).

TO [EDWARD EVERETT]

May 31. 35

Dear Sir,

I must not omit to express my thanks for the Resolutions; [1] &, more especially, to signify my entire & hearty concurrence in their tone & spirit, without reference to the particular nomination. The Citizens of Boston, I think, have placed their feet on solid grounds of principle & patriotism, & whatever may betide the Country, they will have no dereliction, or backsliding, wherewith to reproach themselves. I am bound off for Washington, on Tuesday morning.[2] There being two or three things to speak about, I intend calling at your House this Eve', between six & seven oclock, for a few minutes. I desire this the more especially, as I may now hope to see Mrs E. But there are several friends in town, & as they may call in, in the P.M. it is quite uncertain whether I may be able to leave home; so that if you have any engagement out, pray do not keep yourself in, in expectation of my call.

Have you thought of the expediency of writing a pretty *stringent* letter to G[ales] & S[eaton] to accompany the Resolutions?[3] Yrs truly

D. Webster

ALS. MHi. Published in Van Tyne, pp. 195–196.

1. At a Whig rally in Faneuil Hall on May 28, 1835, Charles P. Curtis had offered resolutions concurring in the Massachusetts legislature's nomination of Webster for the Presidency. Seconded by speeches from Robert Winthrop, Rufus Choate, and Francis C. Gray, the resolutions were unanimously adopted. *Boston Courier,* June 1, 1835.

2. Webster's hurried trip to Washington was to represent claimants before the French claims commission. *Columbian Centinel,* June 10, 1835.

3. The *National Intelligencer* published an announcement of the Faneuil Hall rally on June 2, and two days later, on June 4, it printed the fifteen resolutions adopted by Boston Whigs on the front page.

TO EDWARD EVERETT

[July 2, 1835]

My Dr Sir

I return your letters. It would be very well, if, on the 4th, in various places, Genl. Harrison should be toasted, as Whig Candidate for the Vice Presidency.[1]

I am for Marshfield today, & shall hardly be home, unless called back by some occasion of business, till the middle of next week. I think Mr. [Robert Benny?; Henry Young?] Cranston, of Newport, will be this way, in a few days, with a wish to see you & other friends.

Yrs ever   D. Webster

ALS. MHi.

1. Webster and his Massachusetts supporters were making a strong and concerted effort to force Harrison to defer to Webster's candidacy by running for the Vice Presidency. For example, the *Columbian Centinel,* April 18, 1835, had carried an article, reportedly correspondence from a Cincinnati citizen to the *Portland Advertiser,* supporting DW for the

Presidency and Harrison for the Vice Presidency. Moreover, Everett had urged this policy upon Biddle in June, stating that "if the Whigs at Columbus would nominate Mr. Webster and General Harrison as Vice President it would have a very decisive effect." Quoted in James A. Green, *William Henry Harrison: His Life and Times* (Richmond, 1941), p. 294.

FROM WILLIAM W. STONE, DANIEL D. BRODHEAD, AND WILLIAM GRAY

Boston August 14th. 1835

Dear Sir

At a preliminary meeting of a number of Gentlemen opposed to the late proceedings of the advocates for the immediate abolition of slavery at the south, of which meeting the Hon Harrison G. Otis was chairman, it was voted, that a public meeting of those citizens of Boston who do not approve of those proceedings should be called at Faneuil Hall on Friday afternoon the 21st instant at 4 O'Clock.[1] We were appointed to make arrangements for that meeting, and knowing the desire of the community to hear you on the very important occasion we respectfully invite you to be present, and to address the citizens.

We have the honor to be with great respect Your Obt Servants

Wm. W. Stone }
Danl D. Brodhead } Committee
Wm Gray }

ALS. NhHi. Published in Van Tyne, p. 196. Stone was a Boston and Lowell businessman, an incorporator of the Middlesex Manufacturing Company. Brodhead was a director of the Merchants' Bank and a stockbroker. Gray (1810–1892; Harvard 1829) was a Boston attorney and later United States District Court judge.

1. Some 1500 Boston citizens signed the call for the August 21 Faneuil Hall meeting to discuss antislavery agitation. Richard Fletcher, Harrison Gray Otis, and Peleg Sprague all delivered antiabolitionist speeches, but Webster was conspicuously absent.

TO JAMES HERVEY BINGHAM

Boston, August 24, 1835.

My Dear Sir,

I have received your letter of the 15th,[1] and am quite obliged to yourself and friends for the interest you manifest in what relates to myself.

As to the object of your inquiry, I can only say that it is not possible for me to remember what I wrote to Mr. [John C.] Chamberlain in 1814, respecting the Hartford Convention, or whether I wrote at all.[2] This pretence that there are letters which if published would shed light on the past conduct of individuals is a stale device; it has been frequently put forth both in regard to myself and others. For my own part, I have steadily refused permission to publish private letters, of which I did not recollect the contents; because if consent were granted in one case, it would be presumed in all others, and thus a man's private letters through the whole course of his life, garbled and mutilated to suit the occasion, would be made public. I have therefore always thought it wisest, if confidence is betrayed and private letters published, to let the publication take place under the odium of a breach of confidence.

I take it for granted, however, that if there be a letter of mine in such hands as you describe, it would have been published before now, if it

had proved any thing. If you recollect dates, my dear Sir, you will remember that I left home for the session of Congress early in the autumn
of 1814, before any movement was made for a convention, and there I
remained till that convention adjourned.

If it would gratify yourself and friends, I would give you sundry facts
and dates, which show, what is strictly true, that I had no hand or part
whatever in the Hartford Convention, and it is true that I expressed an
opinion to Governor [John Taylor] Gilman, that it would not be wise in
him to appoint delegates.[3] Further than this I have no recollection of
interfering in the matter. At the same time, it is true that I did not
regard the proposed convention as seditious or treasonable. I did not
suppose that Mr. [George] Cabot, Mr. [Benjamin] West, Judge [William]
Prescott,[4] and their associates, were a knot of traitors.

I am, dear Sir, with long-continued and sincere regard, Your friend,
Dan'l Webster.

Text from *PC*, 2: 10–11. Original not found. Bingham (1781–1859; Dartmouth 1801), one of Webster's Dartmouth classmates and lifelong friends, was at this time a lawyer and banker in Claremont, New Hampshire. In the early forties, he settled in Ohio, where he remained until 1849, when with Webster's influence he received an appointment as a commissioner in the Land Office in Washington.

1. Not found.

2. Webster-Chamberlain correspondence relating to the Hartford Convention has not been found.

3. No manuscript record of this "opinion" has been found.

4. West (1746–1817; Harvard 1768), was a Charlestown, New Hampshire, lawyer (with whom Bingham had read law) and a delegate to the Hartford Convention; Prescott (1762–1844; Harvard 1783) was a Boston lawyer, delegate to the Hartford Convention and to the Massachusetts Constitutional Convention, and judge of the Boston Court of Common Pleas.

TO EDWARD EVERETT

Sep. 2. [1835]

My Dr Sir

I am obliged to renew this note,[1] once more, (renovare dolerem)—
but you perceive I have given it a short time to live. I have hopes it may
then die a quiet death.

I should be glad to see you, if you should be in town today, or tomorrow before 10.

Meantime, I send you a letter, for perusal.[2] Yrs   D. Webster

ALS. MHi.   2. Not found.

1. Not found.

AGREEMENT BETWEEN DANIEL WEBSTER AND JOHN TAYLOR, JR.
SEPT. 14TH. 1835

The said parties agree the said Taylor shall carry on the said Websters farm called the Elms farm in Franklin and to include the Punch Brook pasture for one year, & as much longer as the parties shall agree—the said Taylor has become owner of one undiv[id]ed half of all the stock and produce now on the farm and the income, profits, & increase, of the farm & stock are to be divided equaly between the parties. The said Taylor agrees to cultivate the farm in a farmerlike manner, to furnish all the labour, to take good care of the stock & to account to said Webster anually for one half the income. Taxes on the farm, the cost of grass seed, plaster, & any other manure that may be purchased, to be paid for out of the common stock. The said Taylor is to furnish his own tools. He is to have liberty to keep his own family horse on the farm free of expense—of the swine he is to have two thirds the produce & to account to the said Webster for one third—he is to take to his own use all the milk, butter, & cheese, but is to account to said Webster for one half. The said Taylor is to occupy all the dwelling house except the four rooms lately repaired and finished & furnished at the east end being two lower rooms & two chambers and the cellar under them, and the said Taylor especially agrees to take the best possible care of the four rooms & the furniture in them, to suffer nobody to use either rooms or furniture, to cause the rooms & also the bedding to be kept well aired and at all times in perfect order. The front entry is also reserved with the four rooms, and is also to be kept in as like good order, a china closet up stairs is also reserved —the said Taylor is to keep the fences in good repair & for that purpose may cut timber on the farm, and he is to have fire wood free of expense. It is not expected that the said Taylor will keep a particular account of the milk, butter, & cheese, but he is to allow a reasonable sum for one half the use of the cows.
John Taylor Jr.   Danl Webster

> John Taylor Jr
> one undivided [half of all the stock and produce?]
> Articles, viz—
> Six oxen, val [?]
> Two French Hor[ses]
> Two fat cows
> Nine other co[ws]
> Four three yea[r] [olds]
> Five two year [olds]

Twelve yearl[ings]
Four calves
Three other yearl[ings]
One other cow
One bull
Two hundred & e[ighty sheep]
Hay & fodder pro[duce]
Farm in Fra[nklin]
Prod[uce][1]

DS. NhHi. John Taylor, Jr. (1801–1869), known as "Daniel Webster['s] farmer," managed the Webster farm at Franklin, beginning his work on September 15. *Concord Daily Moni-* *tor,* May 25, 1869.

1. For another list of stock at the Elms, see Entry of September 15, 1835, in Taylor's Elms Farm Accounts, NhFr.

TO CAROLINE LE ROY WEBSTER

Boston, Monday, 3 oclock
Sept. 21. [1835]

Dear Caroline,

The morning after you left home I went to Marshfield, from which place I returned this forenoon, & had the great pleasure of receiving your letter of friday Eve.[1] The weather was so fine the day after you left, & indeed that day, that we all rejoiced in the probability of your having a fine trip. I hope the good weather may last till our friends sail. I pray you to present my most sincere & affectionate love & regards to Mrs [Catherine Augusta Le Roy] Newbold,[2] with the most sincere good wishes for her entire recovery; & to tender my best parting respects to the rest of the party. I wish them all, most devoutly, a happy & prosperous tour.

It gives a pleasure to hear so favorable an account of your father's health. I think much more of that, than of the probable gains of his new speculation in Western lands; although from what you say, & what I know of the value of those lands, I have no doubt at all but he has made an advantageous operation. It is a subject he is quite well acquainted with, & not likely to be mistaken about.[3] I pray you remember me to him, kindly & affectionately.

I left all well this morning at Marshfield. Edward[4] brought me to the Boat, & took the Chaise back. I carried Sarah Hale[5] down on friday. They expect to be somewhat lonesome this week; but have plans for riding & driving, which I think will keep them occupied, if the weather should hold fair.

Tuesday morning.

The weather is fine, & I propose to take the Boat, at 5. this P.M. My cold has been gradually wearing off, & I am now pretty well. I shall address you next at Boston. Ever truly Yrs   Danl. Webster

ALS. NhHi.

1. Not found.

2. Mrs. Newbold (1790–1835), Caroline's sister, who died in December in Paris, France.

3. Caroline's father, Herman Le Roy, was then engaged in efforts to purchase, in partnership with friends and family, some 89,000 acres of the Holland Land Company's holdings in Orleans, Niagara, Genesee, and Erie counties for almost

$2,300,000. See Herman Redfield and Jacob Le Roy to J. J. Vanderkemp, April 30, 1835; Van Eeghen & Co. to J. J. Vanderkemp, 29 June 1835, in Holland Land Company Papers, Gemeente-Archief van Amsterdam, Amsterdam, Holland.

4. Edward (1820–1848; Dartmouth 1841) was Webster's youngest son.

5. Mrs. Nathan Hale was the sister of Edward and Alexander H. Everett.

Webster set off for Maine on September 22 to argue the case of Veazie *v.* Wadleigh, 11 *Peters 55 (1837), before the United States Circuit Court in Bangor. En route, he used the occasion to renew old acquaintances, make new ones, and strengthen his support among voters, which culminated on September 29 with a large public dinner in his honor hosted by the citizens of Bangor.* Columbian Centinel, *September 23, October 7, 14, 1835.*

TO CAROLINE LE ROY WEBSTER

Hallowell, Wednesday
Eve'—Sep. 23. 1835.

Dear Caroline,

You will easily find Hallowell on the map, & here I am, in less than 24 hours from Boston. The weather has been remarkably fine, & the Boats go well, tho', to be sure, for accomodations they bear but a poor comparison with the Southern Boats. I was in Portland this morning from 4 to 8 oclock—of course I saw nobody. My friend Mr [Samuel Ayer] Bradley,[1] I learned, was not in town. The Boat comes no farther than Gardner, half a dozen miles below this place, where Mr [Robert Hallowell] Gardner,[2] & also Mr [George] Evans lives. Mr Evans heard of my arrival, & came to me at the Boat. Mr Gardner met me also, & I called to see the Families of both these Gentlemen. Mr Gardner's family is in great affliction from the sickness of his daughter, Mrs [Delia Tudor Gardiner] Jones.[3] She was married, you know, about the time we saw the family at Washington, & is now thought to be far gone in a decline. They live in a Cottage, while they are building a new & most elegant House. Mrs [George] Evans[4] is gay as usual. She inquired much for you, & says you were confidently expected this way. Mr Evans brought me from the Boat here in his Barouche, & offers me his company tomorrow to call on a few old friends, of an elderly class. I mean, among other calls, to go & see Dr. [Thomas] Sewall's mother,[5] and Mrs [Emeline Colby Webster] Lindsley's.[6]

I have many friends in the Town, who will of course call to see me. On friday I intend going to Bangor, if the weather should be fair. Adieu! I have written to Julia, & shall make out a line to Mr. [James William] Paige that he may hear of my arrival in safety thus far, if this should not find you in Boston. Yrs ever truly   Danl Webster

ALS. NhHi. Published in Van Tyne, p. 623.

1. Bradley (1774–1844; Dartmouth 1799), another of Webster's friends from Dartmouth and Fryeburg, was a Portland attorney.

2. Gardiner (1782–1864), a descendant of Silvester Gardiner, was one of the inheritors of the property of the Kennebeck Company.

3. 1812–1836.

4. Ann, née Dearborn, whom George Evans had married in 1820.

5. Sewall (1786–1845; Harvard Medical School 1812) was a prominent Washington physician and later Webster's personal physician. His mother was Priscilla Cony Sewall (1749–1836).

6. Mrs. Lindsly's mother was Rebecca Guild Sewall Webster (1780–1870), a sister of Thomas Sewall.

TO CAROLINE LE ROY WEBSTER

Bangor, Friday Eve'
Sep. 25. 1835

My Dear Wife,

I reache[d] Bangor this afternoon at four oclock, having left Hallowell a little before 7; & having travelled the whole distance, 70 miles, in a chaise. The Stages were crowded to excess, & one of the agents undertook to bring me along in a Chaise, which he accomplished, with great speed. The Country is somewhat hilly, but the road is smooth, & it is the fashion to drive like Jehu. I am a good deal tired, & shall go early to bed. Mr [Jacob] McGaw,[1] & a few other friends have called, & I believe I may expect more at Eve'; but I am quite too much fatigued to see much company. Yesterday I spent at Hallowell, Augusta, & Gardner, in seeing the people & the places. I called on Mr [Benjamin] Vaughan, Dr [Robert] Cary,[2] & some other elderly people, & took some pains to go & see Dr. Sewall's mother, and also Mrs Lindsley's mother. They both appeared gratified with the attention. Mr Evans devoted the day to me, &

was very kind. I have two College Classmates who are settled in the place, both with families.

Mrs Evans does not go to Washington, till the Spring.

What I shall do tomorrow I do not yet know; but I expect to go up the River, about twelve miles, to see the spot about which the law suit is. As yet, I have heard nothing from home; it is hardly time.

Adieu; with love to the family. Yrs Ever   Danl Webster

ALS. NhD. Published in Van Tyne, pp. 589–590.

1. McGaw (1778–1867; Dartmouth 1797), one of Webster's Dartmouth and Fryeburg friends, was at this time an attorney in Bangor.

2. Vaughan (1751–1835) was a native of Hallowell; Dr. Cary has not been further identified.

TO NICHOLAS BIDDLE

Sep. 30 1835

My Dear Sir,

Mr [Herman] Le Roy, his son Mr Jacob Le Roy,[1] and several other Gentlemen, have made a large purchase of the Holland Land Company, and are desirous of raising, by way of loan from the Bank of the U.S. a considerable sum towards the amount of the purchase money. Mr Jacob Le Roy will visit Philadelphia to lay his proposals before your Board. The collateral security, as I understand, which is proposed to be offered, is the scrip of the New York Trust Company. In their behalf, I have to ask your favorable consideration of their application. The money will not be needed for ninety days, or thereabouts & would be taken for such length of time as might suit the convenience of the Bank. Mr Le Roy will of course make you & the Directors fully acquainted with any other necessary particulars. Yrs, with entire regard,   Danl Webster

ALS. DLC.

1. Jacob Le Roy (1794–1868; attended Yale), the second surviving son of Herman Le Roy, became a partner in his father's business in 1820. He also served as a director of the Bank of New York and managed the family holdings in the Holland Land Company. On the purchase of that land, see above, DW to Caroline Le Roy Webster, September 21, 1835.

TO [HENRY WILLIS KINSMAN]

Wiscasset,
Oct. 3. Saturday Morning [1835]

My Dear Sir

I fear I may be detained here longer than I expected. Our cause looks as if it might run into next week;[1] &, in addition to that, I do not see how I am likely to get thro. Portland, without some delay. I am very desirous of being in Boston, on the 7th, to attend the Meeting in F[aneuil] Hall;[2] but I am very much afraid I shall not be able. I wish you would see Mr. Edmund Dwight, & Mr. [George?] Bond,[3] and signify to them that it is hardly probable I shall be able to reach Boston, in season for the meeting. It will not be necessary that you should show this letter, or give them any other reason than probable retention by the Court. The truth is, I shall escape from Portland if I can; but I fear it will not be possible, without giving offence.

On receipt of this, I wish you would write me, addressed to Portland. I fear some things may need attention. I forgot a check for $431. which Mrs. Webster took to N York. I hope it was provided for, on its return. There is also a note, in[dorse]d by Perkins & Marvin.[4] Does not that come round, ab[ou]t this time? If so, please get it renewed for a month. I send a blank signature, & a blank ind[orsemen]t. Yrs truly

D Webster

ALS. NhD.

1. *Veazie* v. *Wadleigh*, 11 Peters 55 (1837). *Columbian Centinel*, October 7, 1835.

2. The meeting scheduled for Faneuil Hall but transferred to the Odeon had been called by friends to present Webster with a silver vase. *Columbian Centinel*, October 10, 14, 1835.

3. Bond was a prominent commission merchant in Boston.

4. Perkins & Marvin was the printing and bookselling firm of Benjamin Perkins and Thomas Rogers Marvin (1796–1882), the establishment which had printed Webster's *Speeches and Forensic Arguments*.

As Pennsylvania Whig politicians prepared to make their presidential nomination, Webster's candidacy came under its most crucial test. Throughout the year, Webster and his campaign manager, Edward Everett, had concentrated upon winning the backing of the Pennsylvania Anti-Masons, and they had succeeded with the faction known as "Exclusives," men like Harmar Denny, Thaddeus Stevens, and William W. Irwin who wanted to remain independent of the two major parties. But while winning the "Exclusives'" support, Webster and his advisers failed to outdistance Harrison with Whigs and the Anti-Masonic "Coalitionists," and in mid-December, the latter two factions so managed the caucus as to nominate Harrison. By then, even Nicholas Biddle had concluded to support the Hero of North Bend. When Maryland followed Pennsylvania in endorsing General Harrison, "Webster's candidacy for 1836 was over." Sydney Nathans, Daniel Webster and Jacksonian Democracy (Baltimore, 1973), p. 98. See also Charles McCool Snyder, The Jacksonian Heritage: Pennsylvania Politics, 1833–1848 (Harrisburg, 1958), pp. 65–70; and Charles McCarthy, "The Antimasonic Party: A

Study of Political Antimasonry in the United States, 1827–1840," Amer-ican Historical Association, Annual Report, *1 (1902): 428–483.*

TO [EDWARD EVERETT]

Monday Morning
[November 2, 1835]
Dr Sir
I see by the Gazette of this morning that a Harrison Meeting is adver-tized in Philadelphia for the 10th. inst. Our friends in that City have al-ways been unaccountably inattentive to the movements & wishes of the Anti-Masons. As you probably know more of the designs & feelings of the Anti-Masons in Pa. than all Philadelphia, a letter or two from you, calculated to put Gentlemen on their guard, would do good. I think you might safely express the opinion that the Anti Masons would never go in that direction, & suggest inexpediency of attempting any thing, in Pa, in which they did not take the lead. A letter of this sort to our *timid* friend [Nathan] Sargent, & a hint to our *wise* friend Mr Biddle, might be well. I only suggest the matter for your consideration.[1] Yrs truly
D. Webster

ALS. MHi.
1. According to Webster's sugges-tion, Everett wrote Biddle and Sar-gent on November 3 concerning the Philadelphia Anti-Masonic meeting.

See Everett Letterbook (Reel 25, Frame 929), and also Everett to Thaddeus Stevens, November 2, 1835 (Reel 25, Frame 925), Everett Pa-pers, MHi (Microfilm).

TO [EDWARD EVERETT]

Nov. 4. [1835]

Dear Sir
Would it not be well to write strong letters to our friends Isaac Mun-roe,[1] Hezekiah Niles, Mr [William] St[e]uart,[2] Mr [Robert Henry] Golds-bo[rough] &c—before the meeting at Baltimore on the 11th. inst. That meeting ought well to understand the fixed purpose of Massachusetts, & the probable decision of the Anti M[ason]s of Pa.[3] Yrs   D Webster.

ALS. MHi.
1. Munroe (1784–1859), a native of Massachusetts, was the proprietor of the *Baltimore Patriot & Commer-cial Advertiser. Maryland Historical Magazine,* 20 (September 1925): 249.
2. Steuart (1780–1839), a marble-worker, stonecutter, and builder, for-

mer mayor of Baltimore, was one of the vice presidents of the Baltimore Whig festival.
3. Evidence that Everett corre-sponded with these men has not been found. Webster declined an in-vitation to attend their festival, and on December 23, the Baltimore Whigs nominated William Henry Harrison

and John Tyler for President and Vice President. At Webster's suggestion, Cushing attended this December convention, but failed in persuading delegates to defer a nomination.

Caleb Cushing to Edward Everett, December 22, 24, 1835 (Reel 6, Frames 246–247), Everett Papers, MHi (Microfilm); *National Intelligencer*, December 29, 1835.

FROM HARMAR DENNY

Pittsburg Novr 5. 1835

Private

Dr Sir

I was highly gratified by receiving your favor of the 26 Octr with the communications from Mr. [Henry Willis] Kinsman & other gentlemen.[1] I have shewn them privately to the friends from whose minds I was anxious, to remove the erroneous impressions which had been made by a hostile influence. I am happy in the belief that I have not been disappointed. My own opinion of the matter & which I frequently expressed corresponds with the representations given by the gentlemen who were in the Legislature. Being now in possession of evidence conclusive & satisfactory, the allegations can be met, & repelled with more success, than could be effected by asserting merely my opinions or firm convictions. The position which your friends in the antimasonic party have taken is strengthening every day. By a prompt movement we have stolen a march on the V. B. men among us. In a word I may say the whole party is now decidedly anti Van Buren. Editorial responses & private communications which I have received place this matter beyond all doubt. With regard to Genl Harrison's interest I am not so clear. There are some antimasons of influence among us who yet incline to make him the candidate of our party, because of his services during the war. They would unhesitatingly give the preference to yourself, they declare, but are fearful of the arguments derived from your early course in Congress during the war. They forget that antimasonry has risen into importance since the elevation of Genl Jackson on the hobby of military fame & services and has entirely changed the votes of several of the strongest Jackson counties. The people are no longer carried away by military glory, & I think we have nothing to fear on the score of Genl H's glory. It is rather too dim to dazzle. And at any rate the people look to more recent exploits & events. Under existing circumstances Genl H. cannot obtain our nomination. He must first explain away his letter to the Antimasonic Comm[itt]ee.[2] To do this & avoid falling into degrading inconsistency & perhaps making himself ridiculous, I am at a loss to understand. Some say he must be made an antimason. All this shews the difficulties which, even those who seem to be his friends admit are in the way of his receiving an antimasonic nomination. The majority is now clearly against it. A party not connected with the antimasons is forming to support the Genl. To what size it may grow we cannot yet say. It certainly has hard struggling in its present condition—it seems rather rickety. And unless the antimasonic party unexpectedly take it by the hand it will in my opinion never come to much importance. We shall proceed with our State antimasonic convention as preparatory to the *National convention* at which the nominations will be made. If we succeed in obtaining for the State convention favorable materials, we shall then I think have very little difficulty. Efforts are making to accomplish this object. Although you have already in the Senate Chamber, publicly spoken of the antimasonic party & its principles in terms, highly gratifying to all, & perfectly satisfactory to many;[3] yet I am aware that there are some among us who from no sinister motive, will ask for a declaration of your opinions more pointed, in relation to Masonic & Secret Societies & the principles of antimasonry. Some direct expression upon these topics may be requested, as a "sine qua non." Should we not be prepared for this? It is the practice of our conventions to address the individuals proposed as candidates, upon these subjects. But to be able to meet the questions which may be asked "in limine," some friends, of the gentleman named for the consideration of the convention, have always been put in possession of his free sentiments & opinions touching the masonic institution & other Secret Societies so far as he may have formed a judgment of their principles practices, requisitions & influence, upon information & statements of facts; given under oath in courts of Justice & before comm[itt]ees of Legislative bodies, or from other authentic sources, or from the very nature & tendency of such organized associations. These sentiments & opinions are to be communicated privately to members of convention for their information, and if necessary, at an informal or interlocutory meeting.

As your antimasonic friends in Penna wish, with your permission, to bring your name before our antimasonic State convention, which is to meet on 16 Decr. you can greatly strengthen our hopes, & fortify the stand we have taken by an avowal of opinions, upon the subjects I have mentioned, to the full extent to which Mr [William] Wirt went. Any thing short of this would not probably be satisfactory, and to be more clear, direct & positive would preclude all cavils. I submit these matters for your consideration.[4] How far you can venture on this ground without impairing the support which may be expected from another quarter, you are the best judge. A large portion of the Whigs in this part of the country are liberal & honest, & if I can speak from my own experience, would not take umbrage. If you should deem the intimations I have made worthy of your attention I shall be happy to be made with any other friends you shall name the depository of your sentiments & opinions, to be communicated as you may direct, to the members of our convention, privately & individually, or if necessary at a meeting, or in convention. You may consider me now as respectfully, requesting to be informed of your views & opinions on these points which are of much importance in the estimation of antimasons in Penna.

I must ask a thousand pardons for inflicting upon you this prolix letter. I must find my excuse in the deep interest I feel in an affair which concerns Mr Webster & the country. Your Sincere & obt Servt

Harmar Denny

ALS. NhD.

1. Letters not found.
2. For Harrison's response to the Pennsylvania Anti-Masonic party, see *Niles' Register*, 49 (November 14, 1835): 177.
3. Webster's praise of Pennsylvania Anti-Masons had come on June 3, 1834, when Senator Samuel McKean

of Pennsylvania presented the memorial of the Harrisburg Pennsylvania State Convention on the removal of the deposits. For Webster's comments, see *W & S*, 7: 42.
4. See DW to Denny et al., November 20, 1835, below, for Webster's communication to the Pennsylvania Anti-Masons.

FROM HENRY D. SELLERS ET AL.

Pittsburgh November 10. 1835

Sir,

It is made our duty to communicate to you the proceedings of a large meeting of your fellow citizens of Alleghany County, held in this city on Saturday last, nominating you as a candidate for the office of President of the United States. We take great pleasure in forwarding to you this expression of their confidence in your public character; and of their claim to your future services.

We are not called to remark upon the resolutions[1] adopted by our fellow citizens, which are sufficiently explicit on the principles and policy acceptable to Pennsylvania in a candidate for the Presidential office: But we cannot suffer the occasion to pass without expressing our hope that her citizens may be fully informed of the bearing of your political opinions on her prominent interests; as it is not probable that they will be willing to place men in office whose settled views of constitutional, and other questions, are not conformable to those interests.

With cordial wishes for your health and happiness—identified as they are with the best hopes of our beloved country, we are your friends and fellow citizens

Thos. Williams   Henry D Sellers
Charles Avery   Benj Bakewell

William Marks	Wm Bell
David Shields	Samuel Church
James R. Speer	John Tassy
Wm. Eichbaum	M[ichael] Allen
John Irwin	M. B. Lowrie
Robert Hilands	John D. McCord
	Robert Mackie
	O[rlando] Metcalf
	Wm. Wade

ALS by Sellers, signed also by others. DLC. Sellers (1790–1855) was a Pittsburgh physician.

1. The resolutions of the November 5 Pittsburgh convention appear in *Niles' Register*, 49 (November 21, 1835): 201.

FROM HARMAR DENNY

Pittsburg Novr 11. 1835

Dr Sir

The delegates from the antimasonic party of Allegheny County assembled in convention to day, and it gives me great pleasure to say that the utmost harmony of opinion prevailed. There was but one voice that did not concur *fully* to the *object* which the convention has strenuously urged. I hope the same unanimity of sentiment may appear at the State convention.

The delegates from this county are all now your friends—& besides have been instructed by the convention to urge your nomination.

The following are the names of the delegates

N[eville] B Craig Esq Editor of the Pittsbg. Gazt.[1]

Benj[amin] Darlington, a prominent mercht.[2]

W[illiam] W[allace] Irwin Esqr already known to you

J[ames] C. Gilleland Esqr. Editor of the Times[3]

& Harmar Denny.

The statements which we made of our belief that you entertained antimasonic sentiments were founded upon *declarations* made by yourself in the Senate, on presenting the memorial from Harrisbg: *declarations* made by Mr [Benjamin Franklin] Hallet[4] himself in commenting upon that circumstance in his own paper, these, with the assertion by some of your personal friends that they knew you to coincide in sentiment with us, were so far satisfactory. The grounds for this assertion were not mentioned. Some of us understand them to be, conversation with yourself & confidential letters, which had passed some three or four years ago.

In order now to bring our friends in other parts of the State to the earliest possible understanding of your views & thus to satisfy them of your concurrence and most favorably impress their minds, it is very necessary that we should receive some communication from you without much delay.[5] With this view therefore the delegates from this county will address to you a letter, expecting to receive a favorable answer which they can make public at once. By this course we shall anticipate a movement by the friends (not antimasons of V. B.) I think they contemplate some thing of this kind. Our letter to you will be forwarded by the mail of tomorrow or next day.[6]

I hope you received my last under cover to Mr Kinsman.[7] Yours with sincere esteem   Harmar Denny

I will send a Pttsbg. Gazt. containing our proceedings. This is a small beginning but I hope will be the basis of more important and extended action.

ALS. DLC.

1. Craig (1787–1863) owned and edited the *Pittsburgh Gazette* from 1829 to 1841.

2. Darlington, a Chester County, Pennsylvania, native, had settled in Pittsburgh before 1815.

3. Gilleland (d. 1836) began publishing the *Pittsburgh Mercury* in 1811 and took over the *Pittsburgh Times* in 1831.

4. Hallett (1797–1862; Brown 1816) was editor of the *Boston Advocate*, the organ of the Massachusetts Antimasons.

5. See DW to Harmar Denny et al., November 20, 1835, below.

6. See Harmar Denny et al., to DW, November 11, 1835, mDW 12676.

7. Denny was most likely referring to his letter of November 5, above.

FROM JOSEPH WALLACE, SAMUEL SHOCK, AND GEORGE W. HARRIS

Harrisburg November 16. 1835.

Dear Sir,

The Democratic Antimasonic party of Pennsylvania, wishing to ascertain the opinions of the prominent men of the nation on the subject of free-masonry, (which, since the disclosure of its oaths and obligations is in Pennsylvania deemed a subject of great importance,) we, in behalf of the State Committee of that party, take the liberty of addressing to you the following questions, and would respectfully solicit a reply.

1 Do you believe Free-masonry and all other Secret Societies, bound by Secret oaths to be a moral and political evil?

2 Do you believe the exercise of the elective franchise, to be a fair, constitutional and expedient means of removing such evil?

3 When the Chief Magistrate of a State or of the Union, is elected on

antimasonic principles, do you believe it to be his duty, to sustain those principles in his appointments to office? A Democratic Antimasonic State convention will be held on the 14th. of December next, at this place and an answer before that time is respectfully requested if convenient.[1] Yours &c   J. Wallace
                                        Saml. Shock
                                        Geo W Harris
     A copy of this letter has been sent to Messrs [John C.] Calhoun, [John] Forsyth, [Louis] McLane, [Samuel L.] Southard, [Horace] Binney, [John] Sergeant & other distinguished gentlemen.

LS. NhHi. Joseph Wallace of Harris-   a Dauphin County, Pennsylvania,
burg was the state Anti-Masonic   attorney.
party chairman; Samuel Shock (b.   1. For Webster's reply, see letter
1797) was a Harrisburg lawyer,   of November 28, below.
banker, and businessman; Harris was

TO EDWARD EVERETT
                                        [November 19, 1835]
My Dear Sir,
     I send you the letters, recd today, from Pittsburg.[1] I pray you sketch an *answer*, to the letter of the Delegates & let me see you tomorrow. Can you be at my office at 10 oclock?—or shall I come to your House? Yrs
                                        D Webster

ALS. MHi.   ber 11, and from Wallace et al., of
     1. Webster probably enclosed the   November 16, and from Denny et al.,
letters above from Denny, of Novem-   of November 11, mDW 12676.

TO [BENJAMIN BAKEWELL]
                                        Boston Nov. 20. 1835
My Dear Sir,
     Your obliging letter of the 7th instant[1] was duly recd here, but my absence from home on Professional business has prevented an earlier acknowledgement. I am very sensible, My Dear Sir, of the honor done me, by the meeting over which you presided,[2] & feel the full value of the approbation of such a body of men of my public conduct, & their confidence in my attachment to the true interests of the Country. Though the proceedings of the meeting call for no answer or reply from me, I am very desirous, at a proper time, of complying with the wish intimated to me by Mr [Henry D.] Sellers & Mr [Thomas] Williams, in behalf of the

Comm[itt]ee. I write a letter to those Gentlemen to day, which I hope you will see.[3]

It will always give me much pleasure to hear from you, either at home, or at Washington, & I pray you to be assured of the sincere & constant regard, with which I am, Dr Sir, Your friend

AL copy. NhHi. Published in *W & S*, 16: 259. Bakewell (1767–1844) was owner of the Bakewell Glass Works in Pittsburgh.

1. Not found.

2. Bakewell had served as presi-

dent of the Pittsburgh convention of November 5 that nominated Webster for the Presidency. See above, Henry D. Sellers et al. to DW, November 10, 1835.

3. Not found.

TO HARMAR DENNY ET AL.

Boston Nov. 20, 1835.

Gentlemen,

I have the honor to acknowledge your favor of the 11th instant,[1] the receipt of which has been delayed for a few days, by my absence from home.

Permit me, Gentlemen, to express my grateful sense of the respect shown me by my fellow Citizens, the members of the Convention of Democratic Antimasons of Alleghany County, in their recent proceedings, as set forth in your communication. The esteem they are pleased to express for my public character, and their confidence in my attachment to the Constitution of the Country, demand my profound acknowledgements.

Nor do they do me more than justice, in their belief of my entire accordance in their opinions, so far as I understand them on the subject of Secret Societies. You express a wish, however, that for the satisfaction of friends in other parts of the State, I should enable you to make known my sentiments respecting the Order of Freemasonry. I have no hesitation, Gentlemen, in saying, that however unobjectionable may have been the original objects of the Institution, or however pure may be the motives and purposes of individual members, and notwithstanding the many great and good men, who have from time to time belonged to the Order, yet, nevertheless, it is an institution, which, in my judgement, is essentially wrong in the principle of its formation; that from its very nature, it is liable to great abuses; that among the obligations, which are found to be imposed on its members, there are such as are entirely incompatible with the duty of good citizens; and that all Secret Associations, the members of which take upon themselves extraordinary obligations to one another, and are bound together by secret oaths, are, naturally, sources of jealousy and just alarm to others, are especially unfavorable to harmony and mutual confidence, among men, living together under popular Institutions; and are dangerous to the general cause of civil Liberty, and good Government. Under the influence of this conviction, I heartily approved the law, lately enacted in the State of which I am a citizen, for abolishing all such oaths & obligations.

I express these opinions, Gentlemen, with the less reserve on this occasion, inasmuch as they have been often expressed already, not only to some of your own number and many of your friends, but to all others, also, with whom I have at different times conversed on the subject.

Of the political principles and conduct of the Antimasons of Pennsylvania I have spoken freely, in my place in the Senate, and under circumstances which took from the occasion all just suspicion of any indirect purpose. The opinions there expressed, are unaltered. I have ever found the Antimasons of Pennsylvania true to the Constitution, to the Union, and to the great interests of the Country. They have adopted the "Supremacy of the Laws," as their leading sentiment, and I know none more just, or more necessary. If there be among us any so high, as to be too high for the authority of laws, or so low, as to be too low for its regard and protection; or if there be any, who by any means whatever, may exempt themselves from its control, then, to that extent, we have failed to maintain an equal Government. The Supremacy of the Constitution and the Laws is the very foundation stone of Republican Institutions; if it be shaken, or removed from its place, the whole system must inevitably totter to its fall.[2]

Your obliged friend & fellow citizen, Danl Webster

ls draft (by Everett) with revisions by DW. NhHi. Other copies or drafts of this letter are in the Webster Papers, DLC, and in the Buchanan Papers, PHi. One page of an early Webster draft is in the Everett Papers, MHi. Published in PC, 2: 12–14.

1. See mDW 12676.

2. Webster's own draft of this last paragraph is in the Everett Papers, MHi (mDW 12701).

TO JAMES LONGUE

Boston Nov. 21. 1835

Sir,

I have recd your favor of the 17th instant,[1] & am obliged to you for the respectful & friendly sentiments which you express.

My sentiments in regard to Slavery, as it now exists, in the United States, under the guarantee of the Constitution, <were expressed in a letter> have been expressed on many occasions, in & out of Congress. I enclose you the copy of a letter written by me some time ago, <to Mr.> to a Gentleman residing in New York, but formerly connected with Georgia, which contains a brief statement of those sentiments. The letter was published, about the time it was written, in the Newspapers, <but I have not a printed copy on hand> which I now enclose.[2]

<I. These> My opinions on this subject are honestly entertained, & firmly settled. They are founded on what is, in my judgment, the Constitutional right of the Slave holding States, & therefore are not likely to be changed. I can have no objection to repeat the expression of them, <or any occa> at the request of any respectable number of my fellow Citizens; <thou> although this communication <perha> may, perhaps, supersede the necessity of such repetition, in the way intimated by you. On that point, however, <&> I leave it [to] yourself & friends to decide.

With respect, yr obliged fellow Citizen

AL draft. CtY. Longue has not been identified.
1. Not found.
2. Webster was referring to his letter of May 17, 1833, to John Bolton (see *Correspondence*, 3: 252–253).

It had been published in *Niles' Register*, 44 (June 29, 1833): 295. The final clause of this paragraph, "which I now enclose," is not in Webster's hand.

TO EDWARD EVERETT

Nov. 22. [1835]

Dear Sir

I return you Govr. [Joseph] R[itner]'s letter.[1] I hear from Philada that the young men are stirring, & that the feeling for Genl. Harrison is not so fervent as it was.

Would it not be practicable to induce the General to reconsider his resolution not to run for Vice President, in case the Convention should not nominate him for the Presidency? Think of this. Yrs ever

Danl Webster

ALS. MHi.
1. On October 20, 1835, Everett had congratulated Ritner, Anti-Masonic candidate for governor, on the Pennsylvania election (Everett Letterbook, Reel 25, Frame 921, Everett Papers, MHi, Microfilm). Ritner's response has not been found in the Everett Papers, but Everett had probably sent it to Webster, who was now returning it.

FROM WILLIAM WALLACE IRWIN

Pittsburgh 27 Novemb 1835

My Dear Sir

By the mail of this morning I recd your reply to the Delegates from this County & your private letter to myself both dated the 20th inst.[1]

I have shewn the Reply to Dr [Edward D.] G[azzam][2] who agreed with me in suggesting certain slight modifications.

You say

"Nor do they do me more than justice in their belief of my entire accordance in their opinions '*so far as I understand them*' on the subject of Secret Societies."[3]

The remark by Genl Harrison in his letter to the chairman & Secretary of our State Committee that he was unacquainted with the opinions of the Antimasons of Pennsa gave very great offence to numbers of our friends throughout the state.[4] And inasmuch as the opinions of the Antimasons of Pennsa have been repeatedly expressed in their Conventions and publically made known for the last six years, exception might possibly be taken to the words which I have underscored in the sentence quoted: I would for this and other reasons suggest the propriety of striking out the words "*so far as I understand them.*" As the expression is not material to the sense of the passage I presume you will readily assent to the proposition.

In another part of your letter you observe,—"Under the influence of this conviction, I heartily approved the law lately enacted in the State of which I am a citizen for abolishing all such oaths and obligations."

It occurs to me that the law referred to did not give general satisfaction to the antimasons of Massachusetts, and that differences of opinion existed as to its efficacy to accomplish the suppression of secret associations. I am not exactly certain on this point, but if my impression be correct, it would be prudent to make no mention of that law.

The sentence might be thus modified. "Under the influence of this conviction, it is my opinion that the future administration of all such oaths and obligations should be prohibited by law."[5]

With these slight alterations, I trust that your letter will be as satisfactory to every antimason in Pennsylvania, and throughout the Union, as I take pleasure in assuring you it has proved to our mutual friend Dr. Gazzam and myself.

Mr. Denny and Mr. Gilleland (two of the Delegates from this County) left home for the eastward a few days since, and I deem it prudent not to exhibit your reply to the other gentlemen composing the Delegation, until after I shall have the pleasure of again hearing from you.

The severe illness of my family has delayed my departure to Harrisburgh, and I shall probably not be able to leave home before the first of December. Circumstances may detain me here until after that period, or compel me to go to Philada. before I visit Harrisburgh. If I visit Philada. first, I shall be there on Friday or Saturday the 3d. and 4th. Decr. To guard against all contingencies, be pleased to write me in triplicate addressed to me at Pittsburgh, Harrisburgh, and Philada.

Dr. Gazzam desires to be remembered to you. Very truly yours

W W Irwin

I have sent duplicates to Boston & Philada.

ALS. DLC.

1. For Webster's reply to the Allegheny County delegates to the Democratic Antimason Convention of Pennsylvania, see above, DW to Harmar Denny et al., November 20, 1835. DW's "private letter" to Irwin has not been found.

2. Gazzam (b. 1803), a Pittsburgh doctor, lawyer, and associate editor of the *Pittsburgh Times*, became a Free Soiler and later a Republican. He served in the Pennsylvania state Senate in 1856. See *Correspondence*, 3: 364–366, for an 1834 letter from Gazzam.

3. See above, DW to Harmar Denny et al., November 20, 1835.

4. Harrison had written: "As I am not informed of the principles which govern the anti-masonic party of Pennsylvania, otherwise than that they are opposed to masonry, I must

leave you to judge of my principles and opinions in relation to that order, from the fact, that neither myself nor any of my family have ever been members, and from that of my having been in situations where the strongest inducements existed to become a member, arising from the example of my intimate friends and associates, and that too at a time when the society had never been impeached either in relation to its general tendency or to the conduct of any of its members.

"You will readily conclude, gentlemen, from this statement, that I have never been partial to the masonic order." *Niles' Register*, 49 (November 14, 1835): 177.

5. In a final draft (mDW 12702) Webster deleted both objectionable passages, and inserted in the second passage Irwin's suggested phrasing.

TO EDWARD EVERETT

Saturday Morng

[November 28? 1835]

My Dear Sir,

I send you a letter, recd from Harrisburg, & the answer which I propose to return[1]—also the dr[a]ft of a letter to Mr. Irwin.[2]

Would it be possible for you to be at my House, at ½ past 6. this Eve', for half an hour, if I were to send a coach for you?

There are two or three things, I must see you about; and as to some of them, I want other friends to be present also. Yrs   D.W.

ALS. MHi.

1. See above, Joseph Wallace, Samuel Shock, and George W. Harris to DW, November 16, 1835; and DW to

the same, November 28, below.

2. See DW to William W. Irwin, November 30, 1835, below, and mDW 12702.

TO JOSEPH WALLACE, SAMUEL SHOCK, AND GEORGE W. HARRIS

Boston Nov. 28. 1835.

Gentlemen,

I have recd. your letter of the 16th. instant.[1] A desire to know my opinions, concerning any public question, which proceeds from so highly respectable a source, would at all times command my respectful & prompt attention. Before the receipt of your letter, however, a correspondence had taken place between friends of yours in another part of Pennsylvania, & myself on the same general subject. That correspondence, I presume, is to be laid before the Convention at Harrisburg, & may render a particular answer to your letter unnecessary. I will observe, however, that on the subject of all Secret Societies, bound by secret oaths I concur entirely with what I suppose to be the sentiments of the Antimasons of Pa. as I have said on various occasions, heretofore; and there can be no question of the constitutional right of those who believe such Societies to be either moral or political evils, to seek the removal of such evils, by the exercise of the elective franchise, as well as by other lawful means. The expediency of such exercise of the elective franchise, in a given case, must be decided by the electors according to their own sense of the magnitude of the evil, which they seek to remove, & with a conscientious regard to those other great interests of the community, which are necessarily more or less affected by every exercise of that franchise.

I pray you, Gentlemen, to accept the assurance of my personal regard & cordial good wishes.

Your obliged friend & fellow Citizen,

AL draft. NhHi. Published in Curtis,   1. See above.
1: 510.

TO WILLIAM WALLACE IRWIN

Boston Nov. 30th. 1835.

My Dear Sir,

I enclose you, copies of a letter received by me from members of your State Committee & my answer.[1]

If my letter to yourself & your associates had not appeared to supercede the necessity, I should have found no difficulty in answering the two first questions proposed to me in this letter. But I should doubt the prudence of directly replying to the third; because, in the situation in which I stand, that question might appear to others to be little else than asking me, whether, on the happening of a certain event, I would confine myself to Antimasons, in nominations, to office. Altho the question, in form, asks only what I think would be the duty of a chief magistrate, yet, in effect, it might be thought, or represented, as a mere request of a *promise* from me. I wish, My Dear Sir, you would take occasion to explain this point, in conversation, with the writers of the letter, and with other friends. What a Chief Magistrate must do, & ought to do, so far as he is elected on Antimasonic principles, and in regard to portions of the Country where these principles prevail, can be no matter of doubt, to you, or to me; or to any man, who reflects, & who means to act with candor, & honesty towards those who support him. I hope no one hesitates to believe that I am altogether incapable of disappointing, in that respect, any natural & just expectations, which friends may form. But it does not consist with my sense of duty to hold out promises, or any thing which might be regarded, as equivalent to promises, particularly, on the eve of a great election, the results of which are to affect the highest interests of the Country, for years to come.[2] I authorize you, My Dear Sir, to make the substance of this letter known to your friends, & mine; but it is still to be regarded, of course, as a private and confidential letter. Yrs truly

Danl. Webster.

LS. DLC. Published in Curtis, 1: 510–511.

1. See above, Joseph Wallace, Samuel Shock, and George W. Harris to DW, November 16; and DW to the same, November 28, 1835.

2. Harrison's response on this question of appointing Anti-Masons to office was almost the same as Webster's. See William Henry Harrison to William Ayres, November 23, 1835, William Henry Harrison Papers, DLC.

FROM CALEB CUSHING

Washington Dec. 2. 1835

Dear Sir:

The article in the Intelligencer of today[1] I have had in my head some time, but its appearance has been delayed, partly by the pressure of other engagements which stood in the way of my writing it off, and partly by doubts as to the true time & mode of publication. I think it is needed at this moment; and that Washington is on the whole the best point of departure for it. Mr [Joseph] Gales informs me that he shall have it reset immediately for publication in a pamphlet;[2] and if there is any class or field of persons, to and into which to send it, I shall attend to any wishes of yours in that respect with great pleasure.

Very respectfully, Your obedient servant, C. Cushing.

ALS. DLC.

1. The *National Intelligencer*, December 2, 1835, published Cushing's six-column biography of Webster, which emphasized Webster's role in the War of 1812, the Dartmouth College case, and the Webster-Hayne debate.

2. No copy of Cushing's essay in pamphlet form has been found.

TO CALEB CUSHING

New York Decr. 6. 1835

My Dear Sir

I recd your friendly letter,[1] on my arrival in this City yesterday morning. At that time I had not seen the article in the Intelligencer. I have since read it, & am bound to express my grateful [appreciation] to its author. It is much read & talked about here. In dates & facts, it is correct, in an uncommon degree. For the rest, I can only say it appears to me much too commendatory.

I think of but one thing which might be added, & perhaps that is of no great consequence. It refers to the period of the late war. Something like what follows might be said with truth.

"In the recess of Congress, in the Summer of 1814, when the whole seaboard was threatened by invasion Mr W. gave the principal part of his time in cooperating with others for preparing for defence, in case of an attack by the enemy in his neighborhood. By the citizens of Portsmouth, & on the nomination of that venerable Republican John Langdon, he was placed at the head of the principal Com[mitt]ee raised to concert means of defence, & he offered his personal services to the Governor of the State, to be commanded in any mode in which they might be thought to be useful." &c &c.

I expect to be in Washington in the course of the week, & earlier, if any thing should occur of a *hastening* nature.

Yrs, with very sincere regard   Danl Webster

ALS. NN. Published in Fuess, *Cush-*   1. See above, Cushing to DW, De-
ing, 1: 172–173.   cember 2, 1835.

TO EDWARD EVERETT

New York Decr. 7. 1835

My Dear Sir

I have recd yrs of the 4th.[1] The affair of the signatures turns out much as I expected, not quite fraudulent, & not quite fair.[2] It lies in that medium between honesty & dishonesty, which is commonly called management. I am exceedingly glad that Mr [Thomas] H[artley?] is going to Harrisburg, & shall be glad to see him on his way.[3] Nerr Middleswarth is chosen Speaker of the Assembly. He is an important man, & if you know him, it would do good for you to write to him. I hope you do not forget your fast friend Joseph Lawrence.

I believe the Meeting here on Friday Eve' quite exceeded the expectation of those who called it.[4] I am told it was large, beyond precedent, & that it was quite spirited & hearty. Our friend Col [James Watson] Webb says New York (the State) offers fair to go agt. Mr. V. Buren.

I hear nothing important from Washington. Rumours are belligerent, one hour, & pacific the next.

You may expect to hear from me again at Philadelphia. In the meantime, I pray you accept my thanks for your effective good offices, & unwearied friendship. Yours   Danl. Webster

ALS. MHi.

1. Not found.

2. The significance of this discussion of "signatures" has not been determined.

3. At a meeting of Philadelphia Whigs on December 1, Hartley had been appointed delegate to the Harrisburg, Pennsylvania, Whig convention of December 14. *Niles' Register*, 49 (December 5, 1835): 230.

4. The New York Whigs held a meeting in Masonic Hall on December 4, 1835, at which they passed resolutions supporting Webster for president. *Columbian Centinel*, December 9, 1835.

TO CAROLINE LE ROY WEBSTER

N. York Decr. 7. 1835

Dear Caroline,

I recd your letter yesterday,[1] & all here were very glad to hear from you. This leaving home is a pretty hard matter, to those who go, & to those who stay. It may render a reunion more agreeable & more valued.

I went to Church yesterday morning with Mrs [William] Edgar,[2] & for the rest of the day, except a short call at Mr [Edward] Curtis's sat over the fire. Today, I have calls to make, & business to attend to, besides a dinner to eat with the sons of St. Nicholas.

We did <not> wrong in not sending your father some of our apples. He wants two barrels of our *Greenings*. If there come a moderate turn of weather, you must send them on to him. Mr [James William] Paige will advise Fletcher about the time & mode of shipping them. The Captain [Charles Henry Thomas] must be charged to keep them from Frost.

I have paid your butter bill, which is enclosed. Also your bonnet bill —$26.25. For both these amounts please give me credit, & charge household expenses. The butter cost 30 cts, here, as you will see. The honor of New England forbids us to send again to N. Y. for butter. Bonnets, you may get where you please.

Father desires his best regards, & will send you the letters from Mrs. [Catherine Augusta Le Roy] Newbold, as soon as they have been read by friends here.

Adieu, for today   D. Webster

I enclose two little bills which do not pass here.

ALS. NhHi. Published in Van Tyne, p. 591.

1. Not found.

2. Cornelia, née Le Roy (1787–1860), Caroline's sister, then a widow.

FROM [JOSEPH LAWRENCE?]

Harrisburg, Decr. [c. 10, 1835]

Dear Sir,

I must take leave to ask you one question, not for my own satisfaction, but in order to enable me to satisfy others. Although it has been so often, & so authentically denied, you [are] not aware how many People in Pa. still believe that you were a member of the Hartford Convention. Will you do me the favor, therefore, to say under your name, whether you were, or were not a member of that body, & give me leave to make such use of your answer, as I may judge expedient.

Yrs with much regard

AL draft (in DW's hand). NhHi. Published in Van Tyne, pp. 49–50.

TO [JOSEPH LAWRENCE?]

[c. December 10, 1835]

Dear Sir

I have recd your letter, & very cheerfully answer its inquiry. I was not a member of the Hartford Convention, & had no agency in it, nor any correspondence with any of its members. If you will refer to the Journal of Congress, & to the dates of the proceedings relative to that Convention, you will find, My Dear Sir, that I was in my seat in the House of Representatives in Congress, which was before any proposition to hold such a Convention was brought forward, & that I remained in that seat, until after the Convention had met & dissolved.

AL draft. NhHi. Published in Van Tyne, p. 50.

FROM CHARLES MINER

Harrisburg Decr. 17 1835

My Dear Sir,

The Anti-Masonic Convention has just nominated Major Gen. W. H. Harrison 80 to about 20. The Alleghenny Delegation, Mr. [Thaddeus] Stevens and some others having, last night, withdrawn.[1]

Our Convention, which has done nothing but wait the movement of our Rev[ere]d and most excellent master's balance, will receive and register their edict to night.[2] What a farce! All agree, "Mr. Webster is my first choice," but we cannot carry him. Why? It seems strange that he who is the *first* choice of every one should be *less* popular than the man who is only the *second* choice, & confessedly his inferior. Ah, but he was a Federalist? Damning sin! Never to be forgiven: But he was opposed to the war! Let no statesman or patriot hereafter, dare to interpose his voice to save his Country from the Horrors of war! Let no one dare raise his voice against men in power, however rich, who have sacrificed the Peace of the Country. Let no Representative withhold his vote for appropriations however wicked or foolish, in time of war. Condemn Chatham and Fox [3] to infamy; and disfranchise Webster. General Harrison cannot be made President; His nomination only increases the chances of Mr. V. B. and Judge White.

Perhaps a time-serving wisdom would persuade to submission, but neither my honest principles nor my proud spirit can allow me to advise it. I say in coolness to day at noon what I said last evening—you are *sacrificed*, and that not temporarily but on grounds & principles that affect you with this mongrel party now and forever. I am faithfully your friend

Charles Miner

ALS. DLC.
   1. For a discussion of the proceedings of the convention, see Snyder, *The Jacksonian Heritage*, pp. 69–70.
   2. Led by James Todd (b. 1786) and Joseph Lawrence, the Coalitionists delivered 98 votes for Harrison and only 29 for Webster. Snyder, *The Jacksonian Heritage*, p. 70;

Niles' Register, 49 (December 26, 1835): 288.
   3. William Pitt (1708–1778), the Elder, first Earl of Chatham, made numerous speeches in Parliament opposing the use of military force against the American colonies. Charles James Fox (1749–1806) had also taken a leading role in opposing Lord North's American policy. *DNB*.

TO NICHOLAS BIDDLE

Washington Jan. 15. 1836

My Dear Sir

The President is driving for War: at least, he is for going ahead, not caring if war be the consequence, but resolved, at all events, to get a *triumph*, in some way, over France. A. B. & C. hold back: D. E. & F. follow on. My belief is, we shall get a sort of *bragging* message, but no *specific* recommendation of any measure of redress.[1] The war feeling is not high, in Congress; yet, in the H.R. there are more ready to follow, if the P. leads off in that direction, than is generally supposed.

The Senate (while it lasts) I hope, will observe *the just medium*.

As the probability of war increases, the *project* of a "third term" *projects* itself. Mr. V. B. would as soon see the proboscis of an elephant pointed towards him. In his opinion "the true policy of the Country is decidedly pacific."

On the whole, we shall have no war; at least not for a good while to come. France has no occasion to attack us: we shall not be willing, at present to attack her; if we get suddenly [caught] by the ears, it must be in consequence of some "untoward" event—like that of Navarino. Yrs

D. Webster

ALS. DLC.

1. Since Jackson's discussion of the French reparations question in his annual message of December 7, 1835, the United States government had suspended diplomatic intercourse with France because of France's failure to appropriate funds to carry out the provisions of the treaty of July 4, 1831. France demanded that the United States apologize for the misunderstanding that had developed between the countries, but Jackson refused to comply with the condition; and he was, on January 15,

preparing a statement of the situation for presentation to Congress on January 18. As Webster anticipated, Jackson's message urged retaliation, requesting Congress to prohibit French vessels and products in American ports and to appropriate funds for strengthening the navy and coastal defenses to ward off a French attack. *Senate Journal*, 24th Cong., 1st sess., Serial 278, pp. 98–102; Richard Aubrey McLemore, *Franco-American Diplomatic Relations, 1816–1836* (University, La., 1941), pp. 132–176.

TO DANIEL FLETCHER WEBSTER

Washington, January 15, 1836.

Dear Fletcher,

I am sorry for your disappointment about the aid-ship;[1] but never mind, I believe you are as well without it; if you think not, I will see more about it, when I get home. I believe the military honors of our family terminated with my father. I once tried to be captain, and failed; and I canvassed a whole regiment to make your uncle an adjutant, and failed also. We are predestinated not to be great in the field of battle. We are not the sons of "Bellona's bridegroom"; our battles are forensic; we draw no blood, but the blood of our clients.

Your notions of matters and things are quite right, as applicable to your own condition. You must study practical things. You are in the situation of the *haud facile emergunts*, and must try all you can to get your head above water. Why should you botanize, who have not field enough to bear one flower? Why should you geologize, who have no right in the earth, except a right to tread on it? This is all very well; I thought so, at your age, and therefore studied nothing but law and politics. I wish you to take the same course; yet still save a little time, have a few "*horas subsecivas*" in which to cultivate liberal knowledge; it will turn

to account, even practically. If, on a given occasion, a man can, grace-
fully, and without the air of a pedant, show a little more knowledge than
the occasion requires, the world will give him credit for eminent attain-
ments. It is an honest quackery. I have practised it, and sometimes with
success. It is something like studying an extempore speech; but even
that, done with address, has its effect. There is no doubt at least that
the circle of useful knowledge is much broader than it can be proved to
be, in relation to any particular subject, *à priori.*

We find connections and coincidences, helps and succors, where we
did not expect them. I have never learned any thing which I wish to forget; except how badly some people have behaved; and I every day find,
on almost every subject, that I wish I had more knowledge than I possess, seeing that I could produce it, if not for use, yet for effect.

I have a letter from your mother to-day,[2] which I shall try to answer
to-morrow. I am troubled and perplexed with a few small cases in court.
I cannot bring them on, so as to try them, nor put them off, so as to
leave them and go home. They stick, like a half-drawn boot.

We had a debate yesterday in the Senate, pretty warm. I made a
speech, rather good.[3] A quarrel between Mr. [Robert H.] Goldsborough
and Mr. [Thomas Hart] Benton; I hope no fight will grow out of it,
though the language was very rough.[4]

I understand there is a man here from Missouri, a Colonel [George
French] S[trother], who means to have a fight with Mr. Benton, and if
Mr. Benton will not have a regular duel, intends to fight him *ex parte.*[5]

                                                                D.W.

P.S. Paper out.

Text from *PC*, 2: 16–17. Original not
found.
　1. On November 22, 1836, Fletcher
succeeded in getting an appointment
as aide-de-camp to Henry Alexander
Scammell Dearborn. Shortly, however, he resigned the position because
of criticism that he no longer resided
in Massachusetts but in the West.
　2. Not found.
　3. Webster had spoken on the Forti-

fications Bill. See *Register of Debates*,
24th Cong., 1st sess., 12: 148–163.
　4. Goldsborough and Benton had
disagreed on the Fortifications Bill.
　5. The dispute between Strother
and Benton grew out of the recent
congressional canvass in Missouri.
See Elbert B. Smith, *Magnificent Mis-
sourian: The Life of Thomas Hart
Benton* (Philadelphia, 1958), pp.
155–156.

TO CAROLINE LE ROY WEBSTER

                                        Washington, Sunday Morning
                                        Jan 24. 36
Dear Caroline
　I wrote to Fletcher on Thursday.[1] Yesterday & Friday, I was so much

occupied in Court, & with Court business, I had no time to write.

You will see that there is a good deal of heat here. Mr Benton, & others of the Senate, have attacked the proceedings of last session. I have felt bound to defend, or help defend the Senate. This has led Mr [John Quincy] Adams to attack us, in the House, in the most violent manner, & to bestow an especial portion of his wrath & bitterness on me.[2] He has the instinct of those animals, which, when enraged, turn upon their keepers, & mangle those who have showed them most kindness. The members of the Mass. Delegation are exceedingly indignant, & most of them will tell him what they think of him, before the matter is over. He may be alluded to, also, in the Senate, but not by me. You will see the debates.

The weather is exceedingly cold & raw. I feel its effects, in that *thumb* which gave me so much trouble, some years ago. I write this morning, not without difficulty. In other respects I am quite well.

I imagine Mr [Samuel L.] Southard, Mr [John M.] Clayton & Mr [Thomas] Ewing may take part, in this Debate that is going on, & say something to, or abt., Mr Adams & his speech. The House, I understand was disgracefully disorderly, on Friday, & when Mr Adams abused *me* well, some of the members, I believe principally those from the State of New York, *clapped him*—& then the galleries hissed. This, you will see, must have been all very decorous & proper.

For a considerable [part] of next week (I mean this week) I must be in Court. My business there now presses me rather hard.

I send you a lot of invitations, that you may see what is going on. I have been to no parties—& like very much the pleasure of staying at home, & sitting by the fire, thro' an Evening, & never find it dull, tho' I am alone.

Some day this week, I must make a dinner for the Mass. Delegation. They will much miss your Ladyship, from the head of the Table.

It is now, I think, four days, since I had a letter from you; but the mails are so irregular, that perhaps the next may bring me three or four. Today, we have no papers from New York.

With love to you all, I am, Dr wife, Ever yrs   D.W.

ALS. NhHi. Published in Van Tyne, pp. 199–200.

1. Letter not found.

2. On January 22, Adams had spoken in favor of the three-million-dollar Fortifications Bill, denouncing Webster and others who "would rather see the enemy battering down the walls of the Capitol than agree to such an appropriation for the defense of the country." *Congressional Globe*, 24th Cong., 1st sess., p. 127. 24th Cong., 1st sess., p. 127. Adams's speech was a direct response to Webster's of January 14, opposing the appropriation.

Washington Jan. 27. 1836

My Dear Sir,

Our prospects have very much changed since we last saw each other. A complete dismemberment of the Whig party must be the inevitable consequence of the occurrences which have taken place; & there seems little now left for us, but to hold on upon Massachusetts. We must retreat into that Citadel, & defend it.

The Senate, I believe, is nearly or quite, revolutionized. Both Louisiana & Mississippi have both gone against us.[1] The Court will be radically changed. There seems, therefore, nothing in which to place reliance, in any branch of the Govt.

In this condition of things, forlorn enough, certainly, Mr Adams, whose ill-starred fortunes we have labored so hard to uphold, has gone completely over to the adversary. But this I recon no addition to our misfortunes. His late speeches have been violent, in the extreme, & especially bitter towards me, as you will have seen. The feeling among our Delegation is that of *the deepest indignation*. You have never seen Govr. [Levi] Lincoln, Mr [John] Reed, & the rest, so much excited, on any subject. They mean to tell Mr Adams pretty plainly what they think of him. His apostacy will do us no hurt, if we can only *keep him off*. But the difficulty is, Mr V. Buren's friends protest they will not receive him, & orders have been peremptorily given to the Globe not to praise him, or notice him. He is likely to become a political vagrant, seeking for a settlement, from party to party. But you will think I, too, am angry, & warm. Not so. I keep cool. I certainly feel great contempt for Mr Adams, & have been obliged to form very bad opinions of the qualities of his heart, but I do not intend to be betrayed into any warmth. Probably, I think, I shall take no notice of his Speech, whatever. I cannot well do so, without following his own bad example of rudeness & disorder. I will leave him, in other hands, at least for the present.

As this attack of Mr Adams will make some impression on the Antimasons of Mass:, we must try to repel its effects. I am desirous that the people should all have an opportunity of reading my Speech, which so much provoked his ire, & also Mr Southards, Mr [Henry A.] Wise's, & those of other Gentlemen, who have, or will have, something to say, to & of, Mr Adams' Speech. Will you do me the favor to send me a *list* of names in Middlesex, as extensive as you well can, & containing especially, all the Anti Ms you can think of, & all the Jackson men, who would be likely to read what I might send.[2]

I thought very well of your Inaugural,[3] & hear with much pleasure that it was well recd by the Legislature. I wish you a useful & agreeable session. Yours always sincerely   Danl Webster

ALS. MHi.

1. Louisiana sent Robert Carter Nicholas, a Van Buren Democrat, to the U.S. Senate; and in Mississippi, Democrats won majorities in both the state House and Senate, paving the way for Robert James Walker's election to the U.S. Senate. *National Intelligencer*, January 23, 26, 1836.

2. Webster made similar requests for lists from others. See DW to Isaac L. Hedge, January 26, 1836, in *MHi Proc.*, 46, Third Series (January 1913): 275, and DW to Solomon Lincoln, January 26, 1836, mDW 12895.

3. Sworn into office on January 13, Everett had delivered his inaugural address on January 15, 1836.

TO SAMUEL FROTHINGHAM

Washington Jan. 28 1836

My Dear Sir,

My two notes, endorsed by Mr John Connell,[1] fall due in Boston February the 13/16. You obtained their discount, & probably will recollect at what Banks they are to be found. If not, Mr [Henry Willis] Kinsman will hear from them in due season, at the office.

The enclosed letter from Mr Connell[2] shows, that an arrangement is made, for the discount at your office of my note, with his indorsement, for $10,000 to pay the other two. I suppose you have been made acquainted with this arrangement as I believe you have been at Philadelphia. I write today to Mr Connell,[3] enclosing a note, for his endorsement, & desiring him to remit it to you; & I now enclose to you the *policy*, unsigned in blank.

I shall further take care to provide funds, to make up the discount, so that you may have the net $10,000, with which to take up the 2 notes.

I hope all this will be regular. I tried hard to find Mr [Chandler] Robbins—but could not, & he did not come to see me, for which omision, since he is your son in law, I wish you would give him a gentle rebuke. Mr [Abbott] Lawrence tells me he left the City earl[ier] than he expected.

It seems to be credited, today, that a *mediation* has been offered by England.[4] What other news there is, has not transpired.

Yours always truly   Danl Webster

ALS. NN.

1. Connell was a Philadelphia merchant who became a director of the United States Bank of Pennsylvania in 1838.

2. Not found.

3. Letter not found.

4. For a discussion of the English mediation between France and the United States, see McLemore, *Franco-American Relations*, pp. 180–211.

Washington Jan. 30. 1836

My Dear Sir,

I am very sorry to hear so bad an account of Texas.[1] It has been my opinion, all along, as you know, that it was best to sell; but I have trusted to your better information, & have not kept the run of events, so as to know whether the value of the scrip was rising or falling. I hope it is not yet altogether run down.[2]

In the course of the last year, I have made great sacrifices, to get rid of debts & pecuniary engagements, of all kinds, & have looked for nothing from Texas, only that the scrip would prove equivalent to the first cost, 2,000, saying nothing about a hundred or two Dollars, paid the Dr. as my contribution towards exploring &c. &c. I have a mortal aversion to trouble either you or myself, with continued drafts, & redrafts. In addition to the trouble, such operations, too often repeated have not a good appearance.

Mr Daniel Le Roy[3] happening to be here, I have obtained his check on New York, payable to your order on the 10th. of Feby. He thinks it probable that his brother & partner, Mr Wm [Henry] Le Roy,[4] to whom he will write, may be able to cash this check for you at once; and desires you to call at the office, to see whether he can do [so], when the money is needed. At any rate, the check is better than my acceptance—I have promised Mr Le Roy to get the money for him again, by the middle of the month. I thought I had better do this, than to give an acceptance of my own, than to put you to the trouble of asking a favor from the Bank, in these scarce times for cash.

Is there any thing that you will give for this scrip, payable at any time?

I am determined, at last, to be rid of it, without any further delay. As you have some of the same, perhaps you would be willing to offer *something* for this, & lay it all bye together, to wait events. If not, let it be sold at auction for what it will bring.

I have no doubt, My Dr Sir, that you have done all you could to make a penny for me, in this matter. Nor do I know that your advice has not at all times been right, according to circumstances; tho' I confess I have been all along strong for selling. Let us finish it, some how, & forget it.

Mr & Mrs [John Collins] Warren arrived here safe, three days [ago]. They speak of you, & yours, with much kindness & gratitude. Yrs truly

Danl Webster

I enclose Messrs Le Roys check, & return your draft unaccepted.[5]

ALS. NhD.   1. Curtis's letter to Webster, if such were the source of "so bad an account of Texas," has not been found. Webster may have been alluding only to newspaper accounts of Mexican troops' invasion of Texas in the fall of 1835.

2. Webster's Texan scrip was probably that issued by the Galveston Bay and Texas Land Company, organized in New York on October 16, 1830, for the purpose of promoting emigration to an area that Mexico had granted to Joseph Vehlein, Lorenzo de Zavala, and David G. Burnet, impresarios. Early associates in the company included George Griswold, Anthony Dey, George and Edward Curtis, William H. Sumner, and Samuel Swartwout. Just when Webster first invested in the scrip has not been established, although the available evidence suggests that it must have been shortly after the company formed, for, as he explains, he had contributed to the exploring of the land. Moreover, Stephen White, December 4, 1833, reported to Webster that various changes in the laws affecting the region of the grants had "bearing on the stock in those companies" (see *Correspondence*, 3: 281–282). Similarly, when Webster finally sold his scrip has not

been determined. On the company and its activity, see David Woodman, Jr., *Guide to Texas Emigrants* (Waco, 1974), a reprint of Woodman's 1835 publication; [W. H. Sumner], *Address to the Reader of the Documents Relating to the Galveston Bay & Texas Land Company . . .* (New York, 1831); Eugene C. Barker, ed., *Austin Papers*, in *Annual Report of the American Historical Association for the Year 1919* (Washington, 1924), pp. 508–883 *passim*; Elgin Williams, *The Animating Pursuits of Speculation: Land Traffic in the Annexation of Texas* (New York, 1949), pp. 17–20, 31, 47, 56–67, 141, 198; James E. Winston, "New York and the Independence of Texas," *Southwestern Historical Quarterly*, 18 (April 1915): 368–385; and Kate Mason Rowland, "General John Thomson Mason, An Early Friend of Texas," *Southwestern Historical Quarterly*, 11 (January 1908): 163–198.

3. Le Roy (1799–1885), son of Herman Le Roy, and Webster's brother-in-law.

4. Le Roy (1795–1888), also the son of Herman Le Roy.

5. Neither found.

With his bid for the Presidency folding, Webster became increasingly despondent over politics, proposing to withdraw from the canvass and to resign his Senate seat. He did neither, however, mainly because his friends and backers strongly opposed. Nevertheless, Webster gave only the minimum attention to the campaign and politics in 1836, preferring instead to devote much of his efforts toward making a fortune in western lands and in developing his Massachusetts and New Hampshire farms.

TO CHARLES HENRY THOMAS

Washington Feb. 4. '36

Dear Henry,

Although I have not [a] letter from you, either yesterday or today, I must still commend your improved habits. You have certainly whipped up your spirit of letter writing to new speed, so that I get two letters a week, at least. This is very pleasing. There have been times, since I saw you last, when I have doubted whether Marshfield & I should hold on together, to the end of my life. I have felt, in those moments, as a *humility* looks, when she spreads out her wings for flight. Even now, some things are unsettled in my brain. I keep them, however, to myself, &, except you, & one other who has recd a slight hint, nobody knows of the existence of any such notions. There are temptations, which, if Marshfield were not what it is, or if it were to cease to be what it has been, might induce me to look upon the last seven or eight years as a bright spot, in the journey of life, which I had passed *through.* All these things, however, are to be buried in the depth of your faithful bosom; & in the meantime, I must say, that even your slightest letters afford me pleasure. Amidst the toil of law, & the stunning din of politics, any thing is welcome, which calls my thoughts back to Marshfield, tho' it be only to be told which way the wind blows. I am suffering from a cold, & for two days have not been out of my room. Last night, I was dreaming of you, all night; which I hope you will consider as a very great compliment. My letters from Boston all speak of your mother.[1] She seems to have made quite a *sensation*, in Summer Street. Capt. John Thomas will find it necessary to put his best foot forward, when he goes to Boston, if he does not mean to have the shine taken off of himself by his spouse.

In regard to farming matters, you appear to be doing well. Some of your kelp-drawing days have showed great results. If I have kept the account right, you have probably secured as much kelp as will be a decent dressing for all the corn land you prepared to plant at Careswell. By the way—let us settle names. I am tired of the Soule place—& the Sprague place—& "the Widow Winslow's thirds," & so many other names. Let us use some names, *uniformly*, & we shall save time & breath. According to the proposed plans, (which I hope are made) there are three places.

1. The Homestead; that is Green Harbour; & any man must be indicted for slander, who gives it any other name.
2. Those parcels which we have set apart for a mulberry farm. This may be called "The Mulberry farm," or it may be called "Winslow Place," without the "*the*," or "Pelham Place," Pelham being a distinguished name, in the pedigree of the Winslow family.
III. The Soule place, that is to say, the House & land bought of Mr [Henry] Soule,[2] & what we have attached to it, from the Sprague

purchase, may be called "Careswell," which I do much like, or "The Lower Farm," which I like better, or "the cottage farm," when we take down the big house.

Consult Capt John Thomas, & Lucy his wife, on these matters. Let me know what they & you, & Edward think; & we will give these places fixed names, & any body who mis-calls them is not to be answered, when he speaks to us.

Was "Careswell" the name of the Winslow property, generally, or did it apply only to a part of it? Ask your mother to explain & expound.

—And now to return to the kelp. I suppose the season may be pretty nearly over, for it, but if it continue to come, you will be ready to seize it, & know what to do with it. When John Taylor comes down next August or September, I want him to lose himself in our cornfields.

I am thinking of using lime, freely, at Green Harbour; but this will depend on the cost. I understand it can often be had at less than a dollar a cask, at Thomastown, sometimes lower than 80 cts. A cask is 5 bushels, of rank lime—of course, when slacked, there will be ten. Suppose the price a dollar a cask, the slacked lime would be ten cents per bushel, or equal to that at the quarry. Now what is the freight worth, for a vessel to go direct, & to bring her cargo to the mouth of Green Harbor River? This, as well as the actual price at Thomastown, you can readily ascertain. Please make inquiries, & let me know. The Thomastown lime is a good deal stronger than the Pennsylvania lime—& yet, in the best Counties of Pa. they will pay 12. or 15 cents a bushel for lime, & haul it 10. 15. or 20 miles, for corn, clover, & wheat. Think of these things, & count the cost.

If I had lime, in addition to using it with mud & other material, I should use it by itself, thus. I should spread it, 30 or 40 bushels to the acre, on old sward land, like Slaughter Island, or the Old Orchard, or the Sheep pasture, plough it in, & plant the land, with corn, potatos, beans, or some other crop, requiring the hoe, according to the natural strength of the land. The hoeing mixes the lime with the land, so that it affects the whole soil. On such land as the Sheep pasture, I should put 25 bushels, of unslacked lime, to the acre;—& on such light land, I think, should plant beans. The next year, apply manure from the barn yard, as plentifully as possible, get a crop of oats, & put in grass seed. Field turnips would do well, instead of oats, or part might be put into each. On strong clayey land, I should plant corn, or potatos. Ponder these matters.

We have made some mistakes, but must hope to grow wiser. *Never again sow small grains on long manure*. Put that down as one maxim.

If I live & am well, I must go home, either in March, or the early part of April. Either time will be in season to settle some things. If I should be in Marshfield in March, I should expect to drive the team once off the beach, with a load of kelp.

The oxen, which you destine for beef, next fall, you will of course ease off, from their work, so soon as you can, when the business of kelp is over. How many, & which is it best to turn out?

1. There are the old oxen; they must be fatted, of course.
2. The *off oxen*, bought of Capt. [Abraham G.] Stevens (I wish we had the black ram, to go with them)—if not sold, these must be fatted.
3. Then there is the Princeton oxen, which are quite old enough to fat well.

Now, I do not see how we are going *to sell* any thing, unless it be stock, & we must contrive to sell something, or we shall all be called on to make an assignment.

These off oxen, I think, will make good beef, for Capt John Thomas, & his wife Lucy, & for me, & wife Caroline. Suppose, therefore, we devote them to the Captain's "powdering tub," together with any other similar likely thing, which John Taylor may happen to send down next fall. And then suppose we fat the old oxen, & the Princeton oxen, for the market—loosing them from the yoke, as early as we can, keeping them as well as we can thro' the summer, & keeping them on roots, in the fall & winter, until they are fat enough to make people at Brighton "open their eyes," as Captain Thomas would say?

All these things you must weigh. I don't mean you must weigh the *oxen*—they are too poor yet, but weigh these hints.

—But I must stop, from these interesting topics, & pursue them no farther.

You owe the trouble of reading this long letter, to my being unable, from my cold, to go either to the Court or the Senate, & to my having positively forbidden Charles [Brown][3] to let any body in, this day. I am tired, too, of reading, & so have run on with this incoherent scribbling. There is another matter, on which I may write you, in a few days; but if I am well enough to go out tomorrow, I shall have no more leisure to trouble you with a long letter, for some time. Mean while, I hope you will not fail to write as often as you can. Give my best regards to your wife, & to Ann, & the Dr.[4]—& to your father & mother—& my love to Edward. I suppose you all receive Charles' communications, in sufficient abundance. Adieu!—my good friend—   D Webster

ALS. MHi. Published in Curtis, 1: 551–554.

1. Lucy Turner Thomas (1771–1849), who had married Captain

John Thomas, March 4, 1806.
2. Webster had purchased the property from Henry Soule on July 21 and October 30, 1834. See deeds transferring the land in Deed Book, 181: 85, and 178: 23, Plymouth County Registrar of Deeds, Plymouth, Massachusetts.
3. Webster had earlier purchased the freedom of Charles Brown, a slave, and for many years, he remained with Webster as his servant. Curtis, 2: 20.
4. Ann Thomas (b. 1808), Charles Henry's sister, and Dr. John Porter (1795–1865) of Duxbury, who had married in 1829.

TO EDWARD EVERETT, WITH ENCLOSURE

Washington Feb. 7. 36
Confidential
My Dear Sir,

I recd your two letters[1] yesterday. On conversing with Judge Story, we were both of opinion, that there would be an impropriety in publishing the letters of the Chief Justice, so recently after his death, without the consent of the family.[2] I have therefore written a letter to his son, Mr Edward C. Marshall, of which I enclose a copy to you.[3] As soon as I hear from him, I will inform you, & if he consent to the publication, I will have it made here.

I had no opportunity of seeing Mr [Levi] Lincoln yesterday, & if I had found one, I do not know whether I should have ventured to speak to him, on the subject mentioned in your letter, & doubt whether I am the channel thro which a hint of that kind could be usefully made.

The war goes on, here, upon poor Mr Adams. I almost compassionate him. A bad cold kept me from the Senate when Mr [John Middleton] Clayton spoke, but I am told he showed no mercy.[4]

Between ourselves, nothing confounds me so much as Mr Adams apparent disregard of *veracity*—see his disclaimer, quoted in Mr [Henry A.] Wise's speech.[5] If I make any remarks at all, myself, on the occurrence, I shall draw the public attention to this hardy denial.

We have nothing of much interest, since the affair of the mediation. Yours with great regard   Danl. Webster

Please preserve the copy of my letter to Mr Marshall.

ALS. MHi.
1. Not found.
2. In 1833, Marshall had discussed in two letters to Everett his support of Anti-Masonry. These two confidential letters, dated July 22 and August 6, which Everett and Webster hoped to publish, can be found in the Everett Papers, MHi (Microfilm), Reel 5, Frames 440–441, 470–471.
3. Edward Carrington Marshall (1805–1882; Harvard 1826) was the fifth surviving son of John Marshall. For the enclosure, see below.
4. For Clayton's comments on Adams, see *Congressional Globe*, 24th

Cong., 1st sess., Appendix, pp. 647–650.

5. For Wise's discussion of the loss

of the Fortification Bill, see *Congressional Globe*, 24th Cong., 1st sess., Appendix, pp. 659–665.

ENCLOSURE: TO EDWARD C. MARSHALL

Washington Feb. 6. 1836

Dear Sir

In the year 1833 the late Chief Justice Marshall wrote two letters to Mr Everett, now Govr. of Massachusets, on the subject of Masonry, & Masonic oaths.[1] These letters expressed opinions, which the Chief Justice is known to have communicated to others, & Mr Everett was desirous of publishing one or both of them, or so much thereof as related to the foregoing subjects. But the Chief Justice desired the letters to be considered as confidential, & that no public use should be made of them.

It has occurred to Mr. Everett that in consequence of the lamented death of the Chief Justice, there probably exists no longer any reason for withholding these letters from publication. Yet he feels a delicacy in consenting to give them to the public, without the permission of the representatives of the Chief Justice. The fact of the existence of such letters is known, & very solicitous application is continually made to Mr Everett for their publication. Mr Everett has recently written to me, upon this matter, and it is in consequence of his letter, that I write you this, for the purpose of asking whether you and your brother see any objection to the publication? I may add my own wish, that the letters might be made public, since the sentiments they express are precisely such as I hold myself. Copies of the letters are in my possession, & if you should think it necessary, in order to guide your judgments in this matter, to peruse them, I will transmit them, for that purpose.

I pray you to accept my sympathy, for the loss of your great & good Parent. Taught to respect him, from my earliest man hood, I have, for twenty years, witnessed his judicial labors, & studied his character, with constantly encreasing admiration.[2] With much regard, Yours

(Signed) Danl. Webster

ALS copy. MHi. Published in *Van Tyne*, p. 202.

1. See above, DW to Edward Everett, February 7, 1836, note 2.

2. This is one of the rare instances in the extant Webster correspondence where he refers to Chief Justice Marshall's death on July 6, 1835. On July 14, 1835, Webster delivered a short extemporaneous eulogy before the Suffolk Bar and presented resolutions calling for a more formal address on the life and character of Marshall, which Joseph Story delivered on October 15, 1835. *Columbian Centinel*, July 15, 1835; William W. Story, *Life and Letters of Joseph Story* (2 vols.; Boston, 1851), 2: 200–203.

[MEMORANDUM BY LEVI LINCOLN OF A MEETING WITH
WEBSTER RE HIS PRESIDENTIAL NOMINATION]

Memo. Feb 19. 1836.

A Meeting of the Delegates from Massachusetts in the Senate and House, with the exception of Mr Webster, Mr Adams, and Mr [Nathaniel Briggs] Borden, having been had at the instance of Mr Webster, for the purpose of considering his position before the Nation, as a Candidate for the Presidency;—after consultation, Mr [Levi] Lincoln, Mr [John] Davis, and Mr [Abbott] Lawrence were appointed a Committee to communicate to Mr W. the results.

On the morning of the 19th of Feby. the above named Gentlemen waited upon Mr W., when Mr Lincoln stated to Mr W., in substance, that in the meeting which had been held, the Gentlemen present, had assembled *at his instance*, and *as his personal Friends*, and in their discussions and in this communication, they, as well as this Committee, expressly disclaimed any authority or pretence for representing the opinions, feelings, or wishes of others. That they regarded their relation to the subject of his nomination to the Presidency, as one only of common interest to those with whom they were accustomed politically to act, and who had delegated no discretionary or advisory power over this subject. Mr L. further stated to Mr W., that the Gentlemen who attended the Meeting, were of opinion, that as his Nomination proceeded from a Convention of Members of the Legislature, it belonged more appropriately to Gentlemen standing in the same relation to him, and to the same party in the State Government, to hold the correspondence and give the advice which might be needed. Still, with the above disclaimer, responding to his recognition of them *as his personal and political friends*, they had regarded with equal interest & concern, the unlooked for arrangements and circumstances which now greatly embarrassed this position in which, by the agency of others, he was placed. That the nomination made by the Whig Party in the State, gave him a claim to the continued support of that Party—that this was due to their own principles, their own consistency of conduct, and their obligations to him, and that it was by no means the desire of the Delegation here, that at this time he should withdraw. This was a matter for his own consideration and decision, upon such views of public duty, and upon such knowledge of political events and prospects, as with better, or the same means of information, he might have. In fine, that the delegation were of the opinion, that, inasmuch, as circumstances had materially changed in reference to the probability of success, since his nomination, this change of circumstances left him at liberty to consult his own judgment, and either to meet, or withdraw from, the canvass as his own sense of propriety should hereafter dictate, and that the members of the Delegation individually, would hold him justified accordingly.   LL. A.L.

AD. MHi.

TO HENRY WILLIS KINSMAN

Washington Feb. 20. 1836
My Dear Sir,
I recd this morning your letter of the 15th,[1] in which you say that a report prevailed of my having declined the nomination for the Presidency.

This is a point, upon which I have neither done any thing, nor said any thing; nor authorized others to do or say any thing in my behalf. You will readily perceive that there is nothing desirable in my present position; yet, I shall not hastily, or inconsiderately, relinquish it. There are interests, perhaps, connected with it, in regard to which *friends* have a right to expect that *their* wishes & opinions should be regarded.

I intend going home, just as soon as the Boats shall commence running, & shall probably be in such season as to find our friends, the members of the Legislature, still in the City. I may have something to say to them. In the meantime, you are authorized to say that there is no foundation for the report; tho' I hope it may not be necessary to make a formal denial of it, under your name. My design is to confer, freely, with Massachusetts friends, on this matter, & to act exactly as, in the general opinion, the interests of *Massachusetts* may require. Yours always truly
Danl Webster

ALS. MH.
1. Not found.

TO HENRY WILLIS KINSMAN

Washington, Feb. 27, 1836.
My Dear Sir:
The Whig Members of the Legislature of Massachusetts, of the last year, saw fit to put me in nomination for the office of President of the U.S.

Events have since occurred, which were probably not anticipated, and which may be thought to have rendered a reconsideration of that nomination expedient. If this opinion should be entertained by the Whig members of the present Legislature I should exceedingly regret that they should forbear to act upon it, from any motives of delicacy towards me. Indeed, in the state of things at present existing in the country, my personal wishes are, to withdraw my name from the place it occupies before the public, in connexion with the approaching election; and I am restrained from so doing, only by the consideration, that there are interests, which might be affected by such a movement, in regard to which the opinions of others ought to be consulted.[1]

I wish you, therefore, my dear sir, to signify to our friends, that not only would it give me no pain to be no longer considered a candidate, but that such a change in my relations to the country would be altogether agreeable to my personal feelings. At the same time, I wish it may also be said to them, that I shall not act in opposition to their judgment, of what is required by the public good. I shall not separate from them, nor from those principle[s] which we have hitherto maintained, and which, I trust, we shall continue to maintain, whether in majorities or minorities, or in prosperous or adverse fortune. If in their opinion, our common principles and common cause, notwithstanding what has occurred, do still require of me, that I remain in my present position, I shall cheerfully abide by their determination, confident that in no events hereafter to happen, can it become matter of regret to me, that I have conformed to what seemed best to their honest patriotism and intelligent sense of public duty.

With this distinct expression of my own personal wishes, therefore, I leave the subject for their decision; desiring them to consider nothing, but what just and consistent principle, sincere, patriotic duty, and the great cause of constitutional Liberty may appear, in the present posture of public affairs, to demand from them and from me.

With very true regard, your ob'dt servant,   Daniel Webster.

Text from the *Columbian Centinel*, March 26, 1836. Original not found. Published in W & S, 16: 272–273.

1. This letter to Kinsman was not made public until March 24, at a Whig meeting in the Massachusetts legislature. In response, the Massachusetts Whigs unanimously adopted resolutions pledging their continued support of Webster. It was printed in the *Columbian Centinel*, March 26, and in the *National Intelligencer*, March 31, 1836.

TO HENRY WILLIS KINSMAN

Washington Feb. 29. 1836

Private

Dear Sir,

When I wrote you last on political subjects, I informed you that I intended to go home, so soon as I could, & that probably I might find the Legislature still in Session.[1] The uncommon protraction of winter makes it uncertain at what time I may be able to execute this purpose. Meantime, I see & hear a thousand rumours, which it is possible may be so far credited at home as to produce some degree of embarrassment.

Under these circumstances, I have addressed a letter to you, which you will receive under another cover.[2] In writing & communicating that letter, I have two objects;

1. To signify my own wish to retire from the position of a candidate;

2. To signify my resolution, nevertheless, to abide by whatever friends at home may think the good of the cause requires.

I do not wish to receive the votes of one or two States, as a mere matter of respect, or proof of confidence; & I desire it may not be considered, now or hereafter, that I remain a candidate, from any such motive.

On the other hand, I do not wish to [do] anything, which shall tend to weaken the Whig cause, or break up our majority in the State.

These are exactly my feelings.

I wish you to peruse the letter, & show it to a few discreet & influential friends. If you & they shall then be of opinion, that it is necessary to communicate its contents to others, you may do so. How far it may be necessary to communicate them, you must judge. If you find it proper, <you> it may be read, in a meeting of friends. Perhaps that may not be necessary, & that it may be enough to let its import be known, less formally. Remember, to let it be distinctly understood, if I remain a candidate, that I do so, because the Whigs of Massachusetts think the cause requires me so to act.

In using the letter, you will act with caution, too, in another respect; that is to say, not suffer its contents to be the means of schism & division, among friends. This is a point of prudence & delicacy, which must be sedulously guarded.

If on the receipt of this letter, friends are prepared to decide & to act, I think, on the whole, that they should do, at once, & before I get home, all they propose to do on the subject. Yrs very truly,   Danl Webster

ALS. MHi.
1. See above, DW to Henry Willis Kinsman, February 20, 1836.

2. See above, DW to Henry Willis Kinsman, February 27, 1836.

TO CHARLES HENRY THOMAS

Mar. 2. 1836

Dr Henry,

Yr arrangement with [Robert H.] Morehead[1] seems all very well; & so does Mr Whitman's[2] proposition about fixing the price of wigwam. In kelp, you appear to have done well; tho' I have not kept the account so as to know how many loads, in the whole, have been secured.

We have a great deal of ground up, this Spring, & it must be kept up, till it is well enriched, cleaned, & so made fit for laying down. I do not see that we shall need break up any more land, for some years. As soon as we can sufficiently increase the crop of English hay, the farm will be in its right state for profit. The pastures at Careswell must be kept free & clear of bushes, & that is all we can do with them. As to the cow pastures at Green Harbour, they must, one after another, be all top dressed, first clearing away all the stones & bushes. This year, we will begin with the pasture near the House. I have found some excellent matters, on this subject, in the recent proceedings of the Scotch Agricultural Societies; Scotland more nearly resembling N.E. in climate & soil than England does, her modes of agriculture are much better suited to us. The top dressing *may be* almost any thing, but if possible, or as far as possible without too much expense, *lime* should be one ingredient. I have caused inquiries to be made of the lime burners at Thomaston, to know at what price, for cash, they will deliver two or three hundred casks at Duxbury. Lime, mixed with what we can get from ponds & ditches, would do excellently well. Leached ashes would do well also, but would not last, in their effect, a quarter part so long.

We are so completely blocked up with snow & ice, it is impossible to say when I may get away. The river here has opened once, but is again frozen up. We have a foot and a half, or nearer two feet of snow, with a good covering of ice on it.

By the time you receive this, you will have seen the Comm[issione]rs. I shall be anxious to know their decision.[3] Yrs truly   D Webster

ALS. MHi.

1. Morehead was a Marshfield blacksmith.

2. Not identified.

3. Webster and others had petitioned the county commissioners for the construction of a road through his Marshfield property, but a Marshfield town meeting had appointed an agent to oppose the road. After hearing both sides, the county commissioners decided to run the road basically as Webster wanted, from near the Winslow house to the Marshfield-Duxbury line. Lysander Salmon Richards, *History of Marshfield* (2 vols.; Plymouth, 1901, 1905), 1: 161.

TO [EDWARD EVERETT], WITH ENCLOSURES

Mar. 12. 1836

Private

Dr Sir

I enclose you Mr [Edward C.] Marshalls answer to my letter, & Mr [Benjamin Watkins] Leigh's endorsement,[1] which will speak for themselves.

I think Mr L. has decided right, tho' I could much have wished for the publication of the Ch[ief] Ju[stice]'s letter. However, the *fact* of the letter will gradually get out, & by & by, the letter itself, perhaps, may properly appear.

I suppose there can be no objection to my showing the letter, occasionally, to a friend.

What do you think of Ben Hardin's Speech?[2] Is it not melancholy, to see a man who has been our friend, & been President of U.S. subject to such mangling, & not a human individual to take his part? I declare my pity struggles hard against my sense of injustice, & my contempt. Yrs

D.W.

ALS. MHi. Published in part in Van Tyne, p. 203.
1. See below.
2. On January 28, 1836, Hardin had delivered a speech on Adams's resolution concerning the loss of the Fortification Bill of the previous session. For Hardin's speech, see *Congressional Globe*, 24th Cong., 1st sess., Appendix, pp. 625–630.

ENCLOSURE: FROM EDWARD C. MARSHALL

Oak Hill. March 4th. 1836

Dear Sir

The necessity of consultation with my brothers, who were remote from each other and at the time of the receipt of your letter[1] at a great distance from me, has caused this tardy reply to your letter making application for our assent to the publication of two confidential letters of our late dear Father to Mr Everett.

Sacred regard for the memory of our Father, and a disposition to render a litteral compliance with his feelings wherever he has indicated them would lead us, were we to follow our own inclinations, to withhold our assent to the publication of letters which he wished to be treated as confidential; but appreciating the delicate consideration with which the application is made and the friendly source from which it emanates, we have determined to sacrifice our inclinations & to request you to submit the letters and the course proposed to be adopted to the examination of Mr Leigh—the near friend & connexion of our Father. Our confidence in his nice sense of propriety and freedom from excitement on this subject induces us to trust this matter to his judgement, asking of him to give it his most mature consideration.

I cannot forbear an expression of my sensibility to your avowed admiration of my lamented Father. Coincidence of Constitutional opinions naturally produced mutual esteem & I cannot repress my desire to say that I have often heard him speak with rapture of your able & eloquent defence of that Constitution, which he loved with his hearts warmest devotion.

I am dear Sir must respectfully Yrs   Edw C Marshall

ALS. MHi.

1. See above, DW to Edward C. Marshall, February 6, 1836.

ENCLOSURE: FROM BENJAMIN WATKINS LEIGH

March 7. 1836

My dear sir

I do not think the letter ought to be published. I know that some of the chief justice's most intimate friends, and many persons who admired and venerated him above all mankind, are masons, and (what is strange) zealous masons. All these would be deeply wounded by the letter. I think it was probably this consideration which made him so particular in expressing his wish that the letter should not be published. You may be aware, that I am not a mason myself, and certainly have no partiality to the Society, tho' I have never seen any thing in it in Virginia, but a piece of mummery, quite harmless as well as useless. Yrs   B. W. Leigh

ALS. MHi.

TO CAROLINE LE ROY WEBSTER

Washington Sunday morning
[March 13?, 1836]

Dear Caroline,

I wish we had a little matchmaking here, too, or something else to keep one alive, for I confess it has become exceedingly dull. There is nothing of interest in Congress, & as I do not go out at all, & for a month have asked nobody to my rooms, life has become a little *too* solitary. I have read every thing in the known world, except *Dr's books*,—botany, geology, chemistry, novels, travels—children's books—Robinson Crusoe &c. &c.—& at last Dr [Thomas] Sewall offers me his *Medical Dictionary* —I hesitate, at this, for the present.

The same old story is to be told about the weather. It is as cold here as the South part of Greenland. The Chesapeake & the Delaware are as yet all solid ice. Sometime between this & dog's days, I hope, they will get a sweat.

I answered Sally's [Jenkins?] letter,[1] asking my consent to her match. I do not remember what I said *verbatim*, but it was or ought to have been pretty much to this effect; that it was an important matter, that it required a good deal of deliberation, & that as an immediate decision was not important, there seeming to be no haste or impatience in the case, I would attend to the matter, soon after the rising of Congress, & let her know the result of my reflections in due season thereafter.

I see from your letter that *one* I[saac] P. Davis[2] is at my house a good deal. Whenever there is a dinner, or a supper, whatever other names are sprinkled round, by way of garnishment, there his stands, always, at the head, or in the middle of the list. I want to know what *Mrs. P. I*[3] has to say to all this?

Neither Fletcher nor Julia has written me for a month. They must be both very busy.

I do not mean to write another word about *ice, weather, boats*, or *roads*. I take *patience*—& so must you, in large portions.

Dates will show that Dr. [John Collins] Warren was feeling your pulse, & looking solemn, & winking, just about the time that Dr. Sewall was bidding me hold out my tongue, & looking at it, from the nearest point to which his nose would let him approach. This I take to be a proof that there exists between us, whether together or apart, the proper degree of matrimonial sympathy.

Good bye. Charles has brought me a little *clear* cider—by way of inducement.

Give my love to Julia—& Sally Jenkins. Yrs   D.W.

ALS. NhHi. Published under date of January 1834 in *PC*, 2: 3–4.
1. Not found. Sally Jenkins of Boston was the widow of Isaac Jenkins.
2. Davis (1771–1855), Boston manufacturer and businessman. In 1841, through Webster's influence as secretary of state, Davis received an appointment as naval officer of Boston, a post he held until 1845.
3. Susan, née Jackson, daughter of Dr. David Jackson of Philadelphia. Presumably, Mrs. P. I. was a "pet" name for Mrs. Isaac P. Davis. See *Correspondence*, 2: 169.

TO [EDWARD EVERETT]

Washington Mar. 14. 1836

Dear Sir

I have recd yrs of the 8th.[1] & do not wonder that your official honors & vexations make you *grow* lean [&] spare. However, I think you will get thro them all, with credit to yourself & usefulness to the State. I was not at all aware of any possible objections to Mr [John] Heard.[2] He has been so long Register, that he seemed naturally to stand heir to the judgeship. I shall be sorry, indeed if any great evil should come from his nomination.

In regard to your nomination, I must confess I take a view of it somewhat different from your own. These Legislative Caucuses are never popular. A Convention gives opportunity for another set of men to come abroad, & obtain notoriety. Whatever the Whig meeting may be called, & whenever it may assemble, it will be certain to nominate you; & I think that a Convention in the fall, made up of Delegates fresh from the People, will be likely to give you a more hearty, & zealous, & unanimous nomination, than a meeting of the members of the Legislature.

If I were you, I should quite as willingly leave the matter to the Convention. All this, however, you, who are on the spot, must have a more correct view of, & that ought to be done by others, which is most agreeable to *yourself*.

Our correspondence, it is true, has not been very brisk, this winter. You have been busy, with your own affairs, & there has been little here, either interesting or agreeable to write you about.

Touching Ch Jus M[arshall]'s letter, we must talk further, when I get home.

I pray you to give my best remembrances to Mrs Everett. I really long to see the Govr's Lady. I bespeak one day of you, to dine with me, when I get home; & I bespeak one *dinner* of you, at your own house, with you & your wife—for the sake of a little talk, & the remembrances of auld lang syne. Yrs truly   D Webster

ALS. MHi.
 1. Not found.
 2. Heard (1775–1839; Harvard

1795) was appointed judge of Probate for Suffolk County on March 15, 1836.

FROM NICHOLAS BIDDLE

Phila. March 14. 1836

My dear Sir

On my return from Harrisburg last evening, I found your favor of the   inst. & shall duly attend to its contents.[1]

Mr. [Joseph Reed] Ingersoll will have mentioned to you before this time the amendment we desire to the Bill about the Bank, so as to authorize the Secretary of the Treasury to *sell* the interest of the Government. This, if it could be accomplished, would be very useful. If you think so I wish you would cause it to be *done* as you used to say that I used to say.[2]

The accumulation of the revenue is now the great nuisance—the real disturber—and since my resignation of the character, the only true monster. Can you not, by the Land bill, or by some other process, make an early division of that fund.[3] Yours always   N. B.

Washn D. Ca. The reports of the Banks to the 1st. of Feby have been sent to the Senate. I wish you would fill up the enclosed table[4] as soon as convenient without waiting 'till it comes from the Printer.

LC. DLC.

1. Biddle left the date blank. The letter has not been identified.

2. As chairman of the Senate Committee on Finance Webster introduced (on April 25) an amendment to the bill "authorizing the Secretary of the Treasury to act as agent of the United States, in all matters relating to the stock in the Bank of the United States." The act, as finally passed on June 23, did contain a pro-

vision complying with Biddle's request. *Senate Journal*, 24th Cong., 1st sess., Serial 278, p. 307; 5 *U.S. Statutes at Large* 56.

3. By one of the provisions of the Deposit Act, also passed June 23, the surplus above $5,000,000 in the United States Treasury was to be distributed to the states. 5 *U.S. Statutes at Large* 55.

4. Not found.

TO [NICHOLAS BIDDLE]

Washington Mar. 16. '36

Dear Sir

I have already brought before the Com[mitt]ee on Finance the suggestion made by Mr [Joseph Reed] Ingersoll, relative to an amendment of the Bill, respect[ing] the agency for U S. ab[ou]t the late Bank, &c. It is under consideration. I know not what the Com[mitt]ee will finally do. In my opinion, the amendment would be, or might be, very useful.

I send you a copy of the returns of Deposite Banks.

Will the thick ribbed ices of the Delaware never melt?

Yrs, however, in all States of the Atmospheric gasses   D. W.

ALS. DLC.

FROM FISHER AMES HARDING

Chicago, March 16th 1836.

My Dear Sir,

I venture to trespass upon your time by presenting to your attention a subject which has very little in common with your duties at Washington. I refer to Real Estate & speculations in Illinois. This part of the country is advancing with very great rapidity, & lands here are in consequence daily rising in value. The attention both of emigrants & of speculators has been attracted particularly towards this section. In addition to this, the Legislature of the State have adopted such measures in relation to the Illinois & Michigan Canal, intended to connect this place with the navigable waters of the Illinois river, as will insure its early commencement & completion. There is reason, therefore, to suppose, & such is the opinion of judicious men, that both lands along the

Canal route, and lots in Chicago & some other smaller towns, will in no long time be worth a very high price. They have indeed risen much of late, especially since the passage of the Canal Bill, but will it is thought rise much higher. There has been, to a considerable degree a want of ready money here. This has prevented purchases from being made to the extent they would otherwise have been effected. This want still continues to a considerable degree, & will do so, till the opening of Lake navigation in the Spring, which is usually late.

My purpose then in writing is to say that if you or your friends have disposable funds which you or <they> would like to invest in land speculations, a very favorable & safe field is offered here, at the present time. If you should be in such a position & should dare trust the matter to me, I would do my best with it. I could have the advice & assistance of one or two friends who are considerably acquainted with such business. It would make no difference to me whether the sum was small, or larger. The probability is that a quick turn might be made of any purchases with a handsome profit. If you should be disposed to invest any money in this way, the earlier it is done, the better.

I have for some time thought of communicating with you on this subject, but have felt a delicacy in trespassing upon your time & attention which has till this time prevented me from doing so.

I have enjoyed very good health this Winter, & have passed my time cheerfully & in content. I have entered into a partnership with Mr. Henry Moore, a lawyer of this place, formerly from Mass., & an acquaintance of Judge [Joseph] Story.[1] Our business as yet is not large.

With great respect, & the most grateful recollections, Yours, ever,
                                        Fisher A. Harding.

ALS. ViU. Harding (1811–1846; Harvard 1833), classmate of Fletcher, had studied law with DW in Boston. After his admission to the bar, he moved to Detroit, where he became assistant editor of the *Detroit Daily Advertiser.* Later he went to Chicago, where he practiced law and worked as agent for eastern land speculators in the upper Midwest.

1. Moore (d. 1844; Harvard Law School 1833), after working in the West for several years, returned to Concord, Massachusetts, where he died.

TO JOHN DAVIS (1787–1854)
                                        Boston March 28. 1836
My Dear Sir
    I recd your letter this morning, & also one from Mr Clay, both dated the 24th.[1] The disposition to *drive on*, manifested in the Senate, was to be expected, whenever a majority was obtained. I am altogether opposed

to the admission of the new States, until they shall have formed Constitutions, pursuant to laws previously passed by Congress, but if the matter is to be settled in the Senate this week, it will be quite impossible for me to be present at the vote. I found my wife quite unwell. She has had an attack of pleurisy, from which she is slowly recovering. If I return immediately, it is impossible for her to accompany me. If, however, my vote would be likely to turn the scale, on these questions, & the decision can be put off a few days, I shall leave her, & hasten back to Washington next week. From what I see, however, of the spirit that possesses the majority, I fear the whole matter may be decided, by the time you receive this, unless Mr [Hugh Lawson] White & the Indiana Senators,[2] & Mr [Samuel] McKean should be found on the right side, in which case, I hope, you will be able to muster 24 votes.[3] If you have strength enough, put off the final vote to April 15th—& I will be present—or sooner, if I can. Be kind enough to make my regards to Mr Clay, & say to him that I thank him for his letter.

I hear that there is a very good spirit in Connecticut, & some hope that the representative from that State in the Senate,[4] may be soon reformed. Here, all things are much as I expected.

Yours always truly   Danl Webster

If you have 24 you are safe, without me; if you have not, I should do you no good—

N. E.	6
N. J.	1
Pa	1
Del	2
Maryland	2
Va	1
N. C.	1
S. C.	2
Alab.	1 —?
Miss	1.
Louisiana	1.
Ten.	1
Ken.	2
Ohio	1
Indiana	2
	25

I hope you may be as strong as the above.

ALS. MWA. Published in part in W & S, 16: 273–274.

1. Neither letter found, but both had probably informed DW that bills

for the admission of Michigan and Arkansas into the Union had been reported on March 22. *Senate Journal*, 24th Cong., 1st sess., Serial 278, p. 236.

2. William Hendricks and John Tipton.

3. The Michigan bill passed, 24 to 18, on April 2, with Davis opposing; the Arkansas bill, on April 4, with Davis abstaining.

4. John Milton Niles had recently been appointed to the Senate vacancy caused by the death of Nathan Smith. From the outset of his senatorial career, Niles was an independent, eventually joining the Republican party in the 1850s.

FROM SAMUEL PRICE CARSON

Department of State
Republic of Texas
March 30th 1836.

(Private)

My Dear Sir,

Texas has assumed a position, among the nations of the Earth. It will be for an enlightened world to judge of the causes, which have combined, to render the step she has taken inevitable; and also to judge of the high and elevated principles, upon which she has based herself in her incipient movements, which I take leave to say, combines all the guarantees of *Liberty*, and the *rights* of *man*.

With regard to climate, soil, and extent of territory—physical, and moral resources, You are doubtless well advised. To a mind *like Yours*, I need only say we wish the countenance, and cheering *recognition* of our dear mother country. From her, her schools, her statesmen, and Philosophers, we draw all our notions of national law; and will look up to her experience for all the lights necessary, to guide us on to the perfection, of institutions, and regulations, which we hope will command the respect, and admiration of the world. Altho' in the state Department, I am too little of a diplomatist, to write with disguised feelings to an old congressional acquaintance, and may I not add friend? for so indeed I am to You; and the space that separates us augments that feeling, in an increased ratio to the distance, that is between us. By all those holy feelings then, and by all the considerations, which make *liberty*, with her glorious train of attributes, dear to man; allow me to invoke Your aid in obtaining an immediate *recognition* of our Independance.

What may not be done for *"millions* Yet unborn" by the voice, Yes Sir the *mighty* voice of Daniel Webster? and who can estimate the loss, if that voice be withheld?

I can write no more—may God protect You and our dear native country, is the sincere prayer of Yours most truly and profoundly

Sam P. Carson

P.S. President [David Gouverneur] Burnet writes you by the same conveyance that bears this,[1] also to Mr Clay, to whom you will please say
that I shall take an early opportunity of writing him. We are *worn down*
with fatigue. S.P.C.
Inclosed is the Inaugural of the President. It was the production of the
moment as he was inaugurated in one hour after Election & between 2
& 3 oclk A.M.

ALS. NhD.

1. Burnet (1788–1870) was elected
president when Texas declared its independence on March 2, 1836. He
served in that post until October 22,

when a new government was formed
under the constitution, and was later
elected vice president of Texas for
three years. Burnet's letter to Webster has not been found.

TO JOHN DAVIS (1787–1854)

Boston April 7. 1836

My Dear Sir
   I think of setting out on my return to Washington tomorrow, if the
weather be good, although, to tell you the truth, I have had more than
half a mind not to return at all. I see no good to be done, & there is little,
either in or out of Congress, to encourage effort. Our people here maintain tolerably good spirits, & will not neglect the fall elections, since the
State Government depends thereon. But for that consideration, the indifference of some, & the disgust of others, would make the State a ready
sacrifice to the Spoils party. There was a meeting on Monday Eve at
Concert Hall of the Whig members of the Legislature, & some other
Gentlemen.[1] [Horace] Mann, [Julius] Rockwell, [Leverett] Saltonstall,
[Myron] Lawrence of Hampshire,[2] [Isaac Chapman] Bates &c &c—addressed the meeting with energy & effect.
   The Governor was present, & told some truths, in a very plain manner. He said we had nothing to hope, now or at any time, either from
the South or the West, in his opinion. The general feeling seemed to be
that Massachusetts must stand alone, if she stand at all.
   I had heard that a Worcester paper had contained a column of cen-
sorious remarks on your vote on Mr Taney's nomination, but I have not
seen any thing, myself, in any of the papers.[3] I have been often asked
for the reason of your vote, on that side, & have always said, that having
lost our majority in the Senate, there was no hope of defeating the nomination, & no arrangement or understanding had been had among
friends, on the subject; & that, besides, you probably thought that if Mr
Taney was rejected, we should probably have a worse man; & also that
other Whig Senators voted the same way. At proper time, friendly papers
here will put the matter right, if the thing does not die away, as it prob-

ably will. I did not think the vote a matter of any consequence at the time, but am now rather sorry that you did not go with a majority of friends in the Senate. Still, I do not apprehend any considerable evil.

As to business—I sent my funds to the late Branch Bank in N York. The cashier has written to me that that office has ceased to take Deposites, & that my money is deposited in the Commercial Bank; but that when my check comes it will be provided for.

My wife is getting well; but she has sense & good taste enough to stay at home; & I feel ashamed to be so deficient, myself, in both, as not to stay at home with her. My best respects to Mrs Davis.[4]

Yrs truly   Danl Webster

ALS. MWA. Published in *W & S*, 16: 274–275.

1. For a brief report of the Concert Hall "social" event, see the *Columbian Centinel*, April 6, 1836.

2. Lawrence (1799?–1852) was a Belchertown lawyer and Massachusetts state senator.

3. On the final vote, March 15, 1836, Davis had favored Taney's confirmation, while most Whigs, including Webster, had voted in the negative. *Journal of the Executive Proceedings of the Senate . . . 1829 . . . to . . . 1837* (Washington, 1887), 4: 520–521.

4. Eliza, née Bancroft, daughter of the Reverend Aaron Bancroft and sister of George Bancroft.

TO EDWARD EVERETT

April 8. [1836]

Private & Confidential

Dr Sir

I did not return in season to pay you the intended visit, on Sunday Eve; & since that day have had no leisure hour at my disposal. I go off this morning.

Your remarks on Monday Evening appear to have given much satisfaction.[1] They have gone far towards removing many doubts & prejudices. I think your course, (& mine too) is clear. We must go *for* & *with* our friends. We cannot propitiate the enemy, if we were foolish enough to try. There is a good spirit among the Whigs, & I think that decision, energy, & preservation of confidence among friends, will carry thro' the fall elections triumphantly.

In my opinion, the sooner the Advocate takes the side of Judge [Marcus] Morton the better.[2] It will take that side; & its movement to that end will do less harm now than just before the election.

I shall be glad to hear from you. Adieu!   D. Webster

ALS. MHi.

1. See above, DW to John Davis (1787–1854), April 7, 1836, and the *Columbian Centinel*, April 6, 1836,

for the substance of Everett's remarks at the Concert Hall gathering.
2. Benjamin F. Hallett's Anti-
Masonic *Boston Advocate*, which had
been vacillating between supporting
Whigs and Democrats. Morton was
the Democratic gubernatorial candidate.

FROM JOHN DAVIS (1787–1854)

April 10. 1836

Dear Sir

Yours of the 4th[1] has just reached me and I hasten to reply doubting
however whether it will be in season to meet you at N. York. I recollect
your very kind proposition to advance two Thousand Dollars or more on
my account. I had however made antecedent arrangements to raise that
sum on my own account which since our conversation I have learned
proved successful. I have dealings with my brother and can very conveniently adjust the matter with him.[2] I thought I should divide the
money sending part to Maumee and part to Detroit. I have written to
that effect on condition it is raised. I will have the title taken in the manner that is most agreeable to you. It can with perfect convenience be
taken jointly or separately. If separate it can be conveyed rather more
readily & in case of death my minor children would not be in your way
—but whether joint or separate I will take care of the whole interest—
and see that it goes along right. I shall see you before any thing more
is done. Yours very truly   J Davis

(over)[3]

ALS. DLC.
1. Not found.
2. Davis had four brothers and it
has not been possible to identify positively the one from which he received the loan.
3. "(Over)" is in Davis's hand, but
if he added a postscript to this letter,
it has not been found. DW's ANS
endorsement reads: "I sent Mr Davis
my check for $3.000. I understand he
sent one half the cash to Detroit, &
the other to Maumee. D.W."

TO EDWARD EVERETT

Washington April 13. 1836

Private
Dr Sir

I hope our friends will not *anticipate* the time for considering the propriety of allowing an agency of the Bk of U.S. in Boston. Any such
measure as I understand is proposed would be regarded merely as a
Jackson triumph. Can you not call the attention of friends to it, in this
aspect, & as the occasion is not urgent, recommend postponement?[1] Yrs
truly   Danl Webster

ALS. MHi.

1. In connection with its extensive investigation of banks, during which some legislators had advocated the revocation of the charters of all those banks that were in violation of their charters, the Massachusetts legislature apparently had under consideration—or Webster feared it might consider—a measure to deny banking in Massachusetts to the branches of the Bank of the United States, since March a Pennsylvania corporation. For a general discussion of the banking investigation, see the *Columbian Centinel*, April 9, 13, 1836.

TO HENRY WILLIS KINSMAN

Washington April 13. 1836

My Dear Sir

I should regret that the Legislature should take any hasty step, in regard to the prohibition of any agency of the Bank of U.S. in Massachusetts. There can be no immediate necessity for such a measure, &, if adopted, it would assuredly be regarded as a *Jackson* triumph. Besides, in the present condition of the money market, every such thing only serves to encrease the pressure upon the Commercial Community. What it may be necessary to do hereafter, I cannot say; tho' it will require consideration, at any time, before it is decided to banish five millions of active Capital from the State. To the Bank itself, I presume, the proposed measure would do no mischief, as it has abundant calls for its capital, especially in the New States, where the legal rates of interest are from 8 to 12 per cent, & where the rapid rise of property makes debts secure. It might nevertheless be willing, hereafter, in proper terms & conditions, to leave a portion of its capital in Massachusetts. For the present, it seems to me to be highly inexpedient to anticipate the proper time for acting on the subject.

Will you have the goodness to confer with Mr [George] Blake,[1] Mr [William?] Foster,[2] Mr [Robert C.] Winthrop & other friends, & take care that nothing be done, without due consideration. Always yrs   D Webster

ALS. NhD.

1. Blake (1769–1841) was a Boston attorney, close friend of DW, and at this time the senior representative of the Boston delegation to the state legislature.

2. Probably the William Foster (1772–1836) who was the Democratic and Anti-Masonic candidate for lieutenant governor in 1835.

FROM HENRY L. KINNEY

[April 13, 1836]

Dr. Sr.

I will not be able to send the certifficates for the land I buy for you until after I make the drfts on you for the purchase money. Inform Messrs

G[urdon] S[altonstall] Hubbard of Chicago[1] or W[illiam] H[ubbard] Brown Cashier of the Chicago Bank[2] that my Drfts on you to the amt. of five thousand Dollars will be honored at 60 or 90 days from the date thereof.[3] It will enable me to draw the money at the time of making the drft, which might result favourably in making a quick purchase.

If your friend should want to make a like arrangment with me that you have, he had better write me at Chicago as I shall go immediately there on my return. In your next letter to me direct where I shall enclose the tittle papers of your land to you.

Respectfully your obt. Servt. H.L. Kinney

ALS. ViU. Kinney (1814–1861?), born near Shusshequin, Pennsylvania, moved to Illinois with his father in 1830, where he engaged in farming, mercantile pursuits, and speculation. In the early forties, he moved to Texas, where he was one of the founders of Corpus Christi; and in the 1850s, he organized and led a filibustering expedition to Nicaragua.

1. Hubbard (1802–1886), formerly clerk of the American Fur Company, 1818–1823, bought out the company's Illinois operations in 1826. Settling in Chicago in 1834, he was a leading banker and town promoter, serving in the state legislature from 1835 to 1839.

2. Brown (1796–1867), a native of Colchester, Connecticut, had read law with his father before he moved to Illinois in 1818, where he served as clerk of the U.S. District Court. Settling in Chicago in 1835, he first served as cashier for the State Bank and later as president of the Manufacturers National Bank and vice president of the First National Bank of Chicago.

3. Webster's endorsement on the letter, "Wrote accordingly, April 14, to Wm. H. Brown, Cashier &c" indicates that he complied with Kinney's instructions.

TO NICHOLAS BIDDLE

April 14. 1836

Dr Sir

We had a meeting of the Com[mitt]ee [on Finance] this morning, but did nothing. The bill repealing the 14th. Sect. will probably be passed thro',[1] if I may judge from what transpired in the House, & the temper of Mr [Silas] Wright, &c.

The fate of the other measure may be more doubtful, but whatever the King wills, will be done.

I think next week will be a good time for you to be here. Mr Clay, Mr [Willie Person] Mangum, & others, will probably be speaking, in the course of the week. Shall we see you? Yrs   D. Webster

ALS. DLC.

1. Section 14 of the act incorporating the Bank of the United States stipulated "that the bills or notes of said corporation originally made payable, or which shall have become payable on demand, shall be receivable in all payments to the United

States, unless otherwise directed by act of Congress." The act repealing this section passed on June 15, 1836.

3 *U.S. Statutes at Large* 274; 5 *U.S. Statutes at Large* 48.

MEMORANDUM OF LETTER TO FISHER AMES HARDING

April 14. 1836. Wrote Mr Harding—that he might invest for me, to amt. of two thousand dollars, if he could do so, by drawing on me at 90 d[ay]s, from date—payable in N. Y. or Boston—to be sent for acceptance to me at W[ashington] or Boston.

Told him to be prudent, &c.

AD. ViU.

TO EDWARD CURTIS

Washington April 15. 1836

My Dear Sir

I wrote to Fletcher to present himself to you, on Tuesday Morning, the 26th inst.[1] He will undoubtedly come to time, if no accident happen. I presume you still remain in the purpose of taking Washington, in your way. If you have ascertained the best mode of providing means, please inform me. Will it be as well as any way to take the money here? Yours truly   Danl Webster

Every body here is *land* mad.

ALS. NhD.
1. Letter not found.

TO EDWARD CURTIS

Washington April 20. 1836

Dr Sir,

I am quite sorry that you are obliged to give up your western trip, but do not well see how you could do otherwise. I have written to Fletcher, that I think it best for him still to go;[1] & have suggested to him that he forthwith render himself, at Washington. He will call on you as he comes along, & I will thank you to give him letters to any friends in Chicago, or else where.

I enclose a dr[a]ft, for 3,000 at 90 d[ay]s which I will thank you to accept & return to me. I want it, to be used only in case some other arrangements fail, which they may do possibly, in consequence of the pressure for money. I will see the acceptance provided for, in due season, if it shall be used. Will thank you to return it by next Post.

The fates act as if they had designed that you & I should never make any money *in co.*, but I think it best to hold on a little longer, & try the matter fairly out.[2] Whenever you are again ready for the west, I should be glad to put in. Yrs   D. Webster

ALS. NhD.
1. Letter not found.
2. Webster may have been allud-

ing to his Texan scrip, which he had discussed in the letter to Curtis above, January 30, 1836.

TO CAROLINE LE ROY WEBSTER

Senate, Friday morning
April 29. '36

My Dear Caroline,

I recd your letter of Monday Eve[1] this morning. Fletcher has not arrived, but I shall look for him this Evening, or tomorrow. We have had a week of mild growing weather—a reasonable mixture of moisture & warmth.

Today we hope to finish the land bill,[2] if Mr Benton should not wear us all out, by an endless speech—which he threatens to do. If we finish the Bill, I think we shall adjourn to Tuesday, to give time for the officers of the Senate to take up the carpet, clean the chamber &c, for warm weather.

I have some thoughts of running down the river, 25 miles, to a place of Genl [George] Mason's where his son John[3] lives—a great shad fishery &c. & to return on Monday. It now looks, however, like rain; & if that should come, I shall stay at home.

I imagine you will find it necessary to establish your head quarters in N York at Mrs [Cornelia Le Roy] Edgars, especially as Mrs Danl Le Roy[4] appears in bad health. It will be agreeable to you to be with your father. I think you will find it pleasant [to] come to N York sometime next week, or the early part of the week after. You will of course let me know where to write you at N York.

Commodore [Isaac] Chauncey had a party to dine yesterday. I did not make one. It is much pleasanter to have the afternoon to walk about—that is, all that is left of it after a short session. My health is at present very good—but I wish I had Sorrel here. I hate to ride a hack horse, & cannot afford the expense of buying one. I think I may hire one, under [Robert] Tweedy's[5] advice, for the session.

I shall of course write to you as at Boston, till I hear to the contrary. Adieu! Love to Julia.

How can you get on, with so small a household. I should think you would do well to break up, as soon as you can conveniently. Yrs ever truly   D Webster

ALS. NhHi. Published in Van Tyne, pp. 207–208.

1. Not found.
2. Clay's land bill to "appropriate,

for a limited time, the proceeds of the sales of the public lands of the United States, and for granting lands to certain States" passed the Senate on May 4, but the House tabled the measure on June 22. The distribution of the surplus revenue, however, was added to the bill to regulate the public deposits and became law on June 23, 1836. *Congressional Globe*, 24th Cong., 1st sess., pp. 342, 460; 5 *U.S. Statutes at Large* 55.

3. John Mason (1766–1849), fourth son of George, had inherited Gunston Hall, his father's plantation. In 1807, Jefferson had appointed him superintendent of Indian Trade, and during the War of 1812 he served as commissary general for prisoners.

4. Elizabeth Susan, née Fish (1805–1892), Caroline's sister-in-law.

5. Tweedy was messenger to the Senate.

FROM FISHER AMES HARDING

Chicago, May 4, 1836.

My Dear Sir

I received yours of the 14th. ult. this morning,[1] together with the authority to draw upon you for money. The roads have been very bad, and it has been rather longer than the usual time on the way. I showed the authority to make a draft to Mr. [William H.] Brown, the Cashier of the Bank here, and learned that he would *cash* one, if I should have occasion to draw. If I find what seems to be a good opportunity for investing, I shall do so. Property has already risen a good deal, but will it is thought rise higher in June. I will endeavour to be prudent. Mr [Henry] Moore, with whom I am connected, & who is a better judge of property, is now absent from town but will return in a few days. I shall consult him.

Lands for agricultural purposes are, at the minimum price, no doubt a very sure investment. It is difficult to get such on the line of the Canal at that rate or about it. Elsewhere, the lands are very good & valuable, but cannot be disposed of so soon at an advanced price. It occurs to me that it might be as well, if opportunity offered, to purchase something in or about town, which would be saleable probably in June at an advance, and then invest the proceeds in farming lands.

I notice what you say in relation to the scarcity of money, and it is well worth being attended to by those who think of retaining in their hands high-priced purchases. I suppose that an unusually large amount is out upon loans by Banks and private individuals; and should any large portion of this be suddenly called in, it might produce a sensation which would be felt even here. Our speculators are depending a good deal upon sales to Eastern men, and a scarcity of money might have a material effect upon the number of the latter.

If I make any investment, I will immediately inform you. I shall be looking for Fletcher with all earnestness. If he shall wish to purchase, I will give all the assistance I can, by introducing him to those who are judges of such things. I am, Yours truly,   Fisher A. Harding

ALS. ViU. DW endorsed the letter: to Harding, printed above, has been
"recd. & ansd. May 17."   found.
    1. Only DW's abstract of his letter

FROM JOSEPH RICKETSON WILLIAMS, WITH ENCLOSURE
                                              Toledo May 4, 1836
Sir,
    Agreeably to the request of Gov [John] Davis I sent you a receipt for $1000, in the investment of which, I shall be guided by his suggestions.[1]
    Land continues to be taken with great rapidity, and if located for four months more at the same rate, the Monroe Ld. Dist. in M[ichigan] T[erritory] may be considered as extinguished. The best opportunities of investment are now in the western part of Michigan.
    I will inform you when the locations or investments are made & forward the titles, upon the receipt of which I would suggest the propriety of your forwarding me a power of Attorney to sell, as every thing turns with such rapidity here one ought always to be prepared.
    Yours ever   Jos. R. Williams

ALS. ViU. Williams (1808–1861; Har-   ran twice for the U.S. Senate against
vard 1831) had studied law with   Lewis Cass and three times as a Whig
John Davis and, after his admission   congressional candidate. In 1860, he
to the bar, moved first to Toledo and   finally won a state Senate seat.
in 1839 to Michigan. In Michigan, he   1. See enclosure.

ENCLOSURE: RECEIPT
                                              Toledo May 4. 1836
$1000.
    Received through Geo. Bancroft One Thousand Dollars to be invested in Govt. Lands or other Real Estate, and to be accounted for to the Hon. Daniel Webster.   Jos. R. Williams

ADS. ViU.

TO JAMES WATSON WEBB
                                              Washington May 6. 1836.
My Dear Sir,
    My son is quite obliged to you, for giving him a letter to your brother.[1]

As to the subject of your two letters,[2] My Dear Sir, all I can say is, that I pray you to follow the course, which you think duty & honor point out. I have certainly no desire that any effort should be made for me, under circumstances which leave no hope that good would be produced by such effort.

I estimate highly your assurances of continued confidence & attachment, & shall never forget the regard & kindness which you have manifested, so long, & so steadily. But in the present state of things, I pray you to feel fully at liberty to act for the good of the country, and the cause, without reference to any expectations, which you may suppose I have heretofore formed, & to be assured that in so doing you will meet my entire approbation. You probably saw my letter to the Whigs of the Massachusetts Legislature.[3] It spoke my undisguised sentiments. I should have withdrawn from the canvass altogether, but for the state of affairs in Massachusetts, & the opinions of friends there.

I could very much desire to pass an hour with you, on this & some connected subjects. Are you not to be this way?

AL draft. NhHi. Published in Van Tyne, p. 208.

1. James Watson Webb had three brothers, Henry Livingston (1795–1876), Stephen Hogaboom (1796–1873), and Walker Wimple (1798–1876). It has not been determined to which of the three James Watson had written on Fletcher's behalf.

2. Not found.

3. See above, DW to Henry Willis Kinsman, February 27, 1836.

TO EDWARD EVERETT

Washington May 7. 1836

Dear Sir,

I was obliged to you for your letter of the 25. of April.[1] The Genl Court appears to have broke up under more favorable circumstances than I feared, & I am happy to learn from Mr [Caleb] Cushing & Mr [George] Grennell, who have lately returned from their respective Districts, that the general feeling seems to be right, & strong. I hope pains will be taken to put many strong men into the next legislature. In the last, there was a great deal too much of radicalism in some, & of a shallow, unthinking spirit of reform in others. This must be checked, or we may as well all go <to> over to the radical party, together, & at once. It appears to me there existed an extraordinary timidity, dignified by the name of policy, among well meaning & sensible men. Such trash as was put forth, in both houses, without manly & decisive contradiction, is really enough to alarm all considerate men.

We are in a peck of troubles here, & I hardly see our way thro'. My greatest fear, at present, is of a war about Texas. I have no faith in [Edmund Pendleton] Gaines' prudence, or, indeed, in his purposes; & if [Antonio de] Santa Anna² does not conduct himself with great caution & propriety, there will be collision. This whole subject appears to me to be likely to bring into our politics new causes of embarrassment, & new tendencies to dismemberment.

The Land Bill has just about an even chance of getting thro the H. of R.; but I presume very little of escaping the Veto.

What will be done with our money is quite uncertain. Great diversity of opinion prevails among the friends of the administration. Some are for dividing, in some way; others deny that there is any thing to divide.

I fear we shall make a long session of it.

I hear of my wife, as far as N. Y. & hope she will show herself here a fortnight hence.

With kindest remembrance to yr wife & children, I am, Dr Sir, truly yrs   D Webster

ALS. MHi. Published in part in PC, 2: 19–20.
1. Not found.

2. Santa Anna (1795?–1876) was then President of Mexico.

With financial backing from Thomas Handasyd Perkins, Webster expanded his land speculation in May 1836. In addition to the letter to Phineas Davis below, Webster sent almost identical instructions to Fisher Ames Harding, Joseph R. Williams, and Henry L. Kinney, thus authorizing investments of $20,000. Each of these agents proceeded quickly to invest the funds.

TO PHINEAS DAVIS

Washington May 16. 1836

Dear Sir

Th[omas] H[andasyd] Perkins Esq of Boston, who is doubtless well known to you, at least by character, & reputation is now here. He & myself have agreed to join in some investments in land in your part of the Country,¹ & we propose to place a sum in your hands for that purpose, to be invested on the same terms & conditions as you invest other funds for me [& for Mr. Davis.]² The sum which we propose to place at your disposal for this purpose is <ten> five thousand Dollars; of which three fourths are to be invested for account of Col. Perkins, & one fourth on my account. Of course, we leave the choice of places to your discretion, looking to safety, & to the hopes of profit. We would not desire you to be too adventurous, in regard to town lots; but if you should see a good prospect of a handsome <profit> advance, in property of that kind, you will embrace the opportunity so to dispose of part of our means. We think that a judicious selection of lands for agricultural purposes, in townships already settled & settling, *near* <as may be> *to great lines of communication*, & taken up at Govt. Prices, <must> cannot well fail to produce handsome returns on the Capital. Still, we should be very glad if you could make a lucky hit, at some point, where the land should soon be wanted for town purposes, or where it would be met by some canal, or other improvement, which should enhance its value.

So far as may be convenient, we think it best to take titles to Col Perkins & myself, separately. This you can probably do, <in regard> without inconvenience, as to lots taken up for cultivation. You will of course take care to do us equal justice, in regard to the quality of the lands; & let the title of three fourths be made out in his name, & of one fourth in mine. Where it is not convenient to take titles separately, you may make the purchase jointly, in the names of both of us, in the above proportions. We will thank you to be as particular as possible in giving us descriptions of the lands which you may purchase, & immediately forward the titles.

As to the mode of remittance, we have thought of no better way than for you to draw on me. I shall be in this City until the early part of June, perhaps later, & then in Boston. You may draw at thirty days, <or longer or sixty days> if you find it convenient; or at any shorter <length of> time, <but if you draw from *date*,> so as that I get seasonable notice. If you draw at a given number of days from *date*, take care <that the Bill be transmitted in such season as to reach me, for acceptance, ten days or a fortnight before its maturity; and whenever you draw,> to give me immediate notice by mail. As <your> commercial transactions in your quarter may center in New York or Philadelphia, your Bills on me may be made payable either at Boston, or "at the Merchants Bank, in the City of New York"; or at the Bank of the U. States at Philadelphia. I presume you will find no difficulty in cashing these Bills, [either at Cleveland, or Detroit.]³ I forward with this, an engagement to accept.⁴ Col Perkins is on a tour to the South & West, but probably will not go so far as to your place. You will of course, write me, on the receipt of this: You will see what day shall be fixed on for the adjournment of Congress, & may take it for granted, that I shall be here till about that time.

If convenient, I should like at least ten days or a fortnight's notice of your drafts, before they fall due, especially if they should be made payable in New York or Philadelphia, <in order that I might be able to remit the funds. This would be less important, if they should be payable in Boston.>

AL draft. MWalB. Davis (1801–1850), a nephew of John Davis and originally of Northborough, Massachusetts, had settled in Detroit by 1827 after being disinherited by his family for going to sea as a youth. In Detroit, he ran a general store and served as agent for eastern speculators.
1. DW instructed his amanuensis to make "3 or 4 copies" of this letter, each of which he sent to a different western agent.

2. These brackets were inserted by DW's amanuensis. As explained by an endorsement in the handwriting of the amanuensis: "<first bracket omitted in only 2 copies—both brackets omitted in 2 copies>/2 brackets omitted in all[;] 1 d[itt]o—in 2."
3. Brackets here were also inserted by DW's amanuensis.
4. See DW's authorization to Phineas Davis to invest $5,000 and to draw on him for that amount, mDW 39835–95.

TO FISHER AMES HARDING

Washington May 16. 1836

Dear Harding

I wrote you on the 14th. April,[1] giving you authority to draw on me for $2.000 to be invested in lands in your Country, but have yet recd no answer. I presume I shall hear from you soon.

By the enclosed letter & authority you will see that Col Perkins & myself propose to employ you in another similar agency.[2] The letter will explain our views fully, except as to one particular. You will observe that I express the intention of allowing you the same compensation &c, as in regard to other funds, invested for me. There was nothing said in my former letter, I believe, on this point. With other agents however, with whom I have entrusted small sums, & to whom also Col Perkins & myself have now sent funds, the agreement has been that they should be allowed 25 per cent on the profits, or increased value, as a compensation for investing. Now, in regard to the 2.000 for which I heretofore authorized you to draw me, & as to this 5.000, if you think you can afford to let your classmate, D[aniel] F[letcher] W[ebster] divide commissions with you, so much the better for him. He will be with you, I presume, about the time this letter reaches you.

I should be very much delighted if this 5.000 should be advantageously invested, so as to please Col Perkins. In addition to the pleasure of seeing him do well with his money, it would very likely open a door for much further communication.

Pray let me hear from you, on the receipt of this letter. Your friend, truly,   Danl Webster

P.S. Are you sure that you are in the right spot? Is there no chance that Michigan will go ahead of Chicago?

ALS. NNC.
1. See above.
2. DW probably enclosed to Har-

ding a copy of the above letter to Phineas Davis, May 16, 1836.

TO PERKINS & CO.

Washington May 16. 1836

Messrs Perkins & Co.
I enclose a letter from T. H. Perkins Esq addressed to yourselves,[1] by which you will see that I am authorized to draw on you for Twenty thousand Dollars. It is not probable that I shall have occasion to draw for the whole sum at once, or at such short sight, as to cause you any inconvenience in raising the money. I shall give you all practicable notice. I am, with regard, Your ob. Servt   Danl Webster

ALS. MHi. Endorsed: "Rec: May   1. Not found.
18, 1836."

FROM FISHER AMES HARDING

Chicago, May 17th 1836.

My Dear Sir,
I have this day drawn upon you at the Phenix Bank, New York, for five hundred & twenty dollars.[1] I have invested it in some land adjoining Michigan City, I[ndian]a, I purchased along with a friend, paying $500 a piece in cash, & receiving time for the rest of the purchase money. Unless greatly disappointed, we shall sell at a considerable advance previous to the next payment.[2]

As I wrote you in my last, the Cashier of the Bank had assured me that the money would be furnished on such a draft as you authorized me to draw. When I had made the bargain, I found on calling at the Bank, that they were then *out of funds*, but would accommodate me, as the Cashier thought, in a few days. Wishing to complete the transaction, I borrowed the money of a friend, for a day or two. This morning I was able to make use of the draft at the Bank, & accordingly paid my friend. Our Bank is very limited in its means.

Some of our Chicago people here returned from New York, & say that money is not so scarce there, as it was a short time ago. The pressure has been oppressive.

Daniel is, I understand, on his way to the West, by the Southern route. I shall look for him here in two or three weeks. Would you like to have him settle in the West? Yours truly,   Fisher A. Harding

P.S. The draft is drawn at 90 days, & will be sent to New York, with directions to be sent to you for acceptance. I was particular in calling Mr [William H.] Brown's (Cashier's) attention to this point. F.A.H.

ALS. ViU.
1. According to DW's endorsement on the letter, this was his "first investment" through Harding.
2. On May 21, Harding wrote Webster of the sale of the land: "We purchased twenty acres, adjacent to Michigan City, I[ndian]a, for $150 per acre—$3000 in all,—the payments being 1/3 in cash—1/3 in 3 months—& 1/3 in 6 months. We yesterday sold the land for $280 per acre—in all, $5760—the payments being $1000 in cash—1/3 of the residue in 3 months—1/3 in 6 months—& 1/3 in 9 months." See mDW 13241.

FROM PHINEAS DAVIS

Detroit May 23d 1836

Dear Sir,

Your favour of the 16 inst. was received this day.[1] I feel much gratified with the confidence you have reposed in me, and you may rest assured I will invest the $5,000 in such a manner as will afford or yield you an interest of at least 50 per cent per annum—and I should think 100 for 10 years to come. As I wrote you a few days ago I have a very judicious man in the country constantly looking [for] land, and expect him in any moment when the purchase for the 1000$ will be completed. I will advise you from time to time in relation to land operations. There is no doubt but what all good farming lands well situated will be worth from 10 to 20$ per acre in 5 or 10 years and many of them 30 & 40$. Perhaps I may be so fortunate as to find a good location for a Village, and then we may make a very large per cent, but that would be all luck. I am going in the country tomorrow and will write you more fully in my next. Your very Obt Servt   Phins Davis

ALS. ViU. Endorsed: "Acknowledging my letter of May 16. (for Col. Perkins   & self)."
1. See above.

FROM HENRY L. KINNEY

Chicago May 24th 1836

Dr. Sir,

I have this day agreeable to our former understanding executed my Draft on you for three thousand Dollars payable at the Phoenix Bank New York at Sixty days after sight.

Emigration to this country has never before been equal to that this Spring—which makes it more difficult to procure choice entries. I shall however be able to make purchases for you that will tell well,—I have some choice situations in view & shall proceed in all possible haste to secure them for you, & forward the title together with a discription of the lands.

Real estate has enhanced in value greatly within 3 months—through-out this northern country.

A large amt of money might be made in the purchase of improved lands in this Country if Capital could be had. My farming lands purchased last July for 1.25 per acre are worth at this time from 10 to 20 Dolls per acre—but slight improvements on them. I can buy lands by turning my attention to it second handed that would pay 100 per ct. in one year. You spoke of having a friend that had money to invest. I could do that well for him.

I have been buying some lands for Mr [Henry] Hubbard (of New-hampshire), in Putnam Co. that are well located—& shall purchase some in that County for you if I am not to[o] late. I have it in view going to Rock Island Co to make investments for you near the mouth of Rock River.[1]

Property at Chicago, Peru & the mouth of Rock River is rising in value more than at any other place in the west. I shall forward on your title papers as soon as convenient.

I remain with due Respect your Obt. Svt.   H. L. Kinney

I should be glad to hear from you.

ALS. ViU. Endorsed: "July 9. recd & ansd. Wrote Mr. Delafield Cashier—to consider me as accepting July 9."
    1. According to the Dubuque *Iowa News*, July 15, 1837, Webster was by then interested in the city of Rock Island "to the amount of sixty thousand dollars."

FROM JOSEPH RICKETSON WILLIAMS

Toledo May 24. 1836

Sir,

I received yours of 16th.[1] this morning with accompanying letter of credit. I will observe your wishes both with respect to the Drafts and the investment.

A few days since I purchased the valuable mill power with a flour mill, two saw mills & two dwelling houses with 550 acres of land in and about the village of Constantine, the head of navigation on the St. Josephs in St. J. County M[ichigan] T[erritory]. The terms were $20.000, $8000 on or before 3d June & balance in six annual paymts. I consider it *a most excellent operation* and think I shall use $2000 of the money which you and Col. Perkins desire me to invest, in this purchase. It may be necessary to make some improvements in order to double & treble the property. I think it the *best point* I have seen in the interior of Michigan.

I lately located for you about 400 acres of land in the County of Hillsdale a description of which is contained in the following abstract from the Receiver's Duplicate Certificate.

No 12.508

E. 1/2 of s.w. fractional 1/4 Sect. 30 Township 9 South, Range 3 West—cont[ainin]g 80 acres.

s.w. fraction 1/4 and w. 1/2 of s.e. 1/4 & e. 1/2 of n.w. frctn'l 1/4 of Sect. No. 31, Township 9 South Rang[e] 3 West cont[ainin]g 319. 65/100 acres = 399 65/100 acres a $1.25 pr. acre $499.56

It is finely timbered good land and being in an exact western course from this point *may* have a Rail Road pass through it which is chartered to extend from Sandusky to Toledo, thence to [the] western line of Ohio. You will perceive it is on the Disputed Territory.[2] I will give you an early account of the investment of all the funds.

I was very glad to have Col. Perkins become also interested in Michigan lands. The Boston people are not aware of the experiment which is going on in Michigan. I have recently returned from the Western part of Michigan. I then found the office thronged with men of all descriptions and particularly by such as were able to purchase from 80 to 500 acres, and even determined to do so for their own use. The whole of the country is inviting and fertile, and I have not the least doubt that the accession of population for the next three years will be enormous. The day is not distant when all the good land in M. will be located, and then it *must* rapidly & continually advance in price for a course of years. I speak of M. particularly because the population is excellent, because it is the favorite country for emigrants from the best portions of the east & because the peninsula must always be a great thoroughfare, and because no *soil* can offer more advantages.

I am glad your son is here at this time because any operations he may enter into before July will be worth 25 pr. ct. more than any subsequent to that time. He is pleased with the appearance of every thing about *Toledo*, and thinks it is the most *commanding point* on this great outlet. [He is] welcome to my experience, and has accepted my invitation to go with me to Constantine[,] Bronson &c for which places we shall start abou[t] the 27th. I remain With great respect yours   Jos. R. Williams

ALS. ViU.

1. Williams probably also received

a copy of the letter above, DW to Phineas Davis, May 16, 1836.

2. The area around Toledo, to which both Michigan and Ohio laid claim. Congress finally settled the boundary dispute on June 15, 1836, with a provision in the Michigan enabling act. 5 *U.S. Statutes at Large* 49.

TO HENRY COLMAN

Washington, May 25. 1836

My Dear Sir

You have my full consent to refer to me in your card, as it always gives me pleasure to be useful to you, in any way.

I do not regard myself as a very competent judge of the practicability or usefulness of your scheme, & perhaps, on subjects of this nature, may have some of the prejudices of an untravelled man. But since you ask my opinion, I must say, that I should prefer that you should educate sons of mine at Deerfield, rather than in Paris, or Switzerland. I am no believer, I confess, in the utility of foreign education for American boys. When they become men, they may travel, & see other countries, doubtless with much advantage; but, in my judgment, it is better they should grow up at home, amidst the opinions & sympathies of their own circle, and among the objects which are most to interest them in after life. After all, there is no part of the education of our young men more strikingly deficient, than that which respects their knowledge of their own Country. And why should these years be passed in a sort of banishment abroad, in which all sorts of affections, personal, social, & local, are taking possession of the heart? I should choose that a boy of mine should grow up *omnis Americanus*—and visit foreign countries, in his early manhood, as an alien & a stranger, travelling for improvement, & general enlargement of his knowledge.

In all this, however, I dare say I may be wrong; &, at any rate, I desire that those who prefer to send their sons abroad may have the good fortune to place them under your care & tuition.

With cordial regard, Yrs   Danl Webster

ALS. DLC.

TO [HERMAN] LE ROY

Washington May 26. 1836

Dear Sir

For your amusement, for a moment, & to show you how things are going at the West, I send you a copy of a letter recd by me today from Mr P[hineas] Davis, at Detroit.[1] It shows the mode, in which he invested

$500, for me, in the purchase of 400 acres in the town of "Commerce."
Yours truly   Danl Webster

ALS. NNebgWM.
　　1. See Phineas Davis to DW, May 18, 1836, mDW 13235.

TO MARTIN VAN BUREN

Sunday, May 29. 1836
My Dear Sir
　　Mr Le Roy[1] has sent me a *salmon*, which I hope may be good *tomorrow*. Will you do me the favor to dine with me, at 5 oclock on that day, taking the chance that the fish may have been well preserved? Do me the favor also of bringing your son[2] with you. Yours truly
　　　　　　　　　　　　　　Danl. Webster

ALS. NhExP.　　　　　　　　　　Smith Thompson—was in Washing-
　　1. Either Daniel or Herman Le Roy.　ton at the time has not been deter-
　　2. Which of Van Buren's four sons　mined.
—Abraham, John, Martin, Jr., or

FROM PHINEAS DAVIS

Detroit May 30th 1836
Dear Sir,
　　I drew a D[ra]ft upon you this day in favour of the Bank of Michigan for 1000$ at 10 days sight payable at the Mechanics Bank in the City of N Y on account of land. I have also entered this day 80 acres for you & 160 for Mr Perkins. I entered these lots on account of the appearances of stone coal of a very superior quality. I have entered 9 lots in all on account of coal 1 for you, 2 for Mr Perkins, 1 for Gov. Davis 1 for Col J[oseph] Davis[1] his brother, 2 for E[urotas] P Hastings President of the Bank of Michigan,[2] and two I owned previously. The understanding is if coal of considerable value should be found upon either of the lots we are to all share in proportion to the lands which we own. I was out to see the lands last week, but was so unwell and the musquitoes were so plenty it was all most impossible to dig. In diging a place 1 1/2 feet deep & 2 wide & long, I obtained 1/2 bushel of as pure Anthracite coal as you ever saw, and there is an appearance of a large quantity of Iron Ore. But if the land does not possess any of these treasures it is worth what we gave, for farming purposes. I was offered in one hour after we had made the purchase 7$ per acre for all the lots. But should there prove to be a large quantity of coal, it would command 100,000$ and I concluded we could afford to run the risk as well as any one. I shall endeavour to have the examination made soon. It is situated about 38 miles from this place

and will be 15 miles from a Rail Road—had I supposed there was a large lot of coal I should have entered it all for you & Col Perkins, but I thought there was considerable doubt upon the subject and did not wish to purchase any but first rate lands for you, and in order to cover all the lands upon which I had any reason to suppose there was coal, I divided among the gentlemen named, knowing they would make a great company if we should conclude to work the mine. Your son called upon me on Saturday Morning and purchased a horse, and started immediately for Chicago, appeared very much pleased with the country. I expect the Duplicates for your land on account of the other 1000$ any day. The office where I have entered the land is 175 miles from here. I had a letter from the man I employed, and have no doubt that he will be in this week and then will give you all the particulars relating to land & prospects &c. &c. The country is over run with people looking for land. The sales at this Office will be 340 Thousand Dollars this month. I shall not be able to obtain the Duplicates for the land I entered today, before tomorrow. The emigration is equal to 1000 per day which arrive at this place. I wish you to inform me if you will consent to *share* in *proportion* to the lands you own as far as *relates* to *coal* and *Iron.* Your very Obt Servt   Phins Davis

P.S. I shall not probably draw for over 1000$ at a time and perhaps shall not use all the money before the first of July. I shall try to make the very best selections. Yrs   PD

ALS. ViU.
    1. Davis (1774–1843) served in both branches of the Massachusetts legislature.

    2. Hastings held that banking post from 1825 to 1836.

FROM FISHER AMES HARDING

Chicago, June 2nd. 1836.

My Dear Sir,

I received your favours of the 16th. & 17th. May,[1] at the same time. I presume you will have received two letters from me,—one apprising you of a draft for $520,—the other informing you of the sale of the land near Michigan City, at some advance.[2]

I have carefully read your letters and directions respecting the investment of $5000 for yourself and Col. Perkins, and will do my best to carry them into effect. I perceive from them that your intention is merely that I should invest and forward the titles to you, without selling at all. I presume now that your intention was the same with regard to the money in which you were alone interested. This did not occur to me till I received your letters respecting the $5000. I was therefore labouring under a mistake in the Michigan City transaction, but as it turned out, the mistake perhaps did no great *harm*. I have not since made any purchase. In the scarcity of money at the East, & every where, & knowing that you had made other disposition of much of your funds, I thought it best not to do so, except upon a very favorable occasion.

Of course, if you prefer, I will invest your money as you direct; but you will not be likely to realize so much from it. I am confident that the most money by far *has been made* by buying & selling again. Most of those who have invested for Eastern friends have done it in this way. If you are lucky enough to hit upon some peculiar location, a large profit might no doubt be made in any way, but such *hits* are rare. Too many sharp eyes have already examined the country. Col. Perkins, and yourself too would not probably feel quite so safe, in having your money passing from one tract of land to another,—no Boston man would; but on the other hand, no *Western man* or at any rate *Chicago* man would think of doing otherwise, if he intended to make money. My advice to *you* at least is, that you allow me to sell, exchange or dispose of in any other way and to invest the proceeds. There are many opportunities for investment which it would be impossible to take advantage of without it. For example, I could not purchase an undivided interest in a town; yet these are often the best investments.

The most usual mode of operation except in government lands is to buy partly with cash & partly on time. It is the most profitable mode, unless you have a large capital. Bonds are given to make deeds when the final payment is made. This may seem a strange and perhaps an unsafe method, yet three fourths of our transfers are made by it.

Your remarks respecting lands upon great lines of communication at Government prices are certainly entirely correct, but it is difficult to get such, at least here. Good lands along the route of our Mich. & Ill. Canal are worth from 5 to 10 dollars per acre. I have some idea of going up during the Summer into Wisconsin; I may find some good points there, but the *claims* of squatters, or rather their assignees cover most of them. These claims must be respected, for they would have the sanction of *Club Law* at least.[3]

I presume you allude to Michigan City, I[ndian]a. when you ask if there is no chance of its going ahead of Chicago. I am sure there is none. When our Canal is made, Chicago will be the outlet of the whole country on the Illinois river & its branches, one of the richest in the West. It will also be connected by a rail-road with Galena & the mining country. The chief advantage of Michigan City is that it is the only town belonging to Indiana on the Lake, & will be sustained, as far as may be, by the Indiana interest. Its means for a harbour & for internal communication are very deficient. I think no place West of Buffalo will rival Chicago, unless it be the mouth of the Maumee in Ohio. Michigan Territory is promising, but lands are high there, & speculation, intense.

The terms of compensation you mention are very liberal & will be entirely satisfactory; I shall consider them still more so, if possible, if D.F.W. will engage with me in the business.

Daniel has not yet arrived, but, I understand, has reached Detroit. Perhaps, he has been delayed there for a steamboat, intending to come round by Lake Huron. I am looking for him every day. What are his plans for the future?

Mr. [Henry] Moore, my partner, has an interest in a very valuable piece of land near our harbour, the title of which is likely to be contested. His title is derived from the pre-emptor and the main question is likely to be, I believe, whether from the manner in which the survey is made, this piece is included in the preemption. The tract is the South portion of the Sand-bar through which our harbour is constructing. A company of influential men in different parts of the State have combined together for the purpose of getting hold of it, by a _float_, that is, a floating claim to enter unoccupied land. Mr. Moore anticipates quite as much danger from the concentration of interest & influence as from the validity of their title. Should this matter come into litigation, he will like to obtain your professional assistance; & will before long submit to you a fuller statement of the case. He would desire that you should not permit yourself to be retained on the other side; & I may perhaps add my own wish that you should not. I think Mr. Moore would very willingly give Daniel & myself an interest in the Sand-Bar, if we should bye and bye desire it, either for your use or otherwise. If the title is made good, the property will be exceedingly valuable. It is thought it would be worth $200,000; Mr. Moore lately sold a _quitclaim_ of an eighth for $16,000.

I have not seen an announcement of the time of the adjournment, & therefore direct to Washington. I shall perhaps hear from you soon. Be so kind as to remember me to your family. Yours truly   F.A. Harding

P.S. June 3rd. My letter having been delayed, I add here that if you should think it adviseable to allow me to dispose of property purchased, it would be necessary for me either to take it in my own name, or to be furnished with a power of Atty. Mr. M. concurs in the opinion that money may be more advantageously employed in this way.   F.A.H.

ALS. ViU.

1. See above for DW to Harding, May 16, 1836; the letter of May 17 has not been found.

2. See above, Harding to DW, May

17, 1836, and Harding to DW, May 21, 1836, mDW 13241.

3. For a discussion of the purpose and practice of claim clubs in Iowa, see Allan G. Bogue, "The Iowa Claim

Clubs: Symbol and Substance," in
*The Public Lands: Studies in the
History of the Public Domain*, ed.

Vernon Carstensen (Madison, 1963),
pp. 47–69.

FROM HERMAN LE ROY

New York June 3d 1836

My Dear Sir

I have received three of your favors[1] which I have been prevented from replying to from various causes and from a slight indisposition which Caroline will explain to you when she sees you which I very much apprehend has not as yet been the case from the incessant and heavy rains that commenced the day after she left us, which was Wednesday morning. We therefore feel very anxious to hear from her, which I am in hopes will be by the mornings mail.

I have with much pleasure perused Mr P[hineas] Davis's letter to you containing a statement of the locations he has made in the town of Commerce in Michigan, and so near to Detroit;[2] the two Lakes adjoining them, and their being such valuable wheat lands renders the purchase a very valuable one, and there certainly cannot be much hazard in holding such lands, and so near a situation for the export of their produce at such moderate prices. Pray is Mr Davis the Brother of the late Governor of your state who, is now in Congress and what occupation is he now pursuing? He really writes like a man of business, and his statement and arguments in relation to investments, do him much credit. I have noticed by the papers that the Government have been purchasing certain Indian Reservations in Michigan, which I presume will be for sale also. Pray where do these lands lay, are they South of Lake Michigan and are they wheat lands similar to those Mr D. purchased for you. If they are such and rather more South they may perhaps be a desireable acquisition. I wish you should try and get some information as to them, and whether they would not prove a good purchase.

I notice your observations as to the Alleghany Pine timber lands;[2] Jacob [Le Roy] has very recently informed me that he had just received a few lines from our agent, who he had authorized to make a considerable investment in them of fine qualities and favorably situated for transportation. The agent who is gone after them is a very judicious man and says, he meets with more competition by eastern speculators than we had any idea of, and we are apprehending that he will not succeed in procuring the quantum of acres we should have been desirous of purchasing on reasonable terms. The agent had however been in the forest one week in making examinations, and was about departing again to make further excursions and expected in 10 to 12 days after to be enabled to give some decisive information as to what may possibly be laid hold of there, so that we must patiently await further advices from Jacob before any thing definitively can be said on the subject.

The American Land Comp[an]y[4] are going to lay before the Share Holders an exposition of their concerns which from what I can learn will prove a very favorable one, and in the course of a fortnight I am in hopes of getting an inspection of it, and where their investments are situated and which will guide me as to further investments, but I have a high opinion of the Alleghany Lands if they can be obtained on fair terms and well situated for transport.

The Patent arms manufacturing compy.[5] has made a call of $5. per share payable on 5 inst. on one hundred and fifty shares that I have subscribed for; 50 of them are intended for you, which at $5. per share is

$250.— to which please add amount of Prince's P[aymen]t for trees
42.25 which you can remit to me at your perfect convenience.
$292.25

These shares are standing in my name, and as it is probable heavy contracts will be made with the Government for some guns and Pistols I thought perhaps you might prefer not to have your name mentioned as a share holder therein; you have doubtless seen that the Secty. of War in his report speaks very favorably of the invention; the manufactory is to be established at Patterson where contracts are making for the erection of the necessary buildings and it is expected that not more than 15 to 20% will be called in; Dudley Selden and the [Thomas A.] Emmet's[6] with many of your other acquaintances are interested therein also.

I am much pleased to notice by the discussions in the Senate that there appears to be some hope of something being done as to the division of the surplus revenue now laying dead as Mr [Silas] Wright & [James] Buchanan both appear in favour of adopting some measure that may prove beneficial to the community and relieve in some measure the great pressure for money now pervading our country; here from what I can learn the calls are very urgent in Wall Street and good paper offering at from two to 3 pct. per month. I hope these lines may find you relieved from the cold you have been complaining of; the weather here for the last 12 days has been very raw and unpleasant and we have had some very heavy rains with a N.E. wind during that period which has prevented any of our vessels from going to sea and they appear from the Battery all at anchor like a forest recently started up. Hannah Newbold[7] I am happy to say is doing well but the weather has prevent[ed] me from seeing her the last ten days though we hear occasionally from her.

I have letters to day from Edward [Le Roy][8] of the 5th May with his

Nephews who were all hearty in London and who complain dreadfully of the inclemancy of the weather they are experiencing there; I expect they will start for home early in July. If Caroline has reached you please remember us all affectionately to her and Julia and Believe me ever truly with sincere esteem   Herman Le Roy by H Le Roy Newbold[9]

P.S. As the Government is going to pay a part of the French indemnity here it puts me in mind of a small share that my late house was concerned in the Ship Govr. Strong which was under the management of Mr. Samuel G. Perkins which perhaps you can inform me to what amount our share may be therein.[10]

LS (by proxy). NhHi.

1. Only one, DW to [Herman] Le Roy, May 26, 1836, printed above, has been found.

2. See Phineas Davis to DW, May 18, 1836, mDW 13235.

3. These Allegheny pine timber lands lay in Tennessee; and through Stephen and John T. Haight, Webster acquired some 250,000 acres. See DW to Virgil Maxcy, May 31, 1842, mDW 22584.

4. The American Land Company, organized by Boston and New York capitalists on July 1, 1835, with a capital of $1,000,000, acquired a considerable portion of land in Arkansas, Mississippi, Illinois, Indiana, Ohio, Michigan, Wisconsin, Georgia, and New York. While many of Webster's financial friends and associates were stockholders, it has not been established conclusively that he himself was.

5. The Paterson, New Jersey, Patent Arms Manufacturing Company, Samuel Colt's enterprise, had been chartered by the New Jersey legislature on March 5, 1836, but, unable to raise the necessary capital and to sell his revolver to the government, Colt went bankrupt in 1841 and the company closed in 1842.

6. Emmet (1798–1863) was a New York lawyer.

7. Hannah Cornell Newbold (1816–1842) was Herman Le Roy's granddaughter. In 1834, she had married William Henry Morris, a descendant of Captain Richard Morris.

8. Edward Augustus Le Roy (1804–1865), Herman Le Roy's youngest son.

9. Herman Le Roy Newbold (1813–1854), Herman Le Roy's grandson.

10. Under the Convention with France, July 4, 1831, several claimants—among them Le Roy, Bayard & McEvers—received an award of $7,188.81 for the ship *Governor Strong. Executive Documents of the Senate of the United States*, 49th Cong., 1st sess., Serial 2337, p. 69.

FROM PHINEAS DAVIS

Detroit June 5th 1836

Dear Sir

Your favour of May the 26 was received this morning authorizing me to draw upon you at 30 or 60 days sight for 5000$ to be invested in public lands.[1]

Your expression of confidence reposed in me I hope will be fully realized. I think I have not got the speculating mania so much but what I can see strait in most cases, and at present prices of Town property, I do not feel any confidence in, and should not feel willing to venture in a purchase unless I had a purchaser before hand. There is one piece of property which I think it an object to obtain if it can be had, and I shall try to obtain it for Col. Perkins & yourself. It is an Incorporated company called the Black River Steam Mill Company, where individual property is not liable for the debts of said company. I am the President of the company and of course know all about it. The company has been in existance 18 months and possesses the following property which is worth the prices anexed. One Wharf in this City which we have been offered $33,000[;] 5600 acres of first rate pine land on Black River situated at the southern bend of Lake Huron worth 10$ per acre[;] One Water Mill with 200 acres of land $16,000[;] One Steam Mill with 22 acres of land in a growing village with other building worth at least 35,000$ together with lumber on land &c &c. We shall make and bring to market this year 3,000,000 feet of lumber which will average 14$ per 1000 ft which is more than half profit. The whole of the above property stands us in less than $40,000. I hope to be able to obtain 1000$ or more of it at par, which will give us a dividend next January of 50 or 75 per cent, and it will do that anually without any trouble. You will probably ask, if it is so valuable why it can be purchased at par? The reason is the Stockholders know nothing at all about it, and all the stock is owned by the directors except that which I hope to purchase. I should not be at all surprised if we sold the whole concern at 150,000$. There are several who want it, at that and all that will prevent, is the first payment which is $50,000. The property is richly worth that price and will pay at this time 16 per cent on 150,000$. In relation to your proposition through Gov. Davis, I do not know as I rightly understand. He assumes you will pay me 25 per cent upon the investment. That I should not be willing to accept of, if I locate the land free of charge, for the cheapest you can employ any one to locate land for is 10$ for every 80 acres and then you run a great risk in obtaining a faithful Agent. I am perfectly willing to do it as cheap as any other faithful and responsible Agent, but do not wish to be under the market in the matter. The terms given by most eastern people are half of the profits the land being located free of charge. I am willing to locate land on better terms than that. I will invest your money in land and allow you 10 p[er] cent upon your money, but should like to have the lands lay 5 or 10 years, unless we sold and reinvested. In my proposition I should expect to have the agency of the lands for which I should make no charge. Notwithstanding what I have said above in relation to terms I am willing to leave the matter entirely to your generosity untill after we get through with our speculations. I hope to have the pleasure of seeing you in Boston next Autumn, and then we can arrange all matters. It is in consideration of the prospect you hold out for considerable investment of funds which would lead me to leave the matter entirely to you. I feel under great obligations to you already for the amount of money placed at my disposal, and I trust I shall be able to make a large amount of money for you. I drew upon you on the 3[1s]t for 1500$ in favour of the Farmers & M[echanics?] Bank of Michigan at 10 days sight [pay]able at the Merchants Bank in NY. All d[ra]f[t]s [?] will be made payable the[re]. The money will be expended in the Bronson land office and has been on the wa[y?   ] days. Yours very respectfully   P. Davis.

ALS. ViU.
    1. For Webster's authorization, see mDW 39835–95.

FROM JOSEPH WARREN SCOTT

New Brunswick 6 June 1836
Sir
    On the first day of this month the Whig Convention of the State of New Jersey assembled at Trenton for the purpose of nominating to the free men of this State suitable persons to be supported by them for the high and honorable offices of President and Vice President of the United States.
    In the present momentous crisis of our publick affairs, you can easily imagine that the deep interests of our common country[,] the stability of Constitutional law, and the preservation of our institutions in their purity and vigor were among others subjects of anxious excitement.
    Many of our publick characters, who have with you for a long course of years breasted the storm, and exerted their mightiest endeavours to stem the torrent of corruption and misrule, were spoken of in that Convention in terms of approbation and pride.
    I am specially charged as their President to communicate to you one of their resolutions in the following words
    "Resolved, that we entertain the highest opinion of the eminent abilities and patriotism of the Hon Daniel Webster."
    Allow me to add that I have great pride and pleasure in communicating to you the approbation and applause of that grave and dignified assembly.
    Without one dissenting voice the Convention proceeded to nominate William Henry Harrison of Ohio for the office of President of the United

States, and Francis Granger of New York for the office of Vice President.
I have the honor to be with the highest respect Your Obedt Sert

J W Scott

ALS. DLC. Scott (1778–1871; Princeton 1798) was a New Brunswick lawyer, gubernatorial candidate in 1833 and again in 1837, and president of the New Jersey Whig convention of 1836.

FROM JOSEPH RICKETSON WILLIAMS

Bronson Kalamazoo Co.
June [7] 1836

Dr. Sir,

I have this day drawn on you for $2017.67 at 60 days date and as you requested made the same payable at the Merchants Bank in the city of New York. A few days since I wrote you concerning a purchase I had made of property at Constantine, St. Josephs Co.[1] I have concluded the bargain and made the first payment of $8000 towards the satisfaction of one quarter which I have now drawn on you for the above sum interest being added. I mortgaged the property for the six annual payments of $2000, and consequently was obliged to take the Deed in my own name. You will know no partners in the operation, except George Howland[, Sr.] a very wealthy merchant of New Bedford and myself.[2] Perhaps Gov. Davis however will have a small share. The rents of the property will make the subsequent payments. But the proper course to be pursued is to expend in mills to a considerable amount say $8000. I think that will double the population which is now about 300 & consequently treble or quadruple the value of the property. On my return there I found that our purchase had given an impulse to property and that it had risen 50 pr. ct. I had previously recommended several pieces of property to your son but when we arrived there, they were sold & held at more than double the prices at which I could have purchased.

The property being under mortgage, and it being necessary that it should all be under the direction of one will, and that small portions should be occasionally sold I would suggest whether the *title* had not better remain in me. I shall suggest the same thing to Mr. Howland and if you accede, I will give *satisfactory bonds* when I return east in July.

It will appear by the returns that *half a million* of dollars were taken at the Land Office in May. The proportion paid by those who actually intend to settle upon the soil is very great. I have no doubt Michigan will receive a greater accession of population during the next twelve months, than any state or territory ever has in the same period. No mercantile or professional business is pursued for its own sake—all is spec-ulation—or rather *scrambling for spoils*, for they all consider the taking up of land *here* as merely putting their hands in the public chest.

When I have entered the Lands in the names of Col. Perkins and your-self I will inform you.

Your son went off northwardly yesterday afternoon on an exploring, land looking expedition with a woodsman, and intends to enter some of the land he examines. I remain with great respect &c &c

Jos. R. Williams

ALS. ViU.   New Bedford whaling merchant and
  1. Letter not found.   banker.
  2. Howland (1781–1852) was a

TO PERKINS & CO.

Washington June 11. 1836

Messrs Perkins & Co.

I enclose you a letter, recd this morning from Col. Perkins.[1]

It is probable that I may soon be called on for money, which I shall have occasion thro' the credit given me by him on you. But as cash seems still to be scarce with you, I shall probably draw at sixty days, & get the dr[a]ft discounted here. I suppose I shall not have occasion to draw for more than 5.000, at present; tho' it is a little uncertain how soon I may need a further sum. I shall take care not to make sudden calls. Yrs re-spectfully   Danl Webster

ALS. MHi.
  1. Not found.

FROM SIMON KINNEY

Peru (Putnam Coy. Ill.)
June 11th 1836

Sir

My son, Henry L. Kinney, who since his return here, has been & still is much engrossed in business, desires me to say to you, for him, that he received your letter dated Washington May 16th. Ult. authorizing him to draw upon you for $5.000.—in behalf of yourself and Col Perkins, with advice to him as to the manner of appropriating the sum or sums when drawn by him.[1] That, in pursuance of that authority and advice, he thinks it quite probable that he will draw a bill, or bills to amt. of the whole or a part, on 30 to 60 days after sight, in the course of seven to ten days from this time, when he expects to be at Chicago.

That the opportunities for purchasing good lands at Government prices in this part of the State, is much reduced compared with last year and during the winter. But he still thinks that very advantageous investments may yet be made in lands, and that your interest in the matter, shall not lack his rigid and careful & timely attention.

That in accordance with a previous arrangement with you, he wrote to you something more than two weeks ago, informing that he had drawn a bill on you for $3000.—which was cashed for him at Chicago.[2] That since that time, he immediately made the best selection he was able to do of *un*entered lands, and employed a confidential agent to proceed directly to the office at Galena, with the money to enter for those selections. He has not heard from the agent, since he left here for Galena, but expects to do so very soon. And as soon as he does so, he will inform you fully, of the success of the expedition.

I am greatly delighted with this beautiful Country. And I have no hesitation in coming to the conclusion, that if Political Union & harmony —the principles of our excellent constitution, and law and moral order *can* continue to prevail, that we shall not need especially to employ a magisterial agent to "carry out (all) the measures of Gen. Jac[k]son" to ensure its prosperity, improvement and happiness, to a measure unparalleled by any other region of the earth. I am sir with great respect Your Obt Servant   Simon Kinney.

ALS. ViU. Simon Kinney has not been further identified.

 1. The letter referred to was probably a copy of the one above, DW

to Phineas Davis, May 16, 1836.

 2. See above, Henry L. Kinney to DW, May 24, 1836.

TO DANIEL FLETCHER WEBSTER

Washington June 12. 1836

My Dear Son

Your letters to Mr [John] Davis & Mr [John] Cramer, (not Kremer) were recd about a week ago, & were very satisfactory to those Gentlemen. They praised them highly, as evincing intelligence, on your part, & attention to the important business in which you are engaged. Mr Edward Curtis happened to be here, & perused them, & still more regretted that he was not with you,

I have no letter from you since you left Toledo; but I learn by a letter from Mr. [Phineas] Davis[1] that you left Detroit, on horseback, about the 27th of May, I suppose for Bronson, White Pigeon, & so on to Michigan City & Chicago. At the latter place, you will have found various letters from us. It is still uncertain when Congress will rise; but various things call me to the North, & it is my purpose to depart between the 24th. June

& 1st. of July. We have nothing very interesting. It has been, on the whole, a dull & barren session, with this exception, that it will have ended with the creation of two new States. The Toledo boundary, I believe, goes according to the Ohio claim entirely.[2]

We hear little from Boston. At last dates Mr [Stephen] White's family [had] not left home, five days ago. I believe he is detained by Mr Delands[3] illness. The East Boston lots, it is said, sold very well.

Under another cover, you will find a communication, upon a particular, & new undertaking.[4] As Mr [Samuel] Upton[5] has brought this about, partly for the reason of giving you business, I doubt not you will do your very best to accomplish the expectation of the parties. You will continue to address me <as at this place for the present> after the receipt of this, supposing this does not reach you till after the 24th, as I presume it will not, as at Boston. Indeed I may be already leaving Washington when this reaches Chicago.

About coming home—when may we look for you? I think, that there is sometimes fever & ague in the lake country, & as you are not yet well (*acclimated*) if that is the word, you would do well not to stay too long, especially if it should be probable that the affairs which you will have on hand will call you back in the fall. It is expected very important sales will take place in Wisconsin, in October, as you will have learned, & a great many people will be present. There is no doubt, that if you come home in August, having done tolerably well so far, you can take back a good deal of money in the fall. What I would suggest is, that, with the advice of [Fisher Ames] Harding, & other friends in Chicago, or of Mr [Daniel] Whitney[6] at Green Bay, you employ one or two good men—say two, & send them in different directions to *explore for* you, in Wisconsin, in the tracts which are expected to be offered for sale. If you then return some weeks before the sale, you will receive their report, & act accordingly. I understand, that where one has the requisite previous knowledge, a favorable opportunity of entering lands exists, just at the close of the public sales, while others are gone into the woods to examine, &c. All these things, however, you will know more about, than I can tell you. Mr [John T.] Haight[7] leaves this place for Wisconsin this week. He will probably find you at Chicago. He thinks you ought, by all means, to attend the sale, as he thinks the Company,[8] assembled on that occasion, will be willing to give *you* one or two prime chances. There is something in this, worthy of being considered.

In all your operations, you should appear to be acting for yourself; or, at least, for yourself & me; and as it is very probable that this business may induce you to make your home in those regions, at least for some time, you should, on all occasions, act as much [as] possible as if you were already a Western man.

Mr [John] Davis intends going to Detroit, immediately on the rising of Congress. Very possibly, you may fall in with him, somewhere. I think it likely you will not receive this letter, till you have seen the waters of the Mississippi.

Adieu! My Dear Son. I shall expect to receive a letter, in 5 or 6 days, announcing your arrival at Chicago. Your affectionate father

Danl. Webster

With other members of Congress, I have taken a small interest in *Winnebago City*.[9] This is *fancy* stock. I expect little or nothing from it. Note. Mr Cramer's address is—

Hon[ora]ble John Cramer—
Waterford, Saratoga Co.
New York.

He will be here of course till the rising of Congress.

ALS. NhHi. Published in Van Tyne, pp. 663–665.

1. See above, Phineas Davis to DW, May 30, 1836.

2. The mouth of the Maumee, including Toledo, claimed by both states, went to Ohio. See the Michigan enabling act, 5 *U.S. Statutes at Large* 49.

3. Not identified.

4. Not found.

5. Upton (1791–1842), a longtime friend of DW, was born in Salem, Massachusetts, but moved to Castine, Maine, in 1816. Subsequently he lived in Bangor, Boston, and Washington, D.C.

6. Whitney (1795–1862), a native of Gilsum, New Hampshire, had

settled in Green Bay, Wisconsin, in 1819, where he was a speculator and businessman.

7. Haight (1813–1853), born in Addison County, Vermont, had settled in Koshkonong, Wisconsin, in 1836, where he was a lawyer, surveyor, and land agent.

8. The "Company," apparently with some $6,000 capital to engage in land speculation, included DW, Fowler & Co., and Samuel Upton. See DFW to DW, July 1, July 6, 1836, below.

9. Located on the northeast shore of Lake Winnebago, Wisconsin Territory, Winnebago City was a paper town, promoted by James Duane Doty and his associates.

FROM JOHN CATRON

Nashville, 12th June, 1836.

My Dear Sir:

An expression of yours in the Senate, when speaking of the propriety of recognizing the independence of Texas, has made a very strong impression in this country that England may endeavor to gain a footing in Texas by purchase from Mexico.[1] A large meeting was holden here yesterday, which resolved that Congress and the Executive should forthwith, and before the close of the session, recognize the independence of Texas; *and* use the means to end the war; and extend our boundary *west*, that is, acquire the country. This is proposed in effect, though not in terms.

England will be drawn into the Texan war in this wise: The Mexican is driven from Texas with a terror upon him inconsistent with further fighting there. If the matter would end at this, it would be well. But the spirit is abroad through the whole valley of the Mississippi to march upon Mexico. All may emigrate to Texas who will. It is lawful. All who choose may buy Texas lands. This is lawful. The golden city presents temptations strong as in the days of Cortez. Men and money are to be had—the former in excess—to march upon it in the fall. The Mexican population consists of, say 7,000,000—3,000,000 native Indians an encumbrance, the like number of the mixed blood, worthless, or nearly so, as defenders, and one million of Spanish descent unmixed, who are poor soldiers, and divided at that between the parties of the priests and liberals. During the whole of the Mexican civil war, hardly a battle was fought respectable as a foraging skirmish of a well-appointed army of respectable size. Mr. Justin Chambers[2] informs me (now here) that the companies of native Indians, and often of the mixed blood, are marched to the seat of war handcuffed by pairs, with a common chain extending through the middle, and when brought into battle put in front, with orders to shoot them in rear if they give way! That convicts always are managed in this wise, and were at the taking of the Alamo. There is not a boy, "whose quiver and bow is scarcely terror to the crow," in this great valley but believes this, be it strictly correct or not; and hardly one that does not ardently long to be of the army that is to conquer the priests, and divide the ill-gotten gold of the temple—to get his slice of the great lamp in the cathedral, or a foot's length of a silver pillar, and fame besides. It is not supposed there will be fighting enough for tolerable sport. My belief is, that this is but too true; but, whether true or fallacious, the effect must be the same. If the war continues, Texas will endeavor to conquer Mexico. England will aid the latter to resist; will aid her to invade Texas in turn; and depend on it, when she puts her hand into this work, Mexico shares the fate of India.

Whether this be an evil-brooding fancy, you are the better judge; if not, now is the time for us to act as a preventive means. The object of this scrawl is to give the state of temperament in the West—uncontrollable as the Mississippi. It may be of use.

The young fellows who fought in the battle of San Jacinto are dropping in daily, and are followed by crowds of young and old—for hardly any of us have escaped the felicity of having divers young kinsmen there of whom we are most anxious to hear—and the first question is, "How did he fight?" with glistening eyes. "Aye, Aye!" says the father, "I thought so." The boy may have run away, as many did; he is now the hero of the family, and all follow him who choose. No monk is needed to preach the crusade. The interference of yourself and Northern friends to check it would, I feel very sure, be a great service to the country. That the recognition of Texas, and the ending of the war, is the proper course, all must concur, and that another equal opportunity, *after* the close of the present session of Congress, to fix our boundary west of the Colorado, will present, I think no well-informed man will believe. Most sincerely, I have the honor to be your friend and obedient servant, J. Catron.

Text from Curtis, 1: 523–524. Original not found.

1. On recognizing Texan independence, Webster had said (on May 23, before the Senate) that "he had received some information from a respectable source, which turned his attention to the very significant expression used by Mr. Monroe in his message of 1822, that no European power should ever be permitted to establish a colony on the American continent. He had no doubt that attempts would be made by some European Government to obtain a cession of Texas from the Government of Mexico." *Congressional Globe*, 24th Cong., 1st sess., p. 394.

2. Chambers, otherwise unidentified, was probably one of the younger American adventurers who had gone to Texas.

FROM PHINEAS DAVIS

Detroit June 16th 1836

Dear Sir

Since I wrote you last I have learnt that the Land Office at Bronson where I sent to invest your funds to the amount of 2200$ for you has been closed and will remain closed untill July 2.[1] My man will remain in the field untill it open and in the mean time will be constantly surveying the country. I have also taken the liberty to send 1500$ of your money to be invested in Wisconsin Territory by a very particular friend of mine who surveyed nearly the whole country, and I hope through him to be enabled to make some of the most choice locations. You may rest assured that I shall use every means to make the most for you that I can. I have been enabled to purchase 600$ of Steam Mill stock which I wrote to you about in my last letter. There is no doubt but it will divide 50 per cent per annum and I think 75—and the property constantly on the rise. I have two other tracts in view which if I can accomplish I would not thank any one to insure me 1000 per cent and I think from 3 to 5000 on one of them. One of [the] tracts I expect to know about next week and the other not untill July 15th. The whole sum required will not ex-

ceed 4000$ for both if I take no more of the property than I now calcu-
late to. I wrote you in my last respecting them.[2] I now wish to be informed if I shall retain the funds which you have placed at my disposal
for the two above objects or shall I invest what I now have in public
lands and you furnish more funds for the above named purposes. I can
assure you there cannot be the slitest risk in either of the purchases, for
should there never a City rise upon the places it will be worth all I shall
pay for cultivation. Only 18 months ago I wish[ed] to purchase a similar
place but could not get any to join me, the part of which was only 6500$
and the same property has been sold since for 350,000$ and I have no
hesitation in saying one of these points which I now intend to purchase
is better than the one which has since sold for the above sum. Was I
certain I could meet you at Washington in the fore part of July I would
visit you and then I could show you all the modes of operrandi in this
country and if you wish, I will try and see you soon after your return to
Mass. I hope to make for you out of the funds already at my disposal at
least 25 or 30,000$ in the course of two or 3 years, and if I succeed as
well as I now anticipate perhaps 100,000$ although you must not cal-
culate on this last sum unless I meet with a lucky hit. In the Town speculation if I succeed it will furnish us ample funds to operate upon after
the first year from the sale of lots. In haste Yours very Respectfully
                                                Phineas Davis

P.S. Please inform me when congress will ajourn. The sales at this Land
Office at 20,000 per day, and the immigration from 800 to 1000 per day.

ALS. ViU.
  1. According to Joseph R. Williams,
the Bronson Land Office closed because "Receivers Bonds were not suf-

ficient." See Williams to DW, June
14, 1836, mDW 13361.
  2. See above, Phineas Davis to
DW, June 5, 1836.

TO FISHER AMES HARDING
                                        Washington June 18. 1836
My Dear Sir,
  I have recd your letter of the 2. of June, with a P.S. of the 3rd.[1]
  As to the money, which you are authorized to lay out for me, say the
original 2.000 (& which you may consider as being 2.000 notwithstanding you have drawn for 520) you may deal with it as you please—buy &
sell, & get gain. The more money you make of it, the better for yourself,
as well as for me.
  As to the 5000 which you are at liberty to invest for Col Perkins & myself, I do not feel at liberty to give you quite so wide a range, without
the Col['s] permission. Our idea was, mainly, to buy Govt. lands, at 1.25

—& to go so far as that good land could be found for that price. For some part of the sum, say one or two thousand Dollars, you may venture to buy, & sell again, if opportunity offers. But as I have already said, our main object is to buy Govt. lands—well selected, & wait for their rise.

I approve entirely what you did with my money, near Michigan.

Fletcher will be with you, I presume, ere now. You & he will of course lay your heads together, & lay such plans as your united wisdom, experience, & gravity may suggest.

When I see Col Perkins, I will show him your letter, & very probably he will be willing to give you all the latitude suggested in your letter.

Give my love to Fletcher, & let me hear from you often. Learn to write to your correspondents often, whether you have any thing to say or not. Depend on it, that is good advice, to a young lawyer going into business. A man likes to know even that there is nothing to tell him. Yrs truly

D. Webster

Can not you & Fletcher go into the Country, & look out & buy up a few *prime* preemptions?

ALS. NNC.
1. See above.

TO PERKINS & CO.

Washington June 20. 1836

Gentlemen

I draw on you for seven thousand Dollars, at sixty days, under the authority given me by request of T.H. Perkins Esqr., and as I intimated in my last.[1]

The Bill will be discounted at one of the Banks in this District.

Col. P. was yet at the Springs, on the 13th inst. I now write to him, at Pittsburg Pa.[2] Yours truly   Danl Webster

ALS. MHi.   June 11, 1836.
1. See above, DW to Perkins & Co.,   2. Letter not found.

FROM HENRY L. KINNEY

Chicago June 20th 1836.

Dr. Sir.

I recd. yours dated may 16th[1] at Washington in which you authorized me to Draw on you for five thousand Dolls for the purpose of investing for you and Col. Perkins in lands. And I have accordingly this day drawn my draft on you for five thousand Dollars payable Sixty days after date at Boston and Recd the money which I shall take the first opportunity to apply according to your directions and interest. I have allso made my Drft. on you of this date for two thousand Dollars which was accepted payable at the Phenix Bank New York—drawn at Sixty days after sight. I have been making Some entries of land for you & have had agts. engaged in Searching out valuable locations that were not taken. I entrusted to my agt who has been engaged in the surveying of this county $2500 to invest in government lands for you. At the time of my leaving home he had not returned. If he has sucksees in getting the numbers he went for, you will be sattisfied with the application of the money. I found a vacant lot of 160 acres, two miles from Indian town, a very important point on Bureau River where there is a town laid out which is improving rapidly. The lot of which I describe is now worth for farming purposes as land an[d] selling [for] ten Dollars per acre & I should not advise you selling it [for] less. You can recommend its being of the first quality of farming land.

After the rec[e]ival of the duplicates of lands bought for you I shall take the earliest opportunity to draw plots of the lands so bought, and give you correct descriptions of their quality situation & value & forward to you by mail together with duplicates.

I learn your Son has been in town & left the day before my arival here for Galena. I shall try & see him soon. If I find he is to return to Boston immediately, I shall send the tittles to your lands by him together with a knowledge of what I have been doing. Peru property is rapidly rising and I have it in view making a purchase of the two 80 acre lots adjoining Section 17 which would be the east half of the east of Section 18 one mile from Peru, for you and Col Perkins. I could have sold your purchase of me in Peru for a hundred per cent advance from what you pd for it or can do so if you should wish it at any time. I am however of the belief that it will pay you an advance of five hundred percent in one year. I have sold land this day on Section 22 at the termination of the canal for $1000. per acre which is low ground & subject to overflow. I send you by this mail a map of the lands on the canal route—embracing a survey of the County.[2] Still farther west which most of the lands that I have as yet bought for you are within in the Survey as represented on s[ai]d Map. A great rush has been made to this country this Spring for government lands which makes it much more difficult to find good locations readily.

You may be well assured of this fact that I shall not make any purchases of lands that are not well worth the money paid for them. Chicago is crowded with Strangers from every quarter, all eager to b[u]y real estate in Illinois. The lots that have been sold to day have went above the

Valuation put uppon them by the Canal Commisioners. A large amount of money might be made in purchasing improved farms and Selling again to emigrants. On my return home I shall send you a list of your lands &c. &c. I am with due respect Your Obt Svt.   H.L. Kinney

P.S. The reason for my drawing for all the money now is in consequence of making an early application of it for lands before the crowd of Speculators gets into the Galena district.

ALS. ViU.   by Kinney's father in his letter of
   1. This letter was probably a copy   June 11, above.
of the one above, DW to Phineas   2. Not found.
Davis, May 16, 1836, and referred to

FROM HERMAN LE ROY
                                          New York June 20 1836
My Dear Sir,
   On Saturday last H. LeR. Newbold addressed you a few lines at my request[1] and as he explained the cause of my not writing it is unnecessary to repeat it again. He enclosed to you Daniel's letter which I perused with sincere pleasure to notice that he had commenced advantageous operations and that he was so much pleased with the country he had thus far visited and most sincerely hope he may successfully accomplish his investments to the greatest advantage and the knowledge he will attain may be the means of introducing him into a path that may insure him a competency as many young men have succeeded in before him. I was extremely sorry to notice that Caroline was again unwell[.] We all feel very anxious to learn how she is and in some way apprehensive that the intense heat you have experienced may have tended further to debilitate her; the thermometer here was up to 100°° in some situations but at Morrissania[2] by confining ourselves to a large entry where there was some draft we were the less annoyed. Hannah Newbold is perfectly recovered and in fine spirits and her little boy improving in every respect in health with the aid of a young & hearty wet nurse who has taken charge of him.
   I am truly thankful to you of your letter of 13th[3] which I have perused over and over again and observe in it with sincere pleasure the handsome investment Mr [Phineas] Davis has made for you in 400 acres of excellent land and in a very desirable situation which cannot but give you a very great profit in a little while; the character you give of that young gentleman is very much in his favour and his proceedings for you fully evince the favorable testimony you give of him. The mode of cultivating the Prairies which Mr [Lucius] Lyon describes was a novelty to

me and enhances very materially their intrinsic value.[4] The operations that he is making for yourself and Col. Perkins cannot but prove highly advantageous to yourself and your worthy friend the Coln. who really merits every blessing that can be afforded in this world.[5]

The Agent of my son Jacob is acting for him and as successfully as your agent Mr Davis is doing for you; it is scarcely credible the large sum he expects to realize in course of this year. As to our speculation in the Pine lands we were in hopes of being in season to have procured 30 or 40.000 acres at very moderate rates, but the reverse I apprehend will be the result and that but a very few thousand and by the dint of cash payments only will I fear be procured; the number of acres are not yet ascertained as our agent was prevented from locating owing to the heavy falls of rain that we have recently had and in consequence will detain him some weeks longer before the result will be known. At any rate the parties who were interested are so numerous that the division among them will be very moderate and as yet quite uncertain as to extent, as I am informed speculators have driven the lands up to 16 or 20 $ per acre. And as you had formed a good opinion of the speculation and would have wished to have taken a good slice if the purchases could have been made upon favorable terms, I should be sorry, that you should be disappointed therein and therefore tender you a loan of $5000. say five thousand Dolls. to enable you to cause investment to be made of it through the sources you have now the command of and are so well acquainted with in the N.W.; my sincere wish is to promote your interest by embracing the bright opportunities now opened to you by persons so well known to you; if I had not already a heavy amount out in purchases making I would most cheerfully have added a large sum and taken a concern jointly with you, but prudence dictates to me that I should not extend myself farther than I may be liable for and which it is impossible for me to say what they may amount to. As I am actually paying interest on some monies that I have loaned at 6 pct. I shall of course expect that you will allow me the same interest payable annually which I am sure you will consider fair. Your account is credited for yr check for $442.90/100 enclosed.[6] I return to you the description you was kind enough to send me of locations made for yr account which I have examined very minutely and am I in great hopes you may realize a little fortune out of them. Please remember me affectionately to Caroline and apologize to her for not having answered her last affectionate letter, and give my love to Julia also & Believe me ever with sincere affection

Herman Le Roy by H Le Roy Newbold

P.S. Please inform me when you may wish to make use of the $5.th[ou-sand] owing to the great scarcity I of course have not much laying idle at a time. Perhaps you may not require it for 30 or 60 days.

LS (by proxy). NhHi.
1. Not found.
2. Morrisania was the home of Herman Le Roy's granddaughter, Hannah Newbold Morris.
3. Not found.
4. DW had written to Lyon (June 10, mDW 13338) asking about the type of plow used on prairie lands.

Lyon's response, which DW had evidently forwarded to Herman Le Roy, has not been found.
5. For a hint of Lyon's activities in Webster's behalf, see DW to Charles C. Trowbridge, June 23, 1836, below.
6. Not found.

TO C[HARLES] C. TROWBRIDGE

Washington, June 23d. 1836.

Dear Sir,

The Hon'ble. Mr [Lucius] Lyon has put in my hands a letter from you to him, of the 14th. instant, in which you are kind enough to say that my acceptances for $10,000, at 90 or 120 days, would be cashed, at your Bank. I am quite obliged to you, for this readiness to do me a favor. My son is in the West and may want money, and some other friends of mine have an authority also, in certain events to make a small investment for me; and on this account, it will be quite convenient to me to be able to place a small fund in your Bank by the discount of my acceptances. It may be sometime before I shall have occasion to send you an acceptance; but in the course of the summer, I believe, I shall find it desirable to do so.

My acceptances will be made payable in New York, which, I presume, will be agreeable to you. I am, with respect, Your obliged & hume. servt.

Danl. Webster

LS. MNS. Trowbridge (1800–1883) was cashier of the Bank of Michigan from 1825 to 1836, president in 1839, and president of the Michigan State Bank from 1844 to 1853.

TO [PHINEAS DAVIS]

Washington June 24. 1836

Dear Sir

I have recd your letter of the 16th.[1] You appear to be going on very well. I am much pleased with your zeal & diligence, & hope that something handsome may be realized, out of your proceedings, for yourself as well as me. I approve of your sending a part of the funds into Wisconsin, presuming that you have employed an able & honest agent.

I observe what you say of two objects, which you say have in view, which may require a sum not exceeding 4000 Dlls. And you wish to know, whether you shall retain the funds which you now have for these two objects, or shall invest what you now have in public lands, & I furnish you more funds, for the above mentioned two purposes. To which I answer, that if you have opportunities which you think decidedly well of, I wish you to invest what you now have in public lands, & you may draw on me for the four thousand Dollars, necessary for the two last objects, when wanted. This last mentioned sum to be on my sole account, unless I shall hereafter direct to the contrary.

You may find some inconvenience in managing such a variety of concerns, & in keeping them distinct; but in this respect you must do as well as you can. So far as the 5.000, on account of Col Perkins & myself is concerned, you must of course do us equal justice. Whether he will be interested farther than the 5.000, I do not know. At present, what was remitted to you by your uncle, & the 5.000, which you were authorised to invest by my letter of the 26th. (26th) May, & the above mentioned sum of $4.000 (which you may make $5.000 if necessary,) is all on my own sole account.

Congress rises July 4th. I should be glad to see you here, but that is not now to be expected. I should be equally glad to see you in Boston; but I understand from Mr J. Davis that he has written to you, proposing to meet you in Va, & then to go to Detroit with you. I have had much conversation with him, & he will inform you of his & my general impressions. I think we can give you full employment, if affairs look promising. It would please me much to see you, & I hope that sometime in the summer you may be in Massachusetts. I can then tell you how far I can go, in regard to funds, & what portion of the funds may be left, for some years, in your hands. On this part of the case, it would be well that we should converse, & have a distinct understanding.

I have but one thing, in particular, to suggest at present; & that is this. I should like land enough, in one piece, to make one good, large, handsome farm; say from 500 to 1000 acres. The soil must be of the first rate, the land well watered, and the situation high & healthy. The nearer to Detroit, or the River Detroit, or to some rail road, the better of course. Whether at present all wild, or part cultivated, I should not care. If a prime farm of this description could be had, for reasonable price, I should like to buy it, & *let it lie.* I suppose you could only find such an one in private hands. If you know, or should hear, of any thing of this kind, which strikes you well, write me what it can be had for.

Please to address me next to Boston. Yrs truly   Danl Webster

ALS. H. Stanton Hill, Altadena,   1. See above.
California.

TO DANIEL FLETCHER WEBSTER

Washington June 25. 1836

My Dear Son

I recd last Eve' your letter from Chicago, of the 13th of June,[1] being your first from that City.

I think you did well to buy the 800 acres in the Kalamazoo County, by what I hear of that region.

In former letters I have said all I had to say, respecting your future proceedings. Take care of your health—Do not stay in the Lake Country too late—& be sure to be home, soon to pass the whole of August, & part of September with me. I approve of your returning in the fall, as I have observed in former letters, & hope you will leave some faithful "land lookers," to explore for you, in your absence. You may go back in the fall, with as much capital as you think you can use to advantage.

I shall probably not write you again, till I hear further from you, unless it be a short note, or so, to Chicago; as I shall not know where to hit you, after the middle of July.

We think of going from Washington for home on the 29th—be home about the 5th. or 6th. July. The Deposite & *Distribution* bill has become a law—& money is already getting to be much *easier*, as the phrase is.

Your mother has not been very well, since her arrival here. I think a journey will do her good. She talks a little of going to the Springs, with Dr [Cyrus] Perkins'[2] family. I must go strait home, but shall go to the Springs for her, if she shall make the visit there.

At last advices, Mr [Stephen] White's family were at Albany, on their way to Tonnawanda.

Gov Davis will go hence on the 4th. (the day of the rising of Congress) to the Va. Springs—thence to Wheeling—Cleveland, & Detroit. Possibly you may meet with him at the latter place. Yrs ever affectionately   Danl. Webster

Your mother & Julia send a great deal of love, & one of them will write you, before we leave Washington.

ALS. NhHi. Published in *PC*, 2: 20–21.   1800), a longtime friend of DW, was
1. Not found.   a physician from New York City.
2. Perkins (1778–1849; Dartmouth

TO PERKINS & CO.

Washington
June 27. 1836

Gent.

I find I may probably have occasion to draw on you for a further sum, of three thousand Dollars, before leaving this City. If I draw at all, I shall draw on some time, as in the other case.

AL (signature removed). MHi.

FROM DANIEL FLETCHER WEBSTER

Chicago July 1st. 1836.

My dear Father,

I have just got in from Galena and Mineral Point. Your letters I have just read.[1]

I am very sorry that I had not received them before I went away.

I wrote you a letter from Galena, but after I had written it, was convinced I had sent you some wrong information for Mr. [John] Cramer, about the Polish Lands and threw it into the fire. I know, my dear Father, that I owe entirely to you the Agency which I undertake for the parties described in the instrument which you sent me.[2] For your sake, as well as my own, I shall be most anxious and careful to do well with the money.

I might have invested extremely well in Iowa County, about Mineral Point. Speculators have not got there; excepting Mr. [Henry] *Hubbard* of New Hampshire M[ember of] C[ongress] who has sent $20.000. there & Mr. W[illiam] S[haw] Russell[3] who has entered about as much. I went in company with the latter Gentleman. Harding entered three hundred & twenty acres for you, up there, & I entered one hundred & twenty. We did not wait to get our certificates, but Mr Russell was to give them to me at Buffalo, & if I should not be there, to send them to my address at Tonnawanda.

I shall, if I can arrange it, invest two thousand dollars for the *Company* in Iowa County. The mineral is very abundant & very rich & almost *universal.* The Land is good, but hilly—timber very scarce. If one takes up tolerable farming land it must be a good investment for it will rise, if only for agricultural purposes; & should mineral be found on it no one can say how much it might be worth.

I will not tell you all I have heard & seen in these countries, for one who had not witnessed it, would think my stories fabulous.

However, there is great risk in all these matters. One might dig ten years & not find lead enough to make a peep shot, and then one might stub his toes over a lump of mineral.

I made an acquaintance with a man of the name of [Hugh R.] Hunter,[4] at Mineral Point a surveyor, to whom I shall write for information as to lands there, and if I can well invest two thousand for you there, by his assistance, I shall do so.

[Joseph R.] Williams wrote me a letter from Michigan advising me of an excellent purchase near New Buffalo, and I shall probably invest two thousand for you there—the rest I shall think upon. I shall start tomorrow for Calumet River, where lives the owner of the land of which Williams advised me and I may go to New Buffalo. I shall, if I have to make a journe[y] or so more, before I start for home, be obliged to draw on you for a little sine qua non; all expenses in this country are extremely great—much higher than in any of the Eastern Cities. Horse keeping is near two dollars a day in Chicago.

I shall avoid it if possible and I hope to get along without.

My own funds are expended—one thousand cash in Toledo—the same in Government Lands in Michigan and the same in St. Joseph's. One hundred & fifty in Mineral Point and I have two hundred & fifty left. One hundred beside my three hundred has gone for expenses. I have been as economical as possible, but I have not been able to get on with less.

I shall get through all my business as soon as possible, for I want to get home.

I think I cannot get away from Grand Island so as to be home before the middle of August. If I come West again in the fall, three weeks, which shall be my limit, will not be too much at the Island. I shall hurry with all my might.

It is difficult getting drafts cashed here—and from that I apprehend the most trouble. I *will* have them however if I want them.

I received several letters from home, two from Julia and one from Mother. Please give my best love to them. Tell them that I have been where writing was out of the question or I should have written to them both.

I write this letter to you in Harding's Office, which is full of men, talking loud on all sorts of things[—]lands, Towns, horses[,] Canals, Indians &c &c. I fear it is very unconnected, but I hope you will not be displeased.

Please may [make?] my best respects to the Gentlemen who are concerned in the six thousand dollar purchase, & assure them, I shall do my best to give you and them satisfaction.

As this is to be a business affair, any expenses which I shall be at in the arrangement of it, I shall borrow money of you to defray and deduct from my amount of the per centage in your favour.

I will write you very soon again.

I am in perfect health, very brown, from the sun on the prairies, but stout & strong. My little mare turns out a first rate horse; I have ridden her two hundred miles in four days & a quarter—forded & swam numerous streams—the Rock, Fox, Kishwaukee, Du Page, Aux Plaines, Pekatoleka & so on, & waded through bogs & marshes, at which a Yankee Horse would be thunderstruck.

I can drink whiskey of a morning, steer across the prairie by a compass, follow an Indian Trail in the woods & sleep on the floor of a log Cabin, with my saddle for a pillow. With great love Yr most affectionate son   D. F. Webster.

ALS. ViU.
1. See above, DW to DFW, June 12, 1836; and DW to DFW, June 15, 1836, mDW 13363.
2. Not found.
3. Russell was a resident of Montgomery County, Illinois, the "largest single purchaser" in the Wisconsin lead region. Joseph Schafer, *The Wisconsin Lead Region* (Madison, 1932), p. 128.
4. Hunter was a pioneer settler at Mineral Point.

FROM FISHER AMES HARDING

Chicago, July 5th. 1836.
My Dear Sir,

I returned a few days since from Galena & Mineral Point, whither I accompanied Fletcher. I found on my arrival yours of 4th. June,[1] & have since received yours of the 18th. of the same.[2]

You will have received intimation of the St. Joseph purchase made in connexion with Fletcher. While at Mineral Point, I put $400 into the hands of a gentleman who travelled in our company and had heretofore made entries in that region, to be invested in a half section of Government lands toward the Wisconsin river. The certificates will be forwarded to you by Fletcher. The gentleman who was to make the entry will furnish me with a little statement of its character, which I shall transmit to you.

Mineral Point, you are aware, lies in the mineral country North of Galena. I think it a valuable country. Its mineral resources are abundant; in addition to immense quantities of lead there are mines of copper, & perhaps of other metals. Much of the land where the mineral is found is quite broken; there is also a considerable quantity of pretty good land for cultivation. This last is the more valuable from having a good market at home among the miners.

I find as you suggest upon making the calculation that I was mistaken in the amount for which the Michigan City land sold. The sum would be $5600. You understand that the purchase was made in connexion with another person. The $400 which I invested in Wisconsin was a part of the $500, which I received in cash on the sale of the land near Michigan.

I note what you say in regard to the investment of money for yourself & Col. Perkins in connexion. I am not sure, upon reflection, but what that sort of investment may be a good one; it is certainly safe. But just at this time there is little desirable land subject to entry. I have reason to think that considerable will be brought into market North of us this Fall. I shall not purchase, I think, with the Perkins money before that sale, unless a very good opportunity seems to offer. With what remains of the money in which you are alone interested I will make a purchase, if I can find a good one. I do not intend to be very bold in the business; it seems to me that after speculations have been continued as long as they have, that "the better part of valour" will be "discretion." Heretofore, random shots have been as effective as any, but that is not a natural state of things and can hardly be permanent.

It is somewhat difficult to get money here even with drafts. Our merchants do not at this season want them, and our Bank which is but a Branch of the State Bank at Springfield has not sufficient funds to purchase all that are offered.

It would be difficult to get any *prime* pre-emptions at this time. Those under the Law now in existence have all been proved up, and of course cannot be purchased more favorably than other property. There are the *claims* of settlers, but I am a little afraid of them. According to present manifestations in Congress, if any pre-emption law should be passed, it is doubtful how indulgent its terms might be. Without such a law it is true that the settlers may enforce their claims to the lands by the potent efficacy of their clubs, as has often been done heretofore, but I should be scrupulous about investing much money upon such security, to say nothing about its doubtful propriety.

Fletcher will leave us in a day or two, in company with his cousin Herman Le Roy. His health is good. My own is very good, & has been improved by the journey into the interior.

Be so kind as to remember me to Mrs. W & Miss Julia. I am, Yours, sincerely,   F. A. Harding.

ALS. ViU.   2. See above.
   1. Not found.

FROM PHINEAS DAVIS

Detroit July 6th 1836

Dear Sir

I have made a d[ra]ft upon you in favour of the Bank of Michigan for two Thousand Dollars due in 10 days after sight. I also enclose your duplicates for land amounting to $1246.75. The Lands are of the very best quality situated in Genesee County, well watered and near to a road now much traveled, and a large part of the land borders upon a road which will soon be made and distant only 4 miles from good Mills, and the country very well settled and settling rapidly. The lands are lightly timbered with White Oak, Walnut, Beach, Maple & White Wood, but easily cleared very high & dry & very gently undulating. I have also secured for you 1000$ worth of Steam Mill Stock which I consider a first rate investment. The land Office at Bronson I understood was opened on the 5 of this month and I hope to obtain the Duplicates for the Lands which I made application for a month ago. I have made some very choice selections there—will forward you the Duplicates as soon as I receive them. I have closed a contract for 3/8 of 160 acres of land upon the Saginaw River oposite of the Town of Saginaw at 2,250$ on which there will be some thing Handsome made I think in the course of a year from this time. We will be able to dispose of 5 or 6000$ worth of Lots and then have a large proportion of it left. I shall expect the deed next week and then I shall draw upon you at 30 or 60 days for the payment. I shall take all titles in your name, and when we are ready to sell you must give me a power to convey for you but I shall see you before that time if nothing takes place to prevent more than I know of at present and then we can make all arrangements which will be necessary for our mutual advantage. I now think I shall leave here after 16th and go to meet Gov. Davis and accompany him to Boston. I recd your favour of the 24 of June[1] a few days ago but my health has been such I have not been able to write untill today. I directed my Agent who went to Wisconsin not to purchase any lands unless they were of the most choice kind in every respect, and if he purchases you may depend upon it they will be good for he surveyed nearly the whole country and knows all about it. Yours Very Respectfully   Phineas Davis

ALS. ViU.

1. See above.

FROM DANIEL FLETCHER WEBSTER

Chicago July 6th. 1836

Dear Father,

I have drawn on you to-day for fifteen hundred dollars. I purchased something like twenty nine acres south of Pigeon Lake in Port Sheldon, for that sum—with a guarantee from Mr. [Henry] Moore that it should produce one hundred per cent in a year—on condition that I gave him half the Surplus over one hundred per cent, & a power of attorney to manage the property for me—during that time.

I would have bought the property for Fowler & Co¹ & [Samuel] Upton but the conditions were such I thought I had better not, wanting the *powers requisite*. I trust you will confirm my acts & if the Company will, perhaps they might as well take it. One hundred per cent per annum *ought* to satisfy any one. I drew on you at sixty days date payable at the Merchants Bank in New York. I have not thought it best to purchase much property for the Company just now.

Edward H. Hadduck² & I have agreed to go out next Fall & buy up preëmptions; he is to tell me of good ones & go with me, if I will do all I can to raise twenty or *ten* thousand dollars for him on *mórtgage* in Boston this Fall—in September. We are to look up affairs some time in October. He knows all about such things; Harding knows him & he is & has been very kind to me. I hope you will approve my purchase. *One hundred per cent* is, generally speaking, a good investment. By buying up preëmptions I mean buying the Claims of settlers in Wisconsin—taking half their land by paying for the whole. I have no doubt but that *such* will be the best thing we can do with the money of Fowler & Co & Upton.

I leave Chicago for Detroit this afternoon. The Roads over Michigan are *horrible*, not a womans horrible; but I cannot wait for a Boat, Herman Le Roy goes with me. We go in a Schooner across to St. Joseph—& then as we can to Detroit. I shall come home as fast as I can. Last night I had a severe attack of homesickness—it lasted long enough to make me resolve to go to day, if I walked & carried my trunk.

My best love to Mother & Julia. I wrote Mother two pages the other day & have been so busy making or trying to make bargains since, that I have not finished it. I am very well.

I would give an acre of Illinois for one snuff of Cut [?] Island.

Your most affectionate Son   D. F. Webster.

ALS. ViU.
1. Not identified.
2. Haddock (1811–1881), brother of Charles B. and Webster's nephew, had moved to Chicago in 1833 where he became a merchant and banker. Under William Henry Harrison, Webster procured for him the appointment of Receiver of Public Moneys at Chicago.

FROM PHINEAS DAVIS

Detroit July 18th 1836

Dear Sir
On the 16th inst I purchased for you $5000. worth of Stock in the

Giberalter & Shiamassic Companies at first cost.[1] And the Stock this day is worth 400 per cent *cash* in the Giberaltar Company. The Scrip will not be issued until next week, for we can not get it in readiness.

I have not the least doubt but what the scrip (which will cost you $15. per share) will sell in 60 days for 100. or 150.$ and in less than a year at $350.[2] I consider the speculation that I have now made is one of the best that has been made for a long time. But I assure you that it was with the *greatest* difficulty that I obtained so much Stock for you. Scarcely any other one got more than $750. worth.

The company is composed of about 30 individuals of capital and enterprise, and the place will surely go ahead. It is one of the best locations for a city in the western country. It is at the mouth of Detroit River and advantageously situated on account of the interior. As soon as we get the scrip made and our articles printed I will send you a copy, together with your scrip. I wish you to write me what I shall do with your scrip, whether I shall send it all to you or keep a part of it here and sell it on your account. I would not dispose of it at present for less than 1000 per cent advance, and I would not sell it all at that price. I have made a draft on you for $5,000. at 60 days from date. I also made one upon you for $119. at 30 days. I now think I shall make another purchase for you of $4,000. worth of Village property where there is a great water power,[3] and on which I have not the least doubt but you will make a large amount. Cash is now *Scarce*, and now is the time to opperate and there are very few who can get drafts discounted on time, In consequence of the Circular issued by the Treasury department with instructions to receive nothing but Gold & Silver at the Land Office after the 15th of August next.[4]

I shall not visit Boston as soon as I expected, for I want to invest all the money I have in lands before that time. I now think I shall make for you from the $16000. which I have received from you & Mr Perkins at least $60,000. and perhaps twice that sum. I think it might be well to dispose of some of your stock, if you can get 1000 per cent, and invest again or let us divide some. I have got more to say than I can write at this time. I enclose you a letter from my man who is looking [for] lands, and you may see the difficulty there is in obtaining duplicates.[5] I have had the money these 70 days to purchase 30 Lots. Yours Respectfully

Phineas Davis

ps) I hope to be in Boston during the month of August when I hope to have all your business done up for the present.

ALS. ViU.

1. When the town-site promoters finally organized on July 30, they named their enterprise the Gibraltar and Flat Rock Company. Nine men— Benjamin B. Kercheval, Elon Farns-

worth, Charles Noble, Henry Conant, Peter Godfroy, James H. Forsyth, Joshua Howard, Enoch Jones, and Phineas Davis (the largest stockholder with 900 shares)—owned the 4,000 shares of stock. Although the initial capitalization of the company was not stated in the articles of association, other evidence suggests that it was about $60,000. Davis's investment of $5,000 for DW, made one day after the incorporators purchased the land on which Gibraltar was to be built, made DW one of the six major stockholders in the company, but the stock apparently was issued in Davis's name, for the articles of association make no mention of DW. *Deed of Trust and Articles of Association of the Gibraltar and Flat Rock Company* (Detroit, 1836). When

the Michigan legislature incorporated the company on April 3, 1838, its capitalization was placed at $400,000, and in 1839, the company was granted the right to increase its capital to $1,000,000. *Laws of Michigan, 1837–38* (Detroit, 1838), pp. 170–175; *ibid., 1839*, p. 127.

2. Shares in the company climbed to $100 by 1838.

3. For this purchase, see Phineas Davis to DW, July 30, 1836, below.

4. On July 11, 1836, Jackson issued the Specie Circular through the Treasury secretary, ordering the receipt of only specie or Virginia land scrip in payment for public lands.

5. Erastus Ingersoll had written Phineas Davis (July 12, 1836) about the backlog of applications in the Bronson land office (mDW 13467).

FROM HENRY L. KINNEY

Peru July 18th. 1836

Dr. Sir,

I herewith enclose four Duplicates Recpts calling for Seven hundred and Sixty acres which is all of the best quality and adjoining lands which have been held at ten Dollars pr Acre & I think myself are well worth that price at this time.

It is becoming very difficult to find choice entries of Govt. land. There are not at this time any large boddies of good lands to be located at govt. price. The good lands unentered are scattering & some what difficult to find. The entries I have made are all good & I am decidedly of the oppinion that time had better be taken to secure the best locations that are in the market. Good selections will always sell readily at a large advance to settlers that are emigrating to the country. I flatter myself that the purchases I have made will be quite sattisfactory. When I enclose other duplicates to you that are in the hands of my agt. I will draw a brief plot setting forth the situation & value of your lands. My agt. and surveyor are now between this and the Mississippi searching for numbers of lands to be bought for you on the line of the State Road from this to Rockislland on the Mississippi River.

I shall proceed to invest the remainder of your money in my hands to the best possible interest of yourself & Col Perkins according to your directions, & forward the duplicates &c. I shall not make any second handed purchases until I hear from you on the subject, but would say that it is my opinion that much greater advances might be made on the amt. invested by purchasing property in towns that are rapidly improving. Emigrants are daily flocking in from all quarters of the best stamp, hardly any come but the most enterprising citizens. And I have not seen a single individual but what expresses more sattisfaction with this flourishing country than could be expected from a native of another soil. Seven acres of land adjoining the 20 acre lot in which you bought an interest of me has this day been sold for fifteen thousand Dolls. I can buy for you the East 1/2 of the last 1/2 of Section 18 about one mile below the termination of the canal for $30. pr acre. The land is as good for farming as any land east of the Alegany mountains—& I think it will sell within a year for $100. pr acre.

Please write at the recpt of this. I shall enclose other tittle papers soon. I am with due respect your Obt Svt.   H. L. Kinney

ALS. ViU.
1. Not found.

FROM DANIEL FLETCHER WEBSTER

Tonawanda July 19. 1836.

My dear Father,

I arrived here last night, after a long & tiresome run down the Lake. I found a letter from Julia, dated Saratoga.

I hope you will have received my last from Chicago.[1]

This deferring of the land sale in Wisconsin, will knock up the plans of many other people as well as myself—beside, at this time people are so much in want of money that there would be less competition. However, as fair for one as it is for another.

I waited three days in Detroit to learn about the great purchase Mr. [Phineas] Davis was to make there. We talked the affair all over. I have named the town that is to be London. He says he likes the name. They have given twenty thousand dollars for the land at the mouth of the river, four hundred & fifty acres, about forty five dollars per acre. He will draw on you for five thousand.[2] He and I made an arrangement to go to Texas together next Spring. That will be a grand opening I think. I hope you will approve my purchase for you at Pigeon Lake.

When at Detroit I entered my name in Mr. [Charles] Cleland's office[3] and subscribed for a newspaper. I was very much pleased with the place & there is nowhere so good an opening for a Lawyer, not a man of talent at the bar.

I will hasten all I can, my dear Father, & be home as soon as possible, but you will perceive that it will be very hard for me to get away from here so as to be in Boston before the middle of August. I know I shall have many things to do at Boston & ought to be home, but I have found so much to do out here.

I did not make many purchases west of Chicago, took up three forties for myself & [Fisher Ames] Harding took I think, four eighties for you. We entered for Mineral. I attended to Mr. [John] Cramer's affair & have written him at length about it.

I am very much pleased with my St. Joseph purchase. Toledo too, will I think do very well. I had a grand offer made me out there, which I may get some one to take up, nine city Lots for $20,000.

I have not yet got an answer from my Lands in Michigan—they shut up the office so often & make so many alterations in their arrangements. [Joseph R.] Williams has a man there, at Bronson, to attend to it, & I expect to hear every day.

[I] was shocked beyond a passion to hear, at Toledo, of Mr. [Jarvis] Gregg's death.[4] I was in great doubt as to what I ought to do; Alice was only seventy miles from me. But I concluded not to visit her.

We are all well here—Mr. [Stephen] White run down with business. I am going to offer him my services while I stay here. Caroline [Story White] sends her best love to you & Mother & Julia. I shall write them both tomorrow. I am my dear Father Y'r. most affectionate son

D. F. Webster.

ALS. ViU.

1. See above, DFW to DW, July 6, 1836.

2. See above, Phineas Davis to DW, July 18, 1836.

3. Cleland was a prominent Detroit lawyer, former editor of the Detroit *Free Press*.

4. Gregg (1808–1836; Dartmouth 1828), who married Webster's niece, Alice Bridge Webster (b. 1814), Ezekiel's daughter, had died on June 28, 1836, in Hudson, Ohio, where he was a professor at Western Reserve College.

FROM PHINEAS DAVIS

Detroit July 26th 1836

Dear Sir

I have been informed that a gentleman from this place has written to his agent in Boston to purchase out your interest in Gibraltar. I would advise you not to sell at present under 1500 per cent advance. Stock sold yesterday which cost 15$ for 135$ cash and I have no doubt but it will be worth 300$ in less than 6 months. The Gibraltar Company met at my Office last evening and have made an additional purchase of 18000$ of a large water power and another village 6 miles from Gibraltar which will be a great advantage and will bring Col Perkins into the operation. I have no hesitation in saying that we shall realize a profit out of the Gibraltar speculation of $60,000 and should not be surprised if we made $120,000 & perhaps more. Doct G[ideon] Barstow of Salem is here and he has made a purchase of 50 shares and he will be in Boston shortly and will give you all the information you want upon the subject. I hope to be in Boston as soon as the 25 of August when I shall have all our affairs closed as far as investments are to be made and if you are satisfied with my agency I should be pleased to make further investments. I am willing.

When I come on I shall bring on your scrip and a map of our cities &c all of which you will be pleased with. It is impossible to get Dfts. discounted through the Banks at this time owing to the circular issued by the Treasury Department. I cannot leave here untill the business of the Gibraltar Company is finished for I am Secretary Treasurer and Director &c. In haste Yours Respectfully   Phineas Davis

ALS. ViU.

FROM HENRY L. KINNEY

Peru July 28. 1836
Dr. Sr.
   I have been disappointed in proving all of the numbers or entries of land for you that I expected through my agt. The lands he went for were taken some time previous. The enclosed duplicates[1] are valuable locations situated ten miles West of the termination of the Canal & within two miles from the Ill River & mostly timber worth at this time Six Dols. pr acre. I start this day for the land Office at Galena to make entries for you, & hope to get the numbers I have selected—as I have been to considerable expense & trouble in finding them. You may be shure of this fact, that what I purchase will be good—I have thought propper (& a little different from what I expected when I last wrote you) to purchase second handed lands. I have bought the W. 1/2 of the West 1/2 of Section 18. for you & Col Perkins. It is but a few rods over one mile from where the Canal intersects the River, & I think a much better investment for making money than can possibly be made at this time in govmt

lands. The prices of land in and about Peru rises like magick. Since the Engineers have concluded their Survey of the canal route property has risen 100 pr. ct a week. This point is now looked upon with as much interest as that of Chicago. Since the final termination of the canal is fixed upon, the Canal Commissioners are to start next week for this place to make arrangements for letting contracts at this end of the canal route. I paid for the hundred & sixty acres I bought for you on 18—three thousand five hundred Dollars. I got the refusal of the place immediately after my return this Spring for two months at that price. I should not have bought that kind of property for you had I not have thought it to your interest as well as my own to do so & I am now offered over 100 pr ct. advance on the purchase. I consider the property (as land is rating) worth sixteen thousand Dollars—in the enclosed plot I will mark the prices that land has sold for within the last four weeks.[2] The deed to the 160 ac[res] I will have made to you individually & enclose the same as soon as it may be recorded & you can make the propper division with Col Perkins. I shall enter some lands for Col Perkins while at Galena & en[close] them to you from that place. I consider the 1 1/4 interest of which I would have in the purchase of the Ferry on 18 worth $5000— which would make the value of the 160 a[cre]s twenty thousand Dols. The advance I have no doubt would seem large to an Eastern man, but it is not so here. I regret that I could not have seen your son before he left this country.

The mail has just arrived—& brings notice that my Drft on you for two thousand Dollars payable at the Phenix Bank N.Y. 60 days after sight has been protested for non acceptance. I hope I shall have no trouble about it as I have drawn the money & invested & made arrangements to invest your money. Let me hear from you at the recpt of this. I remain with due respect I remain Your Obt Servt.   H. L. Kinney

ALS. ViU.   2. Not found.
     1. Not found.

FROM PHINEAS DAVIS

Detroit July 30th 1836
Dear Sir,
   I have this day drawn upon you for 4850$ at ten days sight payable at the Merchants Bank Boston which will complete the amount I was to invest for you, and at this time I will say nothing about profits, but shall expect to see you in Boston by the 20 of August. I shall leave here as soon as I can get the maps of our city drawn, and the stock issued of the Gibraltar & Flat Rock Company. Since I wrote you the company have

added to their purchase a very *extensive water* power which will greatly increase the value of Gibraltar, which place we call Flat Rock. Doct G[ideon] Barstow will give you all the information you will want upon the subject. Yours Very Respectfully   Phineas Davis

ALS. ViU.

TO EDWARD EVERETT

Marshfield Aug 6. 1836

My D Sir

I am quite glad to hear from you,[1] & to learn that you had a pleasant visit to Bristol & Nantucket. I have no doubt yr journey will do good. It would have given us pleasure to have seen you here, if yr convenience had allowed. There are many good people in this & neighboring towns, who would have rejoiced in the opportunity of shaking hands with you.

I notice the Extract from Mr [Julius] Rockwell's letter.[2] Of course, I shall do nothing to influence the proceedings of the Worcester Convention; but if those proceedings should indicate any doubt, or hesitation, as to following up, in the most decided manner, the Resolutions of the Whig members of the Legislature last winter, I should feel at liberty to withdraw, at once & altogether, from the election. Any idea, or notion, of forming an unpledged ticket, can only be entertained, upon the ground, that the good of the cause, in the State, does not require me to remain in my present condition; & that being so understood, I have already said what course my inclination would prompt me to pursue.

I pray the kindest regards to yr wife, & am, D sir, always Yrs

D. Webster

ALS. MHi.

1. Letter not found.

2. Rockwell's letter to Everett, August 1, 1836, from which the extract probably came, has not been found. Everett answered it on August 4, urging Rockwell to use his influence at the September 14 Worcester convention in behalf of DW's candidacy. The Worcester convention voted unanimously to continue to support DW. Edward Everett to Julius Rockwell, August 4, 1836, Everett Papers Microfilm, Reel 25, Frame 1052, MHi; *Boston Courier*, September 19, 1836.

FROM NICHOLAS BIDDLE

Phila. Augt. 13. 1836

My dear Sir

I send officially a statement of a case in which I think it important not merely for the Bank but for the whole Country that just ideas should prevail.[1] If the views of these gentlemen in Alabama are correct, they shake the whole foundations of intercourse between the States. If the Bank of the U.S. cannot contract, how can a Northern Manufacturing Co[mpan]y buy cotton in the South, or a Northern Insurance Coy insure a Southern vessel. I wish therefore that you would put out the strength of your mind, and demolish these fooleries: since it devolves on you more than on any other public man, to show that this is really a Union— not a mere string of beads with a rotten thread to hold them together. Yrs always   N.B.

LC. DLC.
    1. Biddle's statement (not found) was to call Webster's attention to a situation in Alabama, where payment on bills issued in Alabama and purchased or discounted by agents of three non-Alabama banks had been refused on the ground that those banks lacked power to engage in business in Alabama. The issue reached the Alabama Circuit Court in April 1838, whereupon Justice John McKinley (1780–1852) of Alabama ruled that corporations had no right to do business in bills of exchange in states other than those in which they were incorporated. When the Alabama bank cases, 13 Peters 519 (1839), reached the Supreme Court, Webster, David B. Ogden, and John Sergeant appeared for the bank, against Charles J. Ingersoll, William H. Crawford, Jr., of Georgia, and William J. Van de Gruff of Alabama. Justice Taney's ruling reversed McKinley's decision. Charles Warren, *The Supreme Court in United States History* (2 vols.; Boston, 1928), 2: 50–61; Carl B. Swisher, *History of the Supreme Court of the United States: The Taney Period, 1836–1864* (New York, 1974), pp. 115–122.

FROM FISHER AMES HARDING

Chicago, Aug. 16. 1836.
My Dear Sir,
    I received by the last mail yours of the 30th of July.[1] You do not allude to either of mine as mentioning a draft upon you for $1025, with which I purchased an interest at St. Joseph, M[ichigan] T[erritory] along with Daniel F., but I presume you have received such an one.
    I have within a day or two agreed along with a number of others to purchase four townsites in Wisconsin T. & the North part of Illinois. The part I shall take for you will be one eighth. For the four towns we are to give $40,000; one fourth, nearly cash, the remainder in three equal payments of six, twelve & eighteen months. The first payment of $1250, I shall meet by a draft on you at three months from the 15th of Aug. for $1000, and by giving a note of my own for $250, payable in 20 or 30 days. I shall by that time have some funds of yours accruing from the Michigan City sale. For the other payments sales will be made probably so as to meet them at least in part, & if not, there will be some more coming due about that time for Michigan City. I think this operation will

be a pretty good one; at least paying a good interest on the cash invested. Two of the locations are on the Wisconsin river in W[isconsin] T[erritory], one of the others some fifteen miles from the mouth of Rock river, & the fourth near its head. One of the places, situated on Wisconsin river at the Battle ground which will be called *Superior*, it is proposed to try to make of considerable importance—the more sanguine aim as high even as the *seat* of *Government* of the Territory. I beg you not to smile. The other towns have their value, but will not receive so much attention, and will be sold soon & without improvements. I shall give my own notes for the three future payments, and take the title in my own name, but shall transfer it to you, when the Power of Attorney is arranged.

The draft for $1000 will complete the amount which I have to invest for you, making in all about $2500. I trust none of it will be lost. The property which Daniel & myself purchased at St. Joseph for $2000 is worth very nearly or quite $4000; so I am assured. But I will promise for nothing but a handsome interest in future.

In one of your previous letters you say that you would venture to permit me to invest $1000 or $2000 for Col. Perkin's & yourself in other than Goverm't lands, though contrary to the original purpose & agreement; & you express a hope in your last that something may be yet done in time. It has been my intention to invest that money ($5000)—all or a good part,—in Government lands North of us in East Wisconsin, which it was expected would be brought into market this fall, & with reason as the surveys have been made, and the country, filling with settlers as it is, is quite ripe for such sale. But appearances now indicate that no sale will take place. None has been advertised. Other circumstances too seem to indicate a disposition on the part of the Government to curtail as far as possible the sales of public lands. As to the Land Districts, already existing, there is probably considerable good land yet unentered. In ours however there is none, unless it be a stray fragment which has been over looked. The Galena District, I am told, too is well nigh exhausted. There is probably the best opportunity in the Mineral Point office. But there, the timber-wood has been well nigh all taken, at least in the neighborhood of good lands. I know one man (he had his funds from the East) who invested, I think, $30,000 in timber land merely, at the sale last Spring. This would go farther than a stranger would suppose in a country, not of forests but of plains. Still if one could travel round & examine, he would probably find something—nay, considerable. I think if I should meet with a pretty safe purchase at private sale, & could get drafts discounted,—a thing not now to be done—I should venture to lay out 1 or 2000 for Col. P. & yourself, although not in Government land.

You have doubtless noticed the Treasury order requiring payments at the Land Offices to be made in specie in most cases. It will diminish the amount of entries very much, I think. The Western Banks will suffer greatly; I scarcely see how those in the neighborhoods of Gov't lands will be able to get along. Ours in Chicago from that & other causes is doing *nothing*, literally.

I should have prepared a draft of a Power of Attorney, had I not been somewhat indisposed for a short time past. I will do so soon. I forgot to say that the draft, for $1000, although running from Aug. 15th., will probably not be sent on for some weeks, as the title papers have not been made & will require time. I shall direct to send it to you at *Boston* for acceptance; it will be payable at the Merchants Bank, New York. If you should be at Marshfield, Mr. [Henry Willis] Kinsman I presume will look after it.

A visit to New England, which you suggest, would of all things be most agreable to me, but I can[n]ot quite yet allow myself to enjoy it. My partner, Mr. [Henry] Moore, started yesterday for that land. I beg you again to remember me to Mrs. Webster & Miss Julia. I shall esteem it one of the chief solaces of my exile to be retained in their recollections.

I have written a very long letter; I must beg to excuse it. Yours, truly,
Fisher A. Harding.

ALS. ViU.
1. Not found.

TO NICHOLAS BIDDLE

Boston Aug. 23. 1836
Private
Dear Sir

I recd your communication last week,[1] while at Marshfield, where my family now is. I came up yesterday, for the purpose of going to Exeter, N.H. to see one of my boys [Edward] who is at school in that place, under the same ferule, which brought up his father.

This little journey, Commencement at Cambridge, which is next week, & some other engagements & occurences, may delay, for some time, the preparation of an opinion on the case submitted to me. Meantime, I have meditated on the subject, in a solitary walk or two, & have a clear idea of what the law is, on the subject. It is easy, I think, to dispel all these fogs & mists. The doubts, expressed by the Alabama Gentlemen, appear to me to be the effect of the misapplication of the results of research. I think the whole subject may be placed in a plain point of view.

If it be important to your Bank to have an early opinion, please say so, on receipt of this, & I will lay other things aside, & attend to it. Yrs truly   Danl Webster

ALS. DLC.
 1. See above, Nicholas Biddle to DW, August 13, 1836.

FROM NICHOLAS BIDDLE

Phila. Augst. 26th. 1836

My dear Sir
 I have this morning yours of the 23d. inst.[1] Take your own time. I see my way quite clearly enough, not to stop for the Alabama practitioners— but I like always to walk by a broad refulgent light. So shine forth. By the way—while you have the club in hand, I wish you would give a hard knock at the Virginia decision which is, I suppose very P P Barber-ish.[2] Yours always   N. B.

LC. DLC.
 1. See above.
 2. Presumably the allusion is to a strong states' rights decision handed down by Philip P. Barbour while he

was federal judge for the eastern district of Virginia. The specific "Virginia decision" has not been identified.

FROM JOSEPH RICKETSON WILLIAMS

[c. September 28, 1836]

Sir
 Enclosed with this line you will find the accounts I have made out for yourself & Col. Perkins.[1] The deeds of the land taken in my name I have retained and also the duplicates. I will have both deeds recorded in Michigan. I hope the accounts will prove satisfactory. I shall be in New York until Saturday next & should get any thing directed to the care of Grinnell, Minturn & Co.[2] and afterwards at Toledo.
 I understand that Col. Perkins has inquired or sent for me to your office once or twice. I have little to add respecting the proposition I made to take up what vacant land could be had on a line between the head of Lake Erie & the head of Lake Michigan. A small strip of country through that region must inevitably become as great a thoroughfare as any in the United States. I have reason to know that the Rail Road project will be pushed, and with respect to every incipient movement I shall be informed as soon as any others. Indeed before I left Toledo those principally interested in the charter for the Ohio portion of the Road offered to make me a Director. The land to be obtained however is near a continuation of the same line in Indiana. The soil through that country is "Openings" of fine quality & the country inviting to settlers. I think any measures ought to be taken soon, for reasons that will suggest themselves to you. From the information I had when I left the country I think

20.000 acres of land could be obtained which would promise greater returns than any country I know of at the west, especially as there *are few speculators* in it. Indeed I think the profits would be very great. The method I think would be to transport the Specie from New York, which I could undoubtedly raise there by Drafts upon you or Col. Perkins. I think so because if it could be had at all at Detroit or Buffalo, they would take care and demand a good per centage. I think I should have a pretty clear field & if I had a considerable sum of specie could well afford to pay for protection & transportation of it. I hope to hear from you at all events at New York.

I remain with great respect Yours &c &c   Jos. R. Williams

I take the liberty to call your attention to resolutions adopted at a meeting of Whig Antimasons at New Beford on Saturday Evening.[3]

ALS. ViU.
1. Not found.
2. Merchants and shippers in New York City.
3. The New Bedford "Whig Anti-masons," in line with the action of other local political gatherings that preceded the Worcester convention, had probably adopted resolutions supporting Webster.

FROM JOSEPH RICKETSON WILLIAMS

New York Sept. 29. 1836
Sir.

Since I arrived in New York I have ascertained that large quantities of Michigan land have been sold at $2 pr. acre cash, *by those* who take the funds to reinvest, *to those* who are disposed to await the growth of the country. Even though land should be sold at that rate in the winter which could be secured now at Gov't price it would be an excellent operation.

I understand that $20.000 in specie came from Boston the day I left destined for Wisconsin.

I shall remain here till Monday to hear from you and Col. Perkins & name these facts for his & your considerations.

I remain with grt respect &c &c   Jos. R. Williams

I believe I mentioned that I should get a letter directed to care of Grinnell, Minturn & Co.

ALS. ViU.

TO MOSES MCCURE STRONG

Boston Oct. 24. '36
Dear Sir

On my return to town I find your letter of the 17th inst.[1]

Your suggestion, in relation to the proof, in the case of the mineral land, is very correct, & is the only thing, in addition to what is already done, which occurs to me as necessary. It can, doubtless, be shown, that the lands in question were not of the class, marked as containing minerals, by showing, authentically, what lands *did* constitute that class. This, therefore, should be done; altho' I am not prepared to say, or to admit, without further consideration, that if they had belonged to that class, the Register could refuse an application to enter them, *if, in fact, they had been once exposed to sale.*[2]

I shall be glad to hear the result of your arrangements at Washington, & of your further proceedings at Mineral Point. Very respectfully, Your Ob. Servt   Danl Webster

ALS. NhD.
1. Not found.
2. Strong's endorsement of the letter reads: "About proofs that mineral lands applied for were not reserved in proclamation." Webster and others had been assisting Strong in an effort to get the lead-bearing lands placed on the market by the General Land Office. Kenneth W. Duckett, *Frontiersman of Fortune: Moses M. Strong of Mineral Point* (Madison, 1955), pp. 26, 32.

TO JEREMIAH MASON

Oct. 25. 1836

Private & Confidential
My Dear Sir
    I find a very strong desire among your friends that you would consent to go into the Legislature. At every corner, I am met, & solicited to beseech you not to decline. The young men, also, feel a great interest in the matter. They say, they are willing to do the work, but somebody must be willing to be elected to the H. of R. who can go there, occasionally, & prevent mischief. I really hope you will make the sacrifice, for the common good.
    I may say to you, that Ch. Jus. [Lemuel] Shaw spoke to me on the subject, yesterday, & desired me to see you. He thinks it of the highest importance you should not decline. Yrs truly   Danl. Webster

ALS. DLC.

TO JOHN GORHAM PALFREY

Boston Nov. 15. '36

My Dear Sir,
    I have recd yours of the 12th.[1] My lecture, altogether, was a very slight performance, & of what was said, a great part was never written.[2] If it

were in a state to go to the press, you should have it; if I ever put it into such a state, you shall have it; but it is hardly probable I can do that, before I go to W[ashington].

I *dropped the N[orth] A[merican Review] when the Article appeared about Mr Jefferson, & Mr Jefferson's religion.* From that day, I have never looked into a No.[3]

But, in your hands, I am willing to trust it. If you think of it, tell the publishers to send it to me. Ever Yrs   D. Webster

ALS. NhD.
1. Not found.
2. Palfrey had probably asked for a copy of DW's lecture before the Boston Society for the Diffusion of Useful Knowledge, delivered on November 11. For that lecture, see mDW 13593; W & S, 13: 63–78.
3. Webster had discontinued his subscription to the *North American*

Review apparently in response to Andrew Ritchie's review of Thomas Jefferson Randolph's *Memoir, Correspondence, and Miscellanies, from the Papers of Thomas Jefferson* (Charlottesville, 1829). For that review, see *North American Review*, New Series, 21 (April 1830): 511–551.

Devoid of issues, the presidential campaign of 1836 was largely one of personalities. Van Buren won a clear victory with 170 electoral votes as compared with 124 for all his Whig opponents. Webster carried only his home state; Harrison won Vermont, New Jersey, Ohio, and Indiana; White received Georgia and Tennessee; and Willie P. Mangum, South Carolina. The National Republican–Whig opponents of Jacksonian Democracy had made significant gains since 1832, but still too little to carry the election even had they accepted Webster's exhortation to run a single candidate.

TO NATHANIEL SILSBEE

Boston, November 15, 1836.

My Dear Sir,

It appears highly probable that the election of yesterday has terminated in the choice of yourself and the other gentlemen on the same list, as electors of President and Vice-President of the United States in behalf of the State of Massachusetts.

This result, the relation in which I have stood to the People of the commonwealth during the contest, and events which have transpired or are anticipated in other States, have rendered it proper in my judgment that I should address you this letter to be laid before the electors, when they shall assemble.

My purpose is to say that, in the discharge of their high and most interesting trust, it is my earnest wish that they should act with entire freedom from all considerations merely personal to myself; and that they should give the vote of the State in the manner they think most likely to be useful in supporting the constitution and laws of the country, the union of the States, the perpetuity of our republican institutions, and the important interests of the whole country; and in maintaining the character of Massachusetts for integrity, honor, national patriotism, and fidelity to the constitution.

I am, dear Sir, with sentiments of the truest esteem, your friend and obedient servant,   Danl Webster.

Text from *PC*, 2: 22. Original not found.

LAST WILL AND TESTAMENT OF DANIEL WEBSTER
[November 1836]

I, Daniel Webster, of Boston, in the County of Suffolk, do hereby make & declare this my last will & testament, hereby revoking all wills by me heretofore made.[1]

It is my will that all my just debts be paid, a memorandum of which will be found among my papers.[2] In order to raise money for that purpose, I direct my Executors to collect all the debts which may be due to me at my decease, & to sell & dispose of the following described property, viz: the vacant lot in Summer Street in Boston, between the lot on which my house stands, & the house of Mr. [Stephen] White now occupied by Mr. [James William] Paige; my books; my wine; my furniture & other personal property, except as hereinafter excepted; and also all or any of my property in lands, city lots, Companies, Corporations &c, in Michigan, Ohio, Indiana, Illinois & Wisconsin, or such parts thereof as may be necessary & may be sold to most advantage. And for the like purpose, if necessary to sell my land in Derry, New Hampshire, & my farm & lands in Franklin, New Hampshire, &, if further necessary, to sell also such parts of my Marshfield property, as may be thought best for the good of my heirs; I intending to leave it in the discretion of my Executors to sell such of the above mentioned property first, as may be in their judgment best—not confining them to the order in which the parcels are here enumerated; first of all, however, applying to the payment of debts, the proceeds of any policy or policies on my own life, which may be running at my death.

There being a conveyance of my house in Boston in which I now reside, by marriage settlement in trust to my wife for life,[3] & remainder to my heirs, as will appear by the deed, if no other arrangement be agreed on, as better, property must be sold, to pay off a mortgage of nineteen thousand Dollars on the House; so that it may follow the trusts of the settlement unincumbered.

I give to my beloved wife the coach, pleasure waggons, & coach horses, any hundred volumes of my books which she may prefer, & the furniture which she brought into the house with her, two thousand Dollars worth of plate, & two thousand Dollars a year, during the life time of her father, which is to be in full satisfaction of her right to Dower out of my estate.

I give and devise the rest and residue of my property real & personal to my children, equally to be divided among them; except as hereinafter excepted; that is to say, that in regard to articles which are valuable as keepsakes or tokens, I dispose of such articles, as follows—viz—

To my wife, I give the picture of myself by [Francis] Alexander.

To my Son Daniel Fletcher, I give the vase presented to me by citizens of Boston, the watch in my pocket, & the picture of myself by [Gilbert] Stewart.

To my daughter Julia, I give her mother's picture, by [Chester] Harding, her mother's watch, and all the little articles which were her mothers, a small picture of myself taken when young; & the little bust, or head of myself, by [Robert] Ball Hughes.

To my Son Edward, I give the plate presented to me by Amos Lawrence, the snuff box presented to me by Mr. [Samuel Ayer?] Bradley, and the large gold watch which I wore in his mother's life time—and my Washington medals. And as I have advanced seven thousand Dollars to Fletcher on his marriage, the[4] whole of this is to be reckoned & charged, as part of his portion.

I hereby nominate & appoint my wife Caroline Le Roy Webster, & my son Daniel Fletcher Webster, and the survivor of them, Executrix & Executor of this my last will and testament. In testimony whereof I have hereunto set my hand & seal this   day of November in the year Eighteen hundred & thirty six.   Danl Webster

Signed, sealed, published, and declared by said Daniel Webster, as his last will & testament, in the presence of us, who at his request, & in his presence & in the presence of each other, have hereunto subscribed our names, as witnesses—it being on two sheets each of which, bears my name.

D. Webster
Henry W. Kinsman
Charles H. Thomas
Timothy Fletcher.[5]

DS. NhHi. Published in Van Tyne, pp. 593–595.

1. No earlier wills by DW have been found.

2. Memorandum not found.

3. For the details of the marriage settlement, see *Correspondence*, 3: 82.

4. DW's signature on the first sheet appears at this point.

5. Fletcher (1774–1842), brother of Grace Fletcher Webster and half-brother of James William Paige, who often assisted Webster with his Marshfield affairs.

Whigs generally, as evidenced in the letter from Stephen White below, were alarmed by the emerging hard money policies of the Democratic party, a concern shared by some Democrats also. Led by Senators Nathaniel P. Tallmadge of New York and William C. Rives of Virginia, these Conservative Democratic opponents of specie collection cooperated with Whigs in an effort to repeal Jackson's Specie Circular (see DW to Nicholas Biddle, [December 18, 1836], and DW to Franklin Haven, January 21, 1837, below).

As the Democratic party regulars intensified their drive for specie collection and the adoption of an independent treasury during the Panic of 1837, the Conservative Democrats sought a closer alliance and eventual union with the Whig party in 1839–1840.

FROM STEPHEN WHITE

Boston Sunday Eveng
[December 11, 1836]

My Dear Sir

I have just got your welcome lines written at Philadelphia last fridday.[1] We have also gotten this evening the Report of Mr. Secretary [Levi] Woodbury which seems to follow up the insane project of specie currency indicated in the message of the President.[2] Before effecting so violent a change in the pecuniary affairs of the community affecting the income property and prosperity of all who have a stake in its prosperity it might have been well to show wherein the country has suffered by our present system under which it has grown up and prospered to an extent unprecedented in history. I was not I confess prepared to find in Mr Woodburys Report such an unqualified support of all the ultra doctrines of the crackbrained old chief, as crackbrained he evidently is on this subject or else misled by the inveteracy of his hostility to Mr Biddle and the Bank. He sets at defiance all other thoughts than those which tend to gratify his malevolent feelings. Should these recommendations be followed out who can doubt that the country will see a state of suffering totally unprecedented. Already with Specie in the country abundant beyond all precedent the community are suffering from a scarcity of money which makes every considerate man tremble. Can there be any doubt that this scarcity is caused alone by the hoarding of this specie in the *Selected* Banks as Mr Woodbury chooses to call them, and their withdrawing from the monied means of the country the fund which heretofore has supplied so large a portion of its wants. I quarrel with the whole principle of withdrawing small bills as one which is founded in falacy.[3] A certain portion of the smaller circulation if not supplied by bills of the banks must be supplied of course by specie as they propose—but does it follow as the Secretary supposes that this circulation, which is indispensible to be maintained and kept in every-day use for the community, can find its way into the Banks to strengthen them in case of a pressure? What then is to supply the place of it for every-day use? It is indeed true as I have heard you more than once remark that those principles of public policy as well as constitutional law which we have considered as the Settled bases of the government are again and anew brought up for discussion and debate with a recklessness and hardihood that is astounding.

If I mistake not however the time is at hand when the people by great suffering will be awakend to the absurdity of this policy and will turn them gladly to the aid of those who advocate sounder doctrines. The most prejudiced must see that the US Bank has no hand in the matter but that it results from the arbitrary and tyranical course of the president and his subservient cabinet. The *experiment* is I truly believe approaching its termination and the country is about awakening from its slumbers.

You see I am in a scolding humour but I believe there are thousands who if they had the pleasure of approaching you as I have, even so unceremoniously as in this scrawl, would speak louder and certainly much better than I do to the purpose. Ever dear Sir Yours   S W

ALS. NhHi.
  1. Not found.
  2. For the annual report of the Secretary of the Treasury, see *Executive Documents*, 24th Cong., 2d sess.,

Serial 301, Document No. 4.
  3. White was probably alluding to the provisions of the Deposit Act of June 23, 1836. 5 *U.S. Statutes at Large* 53.

FROM EDWARD EVERETT

Charlestown Massts. 16 Decr. 1836

My dear Sir,

I meant to have had the pleasure of seeing you again before your departure; but you left Boston a little earlier than I expected. We are looking with all our eyes to Washington hardly knowing what to look for. Republicans as we are we feel something of the fear of change which perplexes monarchs. Our best consolation is that those things in which the change is expected are already in such a condition, that it is not easy to change for the worse. The Senate cannot surely get any lower. How will you be able to stand it? I should like to know how Mr V Bs Cabinet is composed if you have any light on the subject.

Can you form any opinion whether the distributed surplus will ever be resumed? The administration spare no pains to infuse that bitter drug into the cup of enjoyment, with which it would otherwise be received by the States. I do not see how it can ever be withdrawn. Could I view the matter merely as a party man, I could wish that the Administration would continue to hold precisely the language they do; for at all elections it would be a just subject of care to the People to choose men known to be friendly to the permanent possession of this fund by the States.

Wild plans of disposing of it are already broached here, & I am sorry to say in this State by our friends. Vermont has divided it among the towns. New Hampshire proposes to do the same altho' Gov. [Isaac] Hill recommended a much wiser disposition of it. The Worcester Palladium a whig paper has recommended the same course & set the People of the towns to petitioning. The Northampton whig paper has copied the article. Mr Speaker [Julius] Rockwell has written a letter in favor of such a distribution, mainly on the ground that if we do not propose to give it to the towns, the Van Buren party will. We must then either acquiese & lose the credit of taking the lead in the measure, or oppose at the risk of being defeated on a very popular question.

I hope you will use yr influence if you can do so, with propriety, to have an efficient & intelligent Councillor from Suffolk. I want an able, clear-headed, sweet-tempered lawyer: a judicious, safe man. I have had no controversy with the present venerable incumbent, but he is not qualified to aid a governor in the discharge of his duties. My friends ought to give me an able council.

And now I must tell you in as much confidence as you may think expedient a secret, which I have only hinted & that imperfectly to one other person. My wife's health in her own opinion, her father's & mine is such as to make her uninterrupted residence in this climate dangerous. She has already fastened upon her a cold of very distressing asthmatic character, which will not probably leave her till Spring. She thinks it absolutely necessary for her health to pass two or three winters in the South of Europe & I presume some such change of climate affords the only chance of permanently strengthening her lungs. It is of course out of the question for me to take her abroad this winter; as I should do, if I were free from engagements. But I do not know that I could be justified in contracting a new engagemt. which would make it necessary for me to stay at home another Winter. I am sensible of all the delicacy with which this matter is to be approached. The interests of our friends as a party & my great obligations to them require that I should not by any rashly proclaimed purpose expose them to inconvenience, for some inconvenience of course attends taking up a new Candidate. But the party is left in the result of the late Election, in a sound & well-organized condition, much more to be relied upon that it was a year ago. With you at its head, & the question of your election to come up, there can be no fears in taking a new Candidate, I mean none not as likely to be realized in adhering to me. On the ground stated I suppose it would be generally felt, that I am warranted in withdrawing; should I decide to do so, as I really think I must, it will be a matter of the greatest anxiety with me to time the procedure so as to produce the least embarrassment. I beg you would consider the matter & favor me with your advice.

I hope that now & then during the winter, you will let me have a line from you & believe me ever with the greatest regard, Yours.

LC. MHi.

TO NICHOLAS BIDDLE

Washington Sunday Eve
[December 18, 1836]

My Dear Sir,

We shall take up Mr [Thomas] Ewing's Resolutions tomorrow,[1] & hear a long talk thereon from Mr [Thomas Hart] Benton. I understand he means to answer all who *write*, as well as all who speak, ag[ains]t the Treasury Order.

At present there is a very fair chance of carrying the Resolution thro. the Senate.

I need not tell you that your letter is read by every body. I think you never did any thing better.[2]

Indiana has elected a Whig Senator, to succeed Mr [William] Hendricks.[3] Yrs truly   D. Webster

ALS. DLC.

1. Ewing had introduced a resolution to repeal the Specie Circular on December 12, 1836; but on December 22, William C. Rives offered an amendment proposing that the government accept the paper money of specie-paying banks that did not issue notes below certain denominations. Rives's recommendation, incorporated into a bill "designating and limiting the funds receivable for the revenues of the United States" passed the Senate on February 10, 1837, and the House on March 1, but Jackson pocket-vetoed it. It was not until May 21, 1838, that Congress finally repealed the Specie Circular by joint resolution. Glyndon G. Van Deusen, *The Jacksonian Era, 1828–1848* (New York, 1959), p. 106.

2. In two letters to John Quincy Adams—November 10 and 11, 1836 —Biddle had discussed the fiscal af-

fairs of the country and called for the recharter of the Bank of the United States. *Niles' Weekly Register, 51* (December 10, 17, 1836): 230–231,

243–245.
   3. Oliver H. Smith replaced William Hendricks.

FROM NICHOLAS BIDDLE

Phila. Decr. 18th 1836
Sunday night

My dear Sir

While you are discussing the Specie order you will derive much information from the adoption of the following resolutions, which I have digested with some care & in consequence of *intelligence received tonight,* and which I commend to your early attention tomorrow—if, as I hope, this letter reaches you in time.

Resolved—That the Secretary of the Treasury be requested to communicate to the Senate the latest Statement made at or for the Treasury of the condition of the Deposit Banks—exhibiting among the particulars, the names of all Deposit Banks appointed since the 23d. of June last—their capitals—and the amounts of public moneys actually transferred or under orders to be transferred to them respectively.

There is such a statement recently prepared. From this and from other sources you will see the amount of money sent into States, where, before, there was never any public money deposited, or collected, or disbursed. Then you can make a strong point by showing that the Banks in which this unexpected amount of money was thus suddenly thrown were forced to lend it out to the citizens of those States,—so that these very transfers rendered natural, if not necessary, the expansion of loans and the Speculations which followed.

The second Resolution would be thus:

That the Secretary be requested to furnish a detailed statement of all transfers of public monies ordered since the 23d of June last, for the purpose of executing the distribution law,—showing the dates and amounts of such transfers, from what place to what place—from what Bank to what Bank—and the times allowed for such transfers respectively. Also a similar statement of all transfers made for disbursements other than those under the distribution law.[1]

Let me know—when you know—the probable result, and believe me always Yours very truly   N.B.

LC. DLC.
   1. On December 20, DW introduced these two resolutions, almost

verbatim, before the Senate. *Congressional Globe,* 24th Cong., 2d sess., p. 34.

Washington Decr. 23. 1836

Dear Sir

Allow me to remind you that my acceptance of your drft falls due in Boston, Decr. 27/30—days which are close at hand. H. W. Kinsman Esquire is my agent there, as I believe I informed you. As I rely on your being able to send the means to him, I hope you have been able to dispose of one or both of the [David Lee?] Child notes.[1] Lest you should not have done so, I send you a draft on myself, accepted, for $3,000 in 20 days—to be used in case of necessity. If, in neither of these modes you can get the cash, you must draw on me, here, at 3 days sight, & get the money for the drft, on *some* terms. As there is not time for me to get an answer from you, & then write to Boston, I must rely on your sending the money to Mr. K. in season, though you borrow the money for the shortest time, & at a sacrifice. I *hope* you will be able to get it from the Child notes; but if not, use my acceptance, or draw on me, here, at the short [time] above mentioned.

I have contrived to take up *both* the protested Bills (13,000 each) & if I can get along with this acceptance at Boston, there is nothing else to be attended to, in this pinching moment.

We have broken up Mr Woodbury's Order. Mr. Rives' amendment was but a mode of avoiding what seemed censure on the President.

Nobody, but Mr Benton, appeared to be for continuing the order.

Pray let me hear from you, on receipt of this, as I shall be *nervous*, till I know that some arrangement is made to meet the acceptance.

It would be bad, if the paper of one member of Congress, & of another elect, should meet with mishap. Yrs always truly   Danl Webster

ALS. NhD.
    1. Not found.

Senate-Chamber, Boston,
December 27, 1836.

My Dear Sir:

I have only time to say to you that, at the meeting of the electors yesterday afternoon (for organization, etc.), your letter was laid before them,[1] and *well received* by all of them—it will appear, with the further proceedings of to-morrow, in the newspapers of to-morrow. The consultation which took place between the members of the college yesterday was such as to leave no doubt on my mind that the vote of the members will be unanimous for yourself as President, and Mr. [Francis] Granger as Vice-President. In great haste, Yours truly, Nath. Silsbee

One, P.M. The votes have been taken, and declared as above.

Text from Curtis, 1: 539. Original not found.

1. See above, DW to Nathaniel Silsbee, November 15, 1836.

TO EDWARD EVERETT

Washington, Dec 30th. [1836]
Private
Dear Sir,
My apology for so long delaying the acknowledgement of your highly interesting letter,[1] is an indisposition under which I have been suffering for a week. Nor do I propose now to say anything on the more important part of your communication, but only, manu filiae, as you see to express my thoughts on the subject of the commonwealth's part of the surplus revenue. There are two questions, first, what ought the Commonwealth to do; second, what ought you to recommend. Without having time to state all the grounds of my opinion, I will say on the first point, that a temporary measure like that adopted in Rhode Island, is most expedient. Deposit all the money among all the banks in the Commonwealth, in proportion to their respective capitals, at an interest of four or five per cent, to be called for when needed. This will give time to arrange, if it be possible to arrange, some such large and general scheme of improvement, to be accomplished by the fund, as shall be acceptable to the whole state; and in the mean time, the money will pass at once into the general business of the people, and help to relieve the pressure of the times.[2]
On the second point I am of opinion that your true policy is to abstain from any specific recommendation, and to content yourself with calling the attention of the legislature to the subject, in a very short and general way. Whatever you propose, there will be some to oppose; and as it is altogether uncertain, what may be th[e] opinion then of a majority of our friends, upon a case so novel, I would not advise you to take a lead which might not be followed.
As Julia has a party this evening, she may be very likely to think that this letter ought not to be extended on to another sheet. Accept therefore the kindest regards of us all, and expect to hear from me again in a few days on the other subject of your letter. Very truly and cordially Yours always Danl. Webster per aliam, as aforesaid.

LS by proxy (Julia Webster). MHi.
1. See above, Edward Everett to

DW, December 16, 1836.
2. Everett recommended using

Massachusetts' share of the surplus
revenue to supplement the state's
school fund. Paul Revere Frothing-

ham, *Edward Everett, Orator and
Statesman* (Boston, 1925), p. 136.

FROM DANIEL FLETCHER WEBSTER

Detroit, January 4, 1837.
At a Meeting of the Directors of the Gibraltar and Flat Rock Company,
held at Gibraltar on the 2nd inst. the following Resolution was adopted:
Resolved, That the sum of Thirty Thousand Dollars be called in and be
paid to Henry Conant,[1] Treasurer of said Company at Monroe, Monroe
County, State of Michigan, as follows, to-wit:
One Dollar per share on the 15th of February next.
One Dollar and Fifty Cents per Share on the 15th March next.
One Dollar and Fifty Cents per Share on the 15th of April next.
One Dollar and Fifty Cents per Share of the 15th of May next.
Two Dollars per Share on the 15th June next.
Upon pain of forfeiting the Shares in case of failure in pursuance of
the By-Laws of the Company.

PHINEAS DAVIS, *Secretary.*

[c. January 4, 1837]

Dear Father,
I was wrong in my statements of the times on which the assessments
on shares are payable. This will set you right. On three hundred shares
this will be considerable—you have three hundred & fifty—the assessment will amount to $2625.00. On mine it will be one hundred & twelve
& half dolls. This assessment is laid to build their canal with & meet
some other expenses for matters which the Directors think necessary to
have done—a public House for Instance—a wharf & warehouse. I don't
like this paying but I see no help for it. I have not yet been down to see
Gibraltar. Mr. [Phineas] Davis went down last Monday Jany 2d. but as
it was New Year's day & it is kept with us I thought I had better defer
to some other time.
It is doing well however. There are no shares to be bought even in
these hard times. I have not as yet done any thing about getting a steam
boat to run between Tonawanda & Gibraltar. I want time to get nat-
uralised here. They say that our petitions for a Railroad & Bank Charter
will be granted, though I think the Speaker, a Mr. [Charles W.] Whipple,[2] will do all he can against them.
I have got my sign up as atty & Counsellor & hope before the end of

winter to have business eno: to pay for it. If my books were only here I should be content.

If you would like I can perhaps get a discount of one or two thousand dollars for you when our New Macomb County Bank goes into operation.[3] If Mr. [Stephen] White can only effect to have us connected with some Bank in Boston—& have our Bills redeemable there we shall do a very great business.

Mr. Davis successors, [Elon?] Farnsworth[,] Chatham & [Frederick?] Hall[4] with many others will be our Customers & our bills will be in great demand. I see by the papers that there has been some division among the administration members on a motion of Mr. [Thomas Hart] Bentons for printing some documents from the Treasury, relating to unexpended appropriations. Is it the beginning of a division or only a temporary thing? I should not wonder if Benton was to be obliterated by the new dynasty. Caroline has been quite unwell these two last days & I have been nurse. She is better to day. With much love to Mother & Julia I remain Yr affectionate Son   Daniel F. Webster.

Printed document and ALS. MWalB.

1. Conant (1790–1851; Middlebury 1813) was a Monroe County physician and politician, having settled there about 1818 after spending a couple of years in Ohio.

2. Whipple (c. 1808–1855; West Point), a native of New York, was a Michigan legislator from Wayne County, 1835–1837, and a justice of the Michigan Supreme Court, 1838–1855.

3. The Bank of Macomb County, chartered in August 1836, first opened its doors in February 1837. Among its stockholders were Daniel Fletcher Webster, Caroline Webster, his wife, and Stephen White, Fletcher's father-in-law. Fletcher was also a member of the bank's board of directors. The first business of the bank was the disappearance of some

$40,000, unaccounted for until later when William Vandervoort and Lucius H. Pratt, major stockholders, claimed that they had taken the money to Buffalo to establish the bank's credit. L. M. Miller, "Early Banks and Bankers of Macomb County," *Michigan Pioneer Collections*, 5 (1884): 474–475.

4. Farnsworth (b. 1799), a native of Woodstock, Vermont, had gone to Detroit in 1822, where he ran for governor in 1839, and later served as attorney general, 1843–1845. Hall (1816–1883), also a native of Vermont, had settled in the West in 1835, where he worked as a storekeeper, justice of the peace, register of deeds, receiver of the U.S. Land Office, bank president, and state legislator. Chatham has not been identified.

TO HARRIETTE STORY WHITE PAIGE

Washington Jan. 8. '37

My Dear Mrs P.

I recd your note this morning,[1] with a letter for Fletcher, which I have despatched. It is just about as expeditious a course as any for letters from Boston to Detroit to come this way. So you may as well write thro me, & make use of my frank, *while it lasts.*

You will have heard from Fletcher & Caroline, by letters recd. here & forwarded. They appear to have had a rough journey, from Buffalo to Detroit. But they are young, & can bear hardening; & it will do them no harm to know early that life is not all a flower garden. To be as young as they are, & with the same flow of youthful spirits, I would willingly consent to walk five hundred miles thro' Cataraugus Swamp, & pass forty Maumees, on the ice, & up to my throat in water.

We are all pretty well. The girls complain, a little, that there are no great numbers of parties ahead, yet announced, & Mrs W. complains of cold & wind, that prevent her from walking. You know *I* never complain of any thing.

Mr. [Isaac?] Mansfield[2] is here, & has called on us, & I have called on him, but without seeing him.

Give my love to your husband & children, & believe me most truly & affectionately Yours   Danl Webster

ALS. NhD.
    1. Not found.

2. Mansfield was a dry goods merchant in Boston.

TO JAMES KENT

Washington Jan. 20. 1837

My Dear Sir

I thank you for your beautiful address to the Law Association.[1] I have read it with perfect delight. How glorious it is to dwell among the recollections of the great Dead! Your account of [Alexander] Hamilton—I say *your* account of Hamilton—amply compensates for all the loads of obloquy, that Jacobinism ever heaped upon him.

Will you do me another favor. I have a son, Danl. Fletcher Webster. In 1819, when I first saw you, at Albany, you patted his head, & held him on your knee. He has grown up, been educated at Cambridge, studied the law, was admitted last autumn, married a wife, broke away from Boston, & has gone to settle in Detroit. He has good principles, talents, ambition, & popular manners. On the great range of subjects, which embrace politics, & political morals, *he cannot think wrong.* Will you allow him to enjoy the pleasure of receiving a copy of your Address, from your own hand.

May Heaven preserve you long! Yours, mo. truly,   Danl. Webster

ALS. NNC.
    1. An address *Delivered before the Law Association of the City of New*

York, October 21, 1836 (New York, 1836).

FROM NICHOLAS BIDDLE

Phila. Jany. 20. 1837

My dear Sir,

Let me tell you how delighted I am with your protesting speech—[1] and Commodore [James] Biddle says that the manner was every way worthy of the matter.

What is to come next?

The Senate is now broken down. One thing at least has not sunk before this tempest. The Bank—thanks be to God—survives to scorn and to defy all these wretches. Very truly Yrs   N B.

LC. DLC.
   1. Biddle was referring to Webster's speech of January 16, 1837, against

Benton's expunging revolution. For the text of that speech, see *W & S*, 8: 30–35.

TO FRANKLIN HAVEN

Washington Jan. 21. 1837

My Dear Sir

I was quite glad to receive your letter of the 12th instant, & now enclose the Bill for discount.[1] As I mentioned to you, I wish the proceeds at my credit, Feb. 1.

Mason Greenwood[2] is a Merchant, at Portland. He is a man of known property & punctuality—& one of the Directors of one of the Portland Banks.

Col [David] Webster[3] is undoubtedly a man of large p[ro]p[ert]y; he bought, many years ago, in cheap times, large quantities of land of the heirs of Mr [William] Bingham, & has sold at such advance as to leave a very great profit.

I believe he has very little to do with Banks. Except some things which I know about, I believe his name is in no Bank at all, except it may be for some small affairs at Portland.

As it takes some time to have communication between us, and as the first of Feb. approaches, I will add, that if you, at any time, see reason to desire another name on this paper, or other security, it shall be furnished on demand.

The Bill superseding the Treasury Order will doubtless pass. That for restraining the sales of the public lands, or limiting them to actual settlers, I think will not. There is so much difficulty in detail, that it is next to impossible to get any thing along.

Mr [Thomas] Ewing has a project, which he thinks might pass, & do some good.[4] I hardly know what it is yet.

There will be an attempt to reduce the revenue by encreasing the list of free articles. This perhaps will be carried some length—& may include salt. But Mr [Churchill C.] Cambreleng's Bill, or any thing which strikes directly at the manufacturing interest, will not pass.[5] I am, with much regard, Yours   Danl Webster

ALS. MH-H. Haven (1804–1893) was president of the Merchants' Bank in Boston, a position he held for more than forty-five years. By this time, Webster and Haven had formed a close social and financial relationship: the Boston banker became an important source of political and financial backing while Webster was able to bring governmental business and an occasional appointment Haven's way.

1. Webster's "Bill for discount" has not been found, but it probably related to his efforts to purchase stock in the Ellsworth Land and Lumber Company, in which Greenwood and David Webster, mentioned below, were leading promoters.

2. Greenwood (1798–1844) was a West India dry goods merchant in Portland, Maine, a banker, and a large speculator in real estate. Late in 1837, he failed financially and settled in Savannah, Georgia.

3. Webster, about whom little is known, was a native of Conway, New Hampshire.

4. Ewing's "project," as Webster called it, was actually a move by Ewing, who had before the Senate a resolution to rescind the Specie Cir-

cular, and by other Whig leaders to convince their colleagues to support William C. Rives's substitute amendment of December 22, which would merely annul the circular. Rives's currency bill, so framed to avoid a direct rebuke of Jackson, called for the collection of federal revenue in "legal currency" or in the notes of specie-paying banks and a gradual elimination of bank notes under twenty-dollar denominations. With but few Democratic dissenters, Democrats and Whigs united to pass Rives's bill through the Senate on February 10 and the House on March 1, but Jackson pocket-vetoed it; and not before May 21, 1838, was Congress able to muster enough votes to repeal the Specie Circular. Glyndon G. Van Deusen, *The Jacksonian Era, 1828–1848* (New York, 1959), p. 106; Harold D. Moser, "Subtreasury Politics and the Virginia Conservative Democrats, 1835–1844" (Ph.D. dissertation, University of Wisconsin–Madison, 1977), pp. 87–89.

5. Cambreleng's bill (No. 829), to "reduce the revenue of the United States to the wants of the Government," failed to pass, as Webster predicted.

FROM ROBERT CHARLES WINTHROP

Boston Jany. 21st 1836 [1837]

Private.

My Dear Sir,

Your Protest[1] reached us last evening & is received with great enthusiasm. Great as the effect of it seems to have been in the Senate Chamber, it seems to be calculated to produce even greater effect among the People of the Commonwealth. I hope you will direct a copy of it to each & every member of the Legislature, & to as many of the Citizens as you shall chance to remember. It has been a topic of consideration among your friends here, whether it were worth while to make it the subject of Legislative action & approbation, & to cause its insertion upon the Records of the State, as it is denied admission upon those of the United States. There seems but one objection to such a course. The expunging system is unfortunately not unknown to Massachusetts' Senates. Not only was Mr. [Josiah] Quincy's Resolution of 1814 or 15 expunged by a vote in 1824, but the Clerk of the House informed me to-day, in conversation, that there was a case of actual *erasure* obliteration & mutilation of Journal, some half century or so, ago. All this, as you most justly implied in your allusion to the precedents which had been cited in the Debate, has nothing to do with the great principles in behalf of which you protested. But still the treatment of this subject by Masstts. Whigs is rendered a little delicate by these occurrences in our own history. One is loth unnecessarily to pull a string which will uncover the nakedness & expose the shame of our own beloved Commonwealth. Will you be good enough, if you have any opinions or wishes upon the subject, to put them on paper for my benefit? We need counsel here very much on this & other points. An uncounselled & unconcerted movement of one of our friends on the subject of the Tariff, a few days ago, produced any thing but a good effect. Massachusetts primâ facie was unanimous against Cambreleng's Bill. The vote upon Mr. [John Cochran] Park's order ² exhibited her in a state of great division. I hope Mr. [Abbott?] Lawrence understands that the compliment to him was struck out by his friends, as unusual & unparliamentary. It certainly was both, &, had it remained, might have cost us the good feelings of many of our present friends. What cause it is now advisable to pursue on this subject—whether to let it go by default, or to bring in strong Resolutions of Remonstrance against the Bill, & fight them through, is another moot matter upon which a word from Washington would be exceedingly acceptable. My position on the Committee to whom is referred the North Eastern Boundary Question induces me to trouble you with a question on this topic also. Is any thing doing at Washington? Can anything be done here? We passed Resolutions last year, & it seemed to me that they fell dead both upon the ears of Congress & our own Legislature.

Should you have a moment of leisure & a mature thought upon all or either of these subjects, I would use it in all confidence, but, I am sure, with great effect.

Upon the subject of your resignation, (which I have reason to believe is still upon your mind) we are all—all who have heard it named—of one mind, & I believe such a step would be met at this moment with a

Protest as sincere, though not so well reasoned, as that which we are now admiring. It is acknowledged that we have no further *claim* to you —that you have a perfect *right* to either furlough or discharge, as your own pleasure or convenience may demand. Nobody pretends that, were you never to lift hand or voice in public places again, you could be charged with not having done—nobly, doubly done, your duty to the Commonwealth & the Country. Still they will not consent to dismiss you, nor, let me add, do they deem it for your own personal advantage to be dismissed. Upon this latter point, some of your particular friends, with whom I have conversed in confidence, are very decided. It is difficult to give reasons, or to tell how exactly they come to their conclusion. Doubtless their own wishes help & strengthen their belief. But I find in many of them a steadfast faith that a continuance in the Senate will work, in the end, best for yourself, as we all know it will [be] infinitely best for all beside yourself. I ought in this latter clause, indeed, to except Mrs. Webster & your family, to whom the sacrifice attending such a continuance is well known to be severe.

Be pleased to present me respectfully to her, & to pardon anything of undue familiarity in the expression of my sentiments, or in the demand for yours. I had hoped to have reached Washington during the Winter, but the cold weather set in so severely while I was at New York about the 1st. that I feared all retreat would be cut off, unless entered upon at once. Being now fairly at work in the Council of 500, I give up all thoughts of any escape.

With great respect, Your Obt. Servt. & Friend   Robt. Chas. Winthrop

ALS. MHi.
1. DW's speech against Benton's expunging resolution was delivered in the Senate on January 16, 1837, and reprinted in *W & S*, 8: 30–35.
2. Park (1804–1889; Harvard 1824) was a Boston lawyer, state representative, and district attorney. His "order" was "that a joint committee be appointed to draft and report Resolutions requesting our Senators and Representatives in Congress, to op-

pose . . . the passage of the bill . . . to reduce the revenue of the United States to the wants of the government; also, & a Resolution expressive of the high sense of approbation entertained by this Legislature of the bold, energetic, and talented opposition already evinced by the Representative from Suffolk district, to a bill which wholly destroys the present tariff system." *Columbian Centinel*, January 18, 1837.

FROM SETH GEER

New York January 23rd 1837.
Sir
At a meeting of Gentlemen, subscribers to the "Ellsworth Land & Lum-

ber Company" held at the Astor House in this city on the 19th. Instant, the following persons were unanimously chosen Directors of said company for the ensuing year.

> Daniel Webster
> David Webster
> Seth Geer
> Harvey Raymond [1]
> Samuel Swartwout
> Thadeus A. Lawrence [2]
> and the Treasurer.
> very respectfully Your Ob. Servant
> Seth Geer Chairman

LS. DLC. Geer (1784–1847), of New York, was an architect.

1. Not identified.
2. Not identified.

FROM DANIEL FLETCHER WEBSTER

Detroit Jany 23. 1837.

My dear Father,

I received your kind letter from Washington.[1] Julia had written us that you were unwell with a cold & we were very happy to hear that you were well again. I was glad that the Michigan bill came up, when you were away for I should not have wished to have you vote against us, & you could hardly, under the circumstances I suppose, have done otherwise.

I wrote a letter the other day to Gov. Everett resigning my commission.[2] The [Boston Daily] Advocate has kept up a fire upon the subject of my appointment ever since it came out. The Editor must be hard pushed for matter. Mr. [Phineas] Davis has just written you upon the subject of a petition to Congress for the creation of a Light House at Saginaw—Lower Saginaw.[3] It is an important point & I believe the Legislature are about to memorialize Congress on the subject. I hope the bill may pass as I have bought a small interest there & of course *I* want a light house to the amount of five hundred dollars. If you think the appropriation a proper one, we hope you will not retard it. I wrote Mr. [Thomas Handasyd] Perkins a long letter the other day, full of all sorts of matters— among others that of the establishment of a Banking House in Sandwich in Canada, just over the line. I have no doubt but that with twenty thousand dollars I could make eight thousand per annum paying ten per cent for the money & all expenses besides. Several gentlemen here say that if Mr. Davis & I can get $20000 they will furnish the same & set the thing going right off. Prime, Ward & King[4] offered [Benjamin] Rathbun half a million to do the same thing with at Waterloo, just opposite Buffalo, which he was effecting when he blew up.[5] The plan is this. To borrow the money at ten per cent—if we can get it, if not, *twelve*—have an agent over there as clerk in whose name the bills should issue & then circulate. The money would be good here or if not, we could, by a broker of our own, discount the bills, give Bank of Michigan Money & the greater the discount the better it would make up for any want of circulation here. It would be a grand thing. I need have no further trouble with it than to keep an eye over matters & receive dividends. I wish some such thing could be done. It would give me a regular income (if it were but little) & I should feel safe. I hope Mr. Perkins will like the idea. It is here, as every where, nothing but command of money gives one high standing—*great* talent of course excepted, & they estimate one more by dollars than by wits. I am anxious for these things only as they serve to keep me along, before my practise is much—if I ever get good business I shall not be so anxious about speculations. I think there is a fine opening here & I hope, if my suit against the Stage Company is brought to trial, to make a good speech that will give me some character. It will be a long while first though; not before next November, if at all—I would take a thousand dollars & compromise.

I was asked the other day if I would take $1250. for one of my Toledo lots. I declined for the present. There is to be an application to Congress for a harbour at Pigeon Lake & before the Legislature of Michigan is a petition for a Rail Road Charter from the Rapids of Grand River to that point. It will bye & bye come to something, I think. St. Joseph is doing well. There is some trouble in Illinois about the Canal, but I do not believe any thing that will injuriously affect Peru. I have had several letters from [Fisher Ames] Harding and I told you, I believe, some time since that he proposed coming to Detroit & joining forces with me, in doing nothing. I wrote him that I should be very glad to have him help me. He wanted to know what your opinion of the arrangement was. I answered that you had not said but I had no doubt but that you would be well pleased with it. Do you not think that he & I could do well together? A partner would be very convenient, when one is out the other is in— when I might be East he would be here & vice versa. Harding too is a good student & as you know very steady—& in fine two heads are better than one. Caroline says that she objects only because she fears Harding will do all the work & I know you will say her ideas are too near right; but I flatter myself that if there is any difference Harding is more lazy than I am. I would like to have Harding too as a friend & confidant, in whom I could trust. I feel a good deal alone here from want of some companion to chat with now & then. Mr. [Augustus Seymour] Porter & Mr. Buck[?][6] are very kind indeed, but I have no *chums*.

Gibraltar is doing well as usual. Our charters are not yet granted. The State is going to try & get a *light house* there too. My letter ought to be luminous, with two light houses in it.

I have not done any thing about getting the proprietors of Gibraltar to unite with Tonawanda in building a Steamboat & having it run direct between the two places. It would be a great thing for Gibraltar. It is for the interest of each place to secure to itself as much as possible of what comes from the East, not so much to send it West, though unless it affords facilities for forwarding it can offer no great inducements to Eastern travel. Gibraltar then should in some way appropriate to itself some portion of the stream of commerce & navigation up the Lake. Tonawanda offers us their portion. The proprietors of the Clinton Line of packets have proposed to Tonnawanda that if they will procure some means of direct forwarding West from that place they will stop their Line there & Tonnawanda offers to join with Gibraltar in building a boat to take the transportation from Tonnawanda direct to Gibraltar—To give us a monopoly, odious word, of all the travel & forwarding on that line. If it is an object to have it, it is also an object to own some of the Steamboat Stock; I hope to be able to make the Gentlemen here understand it. Don't you think I am right?

Caroline is very well. We are going to Mr. Davis' tonight to eat some *oysters*, fresh from Baltimore. They bring them up frozen in tin cans & they really are very good.

We wrote Julia a long letter the other day & some time since one to Mother.

I am quite well & in good spirits. Constant inquiries are made of me about you. All are very anxious that you should come & see Detroit.

Please Give Caroline's & my own best love to our dear Mother & to Julia. I need not say how very very often we think of home and all we have left. Please give my regards to Dr. [Thomas] Sewall & Dr. & Mrs [Harvey] Lindsly.[7] I hope they are all well. Julia has said nothing about Mr. Charles Brown. I hope he is still the same Charles. Good night, my dear Father   Your most affectionate son—Daniel Fletcher Webster.

ALS. NhHi.

1. Not found.

2. Daniel Fletcher resigned as aide-de-camp to Henry Alexander Scammell Dearborn, commander-in-chief of the Massachusetts militia. He had

been appointed to that post on November 22, 1836.

3. Letter not found.

4. New York brokerage firm.

5. Rathbun (c. 1789–1873) was a leading developer and promoter of

Buffalo until his arrest on August 3, 1836, for forgery.

6. Not identified.

7. Lindsly (1804–1889) was a prominent Washington physician and longtime friend with whom Webster occasionally boarded in Washington. His wife, Emeline Colby Webster (1808–1892), was the daughter of Rebecca Guild Sewall and John Ordway Webster of Maine. Although Webster generally referred to Emeline as "My Dear Cousin," there is no evidence that the two were related.

In early 1837, Webster seriously contemplated a temporary retirement from the Senate, if not from politics generally. Old and in poor health, he had spent twenty of the last twenty-four years in Congress. He had overextended himself in western land speculation and his personal finances were in disarray, a situation made worse by signs of imminent national and international economic instability. He was also despondent over his own and the Whig party's poor showing in the recent presidential canvass and over the personal rivalries that still existed within his party. As he wrote to friends in the correspondence below, he explained his situation to them and told of his need for rest and relaxation from public life, a need to deal with his own personal affairs. He wanted time to travel, perhaps to Europe, and certainly again through the upper Midwest, where he now had heavy investments.

The response to Webster's retirement was as it had been in the past: his friends, indeed the country, could not afford the loss; he must remain at his station. Massachusetts and New York Whigs rallied behind him, paying him their highest respect at public meetings, and Webster bowed to their wishes. As he made his way northward upon the recess of Congress, he stopped for a few days in New York, where, at Niblo's Saloon on March 15, he delivered a major speech, setting forth his political program for the country. With the enthusiastic backing he found in New York, and later in Boston, Webster's campaign for the presidential nomination in 1840 had been launched. Going on to Marshfield, Webster there completed plans for his western tour.

TO ROBERT CHARLES WINTHROP

Washington Jan. 27. 1837

My Dear Sir

I have recd your kind & friendly letter.[1] Considering the position, in which Mass. stands, at home, on this expunging question, I doubt whether it would be wise to adopt any proceeding in the Legislature, respecting what has been done here.

Besides, the thing is done. There is no present remedy, & I believe it is better to let the transaction have its natural effect on the public mind, without any extraordinary, or unusual interference.

If the good [people] of the State are satisfied with the course adopted by Mr [John] Davis & myself, we shall be very well contented.

There is no difficulty with Mr [Abbott] Lawrence, in regard to the matter which you mention. I think the course adopted was in all respects wise.

On another subject, mentioned in your letter, I shall write you, in a very few days.

I feel, as deeply as man can feel, my obligations, high & solemn, to the People of Massachusetts. But I really need an interval, at least,—a temporary cessation—of my duties here. For fourteen years, I have had no leisure, not enough even to travel thro. my own Country. I want a year or two. If, at the expiration of that period, my services should be required, I certainly should feel bound to render them. But more of this, in a day or two.

Mrs Webster & Julia reciprocate all your kind remembrances, & desire their best regards to your wife & yourself. Will you also make my kindest & best respects to Mrs Winthrop [2]—& say to Miss Gardner, that I shake her hand, by way of congratulation, on what I understand to be a recent occurrence. But if I congratulate her much, I congratulate Mr G. more.[3]

Yours with constant esteem & regard,   D. Webster

I will send the Protest to all the members of the Legislature, as soon as printed in a decent form.

ALS. MHi. Published in PC, 2: 23.

1. See above, Winthrop to DW, January 21, 1836 [1837].

2. Eliza Cabot, née Blanchard (c. 1809–1842).

3. The Gardiners, probably some of Winthrop's in-laws, have not been identified.

TO HIRAM KETCHUM

Washington Jan. 28. 1837.

My Dear Sir

Professional & other engagements have delayed, until now, an answer to your friendly letter of the 14th of this month.[1]

I am glad if my friends think well of my remarks on the Treasury Circular, & obliged to you & others for the pains you take to distribute copies.[2]

As to a collection & publication of my Speeches on Constitutional questions, if it be thought that such a thing would do good, I would aid in the selection, make any necessary revision, & promote the general object, so far as might be in my power.[3]

The frankness & kindness of your letter, however, seem to require a free expression of my opinions, & feelings, & even of personal wishes & purposes. I shall therefore, in this letter, speak without any reserve, while you will consider me as speaking in entire confidence.

On the past, I have little to observe. Certainly, things have occurred, that I did not expect; & of the utter impolicy of the course adopted by our friends, I held a clear opinion, at all times; but my situation necessarily shut my mouth. The result has weakened us, & distracted us; & whether we shall again obtain the character of a strong, united, patriotic party, is a question of some doubt, with me. I am willing, however, to hope for the best, & act with friends, whether few or many, who will stand on ground which they can defend.

My present purpose is to relinquish my seat in the Senate, at the close of this Session. I am aware there may be some objections to that course, but I think, too, there are some political reasons for it, & I am sure there are many personal ones. I have two years yet to serve, & no more, & the Legislature of Massachusetts is so composed, that a good appointment would now be made, in my place. In the course of the next two years, we shall see something of the developments of Mr Van Buren's policy, in regard to Texas, the Tariff, & other great questions; & although we may be sure, that it will not be such as you & I are likely to approve, it may be more or less acceptable, or unacceptable, to the Country. We are to consider, too, that the *Southern* opposition to Mr. V. B. is likely to be founded in principles, to which we must always be as much opposed, as to Mr. V. B. himself.

I do not mean by this, that our friends ought to wait, & hold back from bringing forward any man of our own. That cannot be done. Somebody will move. You see already indications of another attempt to support Genl. Harrison. If there be, therefore, a body of friends, determined, at all events, to maintain some other candidate, they ought, in my judgment undoubtedly to make that purpose early known.

What I have said above, in reference to the probable developments of two years, has regard only to another question; & that is, my return to the Senate, two years hence. If our friends in Mass should then have the power, & the inclination to send me back, & it should be thought proper, on the whole, for me to resume my labours here, I should not object. The two years I propose, (subject to these casualties which belong to human life & human things) to pass, partly in some necessary attention to my own affairs, a good deal in visiting various parts of the Country, &, by possibility, finally in a *very short* visit to Europe.

If my friends should come to a resolution to place my name before the public, I should, of course, act in conformity to their wishes, & their judgment, in whatever might be supposed likely to influence the result. My only request would be, that whatever is agreed on, should be *adhered to.*

Our strength lies in the great Central States, & in the North. New York & Pa. are key stones. Whatever candidate is agreed on, in those States, will receive the support of the party, thro. the U.S. Pa., as we know, is liable to impulses, & to strange & sudden changes; yet there is a great deal of true principle, & true worth in Pa. But my opinion is, that it is among the Whigs of New York, (& beginning in the City, & beginning immediately) that a first, decisive, & *determined* step should be taken. A resolute occupying of the ground, in that quarter, will, assuredly, bring about compliance, in other quarters. Massa. & all the Whigs in the Eastern States, would, of course, if properly addressed, immediately respond to the Whigs of New York. Those of Philadelphia would do the same, with promptness; & the rest of Pa. would not be likely to keep long aloof. Delaware & Maryland, if I am rightly informed, are ready to unite in the object.

It will be easy to open communications with other States, & Cities. For the present, if you have occasion to write to Boston, address R. C. Winthrop Esqr. Albert Fearing Esqr.[4] and H. W. Kinsman Esqr.

In the Village Record, a paper published at West Chester, Chester Co., Pa. I see a large & general meeting of the Whigs, Anti Masons &c., is called for the 7th. of next month. Now this is just one of those meetings, which, if unattended to, are so likely to commit our friends. The County of Chester, one of the largest in the State, was opposed to the nomination ultimately made at Harrisburg. What their views may be, now, I cannot tell. The leading man is Henry S. Evans Esqr. of West Chester.[5] He is a warm personal friend of mine, but has not written me, on this occasion. He heads the Comm[itt]ee. which makes the call. It is of importance, doubtless, that nothing wrong should be done at this meeting; & I think a confidential letter should be written from your City, to Mr Evans, expressing your opinions, & giving a word of friendly caution in regard to any premature movement, for a Presidential nomination. I think a friendly letter would be recd. by him, in the best spirit.

Of the propriety of all this, however, you & others will judge. I only allude to the expected meeting, as one of these local meetings, which make candidates for our party, without due reference to the state of feeling in other parts of the Country. The day of meeting, you perceive, is near at hand. I have thus, my Dear Sir, spoken very freely, as your friendship required I should do. In conclusion, I have only to request, that you will use these suggestions <prudently &> confidentially, & that you & your friends will suffer no considerations of personal kindness to induce you to adopt any course, which in your judgment, the good of the whole may require. Yours very truly   Danl Webster

Mr. Evans address, is Henry S. Evans Esqr.
    West Chester, Chester Co.
    Pa.

ALS. NhD. Ketchum (c. 1792–1870) was a New York City attorney, a close personal friend of Webster, and later a leader of the Webster Whigs in the city.

1. Not found.

2. For DW's speech on the Specie Circular, see *W & S*, 8: 3–26.

3. A publication specifically devoted to Webster's "Speeches on Constitutional questions" has not been found. Ketchum's project possibly was aborted; perhaps, however, Ketchum directed his energies toward either the reissuance of *Speeches and Forensic Arguments* (2 vols., 1838,

1839) or the initial publication of James Rees, *The Beauties of the Hon. Daniel Webster . . .* (New York, 1839).

4. Fearing (1798–1875), a native of Hingham, Massachusetts, had established himself as a ship-chandler in Boston about 1833, where he became active as a Whig politician.

5. Evans (1813–1872), a journalist and legislator, was owner and editor of the West Chester *Village Record.* In the 1840s and afterward, he served in the Pennsylvania House of Representatives and Senate.

TO [EDWARD EVERETT]

Washington Jan 31. 1837

Private
My Dear Sir,
    Some continuance of ill health, after I wrote you last, & very close occupation, since I recovered, must be my excuse for leaving so long unanswered, an important part of your letter of Decr.[1]
    Your desire to go abroad is very natural, & the probability that such a movement would improve Mrs Everetts health seems to raise to the class of duties, what I presume would at all times be to you an agreeable thing. I should feel regret, that you should leave your present situation. We might have trouble in filling your place. Still, I am bound by duty & friendship to say, that if professional advice & your own conviction concur, that Mrs Everetts health requires a visit to Europe, in my opinion you ought to make it. Your declining would probably bring up several candidates, & there might, perhaps, be no choice, by the People. Still I am inclined to hope that we might preserve the State, by concerted action, & a good spirit.
    I have this day written to Mr Kinsman, a letter to be shown to friends, intimating my intention to resign my seat, at the end of this Session.[2] He will show it to you, no doubt. I place my resignation on the ground

of a strong wish for some respite—some leisure—after a continued service of fourteen years.

My purpose is, for the next two years, to travel, in my own Country, &, by possibility, to make a trip of 6 months to Europe. My own affairs, too, require looking after, & I should be glad to be able so to arrange them, as to be able to live, without pursuing, much longer, my profession.

I would as willingly hold on till the fall, as resign now, but have thought it might be better, or be thought better, that the present Legislature should have an opportunity of filling the place.

On the other hand, it is possible our friends may think that the prospect of having a Senator to choose, may create a new interest in the fall Elections, which would be favorable. I hope that friends, & especially that you, will write me fully & freely, in regard to these points.

Your communication, at the opening of the Session, was exceedingly satisfactory to friends here. I am glad to learn that it was so well recd at home. I could have wished, certainly, for another distribution of the money, deposited with the State; but am glad you left it to the Legislature.

Here, we are yet on the Land law, which I do not think will get thro. both Houses, & the bill respecting the *payments*, of revenue, &c which will pass, probably, in some shape. As to the Tariff, Mr [Silas] Wrights bill, with some modifications, may perhaps pass; but there is no danger of any thing's being done, materially affecting the manufacturing interest. There seems to be a general disposition to leave things, for the present, to the operation of the Act of 1833.

We hear not one word yet from the Court respecting the Bridge cause.[3] Yours, always truly   Danl Webster

Do not fail to give my love to yr wife & daughter.

ALS. MHi. Published in *PC*, 2: 24–25.
1. See above, Everett to DW, December 16, 1836.
2. See DW to Henry Willis Kinsman, January 31, 1837, mDW 14008; DW to Kinsman, February 1, 1837, below; and DW to Robert Charles Winthrop, January 31, 1837, mDW 14010.
3. *Charles River Bridge* v. *Warren Bridge*, 11 Peters 420 (1837).

TO HENRY WILLIS KINSMAN

Washington Feb. 1. 1837.

My Dear Sir,

On reflecting on what I wrote you yesterday,[1] it has occurred to me, that there are one or two points, in regard to which I ought to say something more.

It may be thought, possibly, that the notice of my intended resignation is sudden, & unexpected; so that the Legislature may not be prepared to fill the place. Or, perhaps, it may be thought, that the State elections, next fall, would be more safe, if it were known that a Senator were to be elected.

If our friends, generally, should entertain these opinions, or either of them; & should therefore think that it will be better that I should not resign till the fall, I should of course readily adopt that course. I do not wish to throw out these ideas, beforehand; because, in my judgment, it is better that I should resign now. But still, if our friends should think other wise, I shall yield to their judgment.

You will use what I have here said, therefore, if you find it necessary. But if there should be a ready acquiescence in the idea of my present resignation, it will not be necessary, of course.

I hope you & other friends will consult freely—& fully—& gather the general sentiment of all the Whigs—& let me know the result, as soon as you can. Yrs truly   Danl Webster

ALS. MHi. Published in *W & S*, 16:   1. See mDW 14008.
282.

FROM HENRY SHAW

Feb. 8. 37

Dear Sir

My impressions and opinions are altogether opposed to the course indicated in your letter.[1] It will be freely acknowledged by every one that your service has been long and arduous, & at great pecuniary sacrifice— that its course has been marked with patience & patriotick devotion, and that the State, for services always able, and on occasions unsurpassed by none in splendour, is vastly your debtor. But she has given you her confidence, her devotion, & has on no occasion rebuked or distrusted— this is all a State can do. It is after all no poor distinction to hold *such a State* as Massts under obligation, and it is no small reward for service, to feel & know that she acknowledges with gratitude the full extent of her obligations.

I was sincerely pained to hear your decision. But that is revokable— and My Dear Sir let me ask you to reconsider it. There are reasons both Publick, & Personal to yourself, that I think have weight in imposing this request. It is not necessary to give them at length. Your retirement now would discourage the Whigs of the Union—and probably change Massts.

In the State we are now but just alive—the contest for your place would weaken, by souring probably some prominent men. We cannot afford to loose any. Your retirement would be used every where, as a surrender of all hope. Few like a falling Party. The Whig influence, is a moral influence—this would be greatly impaired. In truth I think, Clay, Calhoun & yourself, representing the peculiar opinions, & embodying the general principles of the Whigs, in connexion with your local positions, at this moment constitute the hope & the strength of that Party—future prospects personally & Publickly depend on your remaining, all of you, in the Senate. I have, some time since made the same suggestion to Mr. Clay—the Country is entering upon a new scene—and no one can tell to what crisis the new Ad[ministratio]n may lead us.

I could *say* much more to you than I dare write. But I certainly hope you will recall the decision. Mr. Clay will stay & so will Calhoun—the East must also be represented—and you must stay. If I was not entirely a private Citizen, & look therefore upon Publick affairs, wholly uninfluenced by personal feelings, I should distrust my own judgment when I found it conflicting with yours. But I feel sure I am right on this subject. Our personal relations would hardly authorize even what I have said, but depend upon it I have no sentiments inconsistent with a generous regard for your future prospects, whatever impressions may be entertained to the contrary. Consider you have asked me for an opinion, & the confidence the request involves would alone have made me your friend. The State will not allow you to retire—the Whigs will forbid it, the Country do not expect it.

Excuse the length of this & believe me cordially yours   H: Shaw

ALS. NhD.   DW's letter to Kinsman, January 31,
    1. Shaw was probably referring to   1837, mDW 14008.

TO HIRAM KETCHUM

Washington Feb. 11. 1837

My Dear Sir,

It seems to be the opinion of the most judicious friends here, as well as in Boston, that, without reference to considerations of personal convenience, & looking only to political consequences, it would be wise for me to retire, at least for a time, from the Senate. The reasons of this opinion, are various, some general, & some special.

I feel fully the great importance of keeping myself with the Whigs of your City. I look upon them, not only as containing many of the most valued & important of my personal friends, but as being, in the aggregate, the only source, to which we are to look for any effectual & vigorous first movement to establish a better state of things in the Country.

Will you allow me to make a suggestion—which, if not done in this confidential way, would appear to manifest a desire for tokens of respect, which I certainly do not feel. You observed, in a letter sometime ago,[1] that I must make a *Speech*, before leaving the Senate. Now, would it not be better, that some occasion should be found for my making a *Speech in N. York*? An occasion, which should give that opportunity, might be used, also, for the expressing a hope, that I might not be long absent, from Congress &c.; & a proper reply to this would make known the light in which my resignation is to be viewed; not as a withdrawal from public life, but as a temporary retirement, &c.&c. You will think of this, & let me know how it strikes you. I hope to be in N. York about the 10th. or 12th. March.[2]

Joseph McIlvaine Esqr. late recorder of Philadelphia, & whom you probably know, is now at Harrisburg, & a leading Whig, among the few Whigs in the H. of R. of Pa. He is personally a friend of mine, & should be written to. Mr. W[illiam W.] Irwin, of Pittsburg, & Harmar Denny, of Pittsburg, now a member of Congress, should also be written to, in due time.

At Baltimore, perhaps as good a man as any to open consultation with, is Jno. P. Kennedy Esquire.

James W. McCulloch is also an important man.[3]

I shall be very glad to see Mr [Hamilton] Fish.

At present, I am so much pressed with affairs, & with company, that it is very difficult for me to find time to answer half my letters. This must be my apology for so meager a reply, to *two* of yours, now on hand.[4] Yrs very truly   Daniel Webster

ALS. Warren A. Reeder, Hammond, Indiana.

1. Not found.

2. According to DW's suggestion, a group of New York Whigs invited Webster to address them, and on March 15, 1837, he attended a reception at Niblo's Saloon, where he discussed politics and announced that he had abandoned the idea of resigning. See David Bayard Ogden to DW, March 2, 1837, below; DW to Ogden, March 4, 1837, mDW 14139; and DW to Philip Hone, March 5, 1837, in Curtis, 1: 556. Webster's Niblo's Saloon speech is printed in *W & S*, 2: 193–230.

3. McCulloch, a native of Maryland and former cashier of the Baltimore branch of the Bank of the United States, had been the defendant in *McCulloch* v. *Maryland*, 4 Wheaton 316 (1819).

4. Not found.

TO DANIEL FLETCHER WEBSTER

Washington Feb. 12. 1837

My Dear Son

We have recd your letters, down to the end of last month,[1] & they have given us much pleasure. Some of them I have sent for perusal to friends, elsewhere. My own engagements have been such that I have not been able to write you, for some time past.

We have had the old Bridge cause up again.[2] Its argument was very laborious. It will be decided tomorrow, & we shall *lose* it. The fact is, *political* opinion has got on to the Bench, & it is in vain to deny. The old judges will be one way; the new ones (a majority) the other.

I have got thro all my business in the Court, & doubt whether I shall ever argue another cause in it.

I have written to friends in Boston, signifying my purpose of resigning my seat in the Senate, at the close of the present Session. In all points of view, I think this is judicious. I want leisure, at least for some time.

In the course of the summer, or in the fall, I intend going to Detroit. It is a point of some difficulty to settle what is the best season of the year. Your roads will not be dry till the middle of June; but that is too late to go as far south as I intend. My notion at present is, that I will leave Boston the first day of September—go direct to Detroit—& take Mrs W. & Julia so far—then consider how I can get best on to the Upper Mississippi—& if they cannot go with me, contrive to get them escorted South to the Ohio River—& meet them at Cincinnati. You & Caroline must come East in such season as to make your visit, & be ready to return with us, Sep. 1st.

I have very good accounts from *Peru*, & am looking for Mr [Henry L.] Kinney here, every day. I have also taken an interest in some small purchases in Wisconsin, which look well.

As to the Gibraltar installments, you will manage them as you think best. For whatever is necessary, you will either draw on me, or give me notice, in season, to enable me to remit. I shall not undertake to keep the run of the several times of payment. You must see to all that.

If on the whole you think it advisable that [Fisher Ames] Harding should join you, I shall not object. You must take care that it does not lead you to neglect Office business. I must give you a similar hint, in regard to business not professional. You must remember that *Professional Eminence* is the great point to be aimed at. In a new Country there are other things, which it may be very well to have interest in, so as to have something which shall rise in value with the growth of the Country. But you will find no pursuit permanently gratifying, except your profession.

In some of your letters you suggested an object of speculation at Saganaw, & another in Canada. I have sent those letters to friends, to see if there be any thing in these projects, which they would like to take hold of. I should not recommend you to have any thing to do, unless some great object was to be obtained by it, with any Banking operations in Canada. That would tend to make you, in the end, but a mere cashier. Stick to the law.

As to these large Co's, my opinion is, it is better for us, at least, with our little means, to keep pretty much aloof from them, & if we have any thing to invest, put it where we can control it ourselves.

The land bill—confining sales to actual settlers—has passed the Senate. Its fate in the House is uncertain; perhaps the chances about equal.

The Bill abolishing the Treasury Order has also passed the Senate, & will no doubt pass the House.

I shall give good attention to all your Light House matters.

With much affection for Caroline, always Yrs (with a rascally steel pen)   D Webster

ALS. R. M. Engert, Washington, D.C.   January 23, 1837.
1. See DFW to DW, January 17,   2. *Charles River Bridge* v. *Warren*
1837, mDW 13748, and above,   *Bridge*, 11 Peters 420 (1837).

TO JEREMIAH MASON

Washington Feb. 13. 1837

My Dear Sir

The Bridge cause will be decided today, & decided wrong. The three old judges, [Joseph] Story, [Smith] Thompson & [John] McLean will be for reversing the judgment of the State Court; the four new judges, [Roger B.] Taney, [Henry] Baldwin, [James M.] Wayne & [Philip P.] Barbour for affirming. Perhaps I ought to qualify this remark by saying, that Judge McLean, not doubting on the merits, has doubts about the jurisdiction; which doubts, I believe, nobody else entertains.

The Court is revolutionized. Politics have gotten possession of the Bench, at last, & it is in vain to deny, or attempt to disguise it.

Taney is smooth & plausible, but cunning & Jesuitical & as thorough going a party judge as ever got on to a bench of justice. He is a man who wears his robes for the purpose of protecting his friends, & punishing his enemies. Baldwin is naturally a confused & wrong-headed creature, very opinionated, & intriguing. In some two or three years, he has talked loud about vested rights & constitutional securities; but he has gone back to his first love, is paying all court to the new chief Justice, means to be well with the powers that be.

Wayne is a gentlemanly man, naturally fair enough, & would follow the lead, when on the right side, when such men as [John] Marshall & Story had the power of giving the lead. But he is not of great fame, &

feels, I have no doubt, that on constitutional questions he is not expected to differ from his friends.

Barbour, I really think is honest & conscientious; & he is certainly intelligent; but his fear, or hatred, of the powers of this government is so great, his devotion to State rights so absolute, that perhaps [a case] could hardly arise, in which he would be willing to exercise the power of declaring a state law void.

The Constitution is now in these hands; & God only knows what is to save it from destruction. Three constitutional questions have been argued this term. They will all be decided one way, Story dissenting in all.[1] In a case, which raised the question whether the bills of the Commonwealth Bank of Kentucky were "bills of credit," he read a dissenting opinion, I think decidedly the ablest I ever heard from him. Today he will, I presume, deliver an opinion also, in the Bridge cause.

Judge Thompson, a very honest man, & bred in a good school, for general law learning, but with some original biasses agt. the powers of the judiciary of the Govt, is getting to be an old man; & McLean though tolerably fair, is, after all, not more than half right, on constitutional questions, nor hardly that. Indeed he is a judge by compulsion. It is not his chosen plane, & he is constantly looking out for the chances of obtaining a high popular office.

In this situation of the Court, Judge Story has decided on leaving the Bench, & I think he is right. He can add nothing to his reputation by staying on it, & will only subject himself to continual mortification. He will be expected to conduct all the ordinary business of the Court, & on all great questions will be voted down.

His wish is to get some situation in Boston, like the presidencey of an Insurance office, which may give him 2500 or 3000 Dlls a year; & to live on this, & his income from his professorship. As soon as something of this sort can be arranged, he will resign his commission. Mr [Abbott] Lawrence[2] will write to Mr William Appleton, today, in relation to this matter; & it is the leading purpose of this letter to ask you to confer with Mr Appleton. In the mean time, the Judge, I presume, would wish nothing said on the subject, until such an arrangement shall be made, as shall justify his resignation. The sooner this object can be completed, the better. Yrs with constant regard,   Danl. Webster

Typed copy (incomplete), NhHi; ALS (incomplete), NhD.

1. *New York* v. *Miln*, 11 Peters 102 (1837); *Briscoe* v. *Bank of Kentucky*, 11 Peters 257 (1837); *Charles River*

Bridge v. *Warren Bridge*, 11 Peters 420 (1837).

2. The remainder of this letter is transcribed from the ALS fragment.

TO ROBERT CHARLES WINTHROP, WITH ENCLOSURE

Feb. 15 [1837]

Private

My Dear Sir,

I write a letter, to be shown, if you see fit, to the Comee. & other friends.[1]

You must, at proper time, put the case fairly to them.

If they say, I must hold on, till the fall; *they must take the chances of the next election.* Yours, with cordial Esteem   D.W.

ALS. MHi.

1. See enclosure, below. As indicated in the letter from Winthrop et al., February 15, below, the Whig legislators met on the evening of the same day to discuss Webster's proposed resignation.

ENCLOSURE: TO ROBERT CHARLES WINTHROP

Washington Feb. 15. 1837

My Dear Sir

I am obliged to you for your letter.[1]

I am sorry that our friends should see any objection, to my resignation, at the close of this Session. It has appeared to me, that that time would be suitable & convenient, considering the character of the present Legislature, & the uncertainty of all that is future.

I pray you all to be satisfied, that my desire to resign, for the residue of the term, does not spring from disgust, altho. there is much here to disgust one, nor from despair, altho' there is enough to discourage us. But my real object is to get some little time for my own affairs. I really do not see how I can attend the next Session of Congress.

Of course, I should have no objection to retain my situation till the fall, were it not that it appears to me, & to friends here, that the good of the whole requires that an opportunity should be afforded to the Legislature to fill the vacancy, at the present Session.

As a good deal of time remains, I still incline to think any apparent difficulties, which may now show themselves, will vanish before the termination of your Session.

I shall be pleased to hear from you, and other friends; & pray you all to believe that I retain my zeal for the good cause, undiminished, & my ardent attachment to my friends, in no degree cooled. With great personal regard, Yours   Danl Webster

ALS. MHi. Published in *PC*, 2: 27.

1. Not found. Occasionally on personal and political matters of this nature Webster communicated with

a friend as if he were answering a letter, when, in fact, he had not received one. Such may have been the case here.

FROM ROBERT CHARLES WINTHROP ET AL.

Boston. Feb. 15. 1837.
Sir,

At a meeting of the Whig Members of the Legislature of Massachusetts, held this evening & which has within a few moments been dissolved, the enclosed Resolutions[1] were unanimously adopted.

In discharging the duty of communicating them to you, we beg leave to assure you, Sir, that they were adopted in no spirit of heartless ceremony, but from a strong, deep, unfeigned feeling of the sentiments which they express.

We have the honor to subscribe ourselves Your Friends & Ob. Servts.

Robt. Chas. Winthrop
Charles Hudson
Samuel B. Walcott[2]
Osmyn Baker
} Committee

ALS, by Winthrop, signed also by others. NhD.

1. Not found.
2. Walcott (1795–1854; Harvard 1819) had studied law with DW and also tutored Fletcher before his admission to Harvard. For more than twelve years he represented Hopkinton in the Massachusetts legislature.

TO HIRAM KETCHUM

Washington, February 20, 1837.
My Dear Sir,

I write at this moment, merely to say, that my friends in Massachusetts make so much opposition to my resignation at the present moment, that in all probability I must defer the execution of that purpose till the fall. At the very earliest possible leisure, I shall write you, in answer to your last friendly letter.[1] Yours, with very sincere regard,

Daniel Webster.

Text from PC, 2: 27–28. Original not found.

1. Not found.

TO DANIEL FLETCHER WEBSTER

Washington Feb. 20. 1837
My Dear Son,

I have recd your letters, down to the 11th. instant.[1] In regard to the assessments, on Gibraltar Stock, my wish is that you pay the assessments on my shares, & all standing in my name; & also on Govr. [John] Davis'. That is more convenient, than to draw a small bill on him. You may draw on me, at whatever time you find convenient, & for whatever sums the object may require.

Since I wrote you last, I have altered my plan, for a western tour.[2] I think of leaving home, the latter part of April, & proceeding by way of Pittsburg, Lexington, Louisville, St. Louis &c, work our way northerly, & reach Detroit about the 10. or 15. June, so as to be home, July 1.

On this matter, we shall write you farther hereafter. We are all well. Soon after you receive this, we shall be *in itinere* for Boston. You can after the receipt of this, direct your letters here, for 3 or 4 days; & they will follow me to N. York. Afterwards, direct to Boston. You need not fear the loss of my *frank*, till you hear further. The Whigs of Boston are in commotion, agt. my proposed resignation. Still, either now or in the fall, I must resign—I want some time to myself.

I have made several operations, this winter. If they turn out well, they will come to something. Still, I rely much on Gibraltar. When I reach Detroit, we will look out a farm, on Lake St. Clair.

With all true love to Caroline. Yrs affectionately   D.W. (over)

Gen[era]l [John E.] Swartz[3] has arrived—& dines with me tomorrow.

P.S. Being a land owner in Michigan, & thinking it likely that some controversies may arise, in regard to certain titles, I am desirous of securing for myself, in case of need, the great benefit of your able Professional services.

I therefore enclose a Bank Note, for $100, which I will thank you to enter on your Retainer Book. Yrs respectfully   Danl. Webster

I have sent yr. letter, containing an acct. of the Ball, to Capt [John] Thomas.

ALS. R. M. Engert, Washington, D.C.
1. See DFW to DW, February 11, 1837, mDW 14042.
2. See above, DW to DFW, Febru-

ary 12, 1837.
3. From Swartzburg, Michigan, Swartz was a local tavernkeeper, one of DFW's close friends.

TO ROBERT CHARLES WINTHROP, WITH ENCLOSURE

Washington Feb. 22. 1837

My Dear Sir,

I enclose a letter to the Committee.[1] You will perceive I have concluded to let the matter of my resignation go by the present Session. When I reach home, I shall ask the favor of a personal interview with the

Comee. I hardly know whether it is worth while to say any thing, in the Newspapers, unless it be some such remarks, as, that, "Mr. Webster's friends have strongly solicited him, not to leave the Senate, at the present moment." I have, indeed, recd. an overwhelming number of wishes, to that effect. Of the propriety of causing any remarks to be made in the papers, however, I leave you to judge.[2]

We are exceedingly busy, with the measures before us; but what will be done, & what left undone, no mortal can tell.

We have no mail today from Boston. Yrs, mo. truly always,

Danl Webster

ALS. MHi. Published in *PC*, 2 : 28.
1. See enclosure below.
2. A week later (March 4, 1837), the *Columbian Centinel* reported "that Mr. Webster, at the earnest solicitation of his friends in Boston, and at Washington, has abandoned the idea of resigning his seat in the United States Senate."

ENCLOSURE: TO ROBERT CHARLES WINTHROP, CHARLES HUDSON, SAMUEL B. WALCOTT, OSMYN BAKER

Washington Feb. 23. 1837

Gentlemen,

I duly recd your letter of the 15th inst, communicating certain Resolutions of the Whig members of the Legislature.[1]

My desire to relinquish my seat in Congress, for the residue of the term for which I was chosen, is sincere & strong; & springs from causes, but little connected with the situation of public affairs. Your communication, however, has brought me to a pause. I feel, that I ought not to disregard the wishes of friends, so decisively expressed. Postponing, till I shall have the pleasure of a personal interview, with yourselves & others, a part of what I could wish to say, I will now only observe, that I shall not create the necessity for a new choice, at the present session, of the Legislature, unless, on my arrival in Massachusetts, I should find a change in the opinions & wishes of friends.

I cannot express the gratitude I feel for the confidence & kindness, manifested by the Whig members of the Legislature, & by yourselves. My best & most faithful services are due to the People of Massachusetts; & I regret that I am able to do so little, for her honor & interest, & for the good of the whole Country.

With much & cordial personal regard, I am your friend & ob. servt

Danl Webster

ALS. MHi. Published in *PC*, 2 : 28–29.
1. See above.

FROM DAVID WEBSTER

New York Feb. 22nd 1837

Dear Sir

Yours of the 19[1] I got this morning am quite as sorry of the mistake respecting the acceptance as you can be, will try to make it satisfactory to you when I see you.[2] I send you four scrips of ten thousand dollars each. One of ten I keep to make me a Director. I have fixed the 100 shares that you subscribed as follows. I have given my notes $2000— to be paid 1st. day of April $5000 the 9th day of July[.] I have paid the remainder of the whole out of a part of what was coming to me from land that I sold say on 39—and the whole 100— shares is now paid up and the stock stand to you clear for you to take your certyficates any time by asking Mr [William Pitt] Fessenden. As soon as you can get to Boston pleas write me at Portland and I will come and see you. I assure you that the stock and all things look well of the Ellsworth concern. Should you want any more scrips all you will have to do is to write to Fessenden and he will send them to you. I have this moment had some conversation with him respecting the same. I leave tomorrow for Portland pleas write me if you think of any thing worth your attention. I shall be glad to hear from you at any time when you will take the trouble to write.

I am glad to hear that Col. [Samuel Ayer] Bradley has got to Washington but hope that he will not trouble his friend too much in ta[l]king about Judge [Judah] Dana. I have been to see Mr [Herman?] Le Roy his health is improving.

My best respects to Mrs. Webster & Julia. Yours very truly

David Webster

PS It is said for a certainty that R[e]uel Williams of Augusta is the Senator elected to take the place [of] Dana.   DW

ALS. NhHi.

1. Not found.

2. Most likely Daniel Webster had written David Webster about protested drafts held by the Commonwealth Bank of Massachusetts. In early 1838, just as Congress and the Massachusetts legislature were investigating the affairs of the collapsed bank, the *Washington Globe* charged that the two Websters' financial affairs had been a significant factor in the bank's failure. According to the *Globe*, which probably received its information from William M. Jarvis, Albert Gallup, George W. Owens, and Henry Allen Foster, Daniel Webster had allowed two drafts for $10,000 each on David Webster and another draft by C. S. Fowler on Daniel Webster for $3,057 to lie protested for nonpayment. These drafts had been made to raise funds for the Ellsworth Bank and Lumber Company and were finally paid in the fall of 1837 by Samuel Swartwout, New York customs collector and a stockholder in the company. See [William M. Jar-

vis?] to Albert Gallup, January 18,
Albert Gallup to George W. Owens
and Henry A. Foster, January 28,
[1838], copies misdated 1839 in the

Albert Gallup Papers, NN; *Washington Globe*, January 20, 23, February
2, 1838; *Portland Daily Eastern
Argus*, February 7, 1838.

TO HIRAM KETCHUM

Washington, Friday morning,
February 24, 1837.

My Dear Sir,

The New York mail having failed yesterday, your two letters of the 21st and 22d[1] were received together this morning.

I regret that my note did not reach you a day or two earlier,[2] but we will, nevertheless, endeavor so to manage as to prevent embarrassment. The meeting may go on, under some modification, such as Mr. [David Bayard] Ogden suggested in his letter received by me this morning.[3]

If this should reach you before the official communication shall be despatched, it may be modified to meet the case. The case is, that the Whigs in the Massachusetts legislature, have made a decided objection to my resigning, so early as to make it necessary for them to fill the place, at the present session of the legislature. I have told them in reply, that I would not do any thing which should call on them to choose a successor this session.[4] I shall send you by this evening's mail, their communication to me, in order that you may see that I have not changed my purpose lightly.

If on the arrival of this, the official communication should not be despatched, you may, if you judge proper, alter and accommodate the phraseology, so as to read that "understanding it is my intention now or shortly to resign my seat," &c.[5]

If the communication should be sent, I will examine it, and if necessary can answer it, as if it had read as above mentioned, and the necessary modifications can be made afterwards.

I send this by the express mail, to relieve your embarrassment as soon as I can. Yours, truly,   Daniel Webster.

P.S. I will look over the copy of the resolutions which you have sent,[6] but which I have not had time to read; make any alterations which the case may seem to require, and return it by this evening's mail.

Text from *PC*, 2: 29–30. Original
not found.
   1. Not found.
   2. See above, DW to Hiram Ketchum, February 20, 1837.

3. Not found.
   4. See above, DW to Robert Charles
Winthrop, February 15, 1837.
   5. See David Bayard Ogden to DW,
March 2, 1837, below, the wording of

which conforms to Webster's recommendation.

6. See DW to Hiram Ketchum,
February 24, [1837], below.

TO HIRAM KETCHUM

Senate, 1 oclock. Feb. 24. [1837]

Dear Sir

I have looked over the enclosed [resolutions], & made only two alterations. One near the beginning. You can alter this language, in any manner, which may be judged advisable; so as to leave my resignation a matter, to be expected soon, rather than fixed down to the end of this
Session, precisely.

The other alteration changes the word *indivisible*, into *inseparable*—
to correspond with the expression, used by me, & which is intended to be
quoted.[1] Yrs truly   D Webster

ALS. DLC.
    1. Ketchum's resolutions, prepared
upon consultation with Webster and
adopted by Webster's New York
friends when he addressed them at
Niblo's Saloon on March 15, are conveniently printed in the *National Intelligencer*, March 18, 1837.

TO DANIEL FLETCHER WEBSTER

Washington Feb. 24. '37

My Dear Son,

There is now *some* probability, that both the land bill,[1] & the bill rescinding, in effect, the Treasury Order, may pass. Should that be the
case, there will be a scramble for Govt. lands, till May 1st. when the
land bill will go into operation, & stop the sales. If you have any knowledge, or can obtain any, of good lands, at Govt. prices, it will be well to
be prepared. It will be a week, after you receive this, before you will know
the fate of the bills. Should both pass, & should you know lands, which
could be entered, with prospect of a handsome profit, you may lay out
2.000 Dlls for me, & draw on me for the money. I will give you due
notice. Be careful not to buy poor land, for the sake of buying; but look
sharp, & be sure of good lands, if you buy any.

I will give you early notice, & a regular authority to draw, if the ex-
igency arises. Yrs   D. Webster

ALS. R. M. Engert, Washington, D.C.
    1. The preemption bill failed to pass.

TO FRANKLIN HAVEN

Washington Feb. 27. 1837

Dear Sir

I am obliged to you for your letter,[1] which I recd this morning.

It was my purpose to have called up, today, the Bill for paying off the French Indemnities; but in regard to this, as well as other matters, we are thrown into a state of confusion, by the vote of the H. of R. tacking another *Distribution Bill* to the fortification Bill. The H. passed this amendment, by 23 votes majority. The Comee. on Finance will recommend the Senate *not* to agree to this; & I presume, tho' I am not certain, that the Senate will *not agree*—what will ensue therefore, I cannot foresee. You will lament, with me, that our course of proceeding is so irregular, & that we attach one great measure to the tail of another. But unhappily the state of things in the other House is such, (and is daily growing worse) that no regularity is to be expected.

This vote will very probably have much bearing on the passing of the land Bill. It may prevent it. If the land Bill should fail, I incline to think we may look out for a *veto*, on the Bill rescinding the Treasury Order.

On the whole, My Dear Sir, it is quite uncertain, even at this advanced hour of the Session, what will be the fate of all the great measures.

About the 20th. of April, I expect to leave Boston for the West; & at that time should be glad to obtain a discount at your Bank, pretty large for me, say 10. or 20 thousand dollars. I shall have acceptances, which I doubt not you will think good; I have also my scrip, in the Detroit Land Co. (Mr [Benjamin Berry] Kercheval's[2] Company) & other things, which I would leave as collateral. I mention this now, that you may, with your usual kindness, keep an eye, so far as proper, to the state of your funds at that time, in connexion with this request.[3]

It seems generally understood that Mr [Benjamin F.] Butler is to remain in the Office of Atty Genl—& that Mr. [Joel Roberts] Poinsett is to be Secretary of War. Probably there will be no other changes, in the heads of Departments. Yrs with true regard   Danl. Webster

ALS. MH-H. Published in *W & S*, 16: 286–287.

1. Not found.
2. Kercheval (1793–1855), a native of Winchester, Virginia, had settled in Detroit in the late 1820s, after serving a short stint as pension agent in Fort Wayne, Indiana. Elected as alderman in Detroit in 1830, he later served in the state legislature. In 1835 he was a director of the Detroit to St. Joseph Railroad Company.
3. Haven endorsed this letter as follows:
"This letter refers to a loan for Mr.

Webster[.] All loans proposed by him, were at his request, acted upon by the Directors.

"I have no recollection of the Loan, the letter refers to. If it was made, it was *good*, and was duly paid,—as was all the paper that the Bank ever discounted for Webster. I do not think he owed the Bank at *any one time* an amount so large as $10,000 dollars. If the discount mentioned by him was made it was extraordinary *in amount*, and was perfectly satisfactory.

"I write this memorandum March

1888—51 years after the date of Mr.   "Mt. Vernon Street"
Webster's letter to me.

FROM DAVID BAYARD OGDEN

New York March 2nd. 1837.

Sir

It having been currently reported that you had signified your intention to resign your seat in the Senate of the United States, a number of the Friends of the Union and of the Constitution in this city were convened on the Evening of the 21st. of last month, to devise measures whereby they might signify to you the sentiments which they, in common with all the Whigs in this city, entertain for the eminent services you have rendered to the country. At this meeting the honorable James Kent was called to the Chair and resolutions, a copy of which I enclose to you, were adopted,[1] not only with entire unanimity but with a feeling of warm and hearty concurrence. On behalf of the Committee appointed under one of the resolutions, I now have the honor, to address you. It will be gratifying to the Committee to hear from you, at what time you expect to arrive in this City, on your return to Massachusetts; if informed of the time of your arrival it will afford the Committee pleasure to meet you and in behalf of the Whigs of New York to welcome you and to present to you in a more extended form than the resolutions present, their views of your public services. I am instructed by the Committee to say that whenever you shall appear among us as a public man or as a private citizen, you will be warmly greeted by every sound friend of that Constitution for which you have been so distinguished a champion. Should your resolution to resign your seat in the Senate be relinquished, you will in the opinion of the Committee impose new obligations upon the friends of the Union & Constitution.

I am with sentiments of respect & esteem Your humble sert ·
David B. Ogden

ALS. DLC. Published in *Speeches and*   *National Intelligencer*, March 18,
Forensic Arguments, 3: 130.   1837; and *Speeches and Forensic*
 1. For those resolutions, see the   *Arguments*, 3: 129–130.

FROM DANIEL FLETCHER WEBSTER

Detroit Mar. 2. 1837

My dear Father

I received your kind letter of Feb. 20. to day.[1] How shall I thank you, not only for your present, but your goodness in continually thinking of me with so much affection. The pleasant manner of your gift, too, my dear Father, made it doubly valuable to me. Caroline has taken possession of it to keep for me.

You will have seen before this by my letters what I have done about your Gibraltar Stock & Mr. [John] Davis'. Did Mr. P[hineas] Davis tell you that you had a right to a lot at Gibraltar whenever you might choose, by agreeing to build upon it a house or store costing one thousand dollars? If he did not this will inform you of it & lots have been selling very fast there—some for $600. I intended to have gone down this week & selected one for you. I shall do so next week & if when you write me you decline building on it, I can give it up & no harm done. I should think it would be worth while. Gibraltar will look up very fast in the Summer & Spring and I have no doubt that shares will be worth $200. if not more. You cannot buy a lot here less than $100. *cash.* I, together with a Gentleman named [John?] Norton [Jr.] [2] have written on to New York to buy ten, which he says he can get for $75. per share. I am to have half— can buy on 6. or 9. mos credit. It will be quite a nice thing. As I told you I have written to Col. [Thomas Handasyd] Perkins, advising him to buy all he can under $100. I think that those of our traders & merchants who hold these will want money so much for Spring purchases that they will sell at a sacrifice for cash. If I had money I would give $100. for all I could get.

Perhaps you ought to be informed a little of Mr. P[hineas] D[avis]. Ever since I have been here, I have noticed that people spoke of him in a peculiar way. The fact is that in some of his dealings, especially in his Gibraltar matters he has not behaved very honourably. He purchased the property for the company, & had their funds to do it with, yet took it in his own name & *mortgaged* it. Several other little things too of the same sort he has done. The mortgage was however taken off & transferred, the Company threatening to expose him if it were not done. Mr. P. D. is engaged so much in speculation that he is driven to all sorts of shifts & beside he is very loose in his way of doing business. Now in this matter of Gov D's instalments, he agreed to see the two first paid to cancel a note held by the Govr. against him, but he forgot all about it—he has not paid his own assessments either, & they threaten seriously to forfeit his Stock. Money too, which he held as Treasurer he has not paid over, but has given the Co. a lot of lumber & stuff to sell & raise the money from. I have no doubt but that he has all along dealt very honourably by you, but a strict eye must be kept on him or he may forget & neglect & not *come up to his agreements.* He is very much in debt— under heavy liabilities for his purchases. I have written this that you may know how things go. I was not fully aware of it till told the other day by B. B. Kercheval—the Pres. of the Co., one of the best & most respected men here. All this, of course, I have never mentioned elsewhere.

I think your change of plan for travelling through the West is much for the better. I wrote you in my last also that Cara & I could not make the other go. I should have liked to go through Illinois & Michigan with you myself but will be very well content if I can only see you here. The Detroit people will be most gratified to see you. I have had several notes for collection sent me from N. Y. through the kindness of Mr. Edward Curtis & Herman Le Roy. The whole amount is $1000. & over. My *leg case* will be a very important one. I mean to make a good thing of it. I have been studying on it the last week. The only difficulty I have now is to get the names of the proprietors of the coaches. When this is done I feel sure of succeeding, & even if it is not, it will be only *put off*.

A man by the name of Andrew Borden[3] wants to buy a forty acre lot of your's—he offers $5. per acre—it is thus described—S.E. 1/2 of S.W. 1/4 of Sec. 3. Town of 2 North Range 8. West. Mr. [Phineas] Davis would have sold it to him, but they split on ten dollars in the Interest. It would much oblige him, (a clever farmer) to have it, as it stands between him & the water for his farm & he will give more than any one else. If you can find the certificate you would not do better I think than to let him have it. Mr. Davis terms to him were the purchase money $50. down & the rest in equal annual payments. This is a long story about a small matter but he was so earnest about it, lest his neighbours would get it & speculate on him that I promised to write you—he wants too another 40. and an 80. which also join his farm—but I think you might as well hold on. When he has got what he has under improvement, the adjoining will be worth more. I hope your operations this winter will do well. You are an owner, I believe in Winnebago City. It is really an important point. A Rail Road is chartered from La Fontaine to that place or *some other near* & the owners of the City should take interest enough in the matter to get the railroad to their town.[4] So you see, even this purchase, which some time since you wrote me you thought would prove a bubble turns out well. I hope it may be a presage of the success of all your other operations. As far as I can learn of them they all look well. St. Joseph is a good one. The RailRoad from here there will be finished with all possible dispatch. The State will take it. There have been some doubts about Peru. The owners of Ottawa have been making great endeavours to change the Termination of the Canal from the former to the latter place. It is not yet fully decided which place will at last have it, but all are very confident of Peru. I do not believe there is any need of fear—

but our Western Legislatures are not to be calculated upon at all. *Interest* governs every thing.

We have not heard from Boston for some days. I had a letter from Uncle Fletcher some time since. I wrote Edward & Capt. Thomas last evening. Caroline has not been very well for a week. She has taken a severe cold. The Dr. has been to see her this afternoon. Nothing serious I hope.

A nephew of Gen. [Aaron] Ward's of New York, gave us a supper the other night. Mrs. [William] Wilkins was there. She is a very fine woman —was, I think, a Miss [Mathilda] Dallas.[5]

With our best love to Mother & Julia I am dear Father Your most affectionate son   Daniel F. Webster.

I forgot to acknowledge the receipt of a letter from Gov. [John] Davis. It needs no reply.

ALS. NhHi.

1. See above.

2. A fellow stockholder with DFW in the Bank of Macomb County, and son of John Norton, cashier of the Michigan State Bank.

3. Not identified.

4. The Wisconsin territorial legis-

lature chartered the La Fontaine Railroad Company on December 13, 1836. George F. Kuehnl, *The Wisconsin Business Corporation* (Madison, 1959), p. 14.

5. Mathilda Dallas Wilkins was the daughter of Alexander J. Dallas of Philadelphia.

TO HIRAM KETCHUM

Washington Mar. 4. 1837

Dr Sir

I have recd official communications from Mr Ogden,[1] & Mr [Philip] Hone,[2] which I have answered.[3]

I thank you for your kindness & frankness, manifested in your suggestions as to what the address shall contain, & what the answer from me shall be.[4]

In another sheet you will receive, under certain general heads, a brief statement of what I should probably say, if I said any thing, on the several topics.[5] As many of these may be alluded to in the Address, as may be thought proper. Most of them have been under consideration in Congress, the late Session, & might be brought forward, properly enough, by any general reference to the proceedings of the Session.

I might say a word on the loss of the Bill restoring duties on burned goods, & that for anticipating payment of the French Indemnities. What I think on those subjects (as well as some others) you may learn by looking at the Editorial Article which will be in the Nat. Intell. on Monday.[6]

I expect to be in Philadelphia, on Thursday or Friday, at latest. Please let me know, soon after my arrival there, what will be the general scope of the address; & I will thank you also, my Dear friend, to write me as fully as possible, what opinions you think it well to advance, & on what subjects to be silent. I feel some anxiety on this head, as I shall have no opportunity to confer with friends, after arriving in the City. Let me know, also, for how *long a time* I shall be endured. I am, Dear Sir, Very truly & gratefully Yours   D Webster

I want to say something more practicable—coming more to the point —than the loose generalities of the Inaugural. I should like to make the Speech *good*, for N York, & not *bad* for the rest of the Country.

ALS. NjMoHP. Published in *W & S*, 16: 287–288.

1. See above, David Bayard Ogden to DW, March 2, 1837.

2. Not found.

3. For DW's responses, see DW to David Bayard Ogden, March 4, 1837, mDW 14139; and DW to Philip Hone,

March 5, 1837, in Curtis, 1: 556.

4. Ketchum's letter, with such suggestions, has not been found.

5. Not found.

6. On Monday, March 7, 1837, the *National Intelligencer* carried a lengthy editorial, "Results of the Session," probably written by DW.

TO THOMAS HANDASYD PERKINS

Washington March 7. 1837

My Dear Sir

Our friend [Henry L.] Kinney arrived here three or four days ago, & has addressed to you & me, & delivered to me, a letter, of which a copy is herewith enclosed.[1]

In answer, I have said to him that I elect to take the whole of the 4 acres in Peru, either to my own sole account, or to your & my joint account, and that I am ready to refund that portion of the purchase money paid by him out of his own means. I have no doubt, not only from what he says, but from what I learn from others, that these *City* acres are very valuable. He has been very successful with a small sum, sent to him before you & I made our communication to him, and which he invested in lots in the town. He appears to me to be very prudent & discreet, as well as enterprising, & all say has made a large sum of money for himself, in a few years.

As you probably may not wish to make further advances, it has occurred to me that you might like to <divide the property> adjust the property & titles, between us in the following manner; viz.

Your portion of the original 5.000 is 3.750; which is nearly half the whole cost of the 4 acres, wanting 250 Dlls.

Now, suppose I pay Kinney, & take a deed to you & myself of the 4 acres, & debit you 250 Dlls. And as the 160 acres of farming land stands in my name already, I retain that. This will give us the four City acres, between us, as joint property; & it will be well to cause it to be laid off into lots, for sale. I have no doubt a large profit might be realized.

Or, if you prefer it, the concern may be adjusted thus: My part of the purchase money of the 160 acres, that is, 1/4 of the whole, is 875 Dollars. Your part of the joint fund, laid out in the purchase of the 4 acres, that is, 3/4ths of 1446.67, is equal to 1084.98. You may therefore take the whole of the 160 acres, leave to me the whole of the 4 acres, & charge me the difference between $875, and 1084.98.

These modes have occurred to me; if any other suggests itself to you, I dare say it will be equally agreeable to me.

I shall meet Mr. Kinney, in New York, about 8 or 10 days hence. If you will be kind enough to answer this, by a letter to me at New York within that time, I shall have an opportunity to get the deeds made out, in such manner as may conform to your wishes.

The compensation to Kinney, according to agreement, viz one fourth profits, is of course to be paid to him, out of the proceeds of the property, however it may be divided between us. Yours, always very truly

AL draft. DLC.

1. Not found.

FROM DANIEL FLETCHER WEBSTER

Detroit Mar. 14. 1837

My dear Father

The news has reached us that the bill rescinding the Treasury order has passed & that the Land bill has been laid on the table, of course not to be taken up again this year. But since the one has passed I am anxious to enter into an operation & have I believe a good opportunity. I see no reason or indication why speculations will not go on this year just the same as last. Every body is full of it here—no great check or come down has been experienced & even during the operation of the Treasury order. Speculators who could afford it took gold to buy lands with. I have had an offer of a good investment, & great probability of good sales, from the Mr. [Alfred G.?] Benson[1] who had letters to me from you & Col. David Webster. He has been over the best part of Michigan & says he has found some first sale pine land not taken up. I made the following arrangement with him. He says that if I will find the money he will locate the land & sell it at New York for ten dollars the acre. He says he knows he can do this, & that after paying the amount of the cost of the land & interest, we will divide the profits. Now I think that by this arrangement I might make ten perhaps fifteen thousand dollars.

I want to borrow six thousand dollars. I will give as collateral security to my note, my Macomb Co. Bank Stock, my Tonawanda Stock & my duplicate of 480. acres in Barry Co. in all amounting at least to eight thousand dollars in value & which I would not sell for ten.

Mr. B. has some authority from a N Y. Company to buy for them or can get it & he says that if I please to buy it on these terms he will operate with me. At any rate the investment will be a safe one—any good lands are worth five dollars an acre & will bring it readily.

I thought I would write to you before saying any thing to any one else. I think I could get the money from Col. Perkins, if he was sure of being safe in the loan.

If you will advance $2000—I will treat it for you as though it was my own & will invest it for *you*. As for instance, if with it I bought twenty lots at say $1.25 per acre & sold for ten dollars I would return you $16000. I think it will be a very fine operation indeed.

Mr. Benson wants to see you in N. Y. & perhaps he will meet you there —if he does not, will you my dear Father, as soon as convenient state to some of your friends there, Col. Perkins perhaps what I want & let me know whether or no I can get it. I of course want to operate quickly if at all—for as soon as navigation opens the whole Territory will be filled with Eastern people.

Five thousand acres of Govt Land would cost $6250. If I could get this amount & sell it for eight or ten dollars per acre you see the profit would be immense. I should want the money for a year—at seven per. cent. 5000 acres would cost $6250. Suppose we sold at $10. $50,000. deduct $6250 – 43750 + Int 7 per cent, 437 – 43,303—half – 21.651. Now if I could do this I should have a little fortune & not much trouble about it. I have thought the matter over these two days & I believe it perfectly feasible.

Caroline is quite well now, though she has been a little ill for the last week. I am to make a speech next Friday evening before the Young Men's Society of Detroit. I am almost prepared. I have not had much law business for several days. I made three dollars by writing a deed the other day & took three more for advice. Mr. [Charles] Cleland is retained by the Stage Company as their counsel in my broken leg case. I told him the other day that he was so confident in the justice of my case that I did not think even he could prevent my getting a verdict. I bought a Gibraltar share of him for $75. He was short of cash & had to pay a note.

We have not yet changed our lodgings, but hope to by the end of the week.

I am quite well & for me very stout. I weigh one hundred & thirty six pounds!

Our River is open & the streets six inches deep in mud. I shall direct this to N. Y. for mails are very irregular. The mail due last Saturday has not yet arrived.

Mother & Julia are I suppose in Philadelphia.

Good bye, my dear Father your most affectionate son

Daniel F. Webster

P.S. Mr [Stephen] White sent Caroline yesterday a check for $100. Both your kindness & his were very apropos.

ALS. NhHi.

1. Perhaps Alfred G. Benson, commercial merchant in New York, part-

ner of Charles March, and longtime friend of Webster.

TO VIRGIL MAXCY

N. York, Mar. 17. 1837

Private & Confidential

Dear Sir

I pray you to inform me what is to be done with the Treasury Order, & *when* it will be done. Money matters are wound up so tight here, as to bring all things to a stand. Pray learn what you can, & write me, (addressed to this place) by return of mail, *by Express*. I shall betray no confidence.[1] Yrs truly   Danl Webster

ALS. DLC.

1. Although Jackson had pocket-vetoed Rives's currency bill annulling the Specie Circular, many, including

perhaps DW, believed and hoped that Van Buren, now in office, might reverse Jackson's specie policy.

FROM JOHN T. HAIGHT

Milwaukie March 31. 1837

Dr Sir,

With this I send you duplicates of Land in this Land district of 2312. 22/100 acres amtg to $2890.28.[1] The Land is well situated and of a first rate quality being timber and Pra[i]rie as You will see by the plats of the Townships which I this day send you. I did not take as much Pra[i]rie as my father[2] thought best for the timber that I have selected is good and good timber is very desireable in an open Country[.] All the Land that I have bought for Your self or Messrs [Caleb] Cushing & [John] Davis I have seen and examined my self and know it to be first rate. We shall soon have a new map of this Terr[itor]y which I shall send to you when I can obtain one. Stage fare to Detroit $58.—21 Days Ex[penditure] $42.50 Charge of Bank for Premium and Int on $5000.00 $81.34 amtg in all to $181.84 leaving in my hands $29.88 the money of your self and

Messrs Cushing & Davis. I entered for Mr Davis for the full amt of which I drew on him $1000.00 and have retained $100.00 of Mr Cushings money to pay my expences and the Charge of the Bank the balance I have taken from your money. I was in an error when I wrote you from Detroit that the Bank only charged me 1/2 per cent for the Gold.[3] At that time I had not counted the money but asked the Cashier the premium he should charge me and understood him to say 1/2 per cent for Gold but on taking the money he said he told me 1/2 per cent for silver and 1 per cent for Gold. We are much disappointed here that the President did not approve the Bill recinding the Treasury order of 11th. July. It is a great injury to [the] west but I think that a majority of the west are not sorry that the Land Bill was defeated. The Land I selected for you in T 4 Range 11 has a tolerable good mill site for size of Stream. That in T 5 Range 11 good timber and that in T 6 Range 12 is near the Town of Clinton which I think will be considerable of an inland Town in a few years. I have this day written Messrs Cushing & Davis & my father. Very Respectfully Yours to Serve   John T. Haight.

ALS. DLC.
   1. Not found.
   2. Stephen Haight (1784–1841), John T.'s father, was former sergeant-at-arms of the United States Senate.
   3. See John T. Haight to DW, March 14, 1837, mDW 14155.

FROM GEORGE WALLACE JONES

Galena Ill April 1st 1837.

My dear Sir,

For the purpose of enabling me to meet the demands for steam & other boats for the Jordan's Ferry property[1] & for the purchase of the additional tract of land adjoining Peru if the purchase can be made, I have drawn on you in favour of Messrs Rogers & Corwith[2] at five days after Sight for the sum of twenty five hundred dollars as authorized by your self when we conversed together in the room of Mr [John?] Shackford[3] in Washington.

I have contracted for One eighth part of the property covering the town of Prophet's Town on Rock River in Illinois for twenty five hundred dollars at four months after date for which I will also draw on you. This point is on Rock River at the point where the Central Rail Road of Ill will, *in all probability*, cross that stream and if so the property will become immensely valuable.

Should you not be disposed to enter with me on this speculation I will thank you to honor my draft on the assurance that I will have the amt refunded to you as soon as I hear from you & can write back to my friends in N York. The speculation I feel confident is a good one & I feel no hesitation in entering into it.

You authorized me to draw on you for a few thousand dollars should I meet with opportunities to speculate. Please advise me as to the amt for which I may draw.

I wish you to understand distinctly that any speculation into which I enter & for which I draw on you are to be for our equal benefit. I will pay you 3 1/2 per cent interest on the one half the amt for which I draw on you.

I am very respectfully Your very obt friend   Geo W Jones

ALS. ViU.

1. The Jordan's Ferry property was located opposite Dubuque, Iowa, on the Mississippi River.

2. Not identified.

3. Shackford was sergeant-at-arms of the United States Senate.

TO WILLIAM PITT FESSENDEN

Boston April 8. 1837

My Dear Sir

I propose to make a journey, this Spring, to the West, & casting about for companions, it was suggested to me by Mr. [Hiram] Ketchum,[1] that as your health might be benefitted, & your curiosity gratified, by a tour in that direction, it might not be disagreeable to you, to be one of our party. If such should be your feeling, I should be very glad to have you join us. Our purpose is to set off in such season as to leave Philadelphia on the first of May; to go to Pittsburg, via Harrisburg; thence to descend the River, visit Lexington, Frankfort, Cincinnati, Louisville &c, &c, & arrive at St. Louis about the first of June. From St. Louis, our course will be up the Mississippi & Illinois Rivers, to Peru (now La Salle), Galena, & other places in that neighborhood, & then across to Lake Michigan, & so to Detroit, & home by way of Buffalo, & Utica. Through this tour, or as much of it as may be practicable, it is proposed that my wife & daughter shall accompany me. I believe, also, that Mrs Webster's youngest brother, Mr Edward Le Roy, will go with us. If we accomplish all this, & reach home by the middle of July, we shall have done well.

Mr Ketchum, as I have reason to hope, has suggested something of this subject already to you. It will give me much pleasure to learn that the plan falls in with your wishes. Nothing is likely to prevent my setting forth, at the time mentioned, unless the *times* should be so difficult & squally, as to embarrass me in these preparations, which may be necessary for so long an absence.

I will only add, that if your engagements, or other causes, should render it inconvenient for you to go the whole tour with us, I should still be happy in your company, for such part of it as may suit with your inclinations, or other arrangements. The length of the Journey, & the state of the season, as it will be, by the time we reach the Mississippi, make it prudent, I think, to leave the Atlantic Coast by the first of May.

An early answer will oblige[2] Your friend   Danl. Webster

ALS. MeB. Published in Francis Fessenden, *Life and Public Services of William Pitt Fessenden* (2 vols.; Boston, 1907), 1: 11–12.

1. Fessenden had read law in New York in the office of his uncle, Thom-as Fessenden, Hiram Ketchum's partner.

2. Fessenden did join Webster for part of this western tour. His response, however, has not been found.

TO DANIEL FLETCHER WEBSTER

Boston April 9. 1837

My Dear Son,

I have not written to you, since I left Washington, & the main reason is, I have not had half an hour's leisure. There are now letters from you & Caroline, as late as Mar. 27th.[1]—by which we learn, with much gratification, that you are both well, have got into your new lodgings, &c. and are pleased with the change. We hear of you from many a passing traveller, whose accounts always delight us. If you are well settled, have good prospects before you, & you & your wife are happy, *one* of my *three* remaining objects in life is accomplished.

As to matters of business.

Money is too scarce, & the times too *really distressing*, here, to think of raising any more at present for western operations. It will be quite as much as I can do to get thro. my existing engagements, & to make such provisions for my journey, & necessary absence, as may be expedient. I certainly never saw such hard times as the present, especially in N. Y. The *pinch*, I am afraid, has not, as yet, come to the *tightest*, in Boston. The Southern, & South Western Merchants, pay nothing. Drafts on them, negotiated at enormous discounts, come back protested, with heavy damages, as well as disappointment of payment. These occurrences are causing a vast many failures, in N. Y. What the end will be, or what the nature of the ultimate crisis, I cannot foresee.

I am glad to hear that Gibraltar is going on so well. If I had a good opportunity to sell for cash, I would dispose of a few shares, merely thro. want of money. But I suppose I could not sell, for cash, here, at any price.

Mr [Henry L.] Kinney has been on this side the mountain since Feby, & I believe is now in N. York. He has had great success, in managing my little matters, & as he represents it, my interest in Peru is now quite considerable. I have taken an interest, also, in *Rock Island City*.[2] Winnebago also goes on well, as it is arranged that the Rail Road from La Fontaine shall terminate in the midst of our plat.[3] It will be built, or begun, this season. If I reach Detroit early enough, I have promised that, if you can, you shall go & meet the other Proprietors, on the spot, & lay out the town, &c. I own 1/12.

I shall improve the earliest opportunity of making known the particulars of all these various western matters to you, to the end that you may keep yourself acquainted with them, & pay all necessary attention to them. If I am not mistaken, my purchases, already made, will afford me the means of spinning out the short remainder of my thread of life. As to the little lot of land, that one of your neighbors wanted to buy, I will hold it till I see you, & then dispose of it, as you advise. It strikes me it may be a little lot, that Mr [Phineas] Davis thought had *coal* on it.

As to our journey. We propose to get away from home in such season, as to leave Philadelphia May 1st. Nothing is likely to prevent this, unless it be the difficulty of making money arrangements, for so long an absence, in these horrid times. Suppose us to leave Philadelphia, May 1st. we shall visit Ohio & Kentucky, & reach St. Louis, about the first of June. There, a Boat from Peru, (now called La Salle) will meet us, & take us up the Illinois. From Peru, *I* shall endeavor to make an excursion to the mouth of Rock River, & to Galena, & its neighborhood—probably leaving Mrs W & Julia at Peru. Then our effort will be to get to Detroit. From Peru to Chicago, will be easy enough—but whether Ladies will be able to get across Michigan, I cannot tell; & it may be, therefore, that we shall be obliged to take the Boats, & go down the Lakes. I expect Col [Thomas Handasyd] Perkins to meet us at St. Louis, & journey with us to Chicago. I intend, also, to press Mr [Stephen] White to take Ellen Joy, & her husband,[4] to Detroit and, then, if you can get Caroline's leave, I should be glad you would leave her with her sister & accompany Mr White to Peru. My concerns at that point are likely to be so important, that I am desirous you should have a personal acquaintance with them.

I shall keep you advised, of our progress, & let you know as near as I can, when I shall be at the different points. Many things may delay me, & it may be the end of June, before I shall reach Peru, or Chicago.

I am a little uncertain what will be best for Caroline to do, in prospect of probable events. Our arrival at Detroit may be too late, for her to come this way. All this must be thought of. I wish, upon the whole, you had a comfortable house, & were at house keeping. If that were so, & you had some friends from this way with you, I should incline to think it might be as well to postpone your visit, this way, till after expected events. I should think, that as you are now striving to get foot hold in business, you could not well be absent from the West, so long as from June till October without injury to your prospects. In all these things, however, Caroline must be consulted, & her wishes respected.

You may answer this letter to "Boston"—& so continue to write, for the present. Letters will be forwarded, if they should arrive here after my departure. Julia wrote yesterday,[5] about family matters; & I will write again, in a week. Give my best love to Caroline. Yr Affectionate father,   Danl Webster

ALS. NNC.
1. Not found.
2. See deed transferring land in Rock Island City, Illinois, from Levi C. Turner and others to DW, February 13, 1837, mDW 40348 and mDWs. The purchase price was approximately $60,000.
3. See agreement of owners of Winnebago City, Wisconsin, March

24, 1837, mDW 14177.
4. Ellen Marion White (1812–1861), daughter of Stephen, had married John Benjamin Joy (1814–1864) in 1835.
5. Letter not found. Only a few of Julia's letters have survived. Reports are that she burned most of her correspondence shortly before her death on April 28, 1848.

TO CALEB CUSHING

Boston April 10. 1837

My Dear Sir,

I enclose two letters, one from our friend [Stephen] Haight, & one from his son, Jno. T. Haight.[1]

I have accepted the Bill of Exchange, mentioned in these letters. It is for $3,000, & is due the 21st. of this month. I was sorry to see it, on account of the very great difficulty of raising money; & did not expect it; but as the young man drew it, I thought it would be very bad for him to have it dishonored.

I have not the least doubt that the investment will prove a very advantageous one. The lands, as I understand the matter, lie on the branches of Rock River, the choice spot of that Country. Mr Jno. T. Haight has probably not fixed their present value too high, at 5 Dlls an acre.

But I have run out of money. Other engagements have absorbed my means, and as this comes unexpectedly, I do not see how I can well meet it.

Under these circumstances, I must invoke your aid. I should be glad to retain some interest, in the investment, if I could, as I have had an eye to the matter for some time; but if I cannot raise the money otherwise, I must part with the whole.

What I have to propose is, that you furnish the 3,000 Dlls; & place in the hands of my partner H. W. Kinsman Esq, to meet my acceptance, the 21st. instant. I will then retain 1/2 the interest in the lands, if you will give time till I return from my proposed journey, to make out my half the money. Or, if you prefer, I will consent that you take the whole investment, & I will transfer the receipts to you, so soon as <I> recd.[2] I expect to leave Boston about the 20th. for the West, & North-West, not to be home again before July. This expected absence makes it more difficult to manage money matters. If I could pay for the land, I certainly would not sell it for 3 Dolls pr acre.

Will you, My Dear Sir, whose good dispositions are not obstructed by the rebus angulae domi, consider of this matter, & let me know what you can do.

An early answer will oblige me, as I have many things on hand, preparatory to my departure. If you have any occasions, leading you this way, the first of the week, I should be glad to see you, on one or two things. We were all sorry to have been absent, when you called last week. Yours faithfully   Danl. Webster

P.S. I have mislaid the Judge's letter.[3] Its purport was to beseech me to accept the drft, as its protest would ruin his son, & as the investment was a very good one.

ALS. DLC. Published in Fuess, *Cushing*, 1: 231–232.
  1. Only one of the letters, John T. Haight to DW, March 14, 1837, mDW 14155, has been found.
  2. Earlier in the year Webster had

already transferred eighty acres of land near Milwaukee to Cushing. See memorandum of transfer, February 8, 1837, mDW 39835–122–A.
  3. Not identified.

TO CALEB CUSHING

Boston April 13. 1837

My Dear Sir

I am very glad you are willing to try to help me out, with this drft of Mr [John T.] Haights.[1] I declare I do not see how else I shall get along with it.

My plan is, if I can make the preparations, about which I am somewhat embarrassed by the times, to leave Philadelphia May 1st. go [to] Harrisburg, Pittsburg, & to Lexington—to be at Lexington about May 15. Visiting Frankfort, Louisville & Cincinnati, to be at St. Louis, say June 10; thence to ascend the Miss. & Illinois Rivers to Peru, (now called La Salle)—thence to Chicago, & home by Detroit & Buffalo—to reach home in July.

Every body is going west, this year. If you wish to meet large numbers of your friends, join us, at some point on our rout[e]—Col Perkins, Mr. [Jeremiah] Mason, Chancellor [James] Kent, & twenty others, have suggested that they would meet me, on the lower Ohio, or upper Mississippi.

It would give me great pleasure to have you with us, for as much of our tour as we could.

I shall be at home all next week, after Tuesday, & should be glad to see you. Can you not come up, for a few hours? Haights draft is due, 18/21st. inst. The 21st. will be friday, of next week.

I go tomorrow P. [M.] to Marshfield, to be back Monday, or Tuesday at farthest. Let me hope that I may see you. I have something to talk about. Yrs truly   D. Webster

ALS. DLC. Published in Fuess, *Cushing*, 1: 232–233.
    1. Cushing's letter, in response to

DW's of April 10, offering assistance, has not been found.

Galena Ill April 14th. 1837

My dear Sir,

I now draw on you in favour of Messrs Campbell & Morehouse[1] or their Order for twenty five hundred dollars at four months after date it being the amt for which I have purchased the undivided eighth in the property of Prophet's Town on Rock River at the point where it is believed the Central Rail Road of Illinois *must* cross that stream. Should this be the case the property must immediately thereafter become exceedingly valuable. The property is at all events very cheap at the price I have purchased. I am so well convinced of this that I have no hesitation in joining you equally in the investment or we will go on in this as with our written agreement in the entries & purchases made last summer.[2] Please inform me on this subject as soon as possible.

There is a probability today of my being able to purchase two shares in the Jordan's Ferry property. Should I make these two purchases I will reserve one of them for you as you requested and may draw on you for the amt which shall be the last, however, until you authorise me to make further demands on you.

If you can do so conveniently I would be pleased if you would furnish me with letters of credit—say for five or ten thousand dollars to be invested either on the terms of our article of agreement or for our *equal* benefit without any charge of interest to me as an equivalent for my services. Authority to draw on Boston, New York or Philadelphia will suit me. Please favour me with a reply as soon as possible that I may know how to act.

I have made an effort to purchase an additional interest in the Lapsley [?][3] at Peru property, but cannot do so at any reasonable price. How did you leave that case in Washington?

You will have recd ere this reaches you my drft in favr. of Rogers & Corwith which I hope is satisfactory to you.

I had the honor to receive by the last mail your very kind favour of the 7th March[4] covering a certificate which I forgot with you. Nothing could be more gratifying either to Mrs Jones[5] or myself than the kind terms in which you have alluded to us in your favr. of the 7th. It will afford us great delight to see you at any time and especially at our humble cottage at Sinsinawa Mound.

I have the honor to be, Sir, With very great respect & esteem Your Obt Servt & friend   Geo W. Jones

ALS. ViU.
1. Not identified.
2. For the memorandum of that agreement, dated March 1, 1837, see mDW 39835–125. The original of the "written agreement" has not

been found.
3. Not identified.
4. See DW to George W. Jones, March 7, 1837, mDW 14146.
5. Née Josephine Grégoire (b. c. 1812).

FROM GEORGE WALLACE JONES

Sinsinawa Mound Wisconsin
April 16th. 1837

My esteemed Sir,

I addressed you two days since from Galena informing you that I had, in pursuance of your verbal authority, drawn on you in favr. of Campbell & Moorehouse for twenty five hundred dollars & Rogers & Corwith for the same amount the first at four months after date & the latter at five days after sight.[1]

I was unable in my letter of the 14th from Galena, for want of time, to inform you of the rise in this Territory of the value of the property at Madison alias the "Four Lakes Association" for which Ja[me]s D[uane] Doty Esqr of Astor at Green Bay is the Trustee under the Articles of Association.[2] He writes to me under date of the 20th of Feby that shares were then worth ten thousand dollars. I think I informed you in the Senate Chamber that a share had been contracted for $27.000—by Mr [James A.] Hamilton of the City of N Y. Mr H[ercules] L[ouis] Dousman a gentleman of Pra[i]rie Du Chien[3] a shareholder informed me three or four days since, that these shares were selling at N York & Philada about the 10th ultimo at from 25 to 30000$ each. This is gratifying to me not only because of my own interest but especially because the sale which I made to you proves to be so very valuable.

Judge Doty as the Trustee of the Four Lakes Association writes to me for my consent to a division of the unsold lots in Madison & a reservation of the Water Power for the Company. I have written to him in reply that I shall be content at a division provided it be made by lottery after each shareholder shall have been duly notified to attend in person or by Agent to the drawing. I have also requested him to call a meeting of the Shareholders at Madison say on the 10 or 15th of June next which I will attend if called. Do my views in this matter accord with yours or if not say, if you please how I shall act?

A dividend of $170 on each share from the sale of lots was declared on the 1st of Jany last. The lots the Judge says are worth 200$ each. The tract of land on which the town is located & which is owned by the Association contains 1360 79/100 acres—& supposing there are 4 lots to the acre, the whole tract would bring at $200. for each lot $1.088.000,— I have never seen the situation but if the town prospers as at present it [is] generally believed it will the speculation will be a grand one.

I shall be compelled to remain at home for some weeks to come after which time I intend to visit my purchases made last summer for you & will give you some information in relation to them. I have offers to buy since my return home but shall not sell until I look at the land again & not then without a good advance on cost.

I have much faith in the property purchased of Campbell, Morehouse, & Craig viz 1/8 of *Prophetstown* on Rock River & would not now take double what it cost us.

I would make some purchases at Savanna another town on the Rail Road & about 35 miles below Galena on the Misspi, if I could with propriety draw on you for the payments.

I am, Sir, with very profound respect, Your sincere friend & Obt Servt
Geo W Jones

ALS. ViU.
1. See above, Jones to DW, April 14, 1837.
2. The "Four Lakes Association" was a joint stock land company whose landholdings centered in Madison. Through Doty's influence, Madison had been selected as the capital of Wisconsin Territory. Alice E. Smith, *From Exploration to State-*

hood, vol. 1 of *History of Wisconsin,* ed. William Fletcher Thompson (Madison, 1973), p. 392.
3. Dousman (1800–1868), born at Mackinac Island, Michigan, had eventually settled in Prairie du Chien, Wisconsin, as agent of the American Fur Company, lumberman, land speculator, and businessman.

Boston April 22. 1837
My Dear Son
I have recd. your letter of the 18th. inst.[1] We had a pleasant, though short, visit from Mr. & Mrs. [Charles Brickett] Haddock. Mr Haddock observed, that you seemed to be more interested in your studies, & was making quite respectable progress; which I was most happy to learn. You cannot be too deeply impressed with the importance of giving your whole mind to your business. You must think of nothing else. Time unprofitably spent, at your age, is a loss which can never be repaired. Let me entreat you, therefore, My Dear Son, to double your diligence, & to push forward, with all your power. You will be obliged, hereafter, to earn your own living, in one of the Professions, or by some active business, to which knowledge is indispensable. Your own happiness & reputation for life, therefore, essentially depend on the manner in which you shall improve your advantages, for the next five or six years.

I am sorry to hear you were wounded by a sword; but what had you to do with swords? You would have been safe from this accident, I presume, if you had been about your proper business.

You say you will need more money to pay up your little debts, & to come home with. I shall furnish you, of course, with what is proper, but you do not say how much you want. You speak of having little debts; what are they? I am willing to allow you small but reasonable sums for pocket money, but do not allow you to contract any debts. Your Bills for tuition & board, & your bill also for Books & Stationary will of course all be paid. Your clothes you get here, unless it be an occasional garment, once in a while. I shall pay no bill for any thing not necessary for your comfort or respectability. You are to have nothing to do with horses, dogs, or guns. Your expenses are to be limited to such things as are necessary for a close & diligent student, & for enabling you to appear respectable, among your associates. The least extravagance, or unnecessary expense, I shall not tolerate. On the receipt of this letter, you will write to me, letting me know how much you need, what the amount of your little debt is, & what they were contracted for.[2]

I am sorry to be gone from home, at your vacation; but it will be a short one, & a longer one, we hope all to be at home, or near at hand. In the vacation you may come to Boston, & Marshfield, if you please, or you may pass it at Franklin. You will be sure not to exceed the vacation, but to return precisely at the proper day. If you come to Boston, your uncle [James William] Paige will give you room in his house, & under his advice, you can get such clothes as you may need made at Mr. [John] Earls.[3] The vacation is so short, that it might [be] as well, on some ac-

counts, to spend it at Franklin. Still, you may come to Boston, if you prefer it. We shall go away some day, next week. You must answer this letter as soon as you receive it. Your affectionate father,   Daniel Webster.

AL (incomplete). NhHi. Published in
PC, 2: 30–31, from which "as you
receive it" and the complimentary
close are taken.
   1. Not found.

2. Edward's response has not been
found.
   3. John Earle, Jr., was a tailor in
Boston.

FROM GEORGE WALLACE JONES

Sinsinawa Mound Wisconsin
April 22nd 1837

My esteemed Sir,
   In pursuance of your request I have effected a purchase of another
share of the Jordan's Ferry property at the terms as agreed upon to wit
twenty five hundred dollars—For one *eighth.*
   In one of my late letters I informed you that I should not again trouble you with any further drfts until I should hear from you on the subject. I am still of the opinion that I shall not trouble you before hearing
from you. Necessity, however, may compel me to draw for One thousand
or fifteen hundred dollars at some days sight. When I wrote I did not
know positively that I could effect the purchase in the Jordan property.
I have been enabled by borrowing from friends a few hundred dollars to
pay up the whole & unless I am called on by them to refund I will not
trouble you very soon.
   As soon as Mr [George W.] Harrison[1] returns from the east I will have
the town surveyed, plats engraven or lithographed & advertise lots for
sale say about the 1st of Sept or earlier. I have no doubt but that the first
sale will more than return us our purchase money & a high interest besides and leave us the ferry Tavern Stand &c. with the greatest proportion of lots for private sale.[2] I have doubted as to the propriety of selling
lots before we get our Patent, or Certificate, at least, for the land. I recollect asking your advice on this subject but some other conversation intervening you did not give me any. You will recollect we purchased the
Squatters (Jordan's) right. They occupied & cultivated ever since 1829
or 30, proved up their preemption before the Register & Receiver of the
proper land Office at Galena Ill but because of their having been recd no
plats of survey in the land Office at Galena & this land not having been
proclaimed by the President the Register & Receiver would not issue the
Certificate. We have, now, all the rights of Jordan's heirs & adm[inistra-
tor]s, have had possession since the 1st of Augt last & will of course have
the benefit of any preemption law that may hereafter pass. Our right is

here respected & will be at the Sale even if we should not be admitted to enter under the preemption proven up by Jordan's. Can we run any risk in selling? And do you advise a sale in Augt or Sept next? I yesterday rented the Ferry till the 1st of March next, to Mr Geo. O[rd] Karrick[3] one of the proprietors, for $600. This is without any other than the common Ferry Flat the cost of working which is double that of keeping a horse boat & the crossing of course much less. I think with a horse or Steam Ferry Boat the ferry will rent for $1200 per annum which would be equal to 6 pr ct interest on 20.000$. so that this proves the property to be worth at least 20.000$ without any benefit from the sale of lots here after to be made. I have no doubt but that the whole property will be worth 100 thousand dollars in another year.

I am, very respectfully Sir, Your Obt Servt & Sincere friend

Geo W Jones

ALS. ViU.

1. Harrison, a surveyor from Galena, had completed the survey of Dubuque in 1833.

2. Apparently, in 1840 Jordan's Ferry still consisted of little more than a "tavern, grocery, [and] stable," with the ferry. In January 1840 Jones was authorized "to keep a ferry on the Mississippi at Dubuque for twenty years; he was not to conflict with the ferry charter of Timothy Fanning and was permitted to use either horses or steam." Weston Arthur Goodspeed and Kenneth Cornell Goodspeed, *History of Dubuque County, Iowa* . . . (Chicago, [1911]), pp. 66, 208.

3. Karrick, a native of Potosi, Missouri, hauled lead and mail between Galena and Dubuque.

In February 1837, Webster made his heaviest investments, probably totaling about $100,000, in lands and stocks, almost all on credit. Some three months later, just as eastern banks suspended specie payments and the Panic of 1837 hit full force, his first installments on those purchases fell due. Like debtors everywhere, Webster found it difficult—almost impossible—to meet his obligations at the time. Indeed, the indebtedness that Webster built up in 1836 and 1837 haunted him for the rest of his life—he was never able to pay all his creditors.

The letter below to William Albert Bradley (1794–1867), former mayor of Washington, D.C., president of the Bank of Washington, and at this time president of the Patriotic Bank, marks the beginning of Webster's most trying financial difficulties. Without reference to his speculations with George W. Jones in the Jordan's Ferry property and with Levi C. Turner in Rock Island City lots, Webster alludes only to Maryland Mining Company and Clamorgan Land Association stock.

The amount of stock Webster bought in Maryland Mining has not been established. The company, incorporated by the Maryland legislature in 1835, speculated in coal lands near Cumberland, Maryland, owning some 1,750 acres and initially capitalized at $200,000. The company's major stockholders—Buckner Thurston (spelled Thruston in the Clamorgan documents), William A. Bradley, Louis McLane, Samuel Swartwout, Virgil Maxcy, George W. Hughes, and Matthew St. Clair Clarke—shortly secured from the Maryland legislature an increase of the capitalization to $1,000,000 (later $1,500,000) and banking privileges.

Many stockholders in the Maryland Mining Company were also heavy investors in the Clamorgan, but Webster's involvement in the latter is more easily established. In fact, Webster seems to have been one of the prime movers in the formation of the company. The Clamorgan Land Association had been formed on February 21, 1837, when a group of eastern capitalists—mainly Washington city officials, federal employees, and congressmen—purchased for $53,699 from George F. Strother the interest that Strother, Pierre Chouteau, Sr., and Marie Le Duc had in some 458,963 acres of land in southeastern Missouri and northeastern Arkansas which had originally been granted by a Spanish governor to Jacques Clamorgan. The United States government had not confirmed Clamorgan's title to the land, but on February 14, the day that the sale was made, Webster issued an opinion, in which others concurred, that the title was valid. Organized as a joint-stock company, with 536 shares of 1,000 arpents each, the company organizers named John Glenn and Charles M. Thurston of Maryland as trustees, Bradley, president, and, initially, Webster, Stephen White, Samuel L. Southard, and Roswell L. Colt, proprietors or directors. Shortly, George W. Hughes replaced White on the list of directors.

Stock distribution in 1837 has not been determined, but in September 1838 it was as follows: Samuel Southard, 50 shares; Virgil Maxcy, 124; William A. Bradley, 77; Roswell L. Colt, 75; Francis Markoe, 8; William Hawkins, 1; William S. Derrick, 6; and R. S. Chew, 1, accounting for only 342 out of 536 shares. Strother himself retained a few shares in the company, but most of the 194 remaining probably were owned by Webster, who shared in the purchase with two of his western land agents, Henry L. Kinney and Levi C. Turner. For most of the cost of his shares in Clamorgan ($10,000 on his own account and $5,000 each for Kinney and Turner), Webster was indebted to Ramsay Crooks, agent of Pierre Chouteau, Sr., and of Pratte, Chouteau and Company, fur traders of St. Louis. The $10,000 acceptance that he mentions to Bradley was probably for stock in Maryland Mining. These February 1837 speculations *plagued Webster for the remainder of his life. Their impact can be traced through the printed correspondence in this and succeeding volumes of the* Papers.

TO [WILLIAM ALBERT] BRADLEY

Boston April 27. 1837
Thursday Eve'

Dear Sir

I have this Eve' recd yours of the 24th.[1] My object in desiring to see you in N. York, was, that we might arrange the renewal of my acceptance, in whole or in part. I do not see that it is *possible* for me to meet it. I hope to be able to pay a part, say 1/3rd—& I supposed this would be better for the Bank than for the acceptance to lie over. But I do not know in whose hands it is, in N. York, & therefore to whom I could apply.

I hope to be in N. York on the 1st & to stay there till the Morning of the 3rd. If you could come, or send, so as that I might renew, by making part payment, I would be very much obliged to you, as I should be most deeply mortified to have the paper lie over. But I have not the means of taking it up. No money can be raised here, by any means within my command. My other matters I have managed as well as I could. I believe most of the Banks think they do well, if they get a third, but *if three dollars would buy one*, I would pay up the whole sum. If any securities I have will be useful to you, to the amount of ten thousand Dollars, I will readily loan them to you, though I hardly know whether I have any thing better than your own. I have done nothing with Clamorgan[2] nor with Maryland Mining Co.[3] Pray let me see or hear from you by the morning of the 3rd. As the note cannot be paid, and as I wish to do all I can, I will leave what I can pay wherever you direct. Yours, very truly,

Danl Webster

Direct to me at American Hotel.

ALS. NhD.

1. Not found.
2. The affairs of the Clamorgan Land Association, and of Webster's involvement in it, can be roughly traced in the following: *Title Papers of the Clamorgan Grant of 536,904 Arpens of Alluvial Lands in Missouri and Arkansas* (Washington, 1837; New York, 1837); *Clamorgan's Title to Lands on the Mississippi River, Opinions of DW and others* (n.p., 1837?); *Papers Relating to the Cla-*

morgan Grant (New York, 1838?); *Prospectus of the Clamorgan Land Association* (London?, 1839?); *Clamorgan Land Association Agreement* (London, 1840); *Prospectus for Raising a Loan of 54,000, upon Shares in the Clamorgan Land Association . . .* (London, 184?); in the Galloway-Maxcy-Markoe Papers, DLC, and in the Papers of the American Fur Company, NHi.

3. For information on the Maryland Mining Company, see *Report of*

an Examination of the Coal Measures, Including the Iron Ore Deposits, Belonging to the Maryland
Mining Company . . . (Washington,
1836); Maryland Mining Company
(Baltimore?, 1836?); Memorial of

the President of the Maryland Mining Company to the General Assembly of Maryland . . . (Baltimore?,
1836?); Loan of the Maryland Mining Company (London, 1840?).

TO CALEB CUSHING

Boston April 29. 1837

My Dear Sir

I send you the Certificates of the 24 hundred acres of land.

I have long been desirous of making this purchase, knowing the value of the lands; but my agent, Mr [John T.] Haight (whom you know) never could accomplish it, till lately; & has now drawn on me, at a very unlucky moment, for the purchase money.

The sum is 3.000 dollars.

I am leaving home, this very day, for the Western Country, & money is so scarce here. I do not see how I can provide the funds.

I put the certificates into your hands, endorsed, in the hope that by your own means, or thro some friend, you might raise the money. I was formerly somewhat acquainted with Mr. [Charles?] Bartlett,[1] & always entertained for him the warmest regard. If necessary, will you call on him, make my respects to him, & signify to him that I have an interest, which would be much promoted by a loan of the money till my return.

Yours, with very true esteem,   Danl Webster

ALS. DLC.
  1. Bartlett was teller of the State
Bank, Boston, with which Caleb

Cushing and others in the Cushing
family had close dealings.

In early May, Webster and his family set out on their tour through the Midwest. William Pitt Fessenden joined them at Pittsburgh on May 11, and the party made its way down the Ohio by boat to Wheeling, (West) Virginia. As the crowd gathered on May 17 to honor Webster at a public dinner, the local newspapers carried an account of the failure of New York City banks on May 10; and in his address, Webster attributed the economic crisis to Jacksonian policies. From western Virginia, the Web-sters traveled on to Kentucky, stopping first at Maysville, and then at Lexington for a barbecue and visit with Clay. Following a short visit with General Harrison at North Bend, the Websters were in Cincinnati on June 3, for another celebration and address. By June 9, they had reached St. Louis, escorted by Henry L. Kinney, Webster's agent. Turning east-ward, the Webster party journeyed overland to northern Illinois for an *inspection of his property holdings in Peru and in Chicago. On July 1, they sailed across southern Lake Michigan to Michigan City, then went by land to Toledo, and reached Detroit on July 8. By July 26 they were again in New York City, preparing to leave for Massachusetts. All along the trip, DW had been honored and feted, but he had also declined many invitations, arguing the need to get back east to prepare for the special session of Congress Van Buren had called for September 4. In analyzing the trip, Fessenden wrote that "so far as gaining friends was concerned, Mr. Webster might well, if not better, have stayed at home and left his fame and public service to speak for him." Quoted in Charles A. Jellison,* Fessenden of Maine: Civil War Senator *(Syracuse, 1962), p. 27.*

TO JOHN PLUMMER HEALY

Canal, Miflin Co. May 8 [1837]

Sir,

In one of my trunks in the Bank, I think the black one, are a bundle of shares in the Ellsworth Land & Lumber Co. amounting to 100 shares, in all. I believe these stand in my name; but they are the property of Col David Webster, to whom you may deliver them, on request. If he wishes a transfer, please send me a power to transfer, to be executed by me.

There is another bundle, containing 50 shares, originally issued to Col Webster, but by him transferred. These you will retain for me.[1] Yours

Danl. Webster

ALS. MHi. Healy (1810–1882; Dartmouth 1835) read law with Webster, 1835–1838, and remained in Webster's office as an associate until 1852. During the period from 1838 to 1852, he represented Boston in the Massachusetts legislature on three occasions.

1. Healy apparently passed DW's

letter of instructions on to David Webster, who replied to Healy as follows:

"Mr Healy this was contained in a long letter from Mr Webster[.] I do not know that I shall want any of the shares in his hands belonging to me untill his return[.] Will see you when I can. Yours truly   D Webster"

TO GEORGE WALLACE JONES

Peru, Illinois, June 24. 1837

My Dear Sir

I arrived at this place day before yesterday, with my wife & daughter, having left home the latter part of April. It was my purpose to have proceeded, today, to Galena, but my wife has become fatigued, & the unexpected call of Congress compels me to turn towards home. I very much regret this, as I do not know when I may be again so near your residence.

I met here Dr. John Porter, whom I have often mentioned to you as a particular friend of mine. He will take this letter to you, & I commend him to your kind regard. I have given him the little agreements, between you & me, & asked him to inquire about the property. I have let him have an interest, in our *first* agreement.

My Clerk writes me[1] that a draft of yours came to hand, after I left home, which was protested. Whether I could possibly have paid it, if I had been at home & had accepted it, I do not know, since money affairs have taken such a turn. There is no doing business, now, in the East. We shall meet, I presume, Septr. 1st.

Make my best respects to your wife, & believe me always truly yours
Danl Webster

P.S. As the mail will carry this letter so as that you will receive it sooner than by Dr. Porter, I put it into the mails. The Dr. will reach you, I presume, in about a week.

ALS. Ia-HA.
1. Letter not found.

FROM MORGAN L. MARTIN
Green Bay June 28. 1837.

Dear Sir,

In compliance with your request I have subscribed for a portion of the La Fontaine Rail Road Stock in your name. The Capital Stock of the Company is $50.000; of which we do not think it may ever be necessary to call in over one half. [James Duane] Doty took 20. I put you down for 10 & took the balance myself. I conceived you would prefer that amount since it would then only require to be paid the sum for which you authorized me to draw on you. Our charter is a liberal one in the use to which we may appropriate our small bank[?] funds, and we shall be able at the next session of our Legislature to get it altered to an unlimited one in duration & procure some other privileges not embraced at present. I have not drawn on you and it will not be necessary to do so until next year and then in small sums as the work may progress.

Since my return here I have conversed with the proprietors interested with me in them (*lands along the route*) and I think they are all willing to give you a handsome interest in the property at the original cost. We would do so immediately but the Engineer whom we expect to make examinations has not yet made the survey, and thinking that we may find it necessary to extend our purchase to other lands not now embraced in it, we thought it advisable to wait until the definite route was determined on & all the plans & estimates completed. When that is done if you are still desirous of sharing with us, we shall be pleased to have you do so, on such terms as cannot but prove satisfactory to you.

I had hoped your journey might have extended to Green Bay this season, as all good citizens feel gratified to attract the attention of strangers, and individually would myself be pleased to welcome you to our border home.

I have the honor to be Very Respfy Your obt. Servt.   M. L. Martin

ALS draft. WHi.

   1. See DW to Morgan L. Martin, March 24, 1837, mDW 14175.

FROM GEORGE WALLACE JONES

Sinsinawa Mound *Grant* Co W.T.
July 7th. 1837

My dear Sir,

I did not receive until last evening your fav. from Peru dated 24th. ult. & post marked the 30th.[1] The Doctor, who was to have been here, a week ago has not yet arrived, but when he does I will take much pleasure in riding with him over the Country & showing him such other attentions, in my power, worthy of the friend of Mr Webster.

Your numerous friends in this Section of the Country, but no one more than myself, regreted exceedingly that they could not have the pleasure of seeing you amongst them & of tendering to you their kindest civilities. Mrs Webster & your daughter would have been hailed amongst us also with delight. We still hope to see you next summer.

Your Clerk did not write to me but the Notaries Public & my creditor did, to inform me that my draft on you in fav. of Rogers & Corwith for 2500$ had been protested & that the one in favour of Campbell & Morehouse at 3 or 4 months sight for 2500$ had been *noted* for protest. When I saw in the newspapers the account of your leaving home for the West I feared my drfts might not be honored unless you had made provision for them before your departure. I have been put to very serious inconvenience & cost in consequence of the non acceptance of my drft in fav of R & Corwith. That in fav. of Campbell & Morehouse I have told them would doubtless be paid on your arrival at Boston. Independent of this purchase from Campbell & Morehouse of the property at Prophet's Town, which is an excellent one I think, I have also purchased for you two other shares, as you requested me to do, in the Jordan's Ferry property at the same price I gave you the interest last winter viz 2500$ per share or $5000 for the two.

I am pleased to hear of the relief, in some degree, at the east, & in money matters & hope you may reach home in time to meet my other drft in fav. of Campbell & Morehouse. This will be all you will have to pay for me until I meet you at Washington on the 1st of Sept when I will have to ask you to relieve me. I know you have a mighty weight to carry into the coming contest in the Senate & therefore will not relish my small affairs. But they are all important to me & you must forgive me if I press them too earnestly on your attention.

I am, Sir, With continued regard Your Obt Servt & friend

Geo W Jones

NB Please present our respects to Mrs & Miss Webster & express to them the regrets we feel at their not visiting our *Mound*. G W Jones.

ALS. ViU.

1. See above.

TO [JOHN PLUMMER HEALY]

Detroit July 12. 1837

Dear Sir

We arrived here three or four days ago, & propose to leave in the Boat tomorrow. I was astonished to find protests of Mr Huntingtons[1] acceptances. I saw Mr. [Levi C.] Turner at Chicago. He said the acceptances would undoubtedly be paid.[2] I have full faith in him, & he will be as much surprised as I am. He will be in N. Y. and Boston about as soon as I am, & we must see what can be done. Every body seems to fail. I find funds here, quite as well as I expected, but there is no mode of remittance. My lands in this State, purchased last year at Govt. price, sell now freely at 5 Dollars an acre. But the *pay* is western money, & nothing else. I do not know what we are all coming to.

It is difficult, as yet, to say, on what day I may reach home, but intend to *hasten*, from this point. Fletcher & his wife are well. They are pleasantly situated, & he seems to have a fair chance to get a living. Col Perkins is some where in the South. I have not seen him, yet. Yrs truly

Danl Webster

ALS. MHi.

1. Not identified.

2. Turner (c. 1805–1867), born at Cooperstown, New York, was apparently a land agent in the Old Northwest for eastern speculators (including DW) in the late 1830s. A lawyer by profession, he also wrote for a Cleveland, Ohio, newspaper in the 1840s and served as editor and proprietor of the *Cincinnati Gazette* in the 1850s, while he simultaneously wrote editorials for the *New York Tribune*. At the time of his death, he was judge advocate of the army, stationed in Washington. The acceptances were most likely one for $5,000, held by Ramsay Crooks, and another for $4,075, then held by Samuel W. Beall. See DW to Ramsay Crooks, September 23, 1837; DW to Franklin Haven, October 2, 1837; and Hamilton Fish to DW, January 19, 1838, below.

FROM CALEB CUSHING

Newbury Port July 28th 1837

Dear Sir:

I congratulate you sincerely upon the brilliant tour you have made in the West, & your safe return. It has been a subject of perpetual regret to me that I was unable to accompany you. I was, unhappily, engaged by my cases in court to so late a day in May, that I gave up the idea of over-taking you, or of following in the purpose to do it; and indeed the early convocation of Congress rendered it impossible for me to be absent so long from home.

Meanwhile, I have not been unmindful of your interest, either at New York or in this State, when occasion offered for me to be of service. Re-cently, I have engaged to take charge of a department of the Journal of Commerce, in reference to the Presidential canvass, induced to under-take it by the consideration that my situation at Washington would en-able me to know your views, & thus to be the channel of useful sugges-tions & arguments. And in regard to this, I wish, at some convenient time after your return to Boston, to confer with you as to the details of this scheme, which is of Mr [Hiram] Ketchum's proposing; & should be glad, therefore, to know whether you remain in Boston, & if not, when you are to be found there.

I provided for your draft in a way that I hope will be satisfactory to you. $1000 I was able to spare from my own resources. $2000 I hired of a confidential person on my note secured by your acceptance, at 1 per cent per month discount in addition to simple interest on the note, being a little less than 1 1/2 per cent in all, which was then the current rate of bank post-notes. It was further conditioned by the lender, that the loan should be for *six months* from April, at which time (*October*) he will need the $2000; & I shall not need my $1000 any sooner. So that you have no occasion for solicitude about this matter at present.

With my best respects to Mrs & Miss W., I am, Very truly yours

C. Cushing.

ALS. DLC. Printed in Fuess, *Cushing*, 1: 233–234.

TO CALEB CUSHING

Boston July 29th. 1837

My Dear Sir

I arrived beneath my own roof this morning, and am much gratified by your friendly letter.[1] My journey has been very agreeable. There are many most interesting things in the West, & a very good spirit & feeling prevail, in general, among the People. Your pleasure I hope is but postponed. I can sincerely advise you to pass two or three months beyond the mountains the first opportunity.

I thank you for the very favorable arrangement abt. the acceptance. For the month to come, I shall be principally at Marshfield. In some spot or another, however, I shall want to meet you, in the meantime. Your proposed aid to the J[ournal] of C[ommerce] will be of great importance. That paper has very important influence, & ought to be so conducted as to afford a good lead.

Are you to be at Boston, or at any Court in Salem, within the next three weeks? Yours truly   D. Webster

ALS. DLC. Printed in Fuess, *Cushing*,   1. See above.
1: 234.

FROM HENRY L. KINNEY

Peru August 24th. 1837
My Dear Sir,

On my return from the West I found several letters in waiting.[1] Some of which brought unfavourable tidings in relation to some of my business which you doubtless feel some interest.

Mr [Daniel J.] Townsend[2] (my partner) has been informed by Mr [Augustus] Porter[3] of Buffalo, that, that the $5000 which was to be passed to your Credit[4] at the Bank of Buffalo had been used for an other purpose previous to the 10th inst. and that it was impossible to get hold of it so as to apply it as intended viz—to your Credit by the time required.

Mr Townsend starts this week for Buffalo & Niagara to settle that and other matters there. I feel very much hurt that you should be disapointed in not receiving that money as was anticipated. It seems as if nothing was certain where money is concerned.

We have had a hard time here for the last four weeks in monied matters. On my return to Chicago after parting with you at M[i]c[higa]n C[i]ty I was induced to put out of my hands between seven & eight thousand Dollars, for which I was to have a Bnk drft on the Phenix Bank N. Y. within two weeks of that time, a part of which I intended to remit to you & the remainder to Suydam Jackson & Co.[5] As yet not one dollar has been returned to me. Although I had the most sacred promises from two of the most wealthy and monied men in the State & heretofore considered quite as punctual as any men in the West. So it is the fates seem to have been against all opperative men this year. Since you left this Country all business men have felt the pressure very much. The State Bnk has been curtailing her issues & it seems now as if there was to be no circulation of money, if this state of things should continue. In the course of my absence *My Partner Mr Townsend* has remitted for me to Suydam Jackson & Co. between three & four thousand Dolls. in drfts. And in the course of this week I send them $1500. & Mr Townsend will dispatch a messenger from Buffalo with a sum which I am in hopes will not be less than ten thousand Dollars to place in the hands [of] that firm for them to Redeem the P[hoenix? Patriotic?] B[ank] money with. Any amt over after redeeming the P. Bnk notes will be placed to your Cr in the Merchants Bnk N. Y. and you advised accordingly. I found my [Michigan and Illinois] canaling affairs in a much more embarrassed state than I had expected when you was here, and have been under the necessity of making Cash advances to an amt. not less than ten thousand Dollars since you left. I have however got things corrected with my canalling in a good train, so that it is a source of income instead of loss. My gain on last months work over expenditures was $1800—this month it will be more. I was offered $10,000 premium on one of my canal sections which offer I excepted but as yet have not been so fortunate as to obtain the money or sattisfactory security for the payment of it. In consequence of which I am still going on with the work under my own direction. I am putting my affairs in a train for genl ajustment and have what business I do, a source of income instead of out expense. Since you left here I have lost but little time in settling & bringing my business in some degree to a close. Great distress is felt in Chicago at this time, on account of the terible condition business men have been placed in through the general derangement of all business affairs over our land.

I should have accomplished more if it was not for being a little out of health the last month. I have necessarily had to attend personally to the arranging of the great variety of business in which I am engaged, which is to me no small task.

I wrote you of my having a visit from Fletcher. He is a noble fellow, (& I need not say My Dear Sir) that I am very much attached to him. About the time of his leaving here on his return to Detroit, I conveyed to you the farm where I now live, a little sketch or plat of which I herewith enclose & will forward to you the Deed as soon as Recorded. The deed is now at the office for Record. I have not deeded you quite as large a tract as was, and still is my intention to do. The farm lies in a square form and contains all the improvements and various proportions of different qualities & kinds of land as you wished to have it. There is now under cultivation on (this) yr Salisbury farm about 140 acres, from 50. to 100 of which I shall sow to wheat this fall. I am now building & will soon have finished a good Barn—30 by 40 feet, which is all the addi-

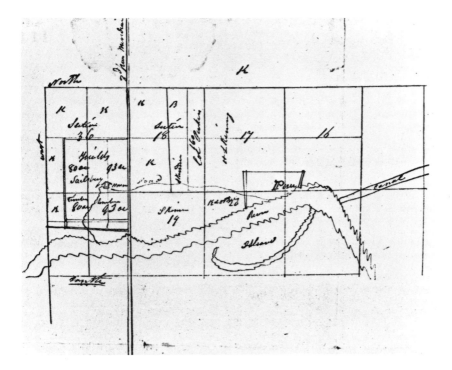

tional improvements that is absolutely ne[ce]ssary to carry on a proffit-able farming interest.

Fletcher seemed much pleased with this country whilst here & ex-pressed to me a willingness to change his location. As I understand it he is decidedly in favour of making this place his permanent residence, & is disposed to make a move this fall, in the event of which every thing will be in re[a]diness for him here. Should he come I am conceited enough to believe him & myself could do things up about right. Should he & yourself conclude it not best for him to settle here, you will permit me to stay at *Salisbury Park* until next spring, as it would change my business plans from what I had wished & hoped would take place.

I am making considerable improvement in my farming interests this Summer, particularly on my Spring creek farm. My crops are excelent, never better than this summer. Not much doing in the way of selling real estate. I have however this week sold three Peru lots & have recd. towards them three thousand Dolls in cash. I have in keeping a few hundred Dollars in Specie that I intend to send to the Patriotic Bnk.

[August 26]

Mr Townsend leaves this day for Buffalo this 26th. august. You may expect to hear some thing favourable from me in a short time, as regards monied matters. I have this day about concluded a sale of some Peru lots to Capt [Harvey?] Wood[6] of L[ower] Canada for which I am to receive from him $5000 to $8000. (*He has the money*). I have written to Mr D[avid] A[iken] Hall[7] & enclosed him three hundred Dolls—we will soon get things right again—you may say to Mr Hall I will sattisfy him for the trouble he has had in my affairs, when I see him. I have about $2200 in Gold I wish I could send to the P.B. You need not be supprized to see me east of the mountains in the course of the next two months. I have been so much engaged in my business that it has been impossible for me to turn my attention to pollitical affairs. I hope to be able to do something soon—towards getting a press established & organizing our party &c. Our Courts will be in session next month. We will then call some pollitcal meetings & send forth an expression. Let me hear from you often. I feel anxious to know how you stand effected these embarrassing times. Things look better here than they did a few days ago. I hope to be able to visit Detroit next month. I shall keep you advised of my movements. I am most sincerely Yours &c   H. L. Kinney

ALS. ViU.

1. Letters not found.

2. Townsend, probably from Detroit, had married Jane S., daughter of Augustus Porter of Niagara and sister of Augustus Seymour Porter, later senator from Michigan. By the summer of 1838, Kinney had broken his partnership with Townsend, and Townsend eventually returned to Niagara.

3. Porter (1769–1849) had been the first judge of Niagara County, was a director of the Bank of Niagara and a prominent landowner and businessman in the area.

4. This $5,000 indebtedness may be the same as that to Ramsay

Crooks, referred to in the descriptive note preceding DW to William Albert Bradley, April 27, 1837.

5. Suydam, Jackson & Co. was a New York mercantile and trading firm, closely allied with the American Fur Company and heavily involved in trade with the Indians of the Old Northwest.

6. Wood (?–1872) settled in Peru in 1837 and remained there until his death.

7. Hall (1795–1870; Middlebury 1815), a native of Grafton, Vermont, was a lawyer in Washington, D.C. At the time of his death, he was regarded as one of the wealthiest men in the city.

FROM DANIEL FLETCHER WEBSTER

Detroit Aug 28. 1837.

My dear Father,

I was forced to make a draft on you the 22d. Inst. for four hundred dollars, very much against my will, but I could not raise a cent in any other way. I had written to Col [Thomas Handasyd] Perkins offering him my property in Michigan & in Toledo at low rates, in the hopes that he would be able to take it of me—but he says in a letter received yesterday that he has suffered severely by the experiment and regrets even his engagements at Peru. I wrote also to Mr. [Stephen] White, telling him that I was very hard pushed & asking him for advice and assistance in raising some funds upon my [Macomb] Bank Stock or Tonawanda, but I have not heard from him. If he does not write soon I shall see what I can do with the Bank Stock.

Since my return from Peru, taking every thing into consideration, I have resolved upon moving there as soon as I can get away. If I can raise the amount of funds necessary to get me clear off from here & something in Pocket besides, I would take my family and all my moveables and reach Peru some time in November. Caroline is ready and indeed anxious to go. She thinks we could do much better where the expenses of living are not so enormously high as they are here & she feels that if we are once well settled at Peru, on your fine farm we shall always be sure of a good living off of that; shall be almost as near home as now & a great deal more independent & respectable. The law business there will soon be as good as it would be here for me—not so much of it, but my share would be the greater half & fees are much higher. I have written to Col [Henry L.] Kinney that I mean to join him at Peru some time this winter if I can & he will be ready for me. I shall take the house as it is— send on all my furniture & a week would see me comfortably settled. Do you approve of this move? The fact is that if I live here much longer, no better business—money impossible to be got for any thing and my family expenses so very large, I shall be ruined in six months more.

I shall write again to Col Kinney today, to learn from him whether or no he has deeded to you the farm on which he now lives, as he was about doing when I was there. If that has been done, I can go on it & by your leave take care of it until you come there next year. If Col. Perkins had been able to buy me out here, I think I should have made a visit East this winter but as he cannot & I don't know who can or will, I must change direction & go West, where if I am not earning much I am not spending a great deal. Caroline is perfectly ready to go, & as I said anxious. We could travel by the first of November.

The draft which I made on you, I will pay myself in some manner— it was at sixty days. I had strong hopes that I should have funds from Col. Perkins. Mr. White will probably say that I may do what I can with my Bank Stock or Tonawanda & I think I can raise some thing on the former.

I hope that you will be able to give me an answer soon & giving me your views as to my project. I should be glad to sell Gibraltar or my Govt. Lands or Toledo Lots pretty cheap—16. shares in Gibraltar at $85. per share—or even $80. Govmt. Lands, which are very good, at four dolls. per acre, & two good lots in Toledo for $3000. for both, one half cash & the rest in six months. If I can get on without selling it would be best for me, as it could be done only at a sacrifice—though I should make a good profit on all but Gibraltar, it is much less than I think I shall be able to get in two years.

I have now told you all my hopes & fears & hope that you will be able soon to send me an answer.

Our Whigs have done grandly in the State. [Isaac Edwin] Crary will be chosen but by less than five hundred majority. Our two days of election in this City were the most exciting ones that I ever saw—Bands of music, Stage Coaches, Flags—a ship on wheels, the Constitution, filled with Sailors & covered with ensigns, one of them bearing in noble capitals "Daniel Webster & the Constitution," together with all sorts of placards & handbills & plenty of rows & fights. We all expected a general engagement with the Irish of the opposite party, but there were only occasional monomachiae. The City was carried by a majority of 85. out of over 1700. votes. In the fall elections we shall beat, I have no doubt. The Whigs all over the State are busy & we find many more of them than any one expected.

Caroline is as usual & we are every day looking for the event. Julia & Ellen [Fletcher][1] are well, the latter has been a little indisposed. We have had several long, kind letters from Mother, which Julia has answered.

I shall direct to Washington, where I suppose you will be by the time this arrives.

Caroline Julia & Ellen join me in much love & [Fisher Ames] Harding desires his regards & respects. Your affectionate son   Daniel F. Webster.

I ought to say that I have become an old stager at Caucus speaking— having addressed "my fellow citizens" for three nights, with *electric effect*. The rules seemed to be to call for [George C.] Bates[2] or [Jacob M.] Howard then [John L.] Talbot,[3] then Webster or [James F.] Joy & then disperse.

ALS. ViU.

1. Ellen Fletcher (d. 1866), Webster's niece, was the daughter of Timothy.

2. Bates (1812–1886; Hobart 1831) had settled in Detroit in 1833 after reading law with John C. Spencer. In 1844, and again in 1849, he was appointed district attorney for Michigan, and in 1871 for Utah.

3. Talbot, also a lawyer and one-time partner of Bates, was, along

with Bates, one of the organizers of   Company in 1836.
the Detroit and St. Joseph Railroad

TO FRANKLIN HAVEN

Marshfield Tuesday Evening
[August 1837]

Dear Sir,

I came down to this place this forenoon, for the purpose of placing my family here for the residue of the Summer; & this evening Mr. Kinsman has sent down Mr. [John Plummer] Healey, to say that he thinks I must come immediately back to town, to see about these most unfortunate *protests* of [Levi C.] Turner's draft.[1] I intended, fully, to have called at the Bank yesterday; but having been out in the morning, I felt unwell, & returned to my House at 11 o'clock, & staid at home thro' the day.

As I informed you, on Saturday, thro J. P. Healey, I saw Mr. Healey in N. York. We conversed on this subject, & I told him I desired to see him & you the moment he came to Boston, & suggested a mode of payment, in case the drawer or acceptor should not take up the drafts. He said he should be at home in a few days, and did not say that it would be necessary for me to see you, before he arrived. However I ought to have seen you, as well as to have sent you word that I had seen Mr. Healey; and should have done so, but for the reason above stated; and I will come, now, to Boston immediately, if you think it will not do to wait for Mr. Healey's return from N. York.

I saw L. C. Turner at Chicago about the 1st of July. He had then no doubt that all the acceptances would be promptly paid. He said the House (the acceptor) had stood firm thro the severity of the pressure; and of course would not fail now. In fact I do not learn that it has failed; but, as happens in other instances, the acceptor, as far as I can learn, *elects*, and pays when he sees fit, and neglects to pay when he sees fit.

At Detroit, about July 10th I first heard of the dishonor of one of the drafts. I wrote to Mr. Turner immediately,[2] and have written again, since. When I left him, he agreed to meet me, in relation to some other matters, in N. Y. or Boston by the middle of August. In N. York I learned that he was expected in that city between the first and fifth. As I know, however, that he was detained in Chicago longer than he expected, I do not think he will be in N. Y. or Boston before the 10th.

I should be glad to stay here, for the residue of this week, for rest; but if necessary will come up immediately. I send this back by Mr. J. P. Healey, and if you suggest to him that my presence will be necessary, or even in any degree useful, he will return, tomorrow, or send me word, and I will come directly to town.

I have still the fullest faith in Turner, both in respect to his integrity and good intentions, and his abundant ability. He may be under the like difficulties, as others, at this moment, if called on to raise large sums suddenly; but I have no doubt of the solidity of his means. Yrs truly

Danl. Webster

Text from *W & S*, 16: 289–290. Original not found.

1. The drafts protested probably had to do with two notes of Webster's, one for $5,000 held by Ramsay Crooks and one for $4,075 held by

Samuel W. Beall. Both notes originated with the joint speculations of DW and Turner in Rock Island City and Clamorgan lands.

2. Letter not found.

FROM DANIEL FLETCHER WEBSTER

Detroit Sept 1. 1837

My dear Father,

I should have written to you myself to inform you of the birth of a daughter to us,[1] but was so much fatigued and overcome by the dreadful night of the 28th. that I have been quite ill ever since.

Julia wrote you immediately on the event.[2] Little Grace Fletcher Webster has blue eyes & light hair & takes after the Story's in appearance. I can see nothing that gives her a claim to Webster blood. I thought at first she had red hair, but was agreeably disappointed. Poor Caroline suffered extremely & the child hardly lived—but thank God! both are now doing well.

I received your kind letter of the 22d. Aug.[3] on the 30th. which reasons above mentioned have hitherto prevented my answering.

In regard to the conditions you refer to as having been mentioned by me, I have changed my mind as to one & as you will have seen by my last letter have intended to go to Peru notwithstanding any doubts on that point. I must raise some money, but I did not intend to ask you to do it for me. I hope I shall be able to do it myself. The object of my removing to Peru would be, not only ulterior benefit, but immediate gain, and I thought that by taking charge of your farm & other property thereabouts, as you suggested to me when here, that I should be sure of a living besides what I could get from the Law and any operations that I might be able to make.

If you think that I could not do this as profitably for you, as any one else could, of course I should not desire to undertake it; though I cannot but flatter myself that I could carry on your farm to as much advantage as any one. All I should want from it would be *board* & no one else would take it so low as that, and that is an object with me, for as I said in my last letter,[4] I cannot live here while every thing is so very high & money not to be had. I find that my expenses, though I save at every leak, are much greater than I can in any manner get along with, & the sooner I get away the better.

My desire would be to take charge of your farm & look after your other property in the State & I think that I could do this as well for you as [any] one could. Col. [Henry L.] Kinney lets his farms at one third for himself, and can do no better with them. I should want no profit, only a living, until my profession should be good enough to support me or a change in times enable me to make some thing on my property. I should like very much to try one year on your farm & see what I could do & if things did not go well I would not ask to try another year. I will carry on the farm for one year for food & clothing & enough to pay wages of men & contingencies & pay over the rest, & if things go well enough during that time to authorize it, we can try the next year.

I think at any rate that I shall go to Peru this winter, if you have no objections, for I shall under any circumstances be better off there than here, where I fear I am every day falling behind hand.

I think under any circumstances I had better go, and I can stay in your house & live along until some one is sent by you to farm the domain. Col Kinney said he was ready to take me immediately in; his sister is going to be married & move off & he will be all alone. So that there will be no immediate trouble on my arrival. I hope you will approve of this move, for I do not see how I can get on longer at Detroit. I would agree to rent the farm & pay as high a price as any one, if I could get some thing to begin on, if you would like that plan better than on shares.

Julia received your kind letter[5] of the same date as mine from you & will leave for home the first opportunity. She is unwilling to go with [Fisher Ames] Harding & indeed I think him but a poor beau. He knows nothing about travelling & would get a lady into all sorts of dilemmas. Besides he is short of funds that he cannot tell how he shall get back or support himself while there. [Henry] Moore owes him a large sum.

Since I began this letter I have been attacked with a severe cold & fever again & a slight touch of the ague. I hope it may pass over for I should be very sorry to be shaking now, when my affairs make it necessary for me to be on my legs.

Please give my best regards to Dr. [Thomas] Sewall & Dr & Mrs [Harvey] Lindsley. All join in much affection & I remain Your most affectionate Son   Daniel F. Webster

ALS. ViU.
1. Grace Fletcher Webster (August
29, 1837–February 7, 1844).
2. Letter not found.

3. Not found.
4. See above, Daniel Fletcher Web-

ster to DW, August 28, 1837.
5. Not found.

FROM HENRY L. KINNEY

Peru Sept 4th 1837

My honored friend

I herewith enclose you Dr Frederick Halls dr[a]ft[1] on his brother D[aniel] W. Hall of Baltimore[2] for $800—which you will please collect —& furnish out of it an amount sufficient to pay the interest on my note given the Patriotic Bank. The amt ought to be paid to our f[rie]nd D. A. Hall Esq. as I suppose he has made some advances.

I sent him about three weeks since $300—which I suppose will more than pay for the last renewal.

Mr F Hall left here to day. I have made some investments for him in Peru. Things begin to brighten up here. I am getting allong with my affairs very much to my sattisfaction.

Some remittances will be made you without doubt for me through Mr [Daniel J.] Townsend from Buffalo.

I have had a line from Fletcher to day he is determined on living among us. I shall have all things ready for him at Salisbury. I have been bringing much of my business to a close. Since I wrote I have been offered by a French Gentleman twenty thousand Dollars for one thousand acres of land directly north of your Salisbury farm. Was it not that I expect to have it occupied some day by the *Websters* I should have sold, as he would pay me for it in Specie—Peru is improving very much at this time. I have had many visitors to see me since you were here—some of whom were disposed to purchase some of my farming interest near Peru. Is it not best to omit selling any of the Kinney estate for the present—I am selling some lots & getting cash. I think I shall be on to see you next month when I will settle every thing with Mr [William A.] Bradley to his sattisfaction & also with S[u]ydam Jackson & Co. I have met with a good [many] of my friends from the ajacent country lately & all agree to go for Webster. I am ever yours with great esteem   H. L. Kinney in great haste as the Stage is waiting.

(please write)

(I have got ten acres of wheat sowed on yr Farm.)

ALS. ViU.

1. Hall (c. 1779–1843; Dartmouth 1803) had served as tutor and professor at Dartmouth and Middlebury colleges before he earned his M.D.

from the Castleton, Vermont, Medical School in 1827. Later, he served as professor of chemistry at Trinity and Columbia colleges before his death at Peru, Illinois. Draft not found.

2. Hall, of Grafton, Vermont, at-

tended Dartmouth, 1805–1806, but did not graduate.

TO EDWARD WEBSTER

Washington Sep. 16. 1837

My Dear Son

I will endeavor to send you a little money, in a few days. In the mean time, I return your letter,[1] in which you will find as many errors, as you see marks.

There are mispellings;

There is no tolerably correct punctuation;

There are instances, in which sentences, after periods, are begun with small letters;

And words, which should be begun with large letters, are begun with small ones.

Write me, immediately, a more careful, & a better, letter.

AL (signature removed). NhHi. Pub-   1. Not found.
lished in Van Tyne, pp. 595–596.

TO RAMSAY CROOKS

Washington September 23d. 1837.

Sir

A note of mine, for $10,000, was given to Mr. [Pierre] Cho[u]teau, of St. Louis, and falls due 1st & 4th of October. Other notes, on account of the same transaction, were given by other gentlemen.[1]

Foreseeing, some time ago, that in the present state of things it would not be practicable to meet the payment, and the notes being secured by mortgage, I applied to Col. [George F.] Strother, with whom, as agent for Mr. Cho[u]teau, the business had been done, to give an extension. He said there would be no difficulty in granting it, and wrote to Mr. Cho[u]-teau on the subject. I have this day received a letter from Mr. Cho[u]-teau,[2] referring me to you, saying the note was in your hands. Col. Stro-ther is in New York, and I shall write him to call on you.[3]

My wish is, that the note may be held by you, till I reach New York, when I will endeavor to make a satisfactory provision for it. I will *pledge* myself, that the endorsers shall admit their responsibility without notice; but if you do not think this sufficient, and their responsibility important, a protest, of course, must take place. Yours, very respectfully

Danl Webster

LS. NHi.

1. At least three notes—one by DW for $10,000, and one each by Turner and Kinney for $5,000 endorsed by DW—represented a part of DW's indebtedness for the Clamorgan lands. See Ramsay Crooks to DW, October 2, 1837, below. Crook's continuing, and often frustrating, ef-

forts to collect these funds from DW, Turner, and Kinney can be traced in the letters between Crooks, DW, W. A. Bradley, Pratte, Chouteau and Company, and Pierre Chouteau, Jr., 1837–1840, in the American Fur Company Papers, NHi.

2. Not found.

3. Letter not found.

FROM HENRY L. KINNEY

Peru Sept. 23d. 1837

Hond. Sir

Your very kind letter of August 25th. from Boston & from N.Y. of 2d. inst.[1] was recd. a few days ago. I have been absent for the last week South & west. Consequently did not read them until some days after their arrival at Peru. It distresses me verry much to know of *your* being troubled on account of my affairs as well as your own. *I stand pledged to you & you only from this time to do any thing in my power as that you may advise for your advancement.* Had your letter from Boston come to hand, before Mr [Daniel J.] Townsend['s] departure to Niagara, I should have made my arrangements to set out for Washington so as to have met you there. It is impossible now for me to leave before he returns. I am expecting daily to hear from him. The time appointed for his return elapses this week. Money is becoming scarce and more difficult to obtain, & should I have to settle the matters with the Patriotick Bnk, I shall not be able to help you to funds to the extent I expected.

I believe I apprised you in my last, of the disappointment I met with in regard to receiving the Bnk drfts for cash advances, that I made in July to the amt of nearly $8000. I go to Chicago next week, as I have a promise of this money or the drfts at that time.

I have negociated a sale of some Bank Stock which I hold of the State Bank of Ill. on which I am to receive $5000. in a short time. I have not made sales to any extent since you were here & there has been no demand for real estate excepting for some of my farming interest near Peru. There is a family of Germans now at Peru that I could sell my Spring Creek farm to & get about twenty thousand Dollars in money down. I shall not sell it, *however* without your advice to do so, even at a greater price than it is worth. I have hinted [to] you the disposition I wished to make of my S[pring] Creek estate. I shall remain unaltered, until there is no hope of the accomplishment of my views in the matter. Then the disposal of S C *estate* or else matters not. Fletcher writes he will be with us at Salisbury this fall if he would not go east. All will be ready for him. All goes on well except these [pressing?] money matters. Timothy[2] tells me there is about 40 acres of wheat sowed & doing well on *Salisbury.* I will write you immediately after I hear from Townsend & know what sucksess he has in making collections. Mr Martin[3] will go east if (he *Townsend*) should get his funds as he expects. You will have heard from him on this I suppose. I shall here after make my remitances to you or Mr [David A.] Hall for the P[atriotic] B[ank] unless I hear from S[uydam] J[ackson] & Co. that all is right or from you that it will not be best to do so.

I shall be able to get drfts or notes discounted next month in our Bank at 90 days If I should want. But these times I feel as if it is well to be cautious about getting into Banks. Please write me what course I should take in my business with the P. B. It will make it tight times with me if I should settle it forth with. Can it not be arranged to pay by instalments. I dislike to trouble you & would not if I did not think it would be in my power to do for you that which would help to pay the many obligations I owe you. I have a prospect of selling Steam Boat & Stage Stock to the amt of thirty thousand Dolls. but shall not get much money down.

[I have not] commenced my dwelling house yet, & shall not probably until I come east. I am making some substantial improvements on my Spring creek farm. I have been building three new farm houses & two new Barns & made other improve[men]ts on the Spring Creek farm since you were here. I was over yesterday it looks very nice.

I am selling some town lots occasionally in Peru. The place has improved very much in the last two months & said to be the most business place in the west now.

I think I could negotiate with the Germans (who are here,) a sale of one thousand acres of land including the west half of Section 17, the remainder north & adjoining Peru for forty Dolls per acre. I was offered last year $100. per acre for a part of the same tract. I should rather not be obliged to sell, as I have about ninety thousand Dollars due me this day, & do not owe fifty thousand altogether, have between 80 and 90 thousand acres of land, over 60 thousand Dolls in Stocks. Is it best for me to sell my best real estate at a great sacrifice, or that which I desire to keep even at a fair price. I have written Mr Hall two letters & expect to hear from him. I am devotedly Yours   H. L. Kinney

Any news from Marshfield would be very interesting to me. My best regards to Mrs & Miss W. I hope Miss Julia got home comfortably. I write Fletcher this evening & you again in a few days. Always affectionately Yours   H L K

ALS. ViU.
1. Neither letter found.
2. One of Kinney's hired hands.
3. Not identified.

Washington Octr. 2. 37
Dr Sir
I recd yr. letter this morning.[1] Mr. [Levi C.] Turner arrived here last Evening. He is in negotiation, at New York for a large sum of money, & I shall return with him to that City at the end of this week, or the beginning of next, & stay there till we provide for all things.[2] We shall pass a Treasury note bill,[3] in some form, & I believe that is all which will be further done. The Sub-Treasuries may, or may not, pass the Senate—but cannot at this session pass the House.[4] Yrs truly
Danl. Webster   (over)

Please send me, at the American House, New York, copy of Mr [Levi] Beardsly's[5] acceptance, with memorandum of interest & damages. Mr Turner will write him (now at Albany) to meet me in N York, & if he does not come, I shall go or send to Albany. He is esteemed a very rich & *monied* man.

ALS. MH-H.

1. Not found.

2. In late October, Crooks reported to Pratte, Chouteau and Company that Webster was in New York negotiating to settle his accounts but was having little success. Turner had not shown up and had allowed his draft to be protested; and Webster had "already asked 6 & 12 months indulgence, but that I would not listen to under any circumstances." Between October 28 and November 1, DW was able to raise $2,000 to apply to his $10,000 account and, according to Crooks, DW had assured him that Kinney and Turner would shortly settle their accounts. "I hope," Crooks concluded, "this will all prove to be gospel, & so it would be, if Mr Webster had the means; but there is very little connexion nowadays between intention and ability." Ramsay Crooks to

Pratte, Chouteau and Company, October 21, 28, November 1, 1837, American Fur Company Papers, NHi.

3. The treasury note bill, approved on October 12, 1837, authorized the issuance of 6 percent interest-bearing notes up to a maximum of $10,-000,000. 5 *U.S. Statutes at Large* 201–204.

4. The subtreasury bill, which called for the deposit of the federal revenue in federal repositories rather than in state banks, passed the Senate on October 4. The House failed to consider the measure during the "special" session. *Senate Journal*, 25th Cong., 1st sess., Serial 308, p. 55.

5. Beardsley (1785–1857), a resident of Cherry Valley, Otsego County, New York, was a lawyer, legislator, and land speculator. Beardsley's acceptance has not been found.

FROM RAMSAY CROOKS

Office of the American
Fur Company
New York, 2 Octr 1837

Sir

Your favor of 23 ult: [1] only came to hand yesterday and in accordance with your wishes we have withdrawn from the Bank your Note for the $10,000 upon the faith of your pledge, and in the expectation that you will soon after your arrival here, make provision for the same.

We also hold the notes of Mr. Levi C. Turner and Mr. Henry L. Kinney, each $5000. with your endorsement, which we have in Bank for collection on the 4th Instant.

I am Very Respectfully your ob Servant   Ramy Crooks
President Am Fur Co

LC. NHi.
    1. See above.

FROM DANIEL FLETCHER WEBSTER

Detroit Oct. 30. 1837.

My dear Father

I received your kind letter of the 21st. Instant this morning [1] and hasten to reply to it.

I am very sorry to see by it that you have not received a long letter from me, stating to you at length my reasons for leaving Detroit & leaving this winter & also saying why I could not come to meet you at New York.[2] In the only letter in which that subject was mentioned by you, you did not appoint any time for me to meet you, nor did you speak decis[iv]ely about my coming, you merely suggested it & I replied to your suggestion, saying, that Caroline was too ill for me to leave & that we were at the time entirely unsettled besides. In my last letter to you, I mentioned what *Mr. [Benjamin B.] Kercheval* said & added, that I thought your letter must have miscarried, as I never received any such notice from you, except what was contained in a letter received from you some time previously & in which you merely said that you should perhaps think it best for me to come on & meet you in New York or Washington, & that you would bear my expenses & to which I replied as I have above said.

In regard to the draft; I had not one shilling, either to go or stay with —& that was the only way in which I could raise any thing & I drew on you with the intention of paying it myself. As I wrote you some time since, Mr. [Stephen] White has not even given me the certificates of my stock in his Canal Co. & has paid in only $400. on my Bank Stock, when he ought to have paid in $1000. The $400. was paid in when I got it. Of course I could get nothing out of what he promised you to give me on my marriage. Property will not sell & *collections* cannot be made. I had already as I wrote you, received more from you than I had any right to ask, & where then was money to come from? I made bold to draw on you, believing that I should be able to pay the draft myself, & you may rely upon it that I will & you need have no uneasiness about it. I drew on you for enough to pay every thing & leave me some thing for need at Peru.

I have been ever since August considering upon removing & have endeavoured to be very careful. I think my prospects there are better, that my expenses will be much less & that I can get on much faster. I go this fall for the sake of saving half a year's expenses. I have over five hundred dollars worth of business in my desk, I mean worth that in *fees*, but it will be a year before I can collect one hundred dollars of it; I have no other resources & how am I to live? I go to Peru with the hope of "earning my bread," which I have not been able to do here. I am much obliged to Mr. White for his kindness in thinking of getting me a place in Buffalo, but I most certainly would never go to that place or have any dependance upon him, while there was a chance any where else. It is now eleven months since I was married & he has not yet fulfilled his agreement; while you have, & much over; & he certainly knew that, whether I absolutely needed what he had agreed to advance or not, it would be very agreeable to me. You know, my dear Father, how extremely unpleasant it would be, to have to depend upon Mr. White, for any thing, & I shall never move East, until I can do so with an independence. Neither Caroline or myself would wish to go back & be exposed to the sneers of ill natured people, especially under the circumstances. We are ready for any hardship or privation, if they are to be undergone by us &, for my own part, I am resolved not to go East until I go there *rich* & can go when I please.

I think our health will be much better after this year & much better too in Peru, than here. We hope that we are pretty much acclimated by this time. The last letter but one which I wrote you was very long & contained all my views upon my proposed removal. I hope it has come to hand before this time. I am very sorry that you think my course precipitate, but really I did not know what else to do: I thought over, for two months, my situation & tried all resources to raise funds, & all of them failed, things looked very well at Peru, we none of us doubted that it would be a good place & I thought that it was my plan to go at once, if at all & I did not see how I was to live in Detroit this winter. I had no means of paying my expenses from any source that I knew of. Time was precious too unless I should try to make a most tedious and expensive journey over land; I consulted with what friends I had here, as it was impossible to do so with you fully. What you had said was that I had better think well before I took the step & I did so; you will understand my situation. I wish I could have seen you very much, but I could not leave Caroline so ill, & for a fortnight I have been quite ill myself. Caroline, with the exception of her removal down here from [?   ] has been confined to the house & almost all the time to her bed for a month, until last Thursday. She was taken ill Oct. 6th. It is two months since her confinement & she had not been comfortable a week before she was ill again. I stated her illness as the reason I could not leave to meet you, in answer to a suggestion in your letter that it might be well for me to do so.

I believe that one of your letters & one of mine to you has miscarried.

I am extremely perplexed, my dear Father, what to do; I would do nothing that should seem to you unadvised & precipitate, as you consider my move for Peru will be: & yet I do not see how I can stay here & I believe my situation there will be very good & that I shall be much better off there. I hope that when you understand my circumstances you will see some propriety in my decision. I was most unwilling to draw on you, but it was the only way left & you shall be at no sort of trouble about it. I hope you will not think I acted wrong, or at least that my situation may be some excuse for me with you.

I think, my dear Father, that we shall be a great deal happier at Peru than we are here & I shall at least have some thing to do. I believe it will be a good move for us & I hope that a few years will convince us all that my choice is a good one.

We expect to go by the Madison to-morrow or next day. The weather on the Lakes has been so boisterous for the last week that the boats have been still for three or four days. The weather [is] fine now & we think it will cont[inue so for a] fine voyage round. This will be our last chance for a boat this year. You must not think we are running any risk. Tis a fine boat & in [this] season of the year we generally have very fine we[ather during] the Indian Summer.

Caroline & the child are pretty well to-night. She sends her best love & affection to you & Mother & Julia, in which Ellen & myself join. Will write a line before I go on board. Your most affectionate son

Daniel F. Webster

I could get not sealing wax & must beg you to pardon wafers.

ALS. NhHi.

1. Not found.

2. See above, Daniel Fletcher Webster to DW, August 28 and September 1, 1837. Fletcher did not discuss in either letter, however, why he could not meet his father in New York.

BOND TO LEVI C. TURNER FOR $50,000

[October 30, 1837]

KNOW all men by these presents that I Daniel Webster of Boston Massachusetts am held and firmly bound unto Levi C. Turner of Otsego County New York in the penal sum of Fifty thousand Dollars current money of the United States to be paid to the said Levi C. Turner or his certain Attorney executors administrators or assigns, to which payment well and truly to be made I bind myself my heirs executors and administrators and every [one] of them by these presents Witness my hand and seal this thirtieth day of October A. D. 1837.

The condition of the above obligation is such, that whereas the said Daniel Webster is indebted to the said Levi C. Turner in the sum of Thirty Thousand Five Hundred dollars, to be paid in ten years from this date with annual interest.[1]

And whereas the said Daniel Webster has conveyed and procured to be conveyed to said Turner a large amount of Real Estate as collateral security—all or any portion of which said Turner has the authority to sell at any time hereafter and apply the proceeds to the payment here of —Now in case said Daniel Webster shall pay to said Turner or his legal representatives, such sum as shall remain due & unpaid, at the expiration of the said ten years, with interest as aforesaid, then this obligation void otherwise in force.

Witness—   Danl. Webster

DS. MWalB.

1. DW gave this bond probably to satisfy his indebtedness to Turner for Rock Island City property. Some three months later, Hamilton Fish, then a New York attorney, representing a client, detailed the story of the Webster-Turner drafts and bond and asked Elbridge Gerry Austin of the Boston Bar for advice. "I send herewith," Fish wrote, "a copy of a draft accepted by Daniel Webster which has been duly protested, & which the holder Mr. Samuel [W.] Beale of Otsego County in this State desires to have prosecuted against Mr. Webster.

"The circumstances attending the making of the draft &c are as I am informed by Mr. Beale as follows: Webster had purchased Western lands of Turner (the drawer) & this acceptance was given in payment. Turner paid it over to Lucius Lyon (of the U.S. Senate) from whom Beale purchased it at a considerable discount before its maturity. Negotiations have been pending for a long time with Turner for a settlement, & Mr. Webster on his return from Washington last October told me that he was then making arrangements with Turner whereby provision would be made for this acceptance. Since then I have been unable to obtain any information from Mr. Webster on the subject. I have written to him but received no answer. Turner has told me that Beale authorized him to make a settlement with Webster in his behalf of this claim; & that he (Turner) had included the amount of this draft in a settlement whereupon Webster had given him a bond for *about* $32,000. & had assigned to him as collateral security Western lands valued at about $67,000. Beale positively denies having ever authorized Turner to make any arrangement whatever in his behalf with Webster and from what I know of his opinion of Turner & from some other circumstances within my knowledge I should think it the *extreme of improbability* that Beale should have *trusted* Turner to make a settlement whereby his hold upon Webster might be discharged.

"I have commenced a suit for Beale against Turner upon the draft as well as some other liabilities. Can this affect his right to proceed against Webster in Massachusetts? Or is Mr. Webster protected by any privileges during his absence at Washington? Beale has been informed that proceedings can be commenced in Massachusetts by attachment against the property of the debtor. He does not desire unnecessarily vexatious proceedings; but wishes the *most summary* process instituted which may be likely to produce the money.

"I would further ask whether you can unite Turner as a defendant. I presume his *interest* is that Webster should be obliged to pay the draft & that would be a sufficient guarantee to exclude any testimony of his adverse to Beale's right of recovery against W. Yet Beale mistrusts him so much (his statements to me have been so contradictory and inconsistent not only with each other but with all probability) that he desires if possible to anticipate the means of excluding his testimony." Fish to Austin, February 16, 1838, Hamilton Fish Papers (typed copy), DLC. Beall's name was misspelled throughout.

TO JOSEPH COWPERTHWAITE

New York Oct. 31. 1837

My Dear Sir

I have been here ten or twelve days, & a great part of that time Mr. [Levi C.] Turner has been negotiating for a large loan of money, to enable him to take up his, & Mr [Levi] Beardsley's acceptances, at your Bank. Mr Beardsley has been here also. As yet, Mr Turner has not accomplished his object. He seems to have abundant means, in bonds & mortgages, but has not found a sale for them, without such *Jewing* as no Christian man can well submit to. Mr. Turner is certainly a man of large & available property, & the comparative amount of his debts is small. He proposes to renew his acceptances, & to pay discounts, &c; in which object, I hope he will meet with success.

Mr Beardsleys 5000 acceptance, discounted for my benefit, will be attended to, & provided for, in some way, ere long.

I have taken of Mr Turner a prime mortgage, for 26.700, in 5 years, interest annually at 7 pr cent. This mortgage covers a portion of the very heart of the City of Chicago, at the Canal Basin. The premises are worth 2 ½ or 3 times the debt, now. The interest is payable annually at the Bank in Detroit.

Can you find me a purchaser, for such a mortgage, on reasonable

Terms? Or would the Bank be willing to take an assesment of it, & let it stand as an *indorser* for me? The title is unquestionable, the mortgagor, Gurdon S. Hubbard, & satisfactory evidence of adequate value is easily given.

I go home today; pray write me a line, touching these subjects.

I cannot sleep anights. The Susquehannah is always before my eyes. Yrs   D. Webster

ALS. PHi. Cowperthwaite was cashier   United States at this time.
of the Pennsylvania Bank of the

AGREEMENT BETWEEN DANIEL WEBSTER AND SAMUEL LEWIS SOUTHARD

Octr. 31. 1837

Danl. Webster having left with S. L. Southard 20 Shares in the Clamorgan grant, as security for D. Webster's note for $10.000 to Morris Canal Co. it is agreed that said Southard may sell said shares, for the purpose of paying said note; & one half of all said shares may sell for, above fifty cents p[e]r arpent, said S. L. Southard shall be entitled to retain, as his compensation.   Danl. Webster   Saml. L. Southard

ADS. NjP. Southard's endorsement of   posited the 20 shares with Cashier
this item is as follows: M. C. & B. Co. as collateral security
"D. Webster to S. L. Southard Author-   for note of $10.000, to be sent by Mr.
ity to sell 20 shares in Clamorgan   W. & our bond or P. Note for $10.500
Grant—2 Novr. 1837. enclosed dupli-   sent to him."
cate of this paper to Mr. W. & de-

FROM EDWARD WEBSTER

Dart. Coll. Nov 6th 1837.

My Dear Father,

I should have written to you a long time since had I not hurt my hand so badly as to render me unable to use the pen.

Our vacation begins the 30th of this month. Cousin Charles [B. Haddock] says that "the faculty will not require me to come back the short term if I study French or any other branch: it will be regarded the same as if I kept school.["]

There has been a writing school here which I should have attended if I had been able. I was very sorry that it happened so, for I am aware what a bad hand I write. I dined at Mr Hadducks a few days since they were all well and desired to be remembered to you and Mother.

We are studying Homers Iliad fourth book and Navigation which are both very interesting studies; and we also have excercises in compositions and declamations every afternoon to Cousin Charles.

I shall require $75 to pay my expenses this term as it is a long vacation[.] I shoud rather pay them before I go home if it would be as convenient to you. I have been as economical as possible but it cost a great deal for furniture &c which last year I hired with my room. I took a ride on your little horse the other day. I like him very much and I think he will make a splendid saddle horse for Julia.

Please give my best love to Mother & Julia & tell Mother I will write in a few days.

I remain my Dear Father your duitiful and affectionate son
Edward Webster

ALS. NhHi.

TO HENRY EDWARDS ET AL.

Boston, Nov. 16th, 1837.

Sir:

If it should be thought advisable to hold a meeting of the citizens, to celebrate, in a proper manner, the recent political success, I shall cheerfully attend it if I should be in the city at the time. Several assemblages have been already convened, which have furnished occasions for mutual congratulations.

Whether any thing more formal or more exclusively confined to the object, ought further to be done, I refer to the feelings and direction of others.

Let us remember, that this great and unprecedented success has been obtained clearly and distinctly on whig grounds. It has been the result of no yielding, no compromise, no abandonment of our principles.

These principles have now received decisive proofs of the approbation of the people; and to our own consciousness that they are just, and calculated to promote the public good, we may add our belief, that they will be more and more generally adopted.

It is, therefore, our duty to adhere to these principles with unwavering steadiness and constancy. Thus far, they have sustained us, and for one, I shall not consent to depart from them.

At the same time, it is equally our duty and our interest, to conduct towards those who have differed from us, with so much moderation and kindness, that they may not be constrained to keep aloof. May we not hope, that many, in all quarters, who see what the actual condition of things is, and how wide and deep is the general dissatisfaction of the people with recent measures of government, will now join us, in carrying on the great work of restoring the government to its well tried and approved policy, and the country to its former prosperity.

To consistency of principle, then let us add all reasonable and practicable conciliation. Let us receive cordially and without reproach, all who will unite with us in upholding and bearing onward, the whig standard.

Will you allow me, sir, to say a word or two, on another, but a connected subject?

We are engaged in an attempt to correct, what we honestly believe to be important errors, in the administration of the government.

To accomplish this object, we can rely on nothing nor do we wish to rely on anything, but the power of the people.

The changes which we have witnessed have been produced by the good sense and patriotism of the people, breaking through artificial barriers of patronage and party, and sweeping away long established political combinations. Our further success must depend on the continued operation of the same causes.

We have nothing, either to carry us forward, or to sustain us where we are, but the justice of our cause, the wisdom of our measures, and the popular approbation.

However, it may be with that of others, our cause is, emphatically, in the hands of the people; and let it be one of our fixed principles, that the people shall be heard; that they shall, in all things, speak for themselves, and that opinions, in regard either to men or measures, shall not be manufactured for the many, by the few. Let the popular voice prevail, and have its free course, fairly and honestly, without control and without elevation.

We have accused others of such arrangements and such combinations in political affairs, as have produced the effect of giving, on important occasions, the people's sanction to that which the people, nevertheless did not really approve. Let us take care that the cause of the whigs, which I believe to be at present the true cause of the country, be never exposed to this reproach. Yours, with very true regard,   Daniel Webster.

Text from *Niles' National Register*, 53 (December 2, 1837): 218. Original not found. Published in *W & S*, 16: 291–292. Edwards (1798–1885), a Boston merchant, was the nephew of Arthur Tappan, under whom he received his mercantile training. With Charles Stoddard of Boston, he dealt in French dry goods. As chairman of the Suffolk County Whig convention, he had invited (November 15) Webster to address a gathering to celebrate the Whigs' resounding victory in the recent state elections. According to Niles, the celebration was deferred, "considering the great number of public meetings that have lately taken place."

FROM FISHER AMES HARDING

Detroit, Nov. 19. 1837.

My Dear Sir,

I had hoped to have seen you when I was at the East, but I felt constrained to leave for the west before you returned from Washington. As Daniel had decided to go to Illinois and as I was a comparative stranger as yet in Detroit, I was unwilling to be absent any longer than was strictly necessary. I had besides some hopes of meeting you on my way in New York.

Since my return, Daniel has started for Illinois & has I presume arrived before this. I have not yet heard from him since his departure, but am daily looking for a letter. I trust he has had a safe passage, though it is not without its risks at this late season.

On my starting for the East, I wrote you a letter,[1] saying that the assurances, which Daniel received from Mr. [Henry] Moore in Chicago that my note for the Superior City &c. property due last August could be extended, had failed, and that as the best that could be done, I had renewed it at the Ann Arbor Bank for $1000 for three months and had drawn on you for the balance $250. My chief object in writing now is to ask you what arrangement you would wish to have made with it. I am inclined to think that a further extension for a part at least could be obtained. I will make the attempt at any rate if you should wish it. I presume money still continues to be scarce at the East. It is emphatically so here.

Daniel joined with me in the renewed note, and Mr. [Phineas] Davis endorsed it.

We have little news here. We have lost the election in this State, but have reduced the majority about one half since August. There is a large addition to the number of Whig members in the Legislature, and some of the new members are men of superior talent and decision. It is thought that their exertions the coming Winter will have considerable influence upon the politics of the State. It is unfortunate that the New York elections did not occur a little earlier, as they would have materially affected the result in Michigan. But we must submit to our fate, as it is, for the present.

Be so kind as to present my regards to Mrs. Webster and Miss Julia. With much regard, Yours truly,   Fisher A. Harding.

P.S. My note falls due Dec. 10th.

ALS. ViU.
1. See Harding to DW, September 12, 1837, mDW 14396.

FROM DANIEL FLETCHER WEBSTER

Peru Dec. 5th. 1837.

My dear Father
I have been intending to write you for the last two days, but have been

prevented. We are getting on very well with all matters. I have considerable business of one kind & another & of some importance—my great
trouble is no stove in my office—though we have had but very little cold
weather as yet—a great deal of *rain* & our roads are almost impassable.
We have had no mail for several days. The river has risen so as nearly
to reach the foundations of some of the buildings on the street at Peru—
it is entirely over the inland & has drowned out all sorts of varmints on
the bottom land—a very large wildcat was killed in the water on Sunday,
just opposite Peru. The Canal is covered & all business stopped. The hay
has nearly all floated off; the Col [Henry L. Kinney] must have lost at
least three hundred tons. Spring creek, where you went fishing was a
foaming torrent yesterday. The water covers all from bluff to bluff at
Peru & looks like a lake. But this material high tide is nothing to the political movement of the waters so unexpected in New York.[1] This is really
a crowning glory. You will have seen before this what sensation it had
made all through the West. Michigan too has completely changed. Gov.
[Stevens Thomson] Mason instead of 5000. had 600: majority and all
the Legislature Whig. I see Massachusetts has as usual done her duty.

We have read the doings in Faneuil Hall with great pleasure.[2] If we
were not so poor and so full of business we would have a jubilee here on
this great occasion.

Caroline has been very well and is as well content as ever with her
situation here. The Col. is all kindness and attention, though very much
occupied and a good deal troubled with money matters. The numerous
matters in which he is engaged and his habit of doing every thing himself from harnessing his horse up to making a Canal contract leave him
but very little time for any thing. He goes to town at nine & returns to
dinner at six. We like it very well; breakfast at half past eight—the Col
& I mount our horses & ride to town, come home at six & have dinner &
spend the evening in reading talking & writing.

I expect to go down to St. Louis to-morrow on business for the Col—
shall be absent about a week. He has several suits of some importance
and I am Crown counsellor on all occasions. I am busy making a couple
of Trust deeds just now, with shifting uses & so on & am employed to
draw up all sorts of agreements amongst the adopted citizens on the
Canal. When my books all get on and my office is nicely arranged & a
good stove in it I shall feel quite a business man.

I believe that I shall not attempt to carry on your farm—& I should be
very glad to see [Nathaniel] Ray [Thomas][3] here in the Spring. He could
do nothing now. I should like to live in the house for the present. We
could all get on together very well.

The Col's men Cornelius [Cokeley][4] & Timothy are his masters but I manage to manage them as far as I want. On the whole I am much pleased with the change from Detroit.

Dr. [John Mark] Smith[5] will see you in Washington & will tell you how we all are.

The Col. has been intending to leave for a month but he cannot say when he shall be able to get away.

Caroline sends you & Mother her best love. She will write to Mother this week. We had a letter from Aunt Harriet [Story Paige] today. Ellen is very well. Grace growing large & very pretty. Your most affectionate son   Daniel F. Webster.

ALS. NhHi.

1. In what was termed a "political tornado," Whigs had swept to victory in the state elections in Van Buren's home state.

2. With Webster, John Bell of Tennessee, and Ogden Hoffman and Edward Curtis of New York present, Massachusetts Whigs had gathered in Faneuil Hall on November 10 to celebrate the election results. *National Intelligencer*, November 16, 1838.

3. Thomas (1812–1840) was the brother of Charles Henry and an employee of Webster's at Marshfield. In 1838, Webster hired him to look after his western investments.

4. Cokeley (d. c. 1850), a native of Pennsylvania, had gone to Peru about 1835 with Henry L. Kinney.

5. Smith, a native of Philadelphia and the brother of Samuel Lisle Smith, lived in Peru and Chicago from 1837 to 1842.

TO CHARLES HENRY THOMAS

N York Decr. 11 '37

Dear Henry

We are here yet—having been to L. Island to make a visit to Mr [David Samuel] Jones.[1] We shall go South about Thursday. There appears to be nothing doing at Washington. Not a word yet from Mr. Kinney, nor from Fletcher since he reached Peru. I suppose I shall find letters at Washington.

I shall write you again, before I leave this City. Yrs   D. Webster

I must have a fish pond. Mr Jones' covers 40 acres. He could rent it for 600 Dlls a year. I saw a little one, not an acre, belonging to one of his neighbors—*full of trout*, & no brook to run into above.

We must have a survey of yellow bog pond. Suppose we excavate, a little, so as, in some places to come down to the gravel. Then raise the dam, so as to flow back towards, but not to, the orchard; then throw up an embankment, so as to define the edge, & make dry walking all round on the Bank—leaving the hassocks, old di[t]ch banks, &c for cover to the fish, & throwing in also some cedar bushes, in the deep places, for the same purpose—not breaking the soil, along the lower part, but letting the water merely flow up, on the grass.

Think of all this, at yr leisure—& see how much we could flow, without much injury, beyond the loss of the fresh grass, which I do not care about—& how *deep* we could make it. Ask Capt Peleg to look at it—perhaps he would like a job. Mr Ford² might take a *level*, if you & the Capt. cannot do it.

ALS. MHi.

1. Jones (1777–1848; Columbia 1796) had served on the New York City Council, 1813–1816, and was at this time county judge of Queens County, Long Island, and a trustee of

Columbia College. In 1827, he had married Susan Le Roy, Caroline's sister.

2. Captain Peleg and Mr. Ford were probably Marshfield neighbors.

FROM HENRY L. KINNEY

Peru December 16th. 1837

My esteemed friend

You will doubtless be a little surprised to learn by this that I am still at Peru.

I have never been more anxious to get away but it seems as if the fates forbade it, allmost every attempt to raise funds, for the last 3 months has proved fruitless. Those on whom I most depended to pay me money have disappointed me. The money affairs of the country for 2 or 3 months past have been in a dreadful condition.

I have thought propper to hold on here a short time longer with the expectation that by staying I shall collect an amount to bring with me that I other wise should not.

On my return last evening from Chicago I found in waiting Mr [William A.] Bradleys letter of the 23d. ulto. in which he says that unless some sattisfactory settlement is made within 30 days from that time a suit will be commenced against you Mr [David A.] Hall & myself on my note to the P[atriotic] Bank. I have done all in my power to arrange my affairs so as to come on and settle the matter with the Bank. But verry much to the injury of myself & friends I have been most sadly disappointed. I should not think the course proposed by the bank would be the quickest and best way of sattisfactorily settling the matter.

I shall do all in my power to have the Bank forthwith paid and will sattisfy those connected with it for any injury sustained by them in consequence of the non compliance with my contract.

I had my arrangements made before leaving the east last Spring to redeem these notes, *which I can show to the Bank*, without depending upon the resources derived from their use.

Notes that I hold against as respons[ible] men as there is in this country for money actually loaned them to be paid on demand remain yet

unsettled in my hands. Some of the best men in the east have authorized me to make investments for them, which I have done and paid in
the notes of the Patriotic Bank—and when I made drft on them for the
amt. they were returned to me protested with the assurance that the
hard times prevented them from taking advantage of the purchase.
These I have been unable to dispose of, for money & the consequence is,
I must lay out of the money. These disappointments lead to verry unpleasant results.

I am verry sorry to give you any trouble about this matter & would
not if I did not consider you were indirectly to be benefited by the loan.
I believe it will be in my power however to reward you well for any trouble you may take in the adjustment of this matter.

I propose to settle the debt in this way. I have placed in the hands of
Messrs S[u]ydam Jackson & Co 4.236.57 sent you by Doct. Smith in
drft 3.363.00 My acceptance or note to be discounted.

The Bal to be made into a 4 or 6 months note to be renewed at maturity by payment of 1/4 the amt with interest. I send my Blank acceptance which [y]ou can make payable in New York Phila or in this State
[here]. I will be prepared to take it up at maturity. I am [i]nclined to believe that Mr [Nicholas] Biddle will have it discounted at his Bank, as
several of my drfts have been discounted there within 6 months. If you
can have this matter settled for me in this way, it will relieve my mind
verry much, besides confering one more great favour to the many already bestowed.

I have had much trouble this summer in keeping my great variety of
business properly going. Our payments average about 20.000 per month.
The revenues from our Canal have been small compared to the heavy
advances that were made to open & prosecute the work. I have written
to Mr. Bradley, this day and refered him to you for the proposition, contained herein.

Fletcher has just returned from St Louis whither he has been on business for me. Mrs Webster Miss [Ellen] Fletcher & little Miss Grace are
all at Salisbury, All well & seem quite contented & happy. Salisbury is a
verry pleasant place to visit I can assure you, altho some what retired &
yet there is a great deal of comfort taken there.

[Daniel J.] Townsend & Kinney will be indirectly concerned in a new
Bank about being established in Wisconsin.[1] This when established will
give us facilaties that we have not heretofore had. It takes time however
to bring these things about especially so when its up hill [in] every direction. I am making some other Banking arrangements with a substantial
institution that will give me command of almost [any] amt of Capital I
may have use for.

I shall do all in my power to get started eastward, & on seeing you will explain all to you sattisfactorly. My friends this way have all been hard pressed, some of which are under strong obligations to me & from whom I had reason to expect much. I have recd nothing—but promises. Those disapointments have given me trouble & all that has prevented my going east before. The amt I have paid in cash for eastern bills since you were here that have not been met, would make me easy now. I have kept all well here. My only trouble is east. I desire to be kindly rem[em]bered to Mrs W & Miss Julia, a package of letters went from Salisbury to them by Capt. Burnett[2] a few days since. With a hope of getting off in a few weeks I remain always affectionately & sincerely your devoted friend

H. L. Kinney

Dec 18. 1837

I have thought proper to enclose the letter to Mr [William A.] Bradley[3] to you that you may read its contents before it goes to Mr Bradley. The reason of my omitting writting so long was in consequence of my having the promises of a Bank dr[a]ft on N. Y. which I was in daily expectation of receiving for 3 or 4 weeks—past. I have been to Chicago & had to extend the time. This expectation is basic[?] on a/c of $8.000 I loaned in Chicago when there with you last July. I am in hopes yet to get it in a week or two.

I shall write you again shortly [from] the west of which I shall soon afterwards leave for Washington. Yours truly   H. L. Kinney

ALS. NhHi.
    1. Kinney was probably referring either to the Bank of Racine or the Bank of Iowa, which the territorial legislature of Wisconsin had char-

tered on January 12, 1838. Both banks failed to open.
    2. Not identified.
    3. Not found.

FROM RAMSAY CROOKS

Office of the American
Fur Company
New York 20 Decr. 1837

Dear Sir

At the time your servant called with your message last friday I expected to have been able to wait upon you, but found it impracticable. I however presume you did not succeed in making arrangements to pay the balance of your Note, which I regret the more as by a letter received this morning from Mr [William A.] Bradley by Mr [Pierre] Chouteau [Jr.] who is now here, he is expected to collect without delay the whole amount of the Notes given his Father in part payment of the Clamorgan Grant.

It will be to me an extremely disagreeable task to make any other than an amicable collection of these Notes, but I cannot see how I can avoid it with propriety, and I really do hope you will at an early day make such arrangements as will relieve me from the necessity of pursuing a course so repugnant to my feelings.

I am with much respect Your ob servant

Ramy Crooks President Am Fur Co

LC. NHi.

FROM DANIEL FLETCHER WEBSTER

Peru. Dec 30. 1837.

My dear Father,

Lowrie & his companion[1] came to hand today, all well—after a very long journey. I did not get your letter in time to have any work cut out for them & our house is so full with the Col's men that they cannot for the present be accomodated up at Salisbury; so I have got a place for them at Peru, until some change shall be made. I was very glad to see them & hope that Lowrie & his friend Alexander Lowrie will behave as well as he used to at Marshfield.

I would advise you however to send no more Irish here—they will be a great source of trouble & vexation as it is. Two such fellows as the Col. has, are enough to ruin a whole settlement. We have great trouble in getting along with them & are in hopes that he will find it consonant with his interest & convenience to remove them soon.

There will be work enough for Lowrie soon, but at present he can't do much except fence in his garden. Two acres will I suppose be enough. I should put it on the East side of the house, about half on the prairie & half on the timber. I have been looking today for a proper site & have not been able to conclude finally which would please you best. I will be careful in my selection, so that it may not be changed. We are all well. Caroline rode on horseback today. Our love to Mother, Julia & Edward and I remain Your most affectionate son   Daniel F. Webster

ALS. NhHi.

1. Alexander Lowrie and "his companion," acquaintances and workers for Webster at Marshfield, had been employed by DW to work at the Salisbury farm in Peru, Illinois. See DFW to DW, December 28, 1837, mDW 14522.

TO RAMSAY CROOKS

Washington Jan. 2. 1838

My Dear Sir

Ill health confined me, both at N. York & Philadelphia, & I arrived here only on the 28th. ult. I find here your letter of the 20th.[1] I had great hopes of being able to pay Mr. [Pierre] Chouteaus note, before this time, but have been disappointed, in every quarter, to which I looked, & had a right to look for funds. I do not complain of Mr Chouteau's impatience. He is entitled to his money. I wish now to prepare such times & terms of payment, as may be met, without further disappointment.

I therefore say, that I will remit to you; viz;

In all February	3,000
In all May	2,500
In all July	2,500; & all int[eres]t—

If this will be satisfactory, the payments shall be made, with precise punctuality.[2] Yours with much regard,   Danl Webster

ALS. NhHi.

1. See above, Crooks to DW, December 20, 1837.

2. In response to DW's suggested repayment schedule, Crooks wrote: "We were in hopes it would have been in your power to discharge the claim at an earlier day, but we never- theless accede to your proposal under the conviction that you will pay us sooner if you can, and at all events that the several amounts will be punctually met at the date[s] specified." Ramsay Crooks to DW, January 5, 1838, mDWs.

FROM DANIEL FLETCHER WEBSTER

Peru Jany 8. 1838

My dear Father

We have been very anxiously waiting & expecting to hear from you. The last news was from you at New York, by Julia's letter of Dec. 3d.[1] I hope that you are well & that nothing but business prevents your writing us a line.

Col. [Henry L.] Kinney is very anxious indeed to hear from you. It is now more than a month since he sent on to you by [Samuel] Lisle Smith's[2] brother, Dr. John Smith, by whom he also sent funds for various purposes & has not heard a word yet either from the Dr. or the funds.

His Patriotic Bank matters trouble him a good deal & he is anxious to hear from you about them. He cannot leave Peru, on account of the urgency of matters here, for though he *does* make everything go while he is here, he dares not leave them to go alone, although it is so important for him to be at the East. He has asked me if I will go on in case he finds it absolutely indispensable either to go or send & I have promised to make the journey. Dr. Smith's conduct appears very extraordinary. Lisle has written several times & says not a word of his brother & in one letter, his last, tells the Col. a note of his for $1200. will be protested the next day at the U. S. Bank, to take up which very note the Col. sent on the money by Dr. John. Things are going well enough here. Money enough & provisions enough. Col. complains a good deal of some of his friends—Suydam & Jackson & Gurdon Hubbard & R [P.] & J[ames H.] Woodworth.[3] We are all well at the Farm.

The Col. has just come into the office. He says that he would come on at any rate if it were [not] necessary for him to remain in order to complete some pecuniary arrangements which he is making by means of several Banks here and in Michigan, & which arrangement, when completed will secure him funds enough for all purposes & give him the control of the money matters of this part of the State.

He is busy too with political affairs, that demand his attention. He has been requested by his friends to stand for Governor—but has pretty much declined. We are to have a County meeting in my office on the 20th. to appoint delegates to the *Gubernatorial*, as Gov. [Levi] Lincoln calls it, & Congressional Conventions.

I was about to say that we were well at the farm. Caroline has been a little bilious, but rides on horseback now & gets better.

Arthur [Wellington] Fletcher[4] wants to come out here & Col K. says he will put him in the way of doing well, especially if he is like his sister Ellen. I wrote him to that effect. Our little girl is very well & grows fast. She is really very pretty indeed—looks like neither of her parents. I have business enough *almost* to do even now, & hope to have more than I can do bye & bye.

Lowrie is fixing the garden—

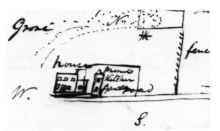

This is the proper site for a house. The garden is placed without reference to the present edifice.

Here is the plan.

It embraces both wood & prairie & is the best place I could find; about four gunshots from the house (240. yrds) for the double barrel, or Mrs. Patrick.[5]

There is a good deal to be done—the fence to be put up & then I don't see how we shall break up the ground properly. Two acres is too much to spade up & it will be difficult to get along with[out] the plough—but I can fix it some how. I am going to have an ice house made in the bank, back of the house, so that you can have a hail storm next summer.

Please give our best love to Mother. Tell her we are very comfortable. We think we shall wait here until you all come on & then go East with you. I wish you could see Grace. She will be able to walk & talk a *little* when you do.

Best love to Julia & Edward & I am, dear Father your most affectionate Son   Daniel F. Webster

ALS. NhHi.

1. Not found.

2. Smith (1817–1854), a native of Philadelphia, had first settled in Peru, but moved to Chicago in 1838, where he pursued law and land speculation and engaged in Whig politics.

3. R. P. Woodworth, probably a brother of James H., has not been

further identified.

4. Fletcher (1814–1874), a native of Portland, Maine, was a son of Timothy Fletcher, DW's brother-in-law.

5. "Mrs. Patrick" was probably the name of a gun. Since DW named his fishing rod (Killall), he probably named his gun too.

When Webster took his seat in the Senate on December 29, 1837, the chief debate was not on financial issues but on slavery and abolitionism. In response to the mob murder of Elijah P. Lovejoy on November 7, 1837, several northern congressmen had returned to Washington with renewed zeal to push the abolitionist cause. On December 18, before the House reenacted the "gag rule," William Slade of Vermont had presented petitions for the abolition of slavery and of the slave trade in the District of Columbia. He had spoken on the subject and moved that the petitions be referred to a special committee charged to report a bill granting the prayer of the petitioners. A day later, Slade's colleague in the Senate, Benjamin Swift, had introduced resolutions from the Vermont legislature on the same general subject. Following a caucus of southern politicians on December 20, Calhoun proposed six resolutions on December 27, in general restating the compact and reserved powers theories of the Constitution and declaring that the general government was obligated to resist all attempts to interfere with slavery. Webster opposed this view of the Constitution, and voted against Calhoun's first two resolutions when they came up on January 3. But he equally opposed Clay's substitutes for Calhoun's fifth and sixth resolves. Clay's resolutions declared that Congress had no jurisdiction over slavery in the states and no power to interfere with the slave trade in the District of Columbia. In the correspondence with Luther Christopher Peck and Hiram Ketchum below, Webster discussed his views of the powers of the general government over slavery and the slave trade, and concluded that both Calhoun and Clay were attempting once again to remake the Constitution.

TO [LUTHER CHRISTOPHER] PECK

Senate Chamber, January 11, 1838.

My dear Sir,

I can have no possible objection to stating to you, in any manner you may desire, my opinions on the various branches of this great and agitating subject of slavery.

In the first place I concur entirely in the resolution of the House of Representatives, passed as early as March, 1790, at a calm and dispassionate period in our political history. That resolution is in the following words:

"*Resolved*, That Congress have no authority to interfere in the emancipation of slaves, or in the treatment of them within any of the States; it remaining with the several States alone to provide any regulations therein which humanity and true policy may require."

In the next place, I entertain no doubt whatever that Congress possessing, by the express grant of the Constitution, a right to exercise exclusive legislation in all cases whatsoever, over the District of Columbia, the same having been ceded by the States of Maryland and Virginia, and become the seat of the government of the United States, have full authority to regulate slavery within the said District, or to abolish it altogether, whenever, in their judgment, humanity and true policy may require it; and that they have full authority also to regulate or restrain the purchase and sale of slaves within the said District, in any manner which they may deem just and expedient.

I am also clearly and entirely of opinion, that neither by the acts of cession by the States, nor by the acceptance by Congress, nor in any other way, has the faith of Congress become pledged to refrain from exercising its constitutional authority over slavery and the slave-trade in the said District.

More than all, it is my opinion, "that the citizens of the United States have an unquestionable constitutional right to petition Congress for the restraint or abolition of slavery and the slave-trade within the said District; and that all such petitions being respectfully written, ought to be received, read, referred, and considered in the same manner as petitions on other important subjects are received, read, referred, and considered; and without reproach or rebuke to the authors or signers of such petitions."

The right of petition, free, unqualified, and untrammelled, I hold to be of the very substance and essence of civil liberty. I can have no conception of a free government, where the people, respectfully approaching those who are elected to make laws for them, and offering for their consideration petitions respecting any subject, over which their constitutional power of legislation extends, may be repelled, and their petitions rejected, without consideration and even without hearing.

Wherever there is a constitutional right of petition, it seems to me to be quite clear, that it is the duty of those to whom petitions are addressed, to read and consider them; otherwise the whole right of petition is but a vain illusion and a mockery. I am, dear Sir, with very true regard, Dan'l Webster.

Text from *PC*, 2: 31–33. Original not found. Peck's letter to DW has not been found.

TO HIRAM KETCHUM

Washington, Jan. 15. 1838

Dear Sir

My Speech on Mr Clays Resolution will appear, I hope, in the Intelligencer tomorrow.[1] I venture to say you will be satisfied with it. We are not slumbering here—but wish to act with circumspection, as well as decision. I consider the proceedings of the Senate as having drawn a line, which can never be obliterated.

Mr Clay & Mr Calhoun, in my judgment, have attempted in 1838, what they attempted in 1833, *to make a new Constitution.*[2]

I am engaged today, up to the chin, in Com[mitt]ee. on the new Sub. Treasury & in Court. Tomorrow, I will write you, on the Hartford Convention] & on the Tariff law of 1833.[3] Yrs   D Webster

ALS. DLC. Published in *PC*, 2: 33.

1. Webster's speech appeared in the *National Intelligencer* of January 23, 1838 (reprinted in *W & S*, 8: 109–114).

2. For Webster's position on Clay's compromise tariff bill in 1833, see *Correspondence*, 3: 202, 209, 213–221, 224.

3. For DW's letter on the Hartford Convention, see DW to [Hiram Ketchum, January 1838], mDW 14613. A discussion of DW and the Hartford Convention question, taken from the *New York Whig*, appeared in the *National Intelligencer*, January 30, 1838. DW's discussion of the tariff appears in DW to Ketchum, January 20, 1838, below.

FROM HAMILTON FISH

New York January 19. 1838

My Dear Sir

When I last had the pleasure to see you in New York, at the request of

Mr. S[amuel] W[ooten] Beall,[1] I mentioned his having placed in my hands a draft for $4.075 drawn by Levi C Turner & accepted by you, which fell due in August last. I understood from you that Mr. Turner was then making some arrangements, of which he would apprise Mr. Beall & whereby the draft would be paid.

I am desired to inform <of> you that no arrangement has been made by Mr. Turner with Mr. Beall, but that after repeated attempts to affect an amicable Settlement Mr. Beall has been obliged to institute a suit against Turner. Mr. Beall is sorely distressed for money to meet his engagements & advises me that unless some arrangement can be made for the Spring payment of this draft or for substituting some New York City Securities (upon which he may receive money) that he shall be under the necessity of resorting to your liability upon the draft. Will you have the goodness to apprise me whether any arrangement can be made to satisfy him & to relieve me from the painful necessity of obeying my clients instructions?[2] With the most sincere respect I have the honor to be Your Obedt. Servt.   H. F.

LC. DLC.

1. Beall (1807–1868; Union College 1827), a native of Maryland, had settled in Green Bay, Wisconsin, about 1829, where he practiced law. Appointed receiver in the Green Bay Land Office in 1835, he engaged in land speculation and reportedly amassed a small fortune, whereupon he settled in Cooperstown, N.Y. Subsequently, he lost his wealth as a result of a Treasury Department investigation that found him in default to the government for some $17,000, much of which he had used to lend to friends. Alice E. Smith, *From Exploration to Statehood*, Vol. 1 of *The History of Wisconsin*, ed. William Fletcher Thompson (Madison, 1973), p. 421.

2. For additional information on this question, see Hamilton Fish to E. G. Austin, February 16, 1838, Hamilton Fish Papers, DLC (partly quoted above, pp. 246–247).

TO [HIRAM KETCHUM], WITH ENCLOSURE
Washington Jan. 20. 1838

My Dear Sir

I enclose you a copy of Mr Clay's bill, in 1833,[1] as originally prepared by him. The copy was made by me, from the original, in Mr C's own handwriting. Some alterations took place, before the measure was formally brought forward, as others, during the progress in Congress. Nevertheless, if you examine the law, it is, now, in truth, an attempt by Congress to surrender the protecting powers, & strike it out of the Constitution. I opposed this bill in every stage, & so did three fourths of the Tariff interest in both Houses. All the South went for it; Mr C's personal friends went for it; & a few good men, from the North & the Center, from various motives, went for it also; for example, Mr [Samuel] Bell, of N. H. & Mr. [Theodore] Frelinghuysen.

The Bill passed at the end of the Session. I took my notes &c. along with me, & staying a day or two in Philadelphia, sat down to write out my Speech at length. A friend happened to come in, & finding out what I was about, dissuaded me from it. He said the act was done—the thing was settled—& the publication of my Speech would only prove a wider difference to exist, among friends. I acquiesced, which I have ever since regretted. When I reached New York, I had conversation, on the subject, with Mr C[harles] King, & *left with him my notes.* I wish they could now be had. I think he once told me he could lay his hands on them. This copy of Mr C's original proposition, I wish you to preserve. I can send you, if you wish it, a list of Ayes & Noes, on the passage of the Bill, in both Houses. All Mass[achusetts] went ag[ains]t it.

I have been expecting for a week to see in the N[ational] Int[elligencer] my remarks on Mr Calhoun's Resolution. I was told yesterday they should certainly appear early next week. Mr [Samuel] Prentiss made a very excellent Speech, on the Vermont Resolutions. Have you read Mr [John] Davis' remarks?[2] Will it not be felt, as a striking fact, that we have had a slave-holder for President, *forty years out of forty eight?* Yrs truly   Danl. Webster

ENCLOSURE: "MR. CLAY'S FIRST PROJECT"

Preamble recites, that differences of opinion have existed, & continue to exist, as to the policy of protecting manufacturing industry, by duties on similar articles, when imported; that this difference is increased, so as to agitate public mind, & threaten serious disturbances; & it being desirable to settle differences &c. enacts.

Sect. 1. existing laws to remain in force till Mar. 3. 1840—then all to be repealed, & hereby are repealed.

S 2. until the 3d of Mar. '40 no higher or other duties than shall now existing to be laid "And from and after the aforesaid day all duties collected upon any article or articles whatever of foreign importation shall be equal, according to the value thereof, & solely for the purpose & with the intent of providing such revenue as may be necessary to an economical expenditure of the Govt. without regard to the protection or encouragement of any branch of domestic industry whatever."

ALS. CSmH. Letter published in Curtis, 1:455–456.

1. See enclosure above.

2. For Prentiss's remarks, see *Con-*

gressional *Globe*, 25th Cong., 2d
sess., pp. 108–109; for Davis's speech

on Calhoun's resolutions, *ibid.*, Appendix, pp. 36–38.

TO BENJAMIN DOUGLAS SILLIMAN

Washington Jan. 29. 1838—

My Dear Sir

I recd your letter this morning,[1] for which I am much obliged to you. I do not know whether I can find here a copy of my Speech, in 1830, on Foote's Resolutions. If I can, I will send it to you.

I think you would be very safe, in adopting, in your House, an Anti Texas Report. As to Slavery, I think it very safe to adopt a Resolution, condemning Mr [John Mercer] Pattons Resolution.[2] Whether it will be best to go farther, you who are on the spot, can best decide. My own opinion is, that the Anti Slavery feeling is growing stronger & stronger, every day; & while we must be careful to countenance nothing, which violates the Constitution, or invades the rights of others, it is our policy, in my opinion, most clearly, not to yield the substantial truth, for the sake of conciliating those whom we never can conciliate, at the expense of the loss of the friendship & support of those great masses of good men, who are interested in the Anti Slavery cause.

I send you enclosed a copy of a letter, lately addressed by me to Mr [Luther Christopher] Peck of the H. of R.[3] It states shortly the opinions, which I hold, and am ready to express, on the general slavery question. I refer you, also, to some remarks of mine, published in the Intelligencer, upon Mr Clays substitute for Mr Calhoun's 5th. Resolution.

We begin the proceeding on the Sub-Treasury Bill tomorrow. It will probably pass this House, without amendment, by 2 or 3 votes. Its fate in the other House is greatly more doubtful. The decision on the Mississippi Election is expected today or tomorrow.[4] The Sub-Treasury bill may, perhaps, be a good [deal] dependent on this decision.

I will look round for a copy of my Speech of 1830, & write you again in a day or two. Yrs truly   Danl. Webster

ALS. NhD. Published in Van Tyne, pp. 211–212. Silliman (1805–1901; Yale 1824), of New York, was a lawyer. A Whig, he was at this time a member of the New York legislature.

1. Not found.

2. On December 21, 1837, Patton had introduced a resolution to the effect "that all petitions, memorials, and papers, touching the abolition of

slavery, or the buying, selling, or transferring of slaves, in any State, District, or Territory, of the United States, be laid on the table, without being debated, printed, read, or referred, and that no further action whatever shall be had thereon." *Congressional Globe*, 25th Cong., 2d sess., p. 45.

3. See above, DW to Peck, January

11, 1838.
4. On February 5, the House of Representatives declared Mississippi's two seats, previously held by John F. H. Claiborne and Samuel J.

Gholson but contested by Sergeant S. Prentiss and Thomas J. Word, vacant. Prentiss and Word subsequently took their seats following a special election in Mississippi.

FROM DANIEL FLETCHER WEBSTER

Peru Jany 29 1838

My dear Father,

I received a very kind letter last evening from Mother & am much obliged to her for the *Loco Foco*. I was in hopes that the next time I heard from you, we should be informed of your having received some of our numerous letters. Col. K[inney] is very anxious indeed about it, as he [has] written to you & sent you funds. I also had a silly letter from Lisle Smith; such as Ned would have been ashamed to write. I am by no means pleased with the young gentleman. He met us in Chicago & stayed three days in the Hotel with us but did not call upon us, or get introduced to Caroline. He has made too some very foolish & impertinent remarks about Julia, which have come to my ears, & for which he deserves to have his own boxed. He has stated too that he would do with me as he pleased & that he would take me into partnership make me serviceable & so on. Foolish & conceited remarks which none but a very self sufficient boy would have indulged in, at least until he knew with whom he had to deal.

Col. K. is by no means satisfied with him & I do not think that Lisle will find things quite as he thinks to have them, if he comes here again. He has neglected business & left every thing at sixes & sevens.

Col K. has just completed the sale of two Canal contracts & says he shall leave here very soon now & come East with funds enough to stop all rumours & complaints. When you hear from him what has detained him, you will I am sure agree with him that he has done the best in staying. He has felt very much pained to hear that you were not exactly pleased with his absence, & has several times expressed himself very much grieved about it as he was confident that you would be aware that he was doing all he could to make matters straight. He feels too that you may think that he has left you to bear the trouble, when he has been & is willing to do any thing at all that will gratify or oblige you & shield you from any kind of uneasiness or embarrassment.

He has been all kindness & attention ever since we have been here & has treated us like his own relations in every thing—both the ladies have become very much attached to him & I feel to him as I would to a brother. Every thing is going pretty well, at the office & at home. We were very much surprised to hear of Mr. [Stephen] White's marriage,¹ & *such* a marriage—the *relict* of a Steamboat Captain, but Caroline is content if her Father is, & has written him a very kind letter, which I hope he will be gratified with. Poor Mrs. [James William] P[aige] does not take it quite so kindly. She speaks of the *"person* whom" & *"Maverick people"* & the *"amiability"* of the lady, & so on—but she will, as we all know, *do* every thing to please her Father.

The first notice we had of his marriage was in a letter from Dr. [Gideon] Barstow, who mentioned having been at his wedding. I hope she will make him a happy & contented man, for he has been very uneasy for a long time.

Lowrie has been very ill, with a bilious attack, but is getting well again. I was afraid we should lose our chance for filling the Ice house in consequence & have engaged several hands to go right to work in finishing it & getting ice, which is now a foot thick in the River & very fine.

It has been quite cold for a week & good sleighing. The Col. has a fine pair of horses & a double sleigh which we make the best use of; it is quite nice over the prairies in any direction.

Grace has been somewhat ill, but is mending. Caroline is quite well & Ellen. We are much troubled about servants—lost our Cook yesterday & the Col's men are, although removed to another house near by, constantly making trouble. I must say they are a rascally lot.

Several Counties have instructed their delegates to the Convention to be holden at Springfield, to nominate the Col. for Governor. I am delegated from this County & so instructed. I think he had better not take it, but go to Congress instead, which he could do without doubt. After he has been in that situation a year or two, he may be Governor & I'll come to Washington.

Canada matters look serious.² I am sorry that we are so near getting involved, but at any rate it's not about Texas this time. We *lead* the Southerners this game. Peru is pretty well out of the World. Mother's letter of the 6th. Inst. arrived only last evening & I have not seen a Washington or a Boston paper since I have been here. Every thing might blow up & we not know it for a long time after. It is very odd that you have not received, at last advices, any of our numerous letters. I owe Mother many thanks for her kind letter so full of news & will answer it forthwith.

I hope Edward will favour me again—his last letter was a very good one indeed—much better & more sensible & manly than Mr. Lisle Smith's.

Please give our best love to Mother & Edward & Julia if she is with you yet & believe me your most affectionate son   Daniel F. Webster.

ALS. NhHi.

1. On December 30, 1837, White had married Mrs. Mary Matthews in New York.

2. On December 29, 1837, in a skirmish over the *Caroline*, which Canadian insurgents had used to transport supplies from the United States to Canada, one American citizen had been killed; and many Americans feared that another conflict between the United States and Great Britain was imminent. Glyndon G. Van Deusen, *The Jacksonian Era, 1828–1848* (New York, 1959), pp. 137–138.

TO [ROBERT CHARLES WINTHROP]

Washington Feb. 7. '38

Private and confidential

Dear Sir

It appears to me to be high time for our friends to be *awake*. You see what has happened in R.I.[1] This is the result of a secret operation, at the same time that there is kept up an appearance of unqualified reference to a National Convention. If we do not look out, & move immediately, the Convention will be no deliberating assembly, but a mere meeting to ratify previous nominations. I enclose you a sensible letter from Mr. [Henry Willis] Kinsman.[2] Yrs truly   D Webster

ALS. MHi.

1. On February 1, 1838, the Rhode Island Whig caucus joined the Kentucky and Maryland legislatures in announcing its support of Henry Clay as the Whig candidate for the presidency in 1840. Although Clay had voiced his support for an open Whig national convention as early as August 1837, he nonetheless worried about the efforts of Webster and other Whigs against his candidacy and he avidly sought preconvention commitments. When, in May 1838, congressional Whigs set December 4, 1839, as the date for their Harrisburg convention, Clay was confident that he would receive the nomination. Glyndon G. Van Deusen, *The Life of Henry Clay* (Boston, 1937), pp. 322–323. For a report on the Rhode Island Whig caucus, see the *National Intelligencer*, February 8, 1838.

2. Not found.

TO HIRAM KETCHUM

Washington Feb. 10. 1838

My Dear Sir

The R.I. affair was a surprise, probably a thing got up by M[atthew?] L[ivingston?] Davis. The Gentlemen here, in either House, knew nothing of it.

Mr [John] Whipple[1] is a very good man, & always friendly with me. He has some peculiarities, however, & I know not what his present opinions are.

It ought to be understood, that if the friends of one Gentleman take so much pains to get people committed, those of others will be driven to the necessity of some measures of counter action.

Your letter to Boston has been sent to me, for my opinion.[2] Gentlemen there seemed pleased with the course suggested by it; & so am I, except that I think Mass, under present circumstances, ought to express a dignified rebuke of these previous commitments, the effect of which, if continued & carried further, will be to make the Convention no deliberative body at all.

Mr [Tristam] Burgess is, I believe friendly, & so is Mr [Benjamin] Hazard,[3] of Newport. I shall see that some letters be written from this place. The man who is able to do the most, to keep R.I. where she ought to be kept, is Ch[arle]s H. Russell of yr City. Charles Potter, of Providence,[4] is also an important man, but I do not know his present opinions exactly. I feel the full importance of exposing, at once, these attempts to take people by surprise.

On the main question, my opinion is unchanged, as yet. I do not think Mr C[lay] *can* get N.H. or Pa. nor that he has any chance of the South. It may, more likely, be found necessary to fall back on Genl. H[arrison]. All this, however, the future must disclose. We shall miss you on the 21st.[5] I trust your Brother[6] will not fail to be here. I have written to Mr [Hugh?] Maxwell, inviting him also.

As to Mr C[lay]'s attacks on me, *the more the better.* The incident referred to embarrasses me, for the moment, because I had intended to invite him & [John Jordan] Crittenden to my dinner.

I hope you will see to N. Jersey. I know nobody there likely to be useful. There must be many persons in yr City, especially yr brother, who understand that ground. Have you communicated with Mr [William B.] Kinney?[7] Yrs truly   D Webster

ALS. NhD.

1. Whipple (1784–1866; Brown 1802), was a Providence lawyer, at this time representing Rhode Island (DW represented Massachusetts) in *Rhode Island* v. *Massachusetts*, 15 Peters 233 (1841). Upon Webster's death, he delivered and later published *A Discourse in Commemoration of the Life and Services of Daniel Webster . . .* (Providence, 1852).

2. Not found.

3. Hazard (1770–1841; Brown 1792) was a lawyer and Rhode Island legislator, serving for thirty-one con-

secutive years from 1808 through 1839.

4. Potter was a merchant.

5. On February 21, Webster was to host a dinner party in Washington, returning the favor of those who had given a dinner in his honor in December 1837, in New York. For a description, see Philip Hone, *The Diary of Philip Hone*, ed. Allan Nevins (2 vols.; New York, 1927), 1: 304–305.

6. Morris Ketchum (1797?–1880) was a prominent New York banker.

7. Kinney, a New Jersey newspaper editor, was later chargé d'affaires to Sardinia.

TO NICHOLAS BIDDLE

Feb. 13. [1838]
Dear Sir

You will see that Mr [Felix] Grundy has come out with a bloody Report, & a more bloody Bill.[1] He proposes to bring the subject up for consideration on Thursday week.

Nobody was looking for any such thing, so far as I know, until it came in. Yrs   D. Webster

ALS. DLC.

1. As chairman of the Committee on the Judiciary, Grundy had presented to the Senate a report on the circulation of notes of the late Bank of the United States and a bill "imposing a fine not exceeding $10,000, or confinement at hard labor in lieu thereof, not exceeding ten years, for issuing, or uttering in any way, the notes, drafts, or other securities of corporations chartered by the United States after their charter had expired." *Niles' National Register*, 53 (February 17, 1838): 390. For Grundy's report and bill, see *Senate Documents*, 25th Cong., 2d sess., Serial 316, Document No. 179.

TO HIRAM KETCHUM, WITH ENCLOSURE

Washington Feb. 13. 1838
Dear Sir,

I have had the propositions, which I now send you on another paper, lying in my desk for some time.[1] I have never prepared them, as formal Resolutions; though I have expressed the substance of them all, very frequently, in conversation, in correspondence, & in debate.

I give them this form, in order to be precise, & to avoid mistakes. The first of the propositions is in the words of the Resolution of the H. of R. in 1790. You will see the same thing referred to, in my Speech on [Samuel Augustus] Foote's Resolution. Yrs truly   Danl. Webster

ENCLOSURE: SLAVERY PROPOSITION

(The first Reso[lution] is in the words of that of the H. of R. of the U. S., March 1790)

1. That Congress have no authority to interfere in the emancipation of Slaves, or in the treatment of them, within any of the States; it remaining with the several States alone to provide any regulations therein, which humanity and true policy may require.

2d. That Congress, possessing by the express grant of the Constitution, a right to exercise exclusive legislation in all cases whatsoever over the District of Columbia, the same having been ceded by the States of Maryland & Virginia and become the seat of the Government of the United States, have full authority to regulate Slavery within the said District or to abolish it altogether whenever in their judgement humanity & true policy may require it; and that they have full authority, also, to regulate, or restrain the purchase & sale of Slaves, within the said District in any manner which they may deem just and expedient.

3d. That neither by the acts of cession by the States nor the acceptance by Congress, nor in any other way, has the faith of Congress become pledged to refrain from exercising its Constitutional authority over Slavery and the Slave trade, in the said District.

4. That the citizens of the United States have an unquestionable constitutional right to petition Congress, for the restraint or abolition of Slavery and the Slave trade, within the said District; and that all such petitions, being respectfully written ought to be received, read, referred, and considered, in the same manner as petitions on other important subjects are received, read, referred & considered; and without reproach or rebuke to the authors or signers of such petitions.

I have put my opinions in this form, only for the sake of precision. The propositions are not resolutions, offered at any time by me.

ALS. Copy, with AN. NhD.
1. See enclosure above.

FROM HENRY L. KINNEY

Lasalle Feby 14. 1838

My Dear Sir

We have all at Salisbury been anxiously waiting a letter from you for some time.

I recd a letter, from Lisle Smith last evening in which I got a pretty hard blow he says you have lost all confidence in me. If it is so I regret it, & that most bitterly. There is nothing that could happen to me, that would give me pain to the verry heart & soul, like that of loosing the friendship & confidence of your self & family. If I have done you wrong it has been through mistaken motives. I will only say, that I am ready to comply with any request you could make of me that comes within the limits of my power. There has been & is still some very important reasons for my staying west, or prolonging my journey east as long as I have. As I view it—our mutual interest might have been advanced for the time being by my going on east early last fall, but it would have been attended with unhappy results in the end, (or that is the view that I take of the matter). In the sucksess which I have had, (and which has been of no little magnitude—for one acting in my humble sphere in life) I have always endeavoured to look to this out come. After parting with you at Michigan Cty I very soon began to discover that monied matters were out of sorts, and endeavoured to guard against the difficulties which I have since had to encounter. I could not have immagined that so great a change could take place in so short a time. Monies that I calculated on receiving with absolute ceartinty, I am now the least likely to obtain. Drfts that I have paid money for have come back protested. Money that I have loaned under peculiar circumstances, has not been returned to me & there seems to have been an entire failure among my friends—& I have had a responsibilaty to shoulder that would be a burden in times like these for any man.

I have had a whole country to keep up & hundreds entirely dependent upon me. If I had left for the east in September it is difficult to tell what the state of things would have been here now particularly if there were many at the east waiting on me, for their marriage outfit.

I have kept my matters going on verry well here & every thing stands fair—which I considered of more importance than going east to pay John Lisle[1] $1250—or to do any thing that I could have done for the Patriotic Bank. Those matters comprise all of a business nature, that required my personal attention east. If I should make as much noise about my matters as my Phila. friends have about those that I have mentioned —this part of the world would be in considerable commotion.

The disappointment my promises have occasioned you has given me more trouble than any thing else which has hapened to me. My engagements to you were founded on the following expectations. My Partner Mr. [Daniel J.] T[ownsend] was to have furnished a sum not less than twenty thousand Dolls a part of which amt he assured me was in the Bnk at Buffalo—he has not as yet been able to realize the first Dollar from any resources of his own—ten thousand Dollars loanded money to Messrs. [Gurdon S.] Hubbard [James H.] Woodworth & others that I was in daily expectation of receiving for more than three months, not the first dollar of it have I yet recd. Not less than fifteen thousand Dollars that I have loanded in smaller sums that I expected with ceartinty to get—of which I have failed to get any part—those disappointments were unloo[k]ed for. In addition to those failures I have been obliged to carry on improvements & keep up & going my various branches of business which has obliged me to use large sums of money. And instead of recving pay from those indebted to me I have been obliged to assist them —& so different has it been from last year—that visitores have been obliged to borrow money West to get home instead of leaving it for investment. I only mention & trouble you with these facts, to show you how impossible it was for me to fore see what was coming, & clear myself from censure.

I have furnished others with money that I might have pd to the P[atriotic] B[ank] & have used large sums in carrying on my business & sustaining my credit here that might have been better applied there. I however did not view it in that light. If a man stands well at home he is very likely to abroad.

I have been very anxious to go east, not so much on a/c of my business there as the desire I have to see yourself & family. I think more of seeing you all, than I do of the injury my credit may sustain by my staying away. I have four Dolls due me in Phila. to one that I owe there.

I have sold a part of my canal contracts to Messrs Lyon & Howard of N.Y.[2] for a Bonus of thirty Eight thousand Dollars—half the amt payable next June the remainder at the completion of the job. Thats one trouble off my mind.

Fletcher & family seem quite contented & hapy at Salisbury. He has been very much troubled lately about the draft he made on you. I have told him I would pay it for him at Detroit. Or if you have paid it, I will send the money to you—as I suppose you would prefer having that paid, to having the amt applied to the P. Bnk. I will however act, according to your advice about those matters. Fletcher is very popular & likely to do quite as well as he could expect among us. We would have elected him to congress if he had been a resident of the district a sufficient length of time to make him eligable. The talk is now in this quarter that I am to be the Whig candidate at the next congressional election. *What do you think about it.* If Mr [John Todd] Stuart of Springfield should decline (who is also talked of as a candidate) my friends look upon my sucksess as ceartin.

Fletcher is very kind to me & seems like a Brother. He does honour to the name of Webster. He is a noble generous hearted young man. So you see, it is not strange that I should be attached to him.

I write this scrawl in some haste as the mail is nearly ready to go out. I will write you soon again & inform you how my Banking matters are coming on & hope then to be able to tell you what time I shall start east.

When I see you I will inform you about all matters to your satisfaction.

I most sincerely hope you will be able to make some sattisfactory arrangement with the Patriotic Bnk. If giving Judgmts mortgages or any thing else that I can do will be of service to you—all you have to do is to inform me.

I enclose you a letter to Mr [Nicholas] Biddle.[3] You can read it & forward to him if you think it worth while. Rember me kindly to Mrs Webster & give my best Love to Miss Julia & believe me ever your sincere friend & svt.   H L Kinney

I am very anxious to hear from you.

ALS. NhHi.

1. Kinney mistakenly combined the names of Dr. John Mark Smith and his brother Samuel Lisle Smith.
2. Not identified.
3. Not found.

TO ROBERT CHARLES WINTHROP

Washington Feb. 16. 38

Dr Sir

I have recd your letter,[1] for which I thank you. A letter went from me to Mr [Richard] Haughton yesterday,[2] expressing my opinions, fully.

I wish the Whig papers in Boston would be kind enough to publish my remarks on Mr Clay's Substitute to Mr Calhoun's 5. Resolutions—as they appear in the Intelligencer of Jany. 23. 1838[3]—as also my Speech, or remarks, on the Preemption Bill, of which I send some copies to you.[4] This last subject is greatly misunderstood, as some of our friends will ere long find out. Yrs truly   D. Webster

ALS. MHi.

1. Not found.
2. Haughton was publisher and editor of the *Boston Atlas*. Letter not found.

3. For DW's speech on Clay's substitute for Calhoun's fifth resolution, see *W & S*, 8: 109–114.
4. DW's speech on preemption also appears in *W & S*, 8: 130–139.

FROM NICHOLAS BIDDLE

Phila. Feby. 18, 1838.
Sunday night.

My dear Sir,

Many thanks for your copy of Mr [Felix] Grundy's foolery! I do not know which is worse—his report or his bill. I wish you would in your own peculiar & steam-engine way, condense about a column of matter to demolish him out & out. If you will do this, it will spare us the necessity which I wish to avoid, of an official declaration on the part of the Bank. I began a few notes on the subject, but am not able to finish them—but hope to add something tomorrow. With great regard Yrs.   N.B.

LC. DLC.

1. See above, DW to Nicholas Biddle, February 13, 1838.

TO [LEWIS F.?] ALLEN

Washington Feb. 23. 1838

Dr Sir

I have recd your letter,[1] & shall be happy to give all due attention to the subject to which it relates. I hope Mr Potter & Mr Allen[2] will make themselves known to me on their arrival.

You are very right, I think at Albany, to keep quiet for the present on the Presidential question. We are in great danger, I fear, of losing all we have now, by premature proceedings in regard to ulterior objects.

Your Anti-Sub Treasury resolutions are excellent. They were presented yesterday, & Mr Wright's attention will no doubt be often called to them.[3] It is supposed the Bill will pass our House by the casting vote of the V.P.

It is believed it cannot pass the H. of R. Yrs truly   Danl. Webster

ALS. Vincent E. Edmunds, Staten Island, N.Y. Allen (c. 1799–1890) was a member of the New York Assembly from Buffalo, Erie County.

1. Not found.

2. Not identified.

3. On February 22, Senator Nathaniel P. Tallmadge of New York had presented before the Senate the resolutions of the New York Assembly against the passage of the subtreasury bill. *Senate Journal*, 25th Cong., 2d sess., Serial 313, p. 245; *Senate Documents*, 25th Cong., 2d sess., Serial 316, Document No. 232.

TO RICHARD HAUGHTON

Washington Feb. 23. 1838

My Dear Sir,

I wrote you some time since,[1] & friends here, I am informed, have since addressed other Gentlemen near you.

Late movements appear to me to be breaking up the Whig party entirely, unless a determined stand be taken somewhere. There is information here this morning of an intended nomination in Maine. I presume you know, if any such thing be in contemplation. A very great effort has been made at Albany, but without effect. A letter now before me, recd. last Evening, says New York will make no nomination at present.[2] The last account from Trenton gives the same assurance of New Jersey; but not with as much positiveness as the letters from Albany speak of New York. The origin of these sudden movements is in the proceeding in R. I.

As to the course proper to be adopted by Massachusetts, I have nothing to add to what was contained in my former letter; except that the opinions therein expressed are greatly strengthened. Nothing but a fair, *deliberative*, & upright Convention, *can save the Whig cause*. I trust, therefore, that Mass. will show that she understands this.

Having made a nomination, on a former occasion, it is proper she should say that, the confidence, which led to that expression of her preference, has not been withdrawn or diminished; but that in the actual state of things, she sees the absolute necessity of Union, & regards the assembling of a Convention as the only means of effecting that object;

but that a Convention, to be useful & competent to its end, must be free, & deliberative, its members acting upon their convictions of the preferences of their constituents, & combining all the considerations which naturally belong to the occasion;—that the Convention should not be held earlier than the fall of 1839;—I think this point of *the greatest importance*, & that Massachusetts ought, by all means to state the *time*;—& that the members should be chosen, in their respective States & Districts, shortly before the time of holding the Convention. All this ought to be put forth, distinctly, & strongly.[3] If there be not that in the Whig *cause*, which can hold us together, there is nothing in any one *name* that can hold us together. It is astonishing to me, that our friends, especially our Northern friends, do not see the difficulty which there will be in supporting the candidate nominated, in these recent proceedings; & the present condition of things leads me to express, in entire & sacred confidence, an opinion, which I fully & completely entertain; & that is, supposing no Mass. candidate to be in the field, I do not believe, that in Novr. 1840, the vote of Massachusetts *can be given* for Mr Clay; nor the vote of any other State, north of Maryland.

I have thought it my duty to speak, thus freely & decidedly, to my friends—& leave the whole matter cheerfully with them. If they entertain my views, they will see the importance of even communicating, *instantly*, with friends in Maine. Please return me the enclosed letter.[4]
Yrs   D Webster

ALS. NhD.
1. Letter not found.
2. Haughton's *Boston Atlas* took note of the New York proceedings in the February 28, 1838, issue, reporting that the Whigs in the New York legislature had determined to recommend a national nominating convention. "This, after all, is the true policy," wrote Haughton. "The premature movements of zealous, impatient

friends in relation to the Presidency are very mischievous."
3. The *Boston Atlas*, March 1, 1838, carried an editorial that emphasized the points Webster made here and implied that Webster remained Massachusetts' choice for the presidency. See also *Boston Atlas*, April 17, 23, 1838.
4. Not found.

FROM RAMSAY CROOKS

Office of the American
Fur Company
New York 23 Feby 1838
Dear Sir
We had this pleasure on the 5 ultimo assenting to the proposition you had the goodness to make us for payment of the balance of your Note,[1] and as the first $3000 will be due 28th current, we beg permission to en-

quire when you purpose making us a direct remittance, and if we are to apply at some place here for the sum in question.

In ordinary times we would not be thus particular, but the present woful condition of business in general, renders it almost impossible to meet our ordinary engagements, and we trust you will therefore pardon the liberty we have ventured to take in thus addressing you.

I am Dear Sir With great respect your ob Servant   Ramy Crooks President Am Fur Co

LC. NHi.
    1. See above, DW to Ramsay Crooks, January 2, 1838.

TO RAMSAY CROOKS

Washington Feb. 24. 1838

Dear Sir

No wonder you should feel doubt, whether I or any body was likely to fulfil pecuniary engagements, at this time. I believe however, that I shall be able to remit you the $3000.—at the day.

What can be done with the next payment, (in May) unless times change, it may be difficult now to say. Yrs with much regard,

Danl. Webster

ALS. NHi.

TO ROBERT CHARLES WINTHROP

Washington Feb. 24. [1838]
Saturday Eve'

Private and Confidential

My Dear Sir

You will see by the enclosed letter that New York will not be persuaded to concur, in certain recent proceedings.[1]

Our intelligence from N. Jersey, today, is, that in that State also there will, certainly, be no movement. There is acknowledged to be no chance of moving either Pa. or Ohio. So that you see, that the great central mass is not agitated by these recent proceedings, nor likely to follow, at least at present, the example which they set.

Let us hold on, where we are, & then we may have a chance for a real popular Convention. I have written to Mr [Richard] H[aughton] lately,[2] quite fully, & you have probably seen the letter. I am Dr sir yrs

D. Webster

You will have heard of the duel, between [William Jordan] Graves & [Jonathan] Cilley, in which the latter fell, this day.[3] I deem it a very unfortunate, as well as a sad affair; & fear evil consequences may result from it.

ALS. MHi.
1. This letter, probably from [Lewis F.?] Allen, has not been found. See above, DW to [Lewis F.?] Allen, February 23, 1838.
2. See above, DW to Richard Haughton, February 23, 1838.
3. For a discussion of the events

that led to the duel, see Charles M. Wiltse, *John C. Calhoun, Nullifier, 1829–1839* (Indianapolis, 1949), pp. 379–380; the Graves-Cilley and Wise-Jones correspondence in *Niles' National Register*, 54 (March 3, 1838): 5–6; and DW to Horatio Gates Cilley, February 25, 1838, below.

TO HORATIO GATES CILLEY

Washington Sunday Evening
Feby. 25. 1838
My Dear Sir,

Before this reaches you, you will probably have read of the death of your Nephew, the Honble Mr [Jonathan] Cilley, member of the House of Representatives from the State of Maine.

This melancholy event was the result of a Duel, fought yesterday afternoon, between him & the Honble Mr [William Jordan] Graves, a member of the same House of Congress, from the State of Kentucky.

I have no authentic information of the circumstances which led to the contest, nor of those which accompanied it. The friends of the Parties will no doubt immediately lay before the public statements of such particulars as they may suppose friends may desire naturally to be informed of. The main object of this letter, is to express my commiseration, with the numerous branches of your family, with whom I have been more or less acquainted, at this afflicting occurrence. Mr. Cilley himself I had not known much. He had so recently become a member of Congress, that our acquaintance was slight. I had heard him speak in his place, once or twice, however, & I thought he spoke with ability. But having known his father, & most of his uncles, either in public or private life, & having had some little acquaintance with his relatives, of his own generation, I have felt it a kind of duty to express towards them condolence, & commiseration; & I ask you to communicate these sentiments, as you may meet with the members of the family, whom I know.

The members of the Delegation from Maine, in both Houses, all of whom are deeply affected by the Event, will do all that remains to be done. The funeral will probably be attended tomorrow. How melancholy it is, My Dear Sir, that neither law nor religion, nor both, can check the prevalence, in society, of the practice of private combat! With friendly regard, Yours   Danl. Webster

Correspondence 1838 [279]

ALS. NhHi. Published in Van Tyne, pp. 742–743. Cilley (1805–1874; Dartmouth 1826) was at this time a lawyer in Deerfield, New Hampshire.

TO RAMSAY CROOKS

Washington D. C. Feby 26 '38

Dear Sir,
I send you a Bank check on New York for Twenty five hundred dollars: also my own check on the Bank of the United States at Philadelphia for Five hundred dollars, which please acknowledge receipt of & endorse on my note. Your Obt. Svt.   Danl. Webster

LS. NHi. Crooks endorsed this letter: "No. 856— "Geo Thomas (Cashr Bank of the Metropolis) check dated Washington DC 26 Feby 1838 order Hon Danl. Webster, on Manhattan Company N. York for $2,500. "Daniel Websters check of 28 Feby 1838 order Ramsay Crooks on Bank of the U. States Philadelphia for $500."

FROM DANIEL FLETCHER WEBSTER

La Salle March 3d. 1838.

My dear Father,
We were all very happy by the receipt of your two letters of Feb[ruar]y 7.[1]
To begin with the last part of it first. I will carefully obey your directions, & write you on the 1. 8. 15. 22. & 29. of every month. I have written to someone of the family nearly as often since I have been here, but our letters somehow miscarry.
Col. [Henry] K[inney] was very glad & greatly relieved to hear from you.[2] Lisle Smith has written to his Father & to him in such a manner as to offend & disquiet him very much. Old Mr. [Simon] Kinney in writing to the Col quotes from one of L. Smiths letters to him as follows "Webster is highly displeased with your son's conduct & says he thinks that he has never meant to come."
I have had a good deal of the Col.'s confidence & I really can with a perfect conviction of its truth say that I believe it would have been very much to his permanent injury to have left. The times have been as bad as possible here & of some thirty thousand dollars of loaned money, to some of the best firms in the State, & long since past due, he has not been able to get one dollar, his Canal matters, calling for $500 per diem, were, until he sold out, which was a few weeks since, of such a nature as demand[ed] his constant presence, some of his important purchases of land were in a very unsettled state & things were so very bad that he felt afraid that if he were to go away every thing here would be broken

up & go to ruin; besides, some of those who *have been* most in his confidence & whom he placed in important places, turn out to be very tricky
& he *dares not* leave them. Mr. [Daniel J.] Townsend, instead of bringing
any capital, has not had the first dollar, the Col. has paid all his travelling & marriage expenses even, & the fact is that the Col. has become
very much afraid of & much disappointed in him. He has put off coming
from day to day in hopes of receiving some of the money due him & in
hopes that he could get matters into a state of safety. When you reflect
that he is the soul & life of every thing going on here, that the whole
country, for ten miles in every direction, just depends on him alone, that
no one else here has a dollar of money & that his affairs have been in
such a state as to require all his exertions to keep them along, you will
I am sure give him credit for having good reasons for not coming on. He
has all along hoped to get some of the money due him, but he has had
to start a bank in Michigan & one in Dubuque, & furnish them with
something to begin on, in order to raise funds to carry his matters along
with.

He would have been East long since had he felt safe at all in leaving
his affairs pure in the hands of Mr. T. The only money we see here is
Wild Cat, as they call Michigan safety fund notes, which would be of no
sort of use East & he has sent on such drafts & notes & Eastern bills to
you as he could get & which he was confident would be cashed.

This $1200. note of Lisle's—its history is shortly this. Lisle & the Col
entered into a contract for building on a pretty large scale & purchased
lumber. Lisle had no funds & the Col set things going—after a while
Lisle wanted to get out of the business & the Col let him off, took the contract on his own shoulders & gave Lisle this note for his interest in the
affair. It was a matter of accomodation & kindness entirely on the Col's
part, & he now holds Lisles notes & has store accounts against, past due
& of long standing to near a quarter of the amount. He has Lisle Smiths
notes long past due for $4000. & accounts for goods furnished John
Smith for $800. All this besides his salary to Lisle Smith, eleven hundred
of which he has paid in cash & maintaining at his own expense every
one of the three & paying all the bills & travelling expenses. If three
people were ever indebted in money & in gratitude to any one, it is these
three people to Col. K.

In confidence between us, I can tell you that Mr. S[mith] is very grasping & full of schemes & plots. He began by offering a *family alliance* to
the Col. which he has all along been trying to bring about & has so managed as to get a great many affairs of the Col's. into his hands. Not content with one half of the canal contracts, an equal interest in the Mer-

cantile matters (all without advancing a dollar of capital) he has got a
large farm from the Col. & a house & lots; the control of all the smaller
matters connected with their business he has always had & he recently
asked from the Col an equal interest, in all his *lands*. He reminds me of
a child sprawled out on the floor & grasping at all the play things far &
near. Of course I do not say all this without knowing what I am about.
If it had not been for his too great precipitancy, which has alarmed &
put Col. K. on his guard, there is no knowing how far he might not have
carried his plans.

As it is he could do a great deal of injury & the party most interested,
since he has had his eyes opened is getting out of the coil as fast & as
quietly as he can.

All this is new to you, no doubt, but I have had a fine opportunity for
watching the movements & have from time to time had several hints
from those who *know* of how things were going.

The Col. has deeded to you the Salisbury farm of four hundred acres
—his men & things are all removed from the premises & every thing is
in readiness for [Nathaniel] Ray [Thomas] to begin—he has not sent you
the deed, because he has meant to come & bring it to you.

Ray ought when he comes to bring a set of good *yankees*, too many
Irish here already—he should have all the tools & implements for carrying on a farm, waggons & horses & cattle & he should have some of the
most necessary articles of house hold furniture.

Provisions are very scarce & high here & barrels of beef & pork & corn
& potatoes, if bought cheap, might very profitably be sent along. Potatoes will bring seventy five cents a bushel here.

Col. Kinney will come by the first boat, certainly, on the opening of
navigation. The weather is now so favourable that we look to see the
River open in a fortnight or at farthest three weeks. He will write you
himself by return mail. Caroline, Ellen & Grace will come along with
him, on their way to Boston. Caroline's health has been very poor the
last three months. She has never entirely recovered from her confinement & wants to see Dr. [John Collins] Warren. I hope that a good long
visit East & seeing all her friends & breathing the salt air will restore
her. She is very weak & faints almost every day. I shall be very glad to
have her among her friends for a time. The child is very well & really
very handsome. It will hold it's own beside of Willie Paige[3] or any other
"hinfant fernomenon" as the Pick Wick papers say.

I shall remain here alone until the last part of the Summer, when I
shall come on for her & her mother. It will be very convenient all round
that my family should be away this summer. Ray will want most of the

house to himself & hands & there is no place for us out of it. Col. K is building a large stone house, which we think of living in with him—if we do not, he will build us a snug place near town, which we will rent of him, & this will not be ready until fall. There will be many things to do here & many changes to be made. We look for a good deal of trouble from the Irish on the Canal & Railroad & are organizing a volunteer corps for our protection. I expect to carry a sword in it. Lowrie is almost well—he reminds me frequently that he is in want of garden seeds of all sorts.

I have been very well all the time, until lately I am a little bilious & have a bad cold on the lungs. I am somewhat full of business, though of late it has been so cold that I could do nothing, except keep warm, or rather try to do so. There will be business enough here soon. Lisle Smith told mother that he had forty suits. I am just making out a declaration in the only one commenced by him that I know of. The remaining thirty nine have not come to my knowledge. Next summer I expect to be pretty much occupied, but I hardly look for so many actions. On Tuesday the 6th. we are all going up to attend a political meeting at Ottawa & on Thursday I am going to attend the Court at Princeton. I mean to have a nice light wagon & a good horse to carry me round the circuit. I have not yet got a green bag. I shall take Putnam, Will, Bureau, La Salle & Henry for my counties & generally attend the Courts, business or not, as is the fashion here. I shall have to be at St. Louis in June to attend a pretty considerable case of the Col's. John Sullivan[4] is established there & I hope he will do well. I was pretty mu[ch] surprised to see him.

[I] thank Julia for her kind letter—with our [love to] Mother & sister & brother I remain Your most affectionate son   Daniel F. Webster.

ALS. NhHi.
  1. Not found.
  2. Letter not found.
  3. James William Paige, Jr. (1835–

1894), son of James William and Harriette.
  4. Not identified.

TO NATHANIEL RAY THOMAS

Washington March 5. 1838

Sir,
    You are now about to proceed to Illinois and other northwestern states as my agent. Your principal duties will be of two kinds.
1st. In the first place you will have the care & disposal of the lands lots & parcels of real estate belonging to me in Ohio, Indiana, Illinois, Michigan & Wisconsin with power to sell excepting the estate or farm called Salisbury near La Salle.[1] You take with you an account of these pieces & parcels of property of which account I also retain a duplicate. You take

2. Daniel Webster, by Chester Harding, c. 1841. Redwood Library and Athenaeum, Newport, R.I.

1. Martin Van Buren, by Miner Kellogg, date unknown. Cincinnati Art Museum, gift of Charles H. Kellogg, Jr.

3. William Henry Harrison, by Albert Gallatin Hoit, 1840. National Portrait Gallery, Smithsonian Institution, Washington, D.C.

4. Hugh Lawson White, artist and date unknown. Reproduction courtesy of the Tennessee State Museum, Nashville.

5. Henry Hubbard, copied by H. M. Knowlton from the original by Wilson, date unknown. State House, Concord, New Hampshire.

6. Henry L. Kinney, photograph by Louis de Planque, date unknown. Corpus Christi Public Libraries, Texas.

7. Levi C. Turner, photograph by Washington G. Smith, c. 1865. New York State Historical Association, Cooperstown.

8. Samuel Bulkley Ruggles, by Henry Inman, date unknown. Columbia University, New York. Photograph courtesy of the Frick Art Reference Library.

9. Caleb Cushing, in 1839. Claude M. Fuess, *The Life of Caleb Cushing* (2 vols., New York, 1923), 1, facing p. 261.

10. Thomas Handasyd Perkins, by Spiridione Gambardella, c. 1837. Samuel Cabot, Beverly Farms, Massachusetts.

11. Ramsay Crooks, by Jules Emile Saintin, 1857. State Historical Society of Wisconsin.

12. William A. Bradley, date unknown. *Records of the Columbia Historical Society*, 6 (Washington, D.C., 1903), facing p. 188.

13. Virgil Maxcy, by Charles Baugniet, 1842. Willis M. Rivinus, New Hope, Pennsylvania.

14. Samuel Lewis Southard, lithograph from life by Charles Fenderich, 1838. National Portrait Gallery, Smithsonian Institution, Washington, D.C.

15. Hiram Ketchum, date unknown. Henry Anstice, *History of St. George's Church in the City of New York, 1752–1911* (New York, 1911), facing p. 442.

16. William Pitt Fessenden, in 1836. Francis Fessenden, *Life and Public Services of William Pitt Fessenden* (2 vols., Boston and New York, 1907), 1, facing p. 12.

17. Daniel Webster, attributed to Bass Otis, date unknown.
White House Collection, Washington, D.C.

18. Julia Webster, by George Linen, 1837. SKT Galleries, New York.

19. Caroline Le Roy Webster, date unknown. *"Mr. W. & I": Being the Authentic Diary of Caroline Le Roy Webster during a Famous Journey with the Honble. Daniel Webster to Great Britain and the Continent in the Year 1839* [New York, 1942], frontispiece.

20. Harriette Story White Paige, by Savinien-Edmé Dubourjal, 1844. Edward Gray, ed., *Daniel Webster in England: Journal of Harriette Story Paige 1839* (Boston and New York, 1917), frontispiece. Original in the possession of Mrs. Reginald Foster, Chestnut Hill, Massachusetts.

21. Queen Victoria, from life by
Thomas Sully, 1838. Metropolitan
Museum of Art, bequest of Francis
T. S. Darley, 1914.

22. John Evelyn Denison, engraved
by F. C. Lewis, 1832, from a drawing by Joseph Slater. National
Portrait Gallery, London.

23. Samuel Jaudon, by Thomas Sully, 1839, from his original painting in 1838. New-York Historical Society.

24. Joshua Bates, by William Edward West, c. 1833. Reproduction courtesy of the Trustees of the Boston Public Library.

also the Patents, Land Office receipts & deeds & agreements of individuals showing my title. There are shares also in incorporations and Joint Stock Companys of which you have the regular evidences.[2] My design is that you should sell this property or any part of it if opportunity should offer which you think favourable. In the course of the ensuing season I hope you will be able to visit most parts of the country where this property lies so as to ascertain its value and be able to act understandingly in the sale of it. You are also authorized to exchange any of it for other property if a favourable opportunity arises, and in case of sale of any part you may reinvest in other purchases in your discretion. It is not my wish to extend my interest in that country, but rather to contract it, and to dispose of a great part of what I own as soon as the times shall be favourable; still you may reinvest in cases that seem to be advantageous. You will take care not to interfere with my agreements with Geo. W. Jones, & Levi C. Turner or other persons who have purchased for me with which agreements you are acquainted. In case of sale you will see the proper commissions paid to those who made the purchases, according to their respective agreements.

2d. Your other main duty will be to carry on my farm called Salisbury. You will look at the Deeds which are said to be sent to Ottawa,—see what land they contain, and see what land they comprise. My wish is to have a very large farm, as large as one active man can well superintend the management of. If this estate be not large enough at present, find out what adjoining lands may be bought and at what prices. Fletcher & his family live in the house, and I presume you will live with them. You will keep an account of whatever produce of any kind he receives and of whatever he contributes towards the pay of any labourers or for other purposes. My object is to realize an income from this farm. You will therefore manage it with economy and to the best possible advantage. The farm must be well stocked—you will employ your own labourers and will have no master over you in whatsoever respects the farm, but will of course consult freely with Fletcher on all important matters, not only in relation to the farm, but in other concerns of mine. You will keep accurate & exact accounts of expenses & income from the farm, as also proper accounts of all sums received & paid on my account in the sale or purchase of property, or otherwise.

You will please write me regularly on the *first, fifteenth,* and *last* days of every month and oftener if occasion requires.

As for compensation it is understood between us that you shall receive *Two thousand dollars* for one year, commencing on the first day of January last. You are to be allowed travelling expenses from Boston to La Salle, and also travelling expenses, on all journeys undertaken from La

Salle, on my business. Your personal expenses Clothing board &c. you will defray yourself. You will be entitled to keep a horse on the farm for your own use. Yours truly   Danl. Webster

LS. NhHi. Published in Van Tyne, pp. 666–667.

1. For the legal specifications of Thomas's duties, see DW's power of attorney to Nathaniel Ray Thomas, March 5, 1838, mDW 39835–170.

2. Neither Nathaniel Ray Thomas's nor DW's inventory of these western holdings, nor the other documents referred to have been found. Thomas's copy may be in a small collection, still in private hands.

FROM NATHANIEL RAY THOMAS

Washington March 5 1838

Dear Sir,

On an examination of your western purchases made by Mr [Fisher Ames] Harding, I find by his letter of Dec 29. 1836[1] that among other parcels of property therein mentioned, he refers to a purchase he had made of 1/8th of four town sites in Wisconsin, including also an improved claim. One of these towns is the City of Superior of which you have certificates for 16 shares of stock.

The object of this letter is to inquire whether you have any title to the other town sites mentioned by Mr H., and whether you are acquainted with their situation & value. I am, with much respect Your Most Obt. Svt.   N. Ray Thomas

ALS. NhHi.
1. See Harding to DW, mDW 13699.

FROM DANIEL FLETCHER WEBSTER

La Salle Mar 14. 1838.

My dear Father,

Col. [Henry L.] Kinney received yesterday your favour of Feb. 24.[1] & desires me to say in answer that on reflection he thought it best not to put all the money in Mr. Lisle's[2] hands, & therefore directed Mr. [Theron D.] Brewster[3] to place the balance, after paying Mr. L. his $2000 in the U.S. Bank to his credit & wrote further to put the certificate of Deposite in the hands of his Father Mr. [Simon] Kinney, & to him, Mr. K. to send you the certificate of deposit. He made this change in the plan in consequence of Lisle's movement & he did not wish to put the money in his hands.

If the Col's Father was in Philadelphia the money was to have been paid to him & he to send it to you, otherwise to send you the certificate of deposit & he hoped & intended to be with you in time to endorse it. He says that he is very sorry not to have been able to leave before this, but that it has been really impossible for him to do so, without great danger. He will come on as soon as the river opens which we hope will take place soon. The ice is going very fast. He will come on immediately, nothing will be allowed to delay him excepting the necessary preparations for departure. We are all well at Salisbury. Caroline will come on with the Col.

We are very sorry to hear of the fatal duel in W. With much love to Mother & Julia & Edward I remain Your affectionate son

Daniel F. Webster.

ALS. NhHi.
1. Not found.
2. Not identified. DFW probably meant Lisle Smith.
3. Brewster, a native of Salisbury, Connecticut, had settled in Peru in

1835, where he first worked in Kinney's store. Later, he engaged in merchandising, grain trade, banking, and the manufacturing of agricultural implements. In 1851, he was elected mayor of Peru.

TO FRANKLIN HAVEN

Washington Mar. 25. 1838

Dr Sir,

I thank you for your letter, & for arranging my note.[1] As to the abuse of the Globe, there is no putting an end to it, & having once exposed its falsity, I must rely on its want of credit.[2]

I send enclosed another little bill on Providence,[3] which please collect, & place to my credit. I expect to be in Boston, abt. the 10th. of April.

I look upon the proceedings in the Senate yesterday, as decisive of the fate of the Sub. Treasury. It was a most interesting & animated day. You will see we struck out all specie payment—this made Mr Calhoun wheel again, & he came out, on the question of engrossment, *agt* the bill, with great earnestness. By this alteration, however, the bill, while it lost Mr C. gained Mr [Alfred] Cuthbert, & Mr [Thomas] Morris. So that a majority of *two* was in favor of the engrossment. No doubt is entertained that Mr C['s] friends in H. of R. will follow him; so that I now regard it as next to certain that the bill cannot pass. Indeed, it is a very incongruous thing, in its present shape. We had the good fortune to [pass] a section; killing the old Treasury Order.[4] I am, Dr Sir, with true esteem, Yrs

D Webster

ALS. MH.
1. Letter not found; note not identified.
2. The *Washington Globe*, in response to Webster's resolution requesting the secretary of the treasury to inquire into the reasons for the

payment of pensions and of fishing bounties in the notes of the collapsed Commonwealth Bank of Boston, had charged that the bank's problems resulted from the indebtedness of many prominent New Englanders. In a partisan tone, the *Globe* leveled specific charges at Webster, alleging that he had had notes protested at the bank for as much as $10,000 at a time. "The above items," the *Globe* added, "constitute but a very small part of the sums borrowed by Mr. Webster of pet banks, to carry on his various speculations." Webster denied his indebtedness to the bank, whereupon Blair and Rives of the *Globe* produced documentary evidence in the form of a letter from David Webster to substantiate their charge. For the specifics of the accusation and Webster's response, see the *Washington Globe*, January 20, 23, February 2, 1838; *Columbian Centinel*, January 27, February 7, 10,

1838; *Congressional Globe*, 25th Cong., 2d sess., pp. 113, 114, 116, 118, 128, 148, 164–166.

3. Not identified.

4. Webster introduced and the Senate approved (37 to 14) an amendment to the subtreasury bill "that it shall not be lawful for the Secretary of the Treasury to make, or to continue in force, any general order which shall create any difference between branches of revenue as to the funds or medium of payment in which debts or dues accruing to the United States may be paid." *Senate Journal*, 25th Cong., 2d sess., Serial 313, p. 314.

TO GEORGE WALLACE JONES

Washington April 6. 1838

My Dear Sir

I foresee that unless some change of times takes place, it will not be in my power to pay my acceptance, now held by Messrs [John] Laidlaw & Co.[1] My friends in Boston write me, that no money can be had, for any thing. Nothing can be sold, & nothing collected. I am going home, to see what arrangements can be made for the future, but I have no hope of obtaining any funds at present.

I hope you will write these Gentlemen, & express the regret I feel—& mortification, too for being obliged to ask them for another renewal. But this thing is unavoidable.

I leave with you a blank acceptance which you will please fill up, & send to them. Let them signify to you the amt. of disc[oun]t & I will send a check for it.

On my return from Boston, I will endeavor to see Messrs L & Co.[2] Yours truly   Danl. Webster

ALS. Ia-HA.

1. Laidlaw & Co. were New York merchants.

2. Jones endorsed the letter: "Attended to & answd in person."

TO NICHOLAS BIDDLE

N.Y. Ap. 9. 1838

Private

Dear Sir

I find a great deal of expectation created here by Mr [Thomas Lyon]

Hamer's movement.[1] It is considered as an Administration forth putting —as a matter showing, that the Adm. means now to abandon Sub. Treasuries, & is making advances towards the Banks.

This is the talk here—but no doubt you are well informed. Hamer is the man of most talent of the party—in the H. of R. Yrs   D.W.

ALS. DLC.
   1. On April 7, Thomas L. Hamer of Ohio, a Democrat, had introduced a motion calling for the federal gov-

ernment to aid banks that resumed specie payments. *Congressional Globe*, 25th Cong., 2d sess., p. 288.

FROM EDWARD EVERETT

Boston 14th April 1838.

My dear Sir,
   The Legislature has adopted some resolves relative to the N.E. Boundary of the U.S. which have been presented to me for my official signature. One of them is in the following terms. "Resolved that no power delegated by the constitution to the government of the United States authorizes them to cede to a foreign nation any territory lying within the limits of any of the U. States."[1] I beg leave to ask whether you consider the principle asserted in this resolve as a well settled doctrine of constitutional law. It appears to me that at any rate it is irrelevant to the question concerning the N. E. Boundary, which is whether a certain territory is within the limits of the U. S. or the British provinces. The principle asserted in the resolution is in the abstract form & to sign it w'd be to commit myself to a doctrine of which as at present advised I have some doubts. I should be very glad to have these doubts removed. If they should not be, I do not feel inclined to send back the resolves with objections but to let them pass *sub silentio* without my signature. I do not wish you to trouble yourself to write a long letter on the subject, but should be gratified to know your opinion in a couple of lines.[2] You can give me the reasons when we meet.

   Yours ever with the greatest regard

P.S. 15th. The mail from N. York I understand confirms the election of [Aaron] Clarke[3] and gives us a majority in nine wards. I shall desire before you return to the South to talk with you on our State Law Suit.[4]

LC. MHi.
   1. These resolutions of the Massachusetts legislature, which Everett signed, appear in *Senate Documents*, 25th Cong., 2d sess., Serial 318, Document No. 434.
   2. For Webster's response, see DW

to Edward Everett, April 20, [1838], below.
   3. Clark, a Whig, served as mayor of New York City, 1837–1839.
   4. *Rhode Island* v. *Massachusetts*, 14 Peters 210 (1840).

Summer Street April 20. 1838
My Dear Sir
I observe the Bill has passed both branches for pay[ing] $30000 to the River Bridge.[1] I have, as you know, a few shares, & shall leave the Certificates with a friend, to receive my part of the money. Will you be pleased to say, in a word, at the foot of this, what sum, or abt what sum, as you suppose, will fall to a Share? Yrs truly   Danl. Webster

ALS. NN.
1. For a discussion of the issue and proposed legislation to allow to the proprietors of the Charles River Bridge "an equitable compensation . . . for the injuries alleged by them to have been sustained by the erec-tion of Warren Bridge," see *Documents . . . of the Senate of the Commonwealth of Massachusetts . . . 1838* (Boston, 1838), Document No. 93. No record of the passage of the legislation in 1838 has been found.

April 20 1 oclock [1838]
Dear Sir
I will certainly find time to see you, in a day or two. Perhaps I will call this Evening, but do not stay in, under that expectation.
Judge [Joseph] Story's remarks are sensible & full of weight; but I think it would be difficult to make a Veto message, on the grounds he suggests.[1]
It would be very unpopular to assert the right in the Genl Government, under any circumstances, to dismember a State, or cede away one part of it; and with the utmost respect for the Judges opinion, it seems to me the case he puts by way of illustration is an extreme one, & must be left to provide for itself, if it should occur.
The Resolution is not well framed; but, even as it stands, I understand it to mean no more than that the Genl Govt. cannot cede away the territory of a State, *without its consent.*
I see embarrassments, in the case, on either side. The question is becoming interesting, in all views. You have reflected deeply upon it, I am sure, & your judgement is better than mine; but if I were called on to act in the case, I should sign the Resolution, trusting that it would be understood with the proper qualification.
This, however, is only my present opinion. I may change it, on conference & further reflection. Yrs truly   Danl. Webster

If you wd. like to send this to the Judge, I will write it off more legibly. D.W.

ALS. MHi.
1. As he had Webster (see above, Edward Everett to DW, April 14, 1838), Everett had asked Story for his opinions on the resolution of the Massachusetts legislature relating to the northeastern boundary. For Everett's letter to Story and Story's reply, see William W. Story, *Life and Letters of Joseph Story* (2 vols.; Boston, 1851), 2: 286–289.

FROM NATHANIEL RAY THOMAS

La Salle April 20. 1838

My dear sir,

You may perhaps be some what surprized to receive a letter from me dated at this place so soon after the reception of mine of the 14th instant;[1] but my contemplated journey to Chicago was prevented by the arrival of a letter from Col. [Henry L.] Kinney, (to his clerk) just as I was going on board the St[eam] Boat, positively directing him to furnish me with a team which he has at length done. This will I am happy to say preclude the necessity of my drawing on you at the present time, although I shall be obliged to do so before many days, for I find my scanty means will not go far in purchasing, corn, oats, potatoes, hay, farming tools, pay of labour, home expenses &. &c. especially when all these things are held at such exorbitant prices. I have sent a man south with what money I brought with me to lay it out in corn, oats & potatoes for seed & for feeding the teams. The sacrifices which we are obliged to make in the commencement of operations here (however limited these operations may be) will be very considerable I assure you; but it only shows the importance of having an abundant supply in the fall, of all things necessary in farming, both in doors & out, and I do hope we shall be able to accomplish this the next.

As I shall be obliged to go to Detroit probably in the course of the summer, I have thought that it might be advisable for me to go to Buffalo, after we get through with our planting, and procure a quantity of tools attend to the shipment of what cattle you may conclude to send out &c., but shall of course wait your advice in regard to it.

If this farm and Fletchers should be put together I think we should keep four yoke of oxen and perhaps we had better say *six* yoke, and at least *six horses*—the latter it seems to me are much the best and most profitable, for all kinds of teaming in this part of the country, where grain can be raised so cheap. We ought also to keep at least 20 cows and a large quantity of hogs. The common cattle (if we keep such) can be purchased cheaper in the southern part of this State; but the horses I think can be better procured farther east. Sheep I should fear might become prey for the *wolves*.

We have had almost incessant snow & rain, ever since Fletcher left here, until yesterday, which makes the ground so extremely wet that it prevents our ploughing.

Lowry is with me & will commence his gardening operations next week. I am, Sir Most Respectfully Your Obt. Svt.   N. Ray Thomas

ALS. NhHi.
1. Not found.

TO WILLIAM PITT FESSENDEN

Boston April 21, 1838
My Dear Sir

I am here on a short visit, & must not omit to write you, before I return to Washington, for the purpose of thanking you for your deeds of respect & kindness, on a recent occasion. Aside, however, from all personal considerations, I think the common cause would have been greatly injured, by the adoption, on the part of our friends, of that course, which you so efficiently opposed.[1]

Events appear already to have made that clear. I learn from Washington that the Whig National Convention is fixed for the first Monday of Decr. 1839; then to be holden at Harrisburg. This is all very well. It will give us a fair & clear field for united exertion, thro this year & the next.

I go back to Washington on Tuesday, but hope not to be kept there long after the first day of June. We must continue to meet, & bring our wives together, in the course of the Summer. I hope you will be able to come this way. If not, I shall try to make a trip to Portland.

Our friend [Hiram] Ketchum was in good health & spirits, as I came thro N.Y.

Col. [Henry L.] Kinney is on his way East, in company with Mrs Fletcher Webster, who is journeying hitherward, to visit her friends.

My wife is at N. York—Julia at Washington—& Edward, whom I believe you have not seen, at Dart[mouth] College. I shall rally the females, & prepare with them to keep house at Marshfield, from the close of the Session, till the autumn. With true & cordial regard, Yrs

Danl Webster

ALS. NhD. Published in part in Francis Fessenden, *Life and Public Services of William Pitt Fessenden* (2 vols.; Boston, 1907), 1: 16–17.

1. The Maine Whig legislative convention, which met in Augusta on March 8 and renominated Edward Kent for governor, made no nomination for the presidency, "but resolutions were adopted pledging the Whigs of the State to abide by the decision of a National Convention."

Maine Whigs, following the example of those in several other states, had apparently wanted to pass resolutions endorsing Clay, but Fessenden had opposed such a course and carried the question for no commitment. *National Intelligencer*, March 13, 1838.

FROM WILLIAM PITT FESSENDEN

Portland. April 30. 1838.

My dear Sir,

Yours of the 21st. inst. was duly recd.,[1] and I thank you, most sincerely, for its expressions of regard.

Apart from any considerations which might be supposed to have arisen from personal friendship, my course, on the occasion alluded to, was such as I believed to be demanded by the best interests of our good cause. In the ultimate success of that cause I have implicit faith, and I would have it succeed under such auspices as will strengthen & secure it.

Unfortunately, the leaven of Loco-focoism is working somewhat among our own friends. Small politicians are acquiring too much power, & narrow views are obstructing, as I think, the course of broad and manly principles. Perhaps this is unavoidable, to some extent. I consider it a duty, nevertheless, to resist such a tide, and, if we cannot stay it wholly, to check its course in some degree. Breakwaters have become fashionable of late—and I think they may be found necessary & useful in more senses than the natural one.

Leaving all these matters, permit me to touch upon another topic. It is highly probable that one of our Whig friends, who is well known to you, will shortly be in Washington, ostensibly, perhaps, as "bearer of despatches" from our Govr. The Gentleman[2] referred to has formerly acted in the same capacity, on a somewhat larger scale, and in reference to the same subject. He will apply directly, and in the first instance, to you, for advice & assistance. He is desirous, moreover, that I should write you, by him, on the subject of his mission, and of the expediency of your standing prominently forth, if occasion presents, in aid of the cause which we are all anxious to promote & advance. It is probable that I may so write. One thing, however, I wish to say, which could not well be said in a letter which must come under his own eye. It is simply to express the hope, that "by-gones may be by-gones." In all things which I have been able to accomplish here, *he* has been my firm and efficient and undeviating supporter & friend. I consider him perfectly sound, and entitled to *cordial* respect & regard—and I have reason to believe that an exhibition of these sentiments from you would be gratifying to him.

Upon hearing of your arrival in Boston, I was extremely desirous to see you there, before your return to Washington. Our Supreme Court, however, was in session, and I could not leave it. I had strong hopes, also, that I might be able to visit Washington before the close of the session. This hope I am likewise compelled to abandon.

We are to have a very exciting political canvass in this State, & particularly in this District, during the approaching summer, and one that, I am fearful, may engross all the time I shall be able to spare from professional engagements & pursuits. Whether, however, I am to lose the long anticipated pleasure of a visit to Marshfield, or not, (and I am not yet prepared to give it up), we shall hope to see Mrs W. & yourself in Portland. I shall not believe that her promise to that effect was made to be broken. Julia, too, is under the same engagement, and I shall abate none of it. And [Thomas Amory] Deblois[3] bids me remind you of sundry claims in the trouting line, which are yet outstanding.

And now, my dear Sir, I pray you to pardon the unfair advantage I have taken of the occasion afforded by your letter.

With most respectful & cordial regards to your wife & daughter, Your friend & Servt.   W. P. Fessenden

ALS. NhHi.
1. See above.
2. Perhaps William Pitt Preble, who went to Washington to discuss the northeastern boundary question.
3. Deblois (d. 1867; Harvard 1813)

had read law with Samuel Ayer Bradley in Fryeburg and shortly settled in Portland, where he became a law partner of General Samuel Fessenden, William Pitt's father.

TO [NICHOLAS BIDDLE]

May 3r. '38

D. Sir,

Mr [Felix] Grundys bill[1] was referred, in the H. of R. to the Jud. Comee. Mr [Francis] Thomas is Chrman, & a majority very hot party men. As yet, however, they have not taken up the Bill for consideration, & I understood yesterday it was doubtful whether they would do so, for some time. I do not think any attempt will be made to bring the matter forward, out of order, by a two third vote. But I shall speak to friends to keep a look out. The impression here, as to the passing the Bill in the Senate, is exactly like your own. The majority was taunted & jeered into it. Mr Grundy told me himself that although the Bill might or would have passed, it would not have passed at *present*, under other circumstances.

You will see Mr [Silas] Wright has introduced a Bill to sell the Bonds.[2] I will try to send you, by this mail, a copy.

The Debate, yesterday, on Mr [Henry] Clays Resolution, did us no great good. It drove the whole party together.[3] "Si sit *prudentia*, nullum numen, &c." What is that Latin? I am not "juvenal" enough to remember "Juvenal." Yrs   D. Webster

ALS. DLC.
  1. See above, DW to Nicholas Biddle, February 13, [1838].
  2. On May 2, 1838, Wright reported from the Senate Committee on Finance, of which DW was a member, a bill (S. 321) to authorize the sale of bonds belonging to the United States. Congress subsequently approved the measure and President Van Buren signed it on July 7. *Senate Journal*, 25th Cong., 2d sess.,

Serial 313, pp. 385, 578.
  3. On April 30, Clay had introduced a resolution stipulating "that no discrimination shall be made as to the currency or medium of payment in the several branches of the Public Revenue," and following the debate on May 2, the Senate Democrats united to refer it to the Committee on Finance. *Congressional Globe*, 25th Cong., 2d sess., pp. 344, 352.

TO [ROSWELL L. COLT]

Washington May 3rd. 1838

Dear Sir

I was sorry not to see you, in N. York, as I wished to have some talk with you.

Imprimis, the *note*, which you put your name to, (holding the Clamorgan Shares) falls due June 12th. which will be here, not long forth. *How can we pay it?*

Item

Do you think well enough of Clamorgan to give an acceptance, payable in Jany, on security of these shares, at 50 pr cent? I spoke to you on this point, I believe when I last saw you. In this, or some other way, I want to raise the wind a little. I have see[n] Mr [William A.] Bradley & Mr [Albert Galliton] Harrison today. They think the Bill will pass. I have little doubt of it, in the Senate; but the H. of R. acts as if it was not likely to pass any thing.[1]

Please let me hear from you. Yours, always, very truly,   Danl Webster
I hope I did not forget to send you a copy of my Speech.[2]

ALS. PHi.
  1. The bill in question was S. 89, "A bill giving effect to the eighth article of the treaty of 1819 with Spain," which recognized grants made before January 24, 1818, by the king of Spain. On February 27, Colt had presented a memorial to the Senate for recognition of his claim (and Webster's, coincidentally) to

the Clamorgan lands in Missouri and Arkansas; and as Webster predicted, S. 89 did pass the Senate, but the House took no action on it. *Senate Journal*, 25th Cong., 2d sess., Serial 313, pp. 71, 124, 289, 327, 332; *Senate Documents*, 25th Cong., 2d sess., Serial 316, Document No. 242.
  2. Webster was probably referring to his second speech on the sub-

treasury, delivered on March 12,   162–237; and *Speeches*, 2.
1838. For that speech, see *W & S*, 8:

TO FRANKLIN HAVEN

Washington May 7. 1838

Dr Sir,

Enclosed I send you a check on the Bk U.S. for $500 Dollars,[1] which please place to my credit.

I want to draw 2 checks on you—one for 500—or thereabouts—& one for 250—or thereabouts—which I hope you will honor, tho' they will overrun my account, some two or three hundred Dollars. I will send along some funds, to make up balance.

This month Mr. [Benjamin B.] Kercheval will be here, to convey to us our respective portions of the lands, purchased by him. My part, costing 10.000 in cash, is still retained by me, & is wholly free & unencumbered. Is it not possible, thro your kindness & Mr [John Plummer] Healeys, that I could, in some way, make an *indorser* of this, so as to get some money at yr Bank? I would leave it in Kercheval's hands, for sale, or to be held as security, or transfer it, in any way, which might most conveniently answer the purpose.

I have a very intelligent young man in the West,[2] taking care of my affairs, (not including this Kercheval business) with directions to sell as fast as practicable; but until he shall be able to dispose of something, I am obliged to live on other means. A line in reply will oblige me.

Congress has had a recess, of three days. The Comee on finance meets this morning, & I propose to say something about Pension Agents. Yrs truly   D Webster

ALS. MH.   2. Nathaniel Ray Thomas.
   1. Not found.

TO ROSWELL L. COLT

Washington May 8. 1838

Dear Sir

I recd yrs last Evening.[1] You will find the *notes*, herewith, drawn & signed, as prescribed.

I know not how I shall get along, without the aid of some credits. I was in hopes you thought well enough of Clamorgan to recon it good security at 50 cts; but if not, I must try you at 37, or 25. What say you, (provided I cannot do better, as I hope to) to become answerable for $5000, taking Clamorgan at 37, 30, or 25?

I send you a Speech or two.[2] I also send to "Mechanics Institute," "Paterson Library," the Inkeepers, &c., at Paterson &c. But "Arch Deacon" —somebody—I could not make out.

I am glad if *you* like the Speech.

Something will be attempted, in one House or the other, to effect a repeal of the Treasury Circular. I told Mr Clay & other friends, before I went home, that on my return, I should move a precise proposition to that effect. Mr Clays proposition had other objects—I think not very necessary—which exposed it to opposition. Of course we will all lend a hand to Mr [Adam Willson] Snyder, if he moves. If nothing prevents—and nobody else moves in the Senate, I shall attempt something in due season.[3]

Shall be very glad to hear from you, Yr's truly   Danl Webster

ALS. PHi.
1. Not found.
2. Probably the second subtreasury speech.
3. On June 12, DW again discussed

banks, bank notes, and the Specie Circular, and introduced at that time a bill that would have nullified the Specie Circular. *Congressional Globe*, 25th Cong., 2d sess., pp. 447–448.

TO ROBERT CHARLES WINTHROP

May 10. 1838

Private & Confidential
Dear Sir

I think these proceedings of Mr. Clay's friends in Philadelphia deserve public remark.[1] They are opposite to the whole spirit of that policy, in which the idea of a National Convention originated. If there are to be Comees, & Meetings, & Caucuses, & Commitments, in favor of Candidates, what will the Convention be able to do? It will have no power of deliberation, whatever. If you think as I do, I hope you will see that some proper suggestion be made, on the subject. Yrs   D. Webster

ALS. MHi.
1. On May 9, at Independence Square in Philadelphia, a group of Whigs, estimated by some to range from 6,000 to 10,000 people, gathered

to express their confidence in and support of Henry Clay as the Whig presidential nominee. *National Intelligencer*, May 10, 1838.

TO NATHANIEL RAY THOMAS

Washington May 11 1838

Dear Ray

I have not heard from you, since you wrote me that you proposed to visit Chicago, for the purpose of obtaining *horse power*, to carry on your farm work.¹ This was all right, & your bill of course will be duly honored. I went home, the early part of April, taking Mrs Webster as far as New York. On our return we met the La Salle party at Philadelphia. They returned with us to Washington, & Fletcher & his wife & Ellen Fletcher have since proceeded to Boston. Col [Henry L.] Kinney is now here, & will wait Fletcher's return, & then they will go West together. I presume they may be expected to leave this City about the 20th. inst. The Col appears to [be] managing his affairs here very well. Indeed I believe he finds little difficulty in arranging matters to his satisfaction.

We hope, here, that times begin to look a little better, but still they are bad enough. Money is very *hard*—all along the coast, from here north.

I have made an arrangement with Mr Kinney, respecting enlarging Salisbury. At present, we wish nothing said upon the subject; as it will require a little time to put all things in proper order. But it is agreed, all round,

That White Hall shall be added to Salisbury;

That the section on the south west of White Hall, along by, or near, Spring Creek, shall also be added; but that there shall be a reservation of the Mill Privilege, on the Creek, as the Colonel does not wish to convey that.

It is also agreed, that the tract, or the greater part of it, which lies between Salisbury & White Hall, on one side, & the River on the other [shall be added]. This extension of the lines will cause Salisbury to comprehend a thousand acres; or thereabouts; & this accords with the original plan, which I entertained, of making a farm of 1000 acres.

When this is accomplished, you will have something to do, in the farming line.

[By] arrangements, which the Col has made, especially with *Cornelius [Cokeley]*, who lives on White Hall, we cannot come into possession of *all* White Hall, until after next year. But there will be enough for you to work on, & still as much left, as the good man Cornelius can take care of.

I perceive, & indeed expected from the first, that you can do little this year, but *prepare* for the future. You will want stock, & tools, & supplies; and I shall endeavor to furnish the means of providing these.

1st. *Stock*. I have agreed with Mr Edward Le Roy for some of his imported stock, if I can find an opportunity to send it on; say half a dozen cows, & a bull. Other neat cattle, it is thought by Mr Kinney, may be had from the South part of Illinois, or adjacent regions.

2. *Tools*. If a list be made of these, they can be sent from Boston; say, Horse power, threshing machine, ploughs, harrows, horse-harness, &c. Or you can obtain these, partly at Boston & partly at Pittsburg, or Cincinnati.

3. Supplies. In the fall, you must have a good supply of *necessaries*. You will want *necessaries* for your own House; & if there were not some objections, it might be well that you should have a quantity of such articles as *salt*, sugar, tea, & coffee, for the accomodation of laborers. This we can think of, hereafter. When Fletcher reaches home, you will be able to compare notes, & judge what is best. It is difficult to find *hands*, to go on, without agreeing to pay enormous wages. [Charles] Henry [Thomas] is seeing what he can do, & Fletcher will see him. It may, very possibly, be found best for you to come East, after harvest, to hunt up men & things, for yourself. This you may think of.

We are all well here. I have not heard from Marshfield, later than the date of a letter from Henry, which I forwarded to you.

We are doing little here—& shall do little. I suppose we shall get away next month. Mrs W. & Julia desire remembrance to you, as does Col K. The Col thinks you are a pretty clever fellow. I tell him not to make up his mind, too soon. Yrs truly   D. Webster

You will take care *to say nothing* about White Hall &c., until Fletcher & Col K. reach home.

ALS. NhHi. Published in *PC*,   1. See above, Nathaniel Ray
2: 36–38.   Thomas to DW, April 20, 1838.

TO RAMSAY CROOKS

Washington May 12. [1838]

Dear Sir,

I have recd yours, of 11th inst.[1] Mr [Henry L.] Kinney is now here. He lives in Illinois, is a very respectable young man, & possessed of a large property. But like others, cannot command ready means. I have spoken to him on the subject of the note, & he is making an effort to arrange it, & will let you hear from him, before he leaves the City. He may probably visit N.Y.

My Dear Sir, you must have patience, not only with him, but with me; for I find it exceedingly difficult to raise money. I went home last month, to arrange some affairs of business, & to provide for what you have a right to expect from me, this month; but I found that nothing could be collected, nothing sold for cash, & nothing borrowed. I shall try not entirely to disappoint you; but I wish I could see an earlier change of times for the better, than I am at present able to discern. Yours with true regard   Danl. Webster

ALS. NHi.
1. See Ramsay Crooks to DW, May 11, 1838, mDWs.

TO HIRAM KETCHUM

May 12, 1838.

Dear Sir:

This Cherokee subject is difficult and delicate.[1] The public sympathies are aroused *too late*. The Whig members of Congress, who have taken an interest in seeing justice done to the Indians, are worn out and exhausted. An Administration man, come from where he will, has no concern for Indian rights, so far as I can perceive. We shall endeavor to do something or to say something. We are all willing.

You think that I ought to do some act to clear myself from the shame and sin of this treaty. My dear sir, I fought it a week in the Senate, on the question of ratification. We came near preventing it, and should have done so, if we had not been disappointed in Mr. [Robert Henry] Goldsborough's vote. We relied on him as a man of honor and religion; but he voted for the treaty, and turned the scale—mortified some of his friends severely—went home, and never returned.[2]

On all occasions, public and private, I pronounce the treaty a base fraud on the Cherokee Indians. What can I do more? Yet, I am willing to do more, if any good can be effected by it. . . . Yours,   D. Webster.

P.S. Please not to mention what I have said about the Cherokee Treaty in the Senate, because I do not know, now, whether the injunction of secrecy was taken off. I will look on Monday, and if it was, will send you a list of *ayes* and *noes*. I think it was taken off, and that the *ayes* and *noes* have already been published.

Text from Curtis, 1: 576. Original not found.

1. Webster was referring to the Treaty of New Echota, negotiated in December 1835 and ratified by the Senate on May 18, 1836, which authorized removal of the Cherokees west of the Mississippi River. A large segment of the Cherokee tribe argued that the treaty had been negotiated by unauthorized persons and that they had never approved it.

2. The vote on the treaty was 31 to 15, with DW voting in the negative. *Journal of the Executive Proceedings of the Senate* (Washington, 1887), 4: 546.

TO [JOSEPH STORY]

Washington May 12. 1838

Dr. Sir

Help me to make a Speech. I wish to say something on this N.E. Boundary; & I desire to be able to resist, in limine, both on English & American authorities, one of the principal preliminary grounds, taken by the English Diplomatists. They say,

That in 1783 the relative position of the two Countries, was this— "The mother Country treating with Colonies, not yet recognized, and the object in view was, not to designate the limits of the Territories reserved to the mother Country, as to assign an appropriate Boundary to the New Power."

They draw important inferences, from these premises.

Now, what I wish, is, to show, that the American Revolution was a division of Empire, & is to be [so] regarded.

You have the cases, English & American, which establish this—please refer me to them.

I must have an answer to this, in 8 days, to be of any use.[1] Yrs

D Webster

ALS. MHi. Published in *W & S*, 16: 298.

1. On June 14, 1838, Webster spoke "at large [on the subject of the Northeastern boundary], chiefly with a view to show that the line desig- nated by the treaty of 1783 was well defined, and easily and readily to be found." *Congressional Globe*, 25th Cong., 2d sess., p. 453. Neither the text of DW's speech nor Story's reply to the above letter has been found.

FROM NICHOLAS BIDDLE

Phila. May 22, 1838

My dear Sir,

I have been prevented by absence from writing to Mr [Richard] Smith[1] about the proposed discount of the note of your self and Mr [Charles?] Nichols,[2] until to day. He will see to it.

Can you tell me any thing further about our old note bill?[3] And

Can you tell me any thing at all about the Speech on the National Bank. What is the meaning of it? What is to be the result of it? Will New York be won by it? Will the South be pleased with it?[4] Here are questions enough from Yrs. always   N. B.

LC. DLC.

1. Smith was cashier of the Washington, D.C., Bank of the Metropolis. He was formerly with the Washington branch of the Bank of the United States.

2. Nichols was a Philadelphia commission merchant.

3. Biddle was most likely referring to Clay's resolution (S. 11), quoted above, DW to Nicholas Biddle, May 3, 1838, note 3.

4. Biddle was questioning Clay's motivation for his speech on a national bank, delivered on May 21. See *Niles' National Register*, 54 (May 26, 1838): 203–204.

TO NICHOLAS BIDDLE

Washington May 24. 1838

Private

Dr Sir

I recd yours last Eve'.[1] It relates to different subjects, & I will put my answers on different papers.

Imprimis, as to the *note*—indorsed by Mr [Charles] *Nichols*. That note was given, in western transactions, will be duly paid, out of a fund appropriated for the purpose, but *I* have no interest in having it discounted. Indeed it is agt. faith, that it is proposed at all for discount any where; but I care nothing about that, except that I do not wish it to be discounted at your Bank, on any idea that such discount would be *a favor to me*. On the other hand, it would suit me much better to let this not receive the effectual declaration "done," & that Mr [Richard] Smith should be told that if I offer him paper, as good or better, in the discount of which I might have an *interest*, he might utter over it the magical word, in his low & soft voice. If 'twere *done*, when 'tis *done* &c. &c.

I hope, however, I may be able to live thro the Session without troubling Mr Smith or yourself. But on some of these things, *ad me pertinentia*, I wrote a letter or two, not long since, to Mr [Joseph] Cowperthwaite.[2] He has not had time to read them. If you think of it, & have leisure—& they who have most do have usually most leisure—pray say [a] word to him about it. In the hope of realizing such advances, as would enable me to live without carrying the Green Bag any longer, I put every thing I could rake & scrape, cash & credit, in lands, at Government price, in Illinois & Wisconsin, in 1836. I am quite sure that the investments were well made, & that as soon as times turn, even a little, those lands will sell at from five to ten times their cost. But at present, I can sell only on long credit, & have preferred not to sell at all. *I am satis[fied]*. Say a word to Mr. C. upon the letter I wrote him. Yours truly   Danl. Webster

ALS. DLC.   22, 1838.
    1. See above, Biddle to DW, May   2. Not found.

TO NICHOLAS BIDDLE
                                    May 24. [1838]
Private
Dear Sir,

The Bank project is a project to *get N. York*. Our illustrious friend[1] seeks his great object, by connecting himself with some one grand idea.

In 1823 that idea was *the establishment of an American System*.

In 1833, the idea was, *to bargain away that system*.

In 1838, it is to make a Bank of U. S. on certain principles (principles!) which see.

This project is an article for the N. Y. market. *I doubt whether it will sell.*

On what is, or may be, before us, in regard to finance, Banks, &c. I exceedingly desire a long talk with you. I would even almost go to Phila-

delphia for the purpose. It is time to come to some *definite* object. Yrs
                                                        D. Webster

ALS. DLC.
  1. Henry Clay.

FROM NICHOLAS BIDDLE

                                        Phila. May 28, 1838
My dear Sir,
    If your amendment passes, I wish you would get your friends to rally
& press its immediate passage by the House: This will be enough to justify early measures for resumption.[1] In haste Yrs   N. B.

LC. DLC.
    1. On May 25, Webster had offered
an amendment to Clay's resolution
(S. 11; see above, Biddle to DW, May
22, 1838, and DW to Biddle, May 3,
1838). The objective of Webster's
amendment, like Clay's original resolution, was to annul the Specie Circular. Congress adopted Webster's
wording, declaring it illegal "for the

Secretary of the Treasury to make or
to continue in force, any general
order, which shall create any difference between the different branches
of revenue, as to the money or medium of payment, in which debts or
dues, accruing to the United States,
may be paid." *Congressional Globe*,
25th Cong., 2d sess., p. 411; 5 *U.S.
Statutes at Large* 310.

TO NICHOLAS BIDDLE

                                        May 29. 1838
                                        Tuesday Eve'
Dr Sir,
    My amendment has passed the Senate, today, 34—to 9.
    I have taken INFINITE pains, to make a rally in the House.[1]
    I fully believe, in 3 days (the period of the French Revolution) it will
be a law.
    I have much—which I could say on this occasion—but the time is
not yet.
    I *pledged myself in N.Y. that if T[reasury] Order was abrogated,
U.S.B. would resume.* It will be abrogated, instanter, as I believe—God
bless you   D.W.

ALS. DLC.
    1. See *Senate Journal*, 25th Cong.,
2d sess., Serial 313, p. 432. The

measure won approval in the House
two days later, on May 31.

TO NICHOLAS BIDDLE

                                        Wednesday, 12 oclock
                                        [May 31, 1838]
Dear Sir,
    The deed is done. I did what I could, last Evening, to rally forces, &

this morning there was force enough to put the Resolution thro the H. of R. like a shot. Nothing remains, but the President's approval, which there is no danger of his withholding.[1] Yrs always truly   D. Webster

ALS. DLC.
1. President Van Buren signed the resolution on the same day.

TO NICHOLAS BIDDLE

[c. May 31, 1838]

Private, or murder

I will tell you a short story. When I left W. for Boston, in April, I signified to my friends that on my return I should bring forward a measure, by itself, for repealing the Treasury Order, & should put it in the same form, as my amendment, introduced for the same purpose, into the Sub-Treasury Bill. They all thought it would be a good move; & one of them said to me, as you have mentioned your purpose, and it will become known, lest you should be *anticipated*, you will do well to mention it to Mr [Henry] C[lay]. Accordingly, with that friend, I walked over to Mr C's lodgings, the Evening before I left Washington, explained my purpose to Mr. C. & assured him that the first day after my return, I should bring forward the measure, if, in the mean time, the H. of R. should not take up the Sub-Treasury Bill.

After I had been heard of, on my return, at New York, & one or two days before my arrival here, Mr C. *brought forward a Resolution himself*—and some considerable bruit ensued, about his promptitude to aid the mercantile interest &c. &c. &c. So the world goes!

Burn this—as it is libellous, in the extreme.

AL. DLC. Printed in McGrane, *Correspondence of Nicholas Biddle*, pp. 310–311.

FROM NICHOLAS BIDDLE

Phila. June 1, 1838

My dear Sir,

Many thanks for your favors, which after being carefully perused, were as carefully destroyed.[1] When the success of *your* amendment reached me yesterday morning, my own course seemed clear. It was to make the most of the Act for the Country's sake—to treat it as the thing which had been waited for, & to adopt it decidedly & instantly—avoiding at the same time all air of triumph, and regarding the Govt. as desirous of measures in which we here incline to cooperate. As the idea of resistance came originally in my letter to Mr. [John Quincy] Adams,[2] I thought the same channel the fittest for declaring our content with the change. Accordingly I wrote the few lines to Mr. Adams,[3] which were immediately printed & sent off to England by the packet. At the same time I thought the occasion apt to yield to our New York friends, & to make the repeal the basis of it.

You see then, that I have endeavoured to turn the Resolution to the utmost benefit of the Country. It remains now to satisfy our friends of the administration that we can serve the public better than any other, or any new concern. To this end we are inclined to do much. What aid can you bring to bear on that point? Our agency at New York can do as well as the new monster projected under the presidency of Mr [Albert] Gallatin—so in Phila.—so in the West & South—so in Europe—so every where.[4] Turn all these things in your mind as it goes round the spacious domain it inhabits, & tell me what may be done. Always Yours   N.B.

LC. DLC.

1. See the two letters above, DW to Biddle, [May 31 and c. May 31, 1838].

2. See Nicholas Biddle to John Quincy Adams, April 5, 1838, in *Niles' National Register*, 54 (April 14, 1838): 98–100.

3. See Nicholas Biddle to John Quincy Adams, May 31, 1838, in *Niles' National Register*, 54 (June 9, 1838): 226.

4. Speaking in the Senate on May 21, Clay had said, "There is but one other person, connected with the banking institutions of the country, in whose administration of a Bank of the United States I should have equal confidence with Mr. Biddle, and that is Albert Gallatin. . . ." Clay did not mean, however, that he advocated either Biddle's Philadelphia bank or Gallatin's New York bank. He thought it "most expedient that a *new* bank, with power to establish branches, be created and chartered under the authority of Congress." *Congressional Globe*, 25th Cong., 2d sess., p. 396. See also Thomas Payne Govan, *Nicholas Biddle: Nationalist and Public Banker, 1786–1844* (Chicago, 1959), pp. 326–338.

TO [EDWARD EVERETT]

[c. June 1, 1838]

Private

My Dear Sir

I think the Measure which has passed both Houses, doing away [with] the Treasury order, may be regarded, not unjustly, as mine.[1] I introduced it, into the Sub-Treasury Bill, & it has now passed, in the same form. I could state circumstances, which might be supposed to show a little want of *ingenuousness*;[2] but I am not disposed to magnify the importance of little things. If Mr [Nathan] Hale, however, who has doubtless noticed the progress of the measure, should see fit to remind his readers that the Resolution, as passed is my original proposition, it might do neither injustice nor harm. Yrs truly,   D Webster

ALS. MHi.
1. Resolution S. 11, annulling the Specie Circular, which passed the Senate on May 29 and the House on May 31.
2. Webster was referring to the res-

olution Clay had introduced on April 30. For a discussion of that "little want of *ingenuousness*," see above, DW to Nicholas Biddle, [c. May 31, 1838].

TO NICHOLAS BIDDLE

Washington, June 4. 1838.

My dear Sir,

I received yours of the first inst. on Saturday evening.[1] Its contents embraced subjects which have recently occupied my thoughts a good deal.

I alluded to them in a late letter to you.[2] It is difficult to say what may be done with the Administration in its present temper. Perhaps it may be brought to see it's own interest. But however this may be it is evident that we must be prepared for something before long. On the general expediency of a National Institution you and I are agreed: but what is to be done ad interim becomes now matter of much importance to be considered. I am trying to form some definite judgment, but at present remain, "multa solvens in animo." Yours truly   Danl Webster

You perceive I am moving for some modifications of Deposite Laws — Is it not important that the law should be made to embrace, not only "Corporations," but "Banking Institutions, established under the laws of any State"?[3]

ALS. James Biddle Collection of the Biddle Family Papers (Andalusia), Philadelphia, Pennsylvania.
1. See above.
2. Perhaps DW was referring to his letter of [c. May 31, 1838] to Nicholas Biddle, above.

3. On June 12, DW introduced a bill "making further provisions for the collection of the public revenue." See *Congressional Globe*, 25th Cong., 2d sess., p. 448; *ibid.*, Appendix, pp. 376–379.

FROM NICHOLAS BIDDLE

Phila. June 5, 1838

My dear Sir,

I have just received your two notes of yesterday, & shall answer forthwith.[1]

1. As to D.W. As this time of my writing is late in the afternoon, & Mr.

[Joseph] Cowperthwait is not in the Bank, I must postpone my talk with him till tomorrow.

2. Come on Tuesday—& then we can talk business, private & public.[2]

3. The project of a Bank is a sad crudity. It is not fit that in this year of our Lord statesmen should talk about foreign capital slightingly—or of men's private concerns disclosed to town meetings &c. &c.

4. My notion is that it is better to take *the* bank until you can make a bank—but this will be best done by friendly arrangement with the Treasury.[3]

5. I would say "Banking Institutions" as well as Corporations.

6. But here are texts enough—so I will make my sixth only Yrs. Very truly   N.B.

LC. DLC.
1. See above, DW to Biddle, June 4, 1838; the other has not been identified.
2. See above, DW to Nicholas Biddle, May 24, 1838, for a discussion of DW's private business.
3. Biddle was probably alluding to his offer of April 30 to John Forsyth to make available immediately to the government some of the $6 million

the Pennsylvania Bank of the United States owed the government on BUS stock. Forsyth rejected the offer, but his successor as secretary of the treasury, Levi Woodbury, had no reservations. In August the Bank advanced $4 million to the government. Thomas Payne Govan, *Nicholas Biddle: Nationalist and Public Banker, 1786–1844* (Chicago, 1959), pp. 333–335.

TO NICHOLAS BIDDLE

Saturday Morning
[June 9, 1838]

Private

My Dear Sir,

When I get to the Senate, today, I will write a short line on public sentiment.[1] My *morning thoughts* have in them something of the *ut ad me revertar.*

H. L. Kinney, of Illinois, is now here. He is well known to members of Congress from the West, & especially well known to Col [Thomas] Mather President of the Illinois Bank,[2] who is probably known to you, but who, at this moment is West of the Alleghany. All the persons, hereabout, who know any thing of Mr K. all would readily certify that he is understood to be, undoubtedly, very wealthy. He is a young man, intelligent, & of excellent character, a Pennsylvanian, well known, with his connexions to Honble Mr [Samuel] McKean.

Now, I can sell to Mr K certain lots of mine in Peru, (La Salle)—& some other property adjoining his Estate, for from 60. to 70 th [?] Dollars, on time, say 2. 3. 4. 5 years. In present state of affairs, and present prospects, he will not agree to buy, on condition of making any considerable payment in *one* year.

I presume he would not buy, on condition to give security by way of Mortgage. 1st. Because he would want the power of selling the City lots, without embarrassment; 2. because he does not give mortgages; his other p[ro]p[ert]y is all clear, & it would astonish the natives, if he were found to give any such security.

Herewith, is a statement, under his hand.[3] I have no doubt that he believes all he has therein said to be clearly *within* the limits of truth.

Now—would such a Bond be a good *basis*, for a loan, for my purposes?—to be strengthened by whatever collateral matters of mine, might be thought useful? I would readily mortgage 50.000 Dlls p[ro]p[ert]y in Mass. & N. Hampshire, if the conveyance could be made to any body not connected with *the Bank*. But I must avoid that, for considerations connected with the *future*, as well as the past.

I shall not go to Philadelphia till *Thursday*. By that day, I hope to be able to take along with me, for the benefit of his health, Mr [Edward] Curtis, who is just recovering from a severe *inflamatory rheumatism.*

If you think such a Bond would be a useful instrument—please say so, (*by return of mail*), as Mr K. will leave here, about Thursday for the West. I do not wish to deal with him, unless I can make use of the Bond; as the p[ro]p[ert]y which I shall part with to him, at the proposed prices, is better than any man's bond, unless the latter can be better brought into the class of *availables.* A word in answer. Yrs   D. Webster

ALS. DLC.
1. Letter not found.
2. Mather (1796–?), a native of Connecticut, had gone west in 1820 as a government agent and later settled in Kaskaskia, Illinois, where he engaged in the mercantile business and served in the state legislature. About 1836 he settled in Springfield, where he shortly became president of the Illinois State Bank.
3. Not found.

FROM NICHOLAS BIDDLE

Phila. June 12. 1838

My dear Sir,

I prolonged my weekly rustication so late into Monday, that I could not answer your favor of the 9th. inst[1] by return of mail. In regard to Mr [Henry L.] K[inney] I should not think it worth while for you to deal with him instantly under the belief that you can easily convert his bonds. This real estate is an excellent thing. Why is it not a little more movable. And just now in the present uncertainty of public affairs we are on the lowest diet and have a ferocious indisposition to lend. But come & talk & we will see if any thing can be done. Till then Yrs always   NB

ALS draft. DLC.
    1. See above.

FROM NATHANIEL RAY THOMAS

La Salle June 15th 1838

My dear Sir,

Since I last wrote you (1st inst) I have received your letter of 21st of May.[1]

I have before me a letter from Mr [Fisher Ames] Harding on the subject of his purchase of the Wisconsin Land Co., a copy of which I enclose.[2] I also send you copy of a letter from Reuben Moore[3] of Chicago written at Mr Hardings request containing some information on the same subject. The *deeds* therein mentioned I have in my possession & shall take them with me to Detroit that Mr H. may deed the property to you. I shall not fail to attend to your wishes in relation to the title of the St. Joseph property, and shall endeavour to get from Mr Harding a full & complete understanding in regard to the several purchases made by him for your account.

I have confidently hoped to have been now on my journey to Buffalo but the non arrival of Fletcher & Col Kinney still keeps me here. I regret this exceedingly, for I know it is all important that I should accomplish my business in that direction, in the interval between planting & haying, which I can now hardly hope to do. If however there should be any one arrive from the east to whom I could confide our farming matters, my absence would not be of so much consequence. I hope this good fortune may await me.

I have planted about 25 acres of corn, but the *draught* the *worms* and the *birds* have made such sad havoc among it that I hardly hope to raise two hundred bushels off the whole of it—indeed I would sell the crop for this amount. But we have done *our* duty, and have only to hope that the future may have better things in store for us. We have had abundant rain for the past week, (accompanied almost daily by tremendous thunder & lightening) and such crops as have not been destroyed from the causes above mentioned are now doing well. *Hail* fell yesterday that was *nine* inches in circumference by *actual measurement*. We experienced no damage from it however—except the breaking of some doz[en] or twenty lights of glass.

The whole neighbourhood (myself among the number) were called to *arms* on Tuesday to quell a Riot among the Irish on the canal. It resulted in securing the ring leaders & taking from the mob some sixty or seventy Guns. There were several of the rioters *shot* in the skirmish—probably six to ten killed & wounded.

My money matters are I assure [you] at a low ebb. I have delayed drawing on you until Fletchers arrival, thinking it possible that other arrangements may have been made to supply [me]. In the hope that I shall soon have the [opportunity?] of bidding both him & Col Kinney I remain, Yours most truly   N. Ray Thomas

Strangers are daily arriving at Peru with the intention to settle here. There is great want of buildings, although there are several constantly in progress of erection. It cannot fail to be a place of much importance.

ALS. NhHi.   2. Enclosure not found.
1. Not found.   3. Not identified; copy not found.

TO NICHOLAS BIDDLE

Washington, Saturday noon
[c. June 16, 1838]

Dear Sir

I have waited a day or two for Mr. [Edward] Curtis. He is now able to travel, but I fear he may find a *clog*, in the Sub. Treasury. It is now supposed the citizen [Churchill C.] Cambreleng may call up that measure, on Monday or Tuesday: so I think I must go without Mr Curtis.

I shall go to Baltimore, tomorrow Eve', & be in Phila on Monday—nothing happening.

I shall bring no *bond* from [Henry L.] Kinney.

My idea, suggested to Mr [Joseph] Cowperthwaite, was, that in the present abundance of money in England, Mr [Samuel] Jaudon might be able to do the needful. Of course, I should prefer to abide nearer home. I do not want any very large sum, at the moment; but I want that parcels should be doled out, at different periods, between this & Jan. or Feb.

All this, is small business for you, who have on your hands the leading money concerns of a whole hemisphere. But if you will say to Mr Cowperthwaite, or Mr M[orris] Robinson,[1] that they, or either of them, may arrange the matter, on good security, I shall be glad; that is to say, provided you think it should be done, & that it can be done, without too much inconvenience. From Phila. I can go to N. York, if there should be reason for it. My wife & daughter will be with me, on their way home.

The Sub. Treasury bill remains in *statu quo*. Calhoun is moving, heaven, earth, & ―― to obtain Southern votes for the measure. He labors to convince his Southern neighbors that it's success will relieve them from

their commercial dependence on the North.[2] His plausibility, & endless perseverance, have really effected a good deal. Even your relative Mr. C[harles Biddle] Shepherd [Shepard] has been, & indeed now is, in a state of doubt. Still, I think the Bill cannot pass; but the majority will be small. The labors of Mr Calhoun, & the power & patronage of the Executive, have accomplished more than I have thought possible. Yrs truly
Danl Webster

ALS. DLC. Published in part in Mc-Grane, *Correspondence of Nicholas Biddle*, p. 301.

1. Robinson, formerly cashier of the New York branch of the Bank of the United States, was at this time president of the Bank of the United States in New York, incorporated in 1838.

2. Calhoun had expressed this view as early as September 1837. "We have now a fair opportunity to break the control of our commercial Shackles," he explained to his brother-in-law, James Edward Calhoun: "I

mean the control which the North through the use of Government credit acting through the banks, have exercised over our industry and commerce." John C. Calhoun to James Edward Calhoun, September 7, 1837, in *Correspondence of John C. Calhoun* (Vol. 2 of *Annual Report of the American Historical Association for the Year 1899*), ed. J. Franklin Jameson (Washington, 1900), pp. 377–378. For a fuller analysis of Calhoun's motives, see DW to Thurlow Weed, June 23, 1838, below.

FROM RAMSAY CROOKS

Office of the American
Fur Company
New York 19 June 1838

Dear Sir

I was duly favored with your esteemed letter of 12 ulto:,[1] and see with regret that you feel in common with the Commercial community, the evils arising from the indiscreet meddling of the Government with the currency of the country.

Were our resources greater than they are, or are likely to be for months to come, I would cheerfully wait your own good time; but the hungry will have bread, and we cannot satisfy their cravings if the Storehouse continues empty. I do not for one instant doubt the sincerity of your intention to meet punctually the engagement you voluntarily made with us by your letter of 2 January last,[2] and I certainly calculated upon receiving the instalments on the days named. That arrangement met the approbation of the party from whom we received your Note in account, but as I have not ventured to advise them of your failure to pay the $2500 on the 31 ulto:, I am in daily fear of their enquiring into the matter. I therefore trust you will soon remit me, if not the whole, at least a considerable portion of the amount I expected last month, with an assurance of an early payment of the balance—and you will also oblige by saying to Mr [Henry L.] Kinney I am anxiously waiting to hear he will soon be able to pay his note, which we still hold: for as an Agent in the matter I shall be compelled to obey the wishes of my constituents however painful the duty may be.

I am, Dear Sir, with much esteem & respect Your ob servant   Ramy Crooks President Am fur Co

LC. NHi.   2. See above.
    1. Not found.

TO RAMSAY CROOKS

Washington June 22. 1838
Dear Sir
    I have recd your favor of the 19th.¹ Is it not possible to make some arrangement *for time*, in regard to this debt of mine, in your hands? I have the property, but whether from that or any thing else, I find infinite difficulty, in getting money. Yours truly   D. Webster

ALS. NHi.
    1. See above.

TO THURLOW WEED

Washington June 23. 1838
My Dear Sir
    When I had the pleasure of seeing you in N York, last fall, I promised to write you, if any thing important should occur, in regard to which you would not be likely to be as well informed from other sources. The knowledge of some facts & circumstances, which are not yet generally known, leads me to regard the present, as a fit occasion for complying with this promise.

As to the fate of the Sub-Treasury Bill, I have nothing to say, beyond what you will have learned, from the communications of other friends. The Bill cannot pass. The majority agt. it is variously estimated, at from 4 to 10.

But the policy, in which the Bill is founded, or rather, that with which it has become connected, *is not to be abandoned*. On the contrary, that policy, is to become, more & more, one great dividing line between parties; & these parties are likely to become, in a greater degree than heretofore, *local*. The mischievous ascendancy of the commercial interest of the North—the unjust & unnatural depression of Southern trade; the necessity of rallying the whole South & South west, against the North, its concentrated capital, its commercial monopoly, its abolition sentiments &c. &c.—these, are to be the leading topics, & leading objects, of the Divorce Party, hereafter.

To carry these purposes forward, you will, within a very short time, see evidence of an arrangement to reorganize a *Democratic Party*, essentially under a Southern lead, which will, or will not, support Mr V. Buren, for another election, according to circumstances. The whole scope, or general object, may be thus stated.

1. To reorganize a Democratic Party, on the strictest doctrines of the State Rights school; & to this end much use will be made of Mr Jefferson's authority, especially his Inaugural Address.

2. To oppose, with "uncompromising hostility," a Bank of U.S. The objections to such an Institution are, its tendency to concentrate Capital, to favor the North, & depress the South, &c. No distinct point will be made on the *Constitutionality* of a Bank, as on that point there will, or may, be some diversity of opinion. But agt. its expediency, all will unite; & this will form one leading & grand characteristic of the party.

3. To complete, at all events, a separation of the Govt. from all State Banks. The party will profess not to be enemies to the State Banks, as such; but only enemies to the policy of using them, for purposes of Govt. They will not consent to such use, & will be, especially, opposed to allowing the public monies to be the basis of commercial discounts, after collection & before disbursement.

4. The fourth & last, & perhaps the main ground, at least one very important ground, on which this Party propose to stand, is their opposition to Abolition, *in every form, & any degree*. They deny the Constitutional power of Congress to touch slavery, or the slave trade, in the District of Columbia; & they, especially, denounce any step of that kind, if taken with a view to give the lead, or set an example to the States, on the subject of abolition.

These are the leading ideas. You will find the party rallying, very much, under Mr Calhoun's lead, & the most active men, in maintaining the ground which will be assumed, will be his friends. Seeing what prominence these operations may give to Mr. Calhoun in the South, Mr V. Buren will make all possible exertions, & all sacrifices to *secure his own standing*, in that quarter also. He, too, will play, & is playing, *for the South*. It is suggested that Mr [James Kirke] Paulding owes his appointment, in part at least, to the fact of having written sundry articles *agt. the Anti Slavery party of the North*. But nothing is likely to save Mr. V.B. if N. York shall go agt. him, next fall. In that event, it is hardly doubtful, that the South, seeing that it must mainly rely on itself, will unite under a leader of its own. Suggestions thro the papers, here and in

S. Carolina, already point to Mr Calhoun, as the next Candidate. You will of course, My Dear Sir, receive this letter as in strict confidence, & having read it, I hope you will write me that it is burnt; as I use that prudent mode, myself, of securing such letter against the chances, which surround human life. With true regard, Yrs [signature removed]

P.S. This letter, My Dr Sir, I need hardly repeat, is entirely for your own information, & I would not wish any such marked reference to its topics, by you in your paper, as might attract attention *here*. You will readily understand the reason of this. After the adjournment of Congress, you will have other evidence of what I have stated, if not before; & in the mean time, this may give you time to prepare for the occasion.

AL (signature removed). NRU.

TO GIDEON LEE

Washington June 30. 1838

My Dear Sir,

I thank you for your letter,[1] which I recd last Evening, & cordially accept your congratulations, on the final defeat of the Sub-Treasury Bill in the H. of R. You will see that we strangled another little Sub-Treasury scheme, in the form of a "Special Deposite" system, in the Senate, yesterday.

We have thus defeated the Sub-Treasury *without the specie clauses*:
We have defeated the Sub Treasury *with the specie clauses*;
And we have defeated the Sub Treasury, in the form of "Special Deposite." My Bill for abolishing the Bank disqualifications, as you will see, was not allowed to pass. Mr [James] Buchanan's Special Deposite Bill was made use of to overlay it; though that enjoyed but a brief existence.

Mr [Silas] Wright will today bring in a Bill to remove these Bank disqualifications; but I fear it will be but an imperfect and scanty measure of relief. We shall amend it, if we are able, & at any rate get all the good out of it we can.

I am truly gratified, My Dear Sir, to know, that our efforts, in these important concerns, meet the approbation of one, who has himself been so much in public life, and who is acknowledged to be so intelligent & well informed, in all that respects the great Commercial interests & business of the Country. With very true regard, Your ob. servt

Danl Webster

ALS. NhD.
1. Not found.

FROM DANIEL FLETCHER WEBSTER

Peru July 16. 1838.

My dear Father,

You will have seen by my letter to Caroline dated Peru—that we have arrived here safely. We found things in pretty much the same state that we left them, a few small houses put up & a good deal of roguery of various kinds done, but with these *improvements* had stopped.

I went directly to Salisbury where were Ray [Thomas] and Arthur [Fletcher]. It looks very well, considering the Season, which has been a very bad one; many were obliged to plant their corn three times. Ray's crops look as well as any body's, but he will not raise more than enough, if enough, to go through the winter with, with all his cattle & horses & men.

We looked over yesterday together your "land papers." Many of your titles were imperfect. None of *L. C. Turners* deeds were either acknowledged or recorded. A great many other titles are imperfect also and Ray will have considerable trouble in making them complete. Your purchase at Toledo of Turner is very singularly described. This title can't be made good till he returns. Ray leaves on Wednesday. I shall go to Chicago with him & on my return shall take charge of the farm during his absence. He will go to Avon for the cattle & I hope Mr. [Herman] Le Roy will have them ready for him as he wants to be as speedy as possible in his movements.

Col. [Henry L.] K[inney] has been very much engaged since his return & is now paying off his men on the Canal. [Daniel J.] Townsend has caused him a good deal of trouble.

I have not yet made any arrangements with him about White Hall, but it shall be done; at any rate you shall have a deed from me of White Hall, & I will get my other farm from him sooner or later. The Stone House of which I spoke to you has not advanced at all & on the whole I do not think that we should get along very well with the old 'Squire & his daughters. I wish we could put a small addition on to *Salisbury.* It would cost about seven hundred dollars to make a building two stories high, with two rooms in it, one above & one below, sixteen feet by twenty & built in the plainest manner. If you come out here with Mother & Julia some such accomodation will be indispensable & I would willingly pay half for the comfort of the thing this winter to Caroline, if we live at Salisbury, as I think we shall have to do. As you recollect the house has only two decent rooms in it & both very low ceilings, only seven feet in the lower story & six feet four inches in the upper. The plan is, if you remember, like this enclosed.[1] You see how much more comfortable and commodious the house would be with this amendment, & if you do not build for yourself a large house, as I suppose you hardly will, upon the farm, some such enlargement is really very necessary. If a few additional acres from the farm I am to have would help do it I should be extremely willing to let them. Ray is of my opinion. We could build an addition of *one* story which would help much. If you will think of this & approve it, we will go right on and do it. The furniture now at the house is what I had in Detroit, with a few additional bed-steads that we got here.

My great anxiety, of course, is at present to have my family comfortable at as cheap a rate as possible & I feel pretty confident that we shall have to refuse to go into the Stone House, though I have not mentioned it yet to the Col, who considers it settled that we shall.

I have understood that I could sell some of my lands near Mineral Point for $10. per acre. I intend to go up there and sell them if I can get that in cash. I must do something of the kind I think to get along. Business promises pretty well. I have made one collecting trip since I have been home, though as yet it is very small. The Col's money affairs improve here since his arrival. The great *Dredging Machines* have come & these will get a good *estimate*. The Col. says that he hopes to make every thing go well & he promises to make a reformation among his Agents & Partners, but I fear that he lacks the nerve to do it. I put him up to it, on every opportunity. Townsend refused to let Ray have a barrel of pork on one occasion, unless he paid the *cash* for it, & as Ray happened to be out just then, it was rather inconvenient to do so. [James] Mulford,[2] who neglected to pay my draft on you to Mr. Welles[3] the cashier of the Detroit Bank has just returned to town. We will settle that matter *today*.

You said that if I would send you the deeds of those lands which were to be added to Salisbury I might draw on you for $500. Will you allow me to anticipate the draft one *half* on condition that I will give you White Hall. I would willingly do it, knowing that I run no risk in waiting for my deed from the Col. of Point Comfort. It would oblige me very much, as I have bought me a horse & have several little bills here, which I would like to pay forthwith.

I have continued writing until the time of closing the mail & have only a moment to spare. With my best love to all at Marshfield I remain Your affectionate son   Daniel F. Webster.

ALS. NhHi.

1. Not found.

2. Mulford went to Peru about 1836 with Henry L. Kinney, where he was a partner with Daniel J. Townsend in the commission business. During the Mexican War he went south, later opening a commission business in New Orleans.

3. Not further identified.

FROM RAMSAY CROOKS

Office of the American
Fur Company
New York 19 July 1838

Dear Sir

After our conversation at Washington I confess I am much disappointed at not hearing from you when here, in relation to your own Note, and that of Mr [Henry L.] Kinney, who in passing through St Louis 2 weeks ago, assured our friend [Pierre Chouteau] you were to provide for his $5000, within 30 days from that time.

Something conclusive must be done in these matters within a reasonable time, and I shall be glad indeed if you will relieve me from the embarrassing situation I am placed in with regard to the claims of the friend we represent, who I fear will now be disposed to conclude we have granted unreasonable indulgences.

I beg the favor of an early, and satisfactory reply,[1] and Am Dear Sir with sincere esteem Most Respectfully yr ob sert—Ramy Crooks President Am fur Co

LC. NHi.
1. For the reply, see DW to Crooks, August 7, 1838, below.

TO JOSEPH COWPERTHWAITE

Boston July 23. 1838

My Dear Sir,

I came up today from Marshfield, where I have been cooling & sleeping one blessed week; & I am a hundred *per cent* better for the operation. With the glorious exception of the afternoon, on which you drove us to "League Island," I have not been cool, before, since the early part of June. If I were well through tomorrow, & my face turned once more to the Sea side, my measure of happiness would be great.

I have just parted with that excellent good man, Mr [Samuel] Frothingham, whom I suppose you will see, by the time you receive this, or soon after. Nobody, except his old friend of the Bk of U.S. could have drawn him from Boston, for love or money. *I* shall miss him, much; as he has done me good, & not evil, continually, for twenty years. But I think he is right to go—Only think of it! 8.000 a year. The Secretary of State gets 6.000! The Chief Jus. of U.S. States gets 5.000. Verily, the monster does things on a monstrous large scale.

Ex dira necessitate, I must ask you, to "call in Mr Pratt,"[1] & put one of the *notes*, to my credit. I shall not draw for proceeds fast, remembering your wishes & suggestions; but cannot get along without drawing 2. or 3. thousand, soon; I shall not call again till 10th. or 20th. of August. [Levi] Turner's acceptances swallowed up so great a portion of my last discount, as leaves little for my own necessities. I hope we may hear from him, thro' Mr [Samuel] Jaudon, in 50 or 60 days.

I am glad you concluded *not to buy* the Borough of Reading.[2] That was a very good hit. Such things tend, happily, to make all this Anti-Bank cry ridiculous. Yours always mo. truly   Danl. Webster

ALS. PHi.

1. Not identified.

2. The town council of Reading, Pennsylvania, requested a $20,000 loan from Biddle's bank, but the request met with the remonstrances of the Safety Committee of Reading, which accused the town council of wanting to sell the town to the Philadelphia bank. Biddle denied having any desire to buy Reading, but said that in consideration of the objections made to the loan, he would decline the town council's request. Nicholas Biddle to the Town Council of Reading, Pa., June 22, 1838, *Niles' National Register*, 54 (August 4, 1838): 355.

FROM NATHANIEL RAY THOMAS

Detroit July 27th. 1838

My Dear Sir,

I arrived at this place the night before last and found that Mr [Phineas] Davis & Mr [Benjamin B.] Kercheval were out of town, but both are expected home to day or tomorrow. [Fisher Ames] Harding I have seen and shall get from him most of the titles to the property he purchased for you. He however knows little about the value of that property and has I should think relied solely in his purchases upon the representation of *interested* persons. I came across the Lake to St Josephs, but having no description of the lots there belonging to you I could not find them. They are however in *north* St Joseph which is mostly *under water* at present, the Lakes having risen about two feet this season. The investment there you will recollect was $2000—which you may conclude is little better than *thrown away*. The opposite side of the river (South St Joseph) is well situated & is quite a flourishing place—destined I should think to be [a] point of considerable importance.

I hastened my journey to this place in order that I might be here with Mr [James McHenry] Boyd of Baltimore[1] who is here for the express purpose of adjusting the interest of Mr [Ramsay] McHenry[2] of Baltimore in the Western Land association,[3] and to get the titles from Kercheval to the property. Harding says that he has all the papers & has directions from Kercheval to make out the deeds which he shall do forthwith. You will remember that in the division of the property one of the Tickets was drawn to you & Mr [Henry] Hubbard; but whether you intend to divide it or have the deed made out jointly I do not know.[4] I understand however that Hubbard is expected here daily and in case of his arrival before I leave for the West which will not be for two weeks at least, I presume we shall be able to make some satisfactory arrangement. Mr Boyd is fearful that Mr Hubbard will be disposed to make some trouble with Kercheval in the adjustment of his compensation; and in a letter which he has recv'd from his Cousin Mr McHenry is contained an extract from one of Mr Hubbards, in which among other things he says "I think Mr Webster must have been misunderstood in being understood to say that it would be competent for any individual to close his business with the Agent. He does not say so now. It is apparent that the whole concern must be closed agreeably to our arrangement in October last or else it goes for nothing. I *shall be authorized by Mr Webster* & Mr Owen[5] to carry out the arrangement made in October last." Now Mr Boyd says that in the arrangements made in October last it was expressly understood that it should be the business of *each individual* to settle with the Agent. I certainly understood it to be your intention that I should get from Kercheval the titles, and I am further advised by Fletcher to do so. At all events it is a safe proceeding and therefore in the absence of advices from you I shall do my best to *get possession of all that I can.* I trust that you will approve of this course and hope that you will not give Mr Hubbard any authority which can interfere with any proceedings of mine regarding it, for I have as yet no doubt that the whole matter may be adjusted without the slightest difficulty—yet not having seen Kercheval I may be mistaken. I will write you how your matters progress.

I shall start for Buffalo as soon as I can get matters in train here leaving the closing of them until my return. I should like to hear from you before I return West and if you would direct a letter to Mr Harding at this place I presume I should get it in season.

While at Chicago I drew on you in favour of E. H. Hadduck for $1060—dated August blank (to be filled up when used) at 60 days date payable at the Merchants Bank in the City of New York. This is for the remaining payment on the Ramsay & Irwin Claim.[6] Mr Hadduck said he has written to you for a Bank Certificate and in case of its arrival before the 10th of August, the draft will be returned to me. Mr Hadduck advanced the money the first of this month. I made arrangements with Mr H. to get in some 40 or 50 acres of wheat on this farm during my absence and I would pay the expense of it on my return. This & some other expenses which I have then to meet will make it necessary for me to raise some more money, but I will see how I can do this when I get to Buffalo.

I do hope that money matters are improving at the east and that it will flow in upon *you* in abundance.

I duly received your letter of the 2d instant from Washington & *took courage.* Very truly & respectfully Yours   N. Ray Thomas

The weather in this Country is *hot* beyond all former precedent.

ALS. NhHi.

1. Boyd (1817–1848) was the grandson of James McHenry, who had served in the Continental Congress and the Constitutional Convention, and as Washington's secretary of war.

2. McHenry (1814–1878), also a grandson of James McHenry, was a "country gentleman," a planter from Monmouth, Hartford County, Maryland, who occasionally sat in the Maryland legislature.

3. The Western Land Association was a speculative enterprise headed by Lewis Cass. Cass's affiliation with the company became an issue in the presidential campaign of 1848. See

Henry Hubbard to DW, August 1, 1838, and DW to Samuel Jaudon, January 12, 1839, below; *Richmond Enquirer*, August 11, 1848; and Joseph G. Rayback, *Free Soil: The Election of 1848* (Lexington, Ky., 1970), p. 237.

4. See Henry Hubbard to DW, August 1, 1838, below; and deed conveying land from Benjamin B. Kercheval and Mark Healey to DW and Henry Hubbard, August 1, 1838, Office of the Register of Deeds, Shiawassee County, Corunna, Michigan, mDWs.

5. Not identified.

6. Not identified.

FROM HENRY HUBBARD

Detroit Augt. 1. 1838

My dear Sir

I hope to make a final arrangement with Mr [Benjamin B.] Kercheval before I leave here. In my bargain with Genl [Lewis] Cass Kercheval was to release to me on certain shares 1/6th of the profits to compensate me for my expenses as I have advanced to Kercheval nearly three thousand dollars already to cover expenses &c. Should you make an arrangement with Mr Kercheval you can propose to him either to pay him what you may consider an equivalent for 1/6th of the profits, or what you may consider an equivalent to one third—if you do the latter Mr K. will hold the half of the third for my use—if you do the former you can hereafter settle with me on as liberal terms for the remaining sixth. I hope to be able to be reimbursed in part at least for my expenses and to be compensated for my services as this is the third journey I have taken to Detroit on this business and sent Mr [Phineas?] Davis[?] here once. By the terms of the contract you were to pay 1/3d. of the profits and be subject to no charges &c. By my agreement with Cass & Mr K. I was to do all the business—pay all the expences &c. and receive a sixth of the profits on certain shares of Mr K.

Should you make any communication to me at this place, your letter will find me here on my return from Wisconsin. I intend to leave for the west by the Boat to morrow. Very truly your's   H Hubbard

ALS. DLC.

TO RAMSAY CROOKS

Boston Aug. 7. 1838

My Dr Sir,

I came up from the Country yesterday, to which I had gone for the benefit of my health.

It is not correct, that I *undertook* to pay Mr [Henry L.] K[inney]'s note.[1] The truth is, a Gentleman, Mr [Simon] Cameron of Philadelphia, had given Mr K. to expect that he would place in my hands, for Mr K's use, a drft with good names, for $4.000 or thereabouts; & that drft I was to apply to his note. But the draft is not yet forthcoming.

I must have a little time to repose, & to reinstate my health—& I will then come to N. York, & some how or other, will adjust these matters. I cannot well go till next month, but in the course of that month, I will make some satisfactory arrangement. I pray you, My Dear Sir, to have a little patience, or I should rather say, a little *more* patience, for you have manifested much patience & kindness already. Yours, with much regard,

Danl. Webster

ALS. NHi.
1. See above, Crooks to DW, July 19, 1838.

TO SARAH GOODRIDGE

Summer St.
Aug. 7. '38

Dear Miss Goodrich

I came up from Marshfield yesterday, & return tomorrow. I had fully intended to call on you, but my health is feeble, & I have had so many things to attend to, that I am fatigued & tired out. I shall come up again next week, toward the end. You must know that I have a grandchild—Miss Grace Fletcher Webster.

She is now at Marshfield—will be up next week—is ten or eleven months old—& before she goes back to Illinois, I want her miniature. It would be convenient, if you could take it the week after next.

I will call & see you, as soon as I arrive next week. Yrs truly

D. Webster

ALS. MHi.

TO JOSEPH COWPERTHWAITE

Boston Aug. 8. 1838

My Dear Sir,

If you have passed one of the notes to my credit, as requested in my last letter, it will give me as much as I shall need at present, or need at all, I hope, if [Levi C.] Turner makes a remittance to reimburse the sums for which I am charged, in order to take up his paper. Pray let me know, as soon as you hear from him. I have been in the Country, for a fortnight, & am getting to be much better, in the matter of health. Next month, I must go to N. York, & may even make my appearance for a single day in Chesnut Street. Yrs truly always   Danl Webster

ALS. NhHi.

FROM EDWARD WEBSTER

Dart Coll., [September 2?,] 1838.

My dear Father

During the winter & spring terms of my Freshman year to gether with other students I got drawn very largely into debt and before I was aware how far I had gone I found myself in debt to a large amount. Knowing that it must of necessity grately hurt your feelings and also asshamed of my own folly & weekness I have let them remain till this time in all they amount to $225. since the time in which these debts were incured I have been trying to pay them with the pocket money which you have been kind enough to give me only spending as much as I was obliged to in order to appear decently and as I know you would wish a son of yours to appear here. It is with great reluctance now My Dear Father that I broach this subject to you. As I am well aware that I disregarded the good advice you had give me and suffered myself to be led away by silly boys & willy store keepers and also knowing the state of your business and money matters I am still more reluctant. You knew the dangers among which I was thrown and warned me but I neglected your warnings but now I come like the Prodigal son of old and ask your help & forgiveness with promises of better conduct and a more rigid compliance to your wishes in future and My dear Father if you would tranmit me money enough to discharge them I should be very thankful to you and I can assure you that I am very sorry for what I have done, and you may res assured that the like will never occur again as this has taugh me a lesson which I never shall forget. And Dear Father I remain your affectionant and henceforth dutiful son   Edward

ALS. NhD. Published in *Dartmouth*   1962): 13.
Alumni Magazine, 55 (November

TO [WILLIAM ALBERT] BRADLEY

Marshfield Sep. 5. 1838

Dear Sir

I send you a letter for Mr [Samuel] Jaudon,[1] in which I have earnestly solicited his aid to Mr [Virgil] M[axcy] in relation both to Clamorgan & the coal property. I have thought it better to seal it.

I should be glad of some of the new scrip, but mine is now at Boston. When I go up, (in two or three days) I will send some. I think also I shall let Mr. M. take some shares, on the same terms as he takes yrs.[2] The idea of getting some relief, even in 4 months, leads me to be willing to make almost any sacrifice. Yrs truly   D. Webster

ALS. CtY.
1. See below, DW to Samuel Jaudon, September 5, 1838.

2. For DW's agreement with Maxcy, see Memorandum, [September 25, 1838], below.

TO SAMUEL JAUDON

Boston Septr. 5. 1838

My Dear Sir,

Mr [Virgil] Maxcy has in charge, for the purpose of sale, certain scrip in the Maryland Mining Co. & certain shares in the "Clamorgan Grant." In regard to the first, the question is one of *value*, merely. From all I know, & can learn, the value of the p[ro]p[ert]y is great.

As to the second, there is connected with that a question of *title*. On this question I have given a Professional opinion, which you will have an opportunity of seeing.[1]

I am very much interested in *both* these matters, & shall be *greatly* benefitted if a favorable sale shall be made. I shall take it therefore as a great personal favor, if you shall be able, without inconvenience to yourself, to give Mr M. useful aid, in his proposed operations.

I have been passing a month at Marshfield, recovering from the exhaustion & fatigue caused by the prolonged Session of Congress.

I am pretty well restored, & am engaged, again, in private & professional affairs.

Mrs W. & Julia desire the most affectionate remembrance to you all. I am, Dear Sir, ever most truly Yours   Danl Webster

ALS. NHi.
1. See *Title Papers of the Clamorgan Grant, of 536, 094 Arpens of*

Alluvial Lands in Missouri and Arkansas (New York, 1837), pp. 14–21.

FROM NICHOLAS BIDDLE

Phila. Sepr. 6, 1838

My dear Sir

I stated to you last year my views in regard to Texas, and you then thought that if the plan of annexation to the U.S. could be abandoned, every consideration of feeling & interest would conspire to make us desire its prosperity. That question is now settled. Mr [Anson] Jones the new minister arrived two days ago in Phila. and he is instructed to withdraw the proposal of Union. This troublesome part of the question being thus disposed of, I am much inclined to think that if their loan of five millions were taken in the United States it would be far better than if they were obliged to seek it in England. I do not however wish to mix myself with the political contests of the day, nor to interfere in matters which have been the subjects of party warfare: and I should like to have the benefit of the opinions of judicious friends before doing anything final in respect to it. Will you then say, whatever you feel at liberty to say on the questions, Whether it would not be greatly for the interest of our common country that Texas should continue independent of all foreign nations—that she should be protected by this country & not be permitted if possible to owe her prosperity to any other aid than ours. Say too whether your opinion is that Texas can maintain its independence or whether in the last extremity this country would permit her to be conquered or reconquered, and being free whether you think a loan to her would be perfectly safe.[1] You will readily understand by the strain of these remarks that I am predisposed to serve Texas because I believe I should benefit our country by it, but before taking any decisive step I should wish to have your judgment because I know that your opinion will be an impartial & a patriotic one. If any circumstance public or private indisposes you to answer I request that you will not answer. But if you incline to speak—speak for I think the occasion worthy of you— and so speak that if when I have decided I should want the benefit of your judgment to sanction my course I may have it & use it publicly or privately. I will only add that what you say I wish you to say quickly.[2] With great regard Yrs   N Biddle

ALS. DLC. Published in Van Tyne, 213–214.

1. According to Govan, *Nicholas Biddle*, p. 354, "Biddle, in an effort to prove to the Texans that the United States was their 'best friend,' invested his personal funds in its lands and bonds. He became the unpaid financial adviser of the republic and did all that he could to aid it to raise funds in the United States and Europe."

2. For DW's response, see his enclosure of September 10, 1838, below.

TO EDWARD WEBSTER

Marshfield Sep. 8. 1838

My Dear Son

I duly recd your letter of the 26 of August[1] & have now yours of the second of this month.[2] It gives us all pleasure to hear of your safe arrival, & of the resumption of your studies. Your account, too, of Mr [John] Taylor, [Jr.,] & of affairs at Franklin was gratifying. We are pretty well here, except myself. I am troubled with my annual cold in my head. Caroline & Julia are at Boston or Nahant. Ellen Fletcher is still with us. I expect your mother & I shall go to Boston, for a few days, either Monday or Tuesday. The weather is again very dry, & every thing, which stood the former drought, seems now likely to be parched up.

Mr Frazer[3] died about ten days ago. Ray Thomas has been so sick, & so long sick, at Tonawanda, that Mrs [Ann Thomas] Porter, & Mr Thomas Ford,[4] have gone on to see him. Our last letters assured us that he was recovering. Fletcher at the last date was at St. Louis. It is uncertain when he will reach Boston.

I expect to hear from you once a week, as you promised. Yr affectionate father   Danl. Webster

Your mother sends her love, & desires you should write her.

ALS. NhHi.
1. Not found.
2. See above. See also DW to Edward, September 8, Edward to DW, September 13, and DW to Edward,

September 21, below.
3. Not identified.
4. Ford was probably one of Webster's Marshfield neighbors.

TO EDWARD WEBSTER

Marshfield Sep. 8. 1838

My Dear Son,

Your letter, respecting your own private affairs, has caused me very great grief.[1] I am shocked, not only at the folly, & guilt, of contracting such a debt, but at the misrepresentations, which you must have repeatedly made; as you have always told me that you owed nothing, which the means I furnished were not competent to discharge. Your letter has remained several days, unanswered, because I had not made up my mind what answer to give. My first feeling was to withdraw you from College, & to let you take care of yourself hereafter. But your letter shows an apparent spirit of repentance, & if I were sure that I could trust *that*, I might be induced to overlook the enormity of your misconduct. But how can I be sure that you have *now* told me the whole truth? How can I trust your present statements? Besides, how was this debt created? Was it by gaming, or other immoral habits,—or by mere thoughtlessness, & folly?

I have concluded to go up to Boston, tomorrow or next day; & then, either to go directly to Hanover, or to write you again. In the meantime,

I want to know more about the manner of contracting this debt; & I expect the whole truth. I would not expose you to public reproach, nor cast you off, for slight cause; but with all my affection, I will not excuse misconduct, and, especially, I will not put up with any degree or particle of misrepresentation, or concealment of the truth. On the receipt of this, you will immediately write to me, directed to Boston; & when I receive your letter, I shall determine what course to pursue.

Your affectionate, but distressed father   Danl Webster

ALS. NhD. Published in Van Tyne, pp. 597–598; and in *Dartmouth Alumni Magazine*, 55 (November 1962): 13.
1. See above, Edward Webster to DW, [September 2?, 1838].

TO NICHOLAS BIDDLE, WITH ENCLOSURE

Marshfield Sep. 9. '38

My Dear Sir,

I recd your letter last Evening;[1] & you have now my answer, which is my wife's handwriting,[2] as I am suffering a little in the matter of eyes. My answer has been hastily written, but the opinions it contains not hastily formed.

Mr [James] Munroes opinion, adverted to in my letter, may be worth looking up. I do not know exactly where it is to be found. You may, however, if you think it worth the trouble, find a reference to it in my Speech on the Panama Mission; which said Speech is in the "Speeches & Arguments of D Webster"—vol 1. as I think.[3]

I go for *our* America—free as possible from all European entangling connexions—"Americanus sum, sed nihil," &c &c.

I am here, in my fourth week of leisure & idleness. My health is greatly improved, & if I could see *into things* a little better, I should be fit to go to Boston, & go to work.

I hope to eat a few grapes with you, in Philadelphia, before Sep. is out. Yrs truly always   D Webster

ALS. DLC.
1. See above, Nicholas Biddle to DW, September 6, 1838.
2. See below.
3. See *Speeches and Forensic Arguments*, 1: 322–350.

ENCLOSURE: TO NICHOLAS BIDDLE

Boston, Septr. 10th. 1838

My Dear Sir

I have recd. your favor of the 8th. instant. The decision of the Govt of Texas to withdraw its application for a union with the U. States is, in my judgment, an event, eminently favorable to both countries. She now stands, as an independent state, looking to her own power, & her own resources, to maintain her place among the nations of the earth; an attitude, vastly more respectable, than that which she held, while solicitous to surrender her own political character, & to become part of a neighbouring country. Seeking, thus, no longer a union with us, & assuming the ground of entire independence, I think it highly important to the interest of the U. States, that Texas should be found able to maintain her position. Any connexion with a European State, so close as to make her dependent on that State, or to identify her interests with the interests of such State, I should regard as greatly unfortunate for us. I could not but regret exceedingly, to see any union between those parts of our continent, which have broken the chain of European dependence & the Governments of Europe; whether those from which they have been disunited, or others. You remember the strong opinion, expressed by Mr. Monroe, that the U.S. could not consent to the recolinization of those portions of this Continent, which had severed the ties, binding them to a European connexion, & formed free & independent governments for themselves; or to the establishment of the European Colonies, in America. The spirit, & reason, of these sentiments, would lead us to regard with just fear, & therefore with just jealousy, any connexions between our near American neighbours, & the powerful states of Europe, except those of friendly & useful commercial intercourse.

It is easy to forsee the evils with which any other connexion, than that last mentioned, between Texas & one of the great sovereignties of Europe, might threaten us. Not to advert to those of a high & political character, one, likely to have a direct bearing on our commerce, & prosperity, is very obvious. I mean the effect of such a connexion on the great staple of our Southern production. Texas is destined, doubtless, to be a great cotton producing country, & while we should cheerfully, concede to her all the advantages which her soil & climate afford to her, in sustaining a competition with ourselves, we could not behold, with indifference, a surrender by her, of her substantial independence, for the purchase of exclusive favors & privileges, from the hands of a European Government.

The competency of Texas to maintain her Independence depends, I think, altogether on the character of her Govt. & its administration. I have no belief at all, in the power of Mexico to re-subjugate Texas, if the latter country shall be well governed. The same consideration decides, also, the question, whether a loan to Texas would be safe. I have supposed, that her new formed Govt was gradually strengthening, & improving, in all the qualities requisite for the respectable exercise of National power. That in institutions so recent, there should be, for a time, some irregularity of action, is to be expected. But if those to whose hands her destinies are now committed, shall look steadily to two great objects, —first, real & absolute, as well as nominal, National Independence—& second, the maintenance of a free & efficient Govt., of which good faith shall, from the beginning, be a marked characteristic, I see nothing to render it less safe to regulate money transactions with her, than with the Govts. of other countries. On the other hand, if a spirit of speculation & project should appear to actuate her councils, & if she should trifle with her public domain, involve herself in contradictory obligations, or seek to establish her prosperity on any other foundations, than those of justice & good faith, there would then be little to be hoped, either in regard to punctuality in pecuniary engagements, or to the probability of her maintaining an independent National character.

My opinion, on the whole, is, that the prospects of Texas, are now far better & brighter than they had ever been before; that the interest of our own country require, that she should keep herself free from all particular European connexion; & that whatever aid can be furnished to her, by individuals, or corporations, in the U. States, in the present state of her affairs, to enable her to maintain a truly independent & national character, would tend to promote the welfare of the U. States as well as of Texas herself. I am, Dr. Sir yours with great [regard]   Danl. Webster

LS. DLC. Published in Curtis, 1: 579–580.

FROM EDWARD WEBSTER

Hanover Sept. 13. 1838

My Dear Father,

I received your letter yesterday.[1] I was aware that it could not but grieve you very much and that was the reason why I never told you before and also made the misrepresentations which you speak of. And Sir I can quiet your fears about my repentance not being real and affected for I certainly do feel very sorry, and penitent and you may rest assured that the like will never occur again. You wish to know how the debts were contracted. I will tell you the *truth* now. You say that you dont know but it was by gaming? It was not for I never gambled for a *cent* in my life nor do I think I ever shall for I never could have been lead away as far as that if any one had tried me, for I detest the practise and always did. A good deal is for such things as nuts & raisins, crockerey, cigars, candy pantaloons chess men backgammon boards knifes and some *wine* a very little of which I can say with a clear conscience I drank my self, riding on horse back and other ways for pleasure. And I am sorry to say very few of the articles were of any use. The *only* immoral thing which I have purchased is wine, the students with whom most of these debts were contracted have graduated so that there would not be the same temptations if I would yield to them which by the help of a firm resolve I hope I never shall!

I should be very sorry to be taken away from college, but if you think best I should be willing to go, with the education you have been kind enough to give me and my bodily strength I feel I should be able to take care of myself. If I do not improve upon trial I do not wish nor ask for any further indulgence, and as to the money part of it if by any means by keeping school or in other way I could make that up to you in a measure or in full I should be most happy to do so, And I remain my dear Father your most affectional and *deeply* penitent son   Edward Webster

ALS. NhD. Published in Van Tyne, pp. 598–599; and in *Dartmouth Alumni Magazine*, 55 (November

1962): 13–14.
1. See above, DW to Edward Webster, September 8, 1838.

TO VIRGIL MAXCY

Boston Sept 17. 1838.
Monday.

Dear Sir,

I have recd. your letter,[1] & am obliged to you, for notice of the time of your departure.

I expect to be in New York, no doubt in season to see you; & think I may probably place some Clamorgan scrip in your hands, on the same terms as those, on which you received Mr [William A.] Bradley's. Yours respectfully,   Danl Webster

LS. DLC.
1. Not found.

TO EDWARD WEBSTER

Boston Sep. 21. 1838

My Dear Son

I recd your letter,[1] two days ago, and have made up my mind to put entire trust in your statements—to clear off your embarrassments—& to give you a fair opportunity to retrieve whatever may have been amiss: & to pursue your studies.

I now trust, My Dear Son, to hear nothing of you, hereafter, except what may be gratifying. You must see, now, that you for your living, & your character & happiness hereafter, you must rely on yourself. If I can get you through with your education, it will be as much as I shall be able to do. I owe a good deal of money, & am at present receiving but a small income from my profession.

If you intend yourself for the *Bar*, you must begin, early, to contract a habit of diligent & ambitious study. You must be emulous of excellence. An ordinary lawyer is not an enviable character. I believe, verily, that you have sense and ability enough to make you quite respectable, & I pray you, My Dear Son, keep your attention steadily directed to your progress in your studies.

Your mother will be glad of your letter, which I received this morning. It has come back from Marshfield, we both happening to be here. She returns tomorrow, & I go to N. Y. this P.M. We look for Fletcher shortly. You will have notice of his arrival—& while here, we shall expect you to come & see him. Some of us will write, to fix the time.

I enclose 3 checks for $100—& 100—& 50—being 250 in all. You may use these, as you have occasion—tho' I should prefer that you should not use the whole of them before the 1st. or 5th of October.

[Your affectionate father, Daniel Webster.][2]

AL (signature removed). NhHi. Published in *PC*, 2: 40–41; and in *Dartmouth Alumni Magazine*, 55(November 1962): 14.

1. See above, Edward Webster to DW, September 13, 1838.
2. The complimentary close is taken from *PC*, 2: 41.

TO JOHN ANDREWS

New York Sep. 22. 1838

Dear Sir,

Mr [Joseph] Cowperthwaite has written to Mr [Thomas] Dunlap,[1] suggesting him to place one of the remaining [Henry L.] Kinney notes to my credit, according to the arrangement heretofore proposed &c. I shall accordingly draw for the proceeds, though probably not very rapidly. Some items of *interest*, &c. having been charged to me, as well as the checks which I have drawn, will you be kind eno. to send me a minute of my acct. as it will stand with this new discount.

Please address me at "Astor House" N. York. Yrs, very respectfully & truly   Danl Webster

ALS. NhD. Andrews was assistant cashier of the Pennsylvania Bank of the United States.

1. Dunlap (1792–1864) was a lawyer and at one time cashier of the Pennsylvania Bank of the United States. From 1839 to 1841, he served as its president.

MEMORANDUM OF AGREEMENT BETWEEN
DANIEL WEBSTER AND VIRGIL MAXCY

[September 25, 1838]

D. Webster has, this 25th. day of September 1838, delivered to V.

Maxcy to be sold by him Twenty Certificates or shares of the Stock of the Clamorgan Land Association of 1000 arpens each, it being agreed between the parties, that a certificate is not to be sold at a less price than Six hundred & twenty five dollars, which is to be paid over, clear of deduction for all commissions & charges whatever, to said Webster; and if sold at a higher price, the surplus is to belong to & be received and appropriated by said Maxcy to his own use as a compensation for effecting the sale, said Maxcy to be at liberty to take to himself any of said Shares at said price of Six hundred & twenty five dollars each.   Danl. Webster   V. Maxcy

If not disposed of by the first of April next the certificates to be returned and the cash raised by the sale or the certificates themselves to be paid or delivered to said Webster or to his written order on this contract.

DS. DLC.

FROM DANIEL FLETCHER WEBSTER

Peru. Sept. 26th. 1838.

My dear Father,

Things occur every day to delay me and every day I rejoice that I am still here to attend to them, although I am indeed most anxious to see you all & my wife & child again. Col. [Henry L.] Kinney is still somewhere on the Mississippi and his return some what uncertain. He has left all affairs connected with his in a very unsettled state and I am unable on that account as well as on some others to get away. If Ray Thomas were here I should be more able to leave, but there is no one to take proper charge of the *farm*; the men are becoming clamorous for pay and I have been obliged to give them all I could raise in any manner & indeed to furnish some supplies beside. Your Farm is not carried on well nor can it be on the present plan. It is too expensive. I have very much to say to you on this subject when we meet. Ray has done all he can & every thing has been made the best of—but I will keep all my remarks until we meet.

I returned from the Mississippi ten days ago & went direct to Ottawa where I passed the Court week. I put off all but one of the judgments against the Col. and defended in a tolerable speech a criminal, who was however convicted, despite my legal acumen, as they always are. I returned here on the 22d. & expected to leave before this but here I am. You remember that I got $3000. of [Nicholas] Boilvin [, Jr.][1] for Col. K. and gave for it my notes endorsed by Judge [Stephen] Haight. One for

$500. has become due—I have not the means of paying it and I cannot come off and leave it. No one is here to answer for the Col. and I cannot get the funds. I must wait his return and get security for the rest of the $3000. or I must sell all I have to pay it. Of course I must not "Levant," but stay and face it.

I have not been able either to make final arrangements for the winter. If I have to move from Salisbury you will have to furnish it, for there is nothing in it but our small array of tables & beds, if I stay some alterations must be made, at any rate the chimneys must be built up. If I do not get away soon I shall not be able to get back this winter and I must try then to have some means to live on at the East. Every thing you perceive is perplexing. I do not write to you my dear Father to have you do any thing at present. I hope you will take no decisive step about matters here till I come on. I am very anxious that Caroline, who I know will be most uneasy about my long delay, should be cheered and made to perceive the benefit and necessity of my deferring my return. She feels, I learn from her letters, rather unhappy and that gives me great pain. I am sure that your talking to her & explaining to her and encouraging her would make her feel much easier. I have told her why for many reasons I could not yet leave, but she never can understand why people don't leave when they say they shall. I say these thing to you, my dear Father, not that I am not aware of all your kindness to her, for she speaks of it in every letter, but knowing that she will try to conceal how she feels from you & thinking that perhaps you might not see how she thought about it.

I shall have made some winter and *summer* arrangements when I leave this place & be sure of returning to some sort of comfortable lodgings. My health continues very good indeed, our men begin to recover. Windsor[2] is nearly well. Arthur [Fletcher] who has been fac-totum, and is really a smart, willing & intelligent fellow, during all the summer, will leave in a few days to join the exploring party under Boilvin. We hear nothing from Ray—no cattle. You have a deed I believe of White Hall.

You must not judge too harshly of Col. Kinney's conduct; I can tell you of many things to extenuate and excuse it. He is a kind hearted man, full of talents—but he cannot endure reverses & has wholly lost his firmness and in some things I think, his wits.

Our corn is nearly all cut; wheat & oats are all stacked, hay got in and preparations making for winter.

With my best love to Mother sister & brother I am your affectionate son   Daniel F. Webster.

ALS. NhHi. Excerpt published in Van Tyne, pp. 667–668.

1. Boilvin, who eventually went west and died in California, was the

son of the Indian agent at Prairie Du
Chien, Wisconsin.

2. Not identified.

TO JOHN DAVIS (1787–1854)

Boston Oct. 2. 1838

My Dear Sir

I thank you for your kind letter of yesterday.[1] It is our full purpose to make a visit to Worcester, shortly, & we shall of course go strait to your House. But whether we shall be able to go next week, is quite uncertain. I have been obliged to go to N.Y. from which I returned only this morning. My wife is at Marshfield, & I must go there tomorrow. Then, again, it is two years since we have been to spend a day in N.H. & I must go to look after my sheep & wool. Perhaps it will be thought best to make the longer excursion first.

I do not know that I can say any thing of New York & Penna. Both sides are confident, in both States, & in N. Jersey also. Our friends real[ly] *feel* confidence; it is possible the other side only affects it. In all these three States the contest will be severe. I hope for the best, & cannot but be encouraged, by the strong assurance of success, manifested by our friends.

I regard the spirit Law of last winter as unfortunate.[2] I fear it was a kind of over-straining, which may hurt the cause which it was intended to aid.

It would do you good to see how I have picked up. If a week had not been lost by this journey to N.Y. I should have made nothing of a five barred fence. There is nothing in this world—or at least for me—like the air of the sea, united to a kind of lazy exercise, & an absolute forgetfulness of business & cares. The mackerel fishing has been glorious. I have had some success, also, in the Tautog way, while in the regular line of cod, haddock, & halibut, business has been steadily cheerful. Little done in duck shooting, but I understand that in my absence last week, a shade of improvement was discernible in this branch. I cannot go extensively into it, this year.

Give my best regards to Mrs Davis. It would do me good to see & hear her laugh. Yours ever truly   Danl Webster

ALS. MWA. Published in *W & S*, 16: 303–304.

1. Not found.

2. On April 19, 1838, temperance forces succeeded in passing through the Massachusetts legislature a bill prohibiting the sale of liquors in less than fifteen-gallon quantities. Arthur B. Darling, *Political Changes in Massachusetts . . .* (New Haven, 1925), p. 239.

TO ROSWELL L. COLT

Boston October 8. '38

Dear Sir

I am very sorry to trouble you again with my notes, & if I could have had the pleasure of seeing you, when in N York, I possibly might have made some bargain or arrangement to take them up without renewal. As it is, I avail myself gladly of your offer, & now enclose two notes, 2.500 each, & will send you the cash balance, viz 194.58 in season.

With much grateful respect Yrs   Danl. Webster

ALS. PHi.

FROM SAMUEL LEWIS SOUTHARD

Jersey City 1 Novr. 1838

Private

Dear Sir,

The p[romissory] notes which we issued for your accommodation become due in 5 or 6 days.[1] In our present situation, it is inconvenient, to be in cash advance to this amount. If you could pay your notes it would be pleasant to us. If you cannot, at this time, we must arrange the matter, in such way, as to be least inconvenient, both to you & us. And unless the notes be paid, we must issue other post Notes which you will negociate & pay us the money for them, with interest &c. to take up those which were issued last year. Will you oblige me by letting me hear from you without delay? As this must be a renewal & as some of our Board, may suppose the collateral of not sufficient value can you not, add to it?[2] I do not wish any question to arise among them respecting accommodation to you. Your friend   Saml L. Southard

ALS draft. MiU-C.
1. Southard was president of the Morris Canal and Banking Company, which issued the promissory note to Webster.

2. DW apparently found it necessary to renew the notes, either in full or in part. See Isaac Gibson to DW, December 11, 1838, mDW 15265.

FROM NATHANIEL RAY THOMAS, WITH ENCLOSURE

Oneonta (Otsego Co)

Dec 4th. 1838

Dear Sir

I have just returned from Unadilla where I spent last evening with Mr [Sherman] Page who I found to be a very agreeable sort of man, and ready to give me all the information in his power regarding the property you purchased of him at the City of Winnebago & at Toledo.[1] He seems very desirous that you should retain the latter, not only (*as he says*) because he shall find it troublesome to raise money in these times to fulfill his obligation to take back the property, but because he is anxious that you should realize *great profits* from the investment, which he is confident you *must* do, if you hold on to the property. In conformity to this desire he has made a proposition a copy of which I annex to this letter.[2] You will I think conclude that he has made a liberal *discount* at least although perhaps it may not prove to be sufficient to cover the loss which you may hereafter suffer. His Bond you may recollect expires on the 22d day of February next, in the mean time something must be decided regarding it. Perhaps we shall know better what to do when I see you in Washington; after I have visited Toledo & seen & ascertained the probable value of the property.

If however you shall think proper to accept the proposition, I will thank you to write me at Toledo that I may enclose Mr Page his Bond & have the endorsement made on *yours* agreeable to his proposition.

I leave this place for Buffalo in the stage, which starts so soon that I have no time left to say anything about other matters which I might wish to refer to.

Please remember me with much kindness to Mrs Webster & Julia & believe me Yours Sincerely   N. Ray Thomas

ENCLOSURE: PROPOSITION BY SHERMAN PAGE (copy)

I make to Mr Webster the following proposition in relation to a parcel of five acres of land which he purchased of me situate in the City of Toledo, in the state of Ohio—to wit—

In consideration of his giving up to me on or before the 22d. day of February next a certain Bond which he holds against me bearing date the 22d. day of February 1837 in which I stipulate to take back the said property & refund to said Webster what may have been paid on account of it; I will endorse on his Bond bearing even date with my own the sum of *Seventeen hundred & ten dollars*;—it being my intention to reduce the price of the said land to *five hundred dollars* per acre at the time I sold the same to Mr Webster (22d February 1837), which will leave a balance due on said Websters Bond of *Eleven hundred & forty dollars*, the payment of which said sum of Eleven hundred & forty dollars I agree to extend two years from the 22d day of Feby. 1839, interest on the same to be computed at 7 per cent per annum: Unadilla 3d. Decr. 1838 (Signed)

Sherman Page
(Witness)
N. Ray Thomas

Memorandum of Mr Page's proposition

There will be two payments due Sherman Page on the 22d. day of Feby. '39

per original contract amounting to $1666.66⅔
2 Yrs interest on $2500. at 7 . . . .   350.00
Add remaining payment 833.33⅓
Amt. due as on Feby. '39 . . . .$2850.00

Mr Page proposes to reduce the price of the land to $500. per acre at the time he sold it to Mr W.

5 acres would be . . . .$2500—
paid in cash . . . . 1500—
which would leave a balance of . .$1000—
add 2 yrs int. to Feby. 22. 1839 . .   140—
—————
1140.00

Amt. of discount proposed by Mr Page . .$1710—

Mr Page agrees to extend the payment of the $1140—to *two years* from the 22d. day of Feby. next   N.R.T.

ALS. NhHi.

1. The record of the Toledo purchase, February 22, 1837, appears in Deed Book 5: 92–94, Office of the

Recorder of Deeds, Lucas County, Toledo, Ohio, mDWs.

2. See above.

FROM NATHANIEL RAY THOMAS

Detroit Dec. 19th 1838

Dear Sir,

I intended to have written to you from Toledo, but the arrival of the stage for Detroit, two hours earlier than usual interrupted me while I was in the act.

I found Toledo to be a place of more considerable importance than I was before aware of, occupying as it seems to me a position far preferable to any other town on the river; indeed it appears from all the information I have obtained from persons who are not interested as well as from those that are, that the question as to which point on the Maumee River is most elligible for a city, seems to be now settled in favour of Toledo, and that Maumee Perrysburg & Manhattan can have no pretensions to an equality—indeed it already numbers nearly or quite as many inhabitants as all three of the others, although the two former had more than two years the start of it. Taking for granted then that this is the point for a city, the next question to be settled is, what is to build it up? In the first place it is surrounded by a rich agricultural *wheat growing* country—it is decidedly the most favourable outlet for the Wabash &

Erie Canal, which by the contracts was to have been completed in October next; but the derangement of the finances and the sickness which has prevailed the past season among the labourers, it is thought will delay its completion, at longest, not beyond the following summer. This Canal together with others which connect with it, that are granted & in progress of construction, it is said comprise an extent of more than a *thousand miles*, a great portion of the business of which it is confidently predicted must center at Toledo or of which Toledo must be the outlet. This of itself it would seem is sufficient to warrant the conclusion that a large town must grow up there, but independent of this the Rail Road chartered from thence to Michigan City when it shall be finished will be another great source of its prosperity as may be inferred from the fact that the 33 miles to Adrian which is in operation has paid an interest the past season of *30 per cent*. This road will of course take most of the business of the Southern portion of Michigan, indeed there has been more flour & other produce passing down the road from Adrian this fall, than with *two* locomotives they could possibly transport & attend to the other business of the road. These facts & opinions are not of course *original*, but I mention them, that we may the better form an opinion of the probable *value of property* at Toledo. There is no such thing as *present* value to such property in the West, and it seems to me we can only arrive at a proper estimate by looking to the probable growth of the Country of which Toledo is the outlet—the vast agricultural resources of which that country is possessed—the numerous Canals & Rail Roads which are proposed, to penetrate it in every direction, and then by comparing it with other towns that *claim* equal advantages.

On the other hand it will be said that the country bordering upon the Maumee River is unhealthy, and although some of the citizens of Toledo insist that the sickness of the past season has been confined chiefly to the canal & labouring people generally, yet I have no doubt that it has been very sickly among *all* classes. But for one I should be very unwilling to base my calculations for the future as regards *sickness* upon the experience of the past season, for if we do, we shall come little short of converting the whole western country into a grand *hospital*. But even admitting the Maumee River to be an unhealthy region, there is a vast country beyond its influence in that respect, of which it must ever be the outlet, and people will go there to transact the business which will be created by it.

The fifteen acre lot in which you are interested with [Levi C.] Turner, is tolerably well situated & will probably come in requisition before the town shall increase to any great extent. The other 5 acre lot purchased of Sherman Page is not so well situated although it may become valuable by & by. At present I should be unwilling to take it even at the reduction which Mr P. proposed to make.

It appears by the record of Deeds at Toledo (which I had the curiosity to examine) that Turner received a deed on only *one* undivided half of the fifteen acres above mentioned, from Gen McKay[1] & John Fitch,[2] which deed he refers to in his contract with you, the consideration for which one half was $16000. You will recollect he sold the same property to you for $7937. It appears also from the record that Mr T. has given a deed of one half of the same property to Robert Campbell[3] of Cooperstown, for which he acknowledges to have received a consideration of $10,000. He may however have subsequently received a second deed from McKay & Fitch which is not recorded.

I saw Mr [Benjamin B.] Kercheval a moment this morning on his way to Ypsalanti—he will return this evening & I shall probably get through with my business with him in the course of tomorrow or next day.

Mr [Phineas] Davis & Mr [Fisher Ames] Harding are also in town, so that I am in hopes to have no delay in the accomplishment of all my business. As soon as I get through & *think I can travel with safety*, I shall start for Washington. We had two or three days ago a slight fall of snow which has made the roads so very slippery that it is dangerous to *limb*, if not to life to travel in a coach. I turned over in one yesterday for the second time since I left New York, but was fortunate in escaping with a very slight bruise on the head. At the same time one of our passengers fractured his arm, another sprained his ancle very badly, two others received slight bruises & two escaped uninjured.

I beg my best regards to Mrs Webster, who with yourself I suppose will arrive in Washington about the time this reaches there, and as I hope in health & safety. I remain Most sincerely Your friend & svt.

> N. Ray Thomas

I may perhaps have to draw on you for fifty or sixty dollars before leaving here for my expenses for I find that stage proprietors dont scruple to charge *ten* cents per mile & break ones limbs into the bargain; and that Inn Keepers have consciences about as convenient. Yrs   N.R.T.

ALS. NhHi.
1. Not identified.
2. Fitch was a judge and merchant from Eschol, Michigan.

3. Campbell (1782–1850) was a Cooperstown, New York, lawyer and banker, and Turner's father-in-law.

RECEIPT FOR LAND CONVEYANCE IN DERRY, NEW HAMPSHIRE, FROM DW TO SAMUEL FROTHINGHAM

> Boston December 31, 1838.

Received of Daniel Webster, this day, a deed of conveyance of three hundred & forty seven acres of land, situate in the Town of Derry, in the State of New Hampshire, which land I hold in trust to sell the same, & to apply the proceeds of such sale to the payment, in whole or in part, as the case may be, of a promissory note for Seventeen Thousand Dollars, given to me by the said Webster, bearing even date with this receipt, & conditioned to be paid in one year from date with interest—Said Land to be sold at any time that I may think expedient without waiting the maturity of the note or otherwise as I may please and the proceeds to be held by me as security in place of the land sold allowing interest therefor.   Sam. Frothingham

ADS. NhHi.

In the winter of 1838–39, Webster made plans to tour England with his family. He had entertained the idea of such a trip since the mid-1820s, when he sought but failed to obtain the ministerial post from John Quincy Adams. Now with his debts pressing heavier than ever, with no prospects for selling his western properties in America, he resolved to go in the hopes of unloading some of his property on English capitalists. When his efforts to go in an official capacity—as a special emissary to discuss the northeastern boundary with British officials—failed, he received financial backing from Massachusetts and New York friends to make the trip as a private citizen. In the correspondence below, Webster made preparations for his departure.

With most of his property placed in trust—probably to protect it from seizure for debts during his absence—Webster, with his wife, Caroline, daughter, Julia, and his sister-in-law, Mrs. James W. Paige, embarked for England on May 18 aboard the Liverpool. *Some two weeks later they arrived to a warm welcome in England. Almost immediately, Webster withdrew from the presidential campaign, as if to emphasize the "private character" of his visit. They remained in England (with only a short side trip to France) for six months, touring the countryside and visiting with English nobility and government officials. Webster met with less success in disposing of his lands than he had hoped, but he did make contacts that facilitated the negotiation of the Webster-Ashburton Treaty in 1842.*

The correspondence below details Webster's reception in England and his response to English society and politics. More intimate accounts of the trip, of the Websters' reception, and of their activities may be found in Julia Webster's diary (manuscript on deposit, MHi); in Caroline Le Roy Webster, Mr. W & I . . . [New York, 1942]; and in Harriette Story

Paige, Daniel Webster in England . . ., *ed. Edward Gray (Boston, 1917), all diary accounts of the trip.*

TO SAMUEL JAUDON

Washington Jan. 12. 1839

Private & Confidential

My Dear Sir

My object in writing you this private & confidential letter, is to communicate a plan, which I have formed, or wish to form, of crossing the water, & visiting you in London. I have a great desire to see England; & if that desire be ever gratified, it must be done without much longer delay. But my circumstances require, that I should connect certain concerns of private business with my voyage; indeed, that some business arrangements should be its leading object.

In the year 1836, finding that I could not leave my seat in Congress without dissatisfying my friends, and seeing that I must do something to secure the means of living hereafter, I entered, as you know, on *Western investments*, partly in company with Mr [Thomas Handasyd] Perkins, partly in a company of which Gov. [Lewis] Cass was the principal proprietor,[1] & partly on my own separate account. These investments were made by faithful & skilful agents, principally in Agricultural lands of excellent quality, in Ohio, Illinois, Michigan & Wisconsin. Prospects of a large rise in value seemed fair, at the time, & I purchased and invested as far as my means, in money & credit, would go.

The events of 1837 checked, for the time, the sale of such property, but have not affected their ultimate value; and the vast emigration into that Country, which has taken place in 1838, being greater, I learn, than in any former year, confirms all expectations, which I ever entertained of the final profits of the investments.

Now, My Dear Sir, if I were certain, that I could *sell* this property in England, or raise money upon it, at a reasonable interest, by putting it into the hands of a trustee here, I would go to England, on the adjournment of Congress. I am aware, that persons on your side, proposing to invest here, naturally prefer public Stocks; but there have [been] instances of Sales of private property; & I have thought it *possible*, at least, that by your kind assistance, I might do something useful to myself, there. I could afford to sell at such prices, as would, in all probability, double the purchase money in ten years, or less.

I could take with me

    1. Regular Govt. titles to 15. or 20. thousand acres of excellent Prairie & timber lands, in various parts of the States & Territories before mentioned.

2. Certificates from the first men in that Country, that these lands would not, now, be rated high, at 5 Dollars an acre, cash; & that they might be expected to be worth twice that price per acre, in less than ten years, perhaps in five.

3. Proof that the titles are perfect, & complete, being derived from Government.

4. Titles to a large property in & near LaSalle, (Peru) consisting of City lots, & extensive agricultural tracts adjoining. This place, you know, is at the head of Steam Navigation on the Illinois, & at the termination of the great Canal from Lake Michigan. Many lines of communication meet here, & for fertility of soil, good climate, centrality of position, & certainty of rapid growth, I prefer this spot to any which I visited, in an extensive tour made through the Country in 1837. The Canal is in progress; means of its completion are secured; it is on the largest scale of any thing in this Country, & is expected to be completed in three or four years.

I own one large tract of most rich & beautiful land, just out of the limits of the town; say a tract of 12 or 13 hundred acres. I never saw finer land, or a better situation. It would not be thought extravagant, I think, to say, that on the completion of the canal, this land would sell for 50 Dollars an acre. I hold also many lots, in this town.

5. A large interest in "Madison City," now become the seat of Govt. in Wisconsin. I have not seen this; but Mr [George W.] Jones, the late, & Mr [James Duane] Doty, the present, Delegate of the Territory, speak of it as property rapidly rising, with the growth of the City, & the Territory.

6. Property in "Toledo"; in the newly laid out town of "Gibraltar," on the N.W. corner of Lake Erie, near the Mouth of the Detroit River; some interest in Mineral lands near Galena, &c. &c. &c.

Can this property be sold in England? If such be the strong probability, I will go over.

But if the prospect be not promising, I cannot afford the expense, nor the loss of time from Professional service. It would hardly be worth while to go for a less sum than $100,000.

I am sure, My Dear Sir, that you will give this subject a little consideration; & if you do not see any strong ground of encouragement, I shall content myself to stay at home, & remain assured, that if it had depended on your kindness & friendship to accomplish my wishes, they would have been accomplished. I have mentioned this to Mr [Morris] Robinson, & only to one person else—& shall not communicate it to others, till I hear from you. This will go by the G[reat] W[estern] & you will probably receive it by the 1st of Feby. In March, I shall hear from you, & if the undertaking should appear to be warranted, I shall sail immediately thereafterwards. Yours with constant regard,   Danl Webster

ALS. NHi.
1. The Western Land Association.

TO SAMUEL JAUDON

Washington Jan. 13. 1839
My Dear Sir
    Altho' I have not written to you,[1] nor recd letters, yet you have been so conspicuous, since you left us, that I seem to have known as much of you, as if you had been all the while in Philadelphia. The last I heard of Mrs Jaudon,[2] was, that she was snugly seated in the Abbey, Coronation day; & without waiting, according to fashion, to put my respects for her at the end of the letter, allow me, thus early, to ask you to give my affectionate remembrance & good wishes to her & the children. I delight to hear of their health & happiness.
    I am but just now arrived here, having staid in Boston to attend to some professional affairs, in as much as nothing important seemed doing in Congress. Mrs W. & Julia are left behind. Edward, who is in College, & who has a long winter vacation, is here with me. We are at Miss Polks,[3] with Mr & Mrs [Richard H.] Bayard,[4] & Mr & Mrs [Edward] Curtis.[5] Judge [Hugh Lawson] White & Lady[6] arrived here but a few days ago. He is feeble, but his health is improving, as I understand, not having seen him myself, as I have not yet been into the Senate.
    Congress has, up to this period of the Session, done nothing of consequence, the House amusing itself with debating abolition questions, & listening to threats of impeachment of Mr [Levi] Woodbury; & the Senate having been engaged in an angry & protracted debate, on the Pub. lands. The Court commences tomorrow. I have two or three old causes to dispose of,[7] but have not recd retainers, for new causes, for some time past. The business in the Court is not now great, nor is the Court itself what it has been.
    On the 15th. instant the Legislature of Mass. will elect a Senator.[8] Under all circumstances, I have concluded not to withdraw my name; & I presume I shall be re elected; but whether I shall ever take a seat, under that election, is uncertain. It will depend on circumstances connected with my personal condition. Very likely, I may go back to Boston, & make *Court* Street the theatre of all my labors for some time to come.
    I saw Mr B[iddle] & Mr [Joseph] Cowperthwaite, on my way hither, &

found them in excellent spirits. Your advices by the R.W. had produced quite animating effects.

Mr B. & the Bank now stand very high, as events have not failed to fulfil his predictions. There was never a moment, I think, in which the credit of the Bank, in this Country, stood better.

You would like to hear something of prospects & probabilities, touching the next Presidential Election. That subject would require something of a chapter; but you shall have it by the next Steam Boat. The *face* of that question is a good deal changed, since last year.

With renewed assurances of attachment & regard, I am, Dear Sir, Yours mo. truly   Danl Webster

I send a parcel of Documents for you to Mr [Morris] Robinson. Whether he will be able to forward them, without incurring too much expense of postage, I do not know.

ALS. NHi. Published in *PC*, 2: 41–42.
1. This letter was most likely one covering the above to Jaudon of January 12.
2. Margaret Peyton Alrichs Jaudon was the stepdaughter of Hugh Lawson White of Tennessee.
3. Boardinghouse in Washington.
4. Mrs. Mary Sophia Bayard, née Carroll, granddaughter of Charles Carroll of Carrollton.
5. Mrs. Mary Curtis (d. 1873) was the daughter of John Cramer, congressman from New York.
6. Mrs. Ann E. White, née Peyton,

whom Hugh Lawson White had married in November 1832.
7. Webster was probably referring to *Rhode Island* v. *Massachusetts*, 13 Peters 23 (1839); *Smith* v. *Richards*, 13 Peters 26 (1839); *Andrews* v. *Pond*, 13 Peters 65 (1839); and *Ocean Insurance Company* v. *Polleys*, 13 Peters 157 (1839).
8. On January 17, the Massachusetts legislature (unanimously in the Senate and by a vote of 330 to 65 in the House) reelected Webster to the United States Senate.

FROM NICHOLAS BIDDLE

Phila Jany 21. 1839

My dear Sir

When Mr [Joel Roberts] Poinsett's report about the Bank matters is printed, please send me one or two copies.[1]

If you think well of it, at the time when the discussion comes up, I should like a view presented resembling what follows:[2]

The Bank was endeavoring to restore specie payments throughout the Union. The Atlantic Bank had begun, or were commencing, (for when the arrangement was made with the Govt., none but the New York Banks had begun their nominal resumption) the West & South was to be assisted and encouraged. In this state of things, the Government wanted several millions. The Bank agreed to advance it; but instead of drawing specie from the Atlantic where the drafts might have broken the Banks, and distributing it in the interior which did not want it, it was arranged that the specie should be left on the Sea Board, and that notes better than specie—preferred to specie, should be given to the interior,—infusing thus into the remote circulation what was wanted to purify it. How it was brought about may not exactly appear; because when a government or an individual sees its error and is anxious to repair it, there is no very great desire to be explicit. We know from Mr Biddle's publication what he thought best to be done.[3] We see from Genl. [Nathan?] Towson's circular[4] what was actually done. The Bank then very naturally said that the Govt. was at last cooperating to restore the currency, and that the resumption might take place, and accordingly it did take place.

Can you do anything for my little friend the Signora Vespucci?[5] I wish you would find a reason for doing so. I would give my share in a right to a ¼ section, rather more readily than to the Poles and the French after Waterloo.

Take good care of Judge [John] McKinley[6] & believe me Yrs always

N.B.

LC. DLC.

1. For that report, see *Senate Documents*, 25th Cong., 3d sess., Serial 339, Document No. 78.

2. On January 28, per Biddle's recommendations, Webster defended the Bank's action in the purchase of the government bonds. For that defense, see the *National Intelligencer*, March 9, 1839.

3. See Biddle to John Quincy Adams, December 10, 1838, in *Niles' National Register*, 55 (December 22, 1838): 259–260.

4. Towson (1784–1854) was a veteran of the War of 1812. His circular has not been identified.

5. Amerigo Vespucci, an Italian "adventuress" and descendant of the

navigator, had come to the United States to "advance her fortunes." Fascinated by her, Biddle "became treasurer of a fund raised for her by private subscription among the representatives and senators in Washington." Thomas Payne Govan, *Nicholas Biddle, Nationalist and Public Banker, 1786–1844* (Chicago, 1959), pp. 346–347. For her memorial to Congress, see the *National Intelligencer*, February 28, 1839.

6. Webster was appearing before the Supreme Court to argue the *Bank of the United States* v. *Primrose*, 13 Peters 519 (1839), one of the Alabama Bank cases, which overturned McKinley's circuit court opinion.

TO [NICHOLAS BIDDLE]

Jan. 25. 39
3 o'clock

My Dear Sir

You will see that Mr [Silas] Wright has called up the subject, & made a speech, defending the Secretaries, in the matter of the sale of the Bonds, &c.[1] He labored hard to prove it a case of necessity; a question, between this mode of proceeding & National Bankruptcy. He commented, but not at great length, on your letter to Mr. [John Quincy] A[dams].[2] Mr [William C.] Rives is now up. I suppose a good deal will be said—it looks as if Mr *Calhoun* meant to say something. *I* shall make a few remarks, the first opportunity. This is the first day I have been an hour in the Senate. My affairs in Court have kept me there. I am looking sharp after Judge McKinly. I understand Mr. C[harles] J[ared] Ingersoll has *volunteered* to support the judge's decision, on account of his hearty coincidence of opinion, & his judgment in regard to the importance of the principles involved. Yrs   D. Webster

ALS. DLC.
    1. On December 19, 1838, Senator William C. Rives of Virginia had introduced a resolution that, in substance, requested the secretary of the treasury to lay before the Senate the government's negotiations with the Bank of the United States. With the report in from the secretary, Silas

Wright led the Senate Democrats, as DW reported, in justifying the bond sale to the Bank. *Congressional Globe*, 25th Cong., 3d sess., pp. 48, 100–101, 113–123, 146.
    2. Biddle to Adams, December 10, 1838, in *Niles' National Register*, 55 (December 22, 1838): 259–260.

FROM EDWARD EVERETT

Boston 14 Feb. 1839

My dear Sir,
    Our friend Clay's speech[1] excites great sensation here, which in the minds of some persons is increased by the remarks, with which Mr Calhoun is said to have followed it up vizt. that "it would consolidate the South," & that "the South was a gainer by this day's work." Is it to be inferred from these expressions that there is a political understanding between Messrs Calhoun & Clay; and that the South is to be consolidated in favor of the latter as a Presidential Candidate.
    Will it not be necessary for you to express yourself on the topics discussed in Mr Clay's Speech? If Mr Clay presents himself on this occasion as the organ of the whig party might not your silence be misconstrued into an acquiescence in his views? The question has been started here whether it will not be necessary that something be done to throw off from Massachusetts the burden of doctrines like Mr Clay's: a burden which it would be hard to carry to the polls next fall. Those with whom I have talked think this could be done no way so effectually or so advantageously as by a speech from you. But of this you can the better judge.

We advance slowly but hope to fall upon some satisfactory adjustment of the Temperance Question, though what it will be does not yet distinctly appear. I have been shut up 8 days with a cold (an unusual event with me) but am now abroad. I write in great haste & should be gratified to get a line from you. With the greatest regard, ever Yours

LC. MHi.

1. On February 7, 1839, Clay had delivered a speech before the Senate denouncing abolitionism and advocating the receipt and referral, but denial of the objective, of abolition petitions. *Congressional Globe,* 25th Cong., 3d sess., Appendix, pp. 354–359.

TO NICHOLAS BIDDLE

Feb 15. 1839

My Dear Sir

I believe we are safe, as to the result of the Alabama Cause.[1] The judgment of the Court will be pronounced, probably, next week. A good many persons have expressed a wish to see a popular sketch of my remarks & I believe Mr [Joseph] Gales who heard them intends to give such a sketch, at some time.[2]

As to mineral lands—it is difficult to say, what is *law*, & what is not, & what is the *remedy*, even if there be legal right, where patents are withheld. All this branch of our system is in a very loose & uncertain state.

I am taking out some patents (by good luck which is a seldom visitor to me, in such matters) of lands containing more or less lead, in the Galena Region, which I am told are worth a hundred Dollars an acre, but I would be glad to sell them for fifty.

We took up last Eve' Mr Wrights bill, for the better security of the public money. The discussion will probably furnish an opportunity to say a few words about Levi [Woodbury]'s negotiations. The committee is sitting in Levi's chambers where our friend [Reuben M.] Whitney used to sit. The Sec[retary] was under examination yesterday, to a late hour. It will probably turn out to be true that great negligence has occurred here, in regard to the examination of the Collectors accounts. The *means* existed at the Department to have learned the true state of things years ago. There have been, I fancy, no false accounts rendered, but the deficiency, for some time past at least, has been covered under loose general heads, of "funds reserved," "Protest money," &c &c, which generalities were permitted by the Comptroller to go along, without being subject to particular inquiry. The Comee. will report about the end of next week & from that time I suppose nothing will be done in the House but debate the Report.[3] Yrs   D Webster

ALS. DLC.

1. *Bank of the United States* v. *Primrose*, 13 Peters 519 (1839).

2. The *National Intelligencer*, March 12, 1839, carried Webster's argument in the Alabama Bank case.

3. On March 2, Levi Woodbury, secretary of the treasury, reported to the Senate on the defalcations of government agents and, a few weeks later, the report to which Webster referred appeared. For those reports, see *Senate Documents*, 25th Cong., 3d sess., Serial 342, Document No. 301; *Reports of Committees*, 25th Cong., 3d sess., Serial 352, Report No. 313.

FROM SAMUEL APPLETON APPLETON

Boston Febry 17th 1839.

My Dear Sir

Your much esteemed letter of the 10th. inst. was duly received.[1] I can but feebly express on paper, the pleasure and gratification I felt in the kind notice you took of my wishes.

Julia has consented to be mine, and it only remains for me to prove by my conduct through life how sincerely and devotedly I love her.

My Uncles wish me to express to you the pleasure it gives them, at the prospect of a closer connection with one whom they have known so long, & esteemed so highly. I hope that the friendship that existed between you and my Father, may be continued to the Son, who will strive also yet to deserve it.

Hoping ere many weeks elapse, I may have the pleasure of seeing you, I remain Dear Sir Most affectionately Yours.   Saml A. Appleton

ALS. NhHi. Appleton (1811–1861), the son of Eben Appleton, was a business partner of James W. Paige and his uncle, Nathan Appleton. Appleton and Julia Webster were married in London on September 24, 1839.

1. Not found.

TO ROSWELL L. COLT

Washington Feb. 26. '39

My Dear Sir

I recd yr letter last Evening.[1] I am in great hopes of hearing something favorable from Mr [Virgil] Maxcy, before I reach N. York. If he shall have made any sale on my account, I shall immediately apply proceeds to my notes. I expect to be in N York about the 11th. of March, & do not mean to leave it until I take up the paper, or make some final arrangement for it. Meantime, if the notes come to maturity, we must continue to meet them, for a few days. Yrs truly   D. Webster

ALS. PHi.

1. Not found.

TO SAMUEL BULKLEY RUGGLES

Washington Mar. 2. 1839.

Private

My Dear Sir

When I had the pleasure of seeing you in N. York, I suggested to you that I should be under a necessity of raising, somewhere, a pretty large sum of money, upon the strength of my Western Lands.[1]

These lands are mostly agricultural, selected with great care, several years ago, & now of much value. I am just now taking out the Patents, and the titles, being Govt. titles, are perfect & complete.

I should be glad of $50,000, but could get along with 40,000. I shall have with me satisfactory evidences of value, & clear exhibits of title; & what I have thought of proposing, is, that some few friends should join in a security to your new Bank,[2] & let a conveyance be made of the property, in trust, to be sold, in reasonable time.

Will you do me the great kindness, My Dear Sir, to think of this a little, so that I may have the benefit of your advice, when I reach N. York about the 8th or 10th inst. Yrs with great regard,   Danl Webster

ALS. MHi.

1. On May 16, two days before he left for England on the *Liverpool*, Webster completed his negotiations with Ruggles, transferring to him and Richard M. Blatchford, on a temporary basis as collateral for this loan of "a pretty large sum of money," a part of his land in Michigan, Wisconsin, Ohio, Indiana, and Illinois. For the deeds transferring this property, see mDW 39835–237, 39835–252, 39835–257, 39835–264, 39835–268, 39835–284, 39835–288,

39835–297, 39835–317, and mDWs. This property was later transferred back to Webster. See DW to DFW, February 7, 1840, mDW 16313, and DFW to DW, June 30, 1840, mDW 16790.

2. Ruggles's new bank, which he and eighteen others had formed in January 1839 and of which he was a director, was the Bank of Commerce. D. G. Brinton Thompson, *Ruggles of New York: A Life of Samuel B. Ruggles* (New York, 1946), p. 39.

MEMORANDUM ON THE NORTHEASTERN BOUNDARY NEGOTIATIONS

[March 9, 1839]

Heads, &c.

1. That the negotiation should be opened, & conducted throughout, in the most friendly spirit, treating all the arguments & suggestions of the Br[itish] Negotiators with entire respect.

2. But that an immediate and final settlement of the question should be urgently pressed, upon considerations and motives, which address themselves equally to both parties.

3. That informal & friendly interviews should be sought, with the Br:

Negrs. & the members of Her M's Cabinet; which interviews should be carefully used, to accomplish the following purposes.

1. To satisfy the English Agents, & the English Govt of the intrinsic weakness of their case, upon the origl. question, under the Treaty of 1783.

2. To satisfy them as far as possible, that they over[r]ate the importance of this Territory to England. To suggest, that England cannot feel anxious for it, merely as so much land, since in the Province of New Brunswick land now is, & for many years to come must be, out of all proportion to population: and that as affording a better communication between Halifax & Canada, it is to be considered that no great communication, by land, between those points can exist, under any circumstances; or at least not for half a century; that England can seldom have occasion to move troops, on that rout[e]; that if she sometimes have such an occasion, there will be no objection to it,[1] in time of peace, although the U.S. should own the land; and that, in time of war, we should prevent such a movement, if we could, whether she, or we, owned the territory. Perhaps, in this connexion, a right of passage, might be thought of, as fit to be made a Treaty Stipulation. I imagine however, that it is not merely a communication from Province to Province that England desires, so much as it is a general strengthening of her frontier, by widening its breadth, East of the St. Lawrence, at this point, and giving compactness & continuity to her possessions.[2]

4. To take an early opportunity, in the formal correspondence, of presenting a clear, & concise view of the merits of the original question. The papers submitted to the Dutch Arbitrator are learned & able, but very prolix. A close, connected & condensed argument, on this original question would not be amiss, if the course of correspondence should seem to make a place for it.

5. To bring England to take her ground; either, that she asserts a line, conformable, as she alleges, to the Treaty, as she did before the Dutch Arbitration; or, that she insists, that the description in the Treaty is so indefinite, that the boundary cannot be found, by any attempt to pursue its requisitions.

6. If she shall take the first course, & set up such a line as heretofore, show how utterly impossible it is to reconcile that line to the plain & clear demands of the Treaty.

7. If she adopt the latter branch of the Alternative, and insist that the Treaty line cannot be found, by the arguments, appropriate to the case & controvert this, showing, among other things, that ridges, or

heights of land, are not of infrequent use, in fixing lines, on this Continent; that the English Govt has, in other cases, prescribed such boundaries; that the U.S. have done the same thing, in many treaties without practical inconvenience; & then urge, as an important matter of fact the actual result of the late survey under the authority of Maine.[3]

8. But however the argument may stand, it is probable that England will not, gratuitously, yield her pretensions; & something must be yielded by us, since the subject has actually become matter of negotiation. A conventional line, therefore, is to be regarded as a leading & most promising mode, of adjustment. With a view to this, <the minister,>[4] before he leaves the Country, should have an interview with the Govr. of Maine, & her Delegation in Congress. He & they should examine the map carefully, & consider the whole subject maturely, & they[5] should be called on to say *what* Conventional line Maine would approve. This interview might be had, without form, or announcement; but it would take time, & should be done as soon as convenient.

If a conventional line should be agreed on, in London, it should be one of the conditions of the Convention, that the Prests. ratification should be postponed here, till Maine had given her consent; & that Her Majestys ratification should be postponed till ratification should be made in U.S.

9. To the suggestion that this Territory cannot be of much importance to Great Britain (which suggestion should only be made in informal conversations) her negotiators would doubtless reply, that, if so, neither could it be of much importance to the U.S.

This would furnish a suitable opportunity to explain the nature of our political Institutions, the limited authority of the Genl Govt, the natural tenacity with which a state clings to what it considers its rights of soil &c &c;[6] & to suggest that for these & similar reasons, the desire for peace, which is really felt by the Cabinet of W. ought not to be measured precisely by what it feels itself authorized to propose, &c &c.

10. In the informal conversations which may take place, suggest & urge strongly the great expense, & perhaps the serious difficulty, to both Governments, of preserving quiet, along the whole line of frontier, thro another Winter, if this controversy be not settled, or some progress made in its adjustment.

11. If a Conventional line cannot be agreed on, propose a joint Commission of survey, &c. of two Commrs on a side, who if *they can agree*, shall ascertain the Treaty line, & mark it, definitely.[7] But this to be without an umpirage.

12. If this be not agreed, propose, that each party shall, by itself, appoint a Commission of Survey, to ascertain the fact, whether the Treaty

line can be ascertained or not; that these Commissions shall act separately; that they shall perform the duty, as early as possible; That each Commision report to its own Government; the reports to be made & copies to be interchanged by <Decr>[8] next, & the negotiation, mean while, adjourned, & transferred to Washington. I suppose, however, that if this course were agreed to, the survey could not be accomplished, the ensuing Summer; as the British Ministry will probably be very much engaged until the close of the Session of Parliament, which will probably not terminate before August; & it may [be] doubtful whether, earlier than that time, any thing could be agreed on.

13. If nothing else can be done, another reference, or a joint Commission with an umpirage, is to be thought of. This however, to be the last resort, unless U.S. Govt. be already committed on the point.

14. Finally, that if an agreement cannot be arrived at, in some of these modes, or in some other which may be suggested, the negotiation to be broken off, with an expression of deep regret, & an intimation that the Govt of U.S. fully believing in the easy practical ascertainment of the Treaty Boundary, will cause a careful & accurate survey to be made, by a Commission of high character, appointed by itself, & acting under oath with authority to explore the country, & following the terms of the Treaty ascertain the Boundary; that in the spirit of amity, it will communicate the result of this survey to the British Govt, expressing, at the same time, its own sense, of what the case, as it shall then be presented, shall demand.

AD draft. NhHi. Copy, with AD insertions, in Martin Van Buren Papers, DLC. Published in part in Van Tyne, pp. 215–218. Except for minor punctuation changes, the differences between the wording of the draft and that of the copy have been explained in footnotes.

1. In the copy, "it" has been stricken and "such a movement" inserted (in DW's hand).

2. In the copy, DW has added: "that is sought by England."

3. Point 7 in the copy reads as follows: "If she adopt the latter branch of the alternative, and insist that the Treaty line cannot be found, controvert this by the arguments, appropriate to the case; and shewing, among other things, that ridges, or heights of land, are not of unfrequent use, in fixing lines, on this Continent; that the English Government, in other cases, has prescribed such boundaries; that the United States have done the same thing, without practical inconvenience, in many treaties; and then urge, as an important matter of fact, the actual result of the late survey under the authority of Maine."

4. For "<the minister>," stricken in the draft, "xxx" has been substituted in the copy.

5. The copy reads "*they.*"

6. "&c &c" deleted in copy.

7. For "definitely," the copy reads "definitively."

8. For "<Decr>," the copy has a blank.

MEMORANDUM OF PROPOSAL FOR SPECIAL MISSION TO ENGLAND

Mar. 10. [1839]

I happened to hear, near the close of the Session, that Mr [Joel Roberts] Poinsett had expressed, in presence of the Pres[iden]t, an opinion favorable to sending me on the Special mission to England.

I heard it intimated, also, abt. the same time, that the President might think my notions too much inclined to a *war* aspect.

I therefore called on Mr P— told him what I had heard, & said that I wished to say a few words to him, expressive of my opinion of the course the minister ought to pursue, merely for the purpose of justifying his favorable opinion.

I read to him this memorandum. He expressed himself as pleased with the suggestions, in general, & asked me for a copy; which I sent him on the 9 Mar.[1]   D.W.

ADS. NhD. Published in Van Tyne, p. 215.

1. DW gave Poinsett the memo-randum of March 9, the draft of which appears above.

TO DAVID BAYARD OGDEN

Washington, March 11, 1839.

My Dear Sir:

I should be very sorry, indeed, to be thought to have become heated on this important subject of the Northeastern boundary, or to have used expressions either leading to war themselves, or manifesting a conviction, on my part, that war was inevitable. You know what I have said on this subject, at different times, through the winter. I have never seen the account of my remarks in the Senate to which you refer.[1] I am certainly of opinion that the controversy should be settled; but I have never contemplated it as a probable event, that two great nations would go to war, to the inevitable sacrifice of so many great interests, and to the agitation of the whole commercial world, on such a question. I have never expected such a result, and do not expect it now. What I meant to say, on the occasion referred to by you, and to say strongly, was this—that it was high time for the two Governments to adjust this controversy; that it had been too long bandied between them as the subject of formal and procrastinating diplomacy; that its condition was every day growing worse and worse, and more and more dangerous to the peace of both nations; that Maine, having explored the country by commissioners, and having ascertained, as she thought, the perfect practicability of finding and marking the true original treaty line, was naturally becoming more and more dissatisfied; that negotiation should now be tried with something of a more earnest spirit; and if, unfortunately, all amicable attempts should ultimately fail—if the two Governments, much as it was to be desired and hoped, should be able to do nothing jointly, to ascertain or fix the boundary, a time must come, of necessity, when the United States must perform that duty for themselves; that they ought, in that case, to explore the country, and to examine the question carefully; and if it should turn out, as I believe it would, that the treaty line could be easily and certainly found, then the United States, in the event above mentioned, ought to mark it and assume it as the true line, and to take possession accordingly; and in this connexion I mentioned the 4th of July as a day in the year of which we often speak as suited to important political decisions. But certainly I could not have intended to say that our Government ought to take possession of the disputed territory on the fourth day of July next, as I was, at the time, favoring a proposition for sending a special minister to England, who could hardly be expected to reach London much before that time.[2]

It may be hoped, my dear sir, that what has occurred, and is still occurring, may have the effect of bringing about an early, satisfactory, and final adjustment of the whole difficulty—a result which no one can desire more sincerely than myself. Yours, with constant regard,

Daniel Webster.

Text from the *National Intelligencer*, March 19, 1839. Original not found. Published in *W & S*, 16: 304–305.

1. On March 9, Ogden wrote that a rumor was abroad, attributed to Webster, "that, if England did not settle this matter [of the northeastern boundary] by the 4th of July next, the disputed territory should be seized by the United States." See David B. Ogden to DW, March 9, 1839, in the *National Intelligencer*, March 19, 1839.

2. For DW's speech on the Maine controversy, see *W & S*, 14: 271–274.

AGREEMENT WITH DAVID A. HALL RE FOUR LAKE COMPANY

Washington Mar. 11. 1839

This witnesseth, that I have this day sold & conveyed unto D[avid] A. Hall Esq one undivided half part of all my interest in the City of Madison purchased by me of G. W. Jones, as by my deeds to said Hall will appear; and I have agreed & do agree, with said Hall, that I will receive the said property from him again, on request, at any time within one year from this date, at the same price which he has stipulated to pay me; viz, the price of ten thousand Dollars. The said Hall has signed a note to me for Eight thousand Dollars, which is indorsed by me, & has gone to my credit at the Patriotic Bank of Washington; & has given me his written obligation for Two thousand Dollars more, in case he should not elect to reconvey said land & property.

Witness my hand, this eleventh day of March 1839   Danl. Webster

The two deeds conveying the said interest within named, bearing date this   day of March 1839, have been placed in the hands of the said D. Webster, to be, by him transmitted to Wisconsin for record.   D.A.H. 11 March 1839.

I have bought of Mr. Webster one moiety of his share in the town of Madison being 1/24th. part of the property of the Four Lake Compy. for the sum of Ten Thousand dollars. I have in part payment, assumed his debt at the Patriotic Bank viz. $8000, and have given him my note for $2000: but the right is reserved to me, within one year, to re[s]cind the bargain, & Mr. W. is to repurchase at the same rate, repaying my advances, at the Bank.   D.A.H.[1]

ADS. NN.

1. Hall's endorsement reads:

"Wrote to Mr. Webster 29 April 1839 to re[s]cind the contract."

TO NICHOLAS BIDDLE

N.Y. Mar. 18. 39
Monday 12 oclock

Private

Dear Sir,

I hear from Maine. They appear to be acting in good faith. Govr—Council—Legislature &c &c. are said to be all one way of thinking, & all earnest.

At any rate, I think I will go to England. As soon as I hear from Mr. [Samuel] Jaudon, I shall come to N.Y. & Phila. If he advises, on the strength of what I proposed to him, that I go, I shall not hesitate. If he thinks he cannot promise any [thing] beneficial, in a pecuniary way, I would still go, if I could fix up sundry matters here, & indications should be such as left it not probable I should be requested to go, on account of others. You shall hear. All seems pacific down East. Yrs.   D.W.

ALS. DLC.

TO SAMUEL BULKLEY RUGGLES

Boston Mar. 23. 1839

My Dear Sir

I am quite obliged to you for your friendly letter from Albany, of the 19th of this month.[1]

Be kind enough, My Dear Sir, to advise me of your return to N. York, as it is my purpose to go to that City immediately, to attend to the subject, about which I wrote you, and which is important to me.[2] I think it will be well to postpone making any proposition to the Bank, until I shall first have arranged the matter of the security.

In a day or two, I will send you an abstract of the property, which I propose to make the basis of the operation.

I will state to you, in entire confidence, that it is my purpose to go to England. You know what rumours are afloat respecting a probable occasion to go thither in a *public* capacity. Of that, I do not allow myself to entertain any strong expectation; but probably we may be able to judge, by indications which will soon be made, what the prospect is. If we should learn that no mission will be dispatched, or, that if there should be a mission, the appointment will fall elsewhere, I should then desire to sail at once, in a private character. I think I can do something useful to myself, in England, and it is possible I might also be in some measure useful to my friends.

I shall proceed to N. Y. soon after learning your return to the City. Yours, with sincere regard,   Danl Webster

ALS. MHi. Published in *W & S*, 16: 306.
  1. Not found.

2. See above, DW to Samuel Bulkley Ruggles, March 2, 1839.

FROM ELIAS PHINNEY

Lexington 25 March 1839

My dear Sir

I send you three of my pigs, of which I beg you will do me the favor to accept. They are of my best breeds—the larger one, a sow, being 3/4 Berkshire & 1/4 Mackey, the two smaller, one a male, the other a female, being 1/2 Berkshire, 1/4 Mackey & 1/4 Moco, a breed which I procurred from the Genesee County (N. York). I find the cross better pigs than the full blood of either kind.

I regret that I could not have sent them sooner, but last Decr. when I had the pleasure of receiving a note from you on the subject,[1] I had none of a suitable age which I considered my best breeds. Should I chance to hit upon a cross, from my various breeds, which will be an improvement upon these I send you, it will give me pleasure to renew your stock, for I hold, that, to one who has done so much to *save our bacon*, every farmer should feel himself bound to furnish him with the best materials for the making of his own.

With proper treatment I have no doubt you will find them to be an ornament to any swinish community. Please direct your farmer not to feed to[o] high least they wax fat & become idle & useless.

With very sincere respect I am Dr Sir yr Obt Servt.   E. Phinney

ALS. NhHi. Excerpt published in Van Tyne, p. 668. Phinney (c. 1781–1849), a native of Lexington, Massachusetts, was, with Webster, a member of the Massachusetts Horticultural Society.

1. See DW to Elias Phinney, December 20, 1838, mDW 15279; and Elias Phinney to DW, *ibid.*, mDW 15282.

TO NICHOLAS BIDDLE

Boston Mar. 29. 1839

My Dear Sir,

Will you [cast] your eye over this, & re-enclose it to me.[1] It seems hardly encouraging enough for me to venture to England, on my own hook.

The property which I gave him a minute of was Western Lands, well selected, good title, & abundant proof of value to $200,000.[2]

The Maine Legislature has adjourned; the hostile armies have retired, & all is peace for the present on the frontier. Mean time, I hear nothing of what Govt. is doing, or expecting to do, abt. the mission. It is not to be denied, that I have a strong will to go to England, in some capacity. I care little what. Yrs   D. Webster

P.S. Mr Jaudon has had my letter but 6 days. I *may* hear further, by the Roscoe.

ALS. DLC.

1. Webster had forwarded to Biddle Samuel Jaudon's letter of February 12 (not found). See DW to Jaudon, March 29, 1839, below.

2. See above, DW to Samuel Jaudon, January 12, 1839.

TO SAMUEL JAUDON

Boston March 29. 1839

My Dear Sir,

I recd. today your letter of the 12th of Feby,[1] by the Siddons, for which I am greatly obliged to you.

I do not take quite courage enough, from what you say, to set forth for England; but my desire to visit your side of the water this year is so great, & so intense, that if I could see how it was to be done without drawing after it a vast expense, & no pecuniary benefits, I should not hesitate a moment.

The Roscoe is in at N.Y. & it is possible I may receive letters from you tomorrow, brought by that ship. She has London dates, as I understand to Feb. 27th. I shall live in hope, at least for a while longer, & until I hear further from you.

The *Maine* business is now all quiet. Nothing of a disturbing character will take place in that quarter, until the two Govts. shall have had ample time & opportunity for bringing the pending negotiation to a close. You have of course heard of the proposition of sending a Special minister to England, & the various rumours which have been in circulation here, as to the person likely to be appointed. For myself, I doubt whether there will be a mission; rather expecting to hear, that before the L'pool Steam Boat arrived out, an arrangement may have been made in London, either for a joint survey of the disputed line, or, perhaps, for transferring the negotiation from London to Washington. If neither of these things shall have happened, & if England shall receive kindly the notion of a Special mission, it will doubtless be despatched. I know not on whom the appointment would be most likely to fall. Maine & Massachusetts, the two States directly interested, would in all probability, be agreed, on the man. But party considerations will doubtless have much influence, & I do not allow myself to expect, that *I* shall see England this year in a public capacity, even if a Special Minister should be sent.[2]

I have transmitted your letter to Mr. Biddle for his perusal.[3] He thinks I ought to cross the water if I can, & I have asked him to peruse yr letter, that he might see what chance there is for my being able to succeed in the pecuniary part of my object. His kindness to me is great, & I feel very true regard for him.

Upon certain of our political affairs, I will write you again soon, *if I do not come.* Our Whig prospects are none of the best, owing to our irreconcilable difference, as to men. My opinion at present is, that our only chance is with Genl. Harrison, & that that is not a very good one.

I am about to lose Julia. She is to be married, I know not when, to Mr. S. A. Appleton, a young man of good character & ability, a member of the family of that name here, but born in England, & for the early part of his life at School in that Country. He has been a partner of N[athan] Appleton, & Mr [James W.] Paige.

Give my love to your wife. I *think* of her much, & *like* her always. I passed two good hours, tete a tete, with her mother at Washington. Judge [Hugh Lawson] White has at last come very right. If there had been on earth no Andrew Jackson, he would always have been a most excellent public character. Adieu! Pray continue to write me—& may God bless you, & yours!   Danl. Webster

ALS. NHi. Published in *PC*, 2: 44–45.
   1. Not found.
   2. For President Van Buren's rejection of Webster as special envoy to England, see his memorandum on the question, [March 1839], Martin Van Buren Papers, DLC.
   3. See above, DW to Biddle, March 29, 1839.

TO SAMUEL JAUDON

N. York April 15. 1839

My Dear Sir

I came hither from Boston three days ago, to await the arrival of the G. Western. She came in this morning, & has brought me your letter of the 22. March.[1]

The general intelligence brought by the G.W. is regarded here as pacific, & favorable. For myself, I rather incline to the opinion, that such instructions have come to Mr. [Henry Stephen] Fox,[2] as will render a *Special Mission* unnecessary.[3] But, with or without a Special mission, I am persuaded the N. Eastern Boundary question will be amicably settled. I have pretty much made up my mind to cross the water; relying on the opinion which you express, that I might expect to sell mineral stock eno. to pay expenses & taking the chance of selling the lands, & some other property.

I send this to Wall Street, to go in the Virginia tomorrow. In a few days, I shall come to a positive conclusion on the subject, & will write you further by the next packet. Yrs very truly   Danl Webster

My wife is here—we are well, & her heart beats with the joy at the faintest hope of seeing you [&] Mrs. J. in London.

ALS. NHi.
1. Not found.
2. Fox (1791–1846) was the English envoy extraordinary to the United States, 1835–1843, having previously served in that post at Buenos Aires and Rio de Janeiro. *DNB*.
3. A memorandum of the agreement between Fox and Secretary of State John Forsyth, February 27, 1839, appears in the Martin Van Buren Papers, DLC.

FROM DANIEL FLETCHER WEBSTER

Salisbury April 26. 1839.

My dear Father,

We are yet busily at work cleaning and repairing the house. We shall paper, plaster, and paint it, almost all over. Both chimnies are in a ruinous condition, one of them indeed all down. The Ravine at the Back of the house is full of all uncleanliness and bones & broken dishes. These matters however are better understood by Caroline and Mother than you & me. Warren Kinney[1] was here the day before yesterday, (Wednesday the 24th) and gave me up the bond for the Miller Farm, of which I informed you. I will send it to you in a few days. The title to the land I sold Col. [Thomas Handasyd] Perkins is good.

I have heard nothing against my title to the [John T.?] Haight & Warren & Miller places.[2] It appears however that Col. [Henry L.] Kinney de-ceived me a good deal as to the terms on which they were let. He told me they were rented to the halves, but I find it was no such thing; on the contrary they have liens on the places for improvements put on them agreeably to contracts made with him. I have not yet learned the exact amount, but Miller claims some thing like four hundred and fifty dollars and the others one hundred & fifty. I think I can arrange with them by selling them some of the Bureau lands and a lot or so in Peru. The White Hall farm is mortgaged for something like two thousand dollars, which will be due about two years from the present time. This is a serious matter; but I think it can be managed well enough by the time it becomes due. The person who holds it, a widow woman is anxious to sell it out and would take part cash & the rest in lots in town. I have learned from Cornelius [Cokeley] himself that the lease by which he holds White Hall *rent free*, was not made by Col. K. till the very night before he went away although it bears date Aug. 10, so that he has no good claim to the occupancy. The writing given him by Col. K. estimates the amount due by him to Cornelius at forty six dollars, & for this he gives him all his cattle, thirty head at the least, and the farm for a year. I can turn him out and take all the cattle on attachment if you so direct. It would certainly be a pecuniary advantage and no one could complain against you. We would have I suppose to pay him for the crops he has put in.

I have had letters sent to the Registers offices of Ottawa, La Salle Co. Hennepin Putnam Co. and Princeton Bureau Co. asking for abstracts of all conveyances to & from H.L.K. to be found on the records—and also to the surveyor at Indian Town to come up & run all the lines. I have all the descriptions except of Salisbury which I would like to have [Nathaniel] Ray [Thomas] copy from your deed.

Peru lots are selling very fast and I understand from Theron Brewster that there will be some hundreds of dollars coming to you on the division. I must have your full power of Atty. signed also by Mother, to act for you and make the necessary conveyances for you. This part of your property which, by the way, was not included, I believe, in Thomas' & my estimate of your Illinois property will be worth something handsome I hope.

Please let Ray forward your deed from May to be recorded & mine from you. The affair as I mentioned in my last, requires *despatch*. As soon as I have got my house & office in order and have been to the Court at Ottawa, I shall go down to see Mr. Walker[3] and consult with him on the [Samuel] Lapsly[4] matters.

I hope to have but little trouble in settling Messrs Lyon & Howards business. Warren Kinney pretends to be very friendly. I shall do nothing hastily, but shall allow no threats or promises to deter me from a pretty straight forward course. I hope you will have time to write me your desires upon the matters I have above mentioned to you.

Caroline has just finished a letter to her Sisters. She wrote Mother from on Board the Canal Boat.

With my best love to all I am dear Father your affectionate Son

Daniel F. Webster.

I wrote you in some haste a day or two since,[5] but find no reason to change my opinions on the necessity of some more funds on our joint account. D.F.W.

ALS. NhHi.

1. Warren Kinney was probably a brother of Henry L.

2. Warren and Miller have not been identified.

3. Not identified.

4. Lapsley (d. 1839), a native of Pennsylvania, had settled in La Salle in 1830, where he farmed and ran a sawmill.

5. See Daniel Fletcher Webster to DW, April 23, 1839, mDW 15463.

TO RICHARD MELVIN

Boston April 29, 1839.

Dear Sir,

I have had conversation with Gentlemen, connected with the Amoskeag Company,[1] respecting the sale of my Derry land to that Company.[2] I am afraid they do not form a just estimate of its value. Two of the Gentlemen, Mr. [John Amory] Lowell[3] & Mr. [William] Amory,[4] go to Amoskeag tomorrow, & I wish that upon receipt of this, you would proceed immediately to that place, & inquire for them. I have told Mr. Lowell, that they might rely on any statements, which you should make, respecting the land, the quantity of wood & timber, &c. I hope nothing will prevent you going over to meet them, as soon as this comes to hand.

I have had no call for taxes this year, & hope the rent of the house, & the few acres of cultivated land, may have paid them. If not, please give me information.

Your Obt. Servant, Danl Webster

LS. NhD. Melvin (1786–1870) was a Derry, New Hampshire, tavernkeeper.

1. The Amoskeag Manufacturing Company of Manchester had been chartered in 1831 but did not commence the manufacture of cotton goods until 1837.

2. On December 31, 1838, Webster had mortgaged at least a part of this

Derry property to Samuel Frothingham for $17,000. See above, Receipt for Land Conveyance, December 31, 1838.

3. Lowell (1798–1881; Harvard 1815) was a member of the prominent Boston and Lowell, Massachusetts, family. Himself a businessman, banker, and manufacturer, he

served as treasurer of the Amoskeag Company from 1836 to 1837.
4. Amory (1804–1888; Harvard 1823), a lawyer, the son-in-law of David Sears, pursued manufacturing rather than law, succeeding Lowell as treasurer of the Amoskeag Company and serving as treasurer of the Jackson Manufacturing Company at Nashua, New Hampshire, from 1831 to 1842.

SUBSCRIPTION FOR WEBSTER

Boston May 1.st 1839. It being understood that Mr Webster in making his arrangements for going abroad is desirous to dispose of his Estate in Summer Street—the Subscribers in consideration of Mr Websters public services are desirous to lessen the loss to him which must be considerable on the Sale of his Estate and to enable him with more ease to complete his arrangements for his visit to England which they think will be useful to the Country and especially so at the present time—they therefore agree to pay the sums affixed to their names respectively for the above objects.

pd Sam[ue]l Appleton paid 500 Dr. Five Hundred Dollars
Rob[er]t G Shaw 500 Dr pd—Five hundred dollars
T[homas] W[ren] Ward 500 pd Five hundred dollars
W[illia]m Oliver 200 – – Two hundred Dollars
John Welles 150—by I. P. Davis—One hundred & fifty
Cash of TWW 100—*paid*.
Joseph W. Revere 250 paid Two hundred & fifty dollars
R[ichard] D. Tucker 100. One hundred dollars—by. I.P.D.

[Second List][1]
Sam[ue]l Appleton—500
Rob[er]t G. Shaw—500
T[homas] W[ren] Ward—500
R[ichard] D Tucker—500
Josiah Bradlee
xJames Read
xJohn Sam[p]son
xE[noch] Train
H[enry] Oxnard

W[illia]m Oliver—200
George Blake
Joshua Blake
Dr. [George C.] Shattuck
xJosiah Quincy Jr
xIgnatius Sargent
xJ[ames] W. Paige
Isaac McLellan
xHenry F. Baker

[Third List]
Sam[ue]l Appleton 500 Five Hundred dollars
Rob[er]t G Shaw 500. Five hundred Ds
T[homas] W Ward 500 Five hundred dollars
Cash 100 T W W
John Welles 150

James Reads Collections
Gov [John T.] Winthrop
J[oseph] W Revere
R[ichard] D Tucker

[Fourth List]

Josiah Bradlee RGS[2]
H[enry] Oxnard x RGS
John Welles—150
Cha[rle]s R Codman
Tho[ma]s Lee
Joseph Tilden
S[amuel] A. Eliot x
J[oseph] C. Warren x
T[homas] Wigglesworth
Eben[ezer] Francis
E[benezer] Tuckerman RGS
H[enry] Codman
T[homas] P Cushing
Jere[mia]h Mason x
F[rancis] C. Lowell x
W[illiam] B Reynolds
B[enjamin] C. Clark
Geo[rge] Blake
Joshua Blake

Dr [George C.] Shattuck RGS
S[amuel] T. Armstrong RGS
Eben[ezer] Breed
Israel Munson
John Parker
T[homas] & J D Bradlee
Horace Gray
John C Gray
Windsor Fay
E. Miller
J H Pearson
Cha[rle]s Amory
W[illia]m Amory
Tho[ma]s Motley
Rich[ar]d Fletcher
Dan[ie]l P. Parker
Phineas Sprague
B[enjamin] C. White
J[ohn] D Bates

[Fifth List]

Train
D C Bacon
Oxnard
Read
Lamson
Baker
H Edwards
J W Revere
John Welles
Jos[eph] W. Revere
Cha[rle]s R Codman
xMartin Brimmer
Tho[ma]s Lee

B[enjamin] C. Clark
xD[aniel] C. Bacon
xFrancis Bacon
Eben[ezer] Breed
Gov. S[amuel] T. Armstrong
xJ[ohn] I. Dixwell
xG[eorge P.] & W. Bangs & Co
Israel Munson
xL[evi] Brigham
John Parker
T[homas] & J D Bradlee
John D. Bates
xH[enry] Edwards

Joseph Tilden
Sam[ue]l A. Eliot
J[oseph] C. Warren
T[homas] Wigglesworth
E[benezer] Francis
xEben[ezer] Chadwick
Henry Codman
E[dward] Tuckerman
Jonathan Phillips
T[homas] P. Cushing
xBenj[amin] Bangs
Jere[mia]h Mason
F[rancis] C. Lowell
W[illiam] B. Reynolds

xCha[rle]s Stoddard
<John L. Gardner>
xP[eter] R. Dalton
xJames Davis
xW[illiam] H. Delano
xSam[ue]l Dorr
Horace Gray
John C. Gray
xStephen Fairbanks
xSam[ue]l Fales
Windsor Fay
xAlbert Fearing
xB[enjamin] Fiske

Those crossed Mr James Read will attend to.

DS. MHi.
1. These lists, except for the fourth and fifth, are preceded by the explanation that heads the first list.

2. "RGS" probably means that Robert G. Shaw will solicit contributions from those by whom his initials appear.

TO NICHOLAS BIDDLE

Boston May 11. 1839

My Dear Sir

I am *really* going to Europe, & have engaged my passage in the Liverpool. I thank you, heartily, for your letter, & the friendly purpose which it indicates.[1]

I intend to be in Philadelphia, Monday Evening, or Tuesday at latest. May you live a thousand years! Yrs, during the whole period—

Danl Webster

ALS. James Biddle Collection of the Biddle Family Papers (Andalusia), Philadelphia, Pennsylvania.
1. See Nicholas Biddle to DW, May 5, 1839, mDW 15493. In this letter,

Biddle pledged "to try to put something in your [DW's] way that will help to pay your expenses &c &c" if Webster were going to Europe.

RECEIPT FOR MONEY TO BE LOANED TO WEBSTER

Received New York May 16th 1839 of Fitzhenry Homer[1] of Boston— Five Hundred—Dollars which together with Twenty seven thousand five hundred Dollars to be furnished by other persons is to be loaned to Daniel Webster for Two Years with interest payable semiannually. As security for the whole of said loan said Daniel Webster is to convey to Samuel B. Ruggles and Richard M Blatchford the property hereinafter named or described, which property is to be held in trust for the repayment of said loan with interest.

Property to be conveyed viz:

1430 58/100 acres of Land in Grant County in Wisconsin,

240 acres in Portage County in Wisconsin,

1531 96/100 acres in Oakland, Genessee, Eaton & St: Clair Counties in Michigan,

399 65/100 acres in Williams County in Ohio.

240 acres in Indiana—being E half of N.E. qr:

Sec. 9 & s.w. qr: Sec 29 Township 37 North Range 9. E.

2 undivided 24th: parts of the City of Winnebago in Wisconsin, the whole 24 parts comprising 421 37/100 acres.

One undivided fourth part of the following lots and blocks in the town of Peru in La Salle County, Illinois. Blocks 54–63–58–34–27–25–South half of blocks 84 & 7. North half of block 86. Lot 10 in block 8. Lots 1 & 10 in block 23. Lot 1 in block 38. Lot 10 in block 53. Lots 7 & 3 in block 88 fractional Lot 6 in block 153. One equal undivided 20th: part of all the real estate which formerly belonged to Lyman D Brewster[2] deceased lying in La Salle County Illinois.

2 acres in lot No 7 of the 20 acre lots in Peru aforesaid

352 shares in the Gibraltar & Flat Rock Company in Michigan.

5 acres in the City of Toledo, Ohio.

200 shares in the Michigan City & Kankakee Rail Road Company, Indiana. 1145 40/100 acres in Bureau County—Illinois.

The above described property is to be conveyed cotemporaneous with the loan and is to be taken by the Trustees, without any other examination or evidence that the title is clear, perfect and unincumbered than the written assurance of Mr Webster to that effect.

There are other valuable properties belonging to Mr Webster in Ohio —Michigan—Illinois—Indiana and Wisconsin, the titles to which are not yet complete in him—those properties he engaged to convey also as security for said loan by himself or by his Attorney as soon as the patents can be procured—the deeds obtained or the titles otherwise perfected in him—but the loan is not to be stayed for such titles or conveyances.

R. M. Blatchford

DS. NhHi.

1. Homer (1799–1856) was a Boston merchant.

2. Brewster (d. 1835), of Nashville, Tennessee, had settled in Peru in 1834.

FROM JOHN EVELYN DENISON

7. Rue de la Chaussee
d'Antin, Paris
June 5. 1839.
My dear Sir

A few days ago I heard from Genl. [Lewis] Cass, the U.S. Minister at this place that you were expected to visit England this summer, and I see by the papers of this morning that you have safely arrived at Liverpool.

It gives me very great pleasure to hear of your having reached English ground, but that pleasure is most materially damped by the impossibility that exists of my welcoming you in person. I was summoned over to Paris a fortnight ago by the alarming illness of Lord William [Cavendish] Bentinck,[1] my wife's uncle and we are now here in attendance upon him, and do not contemplate an early return to England.

It is a matter of real regret to me to be absent from London on your arrival, as I should have had the greatest pleasure in devoting myself to you, and in endeavouring to render your visit agreeable. Not that you will find any want of such attentions as it wd be in my power to afford, as I am sure there will be a universal desire throughout the world of London to pay the fullest tribute of respect to your well known name. I flatter myself however that as an old friend I might have contributed some share of interest beyond the reach of new acquaintances, as I assure you I shd myself have derived extraordinary pleasure from your conversation.

I hope you allow me to wait upon you by deputy through the medium of part of my establishment. My Servants and horses are all idle in the Country, and I have by this post written to my Coachman to hasten to London, where he will put himself under your orders with three carriage horses, and my London chariot. I am sorry that I have not a light open carriage to offer you also for your morning excursions, but you will easily find one to suit you, and I flatter myself my horses will be more efficient than jobs from your hotel. You must not think of refusing me this pleasure. I assure you my horses are doing literally nothing, and my coachman & Postillion will be only too happy to find themselves in London. I shall be obliged to be in England myself toward the end of July as I have to serve the office of High Sheriff for Nottinghamshire this year, & I must attend upon the Judges at the Assizes.

I hope your stay will be prolonged into the Autumn, & that you will so arrange your plans, as to be able to pay me a visit at Ossington, my Country place, before your return. I shall count upon this, & hope you will not disappoint me.

Lady Charlotte[2] begs to be allowed to join me in compliments to Mrs Webster, who I understand accompanies you. Believe me my dear Sir yours very truly   J E Denison.

ALS. MH. Denison (1800–1873), Viscount Ossington, was a member of Parliament. In 1857, he was elected Speaker of the House of Commons. His friendship with DW dated back to 1825, when he made a tour of the United States. *DNB*.

1. Bentinck (1774–1839) had

fought in the French Revolution and later served as governor-general of India. *DNB*.

2. Charlotte Cavendish-Scott-Bentinck, daughter of William Cavendish, duke of Devonshire, whom Denison had married in 1827.

TO [JOHN PLUMMER HEALY]

London June 9. '39

My Dear Sir,

On Monday morning, the 2nd inst, we arrived at L[iver]pool, after a passage of 14 ½ days, or rather less, from Pilot to Pilot. For a great part of the way we had calm, the rest, light winds a head; which same light winds have so retarded the sailing ships, that we were in Lpool several days before the N.Y. Packet of May 1.—tho' we left the 18th. We staid in Lpool 2 days, went to Chester, and thence struck off & hit the Lpool & London Rail Road—& got to London, on the Evening of the 5th. The sixth, it was raining. I went out, quite alone, looked into all the Courts— the whole four were sitting—& saw all their venerable wigs. I staid long enough to hear several Gentlemen speak. They are vastly better *trained* than we are. They speak short. They get up, begin immediately—& leave off when they have done. Their manner is more like that of a school boy, who gets up to say his lesson, goes right through it, & then sits down, than it is like our more leisurely & elaborate habit. I think Sergeant Wilde, who is esteemed a long speaker argued an insurance question in 15 minutes, that most of us would have got an hour's speech out of.[1] The rooms are all small—with very inconvenient writing places—& almost nobody present, except the wigged population. I went to the Parliament Houses—(Houses not in Session). They are very small rooms. Where the Lords sit, I was sure, must be the old painted chamber— where the Com[mitt]ees of conference used to meet. On entering it, I asked the guide, *What Comee's room that was*—he turned, to rebuke my ignorance, & exclaimed, "this is the House of Lords." I was right, however. The H. of C. was burnt, you know, some time ago & the H. of C. now sit in what was the H. of L—and the Lords sit, temporarily, in the old painted chamber. All these accommodations are small & paltry; & new buildings are in progress for the use of both Houses.

The political state of things is quite unsettled. All sorts of expectations exist, as to what shall happen. The ministry, most certainly, are very weak, in public estimation, &, as clearly not very strong in their own. But Lord Wellington,[2] whose weight & influence, are, at this moment, prodigious, does not want Office; & it is said that both he & Sir Robt. [Peel],[3] see the difficulty which they would be obliged to encounter, if in power, in consequence of the state of things in Ireland. Mr. [Daniel] O'Connell[4] is King of Ireland; & it is thought that nothing but military power could keep the peace in that Kingdom of his, under an administration which he should oppose. Some speak of a dissolution of Parliament—others say, the Queen will rather give way to radicalism, than receive the tories into power. A new election, in the opinion of some, would give the Tories a working majority of 70 members. On all these topics, I have seen too little, & know too little, to be able to form any opinion for myself. As yet, I have not attended any Debates in Parliament—but propose to go to the H.C. tomorrow Evening to witness a second Debate on the Jamaica Question. As to private matters, I will write you, if possible, in season for the same conveyance which takes this—if not, I will write by the next. I propose to send this by the Lpool, which sails on the 13th.

June 12. I attended the Debate on the Jamaica Question. The great guns were not fired, but the Debate was handsomely conducted. Sir [Burtenshaw] Ed[war]d Sugden[5] began it. He is not remarkably interesting as a political speaker. Mr [Henry] Labouchere,[6] Mr [William Ewart] Gladstone,[7] & Sir George Grey,[8] all young men, followed & spoke well.

Pray remember me to all friends. Write me often, & tell me all the news. Send my regards to Mr [George] Blake, & let me know how he is. Yrs truly   D. Webster

Be sure to let no one single thing from me ever get into the Newspapers.

ALS. MHi. Published in *W & S*, 16: 309–310.

1. Webster had heard Wilde's argument in *Devaux and another* v. *Steele* before the Court of Common Pleas (*The Times*, London, June 8, 1839). Wilde has not been identified.

2. Arthur Wellesley, first duke of Wellington (1769–1852), hero of Waterloo and former Prime Minister, was at this time a leader of the Conservative opposition in the House of Lords. *DNB*.

3. Peel (1788–1850), also a Conservative leader and former Prime Minister, returned to Downing Street in 1841. *DNB*.

4. O'Connell (1775–1847), a lawyer and Irish politician, was commonly called the "Liberator." *DNB*.

5. Sugden (1781–1875) was a Tory member of Parliament from Ripon and had previously been Irish chancellor, 1834–1835. In 1852 he became Lord Chancellor and was created Baron St. Leonards. *DNB*.

6. Labouchere (1798–1869), a relative of Sir Francis Baring, then Chancellor of the Exchequer, was a member of Parliament who had met Webster in 1825 while on a tour through the United States. *DNB*.

7. Gladstone (1809–1898) was at this time a Conservative member of Parliament from Newark, having previously served in several posts during Peel's ministry. *DNB*.

8. Grey (1799–1882) was a member of Parliament from Devonport. *DNB*.

TO CHARLES HENRY THOMAS

London <May> June 9th 1839

Dear Henry,

I must not permit the Liverpool, which is to depart on the 13th, to return, without a line to Marshfield, to let you all know that we had a most safe, mild, & rapid passage—14 days & a half, less 5 hours—& that we have all arrived in London. The sea was so smooth, more than half the way, that [Seth] Peterson[1] could have rowed me along in my boat. Mrs W. was sick, the early part of the voyage; Mrs [Harriette Story] P[aige] less so, Julia not at all, & with exception of one day, when the sea & other causes laid me up, I was fit for duty the whole voyage.

We have staid a day or two with Mr [Samuel] Jaudon, and are now settled in our lodgings, Brunswick Hotel, Hanover Square.

From Liverpool, we came mostly, not altogether on the Rail Road. We first went to Chester, 20 miles from L.—the oldest town in England—some of its buildings going back for their date to Saxon times, say the 6th or seventh century. We then struck across the Country to the Rail Road, & by it came to London. The usual run from London to Liverpool —200 miles—is 10 1/2 hours.

Two things have struck us very strongly in England, & I will mention them, & they will be the only matters I can now write about.

First, the agricultural beauty and richness of the Country. For many miles together the Country appears to be a tasteful garden. Even the wheat sowing & potato planting is all done so nicely, the ground looks as if it had been *stamped*, as people stamp butter. And then there is the deep green of the Fields, & the beautiful hedges. Of cattle, in driving over so great a part of this little Kingdom, I saw many varieties, & of different qualities. All round Liverpool the Ayrshire breeds abound, & they far surpass any thing else I have seen. In hundreds of flocks [of sheep], every one looks as if Wm Sherburne[2] had been feeding & carding it for 6 months. In parts of Cheshire, & some other places, I saw poor cattle.

The other thing, which struck us, is the ancient ecclesiastical architecture of England. These old vast cathedral churches, & smaller churches, of all sizes & forms, which have stood for ages & centuries, are such objects as we cannot of course see on our side of the Ocean. They are, some of them, most magnificent & grand spectacles.

We have yet not seen much of London. Many persons have called upon us, & we are likely to be busy enough. For the two days we have been here, I have been poking around *incog.*—going into all the courts, & every where else I chose—with the certainty that nobody knew me. That is a queer feeling—To be in the midst of so many thousands & to be sure that no one knows you, & that you know no one. We are apt to feel when we come among great multitudes, that of course we shall recognize somebody. But a stranger in London is in the most perfect solitude in the world. He can touch every body, but can speak to nobody. I like much these strolls by myself. This morning we are all going to breakfast with Mr [John] Kenyon—where we are to meet [Samuel] Rogers, the poet, [William] Wordsworth,³ &c. &c. Yesterday I breakfasted with [William] Sidney Smith,⁴ long known as the greatest wit in England. He is a clergyman, of much respectability. Among other persons, there was [Thomas] Moore, the poet.⁵ An English Breakfast is the plainest & most informal thing in the world. Indeed in England, the rule of politeness is to be quiet, act naturally, take no airs, & make no bustle. If the Queen were to drop into a House to breakfast, the Lady of the House would not alter a thing—but be just as easy, as if it were any other neighbor. This perfect politeness has of course cost a good deal of drill. Fuss & fidgets can be subdued only by strict discipline. We all go to dinner on Tuesday where we are to meet—who do you think? Boz.⁶ The Ladies are delighted—they expect he will look just like Mr Pickwick.

As to many other things, Dear Henry, I must postpone them to another opportunity. I have had no time yet to think of any matters of business. I pray you to give my love to your mother, your wife, & the Drs [John Porter] family. This letter must leave London the 11th. I will leave it open to see if any one will add a Postscript.

June 12. Wednesday Morning. I have nothing to add. We are quite well. *Boz* looks as if he were 25, or 26 years old—is somewhat older—rather small—light complexion—a good deal of hair—shows none of his peculiar humour in conversation—and is rather shy & retiring. We have also met Rogers, Wordsworth, & Moore—so much for the facts.

I have been once to the House of Commons & heard a Debate. Today, we are going to drive out to Richmond Hill.

Adieu—write me, be sure, quite often. Yrs truly   D. Webster

ALS. NhD. Published in Curtis, 2: 6–8.
1. Peterson (1788–1866) was one of Webster's Marshfield employees.

2. Not identified.
3. Kenyon (1784–1856), a wealthy philanthropist and native of Jamaica,

Rogers (1763–1855), and Wordsworth (1770–1850) were all poets.
DNB.
4. Smith (1771–1845) was canon

of St. Paul's. DNB.
5. Moore (1799–1852). DNB.
6. Charles Dickens (1812–1870).
DNB.

FROM JOHN EVELYN DENISON

7 Rue de La Chaussee
d'Antin.
June 10. 1839.
My dear Sir
I trust before this time you will have made acquaintance with my brother, the Bishop of Salisbury.[1] My brethren are only out numbered by those of Joseph, and they have divided themselves among all professions.

I have a brother, an officer at Woolwich,[2] who will be delighted to show you everything to be seen there. Two brothers in the Law in London[3] will introduce you into the penetration of those Regions, whose language & habits are a mystery, but who rule our world by their decrees.

I know you will take especial interest in threading these mazes, all familiar to yourself.

There is to be a great Agricultural meeting & Cattle Show at Oxford. I am inclined to think you ought to attend it, and to take that opportunity of seeing Oxford. One of my lawyer brothers, Henry, will talk to you about this; he is a fellow of Merton College Oxford, & will be able to give you useful information.

I have written to a very good friend of mine, Mr [Henry] Handley,[4] M.P. for Lincolnshire, a great Farmer, & a leading member of the English Agricultural Society to request that he will call on you without the ceremony of an introduction, & tell you abt. the Oxford meeting.

I cannot tell you how much I regret not being able to do with you, all that I am now delegating to others, but I count certainly on seeing you later in the summer. Believe me yours very truly   J E Denison.

ALS. MH-H.
1. Edward Denison (1801–1854).
DNB.
2. Sir William Thomas Denison
(1804–1871). DNB.

3. Henry (1810–1858) and Stephen Charles Denison (b. 1811).
Alumni Oxonienses, 1715–1886.
4. Otherwise unidentified.

TO EDWARD CURTIS

London, June 12, 1839.
My Dear Sir,
I have sent a duplicate of the enclosed to John P. Healy, Esq., Boston,

with directions to have it published in all the Whig papers.[1] If it should not make its appearance in due season, please send him this. We have been in London almost a week; are at the Brunswick House, Hanover Square, and have as much as we can do, to see things and persons. Our heads are rather turned at present, but we hope to get right soon. I have been into all the courts, and both Houses of Parliament; looked at most of the great men, spoken with many of them, and find society more free and easy than I expected. Not that there is not, as I presume there is, a good deal of exclusiveness, but the general manners, when people meet, are void of stiffness, and are plain and simple, in a remarkable degree.

To-day we are to drive to Richmond Hill, as the sun is bright and the day good for prospects.

I find myself kindly remembered by those I have known in America. Sir Charles Bagot, Sir Stratford Canning, Sir Charles [Richard] Vaughan, Mr. [Henry] Labouchere, Lord [Edward George Geoffrey Smith] Stanley,[2] and others, have been prompt to find us out, and to tender us all kinds of attention and civility. [John Evelyn] Denison is in Paris, with his wife's uncle, Lord William Bentinck, who is there ill. On hearing of my arrival, he sent orders for his coach and horses, coachman and postilion, to come to town, and put themselves at my disposal while I remain in London. You are prudent and private in the use of confidential letters, and therefore I may say what I shall say to none but you, that I am already asked whether I will have a conversation with those in high places, on the subjects of common interest to the two countries. More of this another time. As yet, I have delivered no letters of introduction, but have received many calls from persons of consideration. Adieu! I must write a word to [Richard M.] Blatchford.[3] Let no packet come without bringing me a letter from you. The ladies are yet all in bed, but in their behalf, as well as my own, I pray kind remembrance to Mrs. Curtis.

I ought not to omit to say that Mr. and Mrs. [Andrew] Stevenson have received and treated me with great propriety and kindness.[4] Yours,

D.W.

Text from PC, 2: 48–49. Original not found.

1. See "To the People of Massachusetts," June 12, 1839, below.

2. Bagot (1781–1843) had been British minister to the United States, 1815–1820, and was to become governor-general of Canada in 1841. Canning (1786–1880) had been British minister to the United States, 1820–1824. Vaughan (1774–1849) had been British minister to the United States, 1825–1835. Stanley (1799–1869), later earl of Derby, had toured the United States in 1825 with Denison.

3. No correspondence between Webster and Blatchford, dating before 1841, has been found, but there were business transactions between them. See above, Receipt for money lent to Webster, May 16, 1839.

4. Mrs. Sarah Stevenson, née   confirmation as minister to England.
Coles. DW had opposed Stevenson's

TO JOHN PLUMMER HEALY, WITH ENCLOSURE

London June 12. '39
Dr Sir,
Please cause the enclosed to be published, the same day, in all the
Whig Newspapers in Boston—and as soon as you receive it.[1] Yrs
D. Webster

ENCLOSURE: TO THE PEOPLE OF MASSACHUSETTS

London
June 12, 1839
It is known that my name has been presented to the Public, by a meeting of Members of the Legislature of the State, as a candidate for the office of President of the United States at the ensuing Election. As it has
been expected that a Convention would be holden in the autumn of this
year, composed of Delegates from the Several States, I have hitherto
thought proper not to anticipate, in any way, the results of that Convention. But I am now out of the country, not to return, probably, much
earlier, than the period fixed for the meeting of the Convention, and do
not know what events may occur, in the meantime, which, if I were at
home, might demand immediate attention from me. I desire, moreover,
to act no part, which may tend to prevent a cordial & effective union
among those, whose object, I trust, is, to maintain, unimpaired, the Constitution of the Country, and to uphold all its great interests, by a wise,
prudent, and patriotic administration, of the Government. These considerations have induced me to withdraw my name as a Candidate for the
Office of President, at the next Election.   Danl Webster

ALS, DS. MHi. Published in *W & S*,   1. See above.
16: 311.

FROM ALEXANDER BARING, LORD ASHBURTON

Bath House
Piccadilly 12 June [1839]
Dear Sir,
I took the liberty of calling on you yesterday in the hope of having an
opportunity of making your personal acquaintance, and to assure you of
the pleasure it would give me to be of any service to you during your
stay among us. Dispairing of finding you at home will you excuse my

proposing to you to dine here tomorrow at Seven should I be so fortunate as to find you disengaged. I am Dear Sir truly your very ob serv
Ashburton

I risk so short a notice because Lord Brougham[1] dines here & you might perhaps like to meet him.

ALS. MH-H. Baring (1774–1848), financier and statesman, was the British commissioner at Washington in 1842 to settle the northeastern bound-ary question. *DNB*.

1. Henry Peter Brougham, Baron Brougham and Vaux (1778–1868), Lord Chancellor. *DNB*.

FROM DANIEL FLETCHER WEBSTER

Peru June 22. 1839.

My dear Father,

I hardly ever expected to write to you in England, from Peru. We are now almost as far apart as the limited circumference of our little earth will allow, and probably are moving in scenes as diverse as the distance is great. You must now be in London, where I imagine the wilderness of humanity to be as vast as that of the prairies here. I can of course form no idea of the events & occurrences, the sights sounds & actions that you are acting & suffering, grammatically speaking, but I promise myself bye & bye the great pleasure of seeing a letter from you, which shall give us some ideas worth having about England & London.

When I last wrote you, I am aware that my letter was full of troubles & embarrassments; I shall endeavor to write more agreeably at present.

I have been very much occupied with the care of the many interests you have here. We have divided the interests in the [Lyman D.] Brewster estate so far as Ninawa Lots are concerned and your share is a good one. I have endeavoured to make a division between you & me, which of course will always be subject to your approbation; I believe it to be as equal as can be made.

The farms are all doing pretty well and I hope to be able to clear them from most of the incumbrances left on them by [Henry L.] Kinney, without great cost or inconvenience,

I have spent a good deal in fitting up the house at Salisbury and in stocking & improving the farm, which had gone to disorder very much. Caroline & Miss Fettyplace[1] have painted & papered & carpeted & whitewashed with all their might. We enlarged the house, connected the two buildings by a large shed, had a well dug; Lowry had been ditching and draining and [John P.] Tilden[2] planting & hoeing and making fences. My department was that of finance, in which I have made displays of science & tact, worthy a Morris or a Hamilton. I have bought a pair of farm horses; all sorts of farming tools, four nice cows and great quantity of poultry for Caroline.

I have had some business in my profession and have just got home from Hennepin, where I argued a case the day before yesterday. My office is a nice one & I hope to be able soon to earn enough to pay the rent of it.

I have not yet seen Mr. Walker about the Adams [3] & [Samuel] Lapsly claim; but I have written to him & shall soon have an answer appointing time & place to meet him. The Supreme Court sits soon at Springfield & it will be there & then in all probability.

Kinneys affairs turn out very badly. I have not been able to find any property and of course cannot get a judgment worth having. There may [be] hopes of finding some lands *entered* by him, of which there are no conveyances, & which can be discovered by going to the land office at Galena. The first opportunity I have I shall make an investigation. Peru has improved very much and property is rising in value gradually & surely. I hope you will not sell your four farms in England—if you do, get at the least $50. per acre. They will be worth all that in a few years. They are allowed by every one to be the best farms any where in the vicinity of Peru & as good as any in the country—their proximity to town doubles their value. If you can get $10. on 7½ for some of your outlying property it would be as well to sell it: though from all I can learn the selections are generally very good. I have not yet made the tour through Wisconsin & the Northern part of this State. I reserve that for the fall. I believe I have now told you of all our business matters. I keep a strict account of all money paid out which you can examine when you come out to visit me & see lands which only want a small outlay to equal in beauty [all that] can be in England. Our health has been thus far ver[y good.] Caroline is more than contented and takes great pride in her house and her poultry. Grace is very much grown and talks famously. She is going to be a great songstress as well as very pretty. I need not tell you that we think & speak of you every day and *wonder*, of course, what Mother & Julia & Harriet are about. Please tell Julia that we all desire our love to the Queen & will take it out in any thing. I had a letter from Saml. Appleton the other day. He is anxious enough for August to come. Mother I am sure is pleased and I dare say she and Mrs. P[aige] have been to Randell and Bridges and "to the famed Bazaar." You find yourself in the midst of great political excitement, & which with Chartists and changes of Administraton and Court news, have doubtless food enough for thought and speculation. Pray write me, dear Father, bye & bye a short description of men & things. Caroline depends on a letter from

Mother & Harriet & Julia. I have no recent news from Boston, nothing from Ray Thomas since you left. We all desire our best love to Mother & sister and anticipate the greatest pleasure in hearing of the respect & attention which we are sure you must all receive. A *stronger* party we feel could not have been sent. Caroline is as happy in imagining & picturing to herself the enjoyments of the ladies as if she were herself a participator. For my own part I think it would have a greater appearance of reality if I were with you; Julia must therefore make it up to me by one of her best & longest letters. News from the Eastern cities reaches you as soon as us. You were probably not so long going to London as we were coming here.

You will be very sorry to find Sir Charles Vaughan deceased. We heard of it here but a few days since in a letter from Col. [Thomas Handasyd] Perkins. Mr. Saml Cabot[4] and his wife & daughter have just left us, after a visit of a week. They were much pleased with the country & I believe he left directions with his son's partner to buy some of our lots for him, for he has been making some advances.

I have spared paper, my dear Father, for I know your frank won't go in England. I have but room to add that you will have our constant prayers for your happiness while absent & your safe return to home and friends. Good bye, my dear Father. God protect you from all accident & bless you always—Your most affectionate Son   Daniel F.

ALS. NhHi.

1. Not identified.

2. Tilden, a farmer and native of Marblehead, Massachusetts, had settled in Peru, Illinois, in the fall of 1837.

3. Not identified.

4. Cabot (1784–1863) was a partner in Perkins & Co. His wife was Elizabeth (1791–1885), the daughter of Thomas H. and Sally Elliot Perkins.

FROM LEWIS CASS

Paris, le 23d June 1839
Légation des Etats Unis.

My dear Sir,

I perceive by the papers, that you are in England, and I suppose you will take a good look at our father land, before you extend your journey farther. But I trust you intend to visit France, and I write to say I shall be happy to see you here, and to contribute to make your residence agreeable. There is much to interest you in Paris, and I will play guide for you. I am sure you will not regret the little time, which an excursion into France will cost you.

Mr [Alanson?] Fish, who has promised to hand you this letter, is an

American clergyman, at present residing here.[1] I am happy to introduce him to you, for he has high qualities, moral and mental, and is the most eloquent man I ever heard in the pulpit.

Mrs Cass[2] joins me in the tender of respectful regards to Mrs Webster, and in the hope, that we shall have the pleasure of seeing her in Paris.

With sincere regard, I am, Dear Sir, Truly yours   Lew Cass.

ALS. DLC. Published in Van Tyne, pp. 218–219.

1. Fish (1812–1840; Middlebury 1834) was the pastor of the Baptist church at Chelsea, Massachusetts.

2. Elizabeth Spencer (c. 1784–1853), the daughter of Dr. Joseph Spencer, a native of (West) Virginia.

TO [ISAAC P. DAVIS]

London June 24, 1839

My Dear Sir

We have now been in London since the Evening of the 5th; are all quite well, & have been busy enough, in seeing things & meeting persons.

It is the height of what they call "the Season"; London is full, & the hospitalities of friends, the gaieties of the Metropolis, & the political interests of the moment keep every body alive. We have made many acquaintances, & have found those persons whom we have known in U.S. quite over-flowing in their attentions. I have been to the Courts—made the acquaintance of most of the Judges, & attended the Debates in both Houses of Parliament. London dinners, however, are a great hindrance to attendance on the debates in Parliament.

I have liked some of the Speeches very well. They generally show excellent temper, politeness & mutual respect, among the Speakers. Lord [Edward George Geoffrey Smith] Stanley made the best Speech, which I have heard. I was rather disappointed in [Thomas Babington] McCaulay.[1] But so were his admirers, & I have no doubt the Speech I heard was below his ordinary efforts. There is to be a second division tonight on the Govt. plan of National Education. The last division on Lord Stanley's motion resulted in a majority of 5 only for ministers. It is altogether uncertain how the vote will go to night—quite as likely against, as for the ministers. But if it should go agt them, I do not think any great consequences would follow. That the ministry is very weak, in numbers, is quite plain, & all its members admit it, both publicly & privately. Yet I think they will go along, with an uncertain & feeble administration until something shall occur, either to give them new strength, or deprive them of a part of what they now have, so as to give a decided preponderance one way or the other. If there were now to be a dissolution, it seems generally understood that a majority of Conservatives would be returned. A

Conservative Govt, however, would hardly know what to do with Ireland. It was said in the H. of L. the other day, that the constituencies in Ireland were nothing but so many rotten boroughs in the hands of the Catholic Priesthood. I believe there is too much truth in this.

Among the great men here, Lord Wellington stands, by universal consent, far the highest. The publication of his despatches, while it has recalled the recollection of the days of Englands glorious achievement, has shown also the unwearied diligence, steadiness, ability & comprehension, with which he conducted the peninsular campaigns. He is admitted to have no personal motive; to desire no office, & to seek no power. The epithet which all agree to apply to his conduct is "straightforward." If he were now to die, he would depart life in the possession of as much of the confidence & veneration of the British people as any man ever possessed.

We all dined on Saturday with Mr [Joshua] Bates, by whom, & by Mrs B.[2] we have been treated with the utmost attention & kindness. Julia has gone this morning to Richmond & Hampton Court, on horseback. Mrs W. & Mrs P. are going into the City, with Capt [Robert Field] Stockton, to see St. Pauls, & the other City sights. Tell Judge Story, that I have not seen a lawyer or a judge, who has not spoken of him, & praised his writings. If he were here, he would be one of the greatest professional lions that ever prowled through the Metropolis. And tell Mr [William Hickling] Prescott that I have not met with a literary man, that has not spoken in terms of admiration of Ferdinand & Isabella. The circles where I go inquire very much, & very kindly, for Mr & Mrs [George][3] Ticknor, and many remember Governor Everett.

The papers state that The British Queen is to sail from Portsmouth on Monday next; but Mr. [Samuel] Jaudon told me yesterday he believed her departure was postponed to July 12. I send you the papers of this morning; when read, please hand them to Mr. T[homas] W[ren] Ward, or Mr. A[bbott] Lawrence.

We all desire particular remembrance to Mrs. Davis. Remember us also to the good judge. Let us hear from you when you can. As soon as Parliament is prorogued, we shall make excursions into the country. The weather is now very fine, warm, with showers, and the fields round London look delightfully. We have no such deep verdure, unless it be Rhode Island.

It is now the commencement or near the middle of the hay harvest. Yours, adieu, Daniel Webster.

AL incomplete. NhHi. Published in PC, 2: 50–52. Davis (1771–1855) was a Boston manufacturer and businessman. In 1841, through Webster's influence as secretary of state, Davis received an appointment as naval officer of Boston, a post he held until 1845.

1. Macaulay (1800–1859) was a leading historian and politician.

2. Lucretia Augusta Sturgis, whom

Bates had married in 1813.

3. The remainder of the text, for which no manuscript has been found, is taken from PC, 2: 52.

FROM EDWARD EVERETT

Boston 3 July 1839.

My dear Sir

I had yesterday the great pleasure of receiving your letter of the 12th of June.[1] It seems but a few days since you sailed & *vous voila* in London! May the rapid & prosperous voyage prove a happy omen of equal good fortune in all other respects. I am much obliged to such of my old friends as (according to your letter) recollect me. It is twenty years this summer since I was in London, 21 since I passed any time there. At the time of my visit, I was very young; and the smallest of the specks that float in the atmosphere of that mighty capital. If it were not silly to regret the past I could wish I had now at my command one half of the four years & eight months which I passed in Europe at an age too immature to derive real advantage or pleasure. But let me not be ungrateful.

I think nothing of moment has happened since you left us; *at least* no event of interest, that I recollect has occurred within the circle of your acquaintance. At least in my retirement at Watertown, where I write, I have heard of none. I saw Mr [John] Forsyth today. He has been to Portland to hold a conference with Govrs. [Edward] Kent & [John] Fairfield together with C[harles] S[tewart] Daveis & Reuel Williams, on the boundary question. I may mention to you in confidence the purport of Lord Palmerston's[2] proposition. It is to appoint three Commissioners on each side to institute an experimental survey. This proposal is not hampered with the condition heretofore insisted on by the British Government vizt. that the St John's should not be accounted an Atlantic river. But the Commissioners on the two sides would of course split on this point. The Maine gentlemen unitedly recommend a non-concurrence in this proposal & recommend instead a commission to be appointed by some friendly foreign power. This is to be our counter proposition. Neither proposition promises any thing like a speedy adjustment to the controversy. It is quite adroit in the Administration at Washington thus to throw from their own shoulders upon those of the leading men of both parties in Maine the responsibility of this business. They hold a rod over Maine in another matter vizt. the reimbursement of the enormous expenses incurred last Winter.

Mr [Richard] Fletcher has resigned his seat in Congress. It is thought

Mr Abbot[t] Lawrence would be willing to take his place; & if so he will unquestionably be urged to do it. I should be glad to have it settled, for if Mr Lawrence does not go, I fear the Speaker [Robert C. Winthrop] would be taken; & he cannot be spared from the [Massachusetts] house. I wish I could give you a little better account of the good old Bay-State, but the Temperance fever continues to burn. There is to be a mighty celebration tomorrow in Faneuil-hall, without wine; & a great rallying procession of a counteractive character is talked of by the opponents of the law; not tomorrow but some other day soon. Prosecutions for violating the law are multiplied & much excitement exists. Our friends generally are in pretty good heart about the result of the fall elections, & I think myself the good cause has weathered rougher gales; but we shall have our hands full. The President is on a visit to Newyork. A somewhat partizan character was given to the arrangements for his reception in consequence of which the Whigs generally did not turn out. The result in Virginia upon the whole is a drawn game. I think however it shows the prodigious power of the federal patronage & of [Thomas] Ritchie's paper, that Mr [William Cabell] Rives' defection has not proved a greater blow to VB in that State. A Whig convention in Penna. has nominated Mr Clay. If there is to be a schism between his friends & Genl. H. of course that State & with it the election are lost. We shall see what the great national convention will do. I confess I have not much heart about it; and yet it is vexatious to see an Administration so weak kept in existence by the dissensions of its opponents. Genl. [James] Wilson declines being a candidate any longer in New Hampshire & a Mr [Enos] Stevens of No. 4[3] is nominated as a candidate in his place. I must not forget to say that your letter to the People of Massts. is in all the papers today & as far as I have heard is thought just the thing.

Having thus told you all the news (which when I was in Europe used to be the most welcome thing friends could write) I will say a word on business. I have a little land in Wisconsin, I suppose very well chosen. The tracts were selected as first rate lands by my wife's cousin Rufus Parks[4] who is receiver in the Land office at Milwaukee & has explored the territory in person. General [Henry Alexander Scammell] Dearborn who has lately been to Rock River says the influx of emigrants is immense; that the lands, not owned by non Residents are all entered by settlers, except in the interior of the great prairies & that my lands will probably be worth 20 or 30 dollars per acre. I have no idea of such a value except possibly for now & then a choice spot: —at least not for a considerable time to come. Meanwhile I should be willing to sell all I own for much less. Cannot these lands in the West in a case like yours & mine, when the bonâ fide character of the representations of their value could be relied on, find purchasers in London? It was said in my hearing that you contemplated some disposition of a portion of your lands in that great mart of the world. I wish while you are negotiating for yourself you would for me. I do not think it worth while to sell for less than one pound st[erlin]g per acre. I would sell all I own for that, and I should be glad to get as much more as I can. If you can sell for me five thousand acres for five thousand pounds, you shall have a thousand pounds for your pains.

My wife desires her best love to the ladies to which I beg my own most respectful remembrance may be added with the kindest regards of us both to yourself. I know how little time you can have to write; and I do not mean to make my own writing depend on yours, but when you have a quarter of a minute to spare you must bestow it on yours affectionately.

P.S. I am just getting in my hay. What a fine glow it gives one to win a race with a shower! A piece of land next to me in Watertown of 7 acres averaging one inch & a quarter of soil on its superficies (sub soil gravel, which lets every drop of rain right down to the Central Abyss) sold last week for 150 dollars per acre. The lands in Wisconsin which we offer for a song are said to have two or three feet of vegetable mould. As Mr [Samuel] Jaudon is coming home (so the papers say) to whom are your letters to be addressed.

I have just been reading a speech of Mr [Thomas Babington] Macauleys to the electors at Edinburgh. Do not liberal men in England overrate the importance of voting by ballot? It may change a result in a small body nearly divided & voting on some single question (as in our H.R. the choice of Clerk) but I do not think the general complexion of elections in two large counties, in one of which the ballot prevailed & the other not, would differ. In the first place it is plain that if among the tenantry there are persons on both sides of the great questions, the ballot would work both ways if at all. It would release tory tenants from control by Whig landlords as well as whig tenants from the control of tory landlords. But it is assumed I suppose that the tenantry are generally on the Whig side; though I doubt the soundness of such an assumption. Is it credible that if the landlord chooses to establish a political test among his tenantry he will not find the means of doing it? He will exact a pledge. Unless very cumbrous mechanical devises are resorted to the character of the ballot can be detected in the act of giving it. Although unquestionably it is conceivable that in the given case, under a ballot suffrage a shrewd man might generally conceal from the others the way in which he votes, yet it could only be by a previous life of deception & subterfuge too artificial & laborious to be kept up for any length of time or by the mass of the community. Whenever it gets to this, that a people owe the capacity of controlling affairs only to a secret ballot, they will certainly want interest enough in the subject to exercise it at all. If they care enough about their political rights to assert them under the constraint of Mr [George] Grote's [5] mechanical contrivances they will have the spirit & find the means of giving effect to them with even *vivâ voce* voting. It all comes to this under a constitution giving the people the right of suffrage, it is absurd for the landlord to expect to control the tenant's vote. The attempt to do it sooner than anything else would rouse a spirit which sooner than anything else would break down the right of primogeniture, the Corner Stone, I take it of the Monarchy.

LC. MHi.

1. See mDW 15589, and *PC*, 2: 50.

2. Henry John Temple, third Viscount Palmerston (1784–1865), foreign secretary during Lord Grey's administration. *DNB*.

3. Stevens (1780–1864), a native of Charlestown, New Hampshire, had served as town moderator, in the state legislature, and as councillor, before running as the Whig candidate for governor in 1840, 1841, and 1842. No. 4 was an old term designating the area around Charlestown.

4. Parks (1798–1878), a native of Maine, had settled in Milwaukee in 1836, whereupon President Jackson appointed him receiver in the Land Office. Removed by Harrison in 1841, Parks sat in the 1846 constitutional convention and, in 1867, in the Wisconsin legislature.

5. Grote (1794–1871), English historian and philosopher, member of Parliament from London, who had introduced two bills in 1836 and 1837 in favor of the ballot. *DNB*.

TO SAMUEL WILKINSON

London. July 4. 1839

My dear Sir,

I have had the pleasure, since I came to England to make the acquaintance of Mr. Sandback,[1] of the House of Sandback Tinn, & Co. of Liverpool. These Gentlemen are connected with the Colony of Demarara and are desirous of knowing whether free black labor could probably be obtained in the U.S. to be employed in that colony. I have ventured to refer Mr Sandback to you.

He will write you at length upon the subject, and I need only add that he is a gentleman of character & reputation. I am, Dear Sir, With much regard yours   Danl Webster

ALS. NBuHi. Published in Van Tyne, p. 220.

1. Probably Samuel Sandback

(1769–1851), a Liverpool merchant heavily engaged in the West Indian trade.

FROM D. H. NELSON

[July 8, 1839]
Vine Cottage
Hornsby Road

Sir,

Having in contemplation a proposal for the republication in this country of certain speeches delivered by you in the American Senate [1] may I be permitted the honor of a personal interview to confer with you upon this subject. I have not yet hinted of the matter to any publisher, lest it might lead to a hasty, garbled, and unfair representation of sentiment calculated more to influence vulgar prejudice, and widen the breaches of faction, than to rivet in closer moral union two great nations the general features of whose public spirit are counterparts of each other. Trusting that your courtesy will extend thus far even without my being favored with a personal introduction I have the honor to be Sir with great consideration Your obed & Humble Sert.   D. H. Nelson

ALS. DLC. Nelson may have been connected with the well-known publishers, House of Nelson.

1. Nelson probably had in mind an English edition of Webster's *Speeches and Forensic Arguments* (2 vols; Boston, 1830, 1838). Evidence that Webster responded to Nelson's letter has not been found.

TO SAMUEL JONES LOYD, LATER BARON OVERSTONE

Brunswick Hotel,
Hanover Square,
July 9. [1839]

My Dear Sir

I should be quite glad to see you, for ten minutes, on an affair of business, some morning this week, before Saturday, if you should be in town, & should find it convenient to grant me that favor.

I can come to any place which will best suit you. Yours with very great regard,   Danl Webster

ALS. UkBelQU. Loyd (1796–1883), first Baron Overstone (1860), an authority on banking and finance, succeeded to his father's banking business in 1844. *DNB.*

TO HIRAM KETCHUM

London July 23. 1839

My Dear Sir

I am quite obliged to you for your letter by the L'pool, which I recd yesterday.[1] I propose to send this by the return of the same ship. I send you a Newspaper containing an account of the proceedings of the Oxford Agricultural Dinner, & enclosed in the paper you will find a memorandum of some corrections, in the publication of my remarks.[2] If those remarks should be published in N.Y. I wish these corrections might be attended to. Some of them are important.

I believe I may say my remarks were well recd at the time, & have been read with satisfaction.

I could not, with decency, extend them. There were, I knew, to be a great many Speeches, & I had no right but to a little time. Besides, Lord [Frederick] Spencer's[3] remarks, in proposing the toast, did not make a wide opening.

Some Gentlemen here are apparently desirous that I should have an opportunity of saying something, publicly, in London—among others, I think Lord Lyndhurst,[4] & Lord [Henry Peter] Brougham, but it is difficult to find an occasion, in which a foreigner can, with propriety, do more than return thanks, in a very general manner. I do not mean to tresspass on propriety, for the sake of talking.

I must say, that the good people have treated me with great kindness. Their hospitality is unbounded, & I find nothing cold or stiff in their manners, at least not more than is observed among themselves. There may be exceptions; but I think I may say this, as a general truth. The thing in England most prejudiced agt. U.S. is the *Press*. It's ignorance of us is shocking, & it is increased by such absurdities as the travellers publish—to which stock of absurdities, I am sorry to say, Capt [Frederick] Marryatt is making an abundant addition.[5] In general, the *Whigs* know more, & think better of America, than the *Tories*. This is undeniable. Yet my intercourse, I think, is as much with the *Conservatives*, as the *Whigs*. I have several invitations to pass time in the country, after Parliament is prorogued. Two or three of these, I have agreed to accept. Lord Lansdowne & the Earl of Radnor have invited us,—who live in the South[6]— The Duke of Rutland, Sir Henry Halford, Earl Fitzwilliam, Lord Lonsdale &c—who live in the North.[7] ☞ I mention *names*, even in such a way as this, only to you, & [Edward] Curtis, & a few others—for I am dreadfully afraid of something's getting into the papers, on the other side. This fear of publication, is a most despotic restraint, upon the freedom of correspondence.

I see very few American newspapers—& therefore learn what is going on only by letters. I follow your good advice, & say nothing in my correspondence upon topics which now agitate people at home. I am more & more content with my own position, in regard to these questions. You will write me, I trust, by every conveyance, & believe me always with entire regard, Yrs truly   Danl Webster

ALS. NhD. Published in *PC*, 2: 58–59.

1. Not found.

2. Webster had delivered a short speech before the Royal Agricultural Society, Oxford, on July 17. That speech is conveniently printed in *W & S*, 2: 285–289.

3. Spencer, fourth Earl Spencer (1798–1857). *DNB*.

4. John Singleton Copley, the younger, Baron Lyndhurst (1772–1863), previously Lord Chancellor, 1827–1830, 1834–1835. *DNB*.

5. Marryat (1792–1848) had published *A Diary in America, with Remarks on Its Institutions* (2 pts., 3 vols. each, 1839).

6. Sir Henry Petty-Fitzmaurice, third marquis of Lansdowne (1780–1863), formerly Chancellor of the Exchequer; and William Pleydell-Bouverie, third earl of Radnor (1779–1869), Whig politician and friend of William Cobbett. *DNB*.

7. John Henry Manners, fifth duke of Rutland (1778–1857); Halford (1766–1844), a physician; Charles William Wentworth Fitzwilliam, third earl of Fitzwilliam (1786–1857); William Lowther, second earl of Lonsdale, second creation (1787–1872). *DNB*.

FROM EDWARD EVERETT

Boston 26 July 1839

My dear Sir,

Without having a word to say to you, I am unwilling to let the Great Western go without writing a line. My letter of the 3d[1] was intended to go by the Liverpool, but she slipped off without it. We are all much gratified by hearing by the Great Western that John Bull has shown so much of his good sense & of the Old English Hospitality in his attentions to you & yours. You will want to see something of other parts of England, something of the sporting season, something of country life, and something of the continent so that I think you cannot well get home in the autumn or early winter. If I were in your place I would not be in a hurry.

Nothing new in the political world since my last. The elections in several states as you know come on next month. Both sides are sanguine, and calculations before hand are not worth a straw. The Pres. of the U.S. and Mr Clay are both on their way to the Springs. Mr Clay has made a speech at Buffalo, in which he winds up with "Compromise, Concession, & Union." There are points in the speech designed without affrighting the North to conciliate the South. He thinks the Compromise bill establishes a rate of duty, under which by aid of its other provisions, the manufacturers can live, in other words he holds out no hope of a restoration of any protection in 1842; & he intimates that, since the distribution of the surplus revenue, there is no further occasion for expenditure on internal improvements by the Genl. Govt. except to complete the Cumberland road, & construct tide water works. This looks to be like a gentle edging over to Southern ground.

In our own good old State of Mass. the temperance fever still rages.

Men are in a desperate ferment as to the best way of keeping cool. Numerous prosecutions take place. The complaints are generally made & the evidence furnished, by the members of the temperance committees. [Benjamin Franklin] Hallet[t] defends the parties prosecuted. He made a speech of six hours last week on the unconstitutionality of the law & one juror refused to find a verdict, because believing the law unconstitutional, his conscience would not let him convict. Every sort of paltry intrigue is on foot to turn these troubles to political account, but I think we shall beat them, nevertheless.

I see the Merchants of London talk of a dinner. I wish on that, or some other occasion, you may find a chance to say a few words to Johnny B. Capt. [Frederick] Marryatts book, they say, is out and tart as a crab-apple. But I suppose the Hudson will continue to run down hill.

Pray make the kind remembrance of Mrs Everett & myself to your ladies & believe me   Affectionately yours

If you see good Sir C[harles] R[ichard] Vaughan remember me most kindly to him. I answered a letter he was so good as to write me two years ago. But it was sent overland to Constantinople & very likely miscarried. The Marquis of Lansdowne writing to me the 5th of June speaks very kindly of you in anticipation of the pleasure of seeing you.

LC. MHi.
   1. See above, Edward Everett to DW, July 3, 1839.

TO SAMUEL FROTHINGHAM
London July 30. 1839
My Dear Sir
   It is strange enough I have not yet seen Mr [Chandler?] Robbins, nor been able to send him the Portrait. Before I could find out at what House he lodged in London, he had left the City, for the north. I have left word for him, at his former lodgings, & hope I shall see him, some where.

   I saw Mr [Joshua] Bates & Mr [Samuel] Jaudon yesterday. They spoke as if the state of money matters here was *a shade* better. We [are] afraid, however, of bad news from your side, &, for one, it looks to me as [if] we should have bad times, for several months to come. I have become [begun?] to move a little, in some affairs of my own, & have some little hope of success. If the times should really and substantially improve, I think I should find little difficulty.

   We have now been in London two months, and are thinking of departing for the Country. They have been interesting months. London has been quite full, & we have had an opportunity of seeing almost every body, whom we had a desire to see. London is striking, by its immense extent; by its manifestation of the enormous accumulation of wealth; by its Cathedrals, Churches, Hospitals, & Bridges; by the splendor & number of Equipages, met in every street; by its numerous large & beautiful parks & squares, in the midst of the City, as it were; & by its admirable regularity, & good government. Nothing can be better than the system of police, which here keeps 2. millions of people in good order.

Here are many thousands, who do nothing but spend money; & many other thousands who do nothing but earn it; & some, who do a little of both. The men of business work as hard as you do. I can hardly get a sight of Mr Bates, or Mr Jaudon. They live, one in Park Crescent, the other in Portland place, both near Regents Park; but their Counting Houses are near four miles off, away down by the Bank. They seldom get home till six oclock, the common dining hour being seven, or half past.

What I have seen of the *Country*, exhibits a great show of agricultural riches. I have only been as far as Oxford, & home by way of Reading, & Windsor; but every where the cultivation is admirable, & the rural scenery enchanting. The climate is naturally wet, which creates a deep verdure on the fields, exceeding what we can see in U.S. Then the fences are all hedges, & six weeks ago all in blossom.

The last 30 days, the weather has been very wet, & still continues so. If there be no change soon, the crop will be in very great danger. There is apparently a very heavy growth of wheat, but it cannot ripen, unless there is more sun-shine. Very much depends on this crop.

I pray you, My Dear Sir, to remember me with much respect to your family, and believe me to be with very true regard, Yrs   D Webster

ALS. MHi.

TO JOHN JORDAN CRITTENDEN

London, July 31, 1839.

My Dear Sir,

I received yesterday your letter by Mr. [Albert T.] Burnley,[1] whom I was glad to see, and to whom it will give me pleasure to render any service in my power. When I parted with you, I hardly supposed I should ever write to you from London. We have been here now nearly two months, and have been occupied with seeing and hearing. Political excitement, and the state of parties here, made it rather an interesting period. I have attended the debates a good deal, especially on important occasions. Some of their ablest men are far from being fluent speakers. In fact, they hold in no high repute the mere faculty of ready speaking, at least not so high as it is held in other places. They are universally men of business; they have not *six-and-twenty* other legislative bodies to take part of the law-making of the country off their hands; and where there is so much to be *done*, it is indispensable that less should be *said*. Their debates, therefore, are often little more than conversations across the table, and they usually abide by the good rule of carrying the measure under consideration *one step*, whenever it is taken up, without adjourning the debate. This rule, of course, gives way on questions of great interest. I see no prospect of any immediate change of administration. The minority acknowledges itself to be weak in the number of its supporters in Parliament; but their opponents, if they should come into power, would hardly be stronger, without a dissolution and a new election. It is thought that, upon the whole, the conservative interest is gaining ground in the country, especially in England. Still, the leaders of the party feel very little inclined, I think, to be eager for the possession of power. Office here is now *no sinecure.* Business matters have been in a bad state, and money remains quite scarce; but *cotton* has risen a little, and some think the *worst* is over. I expect to hear bad news from the United States. I fear greatly for many of the banks. Nothing can be done with the securities of our States, nor can anything be done with them on the Continent, though money is plenty in *France* and *Holland.* My dear friend, I fear it will be very many years before American credit shall be restored to the state it was in at the time the late administration began its experiments on the country.

My wife and daughter are, of course, much pleased with what is to be seen in London, and Julia was greatly grieved to hear that Cornelia[2] was so near coming the voyage hither and afterwards *gave it up.* The weather is hot,[3] if no change shall come soon, the wheat crop will be in danger.

I am, dear sir, with true regard, Your friend and obedient servant,
Daniel Webster.

Text from Mrs. Chapman Coleman, *The Life of John J. Crittenden* (2 vols.; Philadelphia, 1871), 1: 110–111. Published in *W & S*, 16: 312–313. Original not found.

1. Burnley, a native of Frankfort, Kentucky, emigrated to Texas in the early 1830s and subsequently went to New Orleans; in the late 1840s he established the *Republic*, a Taylor-Whig newspaper in Washington, D.C. Crittenden's letter to Webster has not been found.

2. Cornelia (b. 1816) was Crittenden's daughter.

3. The reference to the weather as "hot" is probably a misreading. It should undoubtedly be "wet." See above, DW to Samuel Frothingham, July 30; and DW to Charles Henry Thomas, July 10, mDW 15889, and to Hiram Ketchum, July 31, printed, *PC*, 2: 61.

TO ISAAC P. DAVIS

London, July 31, 1839.
Dear Sir,
Six days ago, an English gentleman read my speech of last year, in which I gave some account of the productive industry of Massachusetts. Two days afterwards, he sold out some other stocks, and invested £40,000 in Massachusetts 5 per. cents, at 103; stocks of other States, bearing the same interest, might have been had at 88.[1] The Bay State forever!
You may show this to the governor, Mr. [Abbott] Lawrence, &c. &c., but do not let it get into print, as it would be ascribed to wrong motives. Yours, D.W.

Text from *PC*, 2: 61. Original not found.

1. See Edward Kenyon to DW, [July 1839], below.

FROM EDWARD KENYON

[July 1839]
My dear Sir,
We are going into the City with the expectation of procuring funds, not only for the purchase of £30,000 Massachusetts, but of £40,000 if we could get them. Perhaps you would kindly give a line for Mr. [Joshua] Bates to my Brother stating that we will endeavour to procure funds for £40,000 Massachusetts if we can have them, giving to Mr Bates during business hours to day an exact statement of the sum we can pay for in the Course of this week. If you are not at home my Brother will apply directly to Mr. Bates. Truly yrs   Edward Kenyon

ALS. CaOOA. Kenyon, the brother of John and himself a wealthy philan-thropist, was probably also born in Jamaica.

TO BENJAMIN RUSH

Brunswick Hotel
Aug. 3. 1839
My Dear Sir
I am quite afraid, from what I heard intimated by a friend a day or two ago, that I may have been thought remis, in the duty of paying my respects to you, as I should have done. If any appearance of this kind exists, I pray you to be assured, that it is owing to accident, or mistake.
Your attention & kindness to us have been very marked; and any neglect, on our part, would have been quite unpardonable. I pray you to believe, that while I feel that you have been kind to us, I shall feel pleasure, also, in stating, else where and at all times, what I hear & believe of

the acceptable manner in which you have discharged the duties of your station. I am, with regard, your obedient servant   Danl Webster

ALS. NjP. Rush (1811–1877), a native of Pennsylvania and grandson of the signer of the Declaration of Independence, was secretary of the United States legation at London.

FROM VIRGIL MAXCY

Brussels 5. Aug: 1839.

My dear Sir,

My daughter, Mrs [Francis] Markoe [Jr.], who had made up her mind to remain with Mrs. Maxcy[1] & myself till the first of October, in consequence of letters respecting her husbands health, has suddenly determined to go over to England & take passage in the London Packet of the 10th. As she will go under the protection of an uncle & aunt of her husband now here, I have concluded, contrary to my first intention, not to go with her to London, as from accounts of the newspapers, the money market in London seems to be worse than ever. Tho' ever since my return to Europe, it has been glutted with American stocks, it now from my letters seems stuffed to suffocation, and I should have no hope of doing any thing with the Clamorgan Scrip. If by your influence, aided by your Friend, Mr. [Samuel] Jaudon, you can effect an operation in England, I should be most happy to give you an equal participation with myself in all the advantages of it; and if a fair prospect should open of doing any thing—and my presence with the scrip and original papers in my possession should be necessary I would on a day's notice go over to London. All my views of the manner of effecting a sale will be explained in a pamphlet I left with Mr. Jaudon.[2] Altho Mr. Jaudon thought with me that it would be expedient in a prospectus to suggest a price corresponding with the testimony respecting the value of the property, yet I offered the scrip at 10/ per arpent and to put in deposit for every share sold, another share, as security for reimbursement in the course of sales in the next 12 years of the principal & interest at least. The scrip was never brought publicly into market—so that you may fix a higher or lower price—and modify the plan of sale as you think proper.

I have some prospect of disposing of scrip in Holland, whenever money matters shall be more settled—a fair prospect, I think, if the apprehension of war arising out of the complication of affairs in the East should pass off—but these Dutchmen will walk their own pace and will not make a step the faster for hurrying.

I wish much that you may take Brussells in your way to Paris. A steamer will take you from London to Antwerp in less than 24 hours—

and Brussells is by the rail road within an hour & a half of Antwerp—
and there is but little difference in posting from Brussells or Calais to
Paris. Or you may go from London to Ostend by a steamer in 18 hours &
by rail road to Brussels in 5.

If you should decide to pass thro' Belgium, which Mrs. M. & myself
will do our best to make it agreeable to Mrs. Webster & yourself, I shall
be obliged, if you will write to me at this place a week before hand, as I
may spend a part of the two next months in the interesting old cities of
Ghent, Bruges but principally Antwerp. But I should get your letter from
Brussells at whatever place I am in a day. Should you come by way of
Antwerp, & I should be there, I shall probably be at the Hotel d'Angle-
terre—if not an inquiry of the American Consul, Mr. [Thomas H.] Barker,³ will inform you where I am.

Mrs. M. and my daughter join me in best respects to Mrs. W. & your
family. With great regard Truly Yrs   V. Maxcy

ALS. MHi.
1. Mary Galloway Maxcy.
2. The pamphlet was most likely
Prospectus: Clamorgan Land Association ([London], 1839). The Clamorgan land speculators also issued two
other pamphlets in England: Clamor-

gan Land Association Agreement
(London, 1840); and Prospectus for
Raising a Loan of £54,000, upon
Shares in the Clamorgan Land Association . . . (London, [184?]).
3. Barker had graduated from Columbia University in 1827.

TO RAMSAY CROOKS

London Aug 6. 1839

Dear Sir

I was sorry you drew on me for so large a sum as £1000, but the Bill
was accepted, & will be regularly paid. All other things must await my
return. I am now going to Scotland, for a short visit, & then pass a little
time on the Continent; & then home.

This is the sixth day of very charming weather. The price of corn is
now fast falling, & hopes are entertained that commercial affairs will in
some measure recover from their present state of depression. Yours, with
much regard,   Danl Webster

ALS. NHi.

TO [?]

Beaumaris, N[orth] W[ales]
Aug. 15. 1839

Dear Sir

I have recd yours of the 8th instant.¹ I have no objection to your saying, that you would consult me, & take my advice, as to the persons to

be appointed Directors of your proposed Company, in America. <It would not be well to make any further suggestions, at present.> I am, with respect, yr ob. servt   Danl Webster

ALS draft. DLC.
   1. Not found.

TO GEORGE TICKNOR

Lowther Castle.

Aug 21 1839

My Dear Sir,

You will be glad to hear that we have found time to get a *snatch* at the scenery of the Lakes, with which you are so well acquainted, & which Mrs [Anna Eliot] T[icknor]¹ & yourself have so lately visited. We thought of you often, as we had "Scaro Fell," "Helvellen," or "Skiddaw" before us. We have not run the beauty of this scenery into the Details, with the spirit of professed tourists; but have seen enough to convince us that there *is much* of beauty, & something of sublimity in it. Mountain, dale, & lake, altogether, are interesting, & striking, in a very high degree. They are striking to us, who have seen higher mountains & broader lakes. Mr. [William] Wordsworth, in his description of the Lakes, has said, with very great truth, I think, that sublimity, in these things, does not depend, entirely, either on form or size; but much, also, on the position & relation of objects, & their capability of being strongly influenced, by the changes of Light & Shade. He might have added, I think, that a certain unexpected *disproportion*—a sudden starting up, of these rough & bold mountains, hanging over the sweet & tranquil lakes below, in the forms & with the frowns, of giants, produces a considerable part of the effect.

But although we have enjoyed the scene much, some things have been inauspicious. We did not see Wordsworth, as he was not at home; & altho not far off, we did not find it convenient to wait his return. We regretted this the more, as we had the pleasure of making his acquaintance in London, where we met him several times, & were quite delighted with him; so that we were better able to estimate the amount of our loss, in missing him at Ambleside. He had been written to, to meet us here, but had a complaint in his eyes, which prevented him from accepting the invitation. You will have noticed, that he has lately recd an L.L.D. from Oxford. The same honor was conferred at the same time, (the Commemoration) on the Earl of Rippon,² & other distinguished persons—& those persons were cheered, with some heartiness, as their names were announced. But when Wordsworth's was proclaimed, the Theatre rang with the most tempestuous applause. Among the Oxonians, genius & poetry carried it, all hollow, over power & politics. Probably, too, there existed, not only high regard for his private worth, & the good tendency of his writings, but a feeling that injury had been done him, long ago, in a certain quarter.

Nor did we see [Robert] Southey. He was married, as you will have seen, about two months ago;[3] & tho' low spirits be not, of course, the common consequence of such enterprises, yet, if "post hoc, ergo propter hoc," be good logic, his case is an exception to the general rule. He has been quite sad & melancholy, ever since he became the happy bride's groom. Our friends in London, advised us not to call on him; but, in fact, he was not at Keswick. I left your letter, hoping it might gladden his heart to hear from you, when he returned. Finally, we have had better weather, for our visits here. Clouds, mist, & pouring rain, have constituted the succession of atmospheric operations. However, we had great amends, the afternoon we entered Keswick, when the sun came out, in happy moment, & poured a flood of light on the green dale and the smooth Lake; & showed us Skiddaw, veiled only, as majesty should be, with a transparent wreath of mist around his brow. So much for the Country of the Lakes, which we have, truly, very much enjoyed.

We came to this place, on an invitation recd in London, & have been most hospitably & kindly entertained. You know all about Lowther Castle. One may say, safely, of it, what Mr [Jeremiah] Mason said of his house in Portsmouth, that it is a comfortable shelter agt. the Weather! We go hence to Scotland—(not to the Tournament)[4] & expect to see Mr [John Gibson] Lockhart[5] some where near the Falls of Clyde. Our route will be from Glasgow to Edinburgh, perhaps with a little intermediate bend northward, & then to London along the North road. We have not time to see any thing, as it ought to be seen. Yesterday we heard of the arrival of Edward [Webster] & Mr [Samuel Appleton] Appleton in London, by the British Queen.

Adieu! My Dear Sir. Make my particular remembrances to Mrs Ticknor, to whom, as well as to yourself, the ladies desire to transmit their regards. Remember me also to Mr [Benjamin] Guild, & Mr [Edward] Dwight,[6] & their families. Say to Mr Guild, that I do not forget that I am *a farmer*, & therefore look at cattle & turnip fields. This is a bright day, & the harvest needs many such. For a fortnight the weather has been shockingly cold, & wet. I am, Dr sir, very truly, Yrs always

Danl. Webster

ALS. DLC. Published in *PC*, 2: 63–65.

1. Mrs. Anna Eliot Ticknor was the daughter of Samuel Eliot of Boston. She had married George Ticknor on September 18, 1821.

2. Frederick John Robinson, first

earl of Ripon (1782–1859), politician. *DNB*.

3. Southey (1774–1843), poet. He had married Caroline Bowles. *DNB*.

4. On the Tournament, see DW to Hiram Ketchum, August 29, 1839, below.

5. Lockhart (1794–1854), biographer of Sir Walter Scott. *DNB*.

6. Guild (1785–1858; Harvard 1804) was a Boston lawyer and secretary of the Massachusetts Society for the Promotion of Agriculture. Dwight (1780–1849; Yale 1799) was a prominent Boston merchant and manufacturer. Both were Ticknor's brothers-in-law.

TO HIRAM KETCHUM

Glasgow, August 29, 1839.

My Dear Sir,

I thank you for your communications by Mr. Miller;[1] the papers I have not had time to look at, as I received them only this morning. If Mr. [Samuel Griswold?] Goodrich satisfies you, I shall be satisfied. I am now visiting Scotland, and proceed hence to-morrow, a little way into the highlands, if the weather should be fair. But it rains so incessantly, that there is little satisfaction in travelling. Being here day before yesterday morning, we thought we would drive over, and see the "Tournament." The preparation was extensive, but all was spoiled by the rain. From twelve to six the water poured down like a sieve. The jousting was very much impeded, and the dinner, being under a tent or marquee, was overflowed; a like catastrophe happened to the ball-room, so that the company dispersed at six o'clock, without banquet or ball, and provided for themselves as they could. We lodged a few miles off, and went only as spectators for a few hours, not intending to stay to dinner, although we had an invitation, so that we lost nothing but the sight. I quite pitied Lord Eglintoun,[2] who had incurred great expense for a foolish purpose, it is true, and who appeared to suffer much mortification. He appears to be quite a gentleman, and conducted himself as well as possible under the circumstances.

I do not think I shall return until late in the fall. I hear little, and say nothing of American politics. You may manage those things to suit yourselves. I express no opinion to anybody about the pending election. I see enough to convince me that our affairs at home are in a very bad and difficult state, and I do not profess to know who was born to set them right. You are quite correct in your estimate of the importance of the currency question. But what can be done? With the prejudice, the party, the ignorance, and the presumption which prevail, what chance is there of amendment? I have conversed with many of the first men in England on these questions, and think I have learned something, but it will be lost, I suspect, on the followers of —— and ——.

Adieu! I will write Mrs. [Eliza Buckminster?] Lee, but doubt whether I can do it by this conveyance. Yours, ever,   D. Webster.

Text from *PC*, 2: 65–66. Original not found.
    1. Not identified. Communications not found.

2. Archibald William Montgomerie, thirteenth earl of Eglinton (1812–1861).

FROM CHARLES BANCKER JAUDON

London, September 16th 1839

Dr. Sir,

Your letter of the 14th addressed to my Brother[1] who is now in Paris was received at the office this morning, and in his absence was opened by me.

The Newspapers will have apprized you of the most disagreeable business which has called him there, as they are now ringing with the news of Hottinguer & Co. the agents of the Bank, having refused to accept a large amount of the Drafts of the Bank U. States on them. Under what circumstances they resolved to adopt this course was unknown to him on Friday when he left, as no intimation of such an intention on their part, or indeed of the existence of such Drafts reached him until the very day of this Protest, so that he arrived in Paris too late to prevent, but I hope not too late to repair the mischief. This Bill matter did not pass thro this office, but was a direct matter between the Bank & the Paris Agent. We had no advices of the operation till Hottinguer & Co. themselves informed us and of the course they intended in relation to it. As yet I know nothing but the fact of the Protest, & that the probable amount is £200.000.[2] Much evil is anticipated here to American interest, & credit in consequence of this occurrence.

My Brothers absence prevents me giving any other information relative to Mr [William?] Stricklands affair,[3] than that as yet he has paid nothing into this office for your account. The Bill accepted by you to which you allude, falls due on the 23d, Monday next, and will be taken care of by us. This date will be after the return of my Brother, who I expect on Thursday next, and probably after your return to London, so that both may be here in time to make provision for the acceptance, in case any other than the protection it is sure to have from us, is determined upon. I forward two letters to your address recd. this morning.[4] Very respectfully, Your obt Svt   C. B. Jaudon.

Press copy. NHi. Jaudon (1802–1882), the brother of Samuel, was a physician.

1. See DW to Samuel Jaudon, September 14, 1839, mDW 16028.
2. On September 20, 1839, *The*

(London) *Times* reported: "The *Presse* announces that M. Jaudon, agent of the American banks in London, had arrived in Paris. He immediately waited on Messrs. Rothschild and Hottinguer, and, according to that journal, there was every likelihood that the bills drawn by the Bank of the United States would be paid. Our Paris letter states that no definitive arrangement had been made for that purpose, and that the affair would be settled in London, M. Jaudon having set out for our city on Tuesday."

3. DW's relationship with Strickland has not been established.

4. Not found.

TO [JOHN PLUMMER HEALY?]

London Sep. 20. 1839.

My Dear Sir

I have recd your letter, respecting the two acceptances.[1] I had thought they were both provided for. As the Boat goes tomorrow, and as I returned to London only last Eve', I may not be able to arrange so as to write by this opportunity; but by the *very next*, I will cause you to hear from me. We have been absent six weeks, having run over much of England, & something of Scotland. Of course we could stay but little time in any one place, nor were we able to see much below the surface of things. But the agriculture, & the general [aspect?] of things—in England & Scotland, I have looked at, pretty attentively. Taken together, England exhibits a high wrought, exact, elaborate system of art & industry. Every productive power is carried to the utmost extent of skill, & maintained in the most unceasing activity. Constant attention, & close calculation pervade every thing. Rent is high, but prices of produce are high also. About thirty shillings Sterling, say seven dollars, or thereabouts, may be regarded, perhaps, as near the average rent of good land in England. In some parts, it is much higher, say ten dollars, or, rent & tithes together, perhaps fifteen. The land is vastly productive, & prices are high. A Gentleman told me yesterday, that he had sold, some weeks ago, his wheat crop, at eleven pounds Sterling, pr acre, standing, & his oat crop for Eight. This will show you the aggregate of product & price. Forty bushels of wheat, & fifty or even sixty of oats, are not an uncommon yield to the acre. The land is naturally good, & is made the subject of the most careful & skilful cultivation. In the course of forty years, the *turnip* has vastly enriched England. It feeds millions of sheep, whose wool & flesh command high prices, & the feeding of which in the field, during the winter, say ten sheep to the acre, enriches the land, for the succeeding crop of wheat. Then, too, lime is used extensively, & every bone ground up, for bone dust, which is found a most powerful manure. And when the lands require it, a complete system of under ground draining is practised, especially in Scotland, which produces the best effects. Agricultural labor is not more than half as dear in England, as in the U.S.

I shall add a P.S. if I learn any thing before 5 this P.M. of this matter of the U.S. Bank & Hottinguer.

4.P.M. Mr [Samuel] Jaudon has been to Paris. Rothschilds have accepted the Bills of the Bk of U.S. for the honor of the Bank. It is thought the Bank may have drawn, under an understanding with Hottinguer's agt. in U.S. of which his principals were not seasonably advised. It is an unlucky affair, at least, & will much prejudice American interests & credits here.

AL draft. MHi. Published in   1. Not found.
W & S, 16: 314–315.

TO HIRAM KETCHUM

London, September 20, 1839.

My Dear Sir,

I returned to London last evening, after an absence of six weeks, in which period we have seen much of England, and something of the south of Scotland, and as far north as to the commencement of the highlands. While on the journey, I received your several letters and the newspaper sent by Mr. Miller.[1] But to tell the truth, I have found little time since I have been in England, to read American newspapers. My object has been to learn something of England and the English people, and my time has been quite devoted to this, I hope to some little purpose. But I have looked far enough into American political accounts, to see how badly things have gone in Tennessee and Indiana. The latter State has disappointed my expectations. Following your good advice, I write nothing to America concerning American politics, and for good reasons express no opinion here on that subject. Forbearing thus to speak of American politics, and forbearing of course to speak of English politics, my conversation, in my intercourse with English people, is necessarily very general. And for the same reason, as well as for others, those opportunities for saying something in public, which you so much wish that I should improve, but very seldom occur. I heed your good counsel on that subject, and shall be alive to it, but I cannot promise any great results. Nor do I see what I could write upon with a view to publication, which would form an interesting topic. On this point, however, I shall try hard to send you something. What I write, you know, if published in the United States, and known to be mine, would come back here, and for this reason I must be the more careful.

You will see what has happened in Paris in respect to United States bank bills, drawn on Hottinguer. It has caused great concern, almost amounting to consternation here. Mr. [Samuel] Jaudon is now in Paris. I hope we shall hear from him to-day, so that better news may go by The Liverpool to-morrow. I fear the event in business matters in America, if nothing favorable should be in season for this opportunity. In other respects, I am told that money matters are improved in this city.

P.S. 5 o'clock.—Mr. Jaudon has arranged matters in Paris. Rothschild accepts the bills *pro honore*. You will doubtless see it all in the commercial letters.

I have written Mrs. [Eliza Buckminster?] Lee.[2] Mr. Goodwin[3] may call on her. Yours,   D. Webster

Text from *PC*, 2: 69–70. Original not found.

1. Not found.

2. Not found.

3. Not identified.

FROM EDWARD EVERETT

Watertown 23 Septr. 1839

My dear Sir,

I did not mean to let so much time pass without writing to you a few lines, however little of importance I might have to say to you; tho' did I not know by experience that to a traveller abroad any the most trifling token from home is welcome, I should spare you my letters. Of matters of private concern, you will, of course, hear from other pens. In my own domestic circle, things have gone with us this summer, in our usual rusticating style. My wife had the misfortune in coming down stairs about a month ago, to fall & break one of the bones in her left arm, an accident particularly unseasonable, in the present delicate state of her health. It has, however, healed with less inconvenience that I expected. My children are all well.

I lately passed within sight of the groves of Marshfield. On the 3d of Septr. we celebrated the Second Centenary of the settlement of Barnstable; & in passing up & down in the Steamboat, with remarkably fine weather, we caught sight of your plantation. A vessel wrecked in the severe gale of the preceding week, with the loss of eight lives, lay stranded not far from your domain.

We are now in the worry & bustle of our approaching autumnal election, our opponents promising themselves a considerable accession of strength; & our friends, according to custom, croaking a little. The 15 gallon law will probably occasion some defection; other minor questions, not connected with politics, as heretofor, will injure us; but the great difficulty is the dead weight of the Government patronage, & the apathy produced by long & unsuccessful struggles against it. We shall probably succeed, by a diminished majority. A very large & harmonious convention of young men was held at Worcester the other day. Presidential matters were left as found, except that Genl. Harrison's name found a place by the side of Mr Clay's in the resolutions. Messrs [Isaac C.] Bates & [Barker] Burnell were appointed delegates for the State at large to the National Convention. Burnell is known to be friendly to Genl H's nomination. [Nathan] Hale & [Joseph T.] Buckingham greatly reluct at that measure. But I suppose Massachusetts would vote for him if nominated; though Hale doubts. Chief Justice [Artemas] Ward of the Common Pleas resigns. Judge [John Mason] Williams is nominated to his place, & C[harles] H[enry] Warren to Judge Williams'.[1] Mr [Samuel] Hoar was talked of, but declined being a candidate.

You would oblige me by letting me know, as soon as your own mind is made up, whether you shall be at home this winter. If not, I think it will be necessary to associate some one as counsel with the Attorney General in our Rhode Island case; & if it is to come on for argument, this should be done before long.

There is some doubt who will go to Washington in Mr [Richard] Fletcher's place. I think Abbott Lawrence will be the man; but there is a disposition, on the part of some & those not the least active, to send Mr Speaker [John C.] Winthrop. He does not desire it; & I think, myself, he had better stay where he is for the present; but if the People will, he must obey.

The papers give us a glimpse of your movements. Among the last items of information is your dining with the Queen & your being on the way to Eglintoun Castle to attend the tournament. I need not say that I wish all manner of enjoyment to you & your party. You cannot fail of it. We miss you greatly here; but I hope you will stay, till you have seen all that is worth seeing of the glory of European civilization; for all-glorious as it is, I am sure it will not make you love America the less. I have just been reading Lord Brougham's splendid oration at the dinner given to the Duke of Wellington, as warden of the Ang[lican] ports. It was evidently a most gorgeous blaze of eloquence; but did not contain an image or a thought equalling yours, in reference to the Universality of the Martial power of England, hard as it might seem to steer clear of some splendid imagery on that subject, in a speech from such a man, on such a theme.

Praying my kindest regards to Mrs. W. and all the members of your party, I remain as ever Affectionately Yours   E.E.

ALS. MHi.
1. Williams (1780–1868; Brown 1801) was a member of the Bristol

Bar. He served as chief justice of the Court of Common Pleas until he resigned in 1844. Warren (1798–

1874; Harvard 1817), a member of the Plymouth Bar, also served on

that court until 1844, when he resigned.

TO VIRGIL MAXCY

London Sep. 25. 1839

My Dear Sir

I fear I shall not be able to leave London, for three weeks, & can hardly say whether I shall be able to be at Brussells at all. I should be glad to see you here, as I really desire much to realize something out of the Clamorgan property, before I return to America. I have a very excellent letter on that subject, from Dr. [Lewis Fields] Lynn.[1]

Pray inform me whether you think of coming over?

My wife, & family, will go next week to the Hague, & probably thence thro. Brussells to Paris.[2] Circumstances do not allow me to accompany them. I shall take the liberty of giving them a letter, commending them to yr & Mrs Maxcy's kindness. I am, Dr Sir, with great regard, Yours

Danl Webster

ALS. NN. Published in *W & S*, 16: 312.

1. Linn's letter to Webster has not been found.

2. Webster's daughter, Julia, had married Samuel Appleton Appleton on Tuesday, September 24, the day before DW wrote Maxcy.

TO [THOMAS SPRING-RICE, BARON MONTEAGLE]

Sussex Hotel,
Tunbridge Wells
Sept. 29. 1839
7 oclock P.M.

My Lord,

You are doubtless apprised of the occurrences which have lately taken place, respecting the Bank of the United States, & affecting its credit in England.[1]

These occurrences appear to me to have created a crisis, full of danger to the general commercial interests of both countries.

Under the influence of this conviction, although not possessing any official character whatever, I have presumed to ask the favor of a short interview with you, upon the subject. For this purpose I have come down from London; & if your leisure this evening should allow you to see me, I will have the honor of waiting upon you. I should be glad to be permitted to bring with me a respectable Gentleman,[2] recently from the U. States. I am, my Lord, yours very faithfully, Danl. Webster

ALS. ViU. Baron Monteagle (1790–1866) was Chancellor of the Ex-

chequer in Melbourne's second administration, 1835–1839. *DNB.*

1. See above, Charles Bancker
Jaudon to DW, September 16, 1839.

2. Not identified.

FROM THOMAS SPRING-RICE, BARON MONTEAGLE

Wellington Place
29. Sept [1839]

My dear Sir

Mine is at present unfortunately a house of sickness & anxiety to which I am reluctant to ask you to come. But in half an hour after this reaches you, I shall be at the Sussex & shall be happy to talk with you on the important subject to which you allude.[1] I feel the importance of the crisis most deeply. On this money question as upon all others it is of the greatest importance that the two British nations should act together.

Believe me my dear Sir with sincere respect & regard faithfully yours

Monteagle

ALS. MH-H.
1. See above.

TO SAMUEL JONES LOYD, LATER BARON OVERSTONE

Brunswick Hotel
Hanover Square,
Oct. 1. 1839

My Dear Sir

I have learned with the greatest gratification, the interest which you have taken in maintaining the credit of the Bank of the U. States, at the present critical moment. For a week, I have been full of concern; being apprehensive that the most serious evils would fall on the commerce and intercourse of England and America, if Mr [Samuel] Jaudon should not be sustained.

It is not my purpose to make any observations on the case itself, which you understand far better than I do; but only to say, that, in my judgment, the feelings, which I understand you have manifested on the occasion highly become an intelligent friend of the interests of both Countries.[1]

I have not forgotten your kind invitation to visit you, at your residence in the Country, & hope yet for an opportunity of enjoying that pleasure. I am, Dr Sir, with very true regard & esteem, yours

Danl Webster

ALS. UkBelQU. Published in D. P. O'Brien, ed., *The Correspondence of Lord Overstone* (3 vols.; Cambridge, England, 1971), 1: 244.
1. O'Brien explains the matter as follows: "The Bank of the United

States had asked for a loan of £300,000 from the Bank of England and was refused. (Clapham, *The Bank of England* II 160). The U.S. Bank then managed to raise £800,000 from the London market according to G. W. Norman (before the Select Committee on Banks of Issue *Parliamentary Papers* 1840 (602) IV . . .) but Overstone's role in this is not clear. The text of the letter to the Bank of England from the U.S. Bank requesting the loan is in B. Hammond *Banks and Politics in America* *from the Revolution to the Civil War* Princeton 1957 pp. 509–10. The details of the final transaction are given in Overstone's evidence before the Committee on Banks of Issue. . . . The Bank's offer was of securities not money, required personal security from the borrowers, and was for only one month. The loan made by the market was arranged by a consortium who allowed eighteen months or two years, merely on the deposit of American securities" (p. 244).

FROM JOHN HOPE

Bridge of Tilt Inn
Blair Atholl
October 3. 1839

My Dear Sir

I received your letter here, in the heart of the Highlands, yesterday, just before setting out on a, (successful) expedition to the top of Ben Gloe, one of the highest mountains in Scotland. I had time to write to my Bookseller in Edin[burg]h to send to you the Books which I think will in most respects meet your wishes. I am not sure if I have read correctly the sentence as to a Law List as of Books in addition to a List of Judges &c. But I have directed the Catalogue & supplement of the Law Books in the Advocate's Library to be sent—it is a *useful* & *well prepared* Catalogue, tho a general Law Catalogue & if I am wrong as to your meaning, I rather think you will be pleased that I have done so. You will also receive a List of Judges &c which I think will interest you —prepared originally by Sir David Dalrymple, Lord Hailes[1] one of the Judges, well known to you by his Historical annals of Scotland & other works. His Historical notices are curious: It has been continued to the present day by one of the Librarians of the Faculty. As to any View of the Jurisdiction & powers of our Courts, we have nothing which answers your wishes—neither can I do better than refer you to [John] Erskine's *Institutes*,[2] which I think you said you possessed. There is a new & portable Edition by [Alexander] McAllan.[3] On that subject there are 3 remarks applicable to Scotland. 1. We have no separation of Law from Equity, & no separate Courts for either: We have but one Supreme Court Hence every thing as to the Jurisdiction & Powers of the Supreme Judicature, there being but one is very simple, for it possesses every Jurisdiction which supreme courts can possess. The System was made simpler by the changes carried thro under the Duke of Wellington's Administration, which I prepared as Sol[icitor] General, by which we abolished the separate Admiralty & Consistorial Jurisdictions & prepared the way for the future additional (but unimportant) change of Law forcing the Exchequer also to the Court of Session. *We* committed the mistake of *reducing* the Judicial Establishment too low: and I have subsequently acknowledged my mistake in evidence before the House of Commons. But the Consolidation of the different departments of Jurisprudence in one Court (which had united the *power of Review* as an *appellate* court even in Admiralty & Consistorial causes) was an important & useful tho a bold change—has worked well—and has added to the simplicity of our Judicial System. Since if you have but one Supreme Court there is in truth no room for Questions or theories as to the extent of Jurisdiction of the Court. 2. The second important characteristic of our system is a very *valuable* & novel one. After the rebellion in 1746, Lord Hardwicke[4] abolished the Heritable Jurisdictions under wh. the great Barons had exercised within their territories a feudal Jurisdiction both criminal & *Civil*—and in lieu thereof there was instituted for *Each County*—a Sheriff, who must be an advocate, with one or more resident Sheriff Substitutes (according to the size of the County) who exercize a *great criminal* Jurisdiction trying small criminal cases summarily or graver ones with a Jury & with power to inflict punishment *short* of transportation. Their *civil* Jurisdiction is, as to all *personal* causes, I may say unlimited—but not extending to heritable or real property, except in summary matters such as Injunctions of particular kind, but embracing all matters between Landlord & Tenant—but without the power of Jury trial in civil causes: and in all civil & criminal cases (except in the latter when a Jury sits) the decisions are reviewable by the Court of Session, if the cause is not below a trifle in amount. This has been a most invaluable part of our system. I believe in no Country is there any system of local Courts of the *same* or as useful a character. Two disadvantages alone have resulted from the System, one that I believe it has encreased petty litigation & the other that it has drawn unto itself too many important cases from the influence of County Attornies, which are afterwards carried to the Court of Session & so there is *double* Litigation. It was not intended that the Jurisdiction in civil causes shd be so extensively exercised in the Civil Courts—but it *was* not easy & *wd be now* very difficult to draw any limits. I know not that any Book treats properly of the Sheriff Jurisdiction but I have directed one or two to be sent to you wh. may be of use. The principal Sheriff is obliged to attend the Court of Session—is wished to be in practice there, to keep up his knowledge of law &c (tho he cannot take business in wh. any party re-

sidual in his County is concerned)—he must go at times to his County
—& he reviews the Judgments of his Substitutes on written Pleadings,
if he does not decide in the first instance himself. 3. The third pecu-
liarity in our Judicial System is the Ecclesiastical Jurisdiction & discipline of the Church Courts. I think you will like to know more of this &
I have directed a short work by Dr [Matthew] Hale[5] to be sent to you on
that subject. I have ventured to add to the parcel a Publication by myself which I had not completed when I saw you. I am glad that you are
interested in Dr [George] Cook's[6] 1st Work. You will like the continuation much better. There is a third work by Him but of a general character—on the Influence of Divinity on the progress of civilization. He
writes somewhat loosely—but with great sagacity. I shall be glad to answer any other Inquiries connected with any matters of Scotch History
in which you may take an interest—& still more to point out any Works
for perusal for the more you have, they may the longer keep me in your
recollection & lead me the more to hope that if any of your friends visit
Scotland you will oblige me by allowing me to have the pleasure of making their acquaintance. I give myself credit for anticipating the event on
which I beg very sincerely to congratulate you. Lady Morton[7] thought I
was wrong—but in this case a Lady's Eyes were not so quick. Pray offer
Mr & Mrs [Samuel Appleton] A[ppleton] my congratulations. I have the
Honour to be, My Dear Sir most faithfully yours   John Hope

ALS. MH-H. Hope (1794–1858) was
a Scottish judge.
    1. Dalrymple, Lord Hailes (1726–
1792), was also a Scottish judge.
DNB.
    2. The publication, Institutes of
the Laws of Scotland, appeared post-
humously in 1773. Erskine (1695–
1768) was also a Scottish lawyer.
DNB.
    3. Macallan's edition had been

published in Edinburgh in 1838.
    4. Philip Yorke, first earl of Hard-
wicke (1690–1764). DNB.
    5. Hale (1609–1676) had been
Lord Chief Justice.
    6. Cook (1772–1845) was a Scot-
tish church leader.
    7. Frances Theodora, wife of
George Sholto Douglas, seventeenth
earl of Morton.

FROM BARING, BROTHERS & CO.

London, Oct. 12. 1839.

Sir:
    Some public prints in this country having questioned the constitu-
tional right of the individual states of which the North American union
is composed to contract loans, we are happy to be able to avail ourselves
of your visit to this country to refer the point (on which we never entertained a doubt) to you, and to ask your legal opinion on the subject—
an opinion which, we need hardly add, will be conclusive with our-

selves, and most important for all who are interested in state securities. We beg, therefore, that you will favor us with your written answer, at your earliest convenience, to the following inquiry: "Has the legislature of one of the American states legal and constitutional power to contract loans at home and abroad?" We have the honor to be, with great respect, sir, your obed[i]ent servants,[1]   Baring, Brothers & Co.

Text from *Niles' National Register*, 58 (December 28, 1839): 273. Original not found.

1. For Webster's response to Baring, Brothers and Co., see his letter of October 16, [1839], below.

RECEIPT TO VIRGIL MAXCY FOR CLAMORGAN SHARES

This certifies that V. Maxcy has delivered back to me nineteen Shares in the Clamorgan Land Association, heretofore placed in his hands for sale—which shares tho' belonging to me were issued—seventeen in the name of said Maxcy, to wit Nos. 237. from 244 to 252 inclusive and from 283 to 287 inclusive and 296 & 297.—and two in the name of Wm. A. Bradley, to wit, 232 & 235.

London 13th Oct. 1839
13th of October 1839   Danl. Webster
One of the above having been passed away—another without numbers has been substituted.   V Maxcy

ADS by DW and Maxcy. DLC.

TO CHARLES HENRY THOMAS

London Oct. 14. 1839

Dear Henry,

My last letters from you & Ray were about September.[1] I was glad to hear so good account of you all, & of the season & of the harvest. I hope Dr. [John] Porter was not long sick. The storm appears to have done injury, with you as elsewhere. I have been thinking a good deal about Marshfield things, & shall make some changes. I think I have learned something. The English are better farmers than we are. *Turnips have revolutionized English Agriculture.* The sheep are as thick as flies, and mutton is dear. But all these things remain to be talked over.

I go to Paris tomorrow, to meet Mrs W. & the rest of the party. We intend sailing next month—but do not know yet by what conveyance.

Money matters have been in a most horrid state here all summer.

Everything American, stocks and lands, are perfectly flat. Nothing can possibly be sold. By great exertions, I have done enough to pay expenses, so as to go home no poorer than I came, & that is about all. I have sometimes felt half a mind to stay here thro the Winter, but that would have an awkward appearance. On the whole, I have concluded to go home, leaving some things here, & perhaps sending out an Agent in the Spring. You must keep along affairs at the Duxbury & Hingham Banks. Probably the notes will want renewal. I send some Blank signatures. I put this into the bag for the mail at N. York, but shall probably send another by a passenger, containing something for a neighbor, & shall direct this to be left for you at my office.

Ray will not go West, of course, till I get home. Yrs   D Webster

ALS. MHi.
1. Not found.

TO [SAMUEL FROTHINGHAM]
London, Octr. 14. 1839

My Dear Sir

I go tomorrow to France, to bring my wife back to England, & leave this to go to U.S. by the G[reat] W[estern] which sails on the 19th.

The news by the G.W. will gratify you. Your friend Mr [Samuel] Jaudon has got through his difficulties, which have been neither few nor small. There have been periods, in which I could see no glimmer of light, but perserverance has brought about a favorable result.

If we get no bad news by the [British] Queen, which is expected today or tomorrow, I shall feel as if the *pinch* was over. But American credit & American things are all low, & in little repute here. It is impossible to do any thing, at present, with stocks or lands. Indeed, up to this time, my whole effort has been to do some good, if I could, in matters greater than my own. Nevertheless, I mean, in some way or another, to be able to prevent you from the necessity *of selling Marshfield.* The Derry lot, we will sell, as soon as I get home; or if you have an offer, before I reach home, which you think fair & reasonable, you will of course embrace it. We sail next month, but by what conveyance, I do not now exactly know.

Oct. 15. The news by the Sherridan, arrived the 13th tho not very good, is not bad enough to interrupt Mr Jaudon's proceedings. The scrip for his loan is to be deliver'd this day. We look every minute for the B. Queen—very probably she is now in Bristol, & her letters in this City.

Oct. 16. B. Queen is in, & brings, as you know specie & remittances. I trust all is well, now, on this side. The question is, can you hold out on yours. Mr Jaudon completed his loan yesterday, & I am off for Paris. Yrs   D.W.

ALS. MHi.

FROM HARMANUS BLEECKER

The Hague, 15th Oct., 1839.

My dear Sir,

A few days ago, Mr. C. W. Gebhard, of Amsterdam,[1] a brother of Mr. [Frederick] Gebhard[2] of New York, who is one of Mr. [Herman] Le Roy's associates in the claim on the Dutch government called on me with a letter from Mr. Blunt.[3]

Mr. Gebhard has since sent me a copy of the memorial to the king containing an argument of their case, the report of the commissaries of Java, with their reasons, and the decision of the ministers of Justice and the Colonies, made last December. These papers would give you much information concerning the claim. I shall, in a day or two, have some other papers from Mr. Gebhard. Now, whether your presence here, when the case is presented, will be useful, you can decide better than I can. You can judge by my instructions to what extent the government will interfere. Your coming hither on account of the claim would show the interest the claimants take in it; and from the nature of the case, the officers of this government might be disposed to allow you to confer with them; and if this can be done, would it not be better that it should occur before an answer is given to the note presenting the case, than afterwards? I cannot speak more positively.[4]

I have not yet had the pleasure to see Mrs. Webster and her party.

I am, with much esteem and regard, your friend,   H. Bleecker

ALS. DLC.
1. Not further identified.
2. Frederick Gebhard, a native of Switzerland, was a prominent and wealthy merchant in New York City.

3. Not identified.
4. It has not been determined whether DW intervened in the matter.

TO BARING, BROTHERS & CO.

London, Oct. 16. [1839]

Gentlemen:

I have received your letter,[1] and lose no time in giving you my opinion on the question which you have submitted for my consideration. The assertions and suggestions to which you refer, as having appeared in some of the public prints, had not escaped my notice.

Your first inquiry is, "whether the legislature of one of the states has legal and constitutional power to contract loans at home and abroad?"

To this I answer, that the legislature of a state has such power; and how any doubt could have arisen on this point it is difficult for me to conceive. Every state is an independent, sovereign, political community, except in so far as certain powers, which it might otherwise have exercised, have been conferred on a general government, established under a written constitution, and exerting its authority over the people of all the states. This general government is a limited government. Its powers are specific and enumerated. All powers not conferred upon it still remain with the states and with the people. The state legislatures, on the other hand, possess all usual and ordinary powers of government, subject to any limitations which may be imposed by their own constitutions, and, with the exception, as I have said, of the operation, on those powers of the constitution of the United States. The powers conferred on the general government cannot of course be exercised by an individual state; nor can any state pass any law which is prohibited by the constitution of the United States.

Thus no state can by itself make war, or conclude peace, nor enter into alliances of [or] treaties with foreign nations. In these, and in other important particulars, the powers which would have otherwise belonged to the state can now be exercised only by the general government, or government of the U. States. Nor can a state pass a law which is prohibited by its own constitution. But there is no provision in the constitution of the United States, nor, so far as I know or have understood, in any state constitution, prohibiting the legislature of a state from contracting debts, or making loans, either at home or abroad. Every state has the power of levying and collecting taxes, direct and indirect, of all kinds, except that no state can impose duties on goods and merchandise imported, that power belonging exclusively to congress by the constitution. That power of taxation is exercised by every state, habitually and constantly, according to its own discretion, and the exigencies of its government.

This is the general theory of that mixed system of government which prevails in America. And as the constitution of the United States contains no prohibition or restraint on state legislatures in regard to making loans, and as no state constitution, so far as known to me, contains any such prohibition, it is clear that in this respect, those legislatures are left in the full possession of this power, as an ordinary and usual power of government.

I have seen a suggestion, that state loans must be regarded as unconstitutional and illegal, inasmuch as the constitution of the United States has declared that no state shall emit bills of credit. It is certain that the constitution of the United States does contain this salutary prohibition, but what is a bill of credit? It has no resemblance whatever to a bond, or other security given for the payment of money borrowed. The term "bill of credit" is familiar in our political history, and its meaning well ascertained and settled, not only by that history, but by judicial interpretations and decisions from the highest sources.

For the purpose of this opinion, it may be sufficient to say, that bills of credit, the subject of the prohibition in the constitution of the United States, were essentially paper money. They were paper issues, intended for circulation, and for receipt into the treasury as cash, and were sometimes made a tender in payment for debts. To put an end at once, and forever, to evils of this sort, and to dangers from this source, the constitution of the United States has declared, that "no state shall emit bills of credit, nor make any thing but gold and silver a tender in payment of debts, nor pass any law which shall impair the obligation of contracts." All this, however, proves, not that states cannot contract debts, but that, when contracted, they must pay them in coin, according to their stipulation. The several states possess the power of borrowing money for their own internal occasions of expenditure, as fully as congress possesses the power to borrow in behalf of the United States, for the purpose of raising armi[e]s, equipping navies, or performing any other of its constitutional duties. It may be added, that congress itself fully recognizes this power in the states, as it has authorised the investment of large funds which it held in trust for very important purposes in certificates of state stocks.

The security for state loans is the plighted faith of the state, as a political community. It rests on the same basis as other contracts with established governments—the same basis for example, as loans made in the United States under the authority of congress; that is to say, the good faith of the government making the loan, and its ability to fulfil its engagements, the state loans, it is known, have been contracted principally for the purpose of making rail roads and canals: and in some cases, although I know not how generally, the income or revenue expected to be derived from these works is directly and specifically pledged for the payment of the interest and the redemption of the debt, in addition to the obligation of public faith. In several states other branches of revenue have been specifically pledged, and in others very valuable tracts of land. It cannot be doubted that the general result of these works of internal improvement has been, and will be, to enhance the wealth and ability of the states.

It has been said that the states cannot be sued on these bonds. But neither could the U. States be sued, nor, as I suppose, the crown of England, in a like case. Nor would the power of suing, probably, give the creditor any substantial additional security. The solemn obligation of a government, arising on its own acknowledged bona, would not be enhanced by a judgment rendered on such bond. If it either could not, or would not, make provision for paying the bond, it is not probable that it could or would make provision for satisfying the judgment.

The states cannot rid themselves of their obligations otherwise than by the honest payment of the debt. They can pass no law impairing the obligation of their own contracts—they can make nothing a tender in discharge of such contracts but gold and silver. They possess all adequate power of providing for the case, by taxes and internal means of revenue. They cannot get round their duty nor evade its force. Any failure to fulfil its undertakings would be an open violation of public faith, to be followed by the penalty of dishonor and disgrace—a penalty, it may be presumed, which, no state of the American union would be likely to incur.

I hope I may be justified by existing circumstances to close this letter with the expression of an opinion of a more general nature. It is, that I believe the citizens of the U. States, like all honest men, regard debts, whether public or private, and whether existing at home or abroad, to be of moral as well as legal obligation; and I trust I may appeal to their history, from the moment when those states took their rank among the nations of the earth to the present time, for proof that this belief is well founded, and if it were possible that any of the states should at any time so entirely lose her self respect and forget her duty as to violate the faith solemnly pledged for her pecuniary engagements, I believe there is no country upon earth—not even that of the injured creditors—in which such a proceeding would meet with less countenance or indulgence than it would receive from the great mass of the American people.[2]

I have the honor to be, gentlemen, your obedient servant,
Daniel Webster.

Text from *Niles' National Register*, 57 (December 28, 1839): 273–274. Original not found. Printed in *W & S*, 6: 537–540.

1. See above, Baring, Brothers & Co., to DW, October 12, 1839.
2. Webster's written opinion shortly became an issue in American poli-

tics. See Junius (Calvin Colton?),
A Letter to Daniel Webster . . . in
Reply to his Legal Opinion to Baring,
Brothers & Co. upon the Illegality

and Unconstitutionality of State
Bonds, and Loans of State Credit
(New York, 1840).

TO EDWARD EVERETT

London Oct. 16. 1839

My Dear Sir

I have this moment recd your letter by the British Queen,[1] for which
I thank you. I am on the wing for Paris, where I expect to meet my family. They have been to Switzerland, & have left Edward at Geneva. It is
my expectation to embark next month, but by what conveyance, I cannot yet quite say. If anything should occur to change this purpose, I will
give you timely notice. It gives me great pain to hear of Mrs Everett's
accident. I pray to offer to her & the children my love & good wishes.

I have passed my time very agreeably in England—have run over a
good deal of the Country—seen a good many people, & enjoyed much.
But I now feel a strong wish to get home. I feel that my place is not
here; & that I ought not to stay longer than to gratify a reasonable curiosity, & desire to see an interesting part of the world, but not *my* part.
Nevertheless, if I could with propriety, I should like to spend the winter
in Europe. Things have not favored that desire. Every thing connected
with American affairs here has been bad as possible. I do not suppose
any thing, American, could have been sold. At present, we hope the
crisis, or the pinch, is passed. Mr [Samuel] Jaudon has fought manfully
—& we all have done what we could for him—& he has weathered the
storm.

I have a word to say, quite *in confidence*, about the troubles on the
northern frontier, last Winter. I have heard it said, & believe it—that
Lord Palmerston has told Mr [Andrew] Stevenson that if the American
Govt. does not repress or punish these outrages, the British Government
will, & reads us a lecture on the right of pursuing such marauders, into
their own country, out of Mr Monroe's message, Genl Jackson's Florida
Campaign, &c!

Mr Stevenson has written what he thinks a *spirited* reply—& Dr
[Lewis Fields] Lynn, who is now here says he shall call for the corre-
spondence as soon as Congress meets. This is for your *eye* alone. Adieu!
my good friend. I long to see you & to talk with you. I am glad you saw
Marshfield, even at a distance—poor old barren sea beaten Marshfield!
Lowther Castle or Belvoir or Windsor—neither of them is Marshfield.
And so, I am sure, their owners & occupants would think, if they were
to see it. Yrs   D Webster

ALS. MHi. Published in *PC*, 2: 71.
1. See above, Edward Everett to DW, September 23, 1839.

TO JOHN HENRY MANNERS, DUKE OF RUTLAND

London, November 16, 1839.

My Dear Duke,

I am obliged to you for the respectful manner in which, presiding at the meeting of the Waltham Agricultural Association, you were pleased to refer to our conversation at Belvoir, and I have still higher pleasure in noticing the just and liberal sentiments expressed by you on that occasion respecting the relations of our respective countries. Such sentiments, I assure you, will be heartily reciprocated on our side of the Atlantic. England and the United States are not only the two most commercial countries in the world, but they are also those two which have the greatest degree of intercourse with each other. This will strike any one who shall compare the small amount of annual trade between England and France with the great amount of that between England and the United States, and yet France is within sight of England, with thirty-three or thirty-four millions of people, and the United States are three thousand miles off, with half that amount of population; and, notwithstanding the progress which may be expected in some branches of manufactures in America, there is no reason to doubt that this intercourse will continue, and perhaps be increased by the rapid increase of population in America. While the United States continue to import British commodities, it is evidently the interest of England that her customers should increase both in numbers and in the ability to buy and consume her products. On the other hand, every intelligent person in America sees, not only the evils which would ensue from any interruption of the harmony existing between the two countries, but the embarrassments, also, which must be felt in America, whenever any disasters occur sufficient to derange the general prosperous course of trade and business in England.

The intimate relations of commerce subsisting between the two countries, the well-known laws of trade and exchange, and the important fact that both countries use, to a great extent, a representative paper currency, necessarily cause any great embarrassment which may be felt in one to be extended to the other. Your Grace was quite right, I think, in your observations on the subject of corn. America is indebted to England in various ways, and is likely to remain so, while the interest of money remains much lower in the latter country than in the former. We have this year a most abundant wheat crop; and if England should have occasion to import corn or flour, both countries would be benefited by her taking her supply from us. We should be paying so much of our debt, and she would be receiving her supply without the necessity of sending abroad specie; and it is undoubtedly true that the short crop in England last year, leading to so heavy an export of gold and silver to the Continent, most seriously affected commercial business in the United States, as well as in England.

Let us hope, my dear Duke, that between two Christian nations speaking the same language, having the same origin, enjoying the same literature, and connected by these mutual ties of interest, nothing may ever exist but peace and harmony, and the noble rivalship of accomplishing most for the general improvement and happiness of mankind.

Allow me to close this letter with an invitation, which, if given some years ago, would have passed for mere compliment; and that is, that you will come and see us. You are fond of excursions by sea. Eighteen or twenty days will take you from Belvoir Castle to the Falls of Niagara, and you may see much of America this side of the Alleghanies, and something of what is beyond, and return to England in a period hardly longer than an ordinary recess of Parliament. Nature has done much in America which is worthy to attract your notice. Man, I hope, has done something; and at any rate, you and your connections and friends would be sure of receiving that respectful and hearty welcome to which your character and your hospitality to others so well entitle you.

I have the honor to be, my dear Duke, very faithfully yours,

Daniel Webster.

Text from *W & S*, 6: 540–542. Original not found.

FROM JOHN EVELYN DENISON

Ossington
November 17. 39
My dear Sir

I send you the roughest possible scratch, representing the Mole plough at work with a horse, and the skeleton form of the Kurt plough with the two sets of irons. This wd convey little information to any one, who had not seen the instruments, but it may sufficiently refresh your recollections. As it is so great an object in the U.S. to save human labor, I think the double plough, as made by [Robert] Ransome[1] of Ipswich might be found useful. It is in fact two ploughs joined together, cutting two furrows at the same time. It requires four horses, but saves a man—as one man can manage the four horses & the plough. The plough from working on so broad a base, and with wheels, requires in truth no holding, but goes on itself, as you described the ploughs on the Prairies. A large

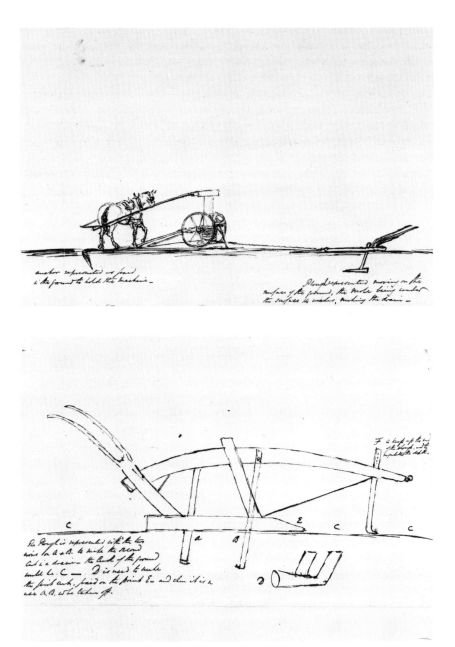

farmer in Lincolnshire showed me some large works he had done on his farm, building stone wall fences &c—and he told me he had done it all by the saving caused by the double ploughs, the men [who] w[oul]d have been ploughing had been turned to all this [oth]er work. It gives me great pleasure to think [tha]t your visit to Ossington suggested some new and int[eres]ting notions on the subject of farming. I feel confiden[t] that separated only by a 12 days voyage we shall before very long see each other again, wh[ich] diminishes the regret with wh[ich] otherwise I sh[oul]d say Adieu.

L[ad]y Charlotte joins me in kindest regards & best wishes to yourself & your whole party. Yours &c   JED:

ALS. NhHi.
1. Robert Ransome (1753–1830), agricultural implement maker. *DNB*.

On November 22, the Webster party boarded a sailing ship for return to the United States. Thirty-six days later, on December 28, they arrived at New York. There, Webster learned that the Whigs, at their national convention at Harrisburg, Pennsylvania, had nominated William Henry Harrison for President and John Tyler for Vice President. By January 1840, Webster was back in Washington, and with other Whigs, gearing up for the second campaign against Van Buren.

TO JOHN PLUMMER HEALY
N York Sunday Morning
Decr. 29. 1839
My D Sir

We all arrived safe, last Evening, having left Portsmouth Nov 22. The latter part of our voyage was rough, & tedious—but quite as comfortable as could be expected. We had one or two blows, on the coast, but the ship took care of us.

I hope to leave for Boston on Wednesday, & to be with you on Thursday. This depends, however, on weather, as I shall wait for a good day. I am Dr Sir truly Yrs   D. Webster

ALS. MHi.

Calendar, 1835–1839

(Items in italic are included in this volume.)

1835

[Jan 1]   To Edward Everett. ALS. MHi. mDW 12166. Sends copy of *Baltimore Patriot* for use by Massachusetts or New Hampshire papers.

Jan 1   *To Israel Webster Kelly.*   3

Jan 1   *To Jeremiah Mason.*   4

Jan 1   To Abraham G. Stevens. Printed. Van Tyne, pp. 190–191. Discusses proposed land purchase, livestock and repairs on the Webster farm, and French spoliations.

Jan 1   To Mrs. Charles Henry Thomas. ALS. MHi. mDW 12170. Hopes that her husband has recovered from his illness; reports that he, Mrs. Webster, and Julia spent Christmas in Baltimore; comments on the severe snowstorm.

Jan 1   *From James H. Causten.*   6

[c. Jan 1]   *To [James H. Causten], with enclosure from James H. Causten.*   8

Jan 1   Deed transferring land in Merrimack County from Benjamin Shaw to DW. DS. Deed Book, 39: 498. Office of the Register of Deeds, Merrimack County, Concord, N.H. mDWs.

[Jan 2]   To Edward Everett. ALS. MHi. mDW 12178. Requests a copy of Everett's Lafayette speech for Mrs. Webster.

Jan 2   Bill for the relief of William Fettyplace and others. AD. DNA, RG 46. mDW 43898.

Jan 3   To Albert Picket, Sr., et al. Copy. NhHi. mDW 12180. Van Tyne, p. 696. Declines invitation to address a group of Ohio teachers.

Jan 3   *From Caleb Cushing.*   8

Jan 5   *To Charles Henry Thomas.*   9

Jan 5   *From Abbott Lawrence.*   10

Jan 5   From Benjamin T. Reed. ALS. DLC. mDW 12190. Discusses his opposition to the customs house bill that would place the weighers on a fixed salary.

Jan 6   Memorial of citizens of Boston for the erection of a new customs house in Boston. DS. DNA, RG 46. mDW 44616.

Jan 6   Deed transferring land in Hillsborough County from Moses and William Gill to DW. DS. Deed Book, 39: 312. Office of the Register of Deeds, Merrimack County, Concord, N.H. mDWs.

Jan 7   To Warren Dutton. ALS. NhD. mDW 12193.

	Reports the nomination of James Moore Wayne to the Supreme Court; urges Dutton to come to Washington.	
[Jan 7]	To Edward Everett.	12
Jan 8	From Eliza Buckminster Lee. ALS. NhHi. mDW 12199. Asks Webster to assist (in some unspecified way) a Mr. Stackpole of Boston, who has been traveling through Europe and Asia for four years.	
Jan 8	From Jeremiah Mason.	13
Jan 9	From Caleb Cushing.	13
Jan 9	From Levi Woodbury. LS. DNA, RG 46. mDW 44353. States that he cannot comply with DW's request for material in time for Congress to act before it recesses.	
Jan 9	Memorial of Zachariah Jellison for a return of duties on tobacco improperly levied on him by the Boston customs office. DS. DNA, RG 46. mDW 45931.	
Jan 10	To Jeremiah Mason. ALS. DLC. mDW 12206. Curtis, 1: 504–505. Discusses the presidential nomination and the election of senator in Massachusetts.	
Jan 10	From Stephen White et al. LS. DNA, RG 46. mDW 44621. Transmit a memorial for the erection of a new customs house in Boston.	
Jan 11	To Israel Webster Kelly. ALS. NhHi. mDW 12210. Asks Kelly to make out another mortgage on land purchased.	
Jan 12	From John B. Manchester. ALS. NhHi. mDW 12213. Thanks Webster for the copies of his speech on Jackson's protest to the censure resolutions.	
Jan 12	Bill making appropriations for the United States Military Academy for 1835. Printed document, with MS insertions. DNA, RG 46. mDW 44163.	
Jan 13	To Warren Dutton. ALS. NhD. mDW 12215. States that the Charles River Bridge case will probably come before the Court in February.	
Jan 13	To [Jacob Merritt Howard]. ALS. MiD-B. mDW 12217. Thanks Howard for letter and expresses the belief that it is about time for Michigan to seek statehood.	
Jan 13	Bill making appropriations for payment of United States pensioners for 1835. Printed document. DNA, RG 46. mDW 44099.	
Jan 13	Bill making appropriations for 1835 expenses of the Indian Department. Printed document. DNA, RG 46. mDW 44108.	
Jan 14	Bill making appropriations for support of the army	

	for 1835. Printed document. DNA, RG 46. mDW 44102.	
Jan 14	Bill making appropriations for the support of naval service for 1835. Printed document. DNA, RG 46. mDW 44111.	
[Jan 15]	To Joseph Gales. ALS. NhD. mDW 12219. Requests Gales to send him reporter's notes on a recent speech so that he may review it before publication.	
Jan 15	To [Henry Willis Kinsman]. ALS. NhHi. mDW 12221. Responds to enquiry from an unidentified person who is interested in purchasing a farm from Webster.	
Jan 15	To Henry Willis Kinsman. ALS. NNC. mDW 12222. Asks for list of his notes at Boston banks; reports resignation of Gabriel Duvall and expected appointment of Roger B. Taney to the Supreme Court.	
Jan 16	*From Caleb Cushing.*	*14*
Jan 17	From George Edmund Badger. ALS. DLC. mDW 12227. Discusses action taken and contemplated in two related court cases.	
Jan 18	*From Henry Willis Kinsman.*	*15*
Jan 18	Petition of John R. Vinton for pay equal to the brevet rank. ADS. DNA, RG 46. mDW 46011.	
Jan 19	To [Henry Willis] Kinsman. ALS. NhD. mDWs. Discusses plans for taking care of certain bank notes.	
Jan 20	To John Forsyth. ALS. DNA, RG 59. mDW 55576. Requests passports to Europe for Thomas Handasyd Perkins, Sr. and Jr.	
Jan 20	From James Watson Webb. ALS. DLC. mDW 12235. Asks DW's assistance in securing a loan.	
Jan 21	From John Forsyth. LC. DNA, RG 59. mDW 55675. Sends the Perkinses' passports.	
Jan 22	*To Jeremiah Mason.*	*17*
Jan 22	To James Watson Webb. AL draft. NhD. mDW 12241. States that he will make some effort to get Webb financial assistance if Webb can make no other arrangements.	
Jan 22	Bill making appropriations for fortifications of the United States for 1835. Printed document with MS insertions. DNA, RG 46. mDW 44119.	
Jan 22	Report from the Committee on Finance on duties refunded under the act of May 19, 1828. AD and printed document. DNA, RG 46. mDW 44349.	
Jan 23	To Charles Henry Thomas. Printed. Gershom Bradford, "The Unknown Webster," *Old-Time*	

New England, 44 (Fall 1953): 57. Expresses
happiness at hearing of Thomas's recovery.

Jan 24 To [Henry Willis Kinsman]. ALS. NNC. mDW
12243. Reports that he "will do anything in my
power to place you in the Post of Adjutant
Genl." short of opposing General Henry
Alexander Scammell Dearborn.

Jan 24 *To Abraham G. Stevens.*   *18*

Jan 24 To [?]. ALS. NhD. mDWs. Comments on the
ability of Thomas A. Deblois and Samuel
Fessenden, two "worthy & respectable" lawyers
in Maine.

Jan 24 From O. S. Phelps. ALS. NhHi. mDW 12249. Asks
Webster to send copy of Adams's eulogy of
Lafayette.

Jan 25 *From James Watson Webb.*   *19*

Jan 26 To Warren Dutton. ALS. NhD. mDW 12259.
Suggests that Dutton and Simon Greenleaf not
come to Washington to argue the Charles River
Bridge case should Roger B. Taney's nomination
to the Supreme Court be rejected.

[Jan 26] *From Charles Pelham Curtis.*   20

Jan 26 *To Edward Curtis.*   *21*

Jan 27 To Edward Everett. Invitation. MHi. mDW 12264.
Invites Everett to dinner.

Jan 29 *To Israel Webster Kelly.*   *23*

Jan 29 Motion by Webster for information relative to
duties on certain articles. AD. DNA, RG 46. mDW
43925.

Jan 30 *To Warren Dutton.*   *24*

[Jan] To Edward Everett. ALS. MHi. mDW 12273. Asks
Everett to check a note on Shakespeare's
Measure for Measure to see if he had "said any
thing ridiculous."

[Jan] Plans for raising money to support the *Annals of
Education*. Printed. *American Annals of
Education* . . . , ed. William C. Woodbridge
(Boston, 1835), 5 (January 1835): vi.

[1835]

[Jan–Feb] From Charles A. Murray. ALS. NhHi. mDW 38732.
Discusses lines from Shakespeare.

[Feb 1] To Edward Everett. ALS. MHi. mDW 12274.
Arranges to see Everett following dinner.

Feb 1 *To Jeremiah Mason.*   *24*

Feb 1 [Editorial on election of John Davis to the Senate
from Massachusetts]. AD draft. NhD. mDW
12276.

Feb 2 From John Forsyth. LS. DNA, RG 46. mDW
44392. Requests increased compensation for the
watchmen of the northeast executive building.

Feb 2	From Noah Webster. Clipping from *Boston Globe*, probably 1852. MHi. Asks Webster to return his long letter on political affairs.
Feb 2	Bill making appropriations for 1835 civil and diplomatic expenses of the government. Printed document, with MS insertions. DNA, RG 46. mDW 44133.
Feb 4	To Charles Henry Thomas. ALS. MHi. mDW 12280. Instructs Thomas regarding repairs at Marshfield.
Feb 4	To Nathaniel F. Williams. ALS. NhD. mDW 12283. Asks Williams to provide for his "acceptance by drawing on me, at 60 or 90 days."
Feb 5	To Mahlon Dickerson. ADS. DNA, RG 45. mDWs. Asks for information regarding the Navy Department's plan to establish a "lithographic press."
Feb 5	To Warren Dutton. ALS. NhD. mDW 12885. Discusses Charles River Bridge controversy.
[Feb 5]	To Edward Everett. ALS. MHi. mDW 12289. Asks for a copy of Colonel Johnson's [?] report on Boston harbor.
Feb 6	*To Jeremiah Mason.* 26
Feb 6	Bill for the relief of Ebenezer Breed. Printed document. DNA, RG 46. mDW 44097.
Feb 6	Bill for relief of Thomas Dixon and company of New York. Printed document. DNA, RG 46. mDW 44087.
Feb 6	Bill for relief of Richard Hargrave Lee. Printed document. DNA, RG 46. mDW 44092.
Feb 6	Bill for relief of S. Morris Waln and Henry Percival. Printed document. DNA, RG 46. mDW 44089.
Feb 7	To Warren Dutton. ALS. NhD. mDW 12295. Reports that the Charles River Bridge case will not be argued before the Court the current term.
[Feb 7]	To Edward Everett. ALS. MHi. mDW 12298. States that he received Johnson's [?] report but not Everett's letter.
Feb 8	To Warren Dutton. ALS. NhD. mDW 12300. Writes of the possibility of a compromise in the Charles River Bridge controversy.
[Feb 8]	To Edward Everett. ALS. MHi. mDW 12303. Asks Everett to send two issues of the *Advocate* to Samuel Prentiss.
Feb 9	*From Caleb Cushing.* 27
Feb 9	From Noah Webster. ALS. DLC. mDW 12308. Henry F. Warfel, *Noah Webster: Schoolmaster to America* (New York, 1936), p. 423. Gives

	permission to use a letter he previously wrote DW.	
Feb 9	Report of Select Committee on Executive Patronage. Copy. DNA, RG 46. mDW 44492.	
Feb 10	From Jonathan Hatch Hubbard. ALS copy. NhD. mDW 12311. Discusses Leland case and requests its continuance to the next term of the court.	
Feb 10	From Theron Metcalf. ALS. NhHi. mDW 12314. Discusses the equity suit between Massachusetts and Rhode Island.	
Feb 11	From Rufus Choate. ALS. DLC. mDW 12317. Seeks to retain Webster for the Rev. George B. Cheever in a libel suit.	
Feb 11	*From John Davis (1787–1854).*	28
Feb 11	From John Forsyth. LC. DNA, RG 59. mDW 56565. Requests return of his letter on the northeast executive building for signature.	
Feb 11	From Stout, Ingoldsby and Company et al. ADS. NhHi. mDW 12322. Ask Webster's attention to the "Bill to prevent evasions of the Revenue Laws."	
Feb 12	[Editorial note on Senate business]. AD. NhD. mDW 12325.	
Feb 14	To Theron Metcalf. AL draft. NhHi. mDW 12327. W & S, 16: 253–254. Sees no need for legislative action regarding the equity case of Rhode Island against Massachusetts.	
Feb 16	*To Charles Henry Thomas.*	29
Feb 16	Amendments by DW to the bill making appropriations for fortifications of the United States for 1835. AD and printed document, with MS insertions. DNA, RG 46. mDW 44122.	
Feb 18	To John Forsyth (enclosures: John Halkett to DW, Dec 26, 1834; Coutts Trotter to Aaron Vail, Dec 21, 1834; Ian R. G. Graham to Coutts Trotter, Nov 8, 1834; Lord Auckland to Coutts Trotter, Nov 8, 1834). ALS. DNA, RG 59. mDW ˜˜˙˙ Encloses papers relating to Trotter and recommends that some "honorable notice could be properly taken of him" for his capture of war pirates.	
Feb 18	To Charles Henry Thomas. ALS. MHi. mDW 12332. Proposes to sell materials at Marshfield to Thomas.	
Feb 19	From Samuel Turell Armstrong. ALS. NhD. mDW 12334. Affirms that he supports Webster's presidential candidacy.	
Feb 20	To [George Bomford?]. ALS. DLC. mDW 12337. Sends instructions for the delivery of a rifle.	

[Feb 20]	To Edward Everett. ALS. MHi. mDW 12338. *PC*, 2: 9. Discusses committee amendments to certain bills before the Senate.	
Feb 21	To Miss [?] Allen. ANS. WaU. mDW 12341. Records his good wishes for Miss Allen.	
Feb 21	*To Samuel Frothingham.*	30
Feb 21	From John Forsyth. LC. DNA, RG 59. mDW 55677. Responds to Webster's letter of February 18 respecting Coutts Trotter.	
Feb 21	From John Forsyth. LC. DNA, RG 59. mDW 56566. Returns his letter of Feb 2, signed.	
Feb 21	*From William Sullivan.*	30
Feb 23	*To William Sullivan.*	32
Feb 23	From Stephen White. ALS. NhHi. mDW 12348. Introduces Charles Parish of Hamburg.	
Feb 24	To Sarah Goodridge. ALS. MHi. mDW 12350. Thanks her for letter.	
Feb 24	To Theodore Lyman, Jr. ALS. NhD. mDW 12352. Reports that the appropriation for Castle Island has passed.	
Feb 24	Motion by Webster for appointing a joint committee to examine private claims. Copy. DNA, RG 46. mDW 43927.	
Feb 25	To [Henry Willis Kinsman]. ALS. NNC. mDW 12354. Discusses financial matters.	
Feb 25	From John Davis (1761–1847). ALS. DLC. mDW 12361. Comments on Congress's attitude toward the Indian and French reparations questions, but mainly discusses the insolvent debtor laws, which he asks Webster to investigate.	
Feb 25	[Opinion on land title of Lewis Cass]. ANS. MiD-B. mDW 12355.	
Feb 26	From Lewis Cass. LC. DNA, RG 46. mDW 44406. Submits estimate of appropriations necessary to carry into effect the provisions of the treaty with the Chippewa.	
[Feb 26]	Amendment to bill for relief of Richard Hargrave Lee. AD. DNA, RG 46. mDW 44095.	
Feb 26	Amendments by DW to bill to regulate the public deposits. Printed. *Senate Journal*, 23d Cong., 2d sess., Serial 265, pp. 196–197.	
Feb 27	To Samuel S. Osgood. ANS. NhExP. mDW 12365. Wishes "to be regarded as your friend, & the friend of all American artists."	
Feb 27	Bill making appropriations for Indian annuities, etc., for 1835. AD. DNA, RG 46. mDW 44170.	
Feb 28	From Nicholas Biddle. LC. DLC. mDWs. Encloses letter to Samuel Jaudon, which he wishes Webster to read and forward.	
Feb 28	From Lewis Cass. LS. DNA, RG 46. mDW 44403.	

	Sends estimate of sum needed to fulfill Article 5 of the treaty with the Pottawatomie Indians of the Wabash.	
Feb 28	From Lewis Cass. LS. DNA, RG 46. mDW 44409. Sends estimate of the funds needed to fulfill the provisions of the treaty with the Pottawatomie Indians of Indiana.	
Feb 28	*From Daniel Fletcher Webster.*	33
Feb 28	*From Stephen White.*	34
[Feb 28]	Amendments to bill making appropriations for the civil and diplomatic expenses of the government for 1835. AD. DNA, RG 46. mDW 44165.	
[March 2]	To Edward Everett. AL (signature missing). MHi. mDW 12372. Van Tyne, p. 195. Reports on complaints in the Senate because the House is tied up with French reparations question.	
March 2	Amendment to bill for making appropriations for minister to Great Britain. Printed. *Senate Journal*, 23d Cong., 2d sess., Serial 265, p. 214.	
March 3	Report of the Committee on Finance relative to the documentary history of the Revolution. AD. DNA, RG 46. mDW 44346.	
March 4	From George Louis Mayer et al. LS. DLC. mDW 12374. Invite Webster to visit Lancaster, Pa.	
March 5	*To Caleb Cushing.*	35
[March 5]	To Edward Everett. ALS. MHi. mDW 12375. Asks Everett to endorse an item, perhaps a promissory note.	
[March 5]	To Joseph Gales and W. W. Seaton. AL. NN. mDW 12378. Encloses comments to be inserted in the *National Intelligencer* on the French reparations matter.	
March 5	*To Stephen White.*	36
[March 5]	[Editorial on the fortification bill]. AD (incomplete). NhD. mDW 12382. *National Intelligencer,* March 7, 1835.	
[March 7]	Memorandum on fees, *Colin Mitchel et al. v. United States,* 9 Peters 711 (1835); 15 Peters 52 (1841).	
[March 8]	*To [Joseph Gales and W. W. Seaton].*	36
March 10	*To Charles Handy Russell.*	37
March 10	To Charles Henry Thomas. ALS. MHi. mDW 12402. Discusses farming operations at Marshfield.	
March 10 [1835]	To Daniel Fletcher Webster. ALS. NhHi. mDW 12405. Urges Fletcher to meet with "men of business" every day.	
[March 10]	[Editorial on United States relations with France]. AD. DLC. mDW 12407.	

[March 10]	[Editorial on the publication of a letter of the French government(?)]. AD. DLC. mDW 12411.
March 17	From John Gardner et al. LS. DLC. mDW 12413. Citizens of York, Pa., tender Webster an invitation to a public dinner.
March 19	From John Strohm et al. LS. DLC. mDW 12422. Invite Webster to a "public entertainment" in Harrisburg.
March 19	To John Strohm et al. Copy. NhD. mDW 12416. Declines invitation to a public dinner.
March 19	*To Charles Henry Thomas.* 37
March 20	From Charles Naylor et al. LS. DLC. mDW 12424. Invite Webster to a public dinner in Philadelphia.
March 21	*To James Buchanan.* 38
March 23	To [Charles Naylor et al.]. Printed. *National Intelligencer*, April 2, 1835. Declines invitation.
March 26	To Charles Henry Thomas. ALS. NSyU. mDW 12429. Suggests he not kill the ox yet.
March 29	To Charles Henry Thomas. ALS. MHi. mDW 12340. Reports arrival in New York, his intention to proceed home; discusses farm affairs.
[c. March]	To Samuel Dunn Parker. ALS. CtY. mDW 12433. Asks to be excused from appearing with Parker in the Bicknell case.
April 2	*To [Edward Everett].* 38
April 4	From Harvey Lindsly. ALS. DLC. mDW 12436. Asks confirmation of proposition that Van Buren men will support DW's choice for Speaker of House of Representatives when Congress reconvenes.
April 6	To Charles Henry Thomas. ALS. MHi. mDW 12438. Reports his arrival in Boston; sends pear limbs for grafting.
April 6	*From Nicholas Biddle.* 39
April 8	*To Tristam Burges.* 40
April 8	To [the Judge of Probate, Suffolk County, Mass.]. ALS. NhD. mDW 12443. Asks that he or Henry Willis Kinsman be appointed administrator of the estate of Daniel Wilde, who was heavily in debt to Webster.
April 8	Power of attorney from Stephen White. DS. MWalB. mDW 39835–243.
April 8	Transfer of power of attorney of Stephen White to DW and from DW to Richard Smith. DS. MWalB. mDW 39835–244.
April 9	*From James Watson Webb.* 41
April 14	From Herman Le Roy. LS. NhHi. mDW 12453. Discusses exchange of correspondence between

	himself and George Law, his attorney, regarding Neapolitan claims.
April 16	To Israel Webster Kelly. ALS. NhHi. mDW 12457. W & S, 16: 255–256. Discusses repairs to the house at Franklin.
April 16	To M[orris] Robinson. ALS. UkLiU. mDW 12459. Sends note for discounting.
April 16	To Charles Henry Thomas. ALS. MHi. mDW 12460. Reports his arrival in Boston, the sale of a horse.
April 18	From John B. Hearne. ALS. NhD. mDW 12462. Requests copies of two of Webster's speeches.
April 19	To R. W. Greene. ALS. MWA. mDW 12464. Asks about a note and what cases are to be before the circuit court in Providence in June.
April 21	Bank draft for $250, payable to Mr. Pratt. DS. PHi. mDW 39835–49.
April 21	From Thomas Handasyd Perkins. Printed. Curtis, 1: 514–515. Discusses reparations in the French Chamber of Deputies.
April 26	To Israel Webster Kelly. ALS. NhHi. mDW 12466. Discusses repairs at Franklin.
April 27	To Samuel Atkinson. LS. MH. mDW 12468. Introduces John P. Bigelow of Boston.
April 27	To David Barton. LS. MH-H. mDW 12470. Introduces Bigelow.
April 27	To Henry A. Bullard. LS. James D. Landauer, New York, N.Y. mDW 12472. Introduces Bigelow.
April 27	To Henry Clay. LS. MH-H. mDW 12473. Introduces Bigelow.
April 27	To James F. Conover. LS. MBevHi. mDW 12475. Introduces a Mr. Loring of Boston.
April 27	To Thomas Ewing. LS. NhD. mDW 12477. Introduces Bigelow.
April 27	To Stephen Fales. LS. MH-H. mDW 12478. Introduces Bigelow.
April 27	To Henry Johnston. LS. MB. mDW 12480. Introduces Loring.
[April 27]	To Charles Henry Thomas. ALS. MHi. mDW 12482. Reports purchase of farm animals.
April 27	From George C. Barrett. ALS. NhHi. mDW 12485. Lists peach trees he has received.
April 28	*To Samuel Lewis Southard.*
[April 28]	To Charles Henry Thomas. ALS. MHi. mDW 12491. Makes arrangements to get his recently purchased cows to Marshfield.
[April 28]	To Nathaniel F. Williams. ALS. NhD. mDW 12496. Comments on the character and ability of Clement Dorsey.

42

April 28   From William Kenrick. ALS. NhHi. mDW 12499.
             Offers to sell Webster more peach trees and
             horse chestnuts.
April 29   To Samuel Frothingham. LS. NN. mDW 12501.
             Asks that checks received during his absence
             from Boston be credited to his account.
April 29   To Charles Henry Thomas. ALS. MHi. mDW
             12502. Arranges to get farm items to Marshfield.
April 30   To Edward Webster. ALS. NhHi. mDW 12505.
             Thanks him for letter and states that they will
             be happy to see him during the vacation.
[April 30]   Receipt to Frederick[?] Smith for $1190.36. ANS.
             MHi. mDW 39835–50.
[April]   From William Woodbridge. AL draft. MiD-B. mDW
             12507. Discusses Michigan's admission to the
             Union as a state.
May 1   To [Edward Everett].   44
May 4   To R. W. Greene. ALS. MWA. mDW 12513. States
             that he will consult with Greene's clients.
May 5   Deed transferring land in Merrimack County from
             Samuel Quimby to DW. DS. Deed Book, 41: 330.
             Office of the Register of Deeds, Merrimack
             County, Concord, N.H. mDWs.
May 8   To Nicholas Biddle. ALS. DLC. mDW 12515.
             Introduces Jacob McGaw.
May 8   Account of S. A. Frazar and DW, re payment of
             Neapolitan claims. ADS. DLC. mDW 39835–52.
May 9   To [Nicholas Biddle].   44
May 9   To R. W. Green. ALS. MWA. mDW 12520. States
             that he will be at Newport, but wants to see
             Greene before going to Rhode Island.
May 12   To [Nicholas Biddle].   45
May 13   Bank draft for $185.92, payable to K. & M. DS.
             NjMoHP. mDW 39835–54.
May 18   To Tristam Burges.   45
May 18   From Daniel Putnam King. ALS. NhHi. mDW
             12526. Sends copy of one of his speeches and
             informs Webster that he has named a son after
             him.
May 18   From Samuel Prentiss.   46
[May 21]   To [Abraham G. Stevens]. AL copy (incomplete).
             NhHi. mDW 12532. Sends instructions
             regarding furniture at Franklin.
May 26   From John Keyes, Josiah Bartlett, Phineas Howe.
             ALS by Keyes, signed also by others. DLC. mDW
             12538. Invite Webster to deliver the bicentennial
             address at Concord in September.
May 30   To [John] Connell. ALS. NIC. mDW 12540.
             Expects to go directly to Washington from
             Boston on June 2.

May 30	To Daniel Putnam King. Draft, with revisions in DW's hand. NhHi. mDW 12541. Van Tyne, p. 697. Thanks King for his address at the Lexington Battle celebration and for the compliment paid in naming his son after him.
May 31	To [Edward Everett]. 47
June 1	To Sarah Goodridge. ALS. MHi. mDW 12545. Hopes to see her at noon.
June 8	Opinion by DW on the Lisbon cases. Printed. Lisbon Cases (Washington, 1835).
June 8	Opinion by DW and F. C. Gray on the Cadiz cases. Printed. Cadiz Cases (Washington, 1835).
June 8	Opinion by DW and F. C. Gray on cases of compromise with captors. Printed. Cases of Compromise with Captors (Washington, 1835).
June 14	To Charles Henry Thomas. ALS. MHi. mDW 12547. Reports his arrival from Washington and his imminent departure for Newport.
June 22 [1835–1852]	To David Aiken Hall. ALS. NN. mDW 38443. Asks Hall to renew a note for $500.
[June 23]	To [Edward Everett]. ALS. MHi. mDW 12549. Suggests that Everett stop by his office.
June 23	To Charles Henry Thomas. ALS. NhD. mDW 12551. Intends to go to Marshfield on June 24.
June 27 [1835?–1852]	To John Agg. ALS. NhD. mDW 38159. Declines dinner invitation.
June 29	To R. W. Greene. ALS. MWA. mDW 12553. Agrees to see a Mr. Mann in his office on July 11.
[July 2]	To Edward Everett. 48
July 3	To R. W. Greene. ALS. MWA. mDW 12556. Discusses case about to be argued before the Court.
July 8	To R. W. Greene. ALS. MWA. mDW 12559. Proposes to see Mr. Mann on Friday.
July 14	Resolutions on the death of John Marshall, presented before the Suffolk Bar. Printed. Columbian Centinel, July 15, 1835.
July 18	To Abraham G. Stevens. ALS. NhD. mDW 12561. Expects to reach Franklin later in the week.
July 21	To Warren Dutton. ALS. NhD. mDW 12563. Had hoped to see Dutton and have his company on the trip to New Hampshire.
July 21	Promissory note for $2500 to Israel Thorndike. DS. ViU. mDW 39835–55.
July 23	From George Grennell, Jr., et al. LS. DLC. mDW 12566. Invite Webster to deliver address on the erection of a monument to commemorate the massacre of Lathrop's company by Indians under King Philip.
July 27	Deed transferring land in Merrimack County from

	Benjamin Shaw to DW. DS. Deed Book, 43: 131. Office of the Register of Deeds, Merrimack County, Concord, N.H. mDWs.	
Aug 1	Deed transferring land in Merrimack County from Samuel Sawyer to DW. ADS. Deed Book, 40: 511. Office of the Register of Deeds, Merrimack County, Concord, N.H. mDWs.	
[Aug 6]	To Edward Everett. ALS. MHi. mDW 12570. Introduces Mr. Robbins, son of Asher Robbins, senator from Rhode Island.	
Aug 9	From Benjamin F. Pepoon. ALS. NhHi. mDW 12572. Discusses paintings and education as a means of developing loyalty among youth of the United States.	
Aug 13	Bank draft for $5000, payable to "my note." DS. NjMoHP. mDW 39835–57.	
Aug 13	Bank draft for $20, payable to Henry Willis Kinsman. DS. NjMoHP. mDW 39835–56.	
Aug 14	*From William W. Stone, Daniel D. Brodhead, and William Gray.*	48
Aug 15	Bank draft for $20, payable to "self." DS. NjHi. mDW 39835–58.	
Aug 20	Bank draft for $300, payable to James Foster. DS. NjMoHP. mDW 39835–59.	
Aug 24	*To James Hervey Bingham.*	49
Aug 26	To [Henry] Wheaton. ALS. MB. mDWs. Introduces George Ticknor.	
Aug 28	Check to "AB" for $100. DS. NjMoHP. mDWs.	
Aug 29	To Seth Weston. ALS. NhHi. mDW 12600. *PC*, 2: 11. Instructs him on the mowing of property bordering river.	
Sept 2	*To Edward Everett.*	50
Sept 3	To Benjamin Abbot. Copy. NhHi. mDW 12604. *PC*, 2: 12. Acknowledges election as a trustee of Phillips Exeter Academy.	
Sept 4	Promissory note for $1200 to Edward Everett. DS. PP. mDW 39835–60.	
Sept 6	From William T. Otto. ALS. DLC. mDW 12606. On the mistaken belief that Webster had delivered a speech at Cambridge in which he discussed political issues important to the southern states, Otto requests a copy.	
Sept [7]	To Charles Henry Thomas, from Daniel Fletcher Webster (for DW). ALS. MHi. mDW 12609. Arranges to meet with Thomas later in the week.	
Sept 14	*Agreement between Daniel Webster and John Taylor, Jr.*	51
Sept 15	Elms Farm Accounts, by John Taylor (runs to 1849, Jan 9). AD. NhFr. mDWs.	

Sept 18	To [Abraham G. Stevens]. ALS. Esther and Mildred Stevens, West Franklin, N.H. mDW 12611. Asks for copies of certain accounts.	
Sept 19	Promissory note for $500 from Nathan Hale. ADS. MHi. mDW 39835-67.	
Sept 21	*To Caroline Le Roy Webster.*	52
[Sept 22]	To Caroline Le Roy Webster. ALS. NhHi. mDW 8964. Discusses his trip to Maine; reports death of Mary C. Silsbee.	
Sept 22	Promissory note for $500 from Nathan Hale. ADS. MHi. mDW 39835-69.	
Sept 23	To Jacob McGaw. ALS. NhD. mDW 12616. Expects to be in Bangor on Friday, but suffers from a "heavy cold."	
Sept 23	*To Caroline Le Roy Webster.*	53
Sept 25	*To Caroline Le Roy Webster.*	54
Sept 25	From John Quincy Adams. LS. NhD. mDW 12626. As one of the readers (along with James Kent and DW) for the American Peace Society prize of $1000, sends copies of four treatises on the subject of a "Congress or a Court of Nations for the amicable settlement of National differences and the abolition of War."	
Sept 25	From Allen Gilman et al. LS. DLC. mDW 12628. Invite Webster to a public dinner in Bangor.	
Sept 29	From Noah Webster. ALS. DLC. mDW 12631. Discusses the copyright law.	
Sept 30	*To Nicholas Biddle.*	55
Sept 30	From Benjamin Vaughan. ALS. NhD. mDW 12635. Sends DW several books.	
Sept	Bill from Moses Noyes for $5.83 for five bushels of rye. ADS. NhD. mDW 29835-71.	
Oct 3	*To [Henry Willis Kinsman].*	55
Oct 5	To [Samuel?] Upton. ALS. NhD. mDW 12640. Sends sketch of his remarks at Bangor.	
Oct 5	To Benjamin Vaughan. AN. PPAmP. mDW 12641. Extends his respects and appreciation.	
Oct 7	From Levi Cutter et al. Printed. *National Intelligencer*, Oct 14, 1835. Invite DW to a public dinner in Portland.	
Oct 7	To Levi Cutter et al. Printed. *W & S*, 16: 257-258. Declines invitation.	
Oct 7	From Abraham G. Stevens. ALS. Esther and Mildred Stevens, West Franklin, N.H. mDW 12643. Reports that he found the farm accounts.	
Oct 10	Bank draft for $33.75, payable to "Office Rent." DS. DLC. mDW 39835-72.	
Oct 10	Bank draft for $700, payable to Mr. Smith. DS. DLC. mDW 39835-73.	

Oct 12	To Edward Everett. Invitation. MHi. mDW 12644. Invites Everett to his house on Summer Street.
Oct 12	To Lemuel Humphrey. Invitation. NhHi. mDW 12646. Invites Humphrey to his house on Summer Street.
[Oct 13]	To [Edward Everett]. ALS. MHi. mDW 12649. Informs Everett that the gathering is a "*Gentleman* party."
Oct 16	Bank draft for $300, payable to Mr. Smith. DS. Charles J. Brockman, Jr., Athens, Ga. mDW 39835–74.
Oct 20	To Morris Robinson. ALS. NhD. mDWs. Sends check for $5000 for credit to his account.
Oct 21	Bank draft for $21.80, payable to Mr. Sawyer. DS. WaU. mDW 39835–75.
[Oct 22]	To William T. Otto. ALS draft. DLC. mDW 12607. Informs Otto of his mistake; his "sentiments on the Constitutional rights & obligations of the States" have long been known.
Oct 22	Bank draft for $8.25, payable to Mrs. Elizabeth Adams. DS. DLC. mDW 39835–76.
[Oct 23]	To Charles Henry Thomas. ANS. MHi. mDW 12651. Comments on the "silk business."
[Oct]	To Edward Everett. ALS. MHi. mDW 12563. Sends James Todd's address and requests him to answer Mr. Chauncey.
[Nov 2]	To Edward Everett. ALS. MHi. mDW 12654. Sends letter for Everett to read and criticize.
[Nov 2]	*To [Edward Everett].* 57
Nov 4	*To [Edward Everett].* 57
Nov 4	To [David Hoffman et al.]. Printed. *W & S*, 16: 258. Declines invitation to Whig festival in Baltimore.
Nov 5	*From Harmar Denny.* 58
Nov 6	To Edward Blake. Copy (from Kinsman, for himself and DW). MBBA. mDWs. Sends names of students reading law in Kinsman's and Webster's law office.
Nov 7	To Nathan Appleton. ALS. MB. mDW 12667. Sends letters (introducing Appleton) for Charles Vaughan, George Lafayette, and John Halkett.
Nov [7?]	To Sir Charles Richard Vaughan. ALS. UkOxU-AS. mDW 12738. Introduces Appleton.
Nov 10	*From Henry D. Sellers et al.* 60
Nov 11	*From Harmar Denny.* 61
Nov 11	From Harmar Denny et al. LS. DLC. mDW 12676. Ask Webster for political opinions.
[Nov 13]	To R. W. Greene. ALS. MWA. mDW 12680. Asks

	Greene if his attendance in the court at Providence on Monday is "indispensable."	
Nov 14	To Edward Everett. Invitation. MHi. mDW 12682. Invites Everett to meet the trustees of the Massachusetts Agricultural Society.	
Nov 15	To R. W. Greene. ALS. MWA. mDW 12684. Reports his arrival at Marshfield and plans to proceed to Boston.	
[Nov 15]	To Charles Henry Thomas. ALS. MHi. mDW 39028. Asks Thomas to prepare for the dinner for the trustees of the Massachusetts Agricultural Society.	
Nov 16	From Joseph Wallace, Samuel Shock, and George W. Harris.	62
Nov 16	Memorandum by Nathan Hale of $500 borrowed from DW. ADS. MHi. mDW 39835–78.	
[Nov 17?]	To Edward Everett. ALS. MHi. mDW 12690. Asks Everett for conference.	
[Nov 17?]	To Sarah Goodridge. ALS. MHi. mDW 9727. Offers to lend her $250.	
[Nov 19]	To Edward Everett.	63
Nov 20	To [Benjamin Bakewell].	63
Nov 20	To Harmar Denny. LS. NhD. mDW 12709. Discusses Pennsylvania nomination.	
Nov 20	To Harmar Denny et al.	64
Nov 20	From Elihu Chauncey. ALS. DLC. mDW 12711. Urges DW to honor invitation from Philadelphia.	
Nov 21	To James Longue.	65
Nov 21	From Daniel Webster, Abbott Lawrence, Joseph Story, Edward Everett et al. Printed. National Intelligencer, Dec 8, 1835. Recommend Sparks's Writings of Washington to the public.	
Nov 22	To Edward Everett.	66
Nov 23	To R. W. Greene. ALS. MWA. mDW 12718. Comments on decision at Providence; suggests that Mann may forward $200 or $300.	
Nov 26	Bank draft for $1140, payable to "interest on my note." DS. Richard E. Meyer, Elmira, N.Y. mDW 39835–80.	
Nov 27	From William Wallace Irwin.	66
[Nov 28?]	To Edward Everett.	68
Nov 28	To Joseph Wallace, Samuel Shock, and George W. Harris.	69
Nov 28	From Horace Binney et al. ALS by Binney, signed also by others. PHi. mDW 12370. Invite Webster to dinner in Philadelphia.	
Nov 30	To William Wallace Irwin.	69
Nov [?]	To Francis Alexander. ALS. NhD. mDW 12735. Thanks him for his picture of the Roman girl.	

Dec 16

Recommends Bryant P. Tilden, Jr., for appointment to West Point.
To John Quincy Adams. ALS. MHi. mDW 12780. W & S, 16: 261. Thanks Adams for his letter of September; states that essays will be forwarded to him in Washington, where he hopes to find time to read them, at which time he will confer with Adams.

Dec 17

From Nicholas Biddle. LC. DLC. mDWs. Introduces John McAran.

Dec 17

From Charles Miner.

73

Dec 19

To [Lewis Cass]. AN. DNA, RG 94. mDWs. Sends papers asking for appointment of Bryant P. Tilden, Jr., to West Point.

Dec 21

To Caleb Cushing. ALS. DLC. mDW 12784. Asks for conference with Cushing.

Dec 21

Motion by Webster relative to merchandise and other property destroyed in the New York fire. AD. DNA, RG 46. mDW 45397.

Dec 22

To John Pendleton Kennedy. ALS. MdBP. mDW 12787. Thanks Kennedy for comments on resolutions relating to the Baltimore and Ohio Railroad.

Dec 22

Memorial of Thomas Aspinwall for compensation for certain expenses incurred as United States consul at London. Copy. DNA, RG 46. mDW 45767.

Dec 22

Memorial of John Crowninshield and other public appraisers of Boston for a salary increase. DS. DNA, RG 46. mDW 45794.

Dec 22

Stock certificates to John Folsom for forty shares in the Massabesick Canal Corporation, Daniel Webster, president. DS. NhD. mDW 39835–82.

Dec 22

Motion by Webster for a statement of the number, extent, and direction of several railroads built or commenced. Copy. DNA, RG 46. mDW 45399.

Dec 22

Motion by Webster relative to the right of the United States to transport mail on several railroads. Copy. DNA, RG 46. mDW 45402.

Dec 23

To Caroline Le Roy Webster. ALS. NhHi. mDW 12788. Van Tyne, pp. 196–197. Comments on her trip to Plymouth, the fire in New York, and affairs in Washington.

Dec 24

To Warren Dutton. ALS. NhD. mDW 12791. Discusses Charles River Bridge matters and the impact Taney and Barbour are likely to have on the ultimate decision.

Dec 24

To John R. Grymes. ALS. MMarsW. mDW 12793.

	Discusses a case to be argued before the Supreme Court.
Dec 24	To Emeline Colby Webster Lindsly. ALS. DMaM. mDW 12795. Sends several gift books for Christmas stockings.
Dec 24	From R[alph] H[askins]. ALS draft. NhD. mDWs. Discusses a Holyoke land claim.
Dec 25	To Edward Curtis. ALS. NhD. mDW 12797. Discusses a bill for the relief of New York and the French reparations matter.
Dec 25	To Caroline Le Roy Webster. ALS. NhHi. mDW 12799. Discusses affairs in Washington and his hope of making a quick trip to Boston in February.
Dec 26	Memorial of Boston merchants requesting a salary increase for weighers and gaugers in the customs office. DS. DNA, RG 46. mDW 45806.
Dec 28	To Sarah Goodridge. ALS. MHi. mDW 12802. Sends her a check for $300.
Dec 28	To Caroline Le Roy Webster. ALS. NhHi. mDW 12804. Van Tyne, pp. 197–198. Discusses several accounts and activities in the Senate and House of Representatives.
Dec 28	From T. L. Savin. ALS. NhHi. mDW 12809. Asks for Webster's opinion regarding the activities of a canal company chartered by the Pennsylvania legislature.
Dec 28	Petition of the inhabitants of Manchester, Massachusetts, for harbor improvements. DS. DNA, RG 46. mDW 45747.
Dec 28	Report of the Committee on Finance on the petition of the owners of the brig Despatch and cargo. Copy. DNA, RG 46. mDW 45650.
Dec 28	Bill for the relief of the owners of the brig Despatch and cargo. Printed document. DNA, RG 46. mDW 45253.
Dec 29	Bill to regulate the deposits of the public money. Printed document, with MS insertions. DNA, RG 46. mDW 45169.
Dec 30	To the Commissioners under the Treaty with France. ALS by S. C. Phillips, signed also by DW. PPAmP. mDW 12813. Urge a rehearing of William Fettyplace's claim.
Dec 30	From Horace Binney et al. LS. DLC. mDW 12815. Ask Webster to name a day when he might join them in a public dinner.
Dec 31	Memorial of Joshua Hatch for a bounty on a lost fishing vessel. DS. DNA, RG 46. mDW 45797.
[Dec]	To Caleb Cushing. ALS. NN. mDW 12817. Wants to see Cushing "for a single moment."

[1835]	To Samuel Turell Armstrong. ALS. MHi. mDW 12824. Requests that he not retire from his post.
[1835]	To [Edward Everett]. AL. MHi. mDW 12827. Expresses the need to take action on some unidentified matter.
[1835]	To [Edward Everett]. AL. MHi. mDW 12828. Sends list of people to whom he would like letters written.
[1835]	To [Edward Everett]. ALS. MHi. mDW 12829. Asks him to confer with an Anti-Masonic leader from New York.
[1835]	To Mrs. Edward Everett. ALS. MHi. mDW 12831. Hopes that her health is restored.
[1835?]	To Mrs. Edward Everett. ALS. MHi. mDW 12842–a. Expresses his high respect and friendship.
[1835?]	To [Charles Henry Thomas]. AL. MHi. mDW 39012. Discusses the use of manure at Marshfield.
[1835?]	To Robert Charles Winthrop. ALS. MHi. mDW 12834. Remarks on the misunderstanding about where they were to meet.
[c. 1835]	"The Crisis" (editorial on Whig policy). AD. MHi. mDW 12835.
[1835–1836]	To Nicholas Biddle. ALS. DLC. mDW 38240. Asks for loan.
[1835–1836]	To Nicholas Biddle. ALS. DLC. mDW 38242. Asks for loan.
[1835–1836?]	To Henry Willis Kinsman. ALS. NNC. mDW 38688. Asks Kinsman to place enclosed letter (not found) in post office.
[1835–1837?]	To Charles Henry Thomas. ALS. MHi. mDW 38958. Plans to come to Marshfield.
[1835–1837?]	To Charles Henry Thomas. ALS. MHi. mDW 38967. Asks Thomas to get his horse at Boyden and Whitings.
[1835–1837]	From Martin Van Buren. Invitation. NhD. mDW 39101. Invites DW to dinner.
[1835–1839]	To Nicholas Biddle. ALS. DLC. mDW 38244. Introduces Mr. Phelps and Mr. Crockett of Kentucky.
[1835–1839]	Opinion in re heirs of James Maxwell. AD. NjP. mDW 39460.
[1835–1842]	To Nicholas Biddle. ALS. DLC. mDW 38252. Introduces Lee White, of Louisville, Ky.
[1835–1843]	To Tristam Burges. ALS. UkENL. mDW 38289. Reports that [John Plummer] H[ealy] will see him in Providence.
[1835–1844]	To Nicholas Biddle. ALS. DLC. mDW 38241. Sends statement of his "professional demands."

[1835–1852] To John Plummer Healy. ALS. MHi. mDW
       38629. Asks him to prepare article for the
       Boston Atlas.
[1835–1852] To [?]. Copy (extract). NhHi. mDW 39294. Van
       Tyne, p. 694. Discusses pain in his arm after a
       long period of shaking hands.
[1835–1852] To Nathaniel F. Williams. ALS. NhD. mDW
       39235. Asks Williams to call upon him at
       Barnum's.
[1835–1852] To Nathaniel F. Williams. ALS. NhD. mDW
       39237. Asks Williams to call on him at
       Barnum's.

1836

Jan 1   To Caroline Le Roy Webster. ALS. NhHi. mDW
       12843. *PC,* 2: 14–15. Wishes the family a happy
       new year; comments on his activities in
       Washington.
Jan 1   Stock certificate for one share in the Boston
       library. DS. MBAt. mDW 39835–83.
Jan 2   To George Washington Lay. ALS. DLC. mDW
       12847. Asks for short conference.
Jan 2   From Stephen Fairbanks. ALS. DNA, RG 46. mDW
       45690. Sends memorial requesting a higher
       salary for weighers and gaugers in the customs
       offices.
Jan 5   To Sarah Goodridge. ALS. MHi. mDW 12849.
       Sends her a check for $150.
Jan 6   To R. W. Greene. ALS. MWA. mDW 12853.
       Suggests that Greene request Mann to forward
       the remainder of his fees.
Jan 6   To [?]. ALS. NjP. mDW 12851. Suggests that
       there will likely be a "full bench" on the
       Supreme Court when the term commences.
Jan 8   From Samuel Smith. ALS. DLC. mDW 12854.
       Sends DW speech on Baltimore trade.
Jan 9   To Samuel Smith. ALS. MdHi. mDWs. Thanks
       him for speech and assures him that
       improvements for Baltimore will receive his
       "favorable consideration."
Jan 10   To [David] Daggett. AL (signature removed). CtY.
       mDWs. Answers Daggett's letter inquiring about
       a Mr. Wright, probably an "Imposter."
Jan 10   To Caroline Le Roy Webster. ALS. NhHi. mDW
       12856. Van Tyne, pp. 198–199. Writes of affairs
       in Washington, especially the French question.
Jan 10   From Nicholas Biddle. LC. DLC. mDWs. Inquires
       about the "French business."

[c. Jan 11]   To Joseph Gales and W. W. Seaton. AD. NhD. mDW 38382. Discusses an insertion to be made in his article on the right of instruction.

Jan 11   To Caroline Le Roy Webster. ALS. NhHi. mDW 12860. Van Tyne, p. 661. Discusses the cheese from Mr. Meacham.

Jan 11   Bill for relief of the sufferers by the fire in New York City. Printed document, with MS insertions. DNA, RG 46. mDW 45225.

Jan 11   Memorial of Boston merchants for a salary increase for inspectors at the port of Boston. Copy. DNA, RG 46. mDW 45817.

Jan 12   From Charles King. ALS. DLC. mDW 12862. Discusses French reparations.

Jan 12   Editorial on instruction of senators by the Virginia legislature. AD. NhD. mDW 12922. *National Intelligencer*, Jan 12, 1836.

Jan 12   Bill in addition to the act of May 24, 1828, entitled "An act to authorize the licensing of Vessels to be employed in the Mackerel fishery." Copy. DNA, RG 46. mDW 45228.

Jan 12   Motion by DW for returns of the Bank of the United States and deposit banks. AD. DNA, RG 46. mDW 45404.

Jan 12   Petition of certain inhabitants of Erie County, Pa., for land from the United States on condition that they settle it. DS. DNA, RG 46. mDW 46019.

Jan 13   Motion to remove injunction of secrecy from the vote on Roger B. Taney. AD. DNA, RG 46. mDW 46399.

Jan 13   From [Samuel J. May], Secretary of the Massachusetts Antislavery Society. Printed (excerpt). Curtis, 1: 525. Urges abolition of slavery in the District of Columbia.

Jan 14   From R[alph] H[askins]. ALS draft. NhD. mDWs. Discusses his land claim matter.

Jan 15   *To Nicholas Biddle.*   74

Jan 15   *To Daniel Fletcher Webster.*   75

Jan 15   To Caleb Cushing. ALS. NN. mDW 12868. Invites him to dinner with Lord Selkirk and others.

[Jan 17]   To Caroline Le Roy Webster. ALS. NhHi. mDW 12871. *PC*, 2: 18–19. Discusses a case to come before the Supreme Court, his dinner party, affairs in Washington, and comments on the death of Grace Webster Everett.

Jan 20   From Mahlon Dickerson. LC. DNA, RG 45. mDWs. Reports that there is no vacancy in the midshipman ranks to which the son of Colonel Brooks might be appointed.

Jan 21   From J. Stephenson. ALS. DLC. mDW 12875. Asks
              for Chinese mulberry seeds.
Jan 23   From J. R. Vinton. ALS. DNA, RG 46. mDW
              46008. Asks for Senate investigation and action
              on his memorial for pay equal to the brevet
              rank in the army.
[Jan 24]   To Joseph Gales and W. W. Seaton. AL. NhD.
              mDW 12884. Requests the insertion of a
              comment in the National Intelligencer.
[Jan 24]   To Joseph Gales. ALS. NhD. mDW 12881. Asks
              that John Quincy Adams's speech be printed in
              the National Intelligencer of Jan 25.
Jan 24   To Caroline Le Roy Webster.   76
Jan 25   To Caleb Cushing. AL. NN. mDW 12890. Invites
              Cushing to dinner.
[Jan 25]   Memorial of clerks of customs of Boston for a
              salary increase. DS. DNA, RG 46. mDW 45810.
[Jan 25]   Memorial of the inspectors of the port of Boston
              for a salary increase. DS. DNA, RG 46. mDW
              45813.
Jan 26   To Edward Everett. ALS. MHi. mDW 12893. PC,
              2: 17–18. Expresses his sympathy for the
              Everetts over the death of their daughter, Grace
              Webster.
Jan 26   To Isaac L. Hedge. Printed. MHi Proc., 46
              (January 1913): 275. Discusses Adams's attack
              on him and asks for list of people to whom he
              might send speeches.
Jan 26   To Solomon Lincoln. ALS. NhD. mDW 12895.
              Asks for a list of people in eastern Massachu-
              setts to whom he might send copies of his
              recent speech.
Jan 27   To Edward Everett.   78
Jan 27   Bill for the relief of Charles I. Catlett. Printed
              document. DNA, RG 46. mDW 45231.
Jan 27   Bill making an additional appropriation for
              repressing "hostilities commenced by the
              Seminole Indians." Printed document. DNA, RG
              46. mDW 45545.
Jan 28   To Samuel Frothingham.   79
Jan 28   Bill for the relief of Henry Wainwright. AD. DNA,
              RG 46. mDW 45232.
Jan 29   To Caroline Le Roy Webster. ALS. NhHi. mDW
              12904. Van Tyne, pp. 200–201. Discusses Great
              Britain's offer to mediate, activities in
              Washington, and the response to Adams's
              speech.
Jan 29   From Charles J. Holmes. ALS. DLC. mDW 12907.
              Praises Webster's fortification bill speech and
              denounces Adams's speech.

Jan 30	*To Edward Curtis.*	80
Jan 30	To John Randolph Grymes. ALS. NhD. mDW 12914. Reports the completion of the argument in the Supreme Court case, *New Orleans* v. *United States.*, 10 Peters 662 (1836).	
[Jan]	To Caleb Cushing. ALS. NN. mDW 12917. Thanks him for the use of certain papers.	
[Jan]	To Henry Willis Kinsman. ALS. NhD. mDW 12920. States that he now intends going to Boston when Congress recesses to arrange some financial affairs.	
Feb 2	To R. W. Greene. ALS. MWA. mDW 12943. Reports receipt of money due on Leland's note.	
Feb 2	To Caroline Le Roy Webster. ALS. NhHi. mDW 12945. Van Tyne, pp. 201–202. Comments on her letter-writing, his health, and Senate speeches on the French question.	
Feb 3	Bill for settlement of state claims against the United States for advances made during the War of 1812. AD draft. DNA, RG 46. mDW 45234.	
Feb 4	*To Charles Henry Thomas.*	81
Feb 4	From Richard Salter Storrs. ALS. NhHi. mDW 12958. Thanks Webster for pamphlets.	
Feb 5	Bill making appropriations for the support of the government in 1836. Printed document. DNA, RG 46. mDW 45435.	
Feb 7	*To Edward Everett, with enclosure to Edward C. Marshall, Feb. 6.*	85
[Feb 8]	From Nicholas Biddle. LC. DLC. mDWs. Asks for several copies of Webster's speech ("one of the very best that *even you* ever made") on the three-million bill.	
Feb 8	Bill to authorize importation of certain bells duty free. Printed document. DNA, RG 46. mDW 45238.	
Feb 9	To Caroline Le Roy Webster. ALS. NhHi. mDW 12968. Van Tyne, pp. 203–204. Thanks her for a letter, reports on his health and Washington society.	
[Feb 10]	[Editorial note on the bank bill in the Pennsylvania legislature]. AD. NhD. mDW 12972.	
Feb 11	To [Henry Willis Kinsman?]. ALS. NhD. mDW 12973. Discusses distributing speeches to Massachusetts legislators.	
[Feb 13]	To Joseph Gales. ALS. NhD. mDW 38380. Sends papers (not found) showing how the Virginia	

legislature handled the expunging resolutions(?).

Feb 15 To Caroline Le Roy Webster. ALS. NhHi. mDW 12976. Van Tyne, pp. 578–579 (under year 1830). Expresses his sympathy over the death of Mrs. Webster's sister, Mrs. Newbold.

Feb 15 To Daniel Fletcher Webster. ALS. NhHi. mDW 12979. States his intention to leave for home "as soon as the boats run."

Feb 15 Motion by DW to obtain pension for James Bohonon. Copy. DNA, RG 46. mDW 45406.

Feb 16 To Mahlon Dickerson. ALS. Bobbie R. Harper, Seabrook, Texas. mDW 12981. Endorses the efforts of a J. W. Boyd to obtain an appointment.

Feb 16 To Mahlon Dickerson (from DW et al.). LS. MHi. mDW 12983. Recommend John Brooks for appointment as midshipman.

Feb 16 To Solomon Lincoln. ALS. Eugene C. Gerhart, Binghamton, N.Y. mDWs. Thanks him for list of people to whom speeches should be sent.

Feb 16 To Caroline Le Roy Webster. ALS. NhHi. mDW 12985. Sends her a "Mass. Bank Bill"; comments on his work at answering letters and preparing to appear before the Supreme Court.

Feb 19 [Memorandum by Levi Lincoln of a meeting with DW re his presidential nomination].   87

Feb 20 To Charles P. Huntington. ALS. MHaDP. mDW 12992. MHi Proc., 57 (February 1924): 271–272. Denies a statement that he and Ezekiel were Masons while at Dartmouth College.

Feb 20 To Henry Willis Kinsman.   88

Feb 20 From Edward Hitchcock. ALS. DLC. mDW 12999. Thanks Webster for the notice of his publication, Report on the Geology, Mineralogy, Botany, and Zoology of Massachusetts (1833).

Feb 21 To Caroline Le Roy Webster. ALS. NhHi. mDW 13006. Van Tyne, pp. 591–592. Discusses the death of Mrs. Newbold.

Feb 22 To Levi Woodbury. Copy. DNA, RG 46. mDW 45684. Inquires on behalf of the Senate Committee on Finance about the indebtedness of the Bank of Steubenville and the German Bank of Wooster.

Feb 23 From Levi Woodbury. LS. DNA, RG 46. mDW 45682. Reports on the indebtedness of the Bank of Steubenville and the German Bank of Wooster to the United States.

Feb 24	From Thomas George Pratt. ALS. NhHi. mDW 13009. Van Tyne, p. 204. Asks DW to clarify what he said in a speech in Baltimore shortly after the removal of the deposits.
Feb 27	*To Henry Willis Kinsman.* 88
Feb 27	To Thomas George Platt. AL copy. NhHi. mDW 13011. Van Tyne, pp. 204–205. Denies that he made any remarks in Baltimore that could be interpreted as starting the recent riots there.
Feb 27	From Mahlon Dickerson. LC. DNA, RG 45. mDWs. Acknowledges DW's letter recommending J. W. Boyd.
Feb 29	To H. Hunt. ALS draft. NhHi. mDW 13014. Van Tyne, p. 205. Discusses the naturalization of foreigners.
Feb 29	*To Henry Willis Kinsman.* 89
[Feb 29]	"The Supreme Court" (editorial). AD. NN. mDW 13021.
March 2	*To Charles Henry Thomas.* 90
March 3	To Samuel Joseph May. ALS. NhD. mDW 13030. Acknowledges receipt of petitions for abolition of slavery in the District of Columbia; will present them as soon as possible.
March 3	Bill to prescribe the mode of paying pensions. Printed document with AN. DNA, RG 46. mDW 45613.
March 3	Bill authorizing the secretary of the treasury to act as agent of the United States in all matters relating to stock in the Bank of the United States. Printed document. DNA, RG 46. mDW 45616.
March 3	Bill authorizing the secretary of war to transfer part of the appropriation for the suppression of Indian hostilities in Florida to subsistence accounts. Printed document. DNA, RG 46. mDW 45626.
March 4	Report of the Committee on Manufactures on allowing a drawback of duties on imported hemp. Printed document. DNA, RG 46. mDW 45950.
March 4	Bill to allow drawback of duties on imported hemp, when manufactured into cordage and exported. Printed document. DNA, RG 46. mDW 45240.
March 4	Opinion of Daniel Webster on the title to land of the Duke of Alagon. Printed. *Legal Opinions of the Honourable Joseph M. White, . . . Daniel Webster, . . . and Edward Livingston, . . . in relation to the Title of the Duke of Alagon* (New York, 1837), p. 20.

Warren Dutton, for Sunday dinner in
Philadelphia.

March 16	*To [Nicholas Biddle].*	96
March 16	*From Fisher Ames Harding.*	96
March 16	From Parker Noyes. ALS. DLC. mDW 13074. Thanks Webster for his speech on the fortification bill.	
March 16	Memorial of citizens of Massachusetts (mDW 45882, 45919, 45877); and Wayne County, Michigan Territory (mDW 45871), for the abolition of slavery in the District of Columbia. DS. DNA, RG 46.	
[March 16]	Petition of B. Aymar & Co. of New York for refund of duties levied on merchandise destroyed by fire. ADS. DNA, RG 46. mDW 45936.	
March 18	From Tristam Burges. ALS. NhD. mDW 13077. Discusses the claim of a Mrs. Davis against France and asks Webster's assistance.	
March 19	To Henry Willis Kinsman. ALS. Dr. Gurdon S. Pulford, Palo Alto, Calif. mDW 13081. Plans to reach Baltimore the next day.	
March 20	From J. Ruggles. ALS. MHi. mDW 13084. Discusses his efforts to purchase lime for Marshfield.	
March 24	To Edward Everett. ALS. MHi. mDW 14174.	
[1836–1839]	Accepts invitation to dinner.	
March 28	To Thomas Aspinwall. LS. NhD. mDW 13085. Asks that he be sent a small, inexpensive machine "for breaking up or grinding *bones* for the uses of Agriculture."	
March 28	*To John Davis (1787–1854).*	97
March 28	To Eliza Adams Upham. ALS. CtY. mDW 13092. Asks her to serve as their cook; tells her that Daniel Fletcher is engaged to Caroline White.	
March 30	*From Samuel Price Carson.*	99
[March]	To Caleb Cushing. ALS. NN. mDW 13103. Fuess, *Cushing*, 1: 230 (excerpt). Sends copies of Clayton's speech, in which he "has seen fit to put a compliment to me in the end."	
[March]	To [Daniel Fletcher Webster?]. ALS. NhHi. mDW 13099. Van Tyne, p. 723. Sends a newspaper clipping reporting Livingston's fee of $25,000 for representing New Orleans before the Supreme Court in *New Orleans* v. *United States*, 10 Peters 662 (1836); states that he expects to receive a "pretty handsome sum."	
March [?]	Motion by DW that memorials on the abolition of slavery presented by him be referred to the Committee on the District of Columbia	

	(memorandum only). AD. DNA, RG 46. mDW 45408.	
April 4	From Walter Lowrie (with ANS by DW, c. April 7, addressed to Joseph Story). ALS. NhD. mDWs. Asks for a copy of the catalogue of books in the Harvard University library.	
April 5	To John Farmer. ALS. NhHi. mDW 13106. States that on the enclosed papers (not found), Farmer will find "all I can say relative to my class-mates, in the particulars required."	
April 6	Acknowledgment of DW's promissory note to John Welch for $4928. DS. NhHi. mDW 39835–86.	
April 6	Bills for the relief of Robert McJimsey (mDW 45531); John Fraser and Company, of Charleston, S.C. (mDW 45533); James Robertson of South Carolina (mDW 45543). Printed documents. DNA, RG 46.	
April 7	*To John Davis (1787–1854).*	100
April 7	To Charles Henry Thomas. ALS. MHi. mDW 13112. Discusses the purchase of land adjacent to the Marshfield farm.	
April 7	From Francis Lieber. ALS. NhD. mDW 13115. Asks Webster to back a memorial he has presented to Congress for support of a statistical study of the United States.	
[c. April 7]	To Joseph Story. ANS. NhD. mDWs. Asks Story to furnish Lowrie with catalogue of the Harvard library.	
April 8	*To Edward Everett.*	101
April 10	*From John Davis (1787–1854).*	102
April 12	Bill repealing Section 14 of the act of April 10, 1816, to incorporate the subscribers of the Bank of the United States. Printed document. DNA, RG 46. mDW 45624.	
April 12	Bills for the relief of Asa Armington et al. (mDW 45535); John F. Lewis (mDW 45540). Printed documents. DNA, RG 46.	
April 13	To John Davis (1787–1854). ALS. DNA, RG 46. mDW 45763. Urges Davis to support the petition of the inhabitants of Duxbury, Plymouth, and Kingston, Mass., requesting that measures be taken to protect their harbor.	
April 13	*To Edward Everett.*	102
April 13	To Timothy Fletcher. ALS. MHi. mDW 13125. Sends fruit trees for Marshfield.	
April 13	To [Andrew Jackson], from John Davis and DW. LS. DNA, RG 59. mDWs. Recommend Andrew Ritchie for consul at Rome.	
April 13	*To Henry Willis Kinsman.*	103

April 13   To [Francis Lieber]. ALS. CSmH. mDW 8659.
                States that he will support Lieber's memorial.
April 13   To James William Paige. ALS. MH. mDW 13130.
                Asks him to take charge of fruit trees he
                purchased in New York.
April 13   From Nicholas Biddle. LC. DLC. mDWs. Discusses
                the status of the Bank as accepted by its
                directors.

April 15   To [Timothy Fletcher]. ALS. MHi. mDW 13139.
                Sends instructions for building a "little summer
                house . . . on Cherry Hill."
April 15   Motion by DW for printing certain bank
                statements. AD. DNA, RG 46. mDW 45409.
April 16   Deed transferring land in Plymouth County,
                Mass., from Elizabeth Whitman to DW. DS.
                Deed Book, 189: 42. Office of the Register of
                Deeds, Plymouth County, Plymouth, Mass.
                mDWs.
April 18   From Thomas L. Winthrop et al. (to DW and John
                Davis, 1787–1854). LS. NN. mDW 13144. Ask
                them to support the claims of the New England
                Mississippi Land Company in the Senate.
April 19   To [Timothy Fletcher]. ALS. MHi. mDW 13147.
                Discusses improvements at Marshfield.

April 21   Bill to remit duties upon certain goods destroyed
                in the fire in New York City. AD. DNA, RG 46.
                mDW 45243.
April 21   Bill making appropriations for the civil and
                diplomatic expenses of government for 1836.
                Printed document, with MS insertions and
                amendments. DNA, RG 46. mDW 45549.
April 22   To Caroline Le Roy Webster. ALS. NhHi. mDW
                13154. Discusses her proposed activities and
                his own in Washington.
April 23   To John Farmer. ALS. NhHi. mDW 13158. Sends
                document and thanks him for a recent petition.
April 23   To R. W. Greene. ALS. MWA. mDW 13160.
                Requests him to draft a closing argument in
                Hammond's case and forward it to him.
[April 24]   To Francis Ormond Jonathan Smith. ALS. MeHi.
                mDWs. Sends him communication on the
                Florida railroad.
April 24   To Charles Henry Thomas. ALS. MHi. mDW
                13163. Discusses purchases for Marshfield.
April 25   Amendment by DW to bill authorizing the

secretary of the treasury to act as agent of the
United States in all matters relating to stock in
the Bank of the United States. AD. DNA, RG
46. mDW 45621.

April 25   Motion by DW relative to the salaries of clerks in
the Executive Department. AD. DNA, RG 46.
mDW 45411.

April 26   Bill providing for the salaries of specified officers
of the government. Printed document. DNA, RG
46. mDW 45628.

April 26   Bill making appropriations for the expenses of the
Indian Department, Indian annuities, etc.
Printed document with MS insertions and
amendments. DNA, RG 46. mDW 45456.

April 28   To [Nicholas Biddle.]. ALS. DLC. mDW 13167.
Asks for his views regarding "the real causes of
the present embarrassment."

April 28   From Lewis Cass. LC. DNA, RG 107. mDWs.
Discusses the problems involved in issuing a
medal commemorating General Ripley's
activities in the War of 1812.

April 28   Account with Linnaean Botanic Gardens of
Flushing, N.Y. ADS. NhHi. mDW 39835–88.

April 29   To [Timothy Fletcher]. ALS. NhHi. mDW 13168.
Van Tyne, pp. 661–662. Discusses trees for his
summer house on Cherry Hill.

April 29   *To Caroline Le Roy Webster.*   *106*

[April 30]   To Lewis Cass. ALS. DNA, RG 107. mDW 57175.
States that he will attend to the matter of
General Ripley's medal.

April 30   From Cary A. Harris. LC. DNA, RG 107. mDWs.
Sends estimate of money needed to fulfill the
provisions of certain Indian treaties.

April 30   From Cary A. Harris. LC. DNA, RG 107. mDWs.
Sends estimate of the amount needed for the
"removal and subsistence of Indians in 1836."

May 4   From Lewis Cass. LC. DNA, RG 107. mDWs.
Requests the attention of the Committee on
Finance to the estimates of the officer of the
Clothing Bureau.

May 4   From Lewis Cass. LC. DNA, RG 107. mDWs.
Discusses the matter of clerks in the War
Department, their compensation, and their
duties.

May 4   *From Fisher Ames Harding.*   *107*

May 4–Sept 12   Abstracts of letters from Fisher Ames Harding. Copy.
ViU. mDW 13178. Details land purchases.

May 4   *From Joseph Ricketson Williams, with enclosure*
of Receipt, May 4.   *108*

May 5   From Lewis Cass. LC. DNA, RG 107. mDWs.

	Sends estimate of the funds needed for the fulfillment of a provision of the Treaty of Oct 26, 1832, with the Pottawatomie Indians.	
May 5	Bill making appropriations for the support of the army for 1836. Printed document with AD amendments. DNA, RG 46. mDW 45447.	
May 6	*To James Watson Webb.*	*108*
May 6	To Mrs. Edward Livingston. Printed. Louise Livingston Hunt, *Memoir of Mrs. Edward Livingston* (New York, 1886), pp. 150–151. Promises to write to New Orleans regarding his and Edward Livingston's fees in the argument of *New Orleans* v. *United States*, 10 Peters 662 (1836).	
May 6	From Peter Force. ALS. DNA, RG 46. mDW 45686. Discusses progress and expenses incurred in preparing his *Documentary History of the American Revolution*.	
May 7	To William Anderson. Printed. *W & S*, 16: 277–278. Informs Anderson that his Murphy farm is for sale through Israel Webster Kelly of Salisbury.	
May 7	*To Edward Everett.*	*109*
May 7	To [Timothy Fletcher]. ALS. MHi. mDW 13196. Discusses farming at Marshfield.	
May 9	To [Timothy Fletcher]. ALS. MHi. mDW 13200. Instructs him on care of trees at Marshfield.	
May 9	To Charles Henry Thomas. ALS. MHi. mDW 13203. Discusses the problems with the town at Marshfield in the construction of a road.	
May 9	Motion by DW calling upon the secretary of war for information relative to the contract for removing the Creek Indians. AD. DNA, RG 46. mDW 45413.	
May 9	Bill making appropriations for the defense of the western frontier. Printed document with AD amendments. DNA, RG 46. mDW 45636.	
May 13	To Daniel Fletcher Webster. ALS. NhHi. mDW 13207. Van Tyne, p. 662. Asks about his progress west.	
May 16	To Benjamin Bakewell. LS. PPiHi. mDW 13210. Introduces Thomas Handasyd Perkins.	
May 16	To Charles Pelham Curtis. LS. OCHP. mDW 13211. Introduces Robert Todd Lytle, surveyor general for Ohio.	
May 16	To Edward Curtis. ALS. Mrs. Chester Hubbard, Wheeling, W. Va. mDW 13213. Introduces William F. Peterson of Wheeling.	
May 16	To Virgil David. ALS. ICU. mDW 13221. Accepts membership in the Lawrenceville Lyceum.	

May 16   To Isaac P. Davis. LS. OCHP. mDW 13222.
              Introduces General Robert Todd Lytle, surveyor
              general of the United States for Ohio.
May 16   *To Phineas Davis.*   110
May 16   *To Fisher Ames Harding.*   112
May 16   *To Perkins & Co.*   113
May 16   To Stephen White. LS. OCHP. mDW 13230.
              Introduces Lytle.
May 17   From Lewis Cass. LC. DNA, RG 107. mDWs. Asks
              that annuities for Indians be taken up by the
              Senate as soon as convenient so that threats of
              hostility may be lessened.
May 17   *From Fisher Ames Harding.*   113
May 18   From Phineas Davis. ALS. ViU. mDW 13235.
              Describes land he has purchased for Webster
              and Davis.
May 19   To William Gaston. ALS. NcU. mDW 13239.
              W & S, 16: 277. Encloses Mr. Vaughan's letter
              to Gaston.
May 19   From Lewis Cass. LC. DNA, RG 75. mDW 57088.
              Discusses the Creek hostilities and the necessity
              of expediting their removal west of the Missis-
              sippi River.
May 20   Bill making appropriations for the suppression of
              hostilities by the Creek Indians. Printed
              document. DNA, RG 46. mDW 45644.
May 21   From Fisher Ames Harding. ALS. ViU. mDW
              13241. Reports the sale of some land he had
              purchased for DW.
May 21   Motion by DW for information relative to the
              northeastern boundary. Copy. DNA, RG 46.
              mDW 45415.
May 23   To [Timothy Fletcher]. ALS. MHi. mDW 13243.
              Discusses Marshfield farm matters.
May 23   To [Israel Webster Kelly]. ALS. NhHi. mDW 13247.
              W & S, 16: 278. Discusses the sale price of his
              Murphy (Londonderry) land.
May 23   *From Phineas Davis.*   114
May 24   *From Henry L. Kinney.*   114
May 24   *From Joseph Ricketson Williams.*   115
May 25   *To Henry Colman.*   117
May 25   From Levi Woodbury. DS. DNA, RG 46. mDWs.
              Senate Documents, 24th Cong., 1st sess., Serial
              283, Doc. No. 385, p. 2. Returns a petition and
              other papers relating to the Union Bank of
              Maryland.
May 26   To H. J. Brown et al. ALS facsimile. PLF. mDW
              13265. Thanks the Goethean Literary Society
              of Franklin and Marshall College for naming
              him an honorary member.

May 26   To [Herman] Le Roy.   117

May 26   Authorization to Phineas Davis to invest $5000
and to draw on him for said amount. ADS.
NhD. mDW 39835–95.

May 26   Motion by DW authorizing the secretary of the
treasury to correct a clerical error in the awards
of the commissioners under the Treaty of 1831
with France. AD. DNA, RG 46. mDW 45381.

May 26   Motion by DW relative to banking charters granted
by the legislative council of Florida. AD. DNA,
RG 46. mDW 45417.

May 27   To R. W. Greene. ALS. MWA. mDW 13267.
Discusses the case of *Allen* v. *Hammond*, 11
Peters 63 (1837).

May 28   To Perkins & Co. ALS. MHi. mDW 13270. Reports
that he has forwarded letters from Thomas
Handasyd Perkins and comments on the
distribution question before Congress.

May 28   From R[alph] H[askins]. ALS draft. NhD. mDWs.
Discusses his land claim.

May 29   To Martin Van Buren.   118

May 30   To Charles Henry Thomas. ALS. MHi. mDW
13273. Discusses affairs at Marshfield.

May 30   From Phineas Davis.   118

May 31   Appointment of Select Committee on Senate Bill
42 to regulate the deposits of the public money.
AD. DNA, RG 46. mDW 45419.

[May]   Memorandum authorizing John Plummer Healy to
accept drafts on DW by William L. D. Ewing
($3000), Felix Grundy ($3000+), Jacob
Bigelow ($1000–1500), DFW ($300). AD. MHi.
mDW 14288.

June 1   From J. Pearce. ALS. DLC. mDW 13284. Queries
Webster about his attribution of the comment,
"Let the people take care of themselves, and the
Government, of itself," to Silas Wright.

June 2   To [?]. LS. Ia-HA. mDW 13286. Introduces George
W. Jones, territorial delegate to Congress from
Wisconsin, in three identical letters.

June 2   From Phineas Davis. ALS. ViU. mDW 13289.
Discusses land purchases in the Detroit area.

June 2   From Fisher Ames Harding.   119

June 3   To [?]. ALS. MHi. mDW 13301. Suggests that the
paragraph in newspapers reporting the sale of
his cheese might be contradicted.

June 3   From Herman Le Roy.   122

June 3   Bill to regulate the deposits of the public money.
Printed document, with MS insertions. DNA,
RG 46. mDW 45256.

June 4   To Charles Henry Thomas. ALS. MHi. mDW
              13306. Comments on the farm and family.
June 4   From Edward Everett. LC. MHi. mDW 13309.
              Discusses an Anti-Masonic attack on him that
              appeared in the *Concord Freeman*.
June 4   From [Henry Willis Kinsman]. AL incomplete.
              NhHi. mDW 13311. Discusses two cases
              involving French claims.
June 5   *From Phineas Davis.*   *124*
June 6   To [Edward Everett]. ALS. MHi. mDW 13317.
              Suggests that Everett meet the attacks on him
              through anonymous publications in newspapers.
June 6   To Henry Willis Kinsman. ALS. NhD. mDW
              13321. Reports on the Fettyplace matter, on
              which he received an answer from the Treasury
              Department.
June 6   To Charles Henry Thomas. ALS. MHi. mDW
              13323. Discusses Marshfield affairs.
June 6   *From Joseph Warren Scott.*   *126*
June 6   From Joseph Ricketson Williams. ALS. ViU. mDW
              13329. States that he has invested $2,017.67 in
              land for DW.
June 7   From Fisher Ames Harding (enclosed with John A.
              Rockwell to DW, July 13, 1836). ALS. ViU.
              mDW 13456. Discusses Rockwell's speculative
              venture.
June [7]   *From Joseph Ricketson Williams.*   *127*
June 9   To [Israel Webster Kelly]. ALS. NhHi. mDW
              13325. Van Tyne, p. 663. Discusses his problems
              with Josiah White on New Hampshire property.
June 9   John Davis to Phineas [Davis], with ANS by DW
              to [Phineas Davis, c. June 9]. ALS. H. Stanton
              Hill, Altadena, Calif. mDWs. Accedes to
              Davis's suggestion regarding coal found on
              land he had purchased for DW.
June 10   To Samuel Ayer Bradley. Typed copy. NhD. mDW
              13336. States that he will pay close attention to
              Captain Porter's petition.
June 10   To Lucius Lyon. ALS copy. MHi. mDW 13338.
              Inquires about the type of plow used for
              planting corn on the prairie lands.
June 11   To Henry Willis Kinsman. ALS. NhHi. mDW
              13340. Sends scrip for distribution to its owners.
June 11   *To Perkins & Co.*   *128*
June 11   *From Simon Kinney.*   *128*
June 12   *To Daniel Fletcher Webster.*   *129*
June 12   *From John Catron.*   *131*
June 13   To Charles Henry Thomas. ALS. MHi. mDW
              13353. Sends copies of correspondence with
              Lucius Lyon regarding the planting of corn in
              Michigan.

June 13   From [Henry Willis Kinsman]. AL draft. NhHi.
             mDW 13354. Discusses a French claims case.
June 14   From Fisher Ames Harding. ALS. ViU. mDW
             13358. Discusses land purchases; comments on
             Daniel Fletcher's activities.
June 14   From Joseph Ricketson Williams. ALS. ViU. mDW
             13361. Discusses land purchases.
June 15   To Daniel Fletcher Webster. ALS. NhHi. mDW
             13363. PC, 2: 20. Discusses land purchases.
June 15   Motion by DW calling upon the secretary of the
             treasury for information relative to marine
             hospitals. AD. DNA, RG 46. mDW 45421.
June 16   To Henry Willis Kinsman. ALS. NhHi. mDW
             13365. Sends packet of French scrip to be
             delivered to its owners.
June 16   *From Phineas Davis.*   *133*
June 16   Bill in addition to the "act making appropriations
             in part for the support of Government for the
             year, 1836." Copy. DNA, RG 46. mDW 45374.
June 17   To John Sergeant et al. LS. MH. mDW 13371.
             Declines invitation from friends of Harrison
             and Granger to celebrate July 4 with them.
June 18   *To Fisher Ames Harding.*   *134*
June 18   To Henry Willis Kinsman. ALS. NNC. mDW
             13377. Asks Kinsman to accept Joseph
             Ricketson Williams's draft on him.
June 20   *To Perkins & Co.*   *135*
June 20   From Phineas Davis. ALS. ViU. mDW 13381.
             Discusses land purchases in Wisconsin and
             Michigan territories.
June 20   *From Henry L. Kinney.*   *135*
June 20   *From Herman Le Roy.*   *137*
June 20   From George C. Washington. ALS. DLC. mDW
             13393. States that he would sell his woodland
             in Georgetown for $450 per acre.
June 20   Report from the Committee on Finance on certain
             banking institutions in Florida. AD. DNA, RG
             46. mDW 45654.
June 20   Resolution by DW respecting certain acts of the
             territorial legislature of Florida. AD. DNA, RG
             46. mDW 45383.
June 20   Bill to disapprove and annul certain acts of the
             territorial legislature of Florida. AD. DNA, RG
             46. mDW 45250.
June 21   To James William Paige. ALS. MHi. mDW 13395.
             Reports the passage of the deposit bill by the
             House of Representatives.
June 21   From [Herman Le Roy]. Dictated letter, unsigned.
             NhHi. mDW 13397. Asks if his son should sell

150 shares of Bank of the United States stock
at their present rate.

June 21   Bill making appropriations for certain fortifications
for 1836. Printed document with AD insertions
and amendments. DNA, RG 46. mDW 45437.

June 22   To Henry Willis Kinsman. ALS. NNC. mDW
13398. Sends certificate in a French claims case.

June 23   *To C[harles] C. Trowbridge.*   *139*

June 24   *To [Phineas Davis].*   *139*

June 24   To Charles King. ALS. MWA. mDW 13403. On
information from Benjamin Watkins Leigh,
recommends John R. Cooke of Winchester, Va.,
for employment.

June 25   *To Daniel Fletcher Webster.*   *141*

June 25   From Henry Willis Kinsman (enclosed with DW
to Levi Woodbury, June 29, 1836). ALS. DNA,
RG 206. mDW 57184. States that Thomas C.
Amory, to whom an award was made, is not a
debtor to the United States.

June 27   *To Perkins & Co.*   *142*

June 28   To Perkins & Co. ALS. MH. mDW 39835–96.
Authorizes payment of $3000 to George Thomas
in sixty days per arrangement with Thomas
Handasyd Perkins.

June 29   To Henry Willis Kinsman. ALS. NhHi. mDW
13410. Discusses French claims matters.

June 29   To Levi Woodbury (enclosure: Henry W. Kinsman
to DW, June 25, 1836). ALS. DNA, RG 206.
mDW 57182. Reports that Thomas C. Amory, to
whom a claim was awarded, is not a debtor to
the United States.

June 29   From Robert Owen. ALS. NhD. mDW 13412.
Introduces Francis Wansey.

June 30   Bill making appropriations for the Military
Academy of the United States for 1836. Printed
document. DNA, RG 46. mDW 45609.

July 1   To Henry Willis Kinsman. ALS. MnHi. mDW
13416. Sends scrip awarded in French claims
cases.

July 1   *From Daniel Fletcher Webster.*   *142*

July 1   From Joseph Ricketson Williams (enclosure:
Williams to DW, July 1). ALS. ViU. mDW
13423. Reports on land purchases in Michigan
Territory.

July 1   Motion by DW respecting payments from the
treasury and monthly statements on the state
of the treasury. AD. DNA, RG 46. mDW 45423.

July 1   Motion by DW calling on the secretary of war for
certain information relating to fortifications,
arsenals, etc. AD. DNA, RG 46. mDW 45425.

	Specie Circular on John T. Haight's land purchases.	
Aug 4	To Henry Willis Kinsman. ALS. NhD. mDW 13501. Makes arrangements to pay bank drafts.	
Aug 5–11	[Opinion of Charles Jackson on the United States citizenship of James Temple Bowdoin, concurred in by DW]. DS. NhD. mDW 13505.	
Aug 6	To Edward Everett.	154
Aug 8	From Henry L. Kinney. ALS. ViU. mDW 13522. Encloses receipts for land purchases.	
Aug 11	To Emeline Colby Webster Lindsly. ALS. DMaM. mDW 13526. Requests her to send letters for Charles.	
Aug 12	To Daniel Fletcher Webster. ALS. NhHi. mDW 13529. PC, 2: 21–22. Urges him to come home as soon as possible.	
Aug 13	From Nicholas Biddle.	154
Aug 16	From Fisher Ames Harding.	155
Aug 16	Deed transferring land in Plymouth County, Mass., from Charles Henry Thomas to DW. ADS. Deed Book, 189: 64. Office of the Register of Deeds, Plymouth County, Plymouth, Mass. mDWs.	
Aug 22	To Perkins & Co. ALS. MHi. mDW 13535. Draws on company for $5000 per authority of Thomas Handasyd Perkins.	
Aug 22	Deed transferring land in Marshfield from Charles P. Wright to DW. DS. Deed Book, 189: 65. Office of the Register of Deeds, Plymouth County, Plymouth, Mass. mDWs.	
Aug 22	Deed transferring land in Marshfield from Asa Hewitt to DW. DS. Deed Book, 189: 66. Office of the Register of Deeds, Plymouth County, Plymouth, Mass. mDWs.	
Aug 23	To Nicholas Biddle.	157
Aug 26	From Nicholas Biddle.	158
Aug 27	To John Davis (1787–1854). LS. MWA. mDW 13540. W & S, 16: 280–281. Suggests that John and Phineas Davis meet him at Marshfield.	
Sept 5	Account of Daniel Webster with Phineas Davis. ADS. NhD. mDW 39835–92. Details investments, April 29 through Aug 3, 1836.	
Sept 7	To Caleb Cushing. LS, by proxy. DLC. mDW 13544. Asks for short conference.	
Sept 12	From Fisher Ames Harding. ALS. ViU. mDW 13546. Discusses land purchases.	
Sept 17	To William D. Lewis. ALS. NN. mDW 13549. Sends him a note (not found) at the request of John Randall, Jr.	
Sept 19	To Albert Collins Greene. LS. MWA. mDW 13551. Acknowledges the receipt of papers relating to	

the Massachusetts–Rhode Island boundary
dispute.

Sept 26   Deed transferring land in Eaton County, Mich.,
           from Joseph Ricketson Williams to DW. DS.
           Deed Book, 2: 136. Office of the Register of
           Deeds, Eaton County, Charlotte, Mich. mDWs.

Sept 26   Deed transferring land in Eaton County, Mich.,
           from Joseph Ricketson Williams to DW. Copy.
           Deed Book, 3: 499. Office of the Register of
           Deeds, Calhoun County, Marshall, Mich. mDWs.

Sept 28   To Edward Everett. ALS. MHi. mDW 13555.
           Discusses again the propriety of making public
           John Marshall's opinion on Masonry.

[c. Sept 28] *From Joseph Ricketson Williams.*   *158*

Sept 29   To John James Audubon. Printed. Francis Hobart
           Herrick, *Audubon, the Naturalist* (New York,
           1917), p. 152. Recommends Audubon to his
           friends.

Sept 29 *From Joseph Ricketson Williams.*   *159*

Oct 3   From Joseph Ricketson Williams (to DW and
           Thomas Handasyd Perkins). ALS. ViU. mDW
           13558. Discusses joint purchase of eighty acres
           in Toledo.

Oct 8   To Edward Webster. ALS. NhHi. mDW 13562.
           Van Tyne, p. 593 (excerpt). Congratulates him
           on his application to his studies.

Oct 22   Memorandum on Elms Farm stock. ADS. NhHi.
           mDW 13564. Inventory of the joint property of
           DW and John Stevens.

Oct 24   To Jesse Buel. ALS. DLC. mDW 13566. Requests
           that the *Cultivator* be sent regularly to
           Marshfield.

Oct 24   *To Moses McCure Strong.*   *159*
Oct 25   *To Jeremiah Mason.*   *160*

Oct 25   To Charles Henry Thomas. ALS. MHi. mDW
           13573. Does not believe he can help Waterman
           Thomas in his court case.

Oct 29   To Samuel Jones. ALS. Samuel J. Wagstaff,
           Vergennes, Vt. mDW 13576. Asks that his
           daughter join the Websters in Washington
           during the session of Congress.

Oct 31   To John Quincy Adams. LS. MHi. mDW 13578.
           Van Tyne, p. 698. Discusses the essays "on the
           subject of the Congress of Nations" for the
           promotion of peace.

Nov 1   To Emeline Colby Webster Lindsly. ALS. DMaM.
           mDW 13585. Asks her to send a letter to Mrs.
           Sally Smith in Washington.

Nov 5   To Edward Everett. LS. MHi. mDW 13587. Reports
           on a conference with James Trecothick Austin.

Nov 5	To Edward Everett. Invitation. MHi. mDW 13588. Invites Everett to dinner to meet the trustees of the Agricultural Society.
Nov 6	From James Trecothick Austin. ALS. MHi. mDW 13590. Discusses the possibility of his appearing in court on behalf of Massachusetts in the boundary dispute with Rhode Island.
Nov 7	To Edward Everett. ALS. MHi. mDW 13591. Forwards letter from James Trecothick Austin.
Nov 8	To Sarah Goodridge. ALS. MHi. mDW 38392. Proposes to call upon her.
Nov 10	To Simon Greenleaf. ALS. MH. mDWs. Discusses some unidentified claim payment.
Nov 14	Receipt for $52.78 for taxes, covering property in Londonderry for 1835. ADS. NhD. mDW 39835–84.
Nov 15	*To John Gorham Palfrey.* *160*
Nov 15	*To Nathaniel Silsbee.* *161*
Nov 20	From Samuel Houston. ALS. NhHi. mDW 13659. Van Tyne, p. 209. Introduces General Santa Anna.
Nov 24	Agreement between John E. Hunt and Daniel Webster regarding collateral for Webster's endorsement of Hunt's promissory note for $1500. DS. MHi. mDW 39835–113.
Nov 28	Petition of John R. Parker, inventor of the "Semaphoric Telegraph," requesting Congress to establish a line of telegraphic communication throughout the United States. ADS. DNA, RG 46. mDW 45841.
[Nov]	*Last Will and Testament of Daniel Webster.* *162*
Dec 1	Petition of Thomas Handasyd Perkins to be released from the payment of certain duties. Copy. DNA, RG 46. mDW 45821.
Dec 7	Deed transferring land in LaSalle County, Ill., from Peter Terry and wife to DW. Copy. Deed Book E: 464. Office of the Register of Deeds, LaSalle County, Ottawa, Ill. mDWs.
[Dec 9]	From M. W. Chapman. ANS. DNA, RG 46. mDW 46159. Asks DW to present petition from the women of Hornby, Steuben County, N.Y.
Dec 10	To Henry Willis Kinsman. ALS. NhD. mDW 13668. Sends check for the payment of a bank note.
[Dec 11]	*From Stephen White.* *164*
Dec 12	Duplicate receipt for eighty acres of land purchased at the Milwaukee land office. DS. DLC. mDW 39835–118–A.
Dec 14	From Daniel Fletcher Webster. ALS. NhHi. mDW

13670. Reports that he and Caroline are still in Buffalo.

Dec 15   From Stephen White. ALS. NhHi. mDW 13674. Discusses the "Galinda affair."

Dec 15   Petition of inhabitants of Boston, Mass., requesting a reduction of the duty on coal. DS. DNA, RG 46. mDW 45959.

Dec 16   *From Edward Everett.*   *165*

Dec 17   To Frances Ann Thompson. ALS. MoSW. mDW 13682. States that he will speak to [Francis?] Baylies about settling his affairs with her.

[Dec 18]   *To Nicholas Biddle.*   *167*

[Dec 18]   To Henry Willis Kinsman. ALS. NhD. mDW 13688. Mentions a claims matter, "Woodbury's Treasury Order"; asks Kinsman to forward the copy of DW's lecture before the Society for the Diffusion of Useful Knowledge.

Dec 18   *From Nicholas Biddle.*   *168*

Dec 19   To Francis Lieber. ALS. CSmH. mDW 13691. Informs Lieber that his lecture before the Society for the Diffusion of Useful Knowledge has not been published.

Dec 20   Motion by DW relative to the transfer of public money. AD. DNA, RG 46. mDW 45427.

Dec 21 [1836?] To Caleb Cushing. Invitation. DLC. mDW 38322. Invites Cushing to dinner.

Dec 22   To Nicholas Biddle. ALS. DLC. mDW 13693. States that, in his opinion, the views expressed in his last letter have been strengthened; mentions that he must be at Annapolis for a court case during the holidays.

Dec 22   Deed transferring land in La Salle County, Ill., from Henry L. Kinney to Daniel Webster. DS. Deed Book E: 494–495. Office of the Register of Deeds, La Salle County, Ottawa, Ill. mDWs.

Dec 23   *To Edward Curtis.*   *169*

Dec 26   Promissory note for $3000. AD. NhD. mDW 39835–119.

Dec 27   *From Nathaniel Silsbee.*   *169*

Dec 29   From Fisher Ames Harding. ALS. ViU. mDW 13699. Discusses land purchases he has made for Webster.

Dec 29   Petition of George Frazar, requesting that he be allowed a bounty on a fishing vessel that was lost at sea. DS. DNA, RG 46. mDW 45845.

Dec 30   *To Edward Everett.*   *170*

Dec 31   From [George] Frazar. ALS. DNA, RG 46. mDW 45849. Sends documents supporting his request for a bounty on the *Quero.*

[1836]	To [Charles Henry Thomas]. AL. MHi. mDW 13713. Instructs him on planting beans.
[1836]	Petition from inhabitants of Concord, N.H., for the repeal of the laws of the District of Columbia which authorize "*the selling of men into Slavery to pay prison expenses.*" DS. DNA, RG 46. mDW 43778.
[1836]	Petition from citizens of Somersworth, Mass. (mDW 43782); from Michigan (mDW 43784), for the abolition of slavery and the slave trade in the District of Columbia. DS. DNA, RG 46.
[1836?]	To [Robert Charles Winthrop]. ALS. MHi. mDW 13715. Asks him to come to Marshfield with Mr. Duncan.
[1836?]	To Warren Dutton. ALS. NN. mDW 13711. Discusses the "Bridge Cause."
[1836?]	Agreement between John Taylor and Daniel Webster for the management of Elms Farm. ADS. NhHi. mDW 39835–120.
[1836–1850]	To Charles Henry Thomas. ALS. NhHi. mDW 39025. Sends nuts for planting at Marshfield.
[1836–1851]	To Sarah Goodridge. ALS. MHi. mDW 38394. Offers her money.
[1836–1851]	To Sarah Goodridge. ALS. MHi. mDW 38396. Proposes to call on her.
[1836–1851]	To Sarah Goodridge. AL. MHi. mDW 38399. Asks when she will be at home.
[1836–1852]	To [Franklin Haven]. ALS. MH-H. mDW 38543. Asks to confer with Haven about Mexican scrip.

1837

Jan 1	From G. Robertson. ALS. DNA, RG 46. mDW 47817. Urges DW to visit Lexington, Ky.	
Jan 1	From Elias Smith. ALS. DNA, RG 46. mDW 47703. Discusses preemption and Whig prospects.	
Jan 3	To E. Ritchie Dorr. ALS. MH-H. mDW 13721. Thanks Dorr for letter and packet of papers.	
Jan 4	To [Henry Willis Kinsman]. ALS. NjP. mDW 13723. Instructs him on the payment of notes.	
Jan 4	Bill for the relief of the owners of the brig *Despatch* and cargo. Printed document. DNA, RG 46. mDW 45376.	
[c. Jan 4]	*From Daniel Fletcher Webster.*	171
[Jan 5]	To Joseph Gales and W. W. Seaton. ALS. NhD. mDW 13731. Sends article for publication on the qualifications of electors.	
Jan 5	From Amos Kendall. ALS. MHi. mDW 13734. Reports, per DW's request, on the removal of	

States that he is sending another letter on his "intended resignation" for friends in the Massachusetts legislature.

Jan 31   To Robert Charles Winthrop. ALS. MHi. mDW 14010. PC, 2: 25–26. Discusses his Senate resignation.

Feb 1   *To Henry Willis Kinsman.*   *186*

Feb 2   Petition of certain authors of Great Britain for Congress to secure to them a copyright on their writings in the United States. Copy. DNA, RG 46. mDW 46024.

Feb 3   To Joseph Hopkinson. ALS. PHi. mDW 14014. Discusses Hopkinson's reports, the question of judges' salaries before Congress, and Hopkinson's argument against the right of instruction.

Feb 3   To James William Paige. ALS. NhHi. mDW 14017. PC, 2: 26. Reports that he intends to resign his Senate seat.

Feb 3   To Jonathan Winship. ALS. MHi. mDW 14020. Thanks him for berries.

Feb 4   To Edward Webster ALS. NhHi. mDW 14022. Van Tyne, p. 595. Asks him to write more often.

Feb 4   From John Quincy Adams. LC. MHi. mDW 14025. Consults on the award for the best dissertation on a "Congress of Nations, for perpetuating Peace."

Feb 4   Bill to amend the act to establish branches of the Mint of the United States, passed March 3, 1835. Printed document. DNA, RG 46. mDW 45646.

Feb 4   Motion by DW to refer amendments to the land bill (S. 20) to the Committee on Public Lands. AD. DNA, RG 46. mDW 45430.

Feb 5   To John McLure. LS. MDeeP. mDWs. Introduces Arthur W. Hoyt.

Feb 6   From Nicholas Biddle. LC. DLC. mDWs. Sends letter from James Ronaldson on the Texas question.

Feb 6   From Maria A. Sturges, Sarah E. Safford, and Lucinda Nye. ALS by Sturges. DNA, RG 46. mDW 46342. Sends petition of 2,925 women of Ohio for abolition of slavery in the District of Columbia.

Feb 6   Twenty-nine memorials for abolition of slavery in the District of Columbia from voters or women of Andover (mDW 46143), Berkley (mDW 46074), Beverly (mDW 46113), Billerica (mDW 46088), Boston (mDW 46118), Boxborough (mDW 46093), Brookline (mDW 46070), Dover (mDW 46100), Dunstable

(mDW 46105), Fall River (mDW 46055),
Framingham (mDW 46084), Marshfield (mDW
46078), New Bedford (mDW 46149), Pepperell
(mDW 46103), Plymouth (mDW 46067),
Rowley & Linebrook (mDW 46080), Shirley
(mDW 46110), South Reading (mDW 46096),
Sudbury (mDW 46091), Wayland (mDW
46082), Westford (mDW 46107), Weymouth
(mDW 46068), Mass.; Bethany (mDW 46044),
Castile (mDW 46048), China (mDW 46034),
Java (mDW 46037), Perry (mDW 46038),
Warsaw (mDW 46051), Genesee County, N.Y.;
and Lycoming County, Pa. (mDW 46034). DS.
DNA, RG 46.

Feb 7	To Hiram Ketchum. ALS. NhD. mDW 38663. Introduces William F. Peterson of Wheeling, an agent for land speculators.	
Feb 7	To [whom it may concern]. ADS. Mrs. W. P. Holloway, Wheeling, W. Va. mDW 14027. Introduces Peterson.	
Feb 7	From M. A. Sturges. ALS. DNA, RG 46. mDW 46333. Sends additional list of names of 333 women for the abolition of slavery in the District of Columbia.	
Feb 8	*From Henry Shaw.*	*187*
Feb 8	Memorandum of transfer of eighty acres of land near Milwaukee to Caleb Cushing. ANS. DLC. mDW 39835–122–A.	
Feb 8	Memorial of merchants and other citizens of New York for the creation of a national bank in New York City. Copy. DNA, RG 46. mDW 46368.	
Feb 11	*To Hiram Ketchum.*	*188*
Feb 11	From Daniel Fletcher Webster. ALS. NhHi. mDW 14042. Discusses payment of property taxes for DW and other eastern investors.	
Feb 11	Draft on Edward A. Le Roy for $5,000. ADS. NN. mDW 39835–123.	
Feb 12	*To Daniel Fletcher Webster.*	*189*
Feb 13	*To Jeremiah Mason.*	*191*
Feb 13	Deed transferring Rock Island City, Ill., land from Levi C. Turner and others to DW. Copy. DLC. mDW 40348. Original in Deed Book A: 321. Office of the Register of Deeds, Rock Island County, Ill.	
[Feb 14?]	From Levi C. Turner. ALS. NhHi. mDW 39091. Sends deed for DW's landholdings in Rock Island City.	
Feb 15	To Jacob Burnett. LS. MDeeP. mDWs. Introduces Arthur W. Hoyt, an engineer from Massachusetts.	

Feb 15	To John Cavender. LS. MDeeP. mDWs. Introduces Hoyt.
Feb 15	To S. Fales. LS. MDeeP. mDWs. Introduces Hoyt.
Feb 15	To [John Plummer Healy]. ALS. MHi. mDW 14056. Proposes settling account with a Mr. Ryder.
Feb 15	To [Henry Willis Kinsman]. ALS. Dr. Gurdon S. Pulford, Palo Alto, Calif. mDW 14058. Instructs him on financial matters.
Feb 15	To M[orris] Robinson. ALS. NNPM. mDW 14059. Sends check on the Merchants' Bank for $4,400.
Feb 15	To Josiah Spalding. LS. MDeeP. mDWs. Introduces Hoyt.
Feb 15	*To Robert Charles Winthrop, with enclosure to Robert Charles Winthrop, Feb. 15.* 193
Feb 15	From Francis Lieber. ALS. MHi. mDW 14065. Asks Webster to recommend him for one of the Lowell chairs at Harvard.
Feb 15	*From Robert Charles Winthrop et al.* 194
Feb 16	From Daniel Fletcher Webster. ALS. NhHi. mDW 14071. Reports the payment of the assessment on DW's Gibraltar stock.
Feb 16	Report of the Select Committee relating to copyrights. AD. DNA, RG 46. mDW 45693.
Feb 17	Draft of Levi C. Turner for $4075 against DW (in Hamilton Fish to E. G. Austin, Feb 16, 1838). Copy. DLC. mDWs.
Feb 17	Eleven petitions for the abolition of slavery in the District of Columbia from voters or citizens of Boston (mDW 46163), Essex County (mDW 46297), Franklin County (mDW 46302), Natick (mDW 46292), Sterling (mDW 46282), West Newberry (mDW 46305), and from "legal voters of Massachusetts" (mDW 46286); of Hornby, Steuben County, N.Y. (mDW 46157); and of Ohio (mDW 46160). DS. DNA, RG 46.
Feb 18	To O. K. Barrell. ALS. N. mDW 14076. Asserts that he was not a member of the Hartford Convention and had nothing to do with it.
Feb 18	To Franklin Haven. ALS. MH-H. mDW 14078. Sends deposit; discusses Congress's lagging on important measures.
Feb 18	To James S. Waters. ALS. PCarlD. mDW 14080. Acknowledges membership in a literary society of Dickinson College.
[Feb 19?]	To Joseph Story. Printed. *Life and Letters of Joseph Story*, ed. William W. Story (2 vols.; Boston, 1851), 2: 269. Calls Story's Charles River Bridge opinion "the ablest, and best written . . . I ever heard you deliver."
Feb 20	To Nicholas Biddle. ALS. PHi. mDW 14081.

	Reports on the action of the Senate Committee on Finance on Biddle's memorial.	
Feb 27	*To Franklin Haven.*	*199*
Feb 27	From John Davis (1761–1847). ALS. NhHi. mDW 14116. Sends DW seeds from the *Pinus pinea.*	
Feb 27	Documents submitted by DW from the Committee on Finance relative to payment for the stock of the United States in the late Bank of the United States. Copies. DNA, RG 46. mDW 45665.	
Feb 27	Resolution by DW authorizing the secretary of the treasury to receive from the Bank of the United States payment for the stock of the United States. AD. DNA, RG 46. mDW 45388.	
Feb 28	From S. W. Ely. ALS. NhD. mDW 14120 (with AD by DW, sending article to "Haddy"). Sends DW a satin-printed copy of his protest against expunging.	
[Feb]	From [Bela] Marsh, [Nahum] Capen, and [Gardner P.] Lyon. Copy. DLC. mDW 14124a. Favor the passage of a law "which shall protect the Foreign author in this Country, so far as he may make contracts with American publishers."	
Feb	Statement of referees (John Quincy Adams, James Kent, and DW) of the American Peace Society recommending that no award be granted. Printed. *Prize Essays on a Congress of Nations* . . . (Boston, 1840), p. v.	
March 1	Memorandum of agreement between Daniel Webster and George Wallace Jones. ADS. Ia-HA. mDW 39835–125. For joint purchase of land on the Mississippi River opposite Dubuque.	
[March 2]	To Nicholas Biddle. ALS. DLC. mDW 13718. Discusses financial questions before Congress.	
March 2	*From David Bayard Ogden.*	*201*
March 2	*From Daniel Fletcher Webster.*	*201*
March 3	Motion by DW to authorize the secretary of the treasury to have printed and sent to the members of the Senate the annual statement of commerce and navigation. AD. DNA, RG 46. mDW 45432.	
March 4	To Edward Everett. ALS. MHi. mDW 14135. Van Tyne, p. 210. Discusses the appointment of a judge for Massachusetts.	
March 4	*To Hiram Ketchum.*	*204*
March 4	To David Bayard Ogden. ALS. NhHi. mDW 14139. W & S, 2: 190–191. Thanks Ogden for resolutions and accepts invitation of Whigs of New York.	
[c. March 4]	"Results of the Session" (editorial). Printed. *National Intelligencer,* March 7, 1837.	

March 4   Draft by John T. Haight on DW for $3000. ADS.
             DLC. mDW 39835–128–A.
March 5   To Philip Hone. Printed. Curtis, 1: 556. Further
             discusses the meeting with New York Whigs.
March 6   From Daniel Fletcher Webster. ALS. NhHi. mDW
             14144. Discusses investment opportunities in
             land.
March 7   To George Wallace Jones. ALS. Ia-HA. mDW
             14146. Sends land certificate that Jones left
             with DW by mistake.
March 7   *To Thomas Handasyd Perkins.*   205
March 8   To Joseph Gales. ALS. DLC. mDW 14151. Gives
             permission for the publication of some article;
             discusses his proposed Senate resignation.
March 11   To Franklin Haven. ALS. MH-H. mDW 14153.
             Sends money for deposit and discusses his
             account.
March 14   From John T. Haight. ALS. DLC. mDW 14155.
             Discusses land purchases in the vicinity of
             Milwaukee.
March 14   *From Daniel Fletcher Webster.*   206
March 17   *To Virgil Maxcy.*   208
March 18   To Charles Rolfe et al. ALS. MeEl. mDW 14164.
             Accepts invitation to visit the Mercantile Library
             Association of New York.
March 18   Certificates for forty-five shares of stock in the
             Ellsworth Land and Lumber Company. Printed
             DS. NhD. mDW 39835–134.
March 20   To Franklin Haven. ALS. MH-H. mDW 14165.
             Sends notes for deposit and reminds Haven that
             he will be needing money soon.
March 21   To Charles Henry Thomas. ALS. MHi. mDW
             14167. Discusses his proposed western trip and
             farming matters.
March 22   From Ebenezer Webster. ALS. MHi. mDW 14173.
             Sends note for $2393.78 with cosigners; urges
             DW to sue if not paid when due.
March 24   To Morgan L. Martin. ALS. WHi. mDW 14175.
             Authorizes Martin to subscribe for him stock in
             La Fontaine and Winnebago Railroad.
March 24   Deed transferring land in La Salle County, Ill.,
             from Henry L. Kinney to DW. DS. Deed Book
             G: 111. Office of the Register of Deeds, La Salle
             County, Ottawa, Ill. mDWs.
March 24   Agreement of owners of Winnebago City, Wis.
             Copy. MWalB. mDW 14177. Agree to give land
             for railroad and depot to the La Fontaine and
             Winnebago Railroad.
March 28   From Henry Clay. ALS. DLC. mDW 14178. Curtis,

Company stocks numbered 1886 to 1900. DS.
NhD. mDWs.

April 14   *From George Wallace Jones.*   215
April 14   Agreement between Simpson & Harrington and
            DW regarding the mortgage on the furniture of
            John E. Hunt. AD. MHi. mDW 39835–148.
April 16   *From George Wallace Jones.*   216
April 20   To Hiram Ketchum. ALS. MHi. mDW 14225.
            Introduces Robert C. Winthrop of Boston.
April 20   Memorandum authorizing John Plummer
            Healy to accept drafts on him. DS. MHi.
            mDW 39835–150.
April 20   Memorandum authorizing John Plummer Healy to
            accept drafts on him by William L. D. Ewing.
            DS. MHi. mDW 39835–153.
April 20   Memorandum authorizing John Plummer Healy to
            accept drafts on him by Jacob Bigelow. DS.
            MHi. mDW 39835–155.
April 22   *To Edward Webster.*   218
April 22   *From George W. Jones.*   219
April 25   Memorandum authorizing John Plummer Healy to
            accept drafts on him by John Connell. DS. MHi.
            mDW 39835–156.
April 26   To Caleb Cushing. AL (signature removed). DLC.
            mDW 14235. Hopes to see him shortly in Boston
            to make some financial arrangements.
April 27   To Nicholas Biddle. ALS. DLC. mDW 14236.
            Reports that he had no success in his negotiation
            with John Amory Lowell.
April 27   *To [William Albert] Bradley.*   222
April 27   To Caleb Cushing. ALS. DLC. mDW 14241. Invites
            Cushing to Boston.
April 28   To William Pitt Fessenden. ALS. MAJ. mDW
            14242. Reports his western itinerary as far as
            Philadelphia, where he expects Fessenden will
            join him.
April 28   To [Herman?] Le Roy. ALS fragment. MHi. mDWs.
            Reports that they are preparing to leave for
            the West.
April 29   *To Caleb Cushing.*   223
May 3   To Edward Webster. ALS. NhHi. mDW 14248.
            Discusses Edward's summer plans.
May 6   To Hiram Ketchum. ALS. NhD. mDW 14250.
            Sends names of Pennsylvania people who are
            to be sent copies of his speeches.
May 8   *To John Plummer Healy.*   224
May 11   To James Ross et al. Printed. W & S, 16: 288–289.
            Declines their invitation to a public dinner in
            Pittsburgh.

May 11	From Boyce McNairy et al. LS. DLC. mDW 14255. Invite DW to a public dinner in Nashville.
May 16	From Warner L. Underwood et al. LS. NhD. mDW 14261. Invite DW to Bowling Green, Ky.
May 17	From Richard Henry Lee et al. LS. DLC. mDW 14264. Invite him to a public dinner at Maysville, Ky.
May 21	To Franklin Haven. ALS. MH-H. mDW 14267. Discusses a bank note supposed to have been paid by Mason Greenwood.
May 24	From George W. Summers et al. LS. NhD. mDW 14270. Invite DW to a public dinner in Charleston, [W.] Virginia.
May 24	From Charles M. Thurston et al. LS. DLC. mDW 14273. Invite DW to a public barbecue in Louisville.
May 27	To John C. Wright. ALS. ViU. mDW 14276. States his plan to visit Cincinnati; urges Wright to thwart any effort to get up a public celebration.
May 29	From Richard Lyles et al. LS. DLC. mDW 14280. Invite DW to Russellville, Ky., to partake in a public dinner.
May 30	From W. Lyle et al. Printed. W & S, 2: 248. Invite DW to a public dinner in Madison, Ind.
May 30	To W. Lyle et al. Printed. W & S, 2: 248–249. Accepts invitation from the Madison, Ind., committee.
May 30	From Jacob Bigelow et al. ALS by Bigelow, signed also by others. DLC. mDW 14284. Invite DW to Michigan City, Ind.
June 1	From Timothy Fletcher. ALS. NhHi. mDW 14292. Reports on his visit to the Salmon River Coal Mines.
June 6	From Noah Noble. ALS. NhD. mDW 14294. Invites DW to visit Indianapolis.
June 9	From William Woodbridge et al. LS. DLC. mDW 14297. Invite DW to a public reception in Detroit.
June 20	From Lewis Bigelow et al. ALS by Bigelow, signed also by others. DLC. mDW 14300. Invite DW to a public festival in Peoria.
June 22	From Vincent Mathews et al. (enclosure: Resolutions of Rochester meeting). LS. DLC. mDW 14304. Invite DW to visit Rochester.
June 23	From George Dawson, Jr., et al. LS. DLC. mDW 14308. Invite him to visit Rochester on his way eastward.
June 24	To J. L. Bogardus. ALS. NhD. mDW 14312. States that he will leave for the East earlier than expected.
June 24	*To George Wallace Jones.* 224

June 28	*From Morgan L. Martin.*	225
June 28	Certificate for twenty-five shares of stock in the Salmon River Coal Company of New Brunswick. DS. MHi. mDW 39835–8.	
June 29	From William Kelley et al. LS. DLC. mDW 14316. Invite DW to visit Erie, Pa.	
[June]	From A. K. Saltry et al. LS. DLC. mDW 14318. Invite DW to visit Upper Alton, Ill.	
July 2	From William T. Otto. ALS. NhD. mDW 14322. Expresses his disappointment that DW was unable to visit Indianapolis.	
July 7	*From George Wallace Jones.*	226
July 9	To Morgan L. Martin. ALS. WGrNM. mDW 14331. Thanks Martin for letter of June 28; expresses his pleasure with what Martin has done.	
[c. July 9]	From Benjamin Franklin Stickney et al. LS. DLC. mDW 14347. On behalf of the citizens of Manhattan, Toledo, Miami City, and Perrysburg, invite DW to a public dinner.	
July 11	To Benjamin Franklin Stickney et al. ALS. OT. mDW 14333. Declines invitation to public dinner but will be happy to meet friends at Toledo.	
July 12	*To [John Plummer Healy].*	227
July 18	To [John Plummer Healy]. ALS. MHi. mDW 14336. Reports that they will leave Buffalo for New York on July 19.	
July 22	To Francis Granger. ALS. NCanHi. mDW 14338. Thanks Granger for invitation but declines because of other engagements.	
July 28	*From Caleb Cushing.*	228
July 29	*To Caleb Cushing.*	228
July 31	To [John H.] Ostrom. ALS. G. Hartley Webster, Harvard, Mass. mDWs. Comments on occurrences at Utica during his visit there.	
Aug 2	Patents to 400 acres of land purchased at the Detroit Land Office. Copy. Deed Book 274: 219. Office of the Register of Deeds, Oakland County, Pontiac, Mich. mDWs.	
[Aug 3]	To John Plummer Healy. ALS. MHi. mDW 14349. Reports that he will return to Boston early the following week.	
Aug 3	To Joel Roberts Poinsett. ALS. PHi. mDW 14351. Introduces J. C. Bates of Massachusetts.	
Aug 4	Deed transferring about two acres of land in Marshfield from DW and Caroline Le Roy Webster to Malatiah Holmes et al. for $100. DS. NhD. mDW 39835–157.	
Aug 5	From William Pitt Fessenden. ALS. NhHi. mDW 14354. Expresses his happiness at hearing of	

	the Websters' arrival in Boston; comments on recent Maine election.	
Aug 5	Certificate for 399 65/100 acres of land in Michigan. DS. MiD-B. mDW 39835–159.	
Aug 6	From Caleb Cushing. ALS. DLC. mDW 14357. Fuess, *Cushing*, 1: 234. Reports that he reached Boston after DW left for Marshfield.	
Aug 8	Deed transferring land in Putnam County, Ill., from Henry L. Kinney to DW. Copy. Deed Book J: 362. Office of the Register of Deeds, Putnam County, Hennepin, Ill. mDWs.	
Aug 9	To [?]. ALS. MLexHi. mDW 14359. Discusses petitioning Congress for relief of the widows and children of those men killed during the battle of Lexington, April 19, 1775.	
Aug 14	To [Henry] Colman. ALS. NhExP. mDW 14361. Recommends means whereby a Mrs. Gale may gain admission of her son, Andrew Bowers Gale, to Phillips Exeter Academy.	
[Aug 16]	To John Plummer Healy. ALS. MHi. mDW 14365. Discusses his mortgage on Hunt's property.	
Aug 19	To John Plummer Healy. ALS. MHi. mDW 14366. Reports that he will be in Boston for three days beginning Monday.	
[Aug 21?]	To Edward Everett. ALS. MHi. mDW 14368. Invites Everett to join him, A. Murray McIlvaine, and Thomas Chambers for dinner.	
Aug 23	To Robert Charles Winthrop. ALS. MHi. mDW 14370. Asks Winthrop for a short conference.	
Aug 24–26	*From Henry L. Kinney.*	229
Aug 25	To [Thomas M.?] Brewer. ALS. MHi. mDWs. W & S, 16: 290–291. Discusses the forthcoming session of Congress.	
Aug 26	From Henry Washburn, Jr. ALS. DNA, RG 46. mDW 46761. Requests DW to present the memorial of Taunton residents against the annexation of Texas.	
Aug 28	From Hannah L. Stickney. ALS. DNA, RG 46. mDW 47666. Sends petitions.	
Aug 28	*From Daniel Fletcher Webster.*	232
[Aug 29]	To [Edward Everett]. ALS. MHi. mDW 14386. Asks Everett to call at his study "for 2 minutes."	
Aug 30	From Andrew Robeson. Printed DS. DNA, RG 46. mDW 46721. Sends resolutions adopted by citizens of New Bedford, Mass., against the annexation of Texas to the United States.	
Aug 30	From H. L. H. Ward. ALS. DNA, RG 46. mDW 47670. Sends petition.	
[Aug]	*To Franklin Haven.*	235

	47664. Sends petition of Albany women against the annexation of Texas.	
[Sept 19]	To [Joseph Gales and W. W. Seaton?]. AD. NN. mDW 14413. *New York Daily Tribune*, Dec 30, 1890. Discusses a "Buckeye" cane, presented to him by citizens of Ohio.	
Sept 21	To Hiram Ketchum. ALS. TxU. mDW 14417. Comments on the Maine election and Washington politics.	
Sept 22	To Edward Everett. ALS. MHi. mDW 14419. Introduces C. C. Trowbridge of Michigan.	
Sept 22	To Hiram Ketchum. ALS. NhD. mDW 14420. Introduces Trowbridge.	
Sept 22	To Harriette Story White Paige. ALS. MH. mDW 14422. Introduces Trowbridge and suggests that she might like to accompany him to Marshfield to visit Mrs. Webster and Julia.	
Sept 23	*To Ramsay Crooks.*	239
Sept 23	*From Henry L. Kinney.*	240
Sept 23	From Nathan Power. ALS. DNA, RG 46. mDW 47660. Sends petition against the annexation of Texas.	
Sept 25	Memorial of women of Hanson, Mass., against the annexation of Texas. DS. DNA, RG 46. mDW 46723.	
Sept 27	From Levi Cook. ALS. DNA, RG 46. mDW 47843. Discusses the financial situation and introduces James Fillson, who plans a trip south for his health.	
Sept 27	Petition of Laura R. Newmarch, daughter of Elisha Phelps, for a pension. ADS. DNA, RG 46. mDW 47499.	
Sept 29	Motion by DW relative to fees on the renewal of merchants' bonds. AD. DNA, RG 46. mDW 46441.	
Sept 30	From William M. Price. LS. DNA, RG 46. mDWs. Discusses fees for the renewal of bonds in New York.	
[Sept]	To Caleb Cushing or Richard Fletcher. ALS. NN. mDW 14430. Asks if Adams's resolutions passed amended or unamended and by what majority.	
Oct 2	*To Franklin Haven.*	242
Oct 2	*From Ramsay Crooks.*	242
Oct 2	Amendment by DW to the bill to regulate the fees of district attorneys in certain cases. AD. DNA, RG 46. mDW 46411.	
Oct 3	From Moses Hanson. ALS. DNA, RG 46. mDW 47672. Sends memorials of the voters of Thorndike, Me.	

Oct 4   Promissory note for $5000 to the State Bank,
                        Boston. Copy. MWalB. mDW 39835–292.
Oct 5   From John E. Hyde & Company. ALS. NHi. mDW
                        14436. Discusses customs bonds.
[Oct 9]   To John Plummer Healy. ALS. MHi. mDW 14438.
                        Sends some unidentified item that Healy should
                        sell to take up DFW's draft.
Oct 10   To Mahlon Dickerson. ALS. DNA, RG 45. mDWs.
                        Recommends Dickerson's attention to the
                        Cassidy case.
Oct 12 [1837?]   To Nathaniel F. Williams. ALS. NhD. mDW 25381.
                        Discusses trouble with his eyes and promises to
                        send draft for $1000 in next mail.
Oct 12   Motion by DW for information relative to the
                        seizure of the ship *Mary* of Baltimore in 1800.
                        AD. DNA, RG 46. mDW 46443.
Oct 12   Memorials against the annexation of Texas from
                        citizens of New London (mDW 46701),
                        Willimantic Village (mDW 46699), Conn.;
                        Thorndike, Me. (mDW 46707, 46709);
                        Abingdon (mDW 46809, 46822), Andover
                        (mDW 46817), Berlin (mDW 46884),
                        Blandford (mDW 46816), Boston (mDW
                        46884), Boston (mDW 46894), Boxborough
                        (mDW 46705, mDW 46718), Bradford (mDW
                        46715), Braintree (mDW 46778), Bristol
                        County (mDW 46926), Brookline (mDW
                        46806), Charlestown (mDW 46924), Dartmouth
                        (mDW 46880), Duxbury (mDW 46922), East
                        Needham (mDW 46882), Groton (mDW
                        46793), Hingham (mDW 46711), Lowell
                        (mDW 46961), Marshfield (mDW 46756),
                        Medfield (mDW 46800), Middlesex County
                        (mDW 46786), Natick (mDW 46918),
                        Newburyport (mDW 46955), Newton Centre
                        (mDW 46781), North Dennis (mDW 46804),
                        Quincy (mDW 46783), Roxbury (mDW 46872),
                        Rowley (mDW 46798), Scituate (mDW 46726),
                        South Weymouth (mDW 46860), Stoughton
                        (mDW 46820), Stow (mDW 46870), Taunton
                        (mDW 46760), West Newton (mDW 46747),
                        Weymouth (mDW 46864), Wrentham (mDW
                        46812), Mass.; Cass County (mDW 46835),
                        Farmington (mDW 46824), Novi (mDW
                        46831), Oakland County (mDW 46829),
                        Redford (mDW 46838), Mich.; Dartmouth
                        College (mDW 46751), Portsmouth (mDW
                        46886), N.H.; Albany (mDW 46856),
                        Bridgewater (mDW 46848), Cayuga County
                        (mDW 46737), Milton County (mDW 46853),

Skaneateles (mDW 46851), N.Y.; Geauga
County (mDW 46891), Hudson (mDW 46842),
Ohio; Wilkes-Barre, Pa. (mDW 46844);
unidentified group (mDW 46801). DS. DNA,
RG 46.

Oct 13 From Mahlon Dickerson. LC. DNA, RG 45. mDWs.
Acknowledges the receipt of DW's letter of Oct
10, with its enclosures.

Oct 14 To Joseph Gales. ALS. NN. mDW 14440. Sends
letter (not found) for Gales's perusal.

Oct 20 To Jacob McGaw. ALS. Lester W. Parker,
Brimfield, Mass. mDW 14442. Inquires if James
Purinton still resides in Bangor.

Oct 23 From Dunbar James Douglas Selkirk. ALS. DLC.
mDW 14444. Sends DW a gun; discusses
American and English politics.

Oct 25 To Franklin Haven. ALS. MH-H. mDW 14449.
Discusses his, Turner's, and Beardsley's efforts
to raise money.

Oct 27 Memorial of 117 women of Newbury, Mass.,
against the annexation of Texas to the
United States. DS. DNA, RG 46. mDW 46988.

Oct 30 To [Joseph Cowperthwaite?]. ALS. NcD. mDW
14450. Informs him that E. Chauncey will
deposit about $3000 to his account and requests
that it be placed to the credit of the Bank of
Illinois at Shawneetown.

Oct 31 Promissory note to Levi C. Turner for $4000. DS.
NhD. mDW 39835–162.

[Nov 1] To Charles Henry Thomas. ALS. MHi. mDW
39038. Reports his arrival from New York.

Nov 2 To Edward Everett. Invitation. MHi. mDW 14462.
Invites Everett to dinner.

Nov 2 To John Kintzing Kane. LS. PPAmP. mDW 14464.
Thanks Kane for the notice of his membership
in the American Philosophical Society.

Nov 2 To Hiram Ketchum. ALS. NhD. mDW 38667.
[1837?–1838?] Sends letter he wrote to publisher of *Boston
Atlas* for Ketchum's comments.

Nov 3 To Benjamin Guild. ALS. DLC. mDWs. Agrees
that the Trustees of the [Massachusetts
Agricultural Society?] may meet at John C.
Winthrop's house if Winthrop so desires it.

Nov 3 From Ferdinand Rudolph Hassler. ALS. DLC.
mDW 14465. States that he is unable to employ

	a Mr. Edgar, whom DW had recommended, in the survey of the coast at New York.	
Nov 4	To Caleb Cushing. ALS. NN. mDW 14469. States that he cannot "take any part in the cause" which Cushing mentioned in his letter of Nov 2 (not found).	
Nov 4	To Caleb Cushing. ALS. NN. mDW 14471. Writes that after Cushing left New York he learned that "the affections of that Lady are already deeply engaged."	
Nov 6	*From Edward Webster.*	248
[c. Nov 6]	To [David A. Hall] (enclosure: Henry R. Daland to D. A. Hall, Nov 4, 1837). ALS. NhD. mDW 14473. In the absence of Stephen White, DW requests the renewal of White's note for $2500.	
Nov 12	To Samuel Lewis Southard. ALS. NjP. mDW 14479. Asks Southard to answer his letter (not found) as soon as he can.	
Nov 13	To Emeline Colby Webster Lindsly. ALS. DMaM. mDW 14481. Asks her help in securing accommodations for the Websters and Curtises in Washington.	
Nov 13	To Charles Henry Thomas. ALS. MHi. mDW 14485. Sends pair of greyhound puppies to Marshfield.	
[Nov 15]	To Franklin Haven. ALS. MH-H. mDW 14548. Reports that he has not yet received his bond from Samuel Lewis Southard and asks Haven to honor a check for $1000.	
Nov 15	From Henry Edwards. Printed. *Niles' National Register*, 53 (Dec 2, 1837): 218. Asks DW if he might attend the Whig victory celebration in Massachusetts.	
Nov 16	*To Henry Edwards et al.*	249
Nov 16	To Samuel Lewis Southard. ALS. NjP. mDW 14487. Asks Southard to answer his letter relating to the Morris Canal.	
Nov 17	To [John H. Ostrom?]. ALS. MBBS. mDW 14489. Praises New York's political "revolution" and expresses the hope that he will see Ostrom in New York.	
Nov 17	From J. William Davis. ALS. DNA, RG 46. mDW 47853. Asks for DW's views on the subtreasury.	
Nov 19	*From Fisher Ames Harding.*	250
Nov 20	To George Washington Lay. ALS. DLC. mDW 14494. Expresses his pleasure with the results of the New York elections.	
Nov 20	From John M. Muscott. ALS. DNA, RG 46. mDW 47748. Asks DW to send him congressional documents.	

[Nov 23]   To Edward Everett. ALS. MHi. mDW 14545.
Informs Everett that he is leaving for New York.

[Nov 26]   From A. Merrymacker, Jr. ALS. DNA, RG 46.
mDW 47849. Discusses the need for
constitutional revisions to allow the direct
election of president, vice president, and
senators.

Nov 27   From John R. Kellogg. ALS. DNA, RG 46. mDW
47795. Requests congressional documents from
DW.

Nov 28   From W. A. Wigton. ALS. DNA, RG 46. mDW
47857. Asks DW to frank him public documents.

Nov 29   To Emeline Colby Webster Lindsly. ALS. DMaM.
mDW 14496. Accepts Mrs. Clemens's offer to
room and board the Websters and the Curtises.

Nov 29   Memorial of Lucy Still for a pension (with LS by
Lucy Still and Eben Farnwell). ADS. DNA, RG
46. mDW 46669.

[Nov–Dec]   To Emeline Colby Webster Lindsly. ALS. DMaM.
mDW 38698. Asks her help in finding rooms in
Washington.

Dec 1   To John Plummer Healy. ALS. MHi. mDW 14498.
Instructs Healy on the payment of certain notes.

Dec 1   From John Jay Kellogg. ALS. DNA, RG 46. mDW
47735. Asks DW to have the *National Intelligencer* and his speech on the subtreasury sent
to him.

Dec 2   From Anthony Lane. ALS. DNA, RG 46. mDW
47132. Sends memorial of citizens of New York
City against the "admission or annexation of
Texas."

Dec 4   To Franklin Haven. ALS. MH-H. mDW 14500.
Sends notes for his account.

Dec 4   From S. L. Hedge. ALS. DNA, RG 46. mDW 47773.
Reports the opening of a Whig reading room in
Plymouth and requests DW to send a Washing-
ton daily paper.

Dec 5   *From Daniel Fletcher Webster.*   251

Dec 5   Memorial of the yearly meeting of the Society of
Friends in New England against the annexation
of Texas to the United States. Copy. DNA, RG
46. mDW 47069.

Dec 6   From William W. Hall. ALS. DNA, RG 46. mDW
47841. Asks DW to introduce a resolution for
establishing a tribunal to adjudicate claims of
citizens against the United States.

Dec 8   From William E. Dunscomb. ALS. DNA, RG 46.
mDWs. Asks DW to give his attention to revision
of the pension laws respecting Revolutionary
soldiers.

[c. Dec 8]	From Josiah T. Marshall. ALS. DNA, RG 46. mDW 47834. Asks DW to place him on his mailing list.
Dec 9	From Moses Decker. ALS. DNA, RG 46. mDW 47813. Asks DW to send him congressional documents.
Dec 9	From Henry Oliphant. ALS. DNA, RG 46. mDW 47793. Requests copies of DW's speeches and other public documents.
Dec 9	From H. C. Van Schaack. ALS. DNA, RG 56. mDW 47809. Asks DW to frank him congressional documents.
Dec 10	From Thomas W. Balch. ALS. DNA, RG 46. mDW 47845. Asks DW for his speech on the sub-treasury.
Dec 11	*To Charles Henry Thomas.* 253
Dec 11	From John A. Hooke. ALS. DNA, RG 46. mDW 47801. Asks DW to frank him documents.
Dec 11	From Samuel Niles Sweet. ALS. DNA, RG 46. mDW 47805. Asks if he might dedicate his work on elocution to DW.
Dec 12	From Luther Humphrey. ALS. DNA, RG 46. mDW 47863. Sends petition on the slavery question.
Dec 12	From George H. Moore. ALS. DNA, RG 46. mDW 47883. Asks DW for copies of his speeches and autographs to add to his collection.
Dec 12	From [George Washington?] Niles. ALS. NhD. mDW 14509. Asks if he might publish Webster's oration delivered before the United Fraternity at Dartmouth College in 1801.
Dec 12	From John Peters & Co. ALS. DNA, RG 46. mDWs. Ask Webster's attention to the law requiring certificates on the values of British currency for all goods imported.
Dec 13	From Robert C. Merrill. ALS. DNA, RG 46. mDW 47833. Asks DW to send him Van Buren's message and accompanying documents.
Dec 14	To Nicholas Biddle. ALS. PPL. mDWs. Introduces Levi C. Turner.
Dec 14	To Joseph Story. ALS. DLC. mDW 14511. Asks if Julia Webster might accompany Story to Washington.
Dec 14	From Virgil David. ALS. DNA, RG 46. mDW 47791. Requests copies of the printed documents accompanying the President's message.
Dec 14	From P. E. Hubbard. ALS. DNA, RG 46. mDW 47803. Asks DW to frank him public documents.
Dec 15	To Joseph Trumbull (with reply to DW, Dec 18, 1837). ALS. NhD. mDW 14514. Sends a new

acceptance for David Webster and a check of
his own for $1031.

Dec 15   From John Kay. ALS. DNA, RG 46. mDW 47855.
          Asks DW to frank him congressional documents.

Dec 15   From Whitmell P. Tunstall. ALS. DNA, RG 46.
          mDW 47831. Asks DW to frank him congres-
          sional documents.

Dec 16   From E. L. Bascom. ALS. DNA, RG 46. mDW
          47885. Asks DW to send him documents.

Dec 16–18 *From Henry L. Kinney.*   254

Dec 16   From Samuel Lord. ALS. DNA, RG 46. mDW
          47789. Sends names of people in Portsmouth
          area to whom DW should send documents.

Dec 17   From Milton Barney. ALS. DNA, RG 46. mDW
          47742. Thanks DW for his frank of several
          congressional documents.

Dec 17   From William Davis. ALS. DNA, RG 46. mDW
          47854. Asks for DW's views on the subtreasury.

Dec 18   From Charles Bailey. ALS. DNA, RG 46. mDW
          47650. Requests a copy of the President's
          message and other public documents relating to
          the public lands.

Dec 18   From M. P. Clossey. ALS. DNA, RG 46. mDW
          47799. Asks DW to encourage Beverly Allen's
          "sample of Literature, 'West of the Mississippi.' "

Dec 18   From Joseph Trumbull. AL copy. NhD. mDW
          39835–81. Accepts Webster's payments and
          proposals, submitted in his letter of Dec 15.

Dec 20   *From Ramsay Crooks.*   256

Dec 20   From S. A. Doolittle. ALS. DNA, RG 46. mDW
          47777. Discusses the preemption question.

Dec 20   From William Jenkins, Arnold Congdon, and
          Samuel Boyd Tobey. Copy. DNA, RG 46. mDW
          47072. Enclose the memorial of the yearly
          meeting of the Society of Friends of New
          England against the annexation of Texas.

Dec 21   From Francis T. Allen. ALS. DNA, RG 46. mDW
          47839. Asks DW to sponsor petitions against
          slavery and the annexation of Texas.

Dec 22   From John Bryant. ALS. DNA, RG 46. mDW
          47786. Discusses the New Hampshire
          gubernatorial election and sends DW a list of
          names to whom documents should be sent.

Dec 22   From M. Shaw. ALS. DNA, RG 46. mDW 47787.
          Sends list of Maine politicians to whom DW
          should frank documents.

Dec 22   From George M. Weld. LS. DNA, RG 46. mDW
          46581. Sends petition requesting the repayment
          of extra duties paid by him on supposedly
          "foreign tonnage."

Dec 26   From George Leet. ALS. DNA, RG 46. mDW
47837. Reports that he is forwarding three
petitions requesting the repeal of the existing
laws relating to slavery and the slave trade in
the District of Columbia.

Dec 26   From J. M. Skinner. ALS. DNA, RG 46. mDW
47750. Asks DW to support a reasonable
preemption law.

Dec 27   From B. Franklin. ALS. DNA, RG 46. mDW 47762.
Sends DW a short article (not found) on the
question of the national currency.

Dec 27   From George E. Pierce. ALS. DNA, RG 46. mDW
47815. Requests the grant of a township of land
to Western Reserve College for the support of
the institution.

Dec 27   Memorial of the Franklin Association of Congre-
gational ministers against the annexation
of Texas. Copy. DNA, RG 46. mDW 47060.

Dec 28   From Robb & Swift (per P. E. Dunnett). ALS.
DNA, RG 46. mDW 47782. Informs DW that
they have shipped him a blue cloth coat.

Dec 28   From James Watson Webb. LS. DNA, RG 46.
mDW 46477. Asks DW's assistance and support
in importing the Napier printing machine duty
free.

Dec 28   From Daniel Fletcher Webster. ALS. NhHi. mDW
14522. Van Tyne, p. 665 (excerpt). Reports on
his trip to St. Louis.

Dec 29   From George Edmund Badger. ALS. DLC. mDW
14530. Sends packet of materials relating to the
case of *Lattimer* v. *Poteet*, 14 Peters 4 (1840).

Dec 29   Bill and accompanying documents relative to
providing greater security for the lives of
passengers on steamboats. Copy, with supporting
ALS. DNA, RG 46. mDW 46482.

Dec 30   To Timothy Fletcher or John Plummer Healy.
ALS. NNC. mDW 14533. Instructs Fletcher or
Healy to remit $2500 to George and Edward
Curtis.

Dec 30   To Franklin Haven. ALS. MH-H. mDW 14535.
Sends deposits to cover check he has issued on
the Merchants' Bank.

Dec 30   From John Kimball. ALS. DNA, RG 46. mDW
47613. Asks DW to frank him documents.

Dec 30   *From Daniel Fletcher Webster.*   257

Dec 31   From Humphrey B. Jones. ALS. DNA, RG 46.
mDW 47712. Informs DW that J. D. Edwards
does not reside in Perry County, Illinois.

[Dec]   To [John Plummer Healy]. ALS. MHi. mDW 14540.

Urges Healy to go to New Hampshire to "put right" political affairs there.

[Dec] From William C. Storrs. ALS. DNA, RG 46. mDW 47811. Requests DW to send him a printed copy of the correspondence relating to the northeastern boundary question.

[Dec] From [?]. Printed. Daniel Webster, *Speeches and Forensic Arguments* (Boston, 1843), 3: 243. Discusses the government's payments to Marblehead fisherman in the notes of the collapsed Commonwealth Bank of Boston.

[1837] To [Timothy Fletcher]. ALS. MHi. mDW 14546. Instructs Fletcher on trimming trees.

[1837] To Hiram Ketchum. ALS. NhD. mDW 38673. Introduces Jacob Bigelow.

[1837] To Robert Charles Winthrop. ALS. MHi. mDW 14550. Thanks Winthrop for letter.

[1837] From Nathaniel W. Howell et al. (to DW and Henry Clay). LS. DLC. mDW 14551. Inform them of a public meeting in Ontario County, N.Y., on the "present deranged State of the currency"; state that they enclose their memorial (not found).

[1837] From Noah Webster (under pseudonym "Marcellus"). Printed. Noah Webster, *A Collection of Papers on Political, Literary and Moral Subjects* (New York, 1843), pp. 269–285. Asserts that knowledge and principle, as well as intelligence and virtue, are important for a republican government.

[1837] Memorandum of DW's lands kept by John T. Haight. AD. WHi. mDW 40668.

[1837–1839] To Samuel Lewis Southard. ALS. NjP. mDW 14555. Urges him to come to the Senate for vote on the subtreasury bill.

[1837–1839?] To John Jordan Crittenden. ALS. NcD. mDW 14542. Invites Crittenden, Henry Clay, and Richard H. Menefee to join him for a dinner of salmon.

[1837–1840] To John Plummer Healy. ALS. MHi. mDW 38637. Asks him to open letters from LaSalle or New York.

1838

Jan 2 *To Ramsay Crooks.* 257

Jan 3 Motion by DW to dispense with consular certificates. AD. DNA, RG 46. mDW 46445.

Jan 3 Petition of John Howard Kyan, of Middlesex,

England, for a United States patent on his method of preserving vegetables from decay. Copy. DNA, RG 46. mDW 46663.

Jan 3   Petition of George M. Weld for the repayment of duties improperly paid by him as "foreign tonnage." DS. DNA, RG 46. mDW 46578.

Jan 4   To James Trecothick Austin. LS. MBU. mDW 14559. Discusses the case of *Rhode Island* v. *Massachusetts*, 12 Peters 657 (1838).

Jan 4   To Joseph Cowperthwaite. ALS. DLC. mDW 14562. Hopes that Thomas Dunlap will "look to my *mortgage*, & put things right."

Jan 4   From Charles L. Hoff. ALS. DNA, RG 46. mDW 47821. Reports on the recent Whig victory in the mayoral election in Wheeling.

Jan 4   Bill to authorize the importation of a Napiers printing press duty free. Copy. DNA, RG 46. mDW 46414.

Jan 4   Motion by DW requesting the secretary of the treasury to communicate to the Senate a statement of customs house bonds executed in the United States between 1827 and 1837. Copy. DNA, RG 46. mDW 46447.

Jan 4   Motion by DW requesting the secretary of the treasury to inform the Senate of the amount of Treasury notes issued since the last session of Congress. AD. DNA, RG 46. mDW 46449.

Jan 4   Documents submitted in support of the bill to import the Napier printing machine duty free (with James Watson Webb to DW, Dec 28, 1837; and R. Hoe & Co. to Webb, Aug 28, 1837). LS and ALS. DNA, RG 46. mDW 46476.

Jan 5   From Ramsay Crooks. LC. NHi. mDWs. Discusses DW's proposal for paying the Kinney note.

Jan 5   From Richard Pickering. ALS. DNA, RG 46. mDW 47829. Thanks DW for his speech on the currency.

Jan 8   From John W. H. Parker. ALS. DNA, RG 46. mDW 47827. Requests DW's autograph.

Jan 8   *From Daniel Fletcher Webster.*   258

Jan 10   From J. I. Brooks. ALS. DNA, RG 46. mDW 47825. Requests copy of DW's speech on Foot's resolution.

Jan 10   From A. W. Fletcher. ALS. DNA, RG 46. mDW 47823. Asks DW to sell him a few hundred acres of land at Peru, Ill., on credit.

Jan 10   From George A. Woodbridge. ALS. DNA, RG 46. mDW 47724. Discusses preemption and French claims questions.

Jan 11   *To [Luther Christopher] Peck.*   261

Jan 11   From Thomas Goodsell. ALS. DNA, RG 46. mDW
47757. Asks DW to assist his son in getting an
appointment to West Point.

Jan 12   From A. G. Holmes. ALS. DNA, RG 46. mDW
47764. Comments on his old age, the years
1775–1776, and his astonishment that recent
elections have not changed the views of Calhoun
and the administration.

Jan 13   From William A. Platt. ALS. DNA, RG 46. mDW
47767. Asks DW to frank him congressional
papers.

Jan 13   From John Renton. ALS. DNA, RG 46. mDW
47737. Asks DW for autograph and public
documents.

Jan 14   From Zalmon F. Robinson. ALS. DNA, RG 46.
mDW 47739. Asks DW for a copy of the
proceedings of Congress.

Jan 15   *To Hiram Ketchum.*   262

Jan 15   From William Burr. ALS. DNA, RG 46. mDW
46619. Sends petition against removing the duty
on woolen blankets.

Jan 15   From Edward Everett (to DW and James
Trecothick Austin). AL draft. MHi. mDW
14564. Asks that DW and Austin write him
on the case between Rhode Island and
Massachusetts.

Jan 15   From William Kent. ALS. DNA, RG 46. mDW
47753. Sends list of residents of Concord, N.H.,
to whom congressional materials should be sent.

Jan 15   From Charles Webster. ALS. DNA, RG 46. mDW
47760. A mechanic out of work, Charles Webster
expresses his appreciation for DW and Clay.

Jan 16   From Daniel Adams. ALS. DNA, RG 46. mDW
47769. States that the Whigs of New Hampshire
are finally organizing to defeat the Jacksonians.

Jan 16   From Anthony Colby. ALS. DNA, RG 46. mDW
47755. Sends list of names to whom newspapers
and public documents should be sent.

Jan 17   From Caleb Atwater. ALS. NhHi. mDW 14572.
Asks DW to assist him in the adjustment of his
claim for compensation.

Jan 17   From G. B. Perry. ALS. DNA, RG 46. mDW 47874.
Asks DW to send him documents, writings, and
speeches that he might use in his newspaper,
the *Canton Herald*.

Jan 17   Motion by DW requesting information from the
secretary of the treasury relative to the payment
of pensions and fishing bounties by the
Commonwealth Bank of Boston and whether

Jan 29   From Samuel A. Eliot (enclosed with Benjamin
Dole to DW, Jan 31, 1838). ALS. DNA, RG 94.
mDWs. Asks DW to assist Benjamin Dole's son
to secure an appointment to West Point.

Jan 29   From David Goodrich. ALS. DNA, RG 46. mDW
47599. Asks DW to use his influence to keep the
mail route from Chicago to Galena through
Rockford.

Jan 29   From William P. Hall. ALS. DNA, RG 46. mDW
47730. Urges DW to support a preemption bill,
a bill for the extension of the National Road,
and one for the improvement of western waters.

Jan 29   *From Daniel Fletcher Webster.*   266

Jan 29   Memorial of Joseph Holmes for the payment of a
bounty on a fishing vessel that was lost at sea.
DS. DNA, RG 46. mDW 46584.

Jan 29   Petition of James Patterson and others, manufacturers of woolen blankets, against any reduc-
tion of duties on them. ADS. DNA, RG 46.
mDW 46618.

Jan 29   Memorial of William S. Freeman and others for an
appropriation for the completion of the frigate
Raritan. DS. DNA, RG 46. mDW 46631.

Jan 30   From J. B. Crowe. ALS. DNA, RG 46. mDW 47877.
Announces that DW has been elected an
honorary member of the Whig Society of
Hanover College.

Jan 31   To Mahlon Dickerson. ALS. MHi. mDW 14602.
Asks Dickerson to place Nathan Allen Cole's
name on the list of applicants for midshipmen.

Jan 31   From Benjamin Dole (enclosure: Samuel A. Eliot
to DW, Jan 29, 1838). ALS. DNA, RG 94.
mDWs. Asks DW to assist his son, William C.
Dole, in securing an appointment to West Point.

[Jan 31]   "Light in the East." AD. NN. mDW 14604.
Editorial (for the *National Intelligencer?*)
discussing the speech of the governor of Maine.

Jan 31   Memorial of the Board of Trade of New York City
for the establishment of a national bank. DS.
DNA, RG 46. mDW 47183.

[Jan]   To [Hiram Ketchum]. AD. NhD. mDW 14613. PC,
2: 184–185. Discusses the Hartford Convention
and asserts that he had nothing to do with it.

Feb 1   To Franklin Haven. ALS. MH-H. 14618. Sends a
deposit of $500.

Feb 1   From Thomas Denny. ALS. DNA, RG 46. mDW
47691. Reports that he is sending the memorial
of the Board of Trade of New York City (Jan
31) requesting the establishment of a national
bank.

Feb 1   From Henry L. Kinney. ALS. NhHi. mDW 14620. Thanks DW for letters; sends DW $1000 and expresses his regret that DW may be dissatisfied with him.

Feb 1   From J. Webster Wiggin. ALS. DNA, RG 46. mDW 47622. Asks if DW might assist him in financing his college education.

Feb 2   To Seth Weston. ALS. NhHi. mDW 14622. *PC*, 2: 33–34. Praises Weston for his meticulous care in keeping the accounts with Charles Henry Thomas.

Feb 2   From Loammi Baldwin. ALS draft. MiU-C. mDWs. Introduces a Mr. Paris.

Feb 2   From S. C. Lyford. ALS. DNA, RG 46. mDW 47879. Sends a list of men in New Hampshire to whom DW should frank documents.

Feb 2   From Daniel L. Miller, Jr. ALS. DNA, RG 46. mDW 47721. Sends memorials (not found) against the annexation of Texas.

Feb 2   From John Thomas. ALS. DNA, RG 46. mDW 47872. Asks DW to send Whig documents to the Rev. Benjamin Whittemore.

Feb 3   From George W. Davis. ALS. DNA, RG 46. mDW 47881. Requests DW's autograph again.

Feb 3   From N. W. St. John. ALS. DNA, RG 46. mDW 47255. Sends antislavery petition of the inhabitants of Wakefield, Ohio.

Feb 3   From Daniel H. Whitney. ALS. DNA, RG 46. mDW 47652. Opposes the transfer of the mail route between Chicago and Galena from Rockford south to the Rock River.

Feb 3   From D. G. Wright. ALS. DNA, RG 46. mDW 47718. Asks if Isaac Hill, governor of New Hampshire, is also a "payer of Pensions" for the United States government; and if any European power or the United States has recognized the independence of Haiti.

Feb 5   Motion by DW requesting the Committee on Finance to inquire into the expediency of relinquishing duties on two chain cables imported into the United States by John E. Lane. AD. DNA, RG 46. mDW 46456.

Feb 5   Memorial of citizens of Hartford, Conn., against the subtreasury. DS. DNA, RG 46. mDW 47177.

Feb 7   To John Plummer Healy. ALS. MHi. mDW 14624. Sends letter from Thomas A. Gold of Pittsfield, Mass., about French claims and asks Healy to answer it.

Feb 7   To Joel Roberts Poinsett. ALS. NhD. mDW 14626.

States that he has not yet delivered the Morgan medal.

Feb 7   To [*Robert Charles Winthrop*].   268

Feb 7   From Charles Griswold. ALS. DNA, RG 46. mDW 47628. Requests a copy of DW's speech on the subtreasury.

Feb 7   From William Rison. ALS. DNA, RG 46. mDW 47698. Requests a copy of DW's speech on the subtreasury.

Feb 8   From Jacob Latting. ALS. DNA, RG 46. mDW 47727. Attributes the nation's economic troubles to the Jacksonians and asks for relief either through the federal distribution of money or the issuance of Treasury notes.

Feb 8   From Warren Marchant. ALS. DNA, RG 46. mDW 47733. Sends two petitions from Barnstable, Mass.

Feb 9   From William M. Kimball. ALS. DNA, RG 46. mDW 47784. Requests documents.

Feb 9   From N. B. Mountfort. ALS. DNA, RG 46. mDW 47611. Reports that he is sending a copy of the constitution and bylaws of the Whig Association of the sixteenth ward of New York City.

Feb 10   To *Hiram Ketchum*.   268

Feb 10   From John Fiske. ALS. DNA, RG 46. mDW 47700. Sends DW a copy of the proceedings of the clerical convention at Worcester on the subject of slavery.

Feb 10   From Samuel Leeds, Jr. ALS. DNA, RG 46. mDW 47694. States that the exchange rates on Tennessee and Mississippi bills are far worse than those DW mentioned in recent remarks.

Feb 12   To Melvin Copeland. ALS. NN. mDW 14632. Acknowledges the receipt of a memorial.

Feb 12   To John Plummer Healy. ALS. MHi. mDW 14634. Discusses the considerations Healy should observe in the selection of a new law office.

Feb 12   To Hiram Ketchum. ALS. NhD. mDW 14636. Curtis, 1: 454–455. Discusses the tariff compromise of 1833.

[Feb 12?]   To Hiram Ketchum (enclosure: extract from the Journal of the House of Representatives on the tariff bill). ALS. CSmH. mDW 14640. Sends information relative to the passage of the compromise tariff of 1833.

Feb 12   From Samuel G. Wheeler. ALS. DNA, RG 46. mDW 47632. Asks DW to assist his stepson, Henry A. Allen, in securing an appointment as midshipman.

Feb 12   Memorials against slavery and the slave trade in

the District of Columbia, from citizens of
Limington (mDW 47293), Thorndike (mDW
47288), Me.; Boston (mDW 47322, mDW
47238), Bradford, West Parish (mDW 47284),
East Bradford (mDW 47282), East Cambridge
(mDW 47286), Gloucester (mDW 47291),
Holliston (mDW 47296), Kingston (mDW
47280), Swansey (mDW 47245), Mass.; Cass
County, Mich. (mDW 47240); Great Falls
Village (mDW 47277), Greenland (mDW
47252), N.H.; Champlain (mDW 47249),
Clinton County (mDW 47298), Peru (mDW
47247), N.Y.; Brookfield (mDW 47263),
Highland County (mDW 47261), Trumbull
County (mDW 47258), Wakeman (mDW
47254), Ohio; Luzerne County (mDW 47275),
Wilkes-Barre (mDW 47270), Pa.; Joseph Clap
and others (mDW 47268).

Feb 12   Memorials against the annexation of Texas from
Cornwall (mDW 47123), Plymouth (mDW
46999), Roxbury (mDW 47120), Conn.;
Macoupin County, Ill. (mDW 47099); Abingdon
(mDW 47074, mDW 47078), Boxborough
(mDW 47083, mDW 47097), Carlisle (mDW
47085), Charlestown (mDW 47008), Concord
(mDW 47125), Dover (mDW 47087), Falmouth
(mDW 47091), Litchfield (mDW 47063),
Mendon (mDW 47066), Milton (mDW 47089),
Pembroke (mDW 47055), Plymouth (mDW
47093), Wayland (mDW 47081), Wendell
(mDW 47057), Mass.; Manchester (mDW
47102), Washtenaw County (mDW 47103,
mDW 47104, mDW 47105), Mich.; New
Ipswich, N.H. (mDW 47002); Clinton County
(mDW 47106), Lawrence (mDW 46993), New
York City (mDW 47130), St. Lawrence County
(mDW 47047), Schenectady (mDW 47038),
Willsborough (mDW 46991, mDW 47041, mDW
47043, mDW 47045, mDW 47051, mDW
47053), N.Y.; Trumbull County, Ohio (mDW
47114, mDW 46997); Kingston (mDW 46995),
Philadelphia County (mDW 47033, mDW
47034, mDW 47035, mDW 47037), Pa.; Orleans
County, Vt. (mDW 47116); Duanesburg Society
of Friends (mDW 47049).

Feb 13 [1838]   *To Nicholas Biddle.*   270
Feb 13   *To Hiram Ketchum, with enclosure, Slavery*
Proposition.   270
Feb 13   From John Ruggles. ALS. DNA, RG. 46. mDW

	46555. Requests an investigation into charges against members of Congress.	
Feb 14	To John Plummer Healy. ALS. MHi. mDW 14650. Asks him to pay interest on a draft and to publicize in New Hampshire that Governor Isaac Hill holds an appointment from the United States.	
Feb 14	From Henry L. Kinney.	271
Feb 14	From J. A. Lowell (enclosed with DW to John Forsyth, Feb 19, 1838). ALS. DNA, RG 59. mDW 55456. Asks DW to send his father's memorial to the secretary of state.	
Feb 15	From A. W. Townsend. ALS. DNA, RG 46. mDW 47635. Urges him to support William C. Rives's bill proposing the selection of twenty-five deposit banks.	
Feb 15	Memorial of D. J. Browne requesting Congress to adopt measures for procuring and preserving a supply of timber for naval purposes. ADS. DNA, RG 46. mDW 46635.	
Feb 16	To Robert Charles Winthrop.	274
Feb 16	From Joseph Cochran, Jr. ALS. DNA, RG 46. mDW 47645. Asks DW to send documents to New Hampshire for distribution.	
Feb 16	From John McLure. ALS. DNA, RG 46. mDW 47687. Discusses the opposition in Pittsburgh to the building of a marine hospital.	
Feb 16	From William Sullivan. ALS. NhHi. mDW 14660. Discusses a report from the War Department and Webster's speech on the subtreasury.	
Feb 16	Tax bill for $53.47 on DW's Londonderry property for 1837. Copy. NhD. mDW 39835–168.	
Feb 16	Motion by DW to appoint a committee to inquire into the charges made in the letter of John Ruggles of Feb 13. AD. DNA, RG 46. mDW 46458.	
Feb 18	From Nicholas Biddle.	274
[Feb 18–19]	From Nicholas Biddle (memorandum). LC. DLC. mDWs. Sends DW points to use in opposing Grundy's bill and report.	
Feb 19	To Nicholas Biddle. LS. DLC. mDW 14664. Asks Biddle to give him an estimate of the debt owed by the United States to Europe.	
Feb 19	To John Forsyth (enclosure: J. A. Lowell to DW, Feb 14, 1838). ALS. DNA, RG 59. mDW 55455. Asks Forsyth to give his attention to Lowell's letter.	
Feb 19	To Samuel Lewis Southard. ALS. NjP. mDW 14666. States that he will "take care that	

	nothing happens to your prejudice in the R. I. & Mass. cause, till yr return."
Feb 19	From McClintock Young. ALS. NhHi. mDW 14668. Reports on the amount of money in circulation.
Feb 19	Petition of Elisha Dunham to be indemnified for spoliations committed by France prior to 1800. DS. DNA, RG 46. mDW 47504.
Feb 19	Memorial of 105 "legal voters" of Boston, Mass., against the annexation of Texas. DS. DNA, RG 46. mDW 47170.
Feb 19	Memorials of citizens of Boston, Mass. (mDW 47320), and Madison County, N.Y. (mDW 47168), against the admission of any new slaveholding state. DS. DNA, RG 46.
Feb 20	From S. A. Holbrook. ALS. DNA, RG 46. mDW 47608. Thanks DW for documents.
Feb 20	From Daniel Hoyt. ALS. DNA, RG 46. mDW 47618. Thanks DW for his several franks.
Feb 20	From James McClelland. ALS. DNA, RG 46. mDW 47859. Asks DW to send him copies of speeches on the subtreasury.
Feb 20	From Charles Osgood. ALS. DNA, RG 46. mDW 47605. Thanks DW for documents.
Feb 21	From J. Bailey. ALS. DNA, RG 46. mDW 47620. Thanks DW for documents.
Feb 21	From Matthew Bridge. ALS. DNA, RG 46. mDW 47639. Asks DW to send documents to Whigs.
Feb 21	From C. P. and B. R. Curtis. ALS. DNA, RG 46. mDW 46602. Send deposition of E. Baldwin, president of the Shoe and Leather Dealers Bank of Boston, and discuss the draft the company was forced to accept in payment from the customs house.
Feb 21	From John H. Ferris. ALS. DNA, RG 46. mDW 47626. Thanks DW for speech on the subtreasury.
Feb 22	To Ashton Alexander. ALS. FrN. mDWs. Declines invitation to dinner for some of Alexander's "New York friends."
Feb 22	From H. Chase. ALS. DNA, RG 46. mDW 47637. Thanks DW for franked documents.
Feb 22	From C. Flanders. ALS. DNA, RG 46. mDW 47615. Thanks DW for speeches on the subtreasury bill.
Feb 22	From John Forsyth. LC. DNA, RG 59. mDW 55679. Discusses the Lowell memorial.
Feb 22	From Luther D. Sawyer. ALS. DNA, RG 46. mDW 47601. Asks that copies of "useful & interesting" speeches be sent him.
Feb 22	From John Thomas. ALS. DNA, RG 46. mDW

47647. Urges DW to send documents to
Benjamin Ellis.

Feb 22   From Thomas Wright, Jr. ALS. DNA, RG 46.
mDW 47676. Requests DW to send him
documents, especially his subtreasury speech.

Feb 22   Memorial of citizens of New York against the
passage of the subtreasury bill and for the
establishment of a national bank. DS. DNA, RG
46. mDW 47188.

Feb 23   *To [Lewis F.?] Allen.*   274
Feb 23   *To [Richard] Haughton.*   275
Feb 23   To [?]. ALS. NhD. mDW 14676. Reports the
decision in some unidentified case.

Feb 23   *From Ramsay Crooks.*   276
Feb 24   *To Ramsay Crooks.*   277
Feb 24   To Mahlon Dickerson (from DW et al.). LS. MHi.
mDW 14679. Recommend the appointment of
Charles Bertody as midshipman.

Feb 24   *To Robert Charles Winthrop.*   277
Feb 24   From John L. Class. ALS. DNA, RG 46. mDW
47682. Requests a copy of DW's speech on the
subtreasury.

Feb 25   *To Horatio Gates Cilley.*   278
[Feb 25] To [Henry Willis Kinsman]. ALS. NhD. mDW
14688. Reminds him that John Plummer Healy
is to attend to the business referred to in a
letter from Colonel [Ebenezer] Webster.

Feb 25   From Jeremiah Mason. Typed copy. NhHi. mDW
14690. Discusses the efforts of Henry Hubbard
of New Hampshire to reopen the investigation
into Mason's presidency of the Portsmouth
branch of the Bank of the United States.

Feb 25   From Elijah Porter. ALS. DNA, RG 46. mDW
47678. Regards DW as "the Senator of the whole
nation"; hopes to see him elected president.

Feb 25   Petition of several officers of the United States
Army for discontinuing the allowance of liquor
to soldiers on fatigue duty. ADS. DNA, RG 46.
mDW 46629.

Feb 26   *To Ramsay Crooks.*   279
[Feb]   To Joseph Gales and W. W. Seaton. ALS. NhHi.
mDW 14698. Asks them to print 1000 copies of
his speech on Clay's substitute for Calhoun's
resolution.

March 1   From John B. Whetten. LC. NHi. mDWs. Acknowledges the receipt of $3000 as payment on
DW's note endorsed for Kinney.

March 1   From Emerson R. Wright. ALS. DNA, RG 46.
mDW 47630. Requests an autographed copy of
DW's subtreasury speech.

March 16 From Nicholas Biddle. LC. DLC. mDWs. Asks DW to work to defeat first section of Senate Bill 257.

[March 17] To Nicholas Biddle. ALS. DLC. mDW 15383. Discusses banks, resumption, and the subtreasury bill.

March 20 [19] To Samuel Lewis Southard. ALS. NjP. mDW 14817. Writes Southard of his previous comments on the banking question, probably for use in a speech on the subtreasury.

March 20 To Charles Brickett Haddock. ALS. NhD. mDW 14821. Sends deed that he has had redrawn.

March 22 From Daniel Fletcher Webster. ALS. NhHi. mDW 14822. Discusses his activities at the Illinois farm and Henry L. Kinney's intentions to travel east.

March 25 *To Franklin Haven.* 285

March 25 Petition of George M. Weld for the remission of the tonnage duty on a cargo of coal imported by him. ADS. DNA, RG 46. mDW 46593.

March 28 To Franklin Haven. ALS. MH-H. mDW 14828. Sends draft for renewal and one for deposit.

March 29 From Jean Baptiste Beaubien. LS. NhHi. mDW 14830. Discusses his case before the Supreme Court.

March 29 Memorial of the Shoe and Leather Dealers Bank of Boston, requesting Congress to indemnify them against loss by depreciation of certain bank bills that they received in payment of a certain customs house draft. ADS. DNA, RG 46. mDW 46598.

March 29 Memorials against the annexation of Texas from citizens of Philadelphia County, Pa. (mDW 47174, mDW 47175, mDW 47176). DS. DNA, RG 46.

March 29 Memorials against the passage of the subtreasury bill from William Banks and others (mDW 47193), H. C. Graham and A. D. Mills (mDW 47197), and citizens of Colchester, Vt. (mDW 47203), DS. DNA, RG 46.

March 30 To Charles Henry Thomas. ALS. MHi. mDW 14833. Discusses farm matters.

[April 2] To Hiram Ketchum. Printed. Curtis, 1: 574. Reports progress on the printing of his speeches.

April 3 To Franklin Haven. ALS. MH-H. mDW 14835. Asks him to honor certain small drafts; states that he regards "the Sub-Treasury as dead."

April 6 To James Silk Buckingham. ALS. NHi. mDW 14837. Acknowledges the receipt of some unidentified communication.

April 6 *To George Wallace Jones.* 286

	also by others. NhD. mDW 14901. Invite DW for the bicentennial of the settlement of Exeter, N.H., in June 1839.	
May 5	To Joseph Warren Scott. Photocopy. NjP. mDW 14903. States that, in accordance with Scott's request, he will gladly attend to the "case of Mrs. Evans" when it comes before the Senate.	
May 7	To Nicholas Biddle. ALS. DLC. mDWs. Discusses legislation relating to the Bank.	
May 7	To Edward Everett. ALS. MHi. mDW 14905. Sends copy of the opinion of the Supreme Court in *Rhode Island* v. *Massachusetts*, 12 Peters 657 (1838).	
May 7	*To Franklin Haven.*	294
May 7	To John Plummer Healy. ALS. MHi. mDW 14910. Sends some unidentified item for the cashier of the Hancock Bank.	
May 7	From Edward Everett (to DW and John Davis, 1787–1854). AL draft. MHi. mDW 14912. Reports that he has been informed of "corruption & surprize" in the treaty recently negotiated at Buffalo and ratified by the Massachusetts legislature, and requests them to give their attention to the reports when the treaty comes before the Senate.	
May 7	Memorial of citizens of Ogdensburg, N.Y., against the passage of the subtreasury bill and for the incorporation of a national bank. DS. DNA, RG 46. mDW 47205.	
May 7	Memorials against executing the treaty made with the Cherokee Indians at New Echota from citizens of Norwich, Conn. (mDW 47462); Portland, Me. (mDW 47459); Andover (mDW 47468), Boston (mDW 47479), Holliston (mDW 47472, mDW 47476), Mass.; Oneida County, N.Y. (mDW 47456). DS. DNA, RG 46.	
May 8	*To Roswell L. Colt.*	294
May 10	*To Robert Charles Winthrop.*	295
May 10	Memorials against executing the treaty made with the Cherokee Indians at New Echota from citizens of Plymouth (mDW 47491), Roxbury (mDW 47493), Mass. DS. DNA, RG 46.	
May 10	Report and resolutions from a committee of the legislature of Massachusetts relating to the northeastern boundary. Printed document. DNA, RG 46. mDW 47506.	
May 11	*To Nathaniel Ray Thomas.*	295
May 11	From Ramsay Crooks. LC. NHi. mDWs. Asks again regarding Kinney's whereabouts.	
May 12 [1838]	*To Ramsay Crooks.*	297

June 4   To John Plummer Healy. LS. MHi. mDW 14969.
Asks him to direct an acceptance for $5000 to
Colonel Ebenezer Webster at Orono, Me.

June 4   To William Kelley et al. AL copy. NhHi. mDW
14971. PC, 2: 35–36. Thanks citizens of Erie,
Pa., for the cane from the timber of Perry's ship.

June 4   *To Nicholas Biddle.*   304

June 4   To Charles Henry Thomas. LS. MHi. mDW 14975.
Informs him to expect a shipment of lumber
from Colonel Ebenezer Webster.

June 5   *From Nicholas Biddle.*   304

June 5   Petition of merchants of New Haven, Conn., for a
repeal of the law that prevents collectors and
receivers from receiving in payment the bills of
those banks that have issued notes of denominations less than $5 since July 4, 1836. DS.
DNA, RG 46. mDW 47214.

June 6   From Joseph Lawrence. ALS. NhD. mDW 10959.
Discusses the role of the Washington County,
Pa., delegates to the 1835 Pennsylvania Whig
convention.

June 6   From Eliphalet Williams et al. (Board of
Commissioners of the Associated Banks of
Boston). DS. DNA, RG 46. mDW 47211. Solicit
DW's attention to their resolves regarding the
receipt of bank notes in denominations of less
than $5 in payment of obligations to the
government.

June 6   Motion by DW for information from the secretary
of the treasury relative to any order or circular
issued to collectors since June 1, 1838. AD.
DNA, RG 46. mDW 46469.

June 6   Memorial of the Board of Commissioners of the
Associated Banks in Boston for a repeal of the
law that prevents collectors and receivers from
receiving in payment the bills of those banks
that have issued notes of denominations less
than $5 since July 4, 1836. DS. DNA, RG 46.
mDW 47210.

[*June 9*]   *To Nicholas Biddle.*   305

June 12   *From Nicholas Biddle.*   306

June 12   Bill (S. 359) making further provision for the
collection of the public revenue. Copy, with AD
insertions. DNA, RG 46. mDW 46419.

June 14   From Samuel Bulkley Ruggles. ALS. DLC. mDW
14983. Praises DW's speech on the repeal of
certain provisions in the deposit law.

June 15   *From Nathaniel Ray Thomas.*   307

June 15   Four promissory notes of Henry L. Kinney, each
for $10,000, endorsed by DW. Copy. MWalB.

mDW 39835–181, 39835–187, 39835–189.
MdHi. mDW 39835–191.

[c. June 16]   To Nicholas Biddle.   308

June 16   From H. Wheeler et al. LS. DLC. mDW 14990.
Invite DW to a public dinner at Massillon, Ohio,
on July 4.

June 17   Agreement between William L. May and Daniel
Webster for the purchase of the Brewster estate
in Illinois. ADS by DW and May. MWalB. mDW
39835–247.

June 18   To Franklin Haven. ALS. NN. mDW 14993. Sends
money for deposit.

June 18   To Charles Henry Thomas. ALS. MHi. mDW
14995. Reports on his activities in Washington.

June 18   From Theodore Dwight. ALS. NhHi. mDW 14997.
PC, 2: 38–40. Reports a conversation he had
with Rufus King in 1804 on the subjects of the
northeastern boundary, King's negotiations in
England, and the Senate's rejection of the
boundary treaty.

June 19   From Ramsay Crooks.   309

June 20   [Certificate of membership in the Archaeological
Association of Athens]. Printed document with
MS insertions. NhD. mDW 14999.

June 22   To Ramsay Crooks.   310

June 22   To Franklin Haven. ALS. MH-H. mDW 15002.
Tells him to charge Taggard's acceptance to his
account.

June 23   To Thurlow Weed.   310

June [23]   To James Whitcomb. ALS. DNA, RG 49. mDW
57072. Asks that a certain Chicago patent be
sent to him when issued.

June 26   To Edgar Needham. ALS. MB. mDW 15012.
W & S, 16: 298–299. Asserts that John Adams
supported independence.

June 27   To Nicholas Biddle. ALS. RNHi. mDW 15016.
Introduces a Mr. Cohen of St. Louis.

June 27   Receipt from William L. May to DW for $1000.
DS. MWalB. mDW 39835–248.

[June 29]   To Caroline Le Roy Webster. ALS. NhHi. mDW
15018. Van Tyne, p. 596. Reports on activities
in Congress.

June 30   To Gideon Lee.   312

June 30   From H. Williams. ALS. DNA, RG 46. mDW 47549.
Sends memorial for the enactment of legislation
regulating steamboat navigation.

[June ?]   To Nicholas Biddle. ALS. DLC. mDW 15022.
Reports on the "Bill of pains & penalties" and
offers suggestions regarding a bank agency in
New York.

July 1   Diary. Printed. *Old Eliot*, 8 (January-March, April-June 1908): 29–32, 64–65. Runs to Dec 10, 1840.

July 2 [1838?]   To Mrs. Edward Everett. ALS. MHi. mDW 38367. Thanks her for "note."

July 2   Bill (S. 386) making provision for the discharge of debenture bonds in certain cases. Copy, with AD insertions. DNA, RG 46. mDW 46425.

July 4   To George Wallace Jones. ALS. Ia-HA. mDW 15032. Asserts that Messrs. Topsall & Co. do not hold an acceptance of his.

July 4   To Caroline Le Roy Webster. ALS. NhHi. mDW 15035. Van Tyne, p. 212. Comments on the interminable discussions in Congress.

July 5   Memorial of citizens of Boston, Mass., for the enactment of laws for the regulation of steamboat navigation. DS. DNA, RG 46. mDW 47548.

July 6   To Caroline Le Roy Webster. ALS. NhHi. mDW 15038. Van Tyne, pp. 212–213. Reports on weather and friends in Washington.

July 6   To Edward Webster. ALS. NhHi. mDW 15041. Van Tyne, p. 597. Reports his departure from Washington; expects to see Edward in Marshfield.

July   To [Ann E. Peyton White]. ANS. NhD. mDW 15044. Sends autograph.

July 7   To Robert Charles Winthrop. ALS. MnM. mDW 15045. Introduces Richard Hickman Menefee of Kentucky.

July 9   Motion by DW for a vote of thanks to the president pro tempore of the Senate. AD. DNA, RG 46. mDW 46471.

July 13   To George Darracott et al. Printed. *Columbian Centinel*, July 18, 1838. Accepts dinner invitation from a group of Boston citizens.

July 13   From John W. Mulligan. ALS. DNA, RG 46. mDW 55416. Discusses map he sold to DW.

July 15   From Nathaniel Ray Thomas. ALS. NhHi. mDW 15047. Discusses his efforts to straighten out DW's landholdings in the Midwest.

July 16   *From Daniel Fletcher Webster.*   313

July 19   *From Ramsay Crooks.*   315

[July 20]   To John Plummer Healy. ALS. MHi. mDW 15058. Asks him to get the official votes of his election to Congress from Suffolk County for 1822 and 1824.

July 21   From Daniel Fletcher Webster. ALS. NhHi. mDW 15062. Discusses Nathaniel Ray Thomas's efforts to correct DW's land claim entries.

[c. July 21]   From [John Plummer Healy]. AD copy. MHi. mDW
                15061. Summarizes the votes for DW and
                opponents in the congressional elections,
                1822–1826.
July 21   Draft from Ebenezer Webster for $1144. DS.
                MWalB. mDW 39835–195.
July 23   To Joseph Cowperthwaite.   315
July 23   From Nathaniel Pitcher Tallmadge. ALS. DLC.
                mDW 15068. Regrets that he will not be able to
                attend the Webster dinner in Boston.
July 27   From Nathaniel Ray Thomas.   316
July 30   From Nathaniel Ray Thomas (enclosures:
                Memorandum by Thomas; B. B. Kercheval to
                Thomas, July 28, 1838). ALS. NhHi. mDW
                15119. Discusses the problems of securing deeds
                to DW's western lands.
[July]   To Caleb Cushing. ALS. DLC. mDW 15132. Asks
                Cushing to send 300 copies of his preemption
                speech to George W. Jones by early afternoon.
Aug 1   To John Plummer Healy. ALS. MHi. mDW 15135.
                Authorizes Healy to accept any draft by Colonel
                Ebenezer Webster and Nathaniel Ray Thomas.
Aug 1   From Henry Hubbard.   318
Aug 1   Deed transferring land in Iowa County, Territory
                of Wisconsin, from Benjamin B. Kercheval to
                DW. Copy. Deed Book J: 335–336. Office of the
                Register of Deeds, LaFayette County, Darlington,
                Wis. mDWs.
Aug 1   Deed transferring land in Portage County,
                Territory of Wisconsin, from Benjamin B.
                Kercheval and Mark Healey to DW. Photostat.
                WHi. mDWs.
Aug 1   Deed transferring land in Grant County, Territory
                of Wisconsin, from Benjamin B. Kercheval and
                Mark Healey to DW. Copy. Deed Book D: 59–60.
                Office of the Register of Deeds, Grant County,
                Lancaster, Wis. mDWs.
Aug 1   Deed transferring land in Green County, Territory
                of Wisconsin, from Benjamin B. Kercheval and
                Mark Healey to DW. Copy. Deed Book A: 333.
                Office of the Register of Deeds, Green County,
                Monroe, Wis. mDWs.
Aug 1   Deed transferring land in Shiawassee County,
                Mich., from Benjamin B. Kercheval and Mark
                Healey to DW and Henry Hubbard. Copy. Deed
                Book D: 225–227. Office of the Register of
                Deeds, Shiawassee County, Corunna, Mich.
                mDWs.
Aug 1   Deed transferring land in Livingston County,
                Mich., from Benjamin B. Kercheval to DW and

Henry Hubbard. Copy. Deed Book 4: 8–11.
Office of the Register of Deeds, Livingston
County, Howell, Mich. mDWs.

Aug 1   Deed transferring land in Portage County,
Territory of Wisconsin, from Benjamin B.
Kercheval and Mark Healey and their wives to
DW. Copy. Deed Book A: 37. Office of the
Register of Deeds, Columbia County, Portage,
Wis. mDWs.

Aug 1   Deed transferring land in Dane County, Territory
of Wisconsin, from Benjamin B. Kercheval and
Mark Healey and wives to DW. Copy. Office of
the Register of Deeds, Dane County, Madison,
Wis. mDWs.

Aug 1   Deed transferring land in Washington County,
Territory of Wisconsin, from Benjamin B.
Kercheval and Mark Healey to DW. Copy.
Office of the Register of Deeds, Washington
County, West Bend, Wis. mDWs.

Aug 2   From Nathaniel Ray Thomas. ALS. NhHi. mDW
15141. Reports on his selection of cattle for the
farm at Salisbury.

Aug 4   To Charles Folsom. ALS. MHi. mDW 15144. States
that he intends to be at Exeter on August 23.

Aug 7   *To Ramsay Crooks.*   319
Aug 7   *To Sarah Goodridge.*   319
Aug 7   Draft from Caleb Rider for $1312.16. DS. MHi.
mDW 39835–197.

Aug 8   *To Joseph Cowperthwaite.*   320
Aug 10   From Jeremiah Smith. ALS. NhHi. mDW 15153.
Expresses the hope that DW will attend the
meeting of the trustees of Phillips Exeter
Academy.

Aug 13   To [?]. ALS. MSaE. mDW 15155. Informs her that
he will be in Exeter.

Aug 13   Authorization to John Plummer Healy to accept
draft on him by Ebenezer Webster. DS. MWalB.
mDW 39835–201.

[Aug 15]   To [John Plummer Healy]. ALS. MHi. mDW 15156.
Gives the itinerary of his trip to Exeter.

Aug 15   From Charles Brickett Haddock. ALS. NhD. mDW
15159. Sends him suggestions for comments at
the Phillips Exeter gathering.

[Aug 16]   To John Plummer Healy. ALS. MHi. mDW 15163.
Offers instructions regarding drafts and acceptances.

Aug 17   Draft for $55.25, payable to J[ohn?] Andrews. DS.
MHi. mDW 39835–199.

Aug 25   To Edward Everett. ALS. MHi. mDW 15169.

Sept 28	Draft by DW for payment of $1500 to Bosworth & Tompkins. ADS. MH. mDW 39835–204.
Sept 29	To Thomas Dunlap. ALS. PHi. mDW 15221. Since Cowperthwaite is ill, DW requests Dunlap to check into the failure to allow Andrews a discount on Henry L. Kinney's note.
Sept 29	To John Plummer Healy. ALS. MHi. mDW 15224. States that he plans to leave New York on Monday.
[Sept 29?]	To Caroline Le Roy Webster. ALS. NhHi. mDW 15226. Informs her of the health of her father; mentions that he expects to hear from Cowperthwaite.
Sept 29	Draft on the Bank of the United States of Pennsylvania for $6000. DS. NN. mDW 39835–208.
[Sept]	To Nicholas Biddle. ALS. DLC. mDW 15229. Introduces Richard Haughton, proprietor of the *Boston Atlas*.
Oct 1	To Roswell L. Colt. ALS. PHi. mDW 15231. Hopes that he can see Colt while in New York.
Oct 2	*To John Davis (1787–1854).*
Oct 8	*To Roswell L. Colt.*
Oct 15	To Roswell L. Colt. ALS. PHi. mDW 15239. Sends $194.58, the interest on his two notes.
Nov 1	*From Samuel Lewis Southard.*
Nov 1	Deed transferring land in Marshfield from Eleazer Harlow to DW. DS. Deed Book, 196: 242. Office of the Register of Deeds, Plymouth County, Plymouth, Mass. mDWs.
[Nov 8]	To Peleg Sprague. ALS. MDuHi. mDW 15243. Urges Sprague to address the Boston citizens at Faneuil Hall.
Nov 12	From Robert Manning. ALS. NhHi. mDW 15245. Sends trees for planting at Marshfield.
Nov 12	Deed transferring land in Merrimack County from John H. Durgin to DW. DS. Deed Book, 55: 80. Office of the Register of Deeds, Merrimack County, Concord, N.H. mDWs.
[Nov 14]	To Edward Everett. ALS. MHi. mDW 15247. Declares that he is doing all he can "to bring about a union, between our Whig Brethren."
Nov 22	To Daniel Moore Bates et al. LS. PCarlD. mDW 15249. Declines invitation to deliver the annual address before the literary societies of Dickinson College.
Nov 25	Memorials from citizens of Mount Carmel (mDW 47572) and Wabash County (mDW 47568),

Oct 2 · 331
Oct 8 · 332
Nov 1 · 332

Ill., for a grant of land from Congress to finish the Mount Carmel and New Albany railroad. DS. DNA, RG 46.

Nov 26   From Ellis Gray Loring. Press copy. MH. mDW 15251. Discusses a claim on the ship *Isabella*.

Nov 28   Promissory note to Isaac Foster for $247. DS. MHi. mDW 39835–309.

[Nov 29]   From A. C. S[mith]. ANS. DNA, RG 46. mDW 47119. Asks DW to frank him documents.

Nov [?]   Memorial of A. M. Stafford and others for the construction of a harbor at Milwaukee, Territory of Wisconsin. DS. DNA, RG 46. mDW 46558.

Dec 4   *From Nathaniel Ray Thomas, with enclosure, Proposition by Sherman Page.*   332

Dec 6   To John Davis (1787–1854). ALS. MWA. mDW 15258. Wants to be notified if something important should come before Congress while he is away.

Dec 7   From George F. Allen et al. LS. DLC. mDW 15260. Invite DW to address the American Society for the Diffusion of Useful Knowledge in New York City.

Dec 7   From Aaron Clark et al. LS. DLC. mDW 15263. Hopes that DW will be able to address the New York Society for the Diffusion of Useful Knowledge.

Dec 10   To Edward Curtis. ALS. CtY. mDW 15264. Introduces a Colonel Cline of the British Army.

Dec 11   To John Forsyth. ALS. DNA, RG 59. mDWs. Introduces a Mr. Langdon, whose brother seeks appointment as consul at Smyrna.

Dec 11   From Isaac Gibson. ALS. NhHi. mDW 15265. Returns DW's note for $10,000 for Timothy Fletcher's endorsement.

Dec 13   To Thomas Hedge. ALS. MoSW. mDW 15267. Sends money for Peter Holmes.

Dec 15   Promissory note to S. J. Sylvester for $1005. DS. MHi. mDW 39835–211.

Dec 17   To James Thacher. LS. DLC. mDW 15269. Agrees with Thacher that the name Duxbury originated in England.

Dec 17   From J. Plympton. ALS. DNA, RG 46. mDW 46626. Forwards petition from army officers on the Upper Mississippi.

Dec 19   *From Nathaniel Ray Thomas.*   334

Dec 19   Promissory note to Joseph Breck & Co. for $261.61. DS. MHi. mDW 39835–213.

Dec 19   Memorial of the General Assembly of Wisconsin Territory asking for a grant of land for the

	improvement of the Pekatonica River. ADS. DNA, RG 46. mDW 46693.
Dec 20	To John Codman. ALS. NhD. mDW 15278. Accepts dinner invitation.
Dec 20	To Elias Phinney. ALS. NhD. mDW 15279. Asks if he might get two of his Berkshire pigs.
Dec 20	From Elias Phinney. ALS. NhHi. mDW 15282. Agrees to give DW two of his Berkshire pigs.
Dec 20	Deed transferring land in Pittsfield, N.H., from DW to Alfred Marston. Copy. Office of the Register of Deeds, Merrimack County, Concord, N.H. mDWs.
Dec 26	Deed transferring land in Plymouth County, Mass., from Charles H. Thomas to DW. ADS. Deed Book, 190: 212. Office of the Register of Deeds, Plymouth County, Plymouth, Mass.
Dec 27	To Nathan Hale. ALS. MHi. mDW 15284. Sends volumes that belong to C. S. Daveis of Portland, Me., who will call for them.
[Dec 30]	To Edward Everett. ALS. MHi. mDW 15286. Says he has asked Hale to call on Everett in the evening.
Dec 31	To Isaac Wayne. LS. NhExP. mDW 15288. States that Dr. Thomas Whipple died shortly after leaving Congress.
Dec 31	*Receipt for land conveyance in Derry, New Hampshire, from DW to Samuel Frothingham.* 336
[1838]	Tax bill for $41.80 for land in Londonderry, N.H. Copy. NhD. mDW 39835–216.
[1838?]	To James Trecothick Austin. ALS. NhD. mDW 38213. Reminds Austin that the argument of their motion will be made the following morning.
[1838?]	To [Nicholas Biddle]. ALS. DLC. mDW 15289. Asks Biddle to look at his letter to Cowperthwaite concerning his need to place his financial affairs in order.
[1838?]	To [Robert Charles Winthrop]. ALS. MHi. mDW 15293. Comments on one of Winthrop's speeches.
[1838?]	To Caroline Le Roy Webster. ALS. NhHi. mDW 39115. Discusses affairs at Marshfield.
[1838?]	Memorandum on the nullification crisis. AD. CSmH. mDW 15294.
[1838–1839]	To Nicholas Biddle. ALS. DLC. mDW 38259. Introduces M. M. Rawlins of Illinois.
[1838–1852]	To John Plummer Healy. ALS. MHi. mDW 38605. Asks Healy to contradict any rumor, growing out of his purchase of property in New Jersey, that he might be planning to move.

1839

Jan 1 Memorial of the citizens of Wabash County, Ill., for an appropriation of land to finish the Mount Carmel and New Albany Railroad. DS. DNA, RG 46. mDW 47568.

Jan 2 To Samuel Turrell Armstrong. ALS. NhD. mDWs. Asks Armstrong to arrange for him to address the Massachusetts legislature on their choice of senator.

Jan 3 Power of Attorney to John Plummer Healy to sell DW's shares in the Salmon River Coal Company. DS. MHi. mDW 39835–218.

Jan 7 Petition of citizens of Pembroke (mDW 46569), Scituate (mDW 46567), Plymouth County, Mass., for improvements in the North River. DS. DNA, RG 46.

Jan 9 To Roswell L. Colt. ALS. PHi. mDW 15301. Arranges settlement of bank loans.

Jan 9 To Franklin Haven. LS. MH-H. mDW 15303. Reports on the investigation of the relationship between the Bank of the United States and the Van Buren administration.

Jan 9 To [John Plummer Healy]. ALS. MHi. mDW 15305. Makes a deposit to and draft on his account.

Jan 10 Petitions from citizens of Hanover (mDW 46571), Marshfield (mDW 46563), Plymouth County, Mass., for the improvement of the navigation of North River. DS. DNA, RG 46.

Jan 12 *To Samuel Jaudon.* 338
[c. Jan 12] To Samuel Jaudon. AL draft. NhHi. mDW 15314. Van Tyne, pp. 723–726. AL draft for letter of Jan 12 and in part (first paragraph) for letter of Jan 13.

Jan 13 *To Samuel Jaudon.* 340

Jan 14 To Peleg Sprague. LS. MDuHi. mDWs. Asks for Sprague's recollections of the Commerce Committee's hearings into the renomination of Samuel Swartwout for New York Customs Collector in 1834.

Jan 14 To Nathaniel F. Williams. ALS. NhD. mDW 15328. Asks for loan of $1000 to $1200.

Jan 15 From John Plummer Healy. ALS. MHi. mDW 15330. Discusses DW's personal finances.

Jan 16 From Nicholas Biddle. LC. DLC. mDWs. Invites DW to join the case of *Bank of Augusta* v. *Earle*, 13 Peters 519 (1839).

Jan 16 To Nathaniel F. Williams. ALS. NhD. mDW 15333. Acknowledges loan.

Jan 17   To Edward Everett. ALS. MHi. mDW 15335. *PC*,
                    2: 42–43. Makes suggestions for legislative
                    resolutions to be adopted regarding the sale of
                    public lands.
Jan 21   *From Nicholas Biddle.*   341
Jan 21   From Levi Fisk (enclosed with John Plummer
                    Healy to DW, Jan 30, 1839). ALS. MHi. mDW
                    15351. Reports on title to land in which DW is
                    interested.
Jan 21   From Peleg Sprague. ALS. DLC. mDW 15339.
                    Responds to DW's inquiry relative to the
                    hearings in 1834 into Samuel Swartwout's
                    renomination as New York customs collector.
Jan 22   From John J. Hardin. ALS. IHi. mDWs. Reports
                    the adoption of resolutions opposing the
                    subtreasury scheme and specie collection by the
                    Illinois House of Representatives.
Jan 25   *To [Nicholas Biddle].*   342
[Jan 25]   To Nicholas Biddle. ALS. DLC. mDW 15344. Asks
                    to what extent payments in the South and West
                    were made in bills of the United States Bank
                    and to what extent in bills from local banks.
Jan 25   Petition of army officers asking that pay and
                    promotion of officers of the line be placed on an
                    equal footing with officers of the staff. DS.
                    DNA, RG 46. mDW 46622.
Jan 25   Memorial of A. M. Stafford and others for the
                    construction of a harbor at Milwaukee. DS.
                    DNA, RG 46. mDW 46558.
Jan 26   To Nathaniel F. Williams. ALS. NhD. mDW 15346.
                    Thanks NFW for his "obliging letter" (not
                    found) and loan.
Jan 28   From Nicholas Biddle. LC. DLC. mDWs. Denies
                    that United States Bank notes were sold for
                    local currency.
Jan 29   From Nicholas Biddle. LC. DLC. mDWs. Inquires
                    about a lead mining claim of Henry Hubbard
                    and others.
Jan 30   From John Plummer Healy (enclosure: Levi Fisk
                    to DW, Jan 21, 1839). ALS. MHi. mDW 15348.
                    Reports DW's claim to land described by Fisk
                    to be unfounded.
Jan 30   Memorial of the General Assembly of Wisconsin
                    Territory for a donation of land for the
                    improvement of the Pekatonica River. DS.
                    DNA, RG 46. mDW 46693.
Feb 1   Power of attorney from DW to Henry Hubbard
                    (to sell lands in Livingston County, Mich.).
                    Copy. Office of the Register of Deeds, Livingston
                    County, Howell, Mich. mDWs.

Feb 2   From Ebenezer T. Fogg, Anthony Collamore, and
             Edward P. Little. ALS by Fogg, signed also by
             Collamore and Little. DNA, RG 46. mDW 46576.
             Enclose petitions from citizens of Scituate,
             Marshfield, Hanover, and Pembroke for
             improvements in the North River.
Feb 4   To Andrew Bowers Gale. ALS. Edwin M. Slote,
             New York, N.Y. mDW 15352. Advises Gale to
             apply himself to his studies at Exeter Academy.
Feb 4   To Mrs. [Ann Maria Bowers] Gale. ALS. CSmH.
             mDW 15353. Says he has written her son.
Feb 4   To Jonathan Prescott Hall. ALS. NhD. mDW
             15354. PC, 2: 43–44. Congratulates Hall on his
             escape from drowning in a carriage accident.
Feb 5   From Samuel Appleton Appleton. ALS. NhHi.
             mDW 15356. Asks permission to marry Julia.
Feb 6   Petition of Clarissa Roach, the widow of Jonathan
             Roach, a marine sergeant during the Revolu-
             tionary War, for a pension. DS. DNA, RG
             46. mDW 46675.
Feb 7   To Nicholas Biddle. ALS. DLC. mDW 15359.
             Reports from the Supreme Court on the progress
             of the Alabama cases.
Feb 11   Memorial of D. Raymond and G. Friend of
             Alleghany County, Md., for a revision of the
             tariff. DS. DNA, RG 46. mDW 46608.
Feb 12   Deed transferring land in Ninawa (or western
             Peru) from William L. May and wife to DW.
             Copy. Deed Book 3: 286. Office of the Register
             of Deeds, LaSalle County, Ottawa, Ill. mDWs.
Feb 14   *From Edward Everett.*   343
Feb 15   *To Nicholas Biddle.*   344
Feb 16   [To Edward Everett]. ALS. MHi. mDW 15372.
             Discusses various matters relating to *Rhode
             Island* v. *Massachusetts*, 14 Peters 210 (1840).
Feb 16   Memorial of Thomas Handasyd Perkins and others
             for the passage of a law to authorize the
             discontinuance of the spirit ration allowed to
             seamen in the public service. DS. DNA, RG 46.
             mDW 46646.
Feb 17   To Nathaniel Ray Thomas. ALS. MWalB. mDW
             15373. Encloses a document containing
             information for anyone interested in occupying
             "the farm."
Feb 17   *From Samuel Appleton Appleton.*   345
Feb 18   From Ramsay Crooks. LC. NHi. mDWs. Urges DW
             to pay his notes.
Feb 19   Two deeds transferring land at Mineral Point,
             Territory of Wisconsin, from the United States
             to DW. Copy. Deed Book O: 551–552. Office of

	the Register of Deeds, Grant County, Lancaster, Wis. mDWs.	
Feb 19	Deed transferring land at Mineral Point from the United States to DW. Copy. Deed Book 30: 338. Office of the Register of Deeds, Columbia County, Portage, Wis. mDWs.	
Feb 22	Deed transferring lots in Rock Island City from George Davenport, DW, and Levi C. Turner to William Dickson. Copy. Deed Book D: 23. Office of the Register of Deeds, Rock Island County, Rock Island, Ill. mDWs.	
Feb 26	*To Roswell L. Colt.*	*345*
Feb 27	To John Plummer Healy. ALS. MHi. mDW 15381. Reports having sent him blank notes; enumerates upcoming cases and states that he has refused others.	
Feb 28	Motion in relation to the distribution of the collection of the laws and official instructions and opinions respecting the public lands. DS. DNA, RG 46. mDW 46473.	
March 1	Petitions for the abolition of slavery and the slave trade in the District of Columbia from citizens of Putnam County, Ill. (mDW 47398); Barnstable County (mDW 47429), Boston (mDW 47418, 47420, 47422, 47424), Bristol County (mDW 47437), Cambridge (mDW 47433), Gloucester (mDW 47452), Newburyport (mDW 47426), Plymouth County (mDW 47416), Wendell Phillips and others (mDW 47408), Mass.; Cheshire County, N.H. (mDW 47404); Madison County (mDW 47380, 47382), Utica (mDW 47384, 47389, 47392), N.Y.; Trumbull County, Ohio (mDW 47378); and Philadelphia County, Pa. (mDW 47376). DS. DNA, RG 46.	
March 1	Petition of citizens of Putnam County, Ill. (mDW 47396); Gloucester (mDW 47435, 47454), and Newburyport (mDW 47449), Mass., against the annexation of Texas. DS. DNA, RG 46.	
March 1	Petition of citizens of Gloucester, Mass. (mDW 47431); and Montgomery County, Pa. (mDW 47374), for the recognition of the independence of Haiti. DS. DNA, RG 46.	
March 2	*To Samuel Bulkley Ruggles.*	*346*
[March 4]	[Notes for *Wilcox* v. *Jackson*, 13 Peters 498, 1839]. AD. NhHi. mDW 15427.	
March 4	Check to Tilden Ames for $150 on the Duxbury Bank. Facsimile. *Official Program, Duxbury Tercentenary, 1637–1937* (Duxbury, Mass., [1937?]), p. 18.	

March 6   To Jean Baptiste Beaubien. ALS. NhD. mDW
15387. Reports developments in Beaubien's
land title case.

March 8   Check to Mr. Lewis(?) for $41.62. DS. NN. mDW
39835–218.

March 9   From David Bayard Ogden. Printed. *National
Intelligencer*, March 19, 1839. Asks for DW's
view on the northeastern boundary question.

March 9   From Joel Roberts Poinsett. ALS. MHi. mDW
38802. Thanks DW for his memorandum on the
northeast boundary controversy.

March 9   [Editorial on *Bank of the United States v.
Primrose*, 13 Peters 519, 1839]. AD. NhD. mDW
15389. *National Intelligencer*, March 12, 1839.

[*March* 9]   *Memorandum on the Northeastern Boundary
Negotiations.*   346

[March 10]   To William T. Carroll. ALS. DNA, RG 267. mDWs.
Writes respecting "the N. Carolina Cause."

[March 10]   To Joseph Gales and W. W. Seaton. ALS. NhD.
mDW 15403. Reports having written out an
account of his part in the debate over the
northeast boundary question.

March 10   *Memorandum of Proposal for Special Mission to
England.*   350

March 11   *To David Bayard Ogden.*   350

March 11   *Agreement with David A. Hall re Four Lake
Company.*   351

March 18   *To Nicholas Biddle.*   352

March 22   To Nathaniel Ray Thomas. ALS. MHi. mDW
15411. Wishes to see him as soon as convenient.

March 23   *To Samuel Bulkley Ruggles.*   352

March 25   *From Elias Phinney.*   353

March 29   *To Nicholas Biddle.*   354

March 29   *To Samuel Jaudon.*   354

March 29   From Nicholas Biddle. LC. DLC. mDWs. Announces
his retirement from the Bank of the United
States of Pennsylvania.

[March]   From Nathaniel Ray Thomas. ALS. MHi. mDW
15413. Proposes to meet DW.

April 1   Unsigned promissory note for $1250. AN. MHi.
mDW 39835.

April 2   To Samuel Bulkley Ruggles. ALS. MHi. mDW
15448. *W & S*, 16: 306–307. Asks to see Ruggles
concerning his proposed trip to England.

April 2   From Nicholas Biddle. LC. DLC. mDWs. Can offer
DW little encouragement regarding sale of his
western lands in England.

April 9   To James Kirke Paulding. ALS. MWalB. mDW
15451. Writes on behalf of J. H. Wright's
application for a commission in the navy.

	money, payable "at the Counting House of Saml. Jaudon." ADS. MHi. mDW 39835–296.
May 12	Deed transferring land in Ninawa (Peru) from DW and wife to Warren Brown. Copy. Deed Book 4: 151. Office of the Register of Deeds, LaSalle County, Ottawa, Ill. mDWs.
May 13	To Ramsay Crooks. AL. NHi. mDW 14543. Inquires whether he has heard from Bradley or Maxcy.
May 13	From Edward Everett (enclosure: DW to the People of Massachusetts, draft by Everett, June 12, 1839). LC. MHi. mDW 15495. Asks to be remembered to various English friends.
May 16	[Power of Attorney to Nathaniel Ray Thomas]. DS. MWalB. mDW 39835–234.
May 16	Deed transferring land in Grant County, Territory of Wisconsin, from DW to Richard M. Blatchford and Samuel B. Ruggles. Copy. Deed Book B: 192–194. Office of the Register of Deeds, Grant County, Lancaster, Wis. mDWs.
May 16	Deeds transferring property to Richard Milford Blatchford and Samuel Bulkley Ruggles in Illinois (mDW 39835–288); Indiana (mDW 39835–264); Michigan (mDW 39835–237, mDW 39835–284); Ohio (mDW 39835–257, mDW 39835–268); Wisconsin (mDW 39835–252, mDW 39835–297, mDW 39835–317). DS. MWalB. NhHi. NhExP.
May 16	[Conveyance to R. M. Blatchford and S. B. Ruggles of property in Peru, Ill.]. AD. DLC. mDWs.
May 16	Deed transferring land in Ninawa (Peru) from DW and wife to Richard M. Blatchford and Samuel B. Ruggles. Copy. Deed Book 4: 160. Office of the Register of Deeds, LaSalle County, Ottawa, Ill. mDWs.
May 16	Deed transferring land in Portage County, Wis., from DW and wife to Richard M. Blatchford and Samuel B. Ruggles. Copy. Deed Book B: 341–344. Office of the Register of Deeds, Columbia County, Portage, Wis. mDWs.
May 16	Deed transferring land in Oakland County, Michigan, from DW to Richard M. Blatchford and Samuel B. Ruggles. Copy. Deed Book 18: 280–282. Office of the Register of Deeds, Oakland County, Pontiac, Mich. mDWs.
May 16	*Receipt for money to be loaned to Webster.* 361
May 17	To John Plummer Healy. AL. MHi. mDW 15498. Settles last-minute financial details before leaving for Europe.

May 17	To Charles Henry Thomas. LS. MHi. mDW 15500. Approves repairs on the Marshfield house.
May 17	To John Ward. ALS. NjP. mDW 15503. Thanks Ward for an initialed snuff-box.
May 18	To Edward Webster. ALS. NhHi. mDW 15504. PC, 2: 46. Bids Edward farewell.
May 18	Contract with Herman and Daniel Le Roy re DW's Boston house. DS. MHi. mDW 39835–304.
May 25	Deed transferring land in Ninawa (Peru) from DW and wife to Henry Hubbard. Copy. Deed Book 3: 288. Office of the Register of Deeds, LaSalle County, Ottawa, Ill. mDWs.
May 25	Deed transferring land in Ninawa (Peru) from Henry Hubbard to DW. Copy. Deed Book 3: 290. Office of the Register of Deeds, LaSalle County, Ottawa, Ill. mDWs.
May	To Thomas Wren Ward. ALS. MHi. mDW 15507. Encloses a document for Ward to amend.
[May]	To Thomas Wren Ward. ALS. MHi. mDW 15509. Proposes to call on Ward.
June 3	To Edward Curtis. Printed. PC, 2: 46–48. Reports their safe arrival in England, gives an account of the voyage and of their reception.
June 5	*From John Evelyn Denison.*
June 5	From Samuel Weller Singer. ALS. MH-H. mDW 15515. Admits DW as a visitor to the Travellers Club.
June 6	Deed transferring land in Ninawa (Peru) from DW and wife to Isaac and Nathaniel I. Abrahams. Copy. Deed Book 2: 418. Office of the Register of Deeds, LaSalle County, Ottawa, Ill. mDWs.
June 7	From Christopher Hughes. ALS. MHi. mDW 15517. Introduces two friends from Baltimore.
June 7	From Christopher Hughes. ALS. DLC. mDW 15519. Introduces Mr. Miller, a London bookseller and stationer.
[June 7]	From Nassau William Senior. AL. MH-H. mDW 15793. Invites DW to breakfast.
June 8	From Sir Charles Richard Vaughan. ALS. MH-H. mDW 15521. Postpones a dinner from the 11th to the 14th so that DW may attend.
June 9	*To [John Plummer Healy].*
June 9	*To Charles Henry Thomas.*
June 9	From Joshua Bates. ALS. MH-H. mDW 15533. Arranges to have DW and his party come to breakfast.
June 9	From William Charles Macready. ALS. MH-H. mDW 15536. Invites the Websters to dinner.
June 9	From Sir Charles Richard Vaughan. ALS. MH-H.

363

364
366

mDW 15539. Wishes to reschedule a dinner party to a date convenient for Sir Charles Augustus Murray.

June 10   To Andrew Stevenson. ALS. DLC. mDW 15542. Accepts an invitation to accompany him to the House of Commons.

June 10   *From John Evelyn Denison.*   368

June 10   From George Grote. ALS. MH-H. mDW 15549. Advises DW to attend the debate in the House of Commons on the National Education Bill.

June 10   From Henry Labouchere. ALS. MH-H. mDW 15553. Invites DW to dinner.

June 10   From Thomas Graham, Baron Lynedoch. ALS. MH-H. mDW 15556. Asks when he might visit DW.

June 10   From John Horsley Palmer. ALS. MH-H. mDW 15560. Invites DW to dinner.

June 10   From Andrew Stevenson. ALS. DLC. mDW 15563. Reports having obtained permission for DW to attend the debates at the House of Commons and offers to accompany him.

June 10   From Sir Charles Richard Vaughan. ALS. MH-H. mDW 15556. Conveys an invitation to dine with his brother, Sir Henry Halford.

June 10   From Petty Vaughan. ALS. DLC. mDW 15568. Encloses a ticket to John Sloane's Museum; offers to accompany DW's party to the Zoological Gardens.

June 10   From W. F. Webster. ALS. DLC. mDW 15572. Inquires whether he might be related to DW through his grandfather's brother.

June 10   Deed transferring land in Ninawa (Peru) from Henry Hubbard and wife to DW. Copy. Deed Book 2: 458. Office of the Register of Deeds, LaSalle County, Ottawa, Ill. mDWs.

June 10   Deed transferring land in Ninawa (Peru) from DW and wife to Nathaniel B. Bullock. Copy. Deed Book 2: 270. Office of the Register of Deeds, LaSalle County, Ottawa, Ill. mDWs.

June 11   From Sir Stratford Canning. ALS. MH-H. mDW 15575. Invites DW to dinner.

June 11   From Sir Montagu Lowther Chapman. ALS. MH-H. mDW 15578. Invites DW to dine at the Clarendon Hotel.

June 11   From E. Magrath. ALS. MH-H. mDW 15581. Invites DW to accept guest privileges at the Athenaeum.

June 11   From Sir George and Lady Philips. AL. MH-H. mDW 15583. Invite the Websters to breakfast June 14.

	MH-H. mDW 15638. Invites DW for dinner with "the leading members of the Bar."
June 14	From Edward Ellice. ALS. MH-H. mDW 15641. Invites DW's party to dinner.
June 14	From Samuel Jones Loyd, later Baron Overstone. ALS. MH-H. mDW 15643. Invites DW to breakfast.
June 14	To Samuel Jones Loyd, later Baron Overstone. LS. UkBelQU. mDW 15630. Accepts breakfast invitation.
June 14	From Sydney Smith. ALS. MH-H. mDW 15645. Advises that he has no open dates in July and invites DW's party for tea on June 23.
June 15	From Henry Richard Vassal Fox, Baron Holland. ALS. MH-H. mDW 15649. Issues a dinner invitation.
June 15	From Henry Hart Milman. MH-H. mDW 15653. Invites the Websters to breakfast.
June 15	From Mary Charlotte Senior. ALS. MH-H. mDW 15657. Invites DW's party for dinner.
June 16	From Sir Charles Augustus Murray. ALS. MH-H. mDW 15660. Reports that the Queen will not attend service at the Royal Chapel that day.
June 17	To Andrew Stevenson. ALS. DLC. mDW 15662. States that he has not received formal invitations to the Queen's Ball that evening.
June 17	From Henry Hart Milman. AL. MH-H. mDW 15665. Asks DW to name a day for breakfast and to see Westminster Abbey.
[June] 17	From Henry Hart Milman. AL. MH-H. mDW 15668. Acknowledges DW's acceptance of his breakfast invitation.
June 17	Deed transferring land in Ninawa (Peru) from DW and wife to John F. Hoyt. Copy. Deed Book 2: 378. Office of the Register of Deeds, LaSalle County, Ottawa, Ill. mDWs.
June 17	Deed transferring land in Ninawa (Peru) from John F. Hoyt and wife to DW. Copy. Deed Book 2: 457. Office of the Register of Deeds, LaSalle County, Ottawa, Ill. mDWs.
June 18	From John Inglis, Bishop of Nova Scotia. ALS. MH-H. mDW 15669. Transmits a dinner invitation for June 22 from the Archbishop of Canterbury.
June 18	From William Lowther, Earl of Lonsdale. AL. MH-H. mDW 15673. Invites DW to dinner.
June 18	From John Stuart-Wortley, later Baron Wharncliffe. ALS. MH-H. mDW 15675. Inquires whether DW might be free on July 1.
June 19	From John Charles Spencer, Earl Spencer. ALS.

MH-H. mDW 15678. Acknowledges a letter of
introduction from [George] Ticknor.

June 20   From Sir William Clay. ALS. MH-H. mDW 15681.
Invites DW's party to spend the weekend at
Twickenham and to see Hampton Court at that
time.

June 21   From Joshua Bates. ALS. MH-H. mDW 15685.
Invites DW's party to call on Lady Wellesley.

June 21   From Samuel Rogers. ALS. MH-H. mDW 15688.
Will provide transportation to and from
Chiswick unless otherwise advised.

June 22   To John Charles Spencer, Earl Spencer. ALS.
MH-H. mDW 15691. Would prefer to visit
Spencer after his return from Winton.

June 22   To Andrew Stevenson. ALS. DLC. mDW 15695.
Inquires whether he should attend the Queen's
levee.

June 22   From Sir Charles Augustus Murray. ALS. MH-H.
mDW 15700. Encloses a card of admission for
the Sunday service in the Royal Chapel.

June 22   From Philip Henry Stanhope, Viscount Mahon.
AL. MH-H. mDW 15698. Invites DW to
breakfast.

June 22   From Andrew Stevenson. ALS. DLC. mDW 15702.
Reports that he is unable to attend the Queen's
levee and advises DW against going without
him.

June 22   *From Daniel Fletcher Webster.*   371

June 23   *From Lewis Cass.*   373

June 23   From Sydney Smith. ALS. MH-H. mDW 15712.
Arranges for the admittance of DW's party to
St. Paul's Cathedral.

June 24   *To [Isaac P. Davis].*   374

June 24   To Hiram Ketchum. Printed. *PC*, 2: 52–53.
Summarizes briefly the progress of his visit to
London.

June 24   To James William Paige. ALS. MH-H. mDW 15718.
Reports Jaudon's opinion that the financial
situation has not improved.

[June 24]   From Dunbar James Douglas, Earl of Selkirk.
ALS. MH-H. mDW 15726. Clarifies a dinner
invitation.

June 24   From Henry Hallam. ALS. MH-H. mDW 15722.
Invites DW to breakfast.

June 24   From William Lowther, Earl of Lonsdale. AL.
MH-H. mDW 15724. Invites DW to dinner.

June 24   From Sir Charles Augustus Murray. ALS. MH-H.
mDW 15744. Comments on what etiquette
should be observed during DW's presentation
to the Queen.

June 24 From Charles Sumner. ALS. DLC. mDW 15729. Van Tyne, p. 219. Refers DW to several friends and acquaintances in England, notably Lord Morpeth.

[June 25] To Andrew Stevenson. ALS. DLC. mDW 15744. Discusses his plan to attend the royal levee.

June 25 From Edward Denison, Bishop of Salisbury. ALS. MH-H. mDW 15736. Invites DW's party to visit Salisbury.

June 26 To Andrew Stevenson. ALS. DLC. mDW 15748. Expects Mr. [Benjamin] Rush at 1:30; must forgo an invitation to the Marquis of Normanby's ball because of exhaustion.

June 26 From Sir Robert Harry Inglis. ALS. MH-H. mDW 15750. Invites the ladies of DW's family to breakfast.

June 27 From Edward Denison, Bishop of Salisbury. ALS. MH-H. mDW 15752. States that consideration of the National Education Bill has been postponed.

June 27 From Robert Knox. LS. DLC. mDW 15755. Invites DW to the Anniversary Dinner of the Newspaper Press Benevolent Association.

June 27 From Sydney Smith. ALS. MH-H. mDW 15757. Advises DW on some reading; recommends Malcolm's *Londinium Redivivum*.

June 27 From T. Walcot. Printed LS. MH-H. mDW 15758. Offers DW the privileges of honorary visitor at the Clarence Club.

June 28 From Philip Henry Stanhope, Viscount Mahon. ALS. MH-H. mDW 15759. Sends DW Macauley's *Indian Code* and a collection of Lord Peterborough's letters.

June 28 From Edward George Geoffrey Smith Stanley, later Earl of Derby. ALS. MH-H. mDW 15762. Requests DW's impressions of various aspects of a libel case—*Stockdale v. Hansard*.

[June 28] From John Stuart-Wortley, later Baron Wharncliffe. ALS. MH-H. mDW 15765. Invites DW and party to visit.

June 29 From George Barton (enclosed with Sir Duncan MacDougall to DW, June 29, 1839). ALS. MH-H. mDW 15769. Offers DW guest privileges at the Colonial Society.

[June 29] From Arthur Buller. ALS. MH-H. mDW 15771. Offers to postpone inviting Daniel O'Connell if DW objects to meeting him.

June 29 From Thomas Denman, Baron Denman. ALS. MH-H. mDW 15775. Extends an invitation.

June 29 From Sir Robert John Wilmot-Horton. ALS. MH-H.

	mDW 15740. Encloses a book; invites DW to dinner.
June 29	From Sir Duncan MacDougall (enclosure: George Barton to DW, June 29, 1839). AL. MH-H. mDW 15779. Encloses letter for DW.
[June]	From Arthur Buller. ALS. MH-H. mDW 15780. Invites DW to dine with his mother and father.
[June]	From Mr. and Mrs. Charles Buller. AL. MH-H. mDW 15782. Offer a dinner invitation.
[June]	From Sir James Clark. ALS. MH-H. mDW 15783. Invites DW to call on him.
[June–Nov]	From Sir William Thomas Denison. ALS. MH-H. mDW 15787. Invites DW to visit the "Military and Naval Establishments at Woolwich."
[June]	From Nassau William Senior. ALS. MH-H. mDW 15790. Introduces Sir R. Wilmot Horton.
[June–Oct]	Invitations, calling cards, etc. Printed documents, and printed documents signed. MH-H. mDW 15794.
July 1	To Virgil Maxcy. ALS. NN. mDW 15841. W & S, 16: 311–312. Outlines his itinerary so he can be reached if Maxcy comes to England.
July 2	From John Gibson Lockhart. ALS. MH-H. mDW 15844. Issues invitation to breakfast and to his brother's home in Scotland.
July 2	From William Lowther, Earl of Lonsdale. AL. MH-H. mDW 15846. Invites DW to dinner.
July 3	To Nathaniel Ray Thomas. ALS. NhHi. mDW 15848. PC, 2: 53–54. Describes the unfavorable financial conditions in England.
July 3	From James Alexander. AL. DLC. mDW 15852. Cancels a dinner invitation.
July 3	*From Edward Everett.*
July 4	*To Samuel Wilkinson.*
July 4	To Edward Curtis. Printed: PC, 2: 55–56. Reports that he has sent Mrs. Curtis a copy of the works of Shakespeare; discusses the money situation.
July 4	From William Harness. ALS. MH-H. mDW 15865. Invites DW's party to breakfast.
July 5	To Hiram Ketchum. Printed. PC, 2: 57–58. Expresses uncertainty over his political future; discusses parliamentary matters briefly, including the manner in which money is appropriated and expended.
July 5	From Lord Arthur Marcus Cecil Hill to [?], for DW. ALS. MH-H. mDW 15868. Suggests that a letter be forwarded to DW and thanks him for obtaining DW's opinion on a legal matter.
July 5	From Ramsay Crooks. LC. NHi. mDWs. Reports that he has drawn on DW for £1000.

July 5   From John Stuart-Wortley, later Baron Wharncliffe.
              ALS. MH-H. mDW 15872. Invites DW's party
              to watch the practice session for a jousting
              tournament.
July 5   From John Stuart-Wortley, later Baron Wharncliffe.
              ALS. MH-H. mDW 15876. Firms up arrange-
              ments to see Apsely House and the jousting
              practice.
July 5   Deed transferring land in Ninawa (Peru) from
              DW and wife to Samuel Cabot. Copy. Deed
              Book 4: 69. Office of the Register of Deeds,
              LaSalle County, Ottawa, Ill. mDWs.
[July 8]   From D. H. Nelson.   380
July 9   To Samuel Jones Loyd, later Baron Overstone.   380
July 9   From Egerton Vernon Harcourt. ALS. MH-H.
              mDW 15885. Thanks DW for offering to supply
              him with letters of introduction for his planned
              trip to the United States.
July 10   To Charles Henry Thomas. ALS. MHi. mDW
              15889. Reports that the wheat crop may be
              endangered by too much rain.
[July 10]   [Memorandum of social engagements]. AD. NhD.
              mDW 15892. Van Tyne, p. 220.
July 12   From Sir Henry Halford. ALS. MH-H. mDW
              15895. Invites DW's party to dinner.
July 12   From John Inglis, Bishop of Nova Scotia. ALS.
              MH-H. mDW 15897. Reports the Archbishop of
              Canterbury can receive DW the following
              morning.
July 12   From Edward George Geoffrey Smith Stanley, later
              Earl of Derby. ALS. MH-H. mDW 15762. Invites
              DW's party to join him in Ireland.
July 12   From Sir Charles Richard Vaughan. ALS. MH-H.
              mDW 15904. Asks if DW plans to accept Sir
              Henry Halford's invitation.
July 13   From Philip Pusey. ALS. MH-H. mDW 15907.
              Regrets being unable to see DW at Worcester
              College.
July 14   To [Joseph Story]. LS (postscript in DW's hand).
              MiU-C. mDW 15909. Introduces Egerton Vernon
              Harcourt, the Rev. Charles Harcourt, and David
              Dundas, who are about to travel to the United
              States.
July 15   From Philip Henry Stanhope, Viscount Mahon.
              ALS. MH-H. mDW 15911. Encloses a copy of
              his latest book.
[July 16]   From Walter Kerr Hamilton. ALS. MH-H. mDW
              15914. Invites DW to breakfast.
[July 16]   From Walter Kerr Hamilton. ALS. MH-H. mDW

July	From William Courtenay, later Earl of Devon. AN. MH-H. mDW 15963. Invites DW to dine.	
[July]	To John Kenyon. ALS. ICU. mDW 15961. Arranges the settlement of a debt owed him by Kenyon.	
[*July*]	*From Edward Kenyon.*	*386*
July	From John David Towse. ALS. MH-H. mDW 15967. Invites DW to dinner on behalf of the Fishmongers Company.	
[July]	[Lines for John Kenyon]. Printed. Allan L. Benson, *Daniel Webster* (New York, 1929), p. 250.	
Aug 1	To Virgil Maxcy. ALS. NN. mDW 15969. *W & S*, 16: 312. Gives his tentative itinerary; wants to see Maxcy in London, especially regarding Clamorgan scrip.	
Aug 1	To Andrew Stevenson. ALS. DLC. mDW 15972. Agrees to accompany Stevenson to Fishmongers Hall.	
Aug 2	From Thomas Denman, Baron Denman. ALS. MH-H. mDW 15974. Invites DW's attendance at parties to be hosted by himself and the Chief Justice of the Court of Common Pleas.	
Aug 3	*To Benjamin Rush.*	*386*
Aug 3	From John Inglis, Bishop of Nova Scotia. ALS. MH-H. mDW 15980. Issues an invitation to DW's party on behalf of the Archbishop of Canterbury and his wife.	
Aug 3	From Edward Kenyon. ALS. NhD. mDWs. Gives reasons for delay in honoring a draft.	
Aug 4	From George Sholto Douglas, Earl of Morton. ALS. MH-H. mDW 15983. Asks to be notified of DW's arrival in Scotland.	
Aug 5	*From Virgil Maxcy.*	*387*
Aug 6	*To Ramsay Crooks.*	*388*
Aug 6	To [?] Ogle. ALS. NhD. mDW 15993a. Agrees to convey Ogle's gift of "Drawings, Directions, etc. . . ." to the U.S. government.	
Aug 7	From Mr. and Mrs. [Fitzowen?] Skinner. AL. MH-H. mDW 15997. Invite the Websters to dinner to meet the judges of assize.	
Aug 8	[Fire Insurance Policy with Massachusetts Fire and Marine Insurance Company]. DS. MHi. mDW 39835-321.	
Aug 14	Deed transferring land in southwestern Wisconsin Territory from George W. and Josephine Jones to Daniel Webster. Copy. Deed Book A: 42–43. Office of the Register of Deeds, Columbia County, Portage, Wis. mDWs.	
Aug 15	*To [?].*	*388*
Aug 19	From William Lowther, Earl of Lonsdale. ALS.	

ram and directs Thomas to buy some American
ewes.

Printed. Edwin Hodder, *The Life and Work of the Seventh Earl of Shaftesbury, KG.* (London, 1887), p. 282. Regrets being unable to pursue their acquaintanceship and proposes they correspond after DW's return to the U.S.

Nov 19   "The Memory of the Heart" (poem). Copy. NhHi. mDW 16185. Bela Chapin, *The Poets of New Hampshire* (Claremont, N.H., 1883), p. 28.

Nov 19   Promissory note for £500 to Joseph Travers. ANS. NhD. mDW 39835–326.

Nov 20   From Anthony Ashley Cooper, Earl of Shaftesbury. ALS. MH-H. mDW 16187. Encloses a copy of one of his parliamentary speeches.

Nov 22   From Daniel Fletcher Webster. ALS. NhHi. mDW 16191. Brings DW up to date on affairs in Illinois.

Nov 25   From John Miller. ALS. DLC. mDW 16195. Extends best wishes to DW on the eve of his return to America.

Dec 5   From Daniel Fletcher Webster. ALS. NhHi. mDW 16198. Advises that he has drawn on DW twice.

Dec 13   Deed transferring property in St. Clair County, Mich., from DW to Richard M. Blatchford and Samuel B. Ruggles. Deed Book K: 290–291. Office of the Register of Deeds, St. Clair County, Port Huron, Mich. mDWs.

Dec 22   From Daniel Fletcher Webster. ALS. NhHi. mDW 16202. Asks DW's advice on the future disposition of DW's Illinois lands.

Dec 29   To Gracie & Sargent (incomplete). AN. MHi. mDWs. Wishes to call on them concerning the subject of a letter enclosed (not found).

Dec 29   *To John Plummer Healy.*   412

[Dec 29?]   To Nicholas Biddle. ALS. DLC. mDW 16214. Will see him in Philadelphia on December 31st.

[1839?]   To John Plummer Healy. ALS. MHi. mDW 16216. Asks him to look into a couple of debts.

[1839]   [Memoranda on sheep raised in England, and on the Bank of France]. AD. NhD. mDW 16218.

[1839–1840]   Memorandum of DW's Wisconsin lands. AD. MWalB. mDW 39835–98.

[1839–1840]   Memorandum on mortgage deed to Samuel Frothingham for John Plummer Healy. ADS. MHi. mDW 38633.

Index

The following abbreviations are used: BUS, Bank of the United States; DW, Daniel Webster; DFW, Daniel Fletcher Webster. The entry for Webster is confined to personal details, avocations, feelings, opinions, political and financial information not readily located elsewhere, and writings and speeches. The reader is referred to specific entries within the main Index for information on Webster's political activities and land speculation. The entries for Boston, New York, and Washington are selective.

Page numbers between 413 and 522 are in the Calendar. Numbers set in bold-face type indicate pages where individuals are identified. Individuals identified in the *Dictionary of American Biography* are denoted by an asterisk immediately following the name. Those identified in the *Biographical Directory of the American Congress* are denoted by a dagger.

Library of Congress Cataloging in Publication Data (Revised)
Webster, Daniel, 1782–1852.
   The papers of Daniel Webster.
   Vol. 3: Charles M. Wiltse, editor, David G. Allen, assistant editor.
   CONTENTS: ser. 1. Correspondence: v. 1. 1798–1824. v. 2. 1825–1829. v. 3. 1830–1834. v. 4. 1835–1839.
   1. United States—History—1801–1809—Collected works.
2. United States—History—1809–1817—Collected works.
3. United States—History—1815–1861—Collected works.
4. Webster, Daniel, 1782–1852. I. Wiltse, Charles Maurice, 1907– II. Moser, Harold D. III. Dartmouth College. IV. Title.
E337.8.W373   973.5′092′4   73-92705
ISBN 0-87451-096-1 (v. 1)